LIFE IN CHRIST

The Original Five Volumes in One

LIFE IN CHRIST

STUDIES IN 1 JOHN

Martyn Lloyd-Jones

CROSSWAY BOOKS

A PUBLISHING MINISTRY OF
GOOD NEWS PUBLISHERS
WHEATON, ILLINOIS

Life in Christ: Studies in 1 John

Copyright © 2002 by Bethan Lloyd-Jones

Published by Crossway Books
    A publishing ministry of Good News Publishers
    1300 Crescent Street
    Wheaton, Illinois 60187

Originally published as five volumes: *Fellowship with God, Walking with God, Children of God, The Love of God,* and *Life in God.*

All Bible quotations are taken from the *King James Version.*

Cover design: David LaPlaca

First printing, one volume, 2002

Printed in the United States of America

ISBN 13: 978-1-58134-439-4
ISBN 10: 1-58134-439-2

VP		16	15	14	13	12	11	10	09	08	07	
17	16	15	14	13	12	11	10	9	8	7	6	5

CONTENTS

VOLUME THREE: CHILDREN OF GOD

VOLUME FOUR: THE LOVE OF GOD

VOLUME FIVE: LIFE IN GOD

VOLUME ONE

Fellowship with God

ACKNOWLEDGMENTS

AS USUAL, THESE SERMONS were edited by Christopher Catherwood, the Doctor's eldest grandson. But as with all the sermons published since the death of Dr. Lloyd-Jones in 1981, a major role was played by the Doctor's eldest daughter, Elizabeth Catherwood, who in her capacity as literary executrix went through all the editing to make sure that it was fully in accord with what the Doctor would have wanted had he been alive to supervise the work. Special thanks are therefore due to her for all her hard work, and also to Alison Walley for copy editing the manuscript and for putting it onto disk ready for the publisher.

1

The Christian and the World

And we know that we are of God, and the whole world lieth in wickedness [or, in the wicked one].

 1 JOHN 5:19

I BEGIN OUR SERIES with this verse because it seems to me to provide us with the background and setting to the teaching of the whole epistle. It is an epistle which, in many ways, people find somewhat baffling and difficult to understand. There are many reasons for that. Its message is essentially a very simple one, but the manner and the style of the writer, the Apostle John (for I take it that he was the author, we need not discuss that), this style, which is so characteristic of him, is one which, unless we are careful to maintain a firm grip of the great principles of his teaching, may very well cause us a certain amount of confusion. Never perhaps is it so true to say of any epistle that we are in danger of missing the wood because of the trees than it is in this particular case.

Some people have said that his style, or method, is kind of spiral; it seems to go round in circles and differs with every turn until he arrives at his ultimate truth and message. It is interesting to contrast the style of the Apostle Paul with that of John. The main difference is that John is not so logical; he is not so clear-cut in his method. He has, of course, exactly the same message, but he states it in a different way. It is said sometimes, loosely and lightly, that John was more mystical than Paul. I cannot admit that, because both of them were, in the truest sense,

Christian mystics, but John's style is more indirect than that of the great Apostle who is always much more direct and logical in his presentation of truth. But, of course, there is a real advantage in having these different styles. Were they to do nothing else, they would remind us of what the Apostle Peter calls 'the manifold grace of God' (1 Pet 4:10), the many different colours. The light of truth is like the natural light; it can be broken up by prism into a large number of subsidiary colours which together form that perfect light. And so it is with the Scriptures, all from God, all in-breathed by the Holy Spirit, all perfectly inspired, and yet differing in these many ways, and thereby reflecting different aspects of the one glorious, ultimate truth. There is a unity, a wholeness about it all.

Another difficulty in understanding the writings of John arises, perhaps, from the fact that when he wrote this, the Apostle was undoubtedly very old. It is agreed by most that this letter was probably written somewhere between A.D. 80 and A.D. 90—you may take A.D. 85 as being perhaps a fairly accurate date—and by that time the Apostle had become an old man. Many things show that: we find him, for instance, speaking of his 'little children', and he uses very affectionate terms. There again, we find another difficulty arising, in that as he is saying one thing, it suggests another thought to him, so he immediately expresses it, and then comes back to the original point he was making. So it is important that we should bear the great central principles in mind, and here in this nineteenth verse we get the essential background to a true understanding of this letter: 'We know that we are of God, and the whole world lieth in wickedness', or 'in the wicked one'.

In other words, the theme of this epistle is the position of the Christian in the world. I always feel that there are three verses in the whole epistle which I would describe as key verses, and this is one of them. The second is chapter 5, verse 13: 'These things have I written unto you that believe on the name of the Son of God; that ye may know that ye have eternal life, and that ye may believe on the name of the Son of God.' And the third is chapter 1, verse 4: 'These things write we unto you, that your joy may be full.' There we have the great and grand objective which was in the mind of the Apostle. The theme is the Christian in this world, what is possible to him; how is he to face it; how is he to stand up to it; what must he do; what is his relationship to this world in which he finds himself?

Now the Apostle, writing as an old man, was addressing people who were in a very difficult world. I do not know how you feel, but I always think that, in and of itself, is a profound source of comfort. Half our troubles arise from the fact that we always seem to think that it is only our world and time that has been difficult. But if history, and the study of history, especially as we find it in the Bible, does nothing else for us, it should always give us a true perspective. When you look back across the story of the Church and of the saints you find that the world has often been as it is today. In a sense we are confronting nothing new at the present time. It has all happened before, and, thank God, there is provision here for us in our perplexities and in our difficulties.

That is why I cannot understand anyone who does not see the utter uniqueness of Scripture; it does not matter at what period of history you may happen to live, nor what may be happening in the world around and about you, you will find that the position has been met and catered for and dealt with somewhere or another in the Bible. And here is a letter written to people who were in an extremely difficult and contradictory world, and the old man, feeling perhaps that his time was short, is anxious that these little ones, these beloved children and grandchildren of his, should know what to do in such a world with all its contradictions and troubles and problems.

Now I do not need to point out how apposite all this is at the present time. I suppose that this is the biggest and most difficult question in many ways that those of us who are Christians today can possibly meet. What is our position in this world? How are we related to it? We are in the same world as everybody else and we are subject to the same things as they are. We do not live enchanted lives; we are all here in the flux of history, and the great question is, what are we to do; what is the difference between us; how are we to adjust ourselves; what is to be our attitude towards current events and affairs; what is our duty with respect to life in this world, and how are we to conduct and comport ourselves?

Those are the great questions that are considered in this epistle. It is by no means the message of this epistle only; indeed a very good case can be made for saying that that is precisely the message of nearly all the New Testament epistles. And in the same way, of course, the book of Revelation was written to comfort and strengthen the first Christians. It was written to people who were suffering persecution and hardship, and it was meant to enable them to overcome their immediate difficulties, as well as to give them a general view of the course of history in the years of the centuries that lay ahead. So let us first look at this message of this epistle in general, before we come to divide it up into its component parts.

Now a time of difficulty and danger is often a time of panic, and there are many ways in which people can show this. It is not only thoughtlessness, alas, because thought can equally be a manifestation of panic. Indeed, even prayer may be a very striking manifestation of panic. Sometimes, panic can be mistaken for true spirituality and a true understanding of the scriptural teaching. But while the effect of the New Testament teaching always is to steady us—and it steadies us of course by presenting us with the truth—it never makes a mere general statement, it is never out just to soothe and comfort us for the time being. No, its message always is that there are certain great principles, and that if we only lay a firm hold upon them and grasp them, if only we base our life upon them and plan the whole of our existence in terms of them, then we can never really go wrong.

Therefore, in a situation of difficulty and of crisis, the first thing we must do is to make sure that we have grasped the New Testament teaching. I do not want to be controversial, and I am particularly anxious not to be misunderstood, but if I may put it in a phrase, in order to call attention to what I have in mind, I would say that in a situation of crisis the New Testament does not immediately say, 'Let us pray'. It always says first, 'Let us think, let us understand the truth, let us take a firm hold of the doctrine.' Prayer may be quite useless and quite void. The Bible has a great deal to tell us about prayer and as to how it should be made. Prayer is not a simple thing in one sense; it may be very difficult. Prayer is sometimes an excuse for not thinking, an excuse for avoiding a problem or a situation.

Have we not all known something of this in our personal experience? We have often been in difficulty and we have prayed to God to deliver us, but in the meantime we have not put something right in our lives as we should have done. Instead of facing the trouble, and doing what we knew we should be doing, we have prayed. I suggest that at a point like that, our duty is not to pray but to face the truth, to face the doctrine and to apply it. Then we are entitled to pray, and not until then.

I mean something like this: if the whole attitude of the Christian in any situation of crisis or difficulty were just to be immediately one of prayer, then these New Testament epistles with all their involved teaching would never have been necessary. No, the New Testament method says, 'You must become certain people before you can pray. There are certain preliminaries to apply, and you must know what you are doing when you pray.'

Now that is something that surely we too need to be very clear about. We need to apply certain great central principles and truths and these are the very things with which John is concerned in this first epistle of his. Therefore, as we look at it we shall be impressed by certain things; we shall be impressed by his realism and by the way in which he does not attempt to gloss over the difficulties and to make light of the problems. Thank God, the Bible always faces things as they are, even at their worst. That is why to me a psychological use of the Bible is of the devil. It is a mis-use of it, because the Bible is not concerned simply to ease a situation. It has a strength and a power; it is concerned about courage, but in terms of its own truth so it looks at the world as it is, at its worst. People say, 'Why, that is depressing!' Well, if it is depressing to you, it is because you do not accept the teaching of the Bible. To be realistic should not be depressing to those who think straightly and clearly, and this is a realistic book.

And then the other great thing that characterises its message is the way in which, having looked at the facts and having faced them squarely and honestly, it applies quite clearly its own great and glorious remedy. And in this verse which we are now considering we are reminded of some of the great characteristic notes of this particular epistle. Firstly, you will find that we come across these words: 'We know.' Then, secondly, we find something about ourselves—that we are of God. And, thirdly, we are told that there are certain things that are always true about the world.

The first thing then, is this great certainty—'*We know.*' John has written these things that they may know that they have eternal life. We need not stay with this, and yet, of course, it is something which is absolutely basic, for this meets the whole position. Christians are not people who are in a state of uncertainty; the very definition of Christians in the New Testament is of people who know where they are, what they are and what they have got; they are not men and women who are hovering in the dark.

Perhaps the days and times through which we are passing are, in that sense, a great advantage to us. There are many senses in which I thank God I am preaching now in this pulpit today and not one hundred years ago or at any time during the nineteenth century. It was so typical of that century for people to talk about the quest for truth and all the excitement that accompanied that quest. You see, in days when life was smooth and easy, then people said how exciting it was to investigate truth and to examine it, and there were people who thought that that was Christianity. It was to be 'a seeker', and you read literature and you compared this with that, and you said how marvellous it all was! But in a world like this of the twentieth century you have no time for this, and thank God for that! We are in a world where black is black and white is white and that is in accordance with the New Testament teaching.

Christians are men and women who are certain, and John writes in order that these people may be absolutely sure. They were sure, but there were certain things that were not clear to them. That always seems to be the position of the Christian in this life and world. We start with the truth which we believe by faith. Then it is attacked and we are shaken by various things but, thank God, these lessons are given to us to strengthen and establish us. That is the first thing to be emphasised in this message, and it is something of which we may be sure. There are certain things that you and I should *know*. Christians have ceased to be seekers and enquirers; they are men and women who have ceased to doubt.

The whole doctrine of assurance and salvation has been heartily disliked in the past hundred years or so. We have heard very little about it and people have thought that it was an unmentionable item. There have been many reasons for that; there is something which can be objectionable about a certain kind of person who claims this knowledge. It can be said in a way that is antagonistic, but that is not what we are commanded here. No, the whole glory of the Christian gospel is that it gives us knowledge; it claims to be the revelation of God; it gives that unique and definite authority, and Christians should know exactly where they are and how they stand. They should have been emancipated and delivered out of the realm of tentative conclusions. There are certain absolutes and we shall see how the Apostle keeps on repeating these. There are certain things possible to you; you must get hold of them and you must hold fast to them.

But about what are we to have this certainty? Firstly, we are to be certain about ourselves. We know that we are of God. What is a Christian? Are Christians just people who pay a formal respect to God and to public worship? Are they just mechanically attached to a church? Do they just try to live a good life and to be a little bit better than others? Are they just philanthropists, people who believe in a certain amount of benevolence? They are all that, of course, but how infinitely more! Now, says John, we know this truth about ourselves as Christians. 'We are of God'; by which he means nothing less than this: we are born of God; we are partakers of the divine nature; we have been born again; we have been born from above, we have been born of the Spirit, we are a new creation.

Now those are the basic postulates of the New Testament position. May I put it like this. I cannot see that the New Testament message has any comfort to give us or any consolation unless we start from that basis; that if we are Christians we are altogether different from those who are not. We know that we are of God—children of God, related to God in that intimate sense, receivers of His very life and nature; in other words, the whole point about Christians is that they are unique and they are aware that they have this new life within them. Paul says, 'I know whom I have believed' (2 Tim 1:12); or he refers to 'the Son of God, who loved me, and gave himself for me', 'Christ liveth in me' (Gal 2:20); 'in Christ' (2 Cor 5:17)—these are his terms as they are the terms everywhere in the New Testament, and the Apostle John starts on this assumption— that we *know Him*. We are not just hoping or just trying to be Christians, it has happened to us, it has all taken place.

Here, then, is the question which we ask ourselves before we proceed any further—do we know that we are of God? Do we know for certain that God has done something in our lives? Do we know that something of the divine life of God is in us? Are we aware of the 'new man' within us, one that is entirely different from the 'old man' that we were by nature? Are we aware that there is something about us which we can only explain in terms of God? Can we say in true humility with the Apostle Paul, 'By the grace of God I am what I am' (1 Cor 15:10)?

Now that is absolutely basic and fundamental. Christians, according to this teaching, are those who have been called out of and delivered from this present evil world; those who have been translated from the kingdom of darkness into the kingdom of light, and who have been taken out of the dominion of Satan and translated into the kingdom of God's dear Son. There is no question about it; that is what has happened to them; that is what makes them Christians and they know it. They are able to say, 'I am aware of this life that is beyond me and within me, and I ascribe it only and entirely to the grace of God in Jesus Christ.' They are aware, not only of a difference between the world that does not believe in Christ, and themselves, but also of this difference between what they were before and what they are now. They can say, 'Though I am amazed and astounded when I consider the sins I have committed and all my unworthiness, I know, in spite of it all, that I am of God; God has had mercy upon me and has worked in me the miracle of the rebirth.'

The second thing we know is the truth about the world. 'We know that we are of God, and the whole world lieth in wickedness' or 'in the wicked one'. What he means by this is that it lies in the power of the evil one. Here again, as we shall see times without number in the study of this epistle, it was an essential part, not only of John's teaching but that of all the Apostles and of the first Christians with respect to the world. They drew this distinction between the Church and the world; the absolute difference between the Christian and the non-Christian; and the truth about the world, according to this teaching, is that the whole world lies under the dominion of Satan, in the grip of outright evil.

Let me emphasise this. The New Testament teaching is that however much the world may change on the surface, it is always under the control of evil and of sin. This admits that the powers of evil can be modified a great deal, and they have been modified during the passing of the centuries. Look back through human history and you will see that there is a kind of grouping. There have been periods when the world has been getting better, but these have been followed by a terrible declension, and the teaching of the New Testament is that the whole time the world has been 'lying in the wicked one'.

Now that is where, it seems to me, we have been so steadily fooled for the last hundred years; and when I say 'we', I mean the Christian as well as the non-Christian. How confident people were towards the end of the nineteenth century that the world was being Christianised! But we must not be deluded by all these changes which are merely superficial; the world, says John to these people, is under the dominion of Satan and sin, it is in the grip of evil, it always has been and it always will be.

And not only that, he goes on, as does the whole of the New Testament, to tell us something of the future of this world, and, of course, this is a vital part of our understanding of our relationship to the world. According to the New Testament (and here we get the realism) the world will always be the world; it will never get better. I do not know the future, there may be another period of apparent reform and improvement, but the world will still be 'lying in the evil one', and indeed the New Testament tells us it may 'wax worse and worse' (2 Tim 3:13). Indeed the evil of the world is so essentially a part of it and its life, that its final outlook will be judgment and destruction. You will find this teaching everywhere. The evil in the world cannot be taken out; it is to be destroyed; there is to be an ultimate climax and there will be a terrible end.

Now Christians start with that view of the world; they are not fooled by it, nor misled by it. The result of this is obvious—Christians have an entirely different view of the world from every other kind of person. Let me put it like this. Christians should not be at all surprised at the state of the world. If they are surprised at it, if they have been deluded by the apparent Christianising of the world in the nineteenth century, then they had better examine their Christian doctrine. No, what is happening today is a confirmation of the New Testament teaching; so Christians are not surprised at it; they do not expect anything different, and they are not, therefore, made unhappy by what they see.

Then, lastly, how are we to relate ourselves to all this? That is John's great message. Let me indicate what he does not say. Does he suggest we reform the world, that we set out to try and improve it—patently that is impossible! Does he, on the other hand, suggest that we turn our backs upon it and withdraw from it completely? Again he does not say that. What he does say is that it is the business of Christian men and women in this world first and foremost to make absolutely sure of themselves, that the world does not come in. They maintain their Christian position; then and then only they turn to the world. What do they do for this world? They restrain the evil as far as they can; they believe that that is God's will, so they pray to Him to have pity and mercy upon the world. But when they are praying they always remember that because of the evil of the world it may be God's will to punish it.

So Christians do not pray lightly and loosely on the assumption that if they pray for God to hold His hand then God will do that. No, the

Old Testament has a great message with regard to that. There was a time when God said in effect to His prophets, to Jeremiah and Ezekiel, 'Stop praying for these people. If Daniel and Noah prayed for them, I would not do it.' That does not mean we do not pray, but it does mean that we pray intelligently and thoughtfully. It means that we pray as seeing God's ultimate plan for this world, and that all our prayers are subject to His holy will. The Christian does not pray so much as a member of a country, but as a member of God's kingdom, as one of those unique people. They are of God, they are out of the world in that sense, yet they ask God to have mercy and compassion.

But, thank God, we are not left like that; we are told, and this indeed is the great message of this letter, that though we are in the world that lies in the wicked one, yet we may live with joy, we may be more than conquerors. There are certain simple principles which we must recognise and implement, and though things are as they are, we, with Christians everywhere, may have a full, abounding and complete joy.

2

Full and Lasting Joy

And these things write we unto you, that your joy may be full.

1 John 1:4

In our consideration of chapter 5, verse 19, we found that the real message of John's letter was the statement: 'And we know that we are of God, and the whole world lieth in [under the dominion and power of] wickedness, [or the evil, or the wicked one].' In other words, we must emphasise the fact that this letter has nothing to say to us unless we accept its definition of a Christian. That is the presupposition of all these New Testament letters; they are not written to the world, but to believers, to Christian people.

I emphasise this point because a failure to grasp it often leads to confusion. In the ministry of the Christian Church there are certain divisions which have, of necessity, to be drawn. The Church of God has a message to the world. To the unbelieving world it is an evangelistic message, and one of the great functions of the Church is to preach that message. But that is not her only message, for she has one for people who have been converted. She must build up the believers; she must talk to the saints and establish them in the faith and give them greater knowledge and understanding. Now if I may speak personally at this point, this is a division that I like to observe. I always preach on Sunday mornings on the assumption that those who are listening are Christians; it is a message to the Church and Christian people, and on Sunday nights my concern is to preach an evangelistic message. So that if there are persons present on Sunday mornings who feel that the message has nothing to give them, then I suggest that they should attend on Sunday evenings as well.

I make that point because of an experience I once had. I remember during a visit to Toronto that on my first Sunday morning, in response to a word of welcome, I announced that that was what I considered the right and wise thing to do. I said that I should be speaking in the morning on the assumption that everyone listening was a Christian and that in the evening I should speak on the assumption that people were not Christians, and that they were there to see how they might become Christians. An incident followed which I felt was significant in this respect. There was a lady present who only attended the services at that church on Sunday mornings; she had never been known to attend in the evenings. To the surprise of the minister, when speaking to him and myself as she left the church, she announced that she proposed to come in the evening. When the minister expressed his surprise, she said that she had now understood that she was not a Christian and would therefore come to learn how she might become one.

So, the basic assumption of this great epistle is that it is for Christians, and it is something which we shall have to hold in our mind constantly as we work through its message. As Christian people we are in a gainsaying, evil world. John has some very strong comments to make about the world in this letter. We must remember constantly that it is a very evil place. According to the Bible the whole mind and outlook of the world is opposed to God; it is under the dominion of Satan and in the grip of the wicked one. Christian men and women must realise that they are living in a world like that; that because it is a world that is opposed to God, it will be doing everything it can to drag them down. It will try to fill their minds here with things that will try to satisfy them and thereby keep them from God and Christ. It is a world in which Christians have to fight for their souls; it is easier to go down than to keep straight. 'We are of God, and the whole world lieth in the wicked one.'

But we see that the Apostle avoids certain errors as he goes on to tell us how we must relate ourselves to that. He does not tell us to start by trying to reform and improve the world. That is of course the tragedy, that so often the Church has imagined that that is her function. That has been the great trouble during the past years, since about the middle of the Victorian period when the Church became a kind of institution; when the line between the Church and the world became so vague as to be almost non-existent, and people talked about 'Christianising' society. There is nothing of that in the New Testament.

On the other hand we are not to turn our backs upon the world in the sense that we are to go right out of it. We are not told to become hermits or anchorites. That also has been an error, and it is very interesting, as you take the long story of the Christian Church from the beginning until today, to find how constantly those two extremes have been very prevalent. There have been those who have set out as Christian social reformers, and then there were those who said that was wrong and that the only thing was to go right out of it. That is the basis of monasticism, and the tendency is perhaps to revive that in certain forms.

But the teaching of this letter, as indeed the teaching of the whole of the New Testament, avoids both these errors and extremes; it is not a programme of world improvement, nor is it a programme of world renunciation. No, it gives us a picture of this kind of position in which we find ourselves, with this opposing spiritual force, this spiritual power that is represented by the world. Our fight is with that, and we are taught in this epistle that we can conquer it, we can rise above it, and we can defeat it, in spite of everything that is so true of it. In spite of the dangers that beset us on all sides, we can triumph and prevail; we can be 'more than conquerors'. And that is summed up very perfectly in this verse which we are now considering.

The Apostle now tells us, 'These things write we unto you, that your joy may be full.' That is it. That is what he is out for. He is anxious that these Christian people, to whom he is writing, should have fullness of joy, though they are in the world which lies under the power of the evil one.

Now that is the amazing thing which is offered us and promised us in the New Testament. It is by no means a message confined to this epistle. We see it in Paul's epistle to the Philippians: 'Rejoice in the Lord always; and again I say, Rejoice' (Phil 4:4). Our Lord promised the same thing in John 16:33: 'In the world ye shall have tribulation,' He said. He described the world as an evil place and He forewarned His followers what to expect from it. He said the world 'will hate you as it has hated me', but His great promise was that He would give them this joy that

He Himself possessed. There was to be a period at the Crucifixion and before the Resurrection when they would be unhappy and miserable, 'But,' He said, 'I will see you again and your heart shall rejoice, and your joy no man taketh from you' (Jn 16:22); and 'These things have I spoken unto you . . . that your joy might be full' (Jn 15:11)—the very words that John repeats here.

This is His promise, and again let us remind ourselves that perhaps there is nothing which is more characteristic of the book of the Acts of the Apostles than this very note. There is no more exhilarating book than that; I always regard it as a kind of spiritual convalescent home, a book to which tired Christian people should always go to be really invigorated and built up. If you are feeling tired and therefore in need of a spiritual tonic, go to the book of Acts and there you will find this irrepressible joy that these people had in confirmation of the Lord's promise!

This is something that is very concrete and definite, which we are offered in the whole Bible. We see something of it even in the Old Testament Scriptures, in Isaiah and in the Psalms, for example. Christian people in this world are meant to be full of joy. That is what we are called to, and we are failing in our Christian witness unless we are experiencing and manifesting it.

What, then, is this joy? What does it mean? Well, first of all let me put it negatively. This desire of the Apostle that our joy may be full reminds me of certain things that are not to be true of us; let me note some of them. As Christian people we have no right to be in a state of melancholy or unhappiness because the world is as it is. Now you see where the background becomes so important, so vitally important. Christians are people, as we have seen, who, above all others, take a realistic view of life in this world; indeed, they should know more about it than anybody else.

Christians do not drug themselves; they are not like the people of the world who think that things are better than they are.

The first thing that must be true of Christian people is that they are honest and realistic; they do not look merely on the surface; they look beneath it. They do not always try to minimise their problems and make out that things are not as bad as they appear to be. They are not always clutching at various possibilities which are suddenly going to remove their troubles and problems; they do not buoy themselves up on various hopes. Christians have seen that all that is wrong; their knowledge of the Bible makes them certain; they have discovered that the world is an evil place.

So here is the danger; the danger confronting people who see things like that is to become melancholy and unhappy. It is the danger of saying that this life and this world are so terrible and hopeless, what can one do? Melancholy, morbidity, a sense of hopelessness and despair—many Christian people have fallen into that. But the person who is feeling melancholy is not one who is experiencing the full joy of the Lord.

In the same way we are not just to resign ourselves to the world as it is in its state and condition. The Christian is not in the position of just making the best of a bad life. There are many again who have fallen into that particular error also. They say, 'Yes, we see that we are not to be guilty of melancholy. Very well then, what is to be our position? Have we to make the best of a bad job and say to ourselves, "We are but strangers and pilgrims here," we have to put up with it for a few years, but we will soon be out of it and there it is?' But that is something which is quite incompatible with this New Testament concept of joy. A person who is resigned to conditions is not full of joy; yet we are told that that is what we should be.

In the same way, John is at great pains to emphasise that we should not be afraid; we must not be in a state of fear, because 'perfect love casteth out fear' (1 Jn 4:18). Paul, in writing to Timothy, said, 'For God hath not given us the spirit of fear; but of power, and of love, and of a sound mind' (2 Tim 1:7). Now it is very difficult for Christians not to be fearful in a world like this. They see the forces of evil; they are aware of the evil and the malignity; they are aware of their own weakness and they are afraid of this mighty power. We need not stay too much with these points, but I think that the kind of legalism that often enters into the life of Christian people is due to nothing but that very spirit of fear. I suggest to you that monasticism is finally based on the same spirit. A man says, 'I cannot stand up to these powers. The only thing to do is to run away from them.' And there are many kinds of monasticism in the spiritual world. People set their rules and regulations—you must not do this, but you may do that—and you live within a confined life. That is the spirit of fear, not the spirit of joy, for if we go through life and this world and are afraid of various things, then we are not filled with joy.

Or let me put it like this. The Christian is clearly not a person who practises what we may describe as a false puritanism, and I want to emphasise the word 'false'. We are not, in the words of Milton, to 'scorn delights and live laborious days'. We are not to give the impression that to be a Christian is an unhappy thing. Or, to sum it up finally, we are not to trudge along in this life painfully; it is a very easy thing to fall into these errors in a world that lies in the power of the evil one, but the very terms of John suggest an entire antithesis to all these things I have mentioned.

Let us, then, look at this word a little more closely. What is joy? 'These things write I unto you, that your joy may be full.' I can see what I am not to be, so what is our definition of joy? This is a question which appears to be simple at first, but the moment you consider it, it is extremely difficult. Can you define joy in a phrase or sentence?

Now it seems to me that we can do nothing better than what we find the Apostle Paul doing in 1 Corinthians 13, that great chapter on the theme of love. Why did Paul write it? The answer is, he had to write the whole chapter because he could not tell us in a sentence what love was. So in defining love he tells us that it does not do this, but it does do that; and the trouble with so many of us in these days, as the result of reading newspapers, is that we have developed small minds! No, these things are too big for that; you cannot define love in a phrase. You have to say quite a number of things about it and you find that you have not explained it even then. Paul, then, has given us a whole chapter on his definition of love, so I suggest to you that we shall have to say a number of things in an attempt to define what is meant by joy.

Another thing we must bear in mind, in any definition we may give of New Testament joy, is that we do not go to a dictionary; we go to the New Testament instead. This is something quite particular which cannot be explained; it is a quality which belongs to the Christian life in its essence, so that in our definition of joy we must be very careful that it conforms to what we see in our Lord. The world has never seen anyone who knew joy as our Lord knew it, and yet he was 'a man of sorrows and acquainted with grief'. So our definition of joy must somehow correspond to that.

Or take it in terms of some of His followers. The Apostle Paul was a man who knew a great joy even in prison. It did not matter where he was, it did not desert him, he was still joyful, and yet in our definition we must include this: 'We that are in this tabernacle do groan, being burdened', 'earnestly desiring to be clothed upon with our house which is from heaven' (2 Cor 5:4, 2). So we must bear those things in mind. The dictionary may say that joy is this, that or the other, but we must have a definition which will cover the joy which was experienced by these great exponents of the Christian faith and above all by our Lord Himself.

It is certainly not flippancy, not a sort of brightness which is overdone, not something which cheaply makes people laugh. I emphasise these negatives because we are such creatures of reaction. I think we all dislike heartily that kind of false puritanism to which I have referred, and it is agreed that there probably was a great deal of that in the Victorian era—the kind of people who said you should not lift the blinds on Sunday, for example, and who imposed some horrible regulations upon those who were trying to be Christians and even upon the children. But the tragedy is, that having seen that that was a false representation of Christianity, people have become a little too superficial. They have gone right over to the other extreme and have put on this flippancy, this superficial joyfulness, in order to say, 'I, at any rate, am not like those Victorians.' But we are not meant to be like this either. Let us beware of these things, let us go to the source itself. In other words joy does not mean lightheartedness, nor does it mean a pleasant emotional feeling.

These, then, are the negatives; so what *is* joy? I suggest it is something like this. The joy about which the New Testament speaks is never something direct and immediate. You cannot make yourself joyful in the New Testament sense; it is always produced by something else. It is a state which is the result of the interactions of various forces and factors playing upon the soul.

What do I mean by that? Well, here, I suggest, are elements of joy. Firstly, a state of complete satisfaction. There is no joy unless I am satisfied; if I am dissatisfied in any respect I am not joyful. My intellect, my emotions and my desires must be satisfied and, more than that, they must all be satisfied together and at the same time.

Let me illustrate that. There are certain things in this life and world which can give me intellectual satisfaction. Indeed, I may be perfectly satisfied intellectually, but my heart may be cold, and if that is so, then, even though my mind is satisfied, I am not in a state of joy. It is exactly the same with desires. There are things I can do which will satisfy my desires, but my mind and conscience condemn me; there is pleasure for the time being, but there is not joy. The satisfaction that is a part of joy is a complete satisfaction—mind, heart, emotions and desires; they are all fully satisfied, and full satisfaction is an essential part of joy.

But it does not stop at that; the next element in joy is a spirit of exultation. What would we say, I wonder, if we were asked to define the exact difference between happiness and joy? The difference, I would suggest, is that joy is more positive than happiness. Let me give you a simple illustration. Look at a little child sitting with its toy; there it is playing, and it is perfectly happy. Then suddenly you come along and from your pocket you produce a new present. The child springs to its feet; there is a brightness, a flush which is exultant—and that is the difference between happiness and joy. Joy is more active; the child was perfectly happy before, but now it is joyful; there is this positive spirit of exultation and rejoicing.

But I want to emphasise the third element which again to me is vital to a true conception of joy. I suggest to you that in joy there is always a feeling of power and of strength. That is why I was at pains to ridicule the false notions of joy; there is never anything flabby or superficial about it. Joy is one of the strongest powers in the world. Someone who is in a state of joy is, in a sense, afraid of nothing. When you are truly joyful, you are wound up by some mighty dynamic power; you feel strong, you are lifted up above yourself, you are ready to meet every enemy from every direction and quarter; you smile in the face of them all; you say, 'I defy them, they can never rob me of it.' The joy of the Lord is your strength; it is a strong power, a mighty robust thing.

There, then, is a very inadequate description and definition, and yet I suggest to you that we cannot get much further than these elements. Joy is something very deep and profound, something that affects the whole and entire personality. In other words it comes to this; there is only one thing that can give true joy and that is a contemplation of the Lord Jesus Christ. He satisfies my mind; He satisfies my emotions; He satisfies my every desire. He and His great salvation include the whole personality and nothing less, and in Him I am complete. Joy, in other words, is the response and the reaction of the soul to a knowledge of the Lord Jesus Christ.

And that is what we are to have. But let me emphasise two words— we are to have it to the limit. 'These things write we unto you, that your joy may be *full*.' Those of you who are interested in Greek terminology will know this word means 'filled full', and our joy in this world is to be full in that sense. Though the whole world lies in the wicked one, and though so many perplexing things are true about us and about our circumstances and conditions, our joy is to be filled to the brim, a real fullness without stint and without limit.

Secondly, 'These things write we unto you,' says the Authorised Version, 'that your joy may be full'; but a better translation would be this: 'These things write we unto you, that your joy may *remain* full', not only that it may be, or become, but that it may remain so. You see what he means? Not only while we are together worshipping God and singing His praises, but also should war come, should the atomic bomb descend, should I be thrown into a concentration camp, my joy must remain full. That is why we emphasised strength. I have not truly got the joy of the Lord if it is going to be variable and dependent upon circumstances and accidents and things that may happen to me. No, I say it is a deep, profound, dynamic thing that enables me to stand whatever may be happening to me, whatever may be taking place in the world, because I know Him, because I see Him and because I know that nothing can separate me from Him and from His love.

Christian people, have you got this joy? Do you know it; have you got this deep intellectual satisfaction; are your emotions satisfied to the full; is your every desire finding completion and all it asks for in the Lord Jesus Christ? That is what we are meant to know; that is what we are meant to have, and, thank God, this epistle has been written in order to tell us how to have it and to hold it, and that it may remain in us, come what may.

3

How to Know
the Joy

*And these things write we unto you, that your joy may be
full.*

1 John 1:4

WE SAW AT THE BEGINNING that 1 John is a practical letter. It is not
a theological treatise, nor is it written from a theological or academic
standpoint; it is meant to aid, encourage and establish Christian people.
So we started with a consideration of the need to realise our basic position: that 'we are of God' and that the whole world lies in the power of
the evil one. Then we saw that we should be experiencing a full and
unshakeable joy, and so now the question is, how we are to have this
joy and how we are to retain it. That was the question confronting those
first Christians as it now confronts us, and the Apostle wrote his letter
in order to tell them how this joy that is in them may remain full in spite
of what may happen to them or come to meet them.

Now it seems to me that the right thing for us to do at this particular point, before we come to a detailed analysis of the letter, is to summarise its argument or message. We have seen that on the surface it is
rather a difficult epistle because of its literary form and because of the
characteristic mentality of the writer. But though his method is spiral,
with each circle leading on to the next, there is very clearly a scheme to
be discerned in the letter. He did not write at random; these are not the
mere ramblings of an old man; there is an order, if we will take the trou-

ble to discover it. It is important, therefore, for us to have an analysis of the letter so that when we do come to the details we shall not be lost in them, but shall remember that the details are part of a great principle.

As we come, then, to an analysis of the letter, we come to something that is extremely interesting. It is a notorious fact (and this has always been agreed) that it is practically impossible to find any two men who have ever themselves agreed in their analysis of this particular epistle. There are people who are like gramophone records; they hear a certain commentator's analysis and they repeat it, but any man who thinks for himself generally ends by having his own analysis. It is very interesting to look at these authorities, such as they are, and to notice the various disagreements, but there are, at any rate, certain broad principles of classification which seem to me to give the best clue to the understanding of this epistle.

There is, I suggest, a division of the letter into three main compartments. The first division consists, in general, of the first three chapters; the second division consists of chapters 4 and 5 to the end of verse 12; and from verse 13 to the end of the fifth chapter you have the conclusion.

In the first division, the Apostle is laying down the conditions which are essential before this joy can be obtained and remain in us. In the second division, he then exhorts these people to practise the principles that he has already laid down, and it is at that point, perhaps, that these divisions of mine deviate most of all from most of the others. But at the beginning of chapter 4 he starts appealing to them: 'Beloved, believe not every spirit'; he is exhorting them, and from there on, as I want to show you, he continues with this exhortation. And then, having done that, he proves his conclusions from chapter 5 verse 13 to the end of the letter.

That is the fundamental division, but again that seems to be subdivided in turn. Take this first great section in which he shows us what is essential before we can ever have and hold this joy. That now is divided up like this. The first thing is the absolute centrality of the Lord Jesus Christ. He starts with Him; the first three verses are devoted to a description of Him: 'That which was from the beginning, which we have heard, which we have seen with our eyes, which we have looked upon, and our hands have handled, of the Word of life; (for the life was manifested, and we have seen it, and bear witness, and show unto you that eternal life, which was with the Father, and was manifested unto us;) that which we have seen and heard declare we unto you, that ye also may have fellowship with us: and truly our fellowship is with the Father, and with his Son Jesus Christ. And these things write we unto you, that your joy may be full.'

Yes, but you will never know any joy until you know Christ. He is the source of joy; He is the fount of all blessings; everything comes through Him. So before John begins to discuss anything else, he talks about Him.

Here again we come to the great watershed which divides Christian preaching and teaching from every other teaching; it is based solely on the Lord Jesus Christ. The Christian Church has nothing to say to the world until it believes on Him. Indeed, the Church's message to the world is one of condemnation until it believes on Christ. Christ is central, He is essential, He is the beginning and the end, and John has nothing to say to these people by way of encouragement unless they are absolutely clear about Him. It is through Him that we have access to God; and it is through Him that we have fellowship with God.

So we start with that as a basic postulate, something that we do not even discuss; namely that if Christ is not the only begotten Son of God and our Saviour, in the way the New Testament indicates, then there is no Christian message and no joy and consolation. Then, says John, if you have believed on Him, the next great thing, in order that you may always have fullness of joy in this world, is that you have conscious fellowship with God—abiding in Him and He in us.

Now that is the great theme in this first section. You will never know this joy, says the Apostle, and it certainly will not remain full, unless you have this fellowship. But how is that to be maintained? John proceeds to deal with that from 1:3 to 2:28 and this is how he puts it to us. There are certain things that tend to militate against that fellowship and to rob us of it; there are certain things which will stand between us and that fellowship which in turn leads to joy.

First of all, there is sin—unrighteousness, and we shall see how he divides that up into committed acts of sin, and the refusal to acknowledge or confess sin. Those are the ways in which sin can come between us and a conscious enjoyment of the fellowship with God. John works this out in an extraordinary manner. He has told us about this possibility of great joy; then comes in a word which almost crushes us to the ground at once: 'This then is the message which we have heard of him, and declare unto you, that God is light, and in him is no darkness at all'

(1:5)—and fellowship seems hopeless. But then, thank God, he tells us how it can be dealt with. If we do recognise and confess sin, then there is the blood which cleanses, and God is faithful and just to forgive us our sins (1:7, 9).

The second hindrance which John talks about in chapter 2 verse 3 is the lack of love to the brethren. If there is anything wrong in my relationship to God, I lose the fellowship and I lose the joy. Yes, but if there is anything wrong in my relationship to my Christian brothers and sisters, I also lose the joy and John works it out in a very subtle way. You lose contact with the brethren and you lose contact with God; you lose your love to God in the same way.

The third hindrance is a love of the world, a positive love for the world, a desire after, a hankering after its pleasures and its whole sinful mentality. This again is an interruption to fellowship with God. You cannot mix light and darkness, you cannot mix God and evil; therefore if you love the world you lose fellowship with God and again you lose your joy.

And the last thing which interrupts fellowship with God, he tells us at the end of the second chapter, is false teaching about the person of Jesus Christ. Obviously if the only way to God is through Christ, if I am in any way wrong about my teaching or my doctrine concerning Him, then automatically I sever the communion and again I lose my joy.

Those, then, are the hindrances—but thank God John does not stop at that. In the first section he tells us that there is a great source of comfort and strengthening: the unction of the Holy Ghost, an advocate within us, as well as an advocate with the Father, who opens our eyes to these things and forewarns us and shows us where we can get release and deliverance.

The second great essential to joy in this life and world is a conscious possession of eternal life. The first was a conscious fellowship with God; now it is a conscious possession of the life of God within us. That is the great theme from the end of chapter 2 verse 28 to chapter 3 verse 24. Again, he tells us, there are certain hindrances to this. In a hurried word he tells us something of what this eternal life within us means, and the hindrances to this are exactly the same things as before.

First is sin—a failure to keep the commandments of God will always rob us of our conscious possession of eternal life. When we live the godly life, we have this assurance and this happiness; but if we fall into sin, we begin to doubt and to wonder, and the devil encourages us in this. There is nothing that so upsets our assurance and confidence as sin; the same thing that breaks fellowship with God leads to uncertainty about the divine life within.

Then the second thing is lack of love to the brethren. He tells us exactly once more what this means and he works it out in detail. In effect he says, 'If you do not love your brethren, you will find that when you go to God in prayer, your heart will be condemning you and you will have no confidence in your prayer. It is interrupting your fellowship and communion and you begin to say, "Well, if I do not love these people who are Christians like myself, I wonder if I am a Christian."' A conscious possession of eternal life is essential to Christian joy, and a lack of love to the brethren again robs us of it because it creates these doubts within us.

And then the next thing once more is false teaching about the Lord Jesus Christ. If for a moment you become unhappy about your understanding of Him, if you once have false notions concerning Him, you immediately lose assurance of salvation; you lose this conscious possession of the life of God within you, and that is why John keeps on repeating these things.

So in a sense you have the three same obstacles as you did in the first section, but, thank God, once more he reminds us of the power of the Holy Spirit; 'He that keepeth his commandments dwelleth in him, and he in him. And hereby we know that he abideth in us, by the Spirit which he hath given us' (3:24). Thank God for the possession of the Holy Spirit who, when we are faced by these enemies which get us down, is always there to do His blessed work and will restore us. So that is the first section; those are the conditions which must be observed before we can have this joy.

We then come to the second section in which John exhorts us and appeals to us to practise these things in an active manner. We now have to apply what he has been laying down for us; that is the theme of the epistle from the beginning of chapter 4 to chapter 5 verse 9, and it can be summarised like this. First of all make certain of the spirits—'Beloved, believe not every spirit' (4:1)—make certain that the spirit within you is the Holy Spirit of God; make certain that you are not being fooled by some false spirit; that is the first exhortation.

Secondly, verses 7—21: make certain that you are dwelling in the love of God; that is absolutely essential. Everything you have got, says the Apostle, has come to you because of the love of God; so make certain you are abiding in and practising that love. Then, thirdly, make certain that you are actively keeping His commandments and that you are overcoming the world that is opposed to you—that is the beginning of chapter 5.

And then, fourthly—you find this in chapter 5 verses 5-9—make certain that you hold right views of Jesus Christ and that you are in the right relationship to Him. Be absolutely certain about His person, because if you are not certain about Him, you will have nothing at all.

Then we come to the last main section. If you do all this, says the Apostle, this will be the result—chapter 5 verse 10 to the end—you will have the assurance that you are a child of God. 'He that believeth on the Son of God hath the witness in himself: he that believeth not God hath made him a liar; because he believeth not the record that God gave of his Son' (5:10). You do these things, says the Apostle, and you will have the witness in yourself.

And the next consequence will be that you will have confidence in prayer. 'This is the confidence that we have in him, that if we ask any thing according to his will, he heareth us' (5:14).

The third consequence is that you will have victory and conquest over sin and over the world; and the final result of it all will be that you will know in the very depths of your life and being that you are a child of God. Though the whole world may be rocking around about and beneath your feet, and though hell may be assailing you from every direction, in the confident, quiet knowledge that you are a child of God, you will have a peace of which nothing can rob you.

There, then, in outline, is the argument of the Apostle; that is the way in which we can obtain joy and maintain it in spite of everything. Now you observe that in doing all that, the Apostle is incidentally doing something else. As we work out this great argument, we shall find that, incidentally, we shall be coming face to face with some of the great central, primary doctrines of the Christian faith. Again I must observe that while this letter is not a theological or doctrinal treatise, it is nevertheless full of theology. These Apostles could never write a practical letter without being full of theology.

The New Testament is never concerned just to administer a little comfort to us; that is why we must constantly emphasise at the present time that psychology is often an enemy to the Christian faith. The only comfort is theological comfort, and notice how the Apostle deals with that in the letter. He starts with the great and mighty central doctrine of the Incarnation, but he is not finished with the first chapter, which is a short one with only ten verses, before he has also dealt with the doctrine of the Atonement.

Then he hurries on to the doctrine of regeneration and the rebirth—it is perhaps one of the classic passages and statements on the doctrine of regeneration in the entire Bible. At the same time he is dealing with the doctrine of sanctification—the third chapter has often been a great battleground for rival theories on this doctrine; but at the same time he has been dealing with the doctrine of sin and the doctrine of the devil. There is no clearer statement about the devil, the adversary of our souls, than you find in this epistle, and at the same time he deals with the whole doctrine of the Second Coming and the return of the Lord.

So in a very short compass we find ourselves confronted with the great eternal principles of the Christian faith. It is like a mighty ocean into which one can dive and swim knowing that one will never cross the border with these great absolutes, with these things that can never be moved, these absolutes in the realm of the spirit and the eternal. In a changing world like this which is so shaky and uncertain and where there seems to be no final principle on which you can base your whole view of life, here we are in the midst of the 'immensities and infinities', as Carlyle called them.

That reminds us, therefore, of the all-importance of theology, of an understanding of the teaching of the Bible. God forbid that we should be so interested in the words of the Bible as to miss the Word itself, or that we should be so interested in our analysis that we miss the message. The message is essentially theological and doctrinal, and 'Apart from this doctrine,' says John, 'I have nothing to give you, or to say to you because you will never know this joy unless you yourselves are solidly based upon the foundation of truth.'

That, then, is the great doctrinal language, but there is, however, one piece of background that is really vital to a true understanding of this epistle. John was not only writing positively, he also wrote negatively, because there was difficulty in the early Church at this time—about A.D. 85, you remember, towards the end of the first century. So he wrote to build up these people, yes, but also to warn and safeguard them against the subtle enemy that had appeared, and he deals with it, in a sense, throughout the epistle. A certain false teaching had come into the Christian Church even in these early days. Let no one think that heresy and apostasy are new. These things came into the Church before the end of the first century, and the Apostle speaks of one of the most famous of them, which called itself *Gnosticism.*

This was a sort of admixture of philosophy and mysticism which had become quite popular, and a number of these people had become Gnostics and had brought this into the early Church. They claimed to have special knowledge. They said that they had a unique revelation, that they could enter into some mystic state in which things were revealed to them that had not been revealed to the ordinary person. That is the meaning of Gnosticism—a special knowledge, a peculiar understanding. They said, 'We special people have seen things, we have an understanding which no one else has got.' But it was really nothing but speculation and they speculated in particular with regard to certain doctrines.

This matter is not only dealt with here: it was the whole theme that the Apostle Paul was dealing with in Colossians 2. That is why, at the end of the chapter, he denounced that false asceticism which these people were practising. It was a contradiction of the Christian faith, but some of them had become deluded as a result of this teaching—you find it referred to in the epistle to the Ephesians also. It was, firstly, a false teaching with regard to the person of our Lord, so you see how essential it is to know this in order to understand John's epistle. It was a false teaching with regard to the reality of the Incarnation, and it really denied the doctrine of the God-man.

This is what it said—there were two views. There were those who said that our Lord did not really have a true body, but it was a phantom one. They said that the Word was not made flesh, but the Word, the eternal Son of God, came and put on a sort of phantom body, so that He never really suffered in the flesh on the cross. That was why Paul said, 'In him dwelleth all the fulness of the Godhead bodily' (Col 2:9)—no phantom body but a real one.

Secondly, there were those who said that we must always draw a sharp distinction between the man Jesus and the eternal Christ, and this is how they did it. They said that the eternal Christ came into the man Jesus when He was baptised of John in the Jordan. Then, they said, on

Calvary Christ went out of the man Jesus and the man remained, so that Christ was not crucified; He certainly did not die for our sins, it was the man Jesus who was put to death on the cross.

That was the strange doctrine which was being taught with regard to the person of our Lord. Indeed, the first three or four centuries of the Christian Church were really spent in great councils arguing about the person of Jesus Christ—God-man, God and man—the reality of the Incarnation, and so on. So John deals with it here.

The second trouble about their teaching was that it was a false view of matter and therefore a false view of sin. It taught that matter was essentially evil and that therefore anything that belonged to matter was in and of itself evil. It said that God had not made the world, because the world was obviously evil. So, how did this world come into being? It said that there were a number of emanations from God and that it was one of these emanations that had created the world. They also talked of various angels which came out from God, and that is why Paul denounced angel worship.

Now we must remember these things as we continue in our study of this epistle, but it worked out like this in practice. Regarding matter as evil in and of itself led to two reactions. The first was a sort of monasticism and rigorism which was designed to destroy the flesh. Paul argues against this, and John does the same thing. These people said that we must spend the whole of our lives in mortifying the flesh; the flesh is evil and therefore we must efface it, we must put on a camel-hair shirt, we must mutilate our body, in a sense, because the flesh is evil—monasticism—and this view has continued throughout the centuries.

The second reaction was quite the opposite to that; it was a sort of liberalism. These people talked like this. They said, 'The flesh is evil, but after all the soul is not in the flesh, so it does not matter what the flesh does. Therefore,' they said, 'there is no such thing as sin. I may do something which is wrong, but it does not matter, the flesh will be destroyed in any case and it is my soul which is going on to God.' That is what is sometimes called 'the sin of the Nicolaitans', and that is why John argues with such strength and force and power against this terrible teaching. These doctrines to John were so vital that he calls these teachers 'liars'. He uses some very strong language; he is the Apostle of love, but this view is so damnable, it is so inimical to the best interest of the soul. These men who do not accept the revelation, who claim such unique under-

standing and initiation into the mysteries—they are of the devil, says
John, they are liars and they must be denounced and avoided at all costs.

There is a great tradition that has come down through the ages that
John was one day visiting a public bath, and as he was about to enter
the water he saw one of the most famous of these Gnostic teachers coming out of the bath and he refused to enter—he would not bathe in the
same water as such a man!

Here, then, is the emphasis of this great truth: the absolute centrality of true doctrine, the central importance of being clear in our view of
the Lord Jesus Christ and His work. You cannot make short cuts in the
spiritual life. If you desire to know this joy, if you are anxious to have it
remaining in you whatever may happen in the world around and about
you, there is only one way and that is to confront these great and glorious truths, to believe and to accept them and to avoid every subtle
heresy, anything that would come along and put itself before us as
human reasoning and understanding and philosophy. That is the way,
says John, and thank God, He instructs us. There are certain absolutes—
the Incarnation, the Atonement, regeneration, sanctification, the doctrine of sin and of the devil and the doctrine of the Second Coming. And
as we believe and understand and practise these things in our relationship to God, in our relationship to one another as Christians, and in our
relationship to the world that is outside, the joy will remain in us.
Indeed, it will increase and continue, and at the end we shall find ourselves standing in His holy presence with joy unspeakable and full of
glory.

4

THE APOSTOLIC DECLARATION

That which was from the beginning, which we have heard,
which we have seen with our eyes, which we have looked
upon, and our hands have handled, of the Word of life;
(for the life was manifested, and we have seen it, and bear
witness, and show unto you that eternal life, which was
with the Father, and was manifested unto us;) that which
we have seen and heard declare we unto you, that ye also
may have fellowship with us: and truly our fellowship is
with the Father, and with his Son Jesus Christ.

1 JOHN 1:1-3

WE SHALL NOT DEAL with this entire statement now, but it is essential that we should read it all, especially the third verse, in order that we might have an understanding of the great message that the Apostle has to convey here to these Christian people to whom he is writing. They had their problems; there is nothing new in the difficulties of the world; it is always full of difficulties and problems. Indeed, our central difficulty today, perhaps, is to fail to realise that all our troubles are, in a sense, exactly the same as the troubles of mankind always in the past, and that there is a common origin of all these things. But it is a part of our human conceit to talk about the problems of the twentieth century as if they were different from those of the first century—but they are not, they are exactly the same. There are differences, I admit, in the local or particular manifestation, but it is the cause of the trouble that counts.

In other words, the problem of mankind is similar to the problem of disease in our physical bodies. We may have one disease with a number of symptoms; they may vary very greatly from case to case, but it is not the symptoms that matter, it is the cause of the disease, it is the disease itself. Now that becomes important, because if we are only concerned with symptoms, we shall only be concerned with treating those symptoms and so we shall probably fail to apply the full message of the gospel. And yet the business of the Church is, in the light of these three verses, to proclaim, to announce the gospel of our Lord and Saviour Jesus Christ.

Let me illustrate what I mean. If I listened to the authorities, even in the Church, today I should be giving an address on the importance of the United Nations Association,[1] and how important it is for all of us to join it and to belong to it and to further this work. God forbid that I should say any word of criticism about the work of the United Nations, or the United Nations Association, but it is not the business of Christian preaching to recommend any such proposal for treating the symptoms of the disease. Our concern is to expose the disease itself, the thing that causes the trouble that leads to the necessity of the United Nations Organisation. That is the business of the gospel, not to be spending its time in treating the symptoms but to tell the world about the one and only remedy that can cure the disease which is the cause of all our local and particular troubles.

The first-century Christians, therefore, were face to face with the same thing as we are today. So the question is, what has the New Testament gospel to say to people living in a world like that? And we have already reminded one another of the answer. It is that in such a world and even under such conditions, it is possible for us to have a joy which is unquenchable, which cannot be defeated, which can prevail and triumph under any conditions whatsoever; a joy that can be brim full whatever these conditions and circumstances may chance to be. In other words, the message of the New Testament is one which comes to individual Christians and to groups of Christian people in that sort of world. It does not tell them how the world can be put right, but it does tell them how they can be put right in spite of that world, and how they can triumph in and over it and have that joy in spite of it. As Professor Karlbach of Switzerland has said, 'It is not the business of the Church to try to discover world unity and order but to witness to the finished work of Christ'[2]—and that is precisely what we are now considering together in these verses.

Having then looked briefly at John's analysis of the whole epistle, we now come to look at it more in detail; and we must start, as John compels us to do, with the first three verses.

Here is the message, so let us analyse it by putting it in the form of some simple propositions. The first is that the gospel is a declaration, a manifestation, a showing. '(For the life was manifested, and we have seen it, and bear witness, and show unto you that eternal life, which was with the Father, and was manifested unto us;) that which we have seen and heard declare we unto you, that ye also may have fellowship with us: and truly our fellowship is with the Father, and with his Son Jesus Christ'—we *show* it unto you, says John.

Now he uses two words there which seem to me to bring us to the very heart of this matter. The gospel is an announcement. We can put that negatively by saying that the gospel of Jesus Christ is not a speculation, nor a human thought or idea or philosophy. It is essentially different, and it must never be put into that category. That is the trouble, alas, with so many of us. We will persist in regarding it as an outlook, as something which results from the meditation and thought of man on the whole problem of life and living. That has been the real tragedy of the last century or so, when philosophy took the place of revelation and people said that the Bible is nothing after all but human thoughts, man's ideas, man's search after God—why should modern man equally not have a place in these matters? So we put forward our modern ideas.

But that is not the gospel! The whole position of the Apostles, John and the rest, is that they have something to declare, something to say. They have seen something, they are reporting it, and that something is so wonderful that John can scarcely contain himself. Have you noticed the interesting point that in a sense there is no introduction to the epistle? There are no preliminary salutations and greetings; John does not even say who he is—you have to deduce that from internal evidence. Here is a man who has something amazing to say; he knows these people have to hear it and so, without any introduction, he suddenly plunges them into the heart of the mighty message he has to deliver. There is nothing uncertain about this message, it is a proclamation; there is an urge and an authority behind it.

In passing perhaps we should observe that it is the loss of this very note in the preaching of the Church, in this century in particular, that accounts for so much of the present state of the Church, and the present state of the world and of society. A man standing in a Christian pulpit has no business to say, 'I suggest to you', or 'Shall I put it to you', or 'On the whole I think', or 'I am almost persuaded', or 'The results of research and knowledge and speculation all seem to point in this direction'. No! 'These things *declare* we unto you'. I know that the old charge which has so often been brought up against the Church and her preachers is that we are dogmatic; but the preacher who is not dogmatic is not a preacher in the New Testament sense. We should be modest about our own opinions and careful as to how we voice our own speculations, but here, thank God, we are not in such a realm, we are not concerned about such things. What we do is not to put forward a theory which commends itself to us as a possible explanation of the world and what we can do about it; the whole basis of the New Testament is that here is an announcement, a proclamation—those are New Testament words.

The gospel, according to the New Testament, is a herald; it is like a man with a trumpet who is calling people to listen. There is nothing tentative about what he has to say; something has been delivered unto him, and his business is to repeat it; it is not the business of the messenger, first and foremost, to examine the credentials of the message, he is to deliver it. We are ambassadors, and the business of the ambassador is not to say to the foreign country what he thinks or believes; it is to deliver the message which has been delivered to him by his home government and the King he represents. That is the position of these New Testament preachers, and that is how John puts it here—'I have an amazing thing to reveal,' he says.

Now this applies not only to men who occupy Christian pulpits and have the privilege of doing so, it is something that clearly applies to all Christians. For as we discuss the world, and its present state and condition, with our fellow men and women, we are all of us individually to behave in the same way. We are to announce this, to proclaim it and not merely to put it forward as an ideas amongst others. All the Apostles did this. Read what the Apostle Paul tells the Corinthians about the way in which he came to them: '. . . not with excellency of speech or of wisdom, declaring unto you the testimony of God' (1 Cor 2:1). So the first thing we have to recapture at the present time is that, in the realm of the

Church, we are doing something which is quite unique. It is unlike every other meeting. You have political meetings and people put forward their ideas; they certainly try to persuade us, and there are things they would have us believe. But there is not this finality; there are rival theories and possibilities. But in the realm of the Church we are out of all that, and we are concerned with a declaration and a proclamation.

It seems to me that it is beyond any doubt whatsoever that the present state of the Church is mainly, if not entirely, due to the fact that we ourselves have become uncertain of our message. Christian ministers have become uncertain about the miracles, uncertain about the supernatural, uncertain about the person of Christ. Hesitancy and doubt have come in, and at last this has become true of the common people everywhere, and there is a querying and a doubting. But the uncertainty began with the preaching, and once we cease to declare and to show, we have departed from the New Testament position. That then is the message for the Church herself at a time like this. She must cease to hesitate or to be nervous or uncertain; we are to stand by these things, and if we stand by them we need not consider the question of falling. The world may fall away from the Church, but let it do so, for she will have to listen again to the message; for the message is a proclamation. That is the first principle.

The second principle is that this declaration of the Church comes to us on the authority of the Apostles, and here again is something that is absolutely fundamental. Peter, in his second epistle, says: 'We have not followed cunningly devised fables, when we made known unto you the power and coming of our Lord Jesus Christ, but were eyewitnesses of his majesty' (2 Pet 1:16)—and that is exactly the same thing as John is saying here. Our only authority is the apostolic witness, and our gospel is based upon what they have said. In these three opening verses, John keeps on repeating it. Three times over he talks about having 'seen' it, twice he says, 'we have heard' it, and he also says, we 'have handled' it. Now he emphasises and repeats that because it is the whole foundation of the preaching of the Church, and there is no message apart from it. The message is what the Apostles have seen, what they have witnessed and what they have experienced and shared together.

Now, one of the first things we must recapture is the essential difference between witness and experience. What is our fundamental authority as Christian people? There are large numbers today who would say that it is experience. A man once wrote that he had been listening to a radio discussion between a Christian and a modern scientific humanist. During this discussion the scientific humanist asked the Christian, 'What is your final proof of the reality and the being of God?' 'And,' said the writer of this article, 'the Christian failed badly in my opinion. He tried to produce certain arguments, but he should have turned to the scientific humanist and said, "I am the proof of the being of God."'

But I would have been entirely on the side of the Christian in that argument, for I am not a proof of the being of God, nor is my experience. The only reality of the being of God is the Lord Jesus Christ. Experience is of value in confirming, in supporting, in helping me to believe these things, but I must never base my position upon it. Once I do that, I really have no reply to make to the psychologists who would explain the whole of the Christian faith in terms of psychology. I do not base my position upon my subjective states and moods and conditions which come and go and are so variable and changing. I have something solid, a solid rock. No, I thank God that I base my position upon certain facts in history: 'that which we have heard, that which we have seen with our eyes, which we have looked upon, and our hands have handled, of the Word of life'.

That is the basis, the apostolic witness and the apostolic testimony. If what we have reported in the Bible by those first witnesses and Apostles and others is not true, if their facts are not true, well then, I have no Christian faith, for to be a Christian is not to believe an idea, nor is it to undergo some subjective experience. All sorts of agencies can give experiences. There are many ideas which we can believe and they may do us a lot of good. The world has discovered that there are all sorts of psychological tests which people can apply to themselves. But that is not the Christian position. The Christian position is that we accept and believe this testimony, that these things here reported have happened. We base it solidly upon the authority and the testimony of these men of God.

Now the argument does not stop at that. You can test the witness of these men. There are many supporting arguments, but, basically, it is what they say, and we are shut down to their witness. Take out the apostolic testimony and what do we know about Jesus Christ apart from it? It is there that the whole arrogance of sin is manifested. It is in the higher critical movement of the nineteenth century when men sat down in their studies to reconstruct their 'Jesus of History'. But what do they know about that apart from these documents? For our knowledge we come back to these; it is a testimony that holds together this complete whole view; take parts out of it and it becomes lop-sided. It either has to be taken as it is or rejected *in toto*.

First and foremost, therefore, there is the report and then my experience as the result of believing the report. Thank God, it is supported by experience, but experience can never do anything beyond supporting it. Do not base your life upon your experience, because you may be sadly disillusioned. Base it upon these facts and then your experience will be a true one.

Then we move on from that to the next matter, which is central. The gospel, I repeat, is a declaration, a showing, and it comes to us on the authority of the Apostles; so what is its message? And the answer that we find here is that the essence of its message is Jesus Christ. 'That is our report,' says John. 'Here we are in this difficult and trying world, so what have I to say to you? Well,' he says, 'I have the most amazing and unbelievable thing that a man can ever say and I have nothing else to add. It is this: the Word of life was made flesh and dwelt amongst us.'

'(We beheld His glory, the glory as of the only begotten of the Father,) full of grace and truth' (Jn 1:14). That is how he puts it in his Gospel, and he really says much the same thing here. This is how he puts it: 'That which was from the beginning'— 'In the beginning,' he says in John 1:1; it is the same thing—before time, away in eternity. There was no beginning; it is endless, it is eternal; that is his way of describing it. We are in time, we are limited in our conception, and we cannot understand eternity; so, because of the limitation of time, when we try to describe eternity we have to say, 'in the beginning'; by which we mean there was no beginning. It sounds paradoxical, but there is no better expression of it. 'That which was from the beginning'; that which has always been, which has come out from that endless eternity. That is the first thing and he also puts it another way: 'In the beginning was the Word, and the Word was with God' (Jn 1:1)—with the Father in eternity.

Then the next thing is that this was *manifested*. We have heard, says John, but also 'we have seen', 'we have handled'. Now these terms are all of the greatest interest, there is a kind of order in them. The first thing it says is that we have heard, then we have seen. We may hear a voice and we think we know whose its is, but we cannot be sure until we have seen.

However, it does not stop at that. John seems to repeat himself, but he does not really. He adds to it—'that which we have seen with our eyes, *which we have looked upon*'. You see, there is a difference between seeing and looking upon. Seeing is the result of something confronting us; we are not looking for it, examining carefully. We may be walking along a street and we suddenly become aware of something— we have 'seen' it. 'Ah,' says John, 'we have not only seen. We have looked upon, we have investigated, and not with a mere cursory glance. We watched and we beheld. We looked at him, we sat in amazement, and we really have examined. And, further, our hands have handled of the Word of life.' It is as if John were saying here, 'I once reclined upon His bosom at a feast we all had together before He left us; I handled Him, I touched Him.' Remember the point which we made about Gnosticism and see how John deals with it here. Christ was not a phantom. No, 'the Word was made flesh', 'we have seen, we have beheld, we have examined, we have handled it'. He underlines the reality of it all. It was not a phantom body. The incarnation is a fact—'from the beginning' but here in time.

But he also reminds us that Christ even rose from the dead in that self-same body. Surely that can be the only adequate explanation of these words here—'and our hands have handled of the Word of life.' You remember the other Gnostic idea: how some of them said that the eternal Christ had entered into the man Jesus at His baptism and left Him on the cross so it was only the man Jesus who died. 'No,' says John, 'the one who died was God and man and He rose from the grave in the same body; and we know that because we have handled . . .' You see the difference? We read in Luke's Gospel that our Lord appeared in the body after His resurrection. The disciples would not believe it—they thought He was a spirit—but He said, 'Behold my hands and my feet.' 'We have handled Him,' says John. 'Handle me,' said the risen Christ, 'and see; for a spirit hath not flesh and bones, as ye see me have' (Lk 24:39). He rose in the body; He was the Son of God, and it was the Son of God who rose again. He is God-man, the one person with the two natures.

That, no doubt, was what was in John's mind as he wrote that prologue to his Gospel: 'And we beheld his glory . . .' (Jn 1:14). I think he is referring to the Mount of Transfiguration for one thing. When Jesus was transfigured He appeared in a transcendent glory—'We saw it,' says John, 'and we have never forgotten it. And then there was the glory of the resurrection; we beheld it, looked upon it.'

That is the whole message of the gospel. He leaves eternity and comes into time, and He goes back into eternity. 'The message we have proclaimed to you,' says John in effect, 'is this in its essence: that on the face of this very earth on which you are still living, with its problems and trials and tribulations, on this very earth the Son of God Himself has come. We have had the amazing privilege of seeing Him, of hearing Him, of examining Him and touching Him and listening to Him—God, the Son of God, was amongst us and it has changed everything. I want to tell you about it so that you may share with us, and our sharing is with the Father and His Son Jesus Christ.'

But let me show you also that John's emphasis here is somewhat different from that of his Gospel. In the Gospel, John's main concern was to prove and to show that Jesus of Nazareth is none other than the eternal Son of God—that is its great message. But that is not the main message in this epistle. It is there, which is why he starts with it, as he must, but here he is concerned to show what that means and what it means *to us*. So he puts it like this. He refers to Him as the 'Word of life'; the Word that not only shows life, but gives life. So his emphasis is like this: 'The Son of God,' he says, 'came on earth not only to show us and to reveal to us the life of the Father. He did do that, for in Him the life of God has been manifested and unveiled. We have seen God in the flesh; as He said Himself, "He that hath seen me hath seen the Father" (Jn 14:9)—look at Him and you see that Father, the divine life.

'But it does not stop at that,' says John. 'Thank God, He came not only to reveal that eternal life, but also to impart it, to give it, to make it possible for us.' The Son of God, as John Calvin put it once and for all, became the Son of man that the sinful sons of men might become the sons of God. He is the Word of Life. The life was manifested, we have seen it, John declares, and that is the great theme of the epistle. That is why he starts with the phrase that has often confused people—'That which was from the beginning'—he is referring to Jesus Christ.

In other words, he already has the great idea in his mind, the great idea that there is possible to us in this world of time a divine life, a divine order of life; we can, indeed, possess the life of God. 'That life,' says John, 'was in Christ to all eternity; He has come and revealed and manifested it.' And he is thinking about the life that you and I can receive, and that is his great and glorious message—that you and I can become partakers of the divine nature and sharers of the divine life itself.

That, then, is the message of the Christian Church to this weary, tired and frustrated world. What is going to happen to it? Let the governments do their utmost—it is their business to do so, for God has ordered governments to keep law and order. So let the government produce order and let all Christian people do their best to be law-abiding citizens in this and every other land. But the message of the gospel is to tell us that though all and every attempt at human order may fail, if we believe on the Lord Jesus Christ we have become children of God and citizens of the kingdom of heaven, a kingdom that can never be shaken and that will last world without end.

5

CHRISTIAN
EXPERIENCE

That which we have seen and heard declare we unto you,
that ye also may have fellowship with us: and truly our fel-
lowship is with the Father, and with his Son Jesus Christ.

1 JOHN 1:3

HERE IN THIS VERSE the Apostle makes the first explicit statement in
the letter of what is one of his main objects in writing to these people.
The fundamental reason, as we have seen, is: 'these things write we unto
you that your joy may be full', and his case is that one of the first essentials and absolute essentials to true joy, in a world such as this, is that
we should realise this wondrous, glorious possibility that lies open to us
of fellowship, of communion, of sharing in the life of God.

So now, we come to what is one of the big, basic themes of the entire
epistle. It is, of course, a great theme also of the whole of the New
Testament; indeed it is one of the profoundest, and at the same time perhaps one of the most difficult of all the New Testament themes. It is the
central core of the New Testament message; but for that reason, and
because there is an adversary of our souls, it is one that, right up to our
own day, has frequently been misunderstood and misinterpreted.

There have been, I suppose, more heresies and more errors with
regard to this epistle, and as to what is meant by this fellowship, than
perhaps with any other matter. Therefore we approach it, not with trep-
idation, nor with fear, but with carefulness, realising that there are pit-

falls and dangers all around us. And yet, it is of all truths, perhaps, the most glorious and the most wonderful. All other doctrines, in a sense, lead to this; all other aspects of truth are destined ultimately to bring us face to face with that which we find here.

Now it is a very large subject, and obviously one which no one should even attempt to deal with hurriedly. It has various aspects and first of all I want to deal in particular with one of them. In doing this, I take my line of approach from what is said by the Apostle himself. Here he is, an old man, at the end of his life, and he is writing to these Christians. Some were old, some were middle-aged, and some were young, and you will find that in the next chapter he divides them up like that and makes a special appeal to them—'fathers', 'young men', 'little children', and so on. He knows about their world; he is in it too, and he is a man who himself has suffered a great deal. He knows what they are enduring; he knows the fight in which they are engaged and he wants to help and encourage them—that is his reason for writing. So he immediately begins to tell them that he has an astounding and extraordinary, almost incredible message to give them.

As we have seen, he has declared to them his certainty about the incarnation and the resurrection. And now the next thing he proceeds to deal with and to emphasise is the fact that the whole point and purpose of the coming of the Son of God into the world in that way was to give to those who believe on Him this amazing gift of eternal life. Now 'eternal' not only concerns duration; it does mean that, but it means something else also. Eternal life means life of a certain quality. Life in this world is not only a temporary limited life; actually, as far as death is concerned, it is always, in a sense, a living death. Life outside God is not life, it is existence, for there is a difference between the two.

You remember how our Lord put it in that great high priestly prayer recorded in John 17:3: 'And this is life eternal, that they might know thee the only true God, and Jesus Christ, whom thou hast sent.' Eternal life always carried that suggestion. Apart from God, life, as we call it, is really death; we are all born in trespasses and sin. We exist, yes, but we are spiritually dead. But eternal life is the true life. It is an endless life, but it is, in addition, a life with a different quality; it is really life in a sense that nothing else is. And that, John tells these people, is what has been made possible to all who believe on the Lord Jesus Christ.

But I am particularly anxious, at this point, to emphasise that in the following way. John, you notice, puts it like this: 'That which we have seen and heard declare we unto you, *that ye also may have fellowship with us*.' Now we shall have to go on to consider his further statement that 'our fellowship truly is with the Father and with his Son Jesus Christ', but the first thing that John says, in effect, is, 'I am writing to you in order that you may share the experience that we have had.' He says that he and the other Apostles, as a result of what they have seen and heard and felt and touched and handled, as the result of their belief on the Lord Jesus Christ, have experienced something, and he wants these people now to share in that experience to the full.

Let us, therefore, consider this Christian experience in a preliminary manner. We must examine it in general before we come to see in detail exactly what it is. And perhaps the best way of doing this is to put it in the form of a number of propositions which seem to me to be quite inevitable. What the Apostle says here about himself and his fellow Apostles is, according to the New Testament, something that should be true of every Christian, and these are the things he says.

The first is that Christians are people who know what they have. The Christian experience, in other words, is a definite and a certain experience—'that which we have seen and heard declare we unto you, that ye also may have fellowship with us.' Now if people do not know what they have, how can they wish for others to share it with them? So that is the starting point—that the Christian experience is not a vague one; it is not indefinite or uncertain. Rather, it is a well defined experience, and true Christians know what they have; they are aware of what they possess; they are in no uncertainty themselves as to what has happened to them and as to their personal position. 'We write these things to you,' says John, 'that your joy may be full', and that you may share what we have got, and you cannot invite someone to share something with you unless you know exactly what you are asking him to share.

This is quite elementary and surely needs no demonstration, and yet I am emphasising it and starting with it because of course we are all aware that not only is this not taken for granted, as it should be by Christian people, but that also it has often been a doctrine that has been much questioned and queried.

We are dealing with what may be called the great New Testament doctrine of the assurance of salvation, and it has been one which has been subjected to considerable criticism. People have regarded it as presumption. They have said that this is something which is impossible, and that no one should be able to claim such a thing. How often have we heard about 'the quest for truth' and all the sentimentality that accompanies such talk. People speak of the thrill and the excitement in this quest and Christians are pictured as mountaineers seeking for some great height.

But there is nothing like that in the New Testament—'these things *declare* we unto you.' 'I am writing,' says John, in effect, 'not because I am looking or seeking for truth, but because I have found it. I would not be writing if I had not found it, and I want you to experience the same thing.' He is not seeking or striving, nor is he just hoping. The position of John when he wrote this letter was not: 'Here I am an old man. I am drawing to the end and I had hoped that sometime this side of death the heavens would be rent and I would suddenly have a clear understanding of these things. Perhaps, however, I may have to wait until I have gone through death and awakened in another world; then I shall begin to see and understand these things.'

Not at all! Here is a man who tells us that he *knows*; and it is because he knows and because of what he has experienced that he is writing. Christians are not men and women who are hoping for salvation, but those who have experienced it. They have it; there is no uncertainty; they 'know in whom [they] have believed' (2 Tim 1:12); and it is because John has possessed this that he writes about it.

So this, surely, is something which is quite fundamental and basic. I verily believe that half our troubles in the Christian life, and indeed most of our unhappiness and our failure to share in the experience of these first Christians, is due to this initial prejudice which we seem to have as the result of sin, and by nature, against the doctrine of assurance of salvation. Yet I suggest to you that you cannot read the New Testament without seeing clearly that all these men and women, the ones who wrote and the ones to whom the letters are addressed, are those who, according to this teaching, know for certain. There can be no true joy of salvation while there is a vagueness or an uncertainty or a lack of assurance with respect to what we have.

Now I am not saying that we cannot be Christians without this assurance of salvation, but I am saying that if we want to have the New Testament experience, if we want to be like the saints of the centuries, then we must have it. Thank God, we, by His infinite grace, are in Christ even if we may remain ignorant about these things. Assurance is not essential to salvation, but it is essential to the joy of salvation.

We can support this by making a second statement. Christians are not only people who know what they have; they are also anxious for all others to have and possess it. And that, of course, is the final proof of their certainty of that which they have: 'That which we have seen and heard declare we unto you'—why?— '*that ye also may have fellowship with us.*' John was anxious that these people should have exactly the same thing he and the other Apostles possessed. That is first and foremost the proof of his certainty as to what he has got. But he also indicates that those who have truly had this Christian experience and who have realised it fully, long for all others to have the same thing.

We are dealing with profound matters here, matters which will test us at the very depths of our whole position as Christian people. Surely this needs no argument or demonstration. Those who have become conscious of the fact that they are sharing the life of God—those who know what it is to rejoice and what it is to be emancipated from certain besetting sins which hitherto always got them down—those who can see through life and who have overcome the world—those to whom death has lost its sting and who know at times what it is even to long to go beyond the veil and to be with Christ in glory—men and women who have had some experience of these things of necessity want others to feel the same.

That is why you find so constantly in the pages of the New Testament that this is one of the tests of the Christian. Am I anxious that others should have what I possess? Am I sorry for men and women in the world around and about me who lack this experience? Some of Paul's great verses express this: he says, 'I am debtor both to the Greeks, and to the Barbarians; both to the wise, and to the unwise. So, as much as in me is, I am ready to preach the gospel to you that are at Rome also' (Rom 1:14-15). He says again, 'For the love of Christ constraineth us' (2 Cor 5:14), and 'Woe is unto me, if I preach not the gospel!' (1 Cor 9:16). He said these things because of the transcendent nature of the experience, and he has a sense of pity and compassion for all who lack it. Christians, in other words, are like their Lord and Master. We are told of our Lord that He looked upon the people and saw them as sheep without a shepherd, and He had compassion upon them. And that is the characteristic of these New Testament disciples. They are sorry for those who are walking in darkness.

Christian people, here is the question that comes to us at a time like this. What is our attitude towards men and women around and about us who are not concerned about these things, who are heedless about them? Have we a sense of compassion for them? Do we know what it is to feel that we will do anything we can in order to make them have what we have got? That is the Christian position, so that, by nature, all who are in Christ have this missionary spirit, this desire for others to have and to share with them the thing that they themselves possess; it is inevitable by definition.

The third principle is perhaps still more important. Christian experience in the life of all believers is always essentially the same experience. I regard this as vital for this reason: that it is because of this that we are able to test our Christian experience, and there are those who would say that the whole purpose of this first epistle of John is to do this. A famous commentary on this epistle written by Robert Law bears that very name—*The Tests of Life*.

Now this is a very important subject. Let us look at it like this. The Apostle tells these people that he longs for them to share with him and the other Apostles the experience that they have. In other words we can lay down this fundamental rule: no one can be a Christian without experiencing what the first Apostles experienced. 'We,' says John in effect, 'were eyewitnesses; we saw, we handled, we touched, we heard. He spoke to us, He breathed the Holy Ghost upon us and we received this blessing from Him. Now,' he says, 'we want you all to come and share this joy and experience with us'; it is the same experience.

This is something, I think, which can be established as a fact of history. It has often been said, and rightly so, that every true revival of religion is a return to the first-century religion; every re-awakening that takes place is just a return on the part of the Church to that which is described in the book of the Acts of the Apostles. That is profoundly true, and if you read the histories of revivals, you will find that in a most extraordinary manner. Revivals repeat one another; there is nothing that is more fascinating than to take the outstanding characteristics of the revivals of the different centuries, and you will find that they are always the same. The same kind of phenomena, the same kind of experience, the same kind of results. It is always a return to that primitive experience, the very thing that John tells us here, sharing, participating in his experience and that of the other Apostles.

We can look at it in another way. Take the biographies or autobiographies of some of the most outstanding saints that the Church has ever known; and again you will find absolutely the same thing, this peculiar sameness, this common element. It is one of the most thrilling things, when reading church history, to observe this constantly being repeated. Let me give one example. When Martin Luther, under the influence of the Spirit of God, was brought to his great experience of salvation, there was nothing that so amazed and thrilled him, as he worked out his Christian doctrine, as the fact that he had been rediscovering for himself everything that St. Augustine had said in his writings; while Augustine found that he had been reiterating the things that had been written by the Apostle Paul! And so it has been throughout the centuries.

Let us emphasise this by putting it negatively: the Christian experience does not vary with the individual. Let me be careful to safeguard that by indicating clearly what I mean. It is not that the means of entry into the experience is always exactly the same. Someone sees God in a service; others tell us that in reading their Bible they found Him. That does not matter; I am speaking of the experience itself, not of the way in which we enter it, and I am at pains to emphasise this because it is our final answer to the attack which is made upon the Christian position by psychology.

'Ah,' says the psychologist, 'these things are a matter of temperament, and people differ from case to case in their temperament and psychology.' But the glorious thing about the Christian experience is that whatever their natural psychology, whatever their natural temperament, all Christians experience essentially the same experience as one another. There are variations even amongst the Apostles; some are impulsive, some are logical, some are morbid, and yet the glory is that they all have the same central experience. The Christian faith can make a morbid man rejoice, it can take a natural pessimist and make him rejoice in tribulation. Regardless of individuality or temperament, all can know this same experience; it does not vary from individual to individual, nor does it vary from century to century.

Our central sin in this twentieth century is, of course, to believe that there have never been people like ourselves. We are essentially people of culture and development and how often do modern men and women say, 'The great people in the past used to believe and experience certain things, but we, with our different background and setting, must not go back to those things because we must have something peculiar to this century.' But this experience is quite independent of centuries; it is the eternal entering into time. Examine these Christians in every century and you will find that the experience is the same, and the greatest need of the twentieth century is to have the experience of the first century.

Why do we stress this? Firstly, because this experience is not primarily something subjective; it is, rather, the result of something which is based upon the belief of an objective truth. Merely subjective experience varies from individual to individual, from time to time and from situation to situation; but here is an experience which is common to all Christians because it is based upon an objective truth. 'That which was from the beginning which we have heard, which we have seen with our eyes, which we have looked upon and which our hands have handled of the Word of life.'

John does not say, 'I have had a marvellous experience and so have the other Apostles.' No, rather John says, 'We have seen, we have heard'—it is all something that comes out of Christ. It is based on objective truth; it is a response and a reaction to that, and because it is not primarily subjective, you have this element of sameness.

Secondly, Christian experience is not only based on objective truth, it is always based upon the *same* truth—it is always based upon Christ, it always emanates from Him. You see, John puts Christ at the beginning; everything is related to Him, and because it is always an experience which results from the same truth, it must be essentially the same experience; the same cause leads to the same effect.

To put it another way, the Christian experience is based upon the receiving of eternal life; God is the giver of eternal life in Christ—the same giver, the same gift and, therefore, the same experience. Now if our Christian experience were based upon our understanding or upon our activities or our efforts, obviously it would differ from case to case. The intelligent and the unintelligent person would not have the same experience; but the glory of this position is that we all receive salvation as a free gift from God. It is the same gift of life, and because it is the same giver and the same gift it must be essentially the same experience.

So if all that is true—and indeed it is profoundly so—then the experience which we have is one which can be tested and examined. Now we shall have to revert to this many times in working through the epistle. John is concerned about testing experience. You will find that later on where he exhorts these people to prove the spirits and to test them.

This is because, as we have seen, there were Gnostics in the early Church and a further part of their teaching was this. They said, 'We have had an experience, with marvellous visions, but you must not question or examine it.' They regarded it as a secret which must be neither questioned nor examined. There are still people like that. They say, 'I am not interested in your doctrine or in your theology and dogma. I have experienced something; something has happened to me, so I must not be examined, because it is very secret.'

But that, according to the New Testament, is the height of error, because this experience which the Christian has is, as we have just seen, always a repetition of the apostolic experience, because it is always based upon the same truth and is the result of the same gift from the same giver. It is an experience that we can test, we can ask it questions, and that is the only way to safeguard ourselves against the false mysticisms and the false teaching which would masquerade as true Christian teaching, but in reality is nothing but something psychological or perhaps even psychic.

And this is as relevant in this modern world as it was in the first century. There are teachers today claiming to know about a 'higher Christian life' for those of us who are but ordinary, average church members. They would have us listen to their teaching, and they tell us that their teaching is something that has come to them because of some wonderful experience they have had. They say no one else can understand it, but they have experienced it. Now this is not what the Apostle is emphasising. His experience is one that is based upon objective truth and teaching. It can be tested, it can be examined; indeed I go further and say it *must* be tested, it must be examined, for there are seducers, there are anti-Christs and there are evil spirits. So test the spirits, prove the spirits, 'prove all things; hold fast that which is good' (1 Thess 5:21). So that far from resenting an examination of our experiences, if we are truly Christian, we will welcome an examination and we will rejoice in it.

And the test of course is none other than that of the Word itself. Here is the test—the apostolic record, the apostolic witness, the apostolic testimony. If my experience does not tally with the New Testament, it is not the Christian experience. It may be wonderful, it may be thrilling, I may have seen visions. But, I say, it matters not at all; if my experience does not tally with this, it is not the Christian experience. How vital it is, therefore, to grasp this central truth.

Lastly, the experience is one which is possible for all. 'That which we have seen and heard declare we unto you, that ye also may have fellowship with us.' Thank God this is an experience, not only for the Apostles because they were with Christ, it is equally possible for us. We must all grasp this. Have we not often felt something like this: 'If only I could have been there when Christ was here in the flesh; if only I could have looked into His eyes and seen and heard Him, why, it would be so much easier to believe!'

But that is an utter fallacy—'What we have seen we declare unto you,' says John. 'The experience is as possible for you as it is for us. You have never seen Him; we saw Him, but you can have the same experience.' So it was not only for the first Apostles but for us also. Never discount the writings of Paul, John and Peter therefore, and say, 'That was all right for them, but it is not meant for me.' It is meant for all; it is meant for us.

Furthermore, it is not only for people with a certain temperament, for those who are said to have a 'religious temperament'; it is for everyone because the sameness of the experience, as we have seen, is due to the sameness of the Giver and of the gift. It is possible to all of us, because it is not in any way based upon us but entirely upon Him and upon His grace and upon His desire and His readiness to give.

Finally, what is the experience? The experience is fellowship 'with the Father and with His Son, Jesus Christ'. To know God! We saw at the beginning that the Christian knows what he has got. So that is the question. Do you know God? And has this knowledge of God given you something in your life that makes you long for others to share it with you? Do you understand the experience outlined in the New Testament? Do you say, as you read it, 'Yes, I know that; I know what it means when he talks of a "new man" and an "old man". I know what he means when he talks about being lifted up above myself and having a knowledge of things unseen, and I know the influence of the Holy Spirit.' This is an experience which is concrete and which can be tested and examined, and it makes us participants of that of which these Apostles wrote so gloriously in the New Testament epistles.

May God give us grace to examine ourselves in the light of these truths. This wonderful experience never varies; it is always essentially the same. Let us make certain that we are sharers in the apostolic experience of a knowledge of God and of receiving eternal life through Him.

6

ALL BECAUSE OF
CHRIST

*That which we have seen and heard declare we unto you,
that ye also may have fellowship with us: and truly our fellowship is with the Father, and with his Son Jesus Christ.*

1 JOHN 1:3

AS MEN AND WOMEN look at the world in which they live, with its
wars, its vicissitudes, its false hopes and all its suffering, those who are
not content with observing these things merely on a superficial level, and
who have any true interest or concern, are bound to ask the questions:
What is the trouble; what is the difficulty; why is the world as it is?

And it is just at that point, of course, that as Christian people we
have something very special and vital to say; it is just there in a sense
that the Christian gospel comes in. And surely, if we as individual
Christians are called upon to do one thing more than any other at the
present time, it is to proclaim the word of the gospel; it is to speak the
word of God in that situation and just in that very connection. That is
the point where the world comes to an end in its thinking; it is baffled,
it does not understand; all its prophecies have been falsified, all its confident hopes have been dashed to the ground, and the world is thus
undoubtedly bewildered.

And if it is just there that we as Christians come in, it is also especially at that point that the message of this first epistle of John comes in
with its specific message. As we have already seen, Christians are not sur-

prised at the state of the world; indeed it is a strange confirmation of their attitude towards life and towards the whole history of the world; for they start, as we have been reminded in our study of this epistle, with the fundamental postulate that 'the whole world lieth in the wicked one'.

Here again, you see, we have one of those illustrations of what the Psalmist meant when he said so perfectly, 'Surely, the wrath of man shall praise thee' (Ps 76:10); and the wrath of man praises God, amongst other things, in that particular way; the very wrath of man that produces a world such as this is a world which is proving the contention of the Bible, that the world is in the power of 'the god of this world', 'the prince of the power of the air'—these various titles which are ascribed to that malign evil power that has set itself in rebellion against God.

Christians, therefore, are not surprised. They understand; they know that there is a radical evil in life as the result of sin and the Fall, and that while that remains there can be nothing in the world except what we have experienced. So they are saved at once from becoming excited about the various false hopes, and they are also saved from the cynicism of this period. This twentieth century is a great reaction from the nineteenth, which was so full of its confident hopes and expectations. Now we are experiencing the reaction, and the average person has become cynical and unconcerned. The philosophy of today is, 'What is the use of anything, the whole world seems to be mad, therefore let us make the best of a bad job.'

Now the Christian is saved from all that immediately, but, thank God, it does not stop at that, it is not merely something negative. The gospel of Jesus Christ gives us a satisfactory explanation of why the world is as it is, and it puts it like this in its essence. It says that all the trouble is due to man's rebellion against God, and to nothing else. We are delivered from the waste of time of trying to analyse political theories. Wars cannot be explained in those terms. You cannot explain wars merely in terms of men like Hitler and others, or of the aggression of one particular nation.[1] Political, economic and social ideas and theories are finally quite inadequate, and with our Christian insight we see things; we know that the explanation is something which is very much deeper. These other things are but the manifestations, for the radical cause of the trouble is that men and women, in their folly, are in a state of rebellion against God.

This is the very essence of the biblical message, that man and woman, placed by God in a state of paradise and perfection, felt that even paradise was an insult to them because there was subjection to God. It was that original act of rebellion that led to all their other troubles—that is the story of the Bible. This initial act of rebellion produced fear in them; once they knew they had done something they should not have done, that caused them to look at each other with jealously and envy. Then the children came, and they were envious and jealous and so on; sorrow came after sorrow. And it can all be traced back to the fact that men and women were really meant to live a life in communion with God, and that happiness, in a full and final sense, is only really possible when they obey the law of their own being; and that as long as they refuse to do that, they can experience nothing but turmoil and unhappiness and wretchedness.

This, says the Bible, is the state of the world away from God. It rebels against God and therefore produces its own miseries. It does not argue about that, it just tells us, and the whole state of the world is just a proof of that. It is no use, says the Bible; you can do what you like, you can organise and scheme as much as you like, but while men and women are in a wrong relationship to God, they can never be better. As Augustine put it: 'Thou hast made us for Thyself, and our souls are restless until they find their rest in Thee.' That is the trouble with the individual and with groups and with society and with nations and thus, ultimately, with the whole world. So, because of sin we are in a world like this, and the world is like this because of sin.

So the questions arise: Is there any hope for us? Can anything be done for us? What is the message of the Christian Church to a world like ours, what has she to say? Here, of course, we come again to the vital question especially for the Church and for the preachers of the Church. Is it the business of Church to try to analyse the situation by putting forward proposals? Is she to throw out suggestions to the statesmen and 'the powers that be' as to how they should order the society of the world? Is she to make application for the adoption of certain Christian principles?

Now, as I understand the Bible, all that is a pure waste of time! Again I suggest that history substantiates and proves my position. The Church has been doing that for many years; she has turned to what has been called the 'social gospel', and we have constantly heard about 'the social application of the gospel'. General statements are made about life; addresses are delivered by archbishops and they are all always recorded in the Press; but still the situation continues. And according to the Bible it must continue. What right have we to expect Christian behaviour from a world that does not believe in Christ? Why should the world apply Christian principles? Does it believe in Christ, does it acknowledge Him to be who He is? Does it accept Him as Saviour?

Indeed, I do not hesitate to say that according to the New Testament it is rank heresy to recommend Christian behaviour to people who are not Christian. They are incapable of it! Before people can live the Christian life they must be made a new creation; if they cannot keep the moral law and the Ten Commandments, the ancient law given to the Children of Israel, how can they live according to the Sermon on the Mount? How can they follow Christ? It is ridiculous! That is not our message; that is not what the Church must say.

No, the Church must address individuals, and her address to them is something like this. It is not for the Church to prophesy what the future is going to be because we do not know. But we do know that whatever the Church may say in the form of these vague generalities it will make no difference. The New Testament, however, comes to me as an individual and says, 'That is the story of the world you are in. If you expect it suddenly to turn over a new leaf, to become perfect and to live the Sermon on the Mount, then your theology is all wrong. In a world that lies under the power of the evil one you can expect nothing but evil and wars.'

'Oh, how depressing,' says someone. But facts can be depressing; and whether they are depressing or not, the business of the wise man and woman is to face those facts. The New Testament is realistic, and it does not hold out hope of a glorious future in terms of the human race and its actions. Rather, it paints a very solemn picture. But it does not stop at that. It comes to us and says, 'In such a world what is possible for you? What is there that you can hold on to? Is there a message that comes to you in such a world, which is going to transform everything for you?' And the answer is, 'Here is the message', and that is the essence of what John immediately plunges into at the commencement of his epistle.

The cause of our troubles, as we have seen, is that we have rebelled against God. We are in the wrong relationship to Him, and we have lost the fact of God. We no longer know Him; we are out of communion and fellowship with Him. That is our trouble, and we have been so made by God that there is something within us that can never be at rest until we get back to that. There is always something lacking until we know God.

The supreme need of the world, and of people as individuals, is a knowledge of God, fellowship with Him and communion with Him, and that, says the Bible, is the central need. We can never be in communion with others until we are in true communion with God. The Apostle Paul says this in Ephesians 2. 'You have been made one,' says Paul, referring to Jews and Gentiles, 'because you have both been put right with God in Christ. The middle wall of partition has been broken down' (Eph 2:11-22).

So man rises against man and nation against nation because each one does not recognise God, and the only way to reconcile man with man is that both should be reconciled to God. The supreme need for every one of us is to know God, to return to that condition of fellowship and communion, to know that centrally I am right with Him. 'That,' says John in effect, 'is the message I have to give you, and it is a glorious one'; that is why he pours it forth without any introduction whatever. 'Because of what has happened,' says John, 'because of the coming of Christ who is the Son of God and the substance of the eternal substance; because of Him and His coming and of what He has done, it is possible for you to be in fellowship with God'—'our fellowship is with the Father and with his Son, Jesus Christ.'

Now there are those who would say that this verse should be read like this—'our fellowship is with the Father, by means of and through His Son, Jesus Christ.' I believe that both ways of looking at the verse are correct; we have fellowship with the Father and with the Son separately, and undoubtedly the great message of the New Testament is that fellowship with the Father is now possible in and through the Son, our Lord and Saviour Jesus Christ. So the question I want to consider now is: how has Jesus Christ made this fellowship with the Father possible? What has He done? In other words, we look back at Him. 'We declare,' says John; 'we remember Him.' Every act of preaching is in a sense nothing but a reminder of Jesus Christ and what He came to do. That is the meaning of the Communion Service also, with the bread and the wine; He told his disciples to remember Him. The whole witness of the Church is a witness to Him, and our business in this world is to tell men and women to remember Jesus Christ, to turn back and look at Him. So thus you see we are raised from the human to the divine level.

What, then, is the basic element of this fellowship? How can we be reconciled to God and have communion with Him; how can we have fellowship with others? In what sense is any sort of peace possible amongst people in a world like this? Well, according to John, it is all something that is based upon our Lord Jesus Christ. It is He who has made it possible.

There are certain things that are essential before you can have fellowship. Firstly, there must be no obstacles or barriers, for if there is anything like that between two persons, there is no true fellowship. If there is suspicion or distrust, if there is a question or query as to motive or whether we can trust one another; if there is a grudge, if there is something that has been done and has wounded or hurt the other, fellowship is immediately impossible. Fellowship demands and insists upon the removal of every barrier and every obstacle, anything that is doubtful or uncertain or that can come between. That is essential before there can be true fellowship, and it is in the light of that that we begin to understand the work of our Lord and Saviour Jesus Christ.

Why is man outside the life of God? The answer of the Bible is that there is a mighty obstacle between God and man, and that obstacle is called sin. Sin came in between man and God. It can be regarded as a terrible cloud of blackness and darkness. Before the cloud man looked into the face of God, but the cloud of sin came in and there it remains. This must be regarded from two aspects, of course. Sin keeps a barrier between God and us, for God is holy and God cannot look lightly upon sin. God had warned man that if he sinned he should die. He told him that if he went where he had been forbidden, he would merit punishment, and the punishment would be nothing but death, spiritual death as well as physical. And spiritual death means the loss of the face of God and communion with Him. Man sinned, and the wrath of God came in. So there is a barrier between God and man.

And that, on the other side, brings in a barrier between man and God in this way, that man with his guilty conscience feels that God is unfair. A disobedient child always begins to dislike the parent. Guilt always has that effect; it always attempts to excuse itself and to put the blame on to the other person. So men and women, in sin and in a state of guilt, begin to have unfair and unworthy thoughts against God. We say that there should not be such laws and, further, that there should never be punishment, even if there are such laws. So we argue and put up this barrier between ourselves and God. We cannot see Him because our guilty thoughts have come between us and Him. There is no friendship and trust; there is an obstacle between God and man in that way. 'The thrilling thing I have to tell you,' says John to these people, 'is that as the result of the coming into this world of Jesus of Nazareth, who is the only begotten Son of God, and as the result of what He has done, I declare unto you that we have fellowship with the Father; the very thing we lost has been restored!'

How then has it been restored? Firstly, He has dealt with the obstacle and barrier of sin—that is why we 'declare the Lord's death till He come'; that is why the Cross must ever be at the centre of Christian preaching. I cannot face God apart from the Cross. That is why the 'mystic' way apart from the Cross is a delusion and a snare; that is why also good works and our good resolutions are something again which lead us astray—the barrier has to be dealt with. The justice and righteousness of the holy God demand that sin should be punished; God cannot say a thing and then withdraw it; God cannot speak and then deny it, and He has said that sinners must be punished. God's law and God's word remain absolute—they cannot be avoided. But Christ has come into the world, and by His infinite act of surrender and consecration He has offered Himself to the Father and called upon the Father to lay upon His holy body, His holy life, the sins of the world. As John says in the next chapter, 'He is the propitiation for our sins: and not for ours only, but also for the sins of the whole world' (1 Jn 2:2). 'The Lord hath laid on him the iniquity of us all' (Is 53:6).

You may not understand it, no one can, but it is the essence of the biblical message. God has done this astounding thing. He has punished your sin and mine there in Christ; our guilt has been removed; that obstacle, that barrier, has been taken away. God is satisfied; His wrath has been manifested upon the head of His only begotten innocent Son. The wrath of God because of sin is already revealed from heaven, says the Apostle Paul in writing to the Romans (Rom 1:18). God revealed His law, but this is the further revelation. It has now been revealed from heaven that God's wrath manifested itself to the full upon the head of Christ who died guiltless and innocent for our sins; and thereby the obstacle has been removed.

In the same way, the moment we come to see that, the other aspect of the obstacle of sin is likewise dealt with; once we look at that cross and realise what happened there, our thoughts of God are entirely changed. We now see that God is a God of love, a God whose love is so amazing and divine that He even brings that to pass. Once we see God truly and Christ dying innocently on the cross for us, then at once we see that God is a God of love. So the obstacle has been taken from the other side also. In Christ there is no obstacle or barrier any longer; friendship has been restored; the enmity, as Paul puts it, has been removed and has been banished. That is the first essential.

The second is that before you can have true fellowship and communion there must be likeness, a fundamental sameness. This is another great theme of the Bible, and it is something we can also prove apart from the Bible. There are many people in this life whom we know, and in a sense we may like them; yet we feel we have no fellowship with them. There is something dissimilar; there is no identity of interests—we have not got this fundamental sameness. Before there can be true fellowship and communion there must be a likeness of nature. Paul has put this once and for ever in 2 Corinthians 6:14 when he says that there can be no fellowship between righteousness and unrighteousness, no communion between light and darkness. There are certain things in this world that cannot mix.

Now that applies to men and women in their relationship to God; before they can really know God and have fellowship and communion with Him they must be like Him. That is an astounding statement, yet it is the very language of the New Testament. The New Testament says that a man can never really know God until he has himself God's own nature, and that is precisely the claim of the Apostle John at this point. 'Our fellowship is with the Father, and with his Son Jesus Christ.' He is going to tell us how we have become 'sons of God', or, as Peter puts it, how we can become 'partakers of the divine nature' (2 Pet 1:4). It is Christ alone who makes that possible to us. John says that in Christ the eternal life was manifested (1 Jn 1:2), but He did not stop at that; He came to give us life. 'I am come,' He said, 'that they might have life, and that they might have it more abundantly' (Jn 10:10). 'Whoso eateth my flesh, and drinketh my blood,' He also said, 'hath eternal life' (Jn 6:54). 'I am that living bread which came down from heaven' (Jn 6:51); 'I am that living manna, that heavenly manna,' He said, 'you must eat and take of Me, and as you do so, you will receive life.'

So before we can have true fellowship with God we must have the nature of God; we must share His life, and in Christ that is made possible to us. We must not think of our Christian life merely as something which produces a doctrine of forgiveness—thank God we are forgiven, that must come first—but I cannot have fellowship with God before I am like Him, and in Christ I can receive a new life, a new nature. I can be born again, I can become 'a new man', and I can say with Paul, 'I live; yet not I, but Christ liveth in me' (Gal 2:20).

And, thirdly and lastly, we must love the same things. We must love one another, there must be no suspicion, there must be a complete understanding, there must be complete confidence and complete trust. Men and women apart from Christ may believe in God as a great power, or as Creator; they may believe in Him as the one who controls everything. We can have such philosophical notions and conceptions of God, but there is no fellowship without love, and it is only as we see Him in the Lord Jesus Christ that we truly come to love Him. 'God commendeth his love toward us in that while we were yet sinners, Christ died for us' (Rom 5:8), and no one ever has loved or can truly love Him until they see Him there in the person of His only begotten Son. God so loved, even unto death, that we guilty sinners might live.

There, says John, is the message I have for you in a world which is as it is because it is not in fellowship with God; a world which is unhappy and miserable and wretched and has its wars and all these things because it is out of communion with Him. The message is that even in a world like that, you can be restored to communion; the guilt of your sin has been removed, the image has been restored, and love for God has been created. And having this fellowship, we can experience what the Lord Jesus Christ Himself experienced. For we are told by the author of the epistle to the Hebrews that He, 'for the joy that was set before him endured the cross, despising the shame' (Heb 12:2). There may be troubles for us, in many ways the cross may come to us, but because of the communion He had with the Father, He was able even to go to the cruel, shameful death of the cross with joy in His heart and was able to despise the shame. And that is the offer of the gospel to all who believe on the Lord Jesus Christ. With this communion and fellowship we may smile, we may carry the cross, we may have perfect joy, though 'the whole world lieth in the wicked one'.

The ultimate question therefore is, do we have this joy of the Lord in spite of what may happen, in spite of grief and sorrow, in spite of uncertainty? Do we have this priceless possession which is offered us in the Lord Jesus Christ?

7

KNOWING GOD

And truly our fellowship is with the Father, and with his Son Jesus Christ.

1 JOHN 1:3

I AM READY TO ADMIT that I approach a statement like this with fear and trembling. It is one of those statements concerning which a man feels that the injunction given to Moses of old at the burning bush is highly appropriate: 'Put off thy shoes from off thy feet; for the place whereon thou standest is holy ground' (Ex 3:5). Here we are given, without any hesitation, a description, the *summum bonum,* of the Christian life; here, indeed, is the whole object, the ultimate, the goal of all Christian experience and all Christian endeavour. This, beyond any question, is the central message of the Christian gospel and of the Christian faith.

The Apostle reminds us of that by this emphatic and vital word *truly*—certainly, beyond a doubt. The word means that, but also something else; it carries in it a suggestion of astonishment. There is no doubt about it and yet the more we realise how true it is, the more amazed we become. It is an amazement of incredulity, one borne of a realisation of something which is a fact certainly, yet astoundingly; to the natural man, incredible, but to the Christian true, yet amazing. 'Truly, our fellowship is with the Father, and with his Son Jesus Christ.' Here, let me repeat, is the very acme of Christian experience and at the same time it is a goal; it is the whole object of Christian experience and of Christian faith and teaching.

Now I am tempted to put this matter in the form of a question. I wonder, as we examine ourselves and our experience, whether we all can say honestly that this is our central conception of the Christian life; whether this is our habitual way of thinking of it and of all that it means and all it represents. Surely as we read a statement like this we must be conscious of utter unworthiness and of failure. However far we may have advanced in the Christian life and experience, as we meet this statement, which John thus introduces without any preamble, do we not find that we are in danger of dwelling on the lower level and of failing to avail ourselves of that which is offered to us in this wondrous faith about which we are concerned?

Let me put it negatively like this: Christians are not simply people who are primarily concerned about the application of Christian principles and Christian teaching in all their relationships and departments of life. They are concerned about that, but that is not the thing that truly makes them Christian. How easy it is today to think of Christianity like that, and how many people do so.

Take a popular classification of a Christian and a non-Christian. Christian people are those who are concerned with the ethics and the teaching of the New Testament and who see the desperate need of applying them to the world today. Now I grant that that is part of the Christian life, but if our conception of it stops at that, we have not, in a sense, got anywhere near the definition given by the Apostle here. No, the Christian life is not essentially an application of teaching; it is a fellowship, a communion with God Himself and nothing less.

Or let me even put it like this: To be a Christian does not merely mean that you hold orthodox opinions on Christian teaching. I put it like that because I think that this is another important emphasis. Perhaps to some of us, and particularly perhaps to those of us who are more evangelical than others, this is the greatest danger of all. We recognise at once that there are certain people who call themselves Christian who hold views that are the antithesis of the Christian faith. There are people calling themselves Christian who deny the unique deity of Christ; to us they cannot be Christian. There are certain things, we say, which are absolutely essential and there can be no parleying or discussion about them. They are essential to the faith, there is an irreducible minimum, but there are people calling themselves Christian who deny some of these things, indeed perhaps all of them together. They may even hold office in the Christian Church and yet be uncertain about the person of the

Lord, denying His miracles, denying the fact of His resurrection, denying the atoning value of His death.

Now to us that is quite clear. We see that someone like that, whatever he may call himself, cannot, according to the New Testament, be a Christian; there are certain things which Christians must believe; there are certain tenets to which they must subscribe; there are certain definitions which they must make their own and about which they say, 'I am certain.' We see that orthodoxy is essential, but my point here, and I am anxious to impress and stress this, is that to hold the right views, to subscribe to the right doctrine, even to be defenders of the right doctrine, does not of necessity make people Christians. No, while the Christian must hold right views and doctrines, that is not the essence of the Christian life and Christian position. Rather, it is to have fellowship with the Father and with His Son, Jesus Christ.

Let me even put it like this: To believe that your sins are forgiven by the death of Christ is not enough. Even to be sound on the whole doctrine of justification by faith only—the great watchword of the Protestant Reformation—that is not enough. That can be held as an intellectual opinion, and if people merely hold on to a number of orthodox opinions, they are not, I repeat, in the truly Christian position. The essence of the Christian position and of the Christian life is that we should be able to say, 'Truly my fellowship is with the Father, and with His Son Jesus Christ.'

That, therefore, is why we should always approach a statement like this with fear and trembling. There have been people in the Church, alas, many times in the past, who have fought for orthodoxy and who have been defenders of the faith and yet they have sometimes found themselves on their deathbeds coming to the realisation that they have never known God. They have only held opinions; they have only fought for certain articles of creed or faith. The things they fought for were right, but, alas, it is possible to stop at that negative position and to fail to realise that the whole object of all the things they claim to believe is to bring them to this central position.

This, let me emphasise again, is the essence, the *summum bonum*, of the Christian life; it is the theme, the objective of everything that has been done by the Lord Jesus Christ, who did not come to earth merely to give us an exalted teaching which we can apply to human relationships, though that is there and it follows; He did not come merely to save us from hell; He came to bring us into fellowship with the Father and with Himself.

This brings us directly face to face with the great question: what then does fellowship mean, what does it represent? 'If this is the great and central thing,' says someone, 'what do you mean by it?' Here again we come to a subject which has often been the cause of controversy. It has led to a good deal of dispute in the long history of the Christian Church, and especially, perhaps, when you come to consider the questions of how it is that one arrives in this state of fellowship and of how one can maintain it. We shall be considering these things later, but let us start now by looking directly at what is meant by this fellowship. We talk about the Christian as being one who has fellowship with God the Father and with God the Son, our Lord Jesus Christ, but what exactly does it mean?

Well, as one understands Scripture and its teaching, it seems to me there are two things at any rate which are true in this connection. The very word that the Apostle uses is an interesting one, this word *fellowship*. Those who are interested in words will know that this word has many different meanings. But a problem like this is not to be faced primarily theoretically. Dictionaries do not provide the answer. No, you have to take a word like this in the light of everything we are told about fellowship with God in the whole of the teaching of the Bible, and there are two things that stand out.

Firstly, to be in a state of fellowship means that we share in things; we are partakers, or, if you like, partners—that idea is there intrinsically in the word. That means something like this: The Christian is one who has become a sharer in the life of God. Now that is staggering and astounding language, but the Bible teaches us that; the New Testament offers us that, and nothing less than that.

Peter writes, 'Whereby are given unto us exceeding great and precious promises; that by these ye might be partakers of the divine nature, having escaped the corruption that is in the world through lust' (2 Pet 1:4). That is it, and there are many other similar statements. Indeed, the whole doctrine of regeneration and rebirth leads to this; born again, born from above, born of the Spirit—all carry exactly the same idea. This, then, is what John is so anxious to impress upon the minds of his readers; that Christians are not merely people who are a little bit better than they once were and who have just added certain things to their lives. Rather they are men and women who have received the divine life.

Now it is just there that the danger tends to come in. 'Is it something physical?' asks someone. 'Does it mean that a kind of divine essence comes into one?' There, you see, you have the whole host of teaching which has come in. The Roman Catholic Church would say that yes, this is something material, and that is why the sacraments are essential. In the application of the water which has been consecrated, the divine life is given to that child, and then as you partake of the mass and receive the host into your mouth, you are literally receiving something of the divine nature and essence. There we have to be careful, and it seems to me that the essence of wisdom at this point is that we should be careful not to go beyond the plain teaching of Scripture. How tempting it is to speculate, to philosophise, to try to work out in our own earthly categories that somehow or another some portion of the divine substance or essence enters into us.

There is only one safe thing to do and say and that is that we do not know; but in some amazing and astounding manner we know that we are partakers of the divine nature, that the being of God has somehow entered into us. I cannot tell you how, I cannot find it in the dissecting room. It is no use dissecting the body, you will not find it, any more than you will find the soul in dissecting the body, but it is here, it is in us, and we are aware of it. There is a being in us—'I live; yet not I, but Christ liveth in me' (Gal 2:20)—how, I do not know. We will understand in glory, but somehow we know now that we are sharers in the life of God, that we are partakers of the life and of the nature of God Himself, that we share it in communion, that we have partaken of it, we have participated in it, and we are in Him. We, somehow, are in God and God is in us; a great mystical conception, staggering to the human mind and yet a reality which can only be expressed in some such term as this—sharing.

The second thing is that as well as being partakers of God, we are partners with Him, sharers in His interests and in His great purposes. That means that we have become interested in the sense of being partners in God's great plan of salvation, in His attitude towards life in this world and in all His wonderful provision for it. Now we who are in Christ have entered into that; that again is something which is emphasised everywhere in the pages of the New Testament, and it is a good test of our whole Christian position. It seems to me that by this definition we cannot truly be Christians unless we are really interested in God's enterprise in this world.

In other words, we know what it is to be grieved by the sin of this world; we do not merely look at the world with a political eye or with a social eye or with an eye of beneficence. No, we see things as God Himself sees them. Evil becomes a reality, sin becomes a reality in the new sense, and we see these powers, these evil forces that are in the world and which are manipulating the life of the world in their enmity against God and we are concerned about that. We feel that God is in it and that we are likewise in it, in that we are concerned to bring the purposes of God to pass. We meditate, we pray; we do everything that we are capable of in furthering the kingdom of light, so that the kingdom of evil may be finally routed. We are sharers in God's thought and in God's enterprise and in God's whole interest in this life and world.

Then let me add something about the second great aspect of this which is the most blessed and comforting and consoling thought for every true Christian. Fellowship always means communion, it always means intercourse, it always means, if you like, conversation—sharing. We talk about having fellowship with people, and that is quite right; it is part of the essential meaning of the word and of its Christian meaning in particular. 'We had a wonderful time of fellowship together,' somebody says, having had conversation with somebody else, and it means that—not only sharing in common but talking about it—this element of communion.

Let us analyse this a bit further. 'Our fellowship is with the Father', and I mean by that that I have communion with God. Now this can be looked at in two ways. First of all it can be looked at from our side, then it can be looked at from God's side. What does this wondrous thing which has been made possible for us in Christ mean from our side? It means, obviously and of necessity, that we have come to know God. God is no longer a stranger somewhere away in the heavens; He is no longer some stray force or power somewhere, some supreme energy. God is no longer some potentate or lawgiver far removed and away from us; God now is someone whom we know.

Consider the Apostle Paul especially as he deals with this; you will find that in writing to the Galatians he talks about their knowing God; 'but now, after that ye have known God, or rather are known of God' (Gal 4:9)—that is the idea. God is now a reality; we know Him, and that is the very essence of this matter. You cannot have communion, you cannot have conversation with a person without knowing that person—there is nothing distant, there is an intimacy and a knowledge.

The Christian, says John, is one who has come to know God, but it is not only that. God not only is a great person—I speak with reverence—the Christian is one who has come to know God as Father. That is why John uses his terms so carefully—'our fellowship is with the Father.' The Christian is one who turns to God and addresses Him as 'Abba, Father'; that is how Paul puts it in Romans 8:15—this spirit of adoption, the result of which is that we know God in that intimate way so that we address Him as 'Abba, Father' because we are His children. So it means that of necessity, but not only that. It also means that we delight in God and that we have joy in His presence. We know God in that way.

But then I think that we can go on to say this: to have communion with God means that we desire to speak with Him and that we have the ability to do that. Let me put it like this: All of us have known what it is to have difficulty in connection with prayer. It is not very difficult to talk to a person whom we love in this world, is it? When we love someone there is no need to try to make conversation, it flows freely; we love that person, and everything in us is stimulated. That is the characteristic of true fellowship and communion. But we all know what it is to get on our knees and to find ourselves speechless, to have nothing to say.

Now if this is our state and condition we do not know God as we ought; true fellowship with God means we desire, we delight in speaking to Him and we have a desire to praise Him. If we love someone, we want to tell him so; we not only say it in actions, we want to say it in words and we do say it. And it is exactly the same with God. The one who is in true relationship with Him praises Him. We do not come to God because we want something. No, rather, we enjoy coming to Him; it is the greatest thing for us—this is the whole idea in this word 'communion'.

Another way is to put it like this: men and women who are in communion with God are those who are sure of the presence of God. I have had people say to me, 'I get on my knees, but I do not feel that God is there'; and you cannot have communion if that is your feeling. No, those who are in communion know that God is there, they realise His presence, it is an essential part of this whole position of fellowship.

Then, of course, all this leads to confidence in speaking to God, in taking our petitions and requests and desires to Him. In other words one of the best ways in which we can test whether we are truly in fellowship and communion with God is to examine our prayer life. How much prayer life is there in my life? How often do I pray; do I find freedom in prayer, do I delight in prayer, or is prayer a wearisome task; do I never know enlargement and liberty in it? For what we are told here is that the Christian in Christ has been brought into fellowship and communion with God, and as you read the psalmists you will find that they enjoyed it, to them it was the supreme thing. Read the statements in the New Testament, read the lives of the saints and of those who have gone before us—that is the characteristic, that is the possibility—conversation with God, an enjoyment of it and a delight in it.

But now let me say just a word on the other side, for as we have seen, there are always two sides in fellowship. 'Truly our fellowship is with the Father, and with his Son Jesus Christ.' How do I know that? I know it because He gives me tokens of His presence and a sense of His nearness. We have said that communion means realising the presence of God, and there is the basic minimum in this matter, that those who can claim that they are in communion with God and say they have fellowship with Him must be able to say, 'I have known that I was in the presence of God who graciously gives me tokens of this; He gives me manifestations.' You can see the dangerous thing I am saying, how it opens the door to fanaticism and excesses; but we have no fellowship with God unless in some way we have known that He was there, that He gave His gracious intimation of His nearness and His presence. He also speaks in His own way to the soul, not always with an audible voice, but He speaks. He gives us consolation, He creates within us holy desires and longings; it is He who does that.

Paul said in writing to the Philippians, 'For it is God which worketh in you both to will and to do of His good pleasure' (Phil 2:13). That is the way to have fellowship with God. You are aware of the surging of those holy desires, and you say to yourself, 'It is God; it is God speaking to me; it is God saying something and calling forth a response in me.' 'We love him, because he first loved us,' says John later in this epistle, and God has fellowship with us in that way.

Not only that, He reveals His will to us. He show us what He would have us to do; He leads us, He opens doors and shuts them; sometimes He puts up barriers and obstacles. You know what I am speaking about. It means that you are aware of the fact that you are in the hands of God and that He is dealing with you, and that as you go forward in this journey called life, God is there. Sometimes the door is shut and you cannot understand it. You say, 'I wanted to go there, but I cannot' and then you say, 'But God is with me and He has shut the door.' Then suddenly you find the door opened and you know it is the One who is walking with you who has suddenly opened it. That is having fellowship with God, knowing that He is there in these various ways in which He manipulates our lives and speaks to us and gives us wisdom and understanding. Every one of these things contains a danger; they all need to be carefully qualified, and yet they are essential to fellowship and communion.

Then He supplies us with strength according to our need and according to our situation. You will find all these things if you read Christian literature; how the saints have been enabled to re-enact what our Lord Himself experienced. Towards the end, He said in effect to the disciples, 'You are all going to leave Me, you will all run away and turn your backs upon Me; in a few hours you will leave Me alone. And yet,' He said, 'I am not alone, for the Father is with Me' (Jn 16:32). And His last words on the cross were: 'Father, into thy hands I commend my spirit' (Lk 23:46). God was there with Him, and the saints all repeat that in their lives and in their experiences. Consider their deathbed testimonies. They will tell you, many of them, how glorious and wonderful it was, that even there they had this fellowship. They were not alone, the presence was there; they could not see God, they could not hear an audible voice, but they knew God was there filling the very atmosphere; they were more certain of God than of anyone else.

Truly, certainly, astoundingly, astonishingly our fellowship is with the Father. Enoch walked with God, and if we are truly Christian, we should be walking with God, speaking to Him, knowing He is there speaking to us, delighting to praise Him, anxious to know Him more and more. Let us test ourselves by this. It is not enough to be orthodox. That is essential, but it is not enough; the vital question for us all to put to ourselves is as simple as this—do I know God?

8

MYSTICISM

And truly our fellowship is with the Father, and with his Son Jesus Christ.

1 JOHN 1:3

WE HAVE BEEN SEEING together that this is really the great offer which is held out to us by the gospel of our Lord Jesus Christ. It is the one thing, the supreme thing that is held before us as that which can enable us to live in a world which, as we have seen so abundantly in the Scriptures, is essentially opposed to God and opposed, therefore, to all who belong to Him. 'If the world hate you, ye know that it hated me before it hated you,' said our Lord in John 15:18, and that is something which as Christian people we should never lose sight of—that the world in its outlook and mentality is opposed to God, and until it becomes converted, until it receives a new life, that will remain its condition.

So the problem confronting us is, how are we to live this Christian, this godly life in a world that is so antagonistic to us in every respect? And the answer of this epistle, as it is the answer of the whole of the New Testament, is that there is only one way in which this can be done, and that is to have this fellowship with God; and that, according to John, is the astounding thing which our Lord came to do; not only to reveal it to us, but to make it possible for us. That is the great emphasis. It is not only a teaching, it is more than a teaching; it is something which He actually does for us.

Now we have been considering this great statement from certain angles; we have been considering certain things that had to take place before it could be possible—the work of Christ—and then we have tried to look at it directly in order to remind ourselves of what exactly it means. But in doing that I have constantly had to utter a word of warning. There is no subject, I think we will all agree, which has led to more misunderstanding perhaps than just this particular question. The whole idea is so exalted and wonderful that once we realise that it is a possibility at all, we must immediately be concerned about having and experiencing it; and in some senses the history of the Church can be described as the history of the various ways in which men and women have tried to arrive at and maintain this communion, this fellowship with God. Some of the greatest adorations in Christian experience have been the result of this particular interest and particular endeavour, so that it is a subject which we must examine rather carefully. There are false ways in which we could seek this fellowship with God as well as true ones.

Now it is impossible to deal with them all, so it seems to me that the most convenient thing to do is to show the two main ways in which men have sought fellowship with God—the evangelical way and the mystical way. That is a pretty general classification. There are many instances in Christian biographies of men and women who seem more or less to combine the two ways, shading one off against the other. There are many sub-divisions of the mystical way, and clearly we cannot hope to deal with them in one discourse. It would take a whole series of discourses. There are large volumes written on many of them; indeed one could say that there are libraries on this whole question of mysticism. It is a most fascinating and absorbing and indeed a most thrilling matter. Clearly I can therefore only deal with what I may describe as the essence of the evangelical position and the essence of the mystical view. (If I may in passing recommend a book that is, I think, one of the most valuable and instructive in this respect, it is a series of lectures that were delivered in 1928 and published under the title of *The Vision of God*, written by Kenneth E. Kirk.)

Here, then, is a subject which must engage our attention, because the mystical and the evangelical in certain respects are so similar, and that is where, perhaps, the danger comes in. The mystic and the evangelical both agree that God does deal directly with our spirits and gives us a knowledge of Himself. They are both agreed that fellowship is not something formal and that the true Christian position is not merely something external and mechanical. The mystic and the evangelical agree that our object and endeavour should be fellowship with God; neither of them is content merely with discharging a certain amount of responsibility, or of conformity to certain moral standards. That, they say, is not the thing; the world can do that, and so can other religions. No, they say, the special thing about the Christian religion is that it offers a man fellowship, an intimacy, a knowledge of God, and they are both concerned with obtaining it.

But as I want to try to show you, it is in the way in which they seek to do this that they tend to part company. Again I would remind you that there have been certain cases where really one must grant that the people concerned have been evangelical and mystical at the same time. There are cases of people who were sufficiently evangelical to see the dangers of their own mysticism, but that does make it rather difficult from the standpoint of classification. Let me give you one example. Take Bernard of Clairvaux. He was clearly mystical and yet we must grant he was evangelical, and there have been other examples of the same thing. There is a great deal of the mystic in Charles Wesley, although he was primarily evangelical, and the same can be said of his brother John. There are such cases which seem to be difficult to classify, so let us deal, therefore, with the big principles.

What is this whole idea of seeking fellowship and communion with God along the pathway of what is described as mysticism? There are, as we have said, many sub-divisions of mysticism. It can be entirely non-Christian; many of the Greek pagan philosophers were mystics in the true sense of the word; there are pagan mystics, as well as religious ones, and as well as, in a sense, Christian mystics. There are certain things which are common to them all; they believe in general that a man can have a kind of immediate intuition of the infinite and the eternal. One definition of the word is: 'Mysticism is the belief that God may be known face to face without anything intervening; the direct knowledge and awareness of God.' Or perhaps better still: 'Mysticism is the theory that the purity and blessedness to be derived from communion with God are not to be obtained from the Scriptures and the use of the ordinary means of grace, but by a supernatural and immediate divine influence, which influence is to be secured by the simple yielding of the soul without thought or effort to the divine influence.'

Generally, we can put it like this, that mysticism makes *feeling* the source of knowledge of God, and not intellect, not reason, not understanding. That is really the differentiating thing about mysticism. The mystic is one who says that this knowledge of God is not something one obtains as the result of understanding or any external objective knowledge; it is something immediate, a direct traffic between one's heart and the Spirit of God Himself, and it happens primarily in the realm of the feelings. God makes known truth to the mystic in some shape or form.

Now that is the big difficulty to the evangelical approach to this subject. The evangelical always asserts the primacy of the Word of God, objective revelation; the mystic tends to depreciate that and says, 'No, what I have to do is somehow or other just submit myself, and upon my spirit in this passive state God will do something by means of my sensations and susceptibilities, and I will come to know God.' Its primacy and emphasis is upon the sensibility rather than upon the understanding.

Now not all mystics are concerned about the same thing. I do not want to spend time with technical terms, but there are three main types. There are what you can call the *theopathic*, the mystic who is concerned about pure feeling and sensation. Then there is the *theosophic*—people who call themselves 'theosophists' today and who are concerned about a knowledge of God resulting from experience and want to examine their knowledge. And there is the *theurgic*, the man who is interested in phenomena, who is anxious to have visions and strange phenomenal experiences; the kind of mystic who delights in seeing balls of light, or illuminations, and likes to talk about trances and 'feeling' the power of God.

Now it is interesting to glance at the history of mysticism. It almost invariably comes in as a protest against a sort of formalism and deadness in the Church. You get this quite as much in the Roman Catholic Church as you do in Protestantism, indeed more so. I think that is very significant in and of itself; the Roman Catholics have always produced more mystics than the Protestants. Mysticism is also a protest against rationalism and a tendency to over-intellectualise the Christian faith. Thus you will find that mysticism has generally tended to show itself at certain periods in the history of the Church. In the early centuries of the Church when there was a good deal of discussion about Christian doctrine and when the doctors of the Church spent their time in working out the arguments against Greek philosophy in order to safeguard the Christian faith, the danger was that the whole gospel might be turned into an intellectual system. And it was at that point that the first

Christian mystics came into being. 'We must be careful,' they said; 'With all our definitions, we are in danger of losing the life.' So mysticism, in a sense, began in the early centuries in Egypt, as a protest against the mere intellectualising of the Christian faith and a kind of formality in the Church.

Then you had another great outbreak of mysticism in the Middle Ages with Bernard and people like that, and again it followed very definitely from the same cause. There was a danger that the Roman Catholic Church of that time was attempting to produce a formal school of philosophy. It had become materialistic and dead and lifeless, and there were certain men, even in the Roman Catholic Church in those dark Middle Ages, who began to say to themselves and to one another, 'We are losing the life; the business of the Christian faith is to bring men into a knowledge of God; here are learned philosophers arguing about the exact nature of angels and how many angels can be suspended at the same time on the point of a nail and all these wonderful philosophical abstracts. That in itself,' they said, 'is a denial of the Christian faith.' So you had an outbreak of mysticism in the Middle Ages just as you had it in the first century.

There is the evidence of this in Protestantism as well. The Reformation came in the sixteenth century and, of course, it led to a great realisation of a kind of spiritual power. But, as almost invariably happens after a revival, it was followed by a period of deadness. Then you came to the age of the theologians, and again there were some people who began to feel that the life had been lost, that this excellent theology had somehow or other become mechanical, and there was a reaction in the direction of mysticism. People of the Puritan period began to put a new emphasis upon the Holy Spirit, and one of the manifestations of the emphasis was what has come to be known as Quakerism.

Here again are mystics, and theirs was a protest against this over-intellectuality of the Christian faith or a merely mechanical statement of certain teaching. So you get the main manifestations of mysticism in Protestantism amongst the Quakers and the others at the end of the seventeenth and the beginning of the eighteenth centuries. One of the most outstanding of these in this country [UK] was William Law with his book *The Serious Call.* Now he had a great influence upon the brothers Wesley, and he was the man who was used of God to bring them into the light and the truth.

Mysticism, then, is concerned to put emphasis upon the reality of the knowledge of God and communion with Him. How does it do so? I have already indicated its method in general, although here again there are two main schools amongst the mystics. The first school believes in quietism, pure passivity. They say you have nothing to do but to be quiet and to relax; this teaching is still popular in various quarters. 'You must not try to think,' they say; 'you must not try to make any endeavour; what you must do is to abandon yourself to God and God will then speak to you and do things to you and you will come to this knowledge of Him'—passivity and quietism. The great exponent of this particular aspect was the famous French woman, Madame Guyon.

That is one way, but there is another type of mystic who is most active. It is most unjust and unfair to think of the mystic as some sort of vague, nebulous kind of person. Someone once said that we must not, if we want to be fair to mysticism, confuse it with the mystical. There is a type of mysticism that is most active, and it says that this vision splendid and this knowledge of God is only to be obtained by a very rigid discipline. You must indulge in introspection, you must examine yourself; then you must go on to meditation; you must think about these things and then you must go on to the stage of where, having meditated and examined yourself, you have a kind of intuition of God. That is what is called 'the mystic way', which calls upon you to purge yourself from sin, and then you may have to go through a period of what is known as 'the dark night of the soul' when you feel you do not know God. But you just remain quiet and you go on with your introspection and meditation and your ascetic practices, and if you do so you will come out into a state of illumination, you will begin to see the truth. You will begin to come to a state when you know, and then you will just have to contemplate, and ultimately you will arrive in a state of union with God when you have more or less lost yourself altogether.

You will find that these mystics have been very active people; their one endeavour has been to come to know God. Most of the men who left life in the world and became monks and anchorites and who went into monasteries were concerned with nothing but that. They put on camel-hair shirts, they deliberately mutilated their bodies, as it were, believing that was the way that would lead ultimately to this state of union with God; and as a result of all this they claimed various experiences. You hear about raptures and visions of joy.

Now what is the evangelical criticism of all this? Let me tabulate it in this way. The main criticism of the evangelical to all this can be put in this form: It is a claim to a continuation of inspiration. The mystic in a sense is claiming that God is dealing as directly with him as He was with the Old Testament prophets; he claims God is dealing with him as He did with the Apostles. Now we as evangelicals believe that God gave a message to the prophets, He gave a message to the Apostles; but we say that because God has done that, it is unnecessary that He should do that directly with us. I do not claim that what I am speaking here has been given to me by a direct inspiration of God. I am here to expound the Scriptures. I claim that the Holy Spirit enables me to do so, but I am not claiming that I have received a direct message from God. No, this is the message, the message that was given to John and his fellow Apostles; I have entered into fellowship with the Apostles and I am repeating their message. But the mystic says he has received a new and fresh message and that he is in a state of direct inspiration.

My second criticism would be that mysticism of necessity puts the Scriptures on one side and makes them more or less unnecessary. You will always find that persons who have a mystical tendency never talk very much about the Bible. They do not read it very much; indeed I think you will find that this is true of most mystical people. They say, 'No, I do not follow the Bible reading schemes; I find one verse is generally enough for me. I take one verse and then I begin to meditate.' That is typical of the mystic. He does not need this objective revelation; he wants something to start him in his meditation and he will then receive it as coming directly from God; he depreciates the value of the Scriptures.

Indeed, I do not hesitate to go further and say that mysticism, as a whole, even tends to make our Lord Himself unnecessary. That is a very serious statement, but I am prepared to substantiate it. There have been people who have been mystical and who claim that their souls have immediate access to God. They say that just as they are, they have but to relax and let go and let God speak to them and He will do so; they do not mention the Lord Jesus Christ.

Not only that, I think we can put it like this. The danger of mysticism is to concentrate so much on the Lord's work *in* us that it forgets the Lord's work *for* us. In other words, it is so concerned about this immediate work upon the soul that it quite forgets the preliminary work that had to be done before anything could be done upon the soul. It tends to forget the cross and the absolute necessity of the atoning death of Christ before fellowship with God is in any way possible.

Or indeed we can go further and put that in a different way. Mysticism is never very strong on the doctrine of sin. The mystic tends to come and say, 'Look here, you have nothing to worry about. If you want to know God just as you are, you have to start getting into communion with Him, and He will speak to you and will give you all the blessings.' They never mention the doctrine of sin in the sense that the guilt of sin is such a terrible thing that nothing but the coming of the Son of God into the world and the bearing of our sins in His own body on the cross could ever enable God to speak to the soul.

Another very serious criticism of mysticism is that it always leaves us without a standard. Let us imagine I follow the mystic way. I begin to have experiences; I think God is speaking to me; how do I know it is God who is speaking to me? How can I know I am not speaking to man; how can I be sure that I am not the victim of hallucinations, since this has happened to many of the mystics? If I believe in mysticism as such without the Bible, how do I test my experiences? How do I prove the Scriptures; how do I know I am not perhaps being deluded by Satan as an angel of light in order to keep me from the true and living God? I have no standard.

Or in other words, my last criticism is that mysticism always tends to fanaticism and excesses. If you put feelings before understanding, you are bound to end in that, because you have nothing to check your experiences with, and you will have no reason to control your sensations and susceptibilities.

'Very well,' says someone, 'if that is your criticism of mysticism, what is the evangelical way in order that I may come to this knowledge and fellowship with God?' It is quite simple, and it is this: It always starts with the Scriptures; it says that the Scriptures are my only authority and final standard with regard to these matters, with regard to a knowledge of God. The evangelical doctrine tells me not to look into myself but to look into the Word of God; not to examine myself, but to look at the revelation that has been given to me. It tells me that God can only be known in His own way, the way which has been revealed in the Scriptures themselves.

I must start with Christ's work for me. There is no true knowledge of God without Christ. 'No man cometh unto the Father, but by me,' said our Lord (Jn 14:6). I must come by Christ, and I must come via the cross. Christ's teaching cannot bring me to God because there is the guilt of my sin. It is Christ's work for me before Christ's work in me; it is what He has done objectively there in that transaction, before He can do anything upon my soul.

So I start with that, and then I believe that having dealt with the guilt of my sin He gives me life. It is a gift from God; it is not something of which I can say I can attain to by following the mystic way; eternal life is the gift of God, and I must realise that it only comes to me on the condition that having seen my sinfulness I believe on the Lord Jesus Christ and thereby trust Him for reconciliation. And therefore as eternal life is the gift of God, I must not seek it directly; it is something that will come to me as the result of following after God. Our Lord put it perfectly once and for ever in the Sermon on the Mount. He did not say, 'Blessed are they who hunger and thirst after spiritual experiences, blessed are they who hunger and thirst after joy and happiness'—not at all! The blessed, the ones who experience a blessing, 'hunger and thirst after *righteousness*: for they shall be filled' (Mt 5:6).

We must not seek this great thing directly; you and I are to seek righteousness and if we do, God will give us the blessing. This wonderful experience of fellowship with the Father and with His Son Jesus Christ is something that He gives to all who truly seek Him in the way He has taught us. It is the whole theme of this first epistle of John; the way to obtain this fellowship, this wondrous experience, is to read this Word, not to take a verse and then fit it into my mystical meditation. No, it is objective revelation, the facts of the incarnation, the life, the miracles, the death, the resurrection, the facts of salvation—'These things,' says John, 'which we have seen and witnessed; these proofs which we have touched and felt and handled.'

The evangelical way of fellowship with God, therefore, is to come straight to the Word, to know its truth, to believe it and to accept it— to pray on this basis and to exert our whole being in an effort and an endeavour to live it and to practise it. 'Blessed are they which do hunger and thirst after righteousness: for they shall be filled'; filled with the fullness of God, with the knowledge of God and such blessings as God alone can give.

Mysticism is an attempt at a short cut to the great experiences; the way of the Scriptures is the other way—simple, indirect but certain, and free from the effects of fanaticism and excesses and leading to a balanced Christian life and living, true to God and His Word, in line with the Apostles and in line with the mighty evangelical tradition throughout the ages and the centuries. May the Lord in His mercy open our eyes to the dangers of these side paths and to all the excesses and fanaticism which ultimately bring disrepute upon the Lord and His great salvation, and keep us ever always to that simplicity which is in Christ Jesus.

9

THE HOLINESS OF GOD

This then is the message which we have heard of him, and declare unto you, that God is light, and in him is no darkness at all.

1 JOHN 1:5

HERE IN THIS VERSE we begin the consideration of the various reasons and causes which John gives his readers for the fact that the fellowship of Christian people with God is not as full as it should be, and is so frequently interrupted. He has announced his great theme, he has reminded them of the great good news, that what is offered to the Christian in this life and world is fellowship with the Father and with His Son, Jesus Christ, or if you like, through His Son Jesus Christ. The Apostle is not concerned in this particular matter to deal with the person of the Lord as such; he has already done that in his Gospel. Not only that, these people, being members of the Christian Church, have already been taught that; John is rather taking it for granted. What he is concerned about here is to enable them to continue in the grace of the Lord Jesus Christ. He is anxious to show them the fullness of this fellowship which is offered and how this fellowship may be maintained in spite of various hindrances and obstacles.

When we gave a general analysis of this letter, we pointed out how that is the scheme on which he works. There are certain things which tend to interfere with the fellowship or to rob us of this true fullness, and immediately he comes to one of them, one of the things which we all so constantly tend to forget. Indeed, here in this verse he holds us face to face with one of the most vital and common things of all. There can be no doubt about that from any standpoint and especially, as I hope to show you, from what can be described as the theological standpoint, there is no more important verse than this one. It immediately concentrates our attention on something that is quite fundamental and primary, and if we neglect it or fail to understand it as we ought, we must of necessity find ourselves overwhelmed with troubles. And therefore we can, perhaps, best consider it together by putting it in the form of a number of propositions.

The first principle is this: we must always start with God. You see how John plunges into this without any introduction; indeed there is something almost surprising about the way in which he does it. He has already said in verse 4, 'And these things write we unto you, that your joy may be full.' Very well, says John, 'this, then is the message which we have heard of him and declare unto you, that God is light and in him is no darkness at all.' The starting point, let me repeat, always must be God Himself.

Now it may sound strange to some that we take the trouble to put that in the form of a principle. 'Surely,' someone may feel like arguing, 'that is something that is self-evident and obvious. Surely the very first and basic thing for Christian people is that they should start with God.' And yet I want to suggest that half our troubles arise in the Christian life because we do not start at this point. It is because we tend to assume that we know the truth about God, it is because we tend to assume that everything is all right in our ideas about God that many, if not most, of our problems occur, because we constantly start not with God but with ourselves. So many people assume that they believe in God and that therefore they need not be concerned about examining their belief. 'I have always believed in God,' says someone, 'it has never occurred to me not to believe in Him.' So in all their thought about these things they tend not to start with God, because they assume that; rather, they tend to start with themselves.

This, of course, has been the outstanding source of trouble since roughly 1860. It had started before that, but it has been particularly true since that time. Man has been put in the centre, and all thinking and all philosophising has tended to start with man; he has been placed at the centre of the universe. Man, if you like, has been placed on the throne and everything, God included, has had to be put in terms of man. Man has set himself up as an authority; it is man and his ideas that count; it is always man in his need and condition that seems to be the starting point. Now that is the very initial error and the source of most misunderstandings. The Bible is constantly reminding us that we must start with God. If ever I start with man, I must ultimately go wrong in all my thinking about truth; because if I start there, everything accommodates itself to my doctrine of man. Yet the doctrine of the Bible is that I can never know man truly unless I look at him in the sight of God and in the teaching concerning God.

So I must always be careful not to start with myself. It is very difficult not to do so; our whole approach to the gospel and to Christianity naturally tends to be from that self-centred and selfish standpoint. We argue like this: Here I am in this world with its troubles and I am ill at ease. I am looking for something I have not got. I am aware of my needs and desires; I am aware of a lack of happiness, and the tendency for most of us is to approach the whole subject of religion, to approach God and Christian truth and everything else, in terms of my desires and my demands. What has He to say to me and to give to me? What can I get out of this Christian faith and religion? Is there something in this that is going to ease my problems and help me in this dark and difficult world?

But that, according to this verse and indeed according to the whole of the Bible, is the root source of error, it is the initial fallacy, it is indeed almost blasphemy against God. The first answer of the gospel can always, in effect, be put in this way: 'Forget yourself and contemplate God.' This, then, is 'the message which we have heard of him'; not that your needs and mine can suddenly be met by the gospel, but rather that 'God is light, and in him is no darkness at all.' Immediately we start with God and not with ourselves.

Furthermore, this is a very valuable test of any teaching or of any doctrine which may confront us. You will find that the great characteristic of the cults and of every religion which is not the true Christian faith is that they tend to come to us in terms of our need. That is why they are always so popular and so successful; they seem to be giving us the thing we want. We have our needs, and they seem to offer us everything just as we want it without any pain or difficulty. There is no more thorough-going test, therefore, of the truth of the faith and of the religion that we may be concerned with than this.

Primarily, the initial test, the characteristic of the revelation of the

Bible, the first crucible, in a sense, of the Christian faith, is that it starts with God. We are silenced, we are put into the background, we are not considering man first and foremost. It is God, it all starts with Him— 'In the beginning, God'—and He is at the centre. The very term *theology* should remind us of that. Theology does not mean knowledge concerning man; primarily it is knowledge of God.

So this is of supreme importance to us as we come to consider the whole question of fellowship and walking with God and of enjoying the life of God. Most of our troubles are due to our self-centredness and concern for ourselves. The psychologists are aware of that and they have their own way of dealing with it, but they do not really meet the situation and the problem. They are only temporarily successful, because the whole time they are pandering to this self within us. No, the way to be delivered from self-centredness is to stand in the presence of God.

According to the Bible the initial cause of man's ills is that, having been created in the likeness and image of God, instead of living a life in subservience to God, man, alas, suddenly exalted himself and claimed a kind of equality with God; and it is his own self-assertion that has led to all his perplexities. Is not the position in which we find ourselves the same situation as that of the people who have gone before us in all ages and at all times? We begin to see that our fallacy is to exaggerate our own twentieth century with its problems. We see we are paying too much attention to our environment and conditions, and we suddenly come back and face this ultimate, absolute truth—that we are all ultimately in the presence of God.

The starting point, then, always must be God and not ourselves and our needs, our desires and our happiness. Before the Bible begins to talk to us about our particular needs, it would have us see ourselves in the sight of God. Its approach to the whole situation is quite unique and entirely different. It does not say it can aid and help us; it confronts us with its own truth, its message from God which comes down to us.

Let me elaborate that a little more. Having reminded us that we must start with God, our text reminds us in the second place that we must accept the revelation concerning God which we have in the Bible and primarily in the person of the Lord Jesus Christ. 'This then is the message which we have heard of him, and declare unto you, that God is light, and in him is no darkness at all.' It is not enough, in other words, for us to say that we must always start with God. The vital question is:

what is the truth concerning God; who is God; what is God; what do we know about Him?

Here again I think we see at once that we are face to face with another of those primary, fundamental questions, and it is tragic to have to remind ourselves of how it is always with regard to these very things that we go astray. 'Oh yes,' people say, 'I have always believed in God.' There are only a very few who actually say they do not believe in God. The average man says, 'Yes, of course I do', and then if you ask him what his ideas of God are—or indeed you need not ask him because he is so fond of expressing his opinions!—he says, 'If God is a God of love, I cannot understand why He should allow conditions like these present ones to exist. Why does God allow wars, why does God . . . ?' Immediately, you see, he is telling you what he thinks of God.

That again, according to the Bible, is one of the first fallacies. To believe in God we must accept the revelation concerning Him, and that revelation is only to be found in the Bible. Now that is a dogmatic assertion, and so is the verse which we are considering. 'This then is the message,' says John, 'which we have heard of him, and *declare*—announce, proclaim—unto you.' John does not say, 'This is the sort of picture I have of God'; he does not say, 'As the result of much thought and meditation and reading, and as the result of my study of the Greek philosophies and contemporary thought, this is the idea I have now arrived at concerning God.' Not at all! He goes out of his way to say the exact opposite.

John says, 'What I am telling you is what my fellow Apostles and I heard from Him and heard about Him.' He has already referred to the Lord Jesus Christ as 'that which was from the beginning, which we have heard and seen and looked upon.' He had to start with Him, 'because,' he says in effect, 'in fact I did not know God and my ideas concerning Him were false until I met Him, until I heard Him and companied with Him for three years. I heard His words; He said on one occasion, "He that hath seen me hath seen the Father. You have been with me and have you not known me, have you not seen and heard me?" He is my authority,' says John; 'He told us certain things and I am just repeating what He said.'

That is the biblical position; so in other words we come to what we may call the watershed in this matter. There are only two ultimate positions; we either regard the Bible as authoritative, or else we trust to human ideas, to what is called philosophy. The whole case of the Bible

is that this is the unique revelation of God and that finally I am shut up
and shut into this particular revelation.

This again has been a matter which has often engaged the minds and
the attention of God's people. What are the so-called proofs or the philosophical arguments for the being and existence of God? Now, according to the Bible I think we must look at it like this: these things have their
place and yet they are not ultimately the final source of truth. Reason
can take me to a certain point, and it is quite right to use it up to that
point, but that will never bring me to a true knowledge of God. I can
argue about the being of God in a purely philosophical manner; I can
say that every effect has a cause, and that cause in its turn is but the effect
of another cause, and I can go back and back until I come to the ultimate cause and that must be God. Well, that is all right as far as it goes,
but to believe that is not to know God.

Again, I can use a moral argument; I can say that I observe in life
that there is bad, good and better; does that not imply that there must
be a best somewhere? Moral arguments lead to arguments about the
absolute, and that is God. This too is all right as far as it goes, it is quite
sound, it is perfectly cogent, and yet when I have worked out that argument and accepted it, I do not know God in the sense that John means
here. What John tells us is that we can have fellowship with the Father
and with His Son, Jesus Christ.

I can use the cosmological argument; I can assert an intellectual
argument as to my existence and my being and show that yet there must
be some ultimate source of this being. Again, all this is quite sound philosophically, but that is not to know God. No, these arguments, these so-
called proofs of the being and existence of God are all right as far as they
go, but they do not bring me to an ultimate knowledge, to a communion, to the fellowship which is offered me in the gospel of the Lord
Jesus Christ.

Here I am left ultimately in this position of relying upon the revelation, and this is the challenging effect of faith; faith calls upon us to come
to this truth as little children, acknowledging our failure, acknowledging our incompetence and impotence, and it confronts us by these dec-
larations, these announcements, and it asks us to accept this truth. I
cannot know God ultimately apart from the revelation that He has been
pleased to give me of Himself; I cannot know God ultimately in the sense
of truly having fellowship with Him except in the Lord Jesus Christ.

Our Lord said, 'I am the way, the truth, and the life: no man cometh unto the Father, but by me' (Jn 14:6). Now I wonder what happens exactly when we test ourselves by that particular statement. Have we found the Lord Jesus Christ absolutely essential in that way, or have we held some view of God which has made us believe we can find God whenever we seek for Him or that we can arrive at God by our own efforts? Our Lord put it like that, and that is the Christian position: 'No man cometh unto the Father, but by me.' He is essential, and we cannot know God truly except we believe this revelation concerning Him. And that is exactly what John says: 'This is the message which we have heard of him and which we declare unto you.' 'I believed things about God,' says John, 'before I met Him. I had ideas concerning God, but when I met Him and listened to Him and knew Him, it was only then I really came to know God.' As Martin Luther put it in his own blunt and striking manner, 'I know no God but Jesus Christ.'

Now there is something, surely, we all must confess, that tends to come to us in rather a startling way. Our tendency is to say that we are all right in our belief of God, but the trouble is our belief in Jesus Christ. But the question is, what has the Christian faith to offer us by way of salvation; and the answer is that it is our thoughts of God that are ultimately wrong; it is in our approach to Him that we go astray; we must start with Him, and we are confined entirely to the revelation which has been given to us. He gave it to the patriarchs of old; He gave it in the Ten Commandments and the moral law and He gave it in the prophets whom He raised up one after another. All these were intended to give us knowledge and understanding of God, but it is only in the incarnate Son that we really come to *know* Him; it is only there that we can possibly know Him as Father and truly have fellowship with Him.

Then the next proposition is that we must start with the holiness of God. There again, surely this fifth verse must come to us as rather a surprise. Surely our first reaction when we read it is to feel it is almost a contradiction. John has just been saying, 'These things write we unto you, that your joy may be full'; so, how is it to be full? Well, 'This then is the message which we have heard of him, and declare unto you, that God is . . .' What would you have expected there? I suggest that most of us would have expected, 'God is love, God is mercy, God is compassion'; but the startling and astonishing thing is that he says, 'God is light, and in him is no darkness at all.' And we want to say to John, 'Have you forgotten what you have been saying? You have been saying that we are to be given an amazing joy, and then you confront us with that.'

But that is precisely what he does say. In other words, we must not start with the power of God or with the greatness of God, though they are perfectly true. We must not start with the knowledge of God, though that is absolutely essential. Nor must we start with God as a source of philosophy. We must not even start with God as love.

Now we can see at once how by putting it like this we just give an utter contradiction to what has been so popular especially, again, since 1860; the great message that has been preached for a hundred years is 'God is love'. That is the thing that has been emphasised, and we have been told that our fathers, and especially the Puritans with their preaching about justice and righteousness and repentance and sin and punishment and death, had been entirely contradicting and denying the gospel of Jesus Christ. We have been told that God is love—that is what we wanted and there He was to meet us; yet what an utter travesty of the gospel that is! This is the message: 'God is light, and in him is no darkness at all.'

I say it with reverence that before I begin to think and consider the love of God and the mercy and compassion of God, I must start with the holiness of God. I go further; unless I start with the holiness of God, my whole conception of the love of God is going to be false, and this of course is what we have been witnessing. We have had the flabby, sentimental notions of God as a God of love, always smiling upon us, and then when wars and calamities come we are baffled and we turn our backs upon religion—this is what millions have been doing since the great wars of this century. And the trouble has actually been due to the fact that they did not start the way the Scriptures start, with the holiness of God. God is utter, absolute righteousness and justice; 'holiness, without which no man shall see the Lord' (Heb 12:14); 'God is a consuming fire' (Heb 12:29); sharing in the light that is unapproachable, everlasting and eternal in the brightness and the perfection of His absolute qualities. Light! And light must not be interpreted as knowledge; light is knowledge, but light essentially stands here for holiness—utter, absolute holiness and purity. And John makes certain that we shall not go astray in our interpretation, by adding this negative: 'And in him is no darkness at all.'

Now it is interesting to observe how the commentators, and even some of the best of them, during the last hundred years, as the result of a modern philosophical approach, are so anxious to interpret this term 'light' in terms of knowledge and truth and enlightenment and understanding. But that is not it; it includes that, but essentially it is the character of God, and the character of God is His holiness.

But why is all this so essential? 'Why,' asks someone, 'is it so vital that we must start with God and not ourselves; why do we start with God and not with our opinions? Why must I be so attuned to this revelation? Why must I start with the holiness of God rather than with His love?'

Let me give you some answers. I suggest that if you do not start with the holiness of God you will never understand God's plan of salvation, which is that salvation is only possible to us through the death of our Lord Jesus Christ on the cross on Calvary's hill. But the question arises; why is that cross essential, why is that the only way whereby man can be saved? If God is only love and compassion and mercy, then the cross is surely meaningless, for if God is love alone, then all He needs to do when man sins is to forgive him. But the whole message is that the cross is at the centre, and without that death God, I say with reverence, cannot forgive.

So what is the trouble? And here is the answer—'God is light, and in him is no darkness at all.' And that means that He is just and righteous; it means that He is of such pure countenance that He cannot behold and look upon iniquity (Hab 1:13); it is the holiness of God that demands the cross, so without starting with holiness there is no meaning in the cross. It is not surprising that the cross has been discounted by modern theologians; it is because they have started with the love of God without His holiness. It is because they have forgotten the life of God, His holy life, that everything in Him is holy; with God love and forgiveness are not things of weakness or compromise. He can only forgive sin as He has dealt with it in His own holy manner, and that is what He did upon the cross.

Therefore it is essential to start with the holiness of God; otherwise the plan of redemption, the scheme of salvation, becomes meaningless and we can see no point or purpose in some of the central doctrines of the Christian faith. But if I start with the holiness of God I see that the incarnation must take place; the cross is absolutely essential, and the resurrection and the coming of the Holy Spirit and every other part of the great plan as well. How important it is that we should start at the right place; how vital it is that we should be led by truth and not by our own ideas.

Let me give you another answer. If we start with the holiness of God we shall find that all the false claims of fellowship with God are immediately exposed. We saw earlier how prone we are to try to have fellowship with God in false ways and that they will not last. John is going to elaborate on that great theme. There is nothing that exposes the false so much as standing face to face with a holy God. Yes, by your own efforts you can have a kind of fellowship in your imagination with that false God whom you construct for yourself. You can practise a kind of hypnotism, but it is not fellowship with God, and in your times of need you will discover that. No, God is light, and any fellowship I may have with Him is in terms of that—it exposes the false. Not only that, it delivers me at once from attempting in a false way to try to find fellowship with Him. If I start with this conception of His holiness, then I see at once that certain things I am prone to do are ultimately going to fail.

But it saves us also from another thing; it saves us from the terrible danger of tending to blame God and to criticise Him in times of trouble and in times of need, and that is one of our greatest dangers—to misunderstand God, to argue and to question, 'Why does God do this; did I deserve this?' But if I start with the holiness of God I will never speak like that. I know at once that whatever may be happening to me is not the result of anything unworthy in God. 'God is light, and in him is no darkness at all', so that whatever may be happening to me is not in any way due to any imperfections in God; it silences me, I put my hand upon my mouth and prevent myself from speaking foolishly and whiningly.

And lastly, it is right and essential that we should start with the holiness of God because actually, in practice and as a matter of fact, it is the only way that leads to true joy. There are false joys, there is a false way of finding peace. You know those great, profound psychologists of the soul, the much maligned Puritans, used to write at great length on what they called a 'false peace'; there was nothing they were more afraid of than having a false peace with God. The most dangerous thing is for people to persuade themselves that all is right with God and then not to find Him in the moment of agony. There is such a thing as a false spirit; that is why the Bible tells us to 'try the spirits' (1 Jn 4:1), to examine ourselves, whether we are in the faith (2 Cor 13:5). There is only one way to true and lasting joy, and that is to start with the holiness of God. If I start there, I shall be delivered from every false peace, from every false joy. I shall be humbled to the dust, I shall see my true unworthiness and that I deserve nothing at the hands of God. I shall come to the only one who can deliver me, the Lord Jesus Christ, and anything I may receive from Him is true; if I receive joy from Christ, it is a true joy, a real and lasting joy.

So you see after all John is not contradicting himself, he is not playing with us and mocking us. 'These things write we unto you, that your joy may be full.' How is my joy to be full? 'The first thing,' says John, in effect, 'is this: if you want that blessing in your life, if you want to be filled, clear out all the rubbish that is in it. If your life is to be full of joy, get rid of everything that is false; then, when it is truly emptied, it can be filled to overflowing with the true joy of the Lord in the Lord Jesus Christ.'

Thank God for the thoroughness of the gospel! Thank God for the heavenly way which starts by holding us face to face with a holy, absolute God and then driving us, leading us to the only Saviour, the Lord Jesus Christ. 'This then is the message that we have received of him and declare unto you, that God is light, and in him is no darkness at all.' We can do nothing better, every time we go on our knees to pray, than just to say that, and when we feel like rushing into our own desires and complaints, just to pause and, like the author of the epistle to the Hebrews, approach him with reverence and godly fear, 'for our God is a consuming fire.'

10

SIN

If we say that we have fellowship with him, and walk in darkness, we lie, and do not the truth: but if we walk in the light, as he is in the light, we have fellowship one with another, and the blood of Jesus Christ his Son cleanseth us from all sin. If we say that we have no sin, we deceive ourselves, and the truth is not in us. If we confess our sins, he is faithful and just to forgive us our sins, and to cleanse us from all unrighteousness. If we say that we have not sinned, we make him a liar, and his word is not in us.

1 JOHN 1:6-10

WE HAVE BEEN LOOKING at verse 5—'This then is the message which we have heard of him, and declare unto you, that God is light, and in him is no darkness at all', and you remember that the way John seems to look at the whole situation can be put like this: Fellowship is a position in which two people are, if you like, walking together along the road; it is a journey, a companionship. There is that key verse in the Old Testament— 'Enoch walked with God' (Gen 5:22). That means he had fellowship with God, and that is a very good way of thinking of it. You see two people walking together down the road, or a husband and wife going together through life, walking through the pilgrimage; that is the idea, and the Christian is one who in that way is walking with God, journeying through this world. So obviously, when you come to consider the nature of fellowship like that, you have at least two things to do. First, you must know something about the character of the two persons who are taking part in the fellowship, and that is why John immediately begins with this very theme and there in that fifth verse he reminds us of the essential nature and character and being of God. 'If you are interested in this fellowship,' says the Apostle in effect, 'if you want to know something about it and to understand what it means; if you want it to persist and continue, then the point at which you have to start is this, the character of God. God is light, and in Him is no darkness at all; utter, absolute holiness, without blemish, without spot, without any admixture of that which is evil and sinful.'

And now in these verses John comes to the other half of the fellowship. It is important that we should know the character of God, but we must also know something about ourselves. There are two parties to this companionship; and there are certain things, according to John, that must be true on both sides before there can be a real fellowship. So here in these verses he comes to this consideration of what must be true of us if we are to enjoy that fellowship with God.

The Apostle here does not merely stop at a consideration of our character and of what must be true of us; he also deals with the limitations and the imperfections that are in us. Obviously we cannot in one study deal exhaustively with all that we are told in these verses, so we shall simply take up one particular aspect of the doctrine now and then subsequently go on to deal with the rest. But here we are confronted at once with what perhaps can be most definitely described as the biblical doctrine of sin. And immediately we come to something which causes, and has always caused, a good deal of difficulty and confusion in the minds of large numbers of people.

The doctrine of sin has never been popular. I suppose also that it is true to say that it has been even more unpopular in the last hundred years, and especially perhaps in the last fifty years, than it has ever been, and there are many people who are utterly impatient at the very mention of the word. Yet it is my whole business and purpose in expounding the Scripture to point out that the doctrine of sin is as integral a part of the biblical teaching as is the doctrine of the holiness of God. It is as true to say that man is sinful as it is to say that God is light and that in Him is no darkness at all.

This is a truth that is to be found everywhere in the Bible. Indeed, I would not hesitate to say that the doctrine of the Bible simply cannot be understood unless we accept this particular teaching, and yet people object to it. There is a kind of general objection; the average person today, without thinking about the doctrine and without examining it, just dismisses it as being soft. 'Ah,' they say, 'that old-fashioned doctrine in which the fathers delighted, with their morbidity and almost perversion! They talked of sin and preached about it, and hasn't that been part of the whole trouble? It made men live a kind of cramped and narrow life; they did not know what life and living meant. They so turned in upon themselves, and so overpainted this picture of our imperfections, that they really put fetters upon mankind.'

Indeed, the argument has been that with our new knowledge and learning, acquired especially in the last century, we have emancipated ourselves out of all this; we have got rid of this talk of sin and of all that would drag and keep us down. Having freed ourselves from the fetters of mid-Victorianism which so delighted in the doctrine of sin, we are now living this freer and much fuller and more glorious life. That has been the tendency. The feeling is that the doctrine of sin has made the whole of life miserable; it has painted it in sombre, dark colours, and all the brightness and the light has been taken out of it. And thus the Church throughout the centuries has been standing between man and his true heritage and has drawn an utterly perverted picture of life. Indeed, the modern view is that men and women who have been canonised by the Church as saints have been monstrosities!

So there is this common deep-seated objection to the whole New Testament doctrine of sin, and, of course, along with that goes the view of life which maintains that really things are not quite as bad as the Bible and the theologians in the past have made it out to be. 'So long as we do our best', people say, 'and look to God occasionally for a little help, then everything can be put right. We must not take these things too seriously; to be a Christian is to be as decent as we can be and to do good and so on, expecting a certain amount of aid from God. So we say our prayers and attend an occasional act of worship and thus we go on; we must not think of all this in those tragic terms of desperate sin and some overwhelming need of the grace of God.'

That is, in general, the modern attitude with regard to this whole subject, and this is the matter with which the Apostle John deals in these verses. He analyses this position, and he deals with it in a very radical and drastic manner. Fortunately, the subject divides itself up in a very definite way in terms of a phrase which John repeats three times. You will find the phrase in the sixth, eighth and tenth verses: 'If we say we have fellowship with him, and walk in darkness, we lie, and do not the truth.' 'If we say that we have no sin, we deceive ourselves, and the truth is not in us.' 'If we say that we have not sinned, we make him a liar, and his word is not in us.'

Now in these verses John teaches that there are three common errors with regard to this whole question of sin. And it is because we go wrong in these three main respects that so many of us, according to the Apostle, fail to enjoy and experience this amazing fellowship with God and with Jesus Christ which is offered to the Christian. So let us look at this, and again, as I do so, let me remind you of what John takes for granted as being the essence of the Christian position. It is: 'If we say that *we have fellowship with him*'—that is what we ought to say. That is what we who use the name Christian should claim; and when we say, 'I am a Christian', that is what we mean. We should not, let me emphasise again, just mean that we are a little bit better than some profligate sinner in the gutters of life, or that we are a little bit better than we once were. We should not mean that we are trying to be decent and moral, or even that we subscribe in a general and vague way to the teaching and the dogma of the Church. No. 'If we say that we have fellowship with him'—that is what we mean, says John. 'You are members of the Church,' he says to these people, 'and that is the claim you are making, that you have fellowship with God', the God whom he has just described.

This, then, is still the claim. That being so, says John, now there are certain things that must follow of necessity, and I put them like this: The first thing that comes between us and this full and glorious fellowship with God that we read of in the New Testament and in the lives of all true saints throughout the centuries is this—it is a failure to realise the nature of sin in general. This is how he puts it. Here is the claim. I say I have fellowship with God and yet I walk in darkness. Well, what of it? It is a lie, says John, and he does not apologise for being blunt and using such a strong term. If I say this and do that, it is a lie, and he goes on to say that I do not tell the truth.

So the question that confronts us is this: what is the matter with people who are in that position? John's answer is that people who are guilty of that have clearly never understood the real nature of sin. Let us take his own description of it at this point. 'If we say we have fellowship with him, and *walk in darkness*'—that is it. We are back again to this picture of companionship, a fellowship of people walking together. If we say that we are walking with him and yet in the meantime are walking in darkness, then we lie. It is not true, it is a false claim, we misinterpret ourselves to our fellow men and women and to the world, and it is all wrong.

Why is this? Well, the New Testament answer is that a person who is in that position is obviously someone who has never realised the gospel and precisely what is meant by sin. Walking in darkness, says John—or in other words, sin—is a kind of realm or atmosphere, and that is the point surely at which so many seem to go astray. They fail to realise that particular truth about sin; they will persist in thinking of it in terms of sins—particular sins and actions. But according to the Bible that is a hopelessly inadequate view of sin. Sin, according to the Bible everywhere, is a realm, a kingdom.

The Bible tells us that there are two kingdoms in this world, the kingdom of God and the kingdom of evil, the kingdom of light and the kingdom of darkness, the kingdom of holiness and the kingdom of Satan and of iniquity. There are two realms in which man can live, so that quite apart from you and me, and quite apart from our individual actions, there is such a thing as sin and evil, a realm, an attitude, an outlook, a mind. Before we were born sin was in the world. The Bible tells us that sin is the explanation of all our ills and troubles and sorrows. God made a perfect world, but then another element, sin, entered in. Man was made perfect by God, but he was tempted and fell, and the result has been that the whole world has been polluted. Thus we are reminded again of these familiar biblical phrases: 'the god of this world' (2 Cor 4:4), 'the prince of the power of the air' (Eph 2:2), that 'we wrestle not against flesh and blood, but against principalities, against powers, against the rulers of the darkness of this world, against spiritual wickedness in high places' (Eph 6:12).

There is another mighty power, a great kingdom, and, according to the Bible there is a mighty contention between these two powers, fighting for supremacy over man in this life and world. The kingdom of God and the kingdom of Satan, heaven and hell—there is a great clash between these forces. And also according to the biblical doctrine, all of us that are born into this world are born under the domination of this kingdom of darkness; and as we are by nature, we tend to live and to think in that way. The kingdom of darkness, or, if you like, 'walking in darkness', represents everything that is opposed to God, everything that is opposed to His holiness and perfection, everything that is opposed to His desires for the world and for man.

'Walking in darkness' means that you live in such a way that you rarely have any thought about God at all; and if you do think about Him, you do not think of Him as 'light [in whom] is no darkness at all'. You think of Him as some benign fatherly person who is ready to smile upon your failures and who is ready to grant you an entry into heaven at the end. That is walking in darkness—the failure to realise that the very organisation of man, the outlook of humanity, is opposed to God, that godlessness is in control and in power and that it dominates everything.

John goes on to describe this in detail in the next chapter: 'Love not the world, neither the things that are in the world. . . . For all that is in the world, the lust of the flesh, and the lust of the eyes, and the pride of life, is not of the Father, but is of the world' (1 Jn 2:15-16). That is it! 'Now,' says John at this point, 'people who have not realised all that are walking in darkness. They do not know it; they are living and thinking and acting in a realm that is the very antithesis to that which is towards God—God is light and in Him is no darkness at all.' We have seen His desires with regard to this world, but here are people who are walking utterly oblivious to all these things; they do not take any interest in them; these things do not affect their lives; they are not striving to live like that—they are walking in darkness.

And what is true of such people? Well, obviously, without any argument, they are not in fellowship with God. This is utterly impossible, for as the Apostle Paul argues in 2 Corinthians 6:14, 'What communion hath light with darkness?' You cannot mix light and dark; both are destroyed, as it were; there are certain things that are utterly incompatible, and this is one of them. Someone whose whole outlook upon life is governed by what you might call worldliness, and who thinks only in human, earthly terms of all that stands for the pride of life, such a one cannot be walking along the same road with God who is light and in whom is no darkness at all. It is impossible. So that is the first essential— that we should realise this whole doctrine about sin as a domination, as a power and as a taint in the world; for if we do not, then we cannot be in fellowship with God.

But John, you notice, goes on to say that not only must we regard it intellectually, we must also practise it—'If we say that we have fellowship with him, and walk in darkness, we lie and do not the truth.' God does what He is. God is not only light, He acts as light, and the same thing applies to man. We really show what we are by what we do; we reveal our doctrine in our practice, and those who have not realised the truth about sin, and certainly those who have a wrong idea about it all, cannot be having real fellowship and communion with God. That is the first thing.

Then the second message is in verse 8: 'If we say that we have no sin, we deceive ourselves, and the truth is not in us.' Let me put it in this way: The second failure is not to realise that our very natures are sinful. That is what John means, and this is a most important point. You see the difference? The reference here is not to acts of sin, but to the nature that produces the acts of sin. He is concerned here about the state which is both the cause and the consequence of what we do, the sinful state, which is a continuous source of influence within us.

Now there are many who are in error about this, generally because we will persist in thinking of sins rather than of a sinful nature. I am sure that the authorities are quite right when they tell us that at this point John was thinking in a particular way and manner of that heresy which was very common in the early Church—we have already referred to it— the heresy of Gnosticism. There were people who argued that if we have become Christians we have been delivered from our sinful nature and we have received a new nature; therefore, because we have received this new nature, there is no sin in us. So, if we do something that is wrong, it is not we who have sinned, the sin is merely in the flesh. Hence the heresy known as *antinomianism*, which means that as long as you are a Christian and claim you know God in Christ, it is immaterial what you do, because you do not sin, it is the flesh or body that sins.

That is the view that John is countering, but it is still fairly common, because we will persist in regarding the matter from the standpoint of action rather than from the point of view of the nature within us that produces the action; and John is very stern about this—'If we say we have no sin, we deceive ourselves, and the truth is not in us.' For someone to say in this way that he has not a sinful nature is nothing but self-deception, and here again I thank God for a word that is so honest and sharp. Are we not rather tired of the popular current writings that are for ever praising us and trying to say that all our troubles are due to somebody else or to our environment? No, says the Bible, the trouble is in you; you are not being honest with yourself.

The question that should confront us all is not simply that we have committed actions that are wrong. No, surely the most important question is, 'Why did I do it; what led me to do it; what is it in me that made me think of it and play with the suggestion?' And there is only one answer; there is something wrong within me, myself; my nature is sinful. I am driven to believe that Paul must have been right when he said, 'For I know that in me (that is, in my flesh), dwelleth no good thing' (Rom 7:18). There is an evil desire, there is something perverted in my essential being, my nature is sinful. That is why we have sinful thoughts, sinful desires, sinful imaginations. There is something in my very being as the result of the Fall that has twisted and perverted everything. There is a kind of fountain within me that gives rise to evil and iniquity; not only do I do wrong, but my nature is sinful. I must never say I have no sin. If I do, I am deliberately deceiving myself.

But how often do we do so; how we try to rationalise our sins; how clever we are at doing it, and yet how easily we see through it when somebody else does it; how easily we can expose them and tell them they are deceivers! The human heart is desperately wicked, and those who look at themselves and face themselves know that this is the simple truth about human nature, that at the centre we are wrong. Our nature is evil and sinful, and not to admit that is self-deceit, and not only that but 'the truth is not in us'.

This again is obvious. The truth is something that always enlightens us. This comes out in Ephesians 5:13: 'Whatsoever doth make manifest is light', and our Lord made this same point when He said, 'This is the condemnation, that light is come [or has come] into the world, and men loved darkness rather than light, because their deeds were evil' (Jn 3:19). People will not come to the light because they love darkness and they know that the light will reveal the darkness and they do not want it to be revealed.

So, says John, if we say we have not sinned, it is obvious that the truth is not in us, because the truth in us is like a great flashlight flashing upon the depths of our being, and all the evil spots and darkness stand out upon the screen and we see and know it and we cannot go on saying that there is no sin in us.

And that brings us in turn to the last point in verse 10: 'If we say

that we have not sinned, we make him a liar, and his word is not in us.'
This is the failure to realise that we as sinners need forgiveness. It is the
failure to realise the nature of sin, to grasp that our own natures are sinful and to understand that we have all actually sinned and need forgiveness.

There are certain people who seem to say, 'Yes, I believe in God and
I like to have fellowship with Him, and yet, you know, I have never been
conscious of my sin. I do not understand that doctrine of yours. If you
were to preach it to people gathered from the streets I could understand
it, but I have been brought up as a Christian, I have always tried to do
good; I have never been conscious of the fact that I am a sinner, that I
need repentance and that I must be converted.'

Well, says John, if that is your position, 'you make him a liar, and
his word is not in you.' If we do not realise that we are sinners and need
the forgiveness of God; if we do not realise that we have always needed
it and that we still need it; if we think that we have always been perfect
or that now we are perfect as Christians; if we do not realise that we
must repent, then, says John, we are making God a liar, for the 'him'
referred to is none other than God Himself. John here is just stating the
whole teaching of the Bible from beginning to end.

What, then, is the teaching? Paul has summarised it perfectly for us
in Romans 3; this is his verdict: 'There is none righteous, no, not one'
(v 10). He says, 'Now we know that what things soever the law saith,
it saith to them who are under the law: that every mouth may be
stopped, and *all the world may become guilty before God*' (v 19). He
goes on, 'For all have sinned, and come short of the glory of God' (v 23).
The Jews, the chosen people, thought they were all right: 'Those others,
the Gentiles,' they said, 'are dogs; they need it, but we do not.' But God
convicts Jew and Gentile; there is none righteous; the whole world, every
mouth, has been stopped. That is the doctrine of the Bible; so if we say
we have not sinned, we are denying the doctrine of the Bible.

But more than that, are we not denying the very doctrine of the
incarnation? Why did the Son of God come into this world of sin? He
came 'to save that which was lost', to provide pardon and forgiveness
of sin by the shedding of His own blood and the breaking of His own
body upon the cross. If I say I have no sin, I am denying the incarnation,
the death and the resurrection—I am making God a liar. Indeed, if I say
I have not sinned, I am thus opposing my view of life to the whole point

and purpose of the grand biblical revelation; and not only am I making God a liar, I am also again proving that His word is not in me, because the word of God always convicts us; it makes us see the necessity of the cross and the atonement and all the wondrous provision that God has made.

Let me sum it up like this: Not to be right about sin, therefore, leads to these results. It means that we are still walking in darkness, that our whole attitude is a lie. If I say I am a Christian and the world knows that I am a Christian and I continue to walk in darkness, I am a liar, I am pretending to be something I am not, I am lying to other people. But, next, I am lying to myself and deceiving myself. Furthermore, I make God a liar, and ultimately I regard as absolutely unnecessary this amazing thing that God has done in Christ. I am laughing in the face of eternal love, which sent His only begotten Son into the world for our rescue and for our redemption. And is it not perfectly obvious, without any need of pressure or of argument, that if I am in that position I have no fellowship with God, for 'God is light, and in him is no darkness at all.' A lie cannot live in the presence of God; it is an utter contradiction of everything that God is, and it just means that I am not a Christian at all.

The doctrine of sin is essential, and unless I realise I am a sinner and must repent, and if my only hope is not in Christ and His death for me on the cross and His resurrection for my justification, I not only have no fellowship with God, but I am dwelling still in utter darkness. Oh yes, to have fellowship with God we must not only be clear about the nature of God, we must be equally clear about ourselves and our own nature.

But, thank God, the Apostle does not leave us at that. Having convicted us of our sin, in the self-same verse he goes on to tell us of the glorious provision—'If we walk in the light as he is in the light, we have fellowship with one another, and the blood of Jesus Christ his Son cleanseth us from all sin. If we confess our sins, he is faithful and just to forgive us our sins, and to cleanse us from all unrighteousness.'

11

WALKING IN THE LIGHT

If we say that we have fellowship with him, and walk in darkness, we lie, and do not the truth: but if we walk in the light, as he is in the light, we have fellowship one with another, and the blood of Jesus Christ his Son cleanseth us from all sin. If we say that we have no sin, we deceive ourselves, and the truth is not in us. If we confess our sins, he is faithful and just to forgive us our sins, and to cleanse us from all unrighteousness. If we say that we have not sinned, we make him a liar, and his word is not in us.

1 JOHN 1:6-10

JOHN HAS SHOWN THAT we must be perfectly clear about certain conditions that must of necessity be observed if we truly are to enjoy fellowship with God. He begins with the character and the being of God Himself; then he shows that we must be equally clear about ourselves. So we have considered what may be called the negative aspect of this—our sinfulness—and now we come to what we may call the positive side of the matter.

You notice that there are certain contrasts which he applies—'If we say that we have fellowship with him, and walk in darkness, we lie, and do not the truth: but if we walk in the light, as he is in the light, we have fellowship one with another, and the blood of Jesus Christ his Son cleanseth us from all sin. If we say that we have no sin, we deceive our-selves, and the truth is not in us'—then, 'If we confess our sins, he is faithful and just to forgive us our sins, and to cleanse us from all unrigh-teousness.' So we are looking now particularly at verses 7 and 9 where he puts all his emphasis on what we have to do in a positive sense. We must see clearly what the positive conditions are which we must fulfil in order to make this fellowship possible, and in order that it may continue.

Here, again, is a statement which must once more be sub-divided into two parts. In order to make this fellowship active we have certain things to do and God must do certain things to us: 'If we walk in the light, as he is in the light, we have fellowship one with another'—that is what we do; 'and the blood of Jesus Christ his Son cleanseth us from all sin'—that is what He does. 'If we confess our sins'—that again is our part; then, 'He is faithful and just to forgive us our sins, and to cleanse us from all unrighteousness.' So it is quite inevitable in the matter of fel-lowship like this that though in a logical sense we persist in dividing up the aspect of fellowship into the two sides—Godward and manward—they are constantly intermixed and intermingled, because it is a sharing together, it is an interaction of the one upon the other.

In other words, fellowship is never mechanical, but always some-thing organic and vital. Yet, of course, if we would understand it truly, for the sake of clarity of thought we are allowed to analyse it in the way we are doing, but we must remember that organic nature. To use an illustration: what we are doing is what the musicians do when they anal-yse a piece of music like a sonata or a symphony. It is right to say that it is composed of various parts and you can make an analysis of it, but if you are truly to appreciate it you must always remember it is a whole and you must take it as such. You cannot stop at an analysis, nor can you leave it at these various bits and portions; they are there, but they are parts of the whole.

Or to take another illustration: the human body consists of sepa-rate parts, and while, of course, you can think of the parts as distinct from the body—you recognise the hand, for example, and the fingers—yet the hand has no meaning in and of itself. So in order to get a good conception of the body it is right to study anatomy and physiology—to divide up the body into various parts, and to study how they all work. But we must never forget that the body is organically a whole; it is an essential, vital unit.

Now that is always essential also in taking any passage of Scripture, but it seems to be particularly true of this first epistle of John with his strange and unusual type of mind. You remember that we described his method of thought as being a spiral one; the steps and stages are not as clear on the surface as they are, say, in the writings of Paul, so in considering his teaching it is very important to bear these two aspects in mind.

Here, then, again is something which is absolutely vital and essential if we are to enjoy true fellowship with God, and first we must consider what we must do with regard to this positive aspect of fellowship. Then we shall consider what God does at this particular point in maintaining the reality of fellowship. But before we begin to do this, let me make some preliminary introductory remarks.

This paragraph is one that notoriously has figured a great deal in theological and religious thought and discussion. There is no passage, perhaps, that is quoted so frequently, when people are concerned about the whole problem and question of sanctification, as this particular one, and that constitutes, in a sense, a danger and adds to our difficulties.

The danger always in interpreting a passage of Scripture like this is that instead of going to Scripture itself and considering what it has to say, we tend to go to it with our ready-made theory and then go on to interpret the statement in the light of that theory and idea. You are familiar with what I mean. What you find is this verse quoted: 'The blood of Jesus Christ his Son cleanseth us from all sin'; and then this other verse: 'He is faithful and just to forgive us our sins, and to cleanse us from all unrighteousness.' Then how often with reference to holiness and sanctification is this verse used: 'walk in the light, as he is in the light.' A great deal is heard about all these verses—they are always popular in this connection—'walking in the light'; 'confessing our sins'; 'the blood of Jesus Christ cleanseth us' and 'he is faithful and just.'

Now it is difficult not to think of these verses in the light of some particular theory of sanctification which we may happen to hold, because the history of this doctrine shows very clearly that we seem to be particularly prone when dealing with it to accept theories based often upon one statement in Scripture and that often taken out of its context. So there is nothing more important in dealing with these verses than that we really should in the first instance make a very special effort to rid our minds of these prejudices and pre-conceived ideas and theories and to consider the statement of Scripture especially in its own particular context.

What adds to our problem, in a sense, is the kind of language of which the Apostle was so fond. Anybody who has ever studied John's Gospel, his epistles and the book of the Revelation will know that John's style is rather characterised by his fondness for certain controlling ideas. He is fond of the ideas of light and of life. He plays with them, and you will find them running constantly right through everything he has ever written; and one of the greatest dangers is that we tend to forget that. John thought pictorially, and the danger is to literalise something which he intended to be just a picture. The result is that you find that most theories with regard to perfectionism tend to base themselves on the writings of John and especially on this first epistle. But I hope to be able to show you that most people have gone astray because they will not recognise his pictures as pictures, and will insist upon materialising them. And thereby they inevitably find themselves teaching a doctrine of perfection in some shape or form.

Those, then, are the preliminary considerations. So coming to the actual statement, what is it that we have to do? Well, according to John, there are two main things: first, we must walk in the light as He is in the light.

Now here I think we come across an illustration of what I have just been saying. John is fond of the phrase, 'walking in the light'; how often it occurs in the Gospel and here it is again. Is it not obvious on the very surface that if you take this in an absolute literal sense it can mean only one thing, and that is absolute perfection. If to walk in the light as God is in the light is taken strictly literally, as it is expressed here, there is only one deduction to draw: as Christians our only hope of forgiveness and therefore of being Christian at all is that we should be absolutely perfect as God Himself is perfect.

But clearly that is impossible! Which of us is perfect, which of us is without sin? 'If we say that we have no sin, we deceive ourselves, and the truth is not in us'; we cannot, therefore, be absolutely perfect. So immediately we find that this phrase of walking in the light as God is in the light must be interpreted in terms of the way in which he customarily employs this picture. And the key to that is to be found in the phrase we have already considered in the previous verse in which we read about walking in darkness—'If we say we have fellowship with him, and walk in darkness, we lie and do not the truth.'

Now we saw that walking in darkness meant living in the realm of darkness, being controlled by the ideas of the world and of sin, belonging to a kingdom, the kingdom of darkness, the kingdom of Satan, the kingdom of this world, the kingdom that is rebellious against the kingdom of God. In other words, the people who walk in darkness are not those who, as it were, are constantly committing some foul sin. They may be highly respectable—indeed, they may be very moral—but they are walking in darkness because they are outside the light of the gospel of our Lord and Saviour Jesus Christ; it is a realm to which people belong; it is an outlook upon life in general.

So when we come to this verse about 'walking in the light', we interpret it as just the antithesis and the exact opposite of 'walking in darkness'. Therefore it does not mean that I claim absolute perfection; but it does mean that I claim that I now belong to a different realm, to the kingdom of light and to the kingdom of God. In that kingdom, alas, I may be most unworthy; but though unworthy, I am in it and I belong to it and I am walking in the realm of light. God is the God of that kingdom, and God is in that kingdom as the King, as the Lord.

So that to 'walk in the light as he is in the light' means that, to use the language of the Apostle Paul in writing to the Colossians, I have been translated from the kingdom of darkness into 'the kingdom of his dear son' (Col 1:13). The Apostle Peter in his first epistle is really expressing the same doctrine when he says, 'Ye are a chosen generation, a royal priesthood, a holy nation, a peculiar people; that ye should show forth the praises of him who hath called you out of darkness into his marvellous light' (1 Pet 2:9). That is it! It is the kingdom to which we belong.

I emphasise this because you will find that certain people with their particular theory of holiness and sanctification are always teaching that the only people who walk in the light are certain very special Christians. Whereas what John is saying is that every Christian of necessity is one who is walking in the light. The non-Christian is the one who is walking in darkness; all Christians, however feeble, unworthy and faltering, are people who are walking in the light; otherwise they are not Christians at all and none of the remarks of the Apostle in any way apply to them.

That is the first point, which we must grasp very clearly. What does it mean in practice? It surely means two things most of all. Firstly, we cannot claim that we are walking in the light unless we have repented. In other words, we are people who have had our eyes opened to the whole of that doctrine of sin that we were considering together earlier. How do I know I am walking in the light? This is one of the best answers: we have come to realise that we were 'born in sin and shapen in iniquity'; that by nature, by birth, 'we are all the children of wrath'. We have come to realise that we were slaves, born under the dominion of sin and of Satan; that we were living in the realm of darkness; that our very nature was sinful and that we have sinned. We have got this new view of sin; we have seen that, and, of course, having seen it, we have bemoaned the fact. We regret it; we have known what it is to feel a godly sorrow because of it. Those who repent are those who have so seen themselves that they have become alarmed about themselves. They know what it is to say, 'O wretched man that I am! who shall deliver me from the body of this death?' (Rom 7:24). This is essential to being a Christian, for no one is a Christian, no one can be walking in the light, who has not seen it.

But you notice it does not stop at that—that is only a kind of initial step. Man, like the prodigal of old, becoming aware of his situation, realises his desperate problem and says, 'I will arise and go to my Father', and he gets up and goes to him; he changes his whole realm and position. The Christian must do this, so it includes positive living; it does not stop at repentance and an acknowledgement and awareness of sin. It means a positive endeavour to live in a manner worthy of one who has been translated into the kingdom of God's dear Son.

What it means, therefore, is that men and women who walk in the light are people who are seeking God. They desire to know God better; they are concerned about the glory and honour of God; they are anxious to please God. They realise that for very many years they have been living in a realm which is antagonistic to God, and their whole idea is to be as different as they can. That is walking in the light, living to the glory and honour of God. God is their Master; they seek righteousness and are concerned about being holy. Now that, I suggest to you, is the teaching of the Apostle at this point.

Let me try to emphasise this as a doctrine. I think you will agree with me that there is, perhaps, no doctrine that has been so frequently misunderstood as this doctrine of what is meant by 'walking in the light'. There have been two misconceptions. The first we have dealt with under the heading of mysticism and monasticism. There are people who, having awakened to the fact that they are sinners and are in the realm of darkness, say, 'Now what we have to do is to walk in the light; how is that to be done?' And their answer is, 'There is only one thing to do; we must segregate ourselves from the world, we must go right out of it. To walk in the light means that we must make this a whole-time job; we must seek God directly by the mystical road, or we must go right away and occupy ourselves fully with certain religious works and thereby we will be enabled to walk in the light.' Read the story of monasticism and mysticism and you will find it was this idea of walking in the light that was at the back of it; that was the idea that led men to take up this vocation of the holy and godly life. That is one error.

The other error is at the other extreme. It is the failure to see the importance of conduct and of behaviour. Let me put this carefully. This is perhaps the besetting danger of those of us who are Protestants and who are most evangelical. We say that the one thing we must avoid is a belief in justification by works, the tendency to say that it is a matter of living a good life that makes us Christians, that it is because we walk in the light that we are Christians. We must not rely upon our works, we say; that is the whole error of Catholicism in its various forms. We say that nothing matters but that we believe on the Lord Jesus Christ and in His death for us and our sin. We are justified by faith only, without deeds.

Yes, but consider also what the Apostle Paul says in 1 Corinthians 6. This is the Apostle of faith, remember, this is the man above all men who preached this doctrine of justification by faith only, and this is what he says: 'Be not deceived; neither fornicators, nor idolaters, nor adulterers, nor effeminate, nor abusers of themselves with mankind, nor thieves, nor covetous, nor drunkards, nor revilers, nor extortioners, shall inherit the kingdom of God' (vs 9-10). 'How do you reconcile these things?' asks someone. Surely the only way to reconcile them is this— and this, it seems to me, is the very thing the Apostle John was anxious to teach at this point. There is only one proof of the fact that I have really seen the truth; there is only one ultimate proof of the fact that I have faith, that my eyes have been opened to the gospel and its message, and it is this: that having seen myself as a condemned sinner, I have forsaken sin, I have repented, and I am striving with all my might and main to 'walk in the light as he is in the light'.

In other words, John is testing our Christian profession. What John is really saying, in effect, is, 'It is no use your saying, "I believe", and then living as if you believed nothing. It is no use saying, "I believe I am such a sinner and that nothing but the death of Christ can save me", and then continuing to live that kind of life. It is impossible,' says John; 'we give a proof of our repentance by the life which we live.' There is no value in a supposed faith that does not lead to action. There is no contradiction between John and Paul; they are both saying the same thing.

So, there are two sides; both are essential, and faith and works are inseparable. That is the way to test the difference between intellectual assent and true faith. There are men and women who accept the Christian teaching as a journal of philosophy, but they do nothing about it. As I understand the New Testament, they are not Christians, they are not walking in the light. A person's acts prove what faith they have; walking in the light means repentance and turning from sin to holiness of life; these are the ultimate proofs of the genuineness of a true Christian profession.

So that is the first thing that John emphasises—that we must walk in the light as He is in the light—and the important declaration therefore which is made is that everyone who is truly Christian is walking in the realm of light and not in the realm of darkness. Let me add once more, I do not say that they are perfect. They may be imperfect, they may be guilty of sin, but thank God they can say, 'I am not like those people in the world; I am not like those men and women who do not believe in Christ. I am essentially different, though in many respects I am guilty of the same things as they are.' You see, therefore, the utter error of those who are outside Christ. They say, 'What is the use of being a Christian? Look at your Christians!' As if that proved it! No. What makes people Christians is the realm in which they are walking; it is the kingdom to which they belong.

The second matter, of course, is confession of sin, and this again is essential. 'If we confess our sins, he is faithful and just to forgive . . . '. Now this, too, is essential, so let me tabulate what seems to be the argument in the Apostle's mind. Why does a refusal on my part to confess my sins break and interrupt fellowship? It does so for these reasons. The light always reveals the hidden things of darkness; so if I refuse to face my sin, it means first of all that I am avoiding the light. I am concealing and refusing to face something, and that breaks fellowship with God, because God is light. Or, to put it another way, it means that I am resisting the Holy Spirit, for it is the work of the Spirit to bring my hidden sins to light, to convict me of that and to lead me to forsake them.

It also means that I am refusing to be honest with myself; and if I am not honest with myself, how can I be honest with God? The person who is dishonest is not in relationship and cannot enjoy fellowship; the man who is dishonest cuts himself off automatically from his partner or friend. If a man is not true to himself, as Shakespeare put it, then he is false to every man; but if you are true, you cannot be false to anyone.

Lastly, not facing my sins means that I dislike the light, and is this not true of us? We dislike the light of the gospel; we want to be told about the love of God, but we dislike the light, and if that is so, how can we walk with God who is light?

Confession is essential. It means that we must remain open to the work of the light, we must let it search us, we must pull down the defences, and we must come to the Word honestly.

Then secondly, we must recognise our sins in particular. This is a painful process; to confess my sins does not just mean that I say in general, 'Well, I am a sinner—I have never claimed to be a saint.' No, rather it comes to the details. I must confess my particular sins, I must name them one by one; it means that I must not gloss over them, I must not attempt to deny them. I must confess them, I must look at them. There must be no attempt to dismiss them as quickly as possible. Confession means facing them, not trying to balance up the sins I have committed and the good deeds I have done. No, I must let the light so search me that I feel miserable and wretched—this honest facing of the things I have done and of what I am; it means that I must confess it to God in words.

Surely it is unnecessary that I should emphasise here that not for one second at this point does John mention my confessing my sins to anybody else. He is not concerned about anybody else; he is concerned about fellowship with God, my walking with God; and what he tells me is that having confessed my sin and confessed it to myself, I confess it to God. 'If we confess our sins, he is faithful and just to forgive us our sins, and to cleanse us from all unrighteousness.'

How often has this verse of John's been used to teach one of the pet theories of holiness and sanctification—that unless you make open confession of your sins to all and sundry at all times you cannot be walking in the light. But John does not say that. He is concerned about my fellowship with God, my walk with God. I am prepared to agree that there are certain conditions and circumstances in which I have to confess my sin to another. If I have sinned against another person, if there are some particular circumstances where another person is involved, I have to do that. But neither here nor anywhere else in Scripture will you find any teaching that tells you you are not walking in the light unless you are all the time exposing all your sins to everybody. No, we must confess our sins to God; we must acknowledge them to Him, mentioning them to Him in detail, baring them, laying them open before Him as David did in Psalm 32, and then, and then only, are we assured of this great and glorious blessing which He is ready to give us.

Yet there is an emphasis upon the human side in this matter. I must walk in the light, and as I see and recognise my sins, as I am convicted of my sins, as I walk with God, as the holiness and the light of His nature reveals them to me, I confess them. I do not care to evade or avoid them; I acknowledge and admit them to Him, and having done that, my side of the fellowship is fulfilled and the glory of the gospel is that if I do that— and how simple it is—then God will do something for me which He alone can do. He will give me joy unspeakable and full of glory!

12

THE BLOOD OF
JESUS CHRIST

*If we say that we have fellowship with him, and walk in
darkness, we lie, and do not the truth: but if we walk in
the light, as he is in the light, we have fellowship one with
another, and the blood of Jesus Christ his Son cleanseth us
from all sin. If we say that we have no sin, we deceive ourselves, and the truth is not in us. If we confess our sins, he
is faithful and just to forgive us our sins, and to cleanse us
from all unrighteousness. If we say that we have not
sinned, we make him a liar, and his word is not in us.*

1 JOHN 1:6-10

WE HAVE SEEN THAT what we must do if our fellowship with God is
to continue can be put like this: We must walk in the light, and we must
confess and acknowledge our sins. It is no use our talking about fellowship with God if we walk in the realm of darkness; no, we must walk
in the light and we must repent, believe on the Lord Jesus Christ, and
follow Him. And in addition to that, we must confess and acknowledge
our sins. But that in and of itself is not sufficient, because we must recognise at once that if we are walking with God and having fellowship with
Him, it follows of necessity that we shall be more conscious than ever
of our sinfulness and our unworthiness; and that is the great problem
always with regard to this whole matter of fellowship with God.

Our first tendency, as we have seen, foolishly and ignorantly, is to think that as we are we have that fellowship with God; but the moment we are convicted of sin we are soon delivered from that. Then the next stage is the one in which we begin to feel hopeless because we are so conscious of our sin and of the holiness of God that we begin to say at once, 'Surely fellowship with God is a sheer and utter impossibility.' Light, we have said, is something that exposes the hidden things of darkness; light always reveals things of which we were unconscious. Light in a room will do that; it will reveal dust and various other things; light on a dark road in the country reveals all sorts of things. It is the character of light to reveal the hidden things of darkness, and this is supremely true of walking with God. When we walk with God and when His Word dwells within us, of necessity we are convicted of sin; everything that is wrong, unworthy and sinful in us is at once brought to the surface.

To use an illustration, we are aware of this very principle when we come into contact with particularly godly and saintly men or women. We cannot be in the presence of such people without at once being conscious of all our defects and all our sins and imperfections. It is not that these godly people draw attention to them in words, nor do they make an analysis of us or point a finger at us; but the effect of saintliness upon us is at once to bring all those things to the surface and we are terribly conscious of them. Well, multiply that by infinity and there you find yourself in the presence of God. The presence of God at once convicts of sin.

In other words, as we have fellowship with God and as we walk with Him in the light, we all experience what the Apostle Peter experienced during one of the first contacts he had with our Lord when our Lord worked a miracle. They had been unable to catch any fish; they had tried, but they had failed, and our Lord sent them back again to the very self-same place and there they had a great haul of fish, and you remember the effect that that had upon Peter. Peter, seeing and realising something of our Lord's Godhead and glory, said, 'Depart from me; for I am a sinful man, O Lord' (Lk 5:8). That is the effect of realising something of the glory of the Son of God incarnate on earth—'Depart from me, O Lord, I am not fit to be in Your presence; I am so conscious of my sin.'

That is what happens when we are truly in the presence of God. So at once the question arises, What can we do? We are trying to walk in the light, we are doing our utmost, we are confessing our sins, but that in and of itself seems to break the fellowship and make it impossible, for our conscience condemns us and we feel we cannot dwell in such a glorious light. And it is in order to answer that question that we must return again to verses 7 and 9. In other words, I want now to emphasise the other side, that which I have already described as the godward side, or the godward aspect. 'If we walk in the light, as he is in the light, we have fellowship one with another, *and the blood of Jesus Christ his Son cleanseth us from all sin.*' 'If we confess our sins, *he is faithful and just to forgive us our sins, and to cleanse us from all unrighteousness.*' And those are the two phrases that we must consider now.

We are confronting here, as we have seen, two statements that have often led to a great deal of discussion and controversy; they are great and glorious phrases, and yet I want to try to show you that they are very often misunderstood and misinterpreted, so that if we are to derive their full benefit and value we must try to discover the meaning that the Apostle was anxious to convey to those people to whom he wrote the letter. There are two main principles here. Firstly, what God has provided to meet our need; and the second is the assurance which we should have in view of God's provision.

What has God provided for us in this matter of fellowship with Him as we become conscious of our sin? The answer is: 'The blood of Jesus Christ his Son cleanseth us from all sin.' 'He is faithful and just to forgive us our sins, and to cleanse us from all unrighteousness.' Yes, but the question is, what do those phrases mean; what is John exactly teaching at that point? Well, in order to concentrate our attention upon it, let me put the question—is John's teaching here with regard to justification only, or does it go on to include sanctification at the same time?

Now we can observe an interesting thing at this point. John does not use the terms justification and sanctification; they are Paul's great words, but, of course, John teaches exactly the same doctrine. Furthermore, I think that much of the trouble with regard to these matters has arisen because people will not see that fact. John, in his own pictorial way, is teaching precisely the same truth as the Apostle Paul teaches in his more logical and legal manner by means of his terms justification and sanctification, righteousness and redemption, and so on. So the best way in which to answer our question is to define the two terms.

What, then, is meant by justification? Justification is the New

Testament term which represents our standing in the presence of God. Justification means not only the forgiveness of our sins, but also that our sins have been dealt with and have been removed from us. Justification states that God regards us as righteous, as if we had not sinned. In other words, it is a stronger term than forgiveness; we may be forgiven and yet our sins remain upon us. But what God does for us in justification is to remove the guilt altogether, to remove the sin. It is not only that He does not punish us for it, but that He looks upon us as righteous, as if we had not sinned; that sin has been removed.

Sanctification, on the other hand, is that condition in which the sin principle is being dealt with. Justification does not deal with the sin principle which is within us; it deals with the sins that we have committed. But after our sins have been forgiven and sin and guilt have been removed from us, the sin principle will remain within us, and what the New Testament means by this doctrine of sanctification is the process whereby the very principle and the activity of sin within us is being taken out of us and removed. Furthermore, we are assured that ultimately that will be completed, and we shall therefore be finally delivered not only from the guilt of sin but also from the power of sin and even from the pollution of sin. So the point to bear in mind is that the difference between justification and sanctification is the difference between dealing with the sins that we have committed and their effect upon us, and dealing with the principle of sin that resides within us.

Now the great question here is which of these two the Apostle John is dealing with in these phrases. This is not just a purely theoretical or academic point. No, the importance of this question arises in this way. I think I can say quite honestly as a pastor and as one who deals with the souls of men and women privately and individually, as well as preaching from a Christian pulpit, that more men and women have come to speak to me on this particular question than on any other. I know of many Christian people who are unhappy or troubled and who have found themselves in great difficulty because of this confusion between justification and sanctification. I do not want to exaggerate this, but I have even discovered many people who have literally been on the verge of a breakdown because of confusion on this point.

There are those who seem to think that the New Testament promises us, as Christians in this life and world, a life which is absolutely free from sin and devoid of any struggle whatsoever. And because they cannot say that they have perfect peace within and that there is no struggle in their life, they begin to feel they are not Christians. Then they begin to fear, and you see them heading for a very bad psychological breakdown. It is, therefore, of vital importance that we should be clear about it. In addition, of course, we can never understand too much of the gracious doctrine of the New Testament.

So, is this justification or sanctification? Let us approach it in this way. What in the New Testament is the meaning of the phrase 'the blood of the Lord Jesus Christ' or 'the blood of Jesus'? What does it refer to? Does verse 7 mean that the blood of the Lord Jesus Christ is cleansing the sin principle right out of me, that it is sanctifying me and that I am being literally purged from sin as a power until I shall be absolutely free from it? Is that what the blood of Christ does? I suggest to you that if you examine every single reference to this phrase in the new Testament you will find that it invariably refers to the death of our Lord—for example, 'In whom we have redemption through his blood, the forgiveness of sins' (Eph 1:7). Take any verse you like and you will find that invariably the blood of Jesus Christ is a reference to the blood shed upon the cross, to his death upon the cross and nothing more.

But it is just there, I think, that confusion has entered. It is not for me to criticise a great teacher and expositor like Bishop Westcott, but there can be no doubt at all that he has been mainly responsible for this confusion. In his commentary on this epistle of John, he taught that the blood represents the life. He quotes the Old Testament, where we are told that the life of the flesh is in the blood (Lev 17:11); so he says that really the effect of the shedding of blood is not so much death as the releasing of life. Therefore, he interprets the blood of Jesus Christ as the life of Jesus Christ—not His death but His life, and what we have here, therefore, he would have us believe, is that the life of Jesus Christ, the life that is in the blood, or the blood that represents the life, is cleansing us and delivering us from the power and the principle of sin that is within us and is responsible for so much.

But in all these passages referring to the blood you will find that every single time, without exception, it clearly refers to death and not to life. The object of Jesus Christ upon the cross was not simply to 'release the life principle'; it was rather to fulfil the law of God which has said that the punishment of sin is death—'the wages of sin is death' (Rom 6:23)—not the releasing of life, but the taking of life, the shedding forth of the life blood. The Apostle Paul says in Romans 5:10: 'If, when we were enemies, we were reconciled to God by the death of his Son'—the blood was shed in that death, and that is the effect—'much more, being reconciled, we shall be saved by his life.' So that surely what the Apostle is referring to here is the death of Jesus Christ, not His life.

That leads us, then, to the second question. What does the death of Jesus Christ achieve? What, according to the New Testament, is the function of the death of our Lord upon the cross, and what has resulted from it? And again I suggest to you that the answer is invariably this: Our Lord's death is that which has purchased our pardon; the death is concerned about reconciliation, about justification, about remission of sins. In other words, I am suggesting that the death of our Lord never goes beyond that.

Take again that great statement of Paul in Romans 5:10 which I have just quoted and you will see the distinction. The death of Christ deals with the guilt of sin, the pollution of sin and its tarnishing effect; sanctification and our perfection is the work of the life of Christ, the work of the risen Christ who has sent the Holy Spirit into us and upon us. The work of sanctification is surely the work of the Holy Spirit who has been given to us as the gift of God by the risen Christ. The death is concerned about the guilt of sin; the life is concerned with the power of sin and our sanctification; and therefore it seems to me that there is nothing which is worse confounded than to say that the blood of Jesus Christ has any reference whatsoever to our sanctification.

It is important we should bear that in mind at this particular point. What John is interested in is fellowship with and a possibility of walking with God. He is not interested in our sinful natures as such, but in the guilt of sin and the tarnishing which sin produces and which interrupts the fellowship. What he is anxious to show us is that though we are guilty of sins, and though we fall into sin, we can still have fellowship with God.

Let us be quite clear about this. The Bible does not teach us anywhere that fellowship with God is made impossible because sin still remains in us; if that were true no man who has ever lived would ever have fellowship with God. For if to have fellowship with God, we must be absolutely perfect and the very sin principle must have been removed, then not one of us has had fellowship with God, for we are aware of sin within ourselves. That is not what John is concerned about. He is concerned about walking with God, and what he says is that though the sin principle remains in us, though we have sinned, we can still have fellowship with God.

'Yes,' says someone, 'but what about the sins I have committed and their polluting and tarnishing effects?' 'Ah,' says John, 'the blood of Jesus Christ cleanses the very guilt and pollution and tarnishing effect and therefore you can continue in the fellowship.' Now there, I suggest to you, is the doctrine of the Apostle at this point. Let no one misunderstand me—I am not stating that sanctification does not matter. Sanctification is of supreme importance, but where sanctification comes in is this: your effort to walk in the light is part of your sanctification, and so is your confessing your sins and recognising them.

John has a great deal to say about sanctification in this epistle. He tells us to love the brethren; he tells us to be kind and loving; he tells us not to live for the things of this world—that is sanctification. But the blood of Jesus Christ has no reference to sanctification; it is, rather, something that has reference to our justification. The question before us is just this question of finding ourselves sinful and then feeling we cannot have fellowship with God. We think we are unworthy of this fellowship, so what can we do about it? And this is John's answer to us in this glorious message.

So if that is the doctrine, then there are certain things that follow immediately, to which we must pay attention. There are certain phrases that one often hears being used in this connection which seem to me to be quite unscriptural. The Christian is not a man or woman who ought to be walking in the light but who so often is walking in darkness. The Christian is one who, by definition here, is always walking in the light even though he falls into sin. By falling into sin you do not return to walking in darkness. The Christian is not a Christian at all unless he is walking in the light.

Let me put it in this way. There are some people who seem to speak in such as way as to give the impression that one moment you are in the kingdom of God and the next moment you are in the kingdom of Satan. But the New Testament does not say that. Christians do not spend their lives walking in and out of the kingdom of God; we are all by nature in the kingdom of darkness, and by becoming Christians we are translated, put into, the kingdom of God. Let me say this, and it is a daring statement in a sense, yet it is scriptural: if I fall into sin I am still in the kingdom of God. I am not walking in darkness because I have sinned; I am still in the realm of light and in the kingdom of God even though I have sinned—the shed blood of Jesus Christ put me there. And it is this shed blood of Christ that still delivers me from the guilt of my sins in the kingdom of God.

Let me also put it like this—you sometimes hear people, in the light of this word, saying something to this effect: 'You know, we have to keep going back to Calvary'; and they draw this picture of the Christian life as a journey. You start at Calvary, and you walk in the fellowship, then you sin, and you have to go back to Calvary. No, you do not go back; in a sense Calvary is always accompanying you. You do not go back in your Christian life; if you fall into sin, you confess it and go on. It is the blood of Jesus Christ that cleanses, and Calvary is something that accompanies us in the grace and mercy of God. It is exactly like the picture which the Apostle Paul draws in 1 Corinthians 10:4, when he talks about the rock that followed the ancient people in the wilderness. That rock was Christ, he says.

Let me take just one other phrase. You have people using this self-same text and saying something like, 'Ah, yes, you must take your sin and put it under the blood.' They talk as if they are being highly scriptural, but actually they are misinterpreting the phrase. You do not find this misinterpretation in Scripture. Surely what our text teaches us is that when we sin we must confess it. We acknowledge it before God, and in His infinite mercy He will put the blood upon it. It is God who applies the blood; He is faithful and just to forgive us our sins. It is the blood of Jesus Christ that cleanses us from the guilt of sin; God has made the provision, and He applies it. We are called upon to walk in the light and to confess our sins, and as we do so He will bring to bear upon our confessed sin the provision He made on Calvary in the death of His only begotten Son. We are delivered from that guilt and pollution and from that tarnishing effect and we are conscious that the fellowship is restored and we can continue. In other words, I suggest to you that sanctification does not enter into this phrase at all, that the whole time the Apostle is concerned about justification, and then the rest of the epistle in a sense is just an elaboration of the great doctrine of sanctification.

Let me, finally, emphasise the assurance which the Christian has in the light of this wonderful provision. This is one of the most comforting statements in the Holy Scriptures. Here am I anxious to have fellowship with God and to walk with Him in the light, but I find myself sinning. Then the devil comes and says, 'You are no Christian; you cannot walk with Him; look at your sin and your guilt!'—and one feels hopeless. But here is the glorious answer to that, and this is our assurance—'The blood of Jesus Christ cleanses us'—it goes on doing so and will continue to do it—'from all sin'. 'He is faithful and just to forgive us our sins, and to cleanse us from all unrighteousness.'

How can I hope to have this forgiveness of my sins? The answer is that the blood of the Son of God cleanses me from it. Look at David in Psalm 51, conscious of pollution and of the need of cleansing. 'This pollution, this tarnished effect of sin,' he cries, 'what can take it from me? Hyssop is not enough; the blood of bulls and of goats is not enough.' No, I need something that can cleanse me and give me assurance, and this is what I am told: it is the blood of Jesus Christ His Son, and I can trust this. Or as the Apostle Peter puts it in his first epistle, where he reminds us that we should be perfect and clear in our minds that we have been delivered from our sinfulness and from our vain conversation inherited by tradition from our fathers, not 'with corruptible things, as silver and gold . . . but with the precious blood of Christ, as of a lamb without blemish and without spot' (1 Pet 1:18-19). All the solutions of the world are insufficient to get rid of the stain of my sins, but here is the blood of the Son of God, spotless, blameless, and I feel that this is powerful.

> *There is power, power, wonder-working power*
> *In the precious blood of the Lamb.*
>
> *His blood can make the foulest clean,*
> *His blood availed for me.*
>
> CHARLES WESLEY

That is our comfort and consolation.

But in addition, 'He is faithful and just to forgive us our sins, and to cleanse us from all unrighteousness.' What does this mean? Well, says John, if you want further comfort and assurance, here it is—it is the very character of God Himself. God has promised that in Christ He has provided the way. He promised it in the old dispensation; He gave us types and shadows, all the ceremonies of the levitical priesthood. But, God said, I am going to provide a perfect sacrifice, and when He comes, sin will be entirely forgiven. And God is faithful; all He has promised has been perfectly fulfilled. He has promised that if we confess our sins, if we look to His Son dying upon that cross, He will forgive us freely. Therefore have no doubts, says John; rely upon the faithfulness of God to His own word and promises.

But even stronger than that, John tells us that God is just, and this is John's way of putting what Paul has said in Romans 3:25. Paul puts it like this: The problem of sin to God, if I may put it with reverence, is, how can He forgive sin and still remain a holy and just God? The answer is in the cross of Christ. He has set Him forth 'to be a propitiation for our sins', and the result is that in the light of the death of Christ upon the cross, God can be 'just and the justifier' (v 26) of the ungodly. The cross of Christ justifies God; he remains holy because He has punished sin in the death, the shed blood, of His Son.

So as I am aware of my sinfulness and my unworthiness and my unrighteousness, I look to the blood of Jesus Christ, and I see there the forgiveness of God. I see the justice of God; I know that there God has forgiven and still forgives and will forgive. It is not that I am to make merchandise of the blood of Christ; not that I am to regard the blood of Christ as a cheap thing which allows me to continue in sin that grace may abound. No, it is that I can have this confidence that the death of Christ upon the cross is the propitiation for my sins—indeed, for the sins of the whole world—and that all my sins have been dealt with and are covered, are removed and banished there in Him.

Knowing thus the faithfulness and justice of God and the power of the blood of Christ to deliver me and to cleanse me from the guilt and stain of my sins, I can with confidence go forward, knowing that all is clear, my conscience has been cleansed, and I can continue to walk with God.

13

JESUS, HIS SON

. . . the blood of Jesus Christ his Son (or, the blood of Jesus his Son) . . .

1 JOHN 1:7

IT IS THE BUSINESS OF Christian preaching at all times, on all days and on all occasions, to be preaching Christ Jesus the Lord. But it is always good for us particularly and specially to remind ourselves of the facts and of the details lest we tend to assume we know them all, instead of constantly reminding ourselves of them. And here, in this one phrase, it seems to me we have a perfect account or epitome of the essential doctrine which is taught in the New Testament with regard to this great and vital subject—'the blood of Jesus his Son.'

Now these New Testament epistles were never written merely for the sake of writing; they were never produced merely as literary effusions of men who were fond of writing or whose vocation in life was that of producing literature. These letters came into being because of a situation that arose in the infant Christian Church; they were written with pastoral intent, and that is particularly true of this first epistle of John.

John is concerned, as we have seen all along, about the vital importance of understanding the doctrine concerning the person of our Lord Jesus Christ. This is, in a sense, the thing that made him write at all. As we go on through this epistle in subsequent volumes we shall find that he makes frequent references to what he calls 'anti-Christs', and he uses very strong language. He says that certain people who are writing about this doctrine are 'liars', and so according to John, it is very important that we should be perfectly clear, without any suspicion of doubt or of hesitation, with regard to the person of Jesus of Nazareth, the Son of God.

This is something that can never be emphasised too frequently; the whole case of the New Testament is bound up with this question. So it is something which we must constantly repeat, because it does seem to be the fatal tendency of mankind, even of the Christian Church herself, to divorce the teaching from the person. Yet the moment you do so, you have no real teaching. That is what differentiates this from everything else; it is not an idea or a proposal, nor is it a philosophy. It is the presentation of a person, without whom we have nothing at all.

I am not saying that there is no value at all in good, uplifting and moral teaching or that there is no benefit to be derived by society from the consideration of noble ideas and exalted conceptions with regard to life. That is all right, but it is just not Christianity. It has nothing to do with it, in a sense, and we can do no greater violence to the New Testament doctrine than to represent the message of Christ's birth[1] as but some vague general message of goodwill and of good cheer and happiness. That is not its message at all.

No, if we do not start with the person of the Lord Jesus Christ, if we are not absolutely clear about Him, then there is nothing. There is no good news, there is no evangel, there is no gospel; there is nothing to cheer us up, there is no hope. We are just living in the darkness of the world, and we are unutterably foolish in trying to persuade ourselves that things are better than they really are. There is no such thing, in a sense, as the 'Christmas spirit'. That is not the Christian message; it is not a vague spirit; it is a message of news concerning Him, so that, therefore, we must of necessity start at this point and be absolutely clear about this matter.

As has often been pointed out, 'Christianity is Christ'. It all centres round Him, and every doctrine that we have and every idea that we possess is something that comes from Him. Therefore, we must of necessity start with Him, and of course John in this letter has already done so. We pointed out, in dealing with the first three verses, that immediately he announced his message: 'That which was from the beginning, which we have heard, which we have seen with our eyes, which we have looked upon, and our hands have handled, of the Word of life . . . that which we have seen and heard declare we unto you.' He started at once with his doctrine, and it was the doctrine of the person. For the whole message which John has to deliver is, simply, that to us there is only one way of fellowship and communion with God, and that is because of the Lord Jesus Christ. It is He alone who can enable us to know this fellowship, for there is 'one mediator between God and men, the man Christ Jesus' (1 Tim 2:5).

So if He is the essential link, if He is the only way of communion with God, how vitally important it is that we should be perfectly clear about Him! And as we saw in those first three verses, John immediately proceeds to correct certain errors that had crept in with regard to His person, even in those early days. 'We have heard,' says John, 'we have seen with our eyes, we have looked upon, our hands have handled.' And there, immediately, he is correcting heresy. Indeed, as you look at this epistle and go through it, you are at once impressed by the great fact, which he goes on repeating, that it is these various doctrines with regard to the person of the Lord Jesus Christ that always tend to be the greatest source of trouble in the Christian Church. So we must be clear about this; otherwise we have nothing whatsoever.

So here in one phrase he again gives the whole doctrine, and to me there is nothing that is quite so wonderful or charming, in the true sense of the word, as the way in which so often in the Scriptures you have the whole of the doctrine put in a phrase like this. These men repeat it; they never apologise for that, they were always preaching the same theme; it was always this wonderful person. They never got far away from Him because He was everything to them, and so they go on repeating their whole doctrine, and here is a phrase which says it all—'the blood of Jesus his Son'.

What does this suggest to you? First of all it reminds us of the historical character of our faith. You see, our faith is concerned about the person of Jesus and there, immediately, we are in the realm of history. The Greek philosophers talk a great deal about their 'ideas'. These began as great ideas up in the heavens; then these great ideas had somehow or another become incarnate, but it was all in the realm of ideas. They were always concerned about thoughts, and so much that still passes as Christianity falls into that ancient error.

Now that is corrected here, because we are concerned about Jesus, 'Jesus his Son'; we are concerned about certain *facts*, and that is the great glory of our Christian faith, that it is something that is based upon a series of historical facts and events, and this very name, Jesus, reminds us of that. 'Jesus'—yes, the baby that was born in Bethlehem in a stable and placed in a manger; Jesus, an actual child that was born into this world; the boy Jesus arguing in the Temple, still right in the realm of history and of facts; a young man working as a carpenter, Jesus.

Then there were three years, the most amazing three years the world has ever known, when, having set out upon His public ministry, He travelled backwards and forwards, up and down that land of Palestine, preaching and teaching and working His miracles and dealing with the people. It is still solid history, yes, quite as definite as 55 B.C. when Julius Caesar conquered Britain; quite as real as 1066 and all other events of history—Jesus a person and all that we know about Him, culminating in the agony in the garden and on the cross and in the burial and the resurrection and the ascension.

Now that is what we are concerned about; it is as real, as realistic as that. Oh! how can one put this so that it may be clear to us once and for ever that we are essentially concerned about something that has taken place in history? When unbelievers or people who tell us that they are not Christians come to us and would have us believe that we are misled or that we have gone astray in believing our Christian faith and gospel, when they come and deny our truth and faith, the real answer to give them is not, 'You can say what you like, but I have felt or experienced something.' No, the real reply is history, the birth of the baby Jesus in the manger, and all the other facts that we have just mentioned.

Experience is not the ultimate proof of our Christian faith and its reality. Thank God, we do have experiences, but, thank God, we have something much more than that. With regard to experiences we must agree with the writer of the hymn who said, 'I dare not trust the sweetest frame'—feelings come and feelings go—

> But wholly lean on Jesus' Name.
> On Christ, the solid Rock, I stand;
> All other ground is sinking sand.

> EDWARD MOTE

Jesus—the person, the one who has entered into history—thank God for a historical faith, thank God for a gospel that is based upon facts. That is the first thing that is suggested to us by this verse.

But let me go on to say a word about the wonder of the incarnation. Having looked in that way at the historicity of the incarnation, let us have a look at the wonder of it. Here, of course, the very words used by the Apostle, and especially these two words in juxtaposition, express the whole doctrine: *'Jesus his Son'*. What an amazing combination of words! You will find the writers of hymns sometimes invoking angels, sometimes wishing that they had the power and voice of an angel to express truth, and that is exactly how I feel as I take these words. Oh, for a thousand tongues to express it! Oh, for an angelic power of expression to bring out the full meaning of such terms, but here they are, put together.

The baby lying in the manger, His Son, God's Son. The boy aged twelve in the Temple reprimanded by Mary and Joseph for not having accompanied them as they went back from the feast at Jerusalem. Jesus—who is He? 'His Son', the Son of God. The carpenter working quietly day by day in His workshop, so much like others to all outward appearance and yet essentially different, doing His work and helping others—Jesus the carpenter of Nazareth? No—'Jesus his Son'. And on you go with the story, and all along it is the same.

What does all this convey to us? Well, here we are face to face with the whole marvel and wonder of the incarnation. The Apostle Paul puts it all in that grand passage of his in Philippians 2:5-11, which surely can never be improved upon: 'Let this mind be in you, which was also in Christ Jesus'—now here is the doctrine—'who, being in the form of God, thought it not robbery to be equal with God: but made himself of no reputation, and took upon him the form of a servant, and was made in the likeness of men; and being found in fashion as a man, he humbled himself, and became obedient unto death, even the death of the cross. Wherefore God hath highly exalted him, and given him a name which is above every name; that at the name of Jesus every knee should bow, of things in heaven, and things in earth, and things under the earth; and that every tongue should confess that Jesus Christ is Lord, to the glory of God the Father.'

But all that is really conveyed by this expression—'Jesus his Son'; the baby is none other than the Son of God. This involves all that Paul has put in that magnificent statement of his; it involves the humiliation of the incarnation; it involves what is there put as 'making himself of no reputation'; 'being in the form of God'—in other words having all the qualifications that make God God—having those essential things that are essential to deity, not an appearance but the thing itself in its essence. But how did one who was thus in the form of God become the baby lying in a manger? And the answer is that He did not hold on to, He did not clutch at all at the prerogatives and the insignia of deity to which he was thus entitled there in eternity; rather, He made Himself of no reputation. He did not cease to be God, He did not divest Himself of His deity; nor did He empty Himself of the content of eternity. No, that is error, that is heresy. But what He did was this: He decided that He would come on earth and not use them or employ them. He decided that He would, as it were, hold them in abeyance. He would live life as a man though He was still God—'Jesus his Son'.

We cannot understand this. It baffles not only the mind and understanding, but also the very imagination itself. But that is the picture that is conveyed of the marvel and the miracle of the incarnation in the New Testament. We have read at times of certain kings travelling incognito. The man is a king or a prince, but he does not let it be known; he lives as if he were an ordinary traveller. And it was something like that, multiplied by infinity, when the Son of God became Jesus. He did not use the powers, He did not exercise His prerogatives, He came in the likeness of man.

He came, indeed, in 'the likeness of sinful flesh' and He lived out His life as a man, but He was still God—God and man, God-man; two natures in one person and yet no co-mingling, not a kind of effusion of the two natures. No, two natures; still Jesus, yes, truly man, but all the time 'His Son', the unique Son of God, the one who has come out of the bosom of the Father. Two natures in one person and therefore that extraordinary person of whom we read in the Gospels and upon whom we meditate. This strange amazing thing—the baby in helplessness—Son of God; the boy with His understanding—Son of God; the carpenter—Son of God; always the two. Jesus, His Son.

Next let us see how this extraordinary phrase reminds us and establishes the reality of the incarnation: 'The blood of Jesus his Son.' Here John is again correcting those heresies that had crept in with regard to the person of our Lord. What he is really telling us in this phrase is that the incarnation does not mean that the Son of God took upon Him a phantom body. It is not that the Son of God put a kind of cloak or covering appearance of flesh and body. Not at all! 'The Word was made flesh' (Jn 1:14). He was not a spirit; this was not a theophany, a mere appearance. It is an *incarnation*—'a spirit hath not flesh and bones' (Lk 24:39); a spirit does not have blood, but it is 'the blood of Jesus his Son'. The incarnation is a reality; it is a fact.

Now there were certain people in that early Church to whom John had occasion to point out that particular heresy. They said that the Son of God could not really have been made flesh. 'It is impossible,' they said, 'for God to dwell on the earth as man and in the likeness of sinful flesh. No, what happened was this: when the eternal Son came on earth he took on this kind of phantom body, it was not a real one.' But John denies that when he says, 'the blood of Jesus'. The baby, the boy, the carpenter—it was an actual incarnation, not an appearance.

But let me put it like this also. There were those, you remember, who taught that Jesus certainly was a human being. They said they believed in the baby in a manger and the boy and so on, but what they tell us at this point is that at His baptism the eternal Christ entered into the man Jesus. 'There is no such thing as the virgin birth,' they said; 'there is no such thing as God actually being born and coming out of the virgin's womb. No, there, in the baptism, the eternal Christ somehow came into the man Jesus, and then He dwelt with Him throughout the three years, but on the cross left Him again. So that the Son of God did not die, it was Jesus the man who died'—that was actually being taught in the early Church.

It is good for us to remind ourselves that every single heresy that we can ever think of had been thought of probably before the end of the first century. There is nothing very modern or up to date in being heretical; it is as old as the gospel itself. Let no one think he is wonderful and modern in denying certain of these essential doctrines!

And this is John's reply: it is 'the blood of Jesus his Son' that cleanses us from all sin. The blood of man cannot do it, nor the blood of bulls and of goats. It was the very Son of God who died, as it was the Son of God who was born, as it was the Son of God who endured the contradiction of sinners against Himself and staggered up Golgotha. It was His blood that was shed. And that is the blood that purchased our pardon and forgiveness and reconciles us to God and opens the door of heaven to let us in. It is actual, it is real, it was not an appearance. The amazing doctrine is that as Jesus was the Son of God, it was the Son of God who died upon the cross. Wonder of wonders, marvel of marvels, even as He was dying, He was still Jesus, His Son, and it is that blood that sets us free.

There is one other deduction. We are reminded by this phrase of the whole purpose of the incarnation. Now the New Testament is never in any difficulty about this; its answer is always perfectly clear and plain and unequivocal. The Son of God was born as Jesus in Bethlehem in order that He might die. He came to die, and we should never speak of the incarnation except in terms of the death; all these doctrines are one and indissoluble. He came to taste death for every man; He came to die because nothing but that death could save us. That is the doctrine, so that as we think of 'the blood of Jesus his Son' we are reminded that nothing less, nothing else, could provide salvation.

God had given the law; God had sent His prophets and patriarchs. He had raised up great men and blessed them, and still there was no true salvation. The best men had failed; none could keep the law; 'every mouth [has been] stopped', 'the whole world [is] guilty before God', all have 'come short of the glory of God' (Rom 3:19, 23). Everything had been tried, and nothing was sufficient. There is only one way whereby man can be saved and reconciled to God; there must be a shedding of blood and a perfect offering and sacrifice. There must be someone who is man and yet more than man. He must be perfect and absolute.

So the Son of God came and took unto Himself human nature, and in this perfect human nature He shed His blood. And the Lord God is satisfied; the sacrifice and offering are perfect, and in Him God can forgive and pardon—'the blood of Jesus his Son.' The purpose of the incarnation is the death and the atonement, the resurrection and the reconciliation.

Last of all, how can we finish without considering, however feebly and unworthily, the love that led to all this. Just think of it; the Son of God, Jesus, the one through whom all things were made, the Word that is in the bosom of the Father, the Word that was God from the beginning, the eternal absolute Son enjoying all the full prerogatives of deity from everlasting to everlasting—lying helpless as a baby in a manger. And all that you and I might be saved and reconciled to God!

Oh, what wondrous love that should stoop so low! But look at the record, follow the story; look at Him suffering the scorn and the derision, the abuse, the jealousy, the envy, the hatred, the malice, the scourging. Look at Him as they put that heavy cross upon His holy shoulder.

As He staggers beneath His load a man, Simon of Cyrene, has to come and help Him. Who is this struggling under this impossible weight? It is the everlasting eternal Son of God, Jesus, His Son! And why is He doing it? That you and I might be redeemed.

Look at Him there upon the cross, in His pain, suffering that agony that is almost unendurable. What does it all mean? Why has He done it all; why does He die; why does He suffer Himself to be buried in a grave? What has produced it all? And there is but one response—'Love, so amazing, so divine.'

God has come Himself in the person of the Son; He has known that humiliation and the suffering and the contradiction of sinners and the agony and the shame, and He has done it so that we might be forgiven, that we might become His children and that we might go on to be with Him in glory for ever and ever. What amazing love, to give us so much, to stoop so low! 'God commendeth his love toward us, in that, while we were yet sinners, Christ died for us' (Rom 5:8).

'The blood of Jesus his Son!'

NOTES

CHAPTER FOUR: THE APOSTOLIC DECLARATION

1 The United Nations Association was an organisation set up in Britain after the Second World War to support the work of the United Nations.

2 Said in 1948 at the gathering of the World Council of Churches—he was accused of having 'thrown a bombshell into the proceedings'!

CHAPTER SIX: ALL BECAUSE OF CHRIST

1 This sermon was preached on Remembrance Sunday 1948.

CHAPTER THIRTEEN: JESUS, HIS SON

1 This sermon was preached on 26th December 1948.

Walking with God

Acknowledgments

THESE SERMONS WERE first preached in Westminster Chapel in 1948/9 and form the sequel to *Fellowship with God*. Eagle-eyed readers will note that the last verse of chapter 2 is not dealt with. This is because the Doctor felt that that verse was better incorporated in the sermons on chapter 3, and so his exposition of verse 29 will appear as the first chapter of volume 3 of this series.

The basic editing of these sermons was carried out by Christopher Catherwood, the Doctor's eldest grandson and Editorial Director at Crossway Books in England. However, as usual, an enormous amount of work on these manuscripts has also been done by Elizabeth Catherwood, the Doctor's elder daughter and literary executrix, and to her go special thanks. (She has also done much unsung on many of his other books, so it is fitting that she should be given her due honour here.) As before, Alison Walley has not only copy edited the manuscript, but typed it onto disk for the publishers, and so full thanks are due to her as well.

Lastly, much of the vision for this series comes from the enthusiasm shown by J. I. Packer, who with his wife heard many of them preached back in the 1940's, and also to Lane Dennis, the publisher for Crossway, whose commitment to the cause of Christian truth has made their publication possible.

1

SIN

My little children, these things write I unto you, that ye sin not. And if any man sin, we have an advocate with the Father, Jesus Christ the righteous: and he is the propitiation for our sins: and not for ours only, but also for the sin of the whole world.

1 JOHN 2:1-2

THERE ARE CERTAIN PERIODS in our lives—New Year's Eve perhaps[1] or certain important occasions—when we find ourselves thinking about life itself, its whole object and meaning and purpose. We think about ourselves, wondering what we have made of life, what are we doing with it and what is the ultimate future that is very steadily facing us all. Probably, quite inevitably, we also look backwards, wondering how we have conducted and comported ourselves hitherto, and probably also we are all aware of a sense of dissatisfaction. We are aware that we have not done what we should have done and what we intended to do. We are aware of a sense of failure and inadequacy, and at the same time we are aware within us of a desire to do better in the days that lie ahead. Those are the thoughts that tend to come to us as we pause at any point in life and look backwards and forward, and perhaps the greatest and the most important thing of all is that we should be quite certain about life itself and its meaning and its purpose.

Now the danger at a time like this always is to take too superficial a view. The trouble, it seems to me, about New Year's and all our other resolutions is that they are resolutions with regard to particular things, but we fail to be concerned about first principles. Our danger is that we deal with the symptoms instead of with the disease, and that is surely the biggest danger as we look back and review the past. We tend to get down immediately to detail before we have really considered the big principles themselves, and thus it is that life so often tends to become rather futile.

One of the real difficulties in life is not to be mastered by it. We all tend inevitably to become victims of circumstances and chance and of accident and thus we go on from day to day perhaps feeling uneasy at times, feeling concerned and then somehow or other getting rid of that feeling or forgetting it, and so we are back where we were before. Then, perhaps, something big and important will take place; a birth, a death, an illness or an accident, some calamity which we read of in the newspapers, or war, something devastating, and again we are pulled up and we begin to think and to meditate. We are once more conscious of this sense of dissatisfaction and lack of ease about ourselves, and we ponder and propose that really something must be done about it. We are genuinely determined to do so and then, somehow or another, that acute state passes and in a few days we are back again exactly where we were at the beginning.

Now that, I suggest, is not an unfair or inadequate picture of the life of the average person; aware from time to time of something centrally wrong and then being confined only to detail instead of to the central thing. And the inevitable result is that the main tenor of life continues more or less as it was before and nothing really vital has been changed.

Now the Bible is very concerned about all that. Indeed, that is its great central concern, and it has one great remedy for the problem. According to the Bible the one big thing that matters is that we should be right with God. The Bible is, primarily, a book of great principles. Of course it does come down to details, but its main emphasis is on these central principles. It looks out upon mankind trying to improve itself, and it says, 'Yes, that is all right, but it will avail you nothing because you are ignoring the centre. You are treating the symptoms, but you have forgotten that the trouble is at the source.' So it always brings us back to that source, which is that the most important thing of all is our relationship to God.

To put it another way, all our troubles in life, according to the Bible, are ultimately due to the fact that we are in a wrong relationship to God.

That has been the Biblical diagnosis for thousands of years and it is as true now as it has ever been—all our ills and all our unhappiness ultimately come back to the fact that we have wandered from God, that we are not in the right relationship to Him. Indeed, the Bible goes further and says that until we do come back to that true and right relationship, nothing will avail us. We can improve ourselves here and there, but if we are centrally wrong, finally we shall be altogether wrong.

That is the great theme of the Bible from beginning to end, and the ways in which it puts that message are almost endless. You get it in plain, direct, unvarnished teaching, but you also get it in some of the people that it puts before us, and we should thank God for them, these characters and illustrations which we have in the Bible, who are, as it were, living representations of its doctrine and teaching.

Take the saints of the Bible, the so-called heroes of the faith; take people like those who are represented in Hebrews 11. They are but samples, just a few of the great list of names that we have in the Old Testament. There are men and women who were in this world exactly as we are, subject to the same vicissitudes, subject to the same things that tend to happen to us in a world like this, and yet, as you look at them, you have to admit that there was something exceptional and outstanding about them. They were people who seemed to be triumphant in life, and their secret, according to the Bible, was only one thing; it was their relationship to God.

Now these were men and women who were independent of their circumstances, and they were what they were because they were right at the centre with God. They suffered terrible trials, they endured adversity in its extremest form, yet you cannot look at them without seeing that they were people who possessed a calmness, a poise and a hopefulness which nothing could destroy. You see things going wrong all around and about them, and yet you see them going steadily forward. And the reason for this, says the author of Hebrews, was their faith. Faith is being in the right relationship to God, knowing Him. Their secret was that they went on 'as seeing him who is invisible' (Heb 11:27); it was because they were right with God that they were made independent of circumstances and chance and conditions and surroundings.

That is typically representative of the Biblical teaching, and the message of the Bible to us is still just that. It is not part of the business of Christian preaching and of the Christian Church just to comment about conditions and circumstances and happenings. It is not part of the preaching of the gospel to try to predict and prophesy what will happen in the future. Many attempt to do that, but it is utterly hopeless. It may cheer us up for the time being to be told that something good is going to happen, but it is the old story and it never leads to anything. Rather, the business of Christian preaching is to tell us that whatever the circumstances may be, whatever may be awaiting us in the future, if we are right with God it will not finally matter, it will not have a devastating effect upon us.

Now that is an all-inclusive challenge; the Bible makes that claim and its whole offer is just that: if we are right at the centre with God we can look to the future and say, 'Come what may, all will be well with my soul.' This message, which it puts to us in so many different ways, places us in this happy position of being more or less independent of circumstances and accidents and chance and environment, anything that may happen. It does not try to improve these particular problems; it puts us right. Its case is that if we are right, then we shall be masters of our circumstances, so it always brings us back to that central and all-important matter.

Here, then, is the thing that primarily counts, that we should be right with God, that we should have fellowship with Him, that we should know Him; so that if God calls us, as He called Abraham, to do something which seems to us at that moment to be shattering, we go forward as seeing Him who is invisible; we do it in faith. Or, like Moses perhaps, we may be presented and confronted by a choice which we cannot quite understand, but we will be in no hesitation, 'choosing rather to suffer affliction with the people of God, than to enjoy the pleasures of sin for a season' (Heb 11:25). That is it! We may be called to do things which come to the natural man in an utterly devastating manner, and yet to us, because we are right with God, we will have an understanding and we will not be afraid.

That is the thing which John deals with in these two verses. This epistle, as we have seen,[2] was probably written about A.D. 85 when John was an old man. The words he uses suggest that he was old: he says, 'my little children,' though he was not addressing little children but adults, members of the Church. But to John they were but little children; some had even come into the faith in his own ministry. At any rate, he had taught them, and now the old man at the end of his life, knowing he has not many more years in this world, sees these people, the young Christian Church, confronted by difficulties and problems and trials and tribulations. What can he say to them? He sees the danger, he knows the frailty of human nature, what is it that matters? So his final bit of advice to them is: 'My little children, these things write I unto you, that ye sin not. And if any man sin, we have an advocate with the Father, Jesus Christ the righteous: and he is the propitiation for our sins: and not for ours only, but also for the sins of the whole world.'

As John looks at those people, and as he looks back across his own life, he sees that there are two main dangers that always confront us— he is writing particularly to Christian people. The first is that of complacency, and the other is the exact opposite, the danger of hopelessness. Or, to put it another way, the danger is compromise on the one hand and depression on the other; and the trouble with most of us is that we tend to oscillate between these two. In certain moods and states we are very complacent; we say we are all right, but in the next moment we are feeling utterly hopeless and full of despair. How difficult it is to maintain an even keel, to keep balance, just to be steady and strong and sure, avoiding these extremes that are always there confronting us. That is John's diagnosis, so he provides something which will cater for that very possibility and he divides his message up into two—command and comfort; exhortation and consolation; objective and promise. And the two parts are: what you and I have to do and what God in His infinite grace is always ready to do for us.

Now these, according to the Bible everywhere, are the two most important things for us in this life and world. They are the two things we must always bear in mind if we are anxious to enjoy true fellowship with God. That is John's advice to these people. 'I am going out of the world,' he says in effect. 'I shall not be with you much longer, and the one thing that matters for you is that you should always be walking with God, that you should always be maintaining that fellowship. If that is right, it does not matter very much what will happen to you.'

How, then, is that to be maintained? This is John's reply. First of all there is the word, the command, the exhortation, the objective which we should never lose sight of, but which we should always keep steadily before us: 'These things write I unto you, that ye sin not.' If you want to know God and maintain fellowship with God, do not sin. We shall look later at these two verses in a more purely practical sense, and I want to put it as simply as I can. There is very high doctrine in these two verses, doctrine that has often led, and will lead, to a great deal of discussion and disputation, but let us just look at it now quite simply as a practical, direct exhortation.

'That ye sin not.' What does this mean? To answer that, let us ask an apparently almost ridiculously simple question: What is sin? Why should we not sin? Well, sin means that we disobey God's holy law which He has revealed to us. Sin is anything that is condemned in the Bible. It does not matter what it is, if the Bible tells us not to do it then we must not do it: 'Thou shalt not kill'; 'thou shalt not steal'; 'thou shalt not commit adultery.' I feel at times we ought to put the Ten Commandments in the forefront of our preaching. There are certain prohibitions which are absolute and about which there is no discussion, and if you are in a condition of querying and questioning and breaking them, then you will never know fellowship with God; these are absolute where God is concerned. Sin is disobedience to God's revealed law.

It also means disobeying conscience. There is within us all that inward monitor; we have no excuse; before we did that thing we knew it was wrong; there was this voice that told us not to do it, that called us to stop and think. It said, 'No, you cannot do that.' It was there and we knew it was wrong and yet we did it. To disobey conscience is to commit sin. The Bible does not only say that if we are doubtful about a thing we must not do it; it says, 'Abstain from all appearance of evil' (1 Thess. 5:22); anything that looks evil, do not do it.

Or, to put it still more generally, sin means that our lives are governed by desires and not by truth. Is this not the very essence of the whole moral psychological problem at the present time? People today are not interested in truth; they say they are entitled to do what they want to do, and if you begin to reason with them they say, 'Why not?'—that is the question—or 'I couldn't care less!' That is the terrible and awful statement that sums it up—this modern spirit of lawlessness, governed by desire, by impulse, by passion and lust and not by standards of truth, not by a clear indication of that which is right and wrong.

We can sum it up like this: to live a life of sin means that we are not governed by God, that thoughts of God are not at the centre of our lives, that we do not ask ourselves, 'What would God have me to do, what does God prohibit?' It means that we are governed by what John, in this self-same chapter, goes on to call 'the world'—the way of the world, the whole attitude of the world. It is that sort of life in which thoughts of God do not come in except perhaps occasionally when men and women are frightened because they have been taken ill or there is a death. It means God has not governed and controlled their lives, that they have been dictated by everything that is apart from God. That is sin, to live and to dwell in that kind of atmosphere and to be living that sort of life; as if God did not exist and as if this were the only world and as if man were the supreme being in the whole universe. That is the negative way of looking at it.

The positive way to view this is, of course, that we live as people who are walking in the light. We must not be content with looking at this question of sin negatively; the best way of not sinning is positively to be living the godly life, and that means walking in the light. In other words, it means living as to God and to His glory.

As the first question in the Shorter Catechism of the Westminster Confession puts it, 'The chief end of man is to glorify God and to enjoy Him for ever.' That is the way to avoid sinning, to start out with this main objective, that I am here to live to the glory of God, that my supreme purpose should be to honour Him and to live in accordance with His holy will. I should ask myself, not 'What do I want?' but 'What does the Lord want? What is the Lord's will? What has He revealed concerning Himself and His purpose?' I start with the great desire to live to His glory, and if I do that I shall not sin.

That, then, is the first way of looking at it; that is what is meant by saying 'that we sin not.' But let me go on to ask a still more practical question—why must we not sin? Let me give you some answers to that question—and I suggest to you that the more we reason these things out, the better it will be for us and the more we shall be unable to sin. Firstly, sin is something which is condemned and hated by God, something which is utterly opposed to Him and His divine and holy nature. That really ought to be enough for us. There is no need to argue about this. I must not sin because God has said I must not; it is abhorrent to Him.

Another reason why I should not sin is that sin is wrong in and of itself and in its own nature. Is this not one of the greatest troubles in life, that we will not look upon these things objectively? Of course we do not do that because we are involved in the process and we are always out to excuse ourselves and to explain away what we have done. But it is important that we should look upon sin objectively, look at its ugliness and its foulness; look at all the misery and wretchedness it produces, look at all the havoc that it makes. If only we could see the real nature of sin, we should hate it, so it behooves us to look at it and examine it. It must be avoided because of its ugliness and because of its twisted and perverted character.

Let me put a still stronger reason to all Christian people. I should not sin because sin is the terrible and foul thing that caused such suffering to my blessed Lord; the thing that brought the Son of God from heaven to earth, in a sense, was just this. The thing that made Him humble Himself and make Himself of no reputation was ultimately the problem of sin. It was sin that made Him endure the contradiction of sinners against Himself; it was the problem of sin that caused Him to sweat drops of blood in the garden of Gethsemane; it was sin that drove the nails into His holy hands and feet; it was sin that produced the agony and the suffering and the shame of the cross—that is what sin does. Can I, as a Christian, go on sinning? 'These things write I unto you, that ye sin not.' You should not desire that which caused Him so much suffering and so much pain.

But let me give you another reason. Sin is dishonouring to the gospel, to its claims and to its power. Here is a gospel which tells us it can give us power; a gospel that offers us life and renewal of strength. So, then, if we sin, we are denying the gospel and bringing it into disrepute, so we must not sin.

Now I put it like this because that is the way in which the New Testament presents its whole doctrine of holiness and the way in which it calls us not to sin. In other words, we are not to be spending our life trying to surrender ourselves, trying to yield ourselves up, trying to let go that God may give us the victory. No! We have to reason it out; we must say, 'I must not sin because God condemns it, because it is wrong in itself, because it caused Christ's suffering, because it is dishonouring to the gospel.' Reason it out—that is the New Testament appeal. 'I write these things unto you, that ye sin not,' and you must know why.

John is concerned fundamentally about our walk with God and our fellowship with Him, and therefore he says, 'My little children, I write these things unto you because sin always ultimately breaks fellowship with God, and therefore immediately casts us off from the source of all our blessedness. It is no use your saying you want to walk with God and then deliberately sinning. The moment you sin, fellowship is broken; the moment you fall into this kind of transgression, you interrupt the fellowship. The one thing that matters is fellowship with God. I do not know what may await you; you may be tried, you may be persecuted, there may be war and calamity, there may be terrible things awaiting you; the one thing that matters is that you are right with God. That being so, do not sin because sin breaks the fellowship.'

Not only that; sin is utterly inconsistent with our profession. It is totally inconsistent with our professed hatred of sin and with our professed desire to be delivered from it. Christians arc people who realise and know that sin is the central problem in life and they therefore say that they want to be delivered and emancipated from it. So if they continue to sin, they deny what they profess to believe. Such a position is completely inconsistent and self-contradictory.

And sin also leads always to an evil conscience. When men and women sin, they are under a sense of condemnation, they are unhappy—I am speaking true to experience, am I not? Look back across the past days. When you did something you should not have done, did you not become miserable with yourself and irritable with everybody? Well, it was because you were unhappy; you knew you were wrong and yet you did it, and there you were, miserable and unhappy. 'Little children, these things write I unto you, that ye sin not.' It will rob you of happiness and joy and will give you a sense of condemnation.

But it will even do worse than that, it will lead to doubts; it will, at times, make you feel uncertain of your relationship to God. But still more important is this: it will make you feel you have no right to pray. Have you not experienced that? You do something that you should not do and you get this sense of condemnation; then something happens and you feel you need strength from God and you say, 'I will pray about it.' And then the thought comes to you that you have no right to pray, you have sinned against God, you are a cad to rush to Him just when you want Him; and when everything goes well you do not want Him and you forget Him—have you not found this interruption to prayer? That is why John tells these people not to sin.

It is so practical. It works like this. When we face the future, we wonder what is going to happen; there are so many things that may happen to any one of us—a terrible illness, loss of money, the illness of a dear one, death, war—who knows? Well, these things may happen; we may be utterly helpless. We see that the world cannot help us with all its wealth, its education and its knowledge. We are left there face to face with one of these trials and crises of life. We say, 'I wonder, what of God?' and we are about to pray and then comes this sense of condemnation and somehow we feel we have no right to approach Him. That is why we must not sin. If we want to enjoy fellowship with Him, if we want to be able to pray in the hour of crisis, we must keep the line of communication clear, keep the pathway open, avoid these obstacles that hinder access to God.

And then, lastly, let me put it like this. Sin always leads ultimately to a sense of utter hopelessness, and that is why these New Testament epistles are written. People in that state and condition may sometimes sin for so long that they feel they can do nothing and they have this sense of devastation and of being forsaken.

Those are some of the reasons why we should not sin—that is the command which the Apostle gives to these people.

But let us finish with just a word about the other side: the comfort and the consolation. Thank God there is this further word: 'And if any man sin'—or has sinned—'we have an advocate with the Father, Jesus Christ the righteous: and he is the propitiation for our sins; and not for ours only, but also for the sins of the whole world.' If, therefore, you see as you look back nothing but sins against God, I assure you that if you believe on the Lord Jesus Christ those sins are forgiven you, they are blotted out. 'Ah, yes,' says someone, 'but you do not know how terribly I have sinned, how much I have sinned.' My dear friend, 'He is the propitiation for . . . the sins of the whole world,' and you and all your sins are included. Do not let the devil therefore depress you, do not let him drive you from that optimistic blessing to despair and hopelessness. If you see your sins, as John has already told these people, you have but to confess your sins, and if you do so, 'He is faithful and just to forgive us our sins and to cleanse us from all unrighteousness' (1:9). For the provision is already made, the propitiation has already been provided. He, the Christ, the Son of God, has once and for ever covered all your past sins, all your present sins, all the sins you may commit; the sins of the whole world are covered; the offering has been made once and for ever.

Very well, it seems to me there is only one thing that matters and that can be put in the very little word, 'we.' 'My little children, these things write I unto you, that ye sin not, and if any man sin *we* have an advocate with the Father.' Who are 'we'? Is that the whole world? No, that is not the whole world; that is Christian people, we who know Him, we who have fellowship with the Father, the people to whom he writes, the Christian members of the Christian Church. That is, therefore, the one thing that matters and that counts. Do we know God? Have we fellowship with the Father and with His Son, Jesus Christ? Do I know for certain that Christ is my advocate? I may see myself in six months hence in a terrible predicament. I may want to pray to God and then comes this condition of sin and I feel I cannot; and the one thing that will matter then will be that I shall be able to go on and to say, 'I have an Advocate and I can turn to Him; and because of His advocacy I shall know that I am in fellowship with the Father, and God will smile upon me and will grant me His blessing.'

That is the thing that matters in life, that we know Him, Jesus Christ, the righteous one, the advocate with the Father, the propitiation for our sins. Do we know Him? If we do, we know God; and if He is our advocate and representative, our continued fellowship with God is certain and assured.

Thanks be unto God for the heavenly advocate who maintains us in fellowship by His life, by the offering He made once and for ever, and by the power and the life He gives us through the Holy Spirit.

2

DOCTRINE AND LIFE

My little children, these things write I unto you, that ye sin not. And if any man sin, we have an advocate with the Father, Jesus Christ the righteous: and he is the propitiation for our sins: and not for ours only, but also for the sins of the whole world.

1 JOHN 2:1-2

WE HAVE CONSIDERED these verses in general, and, as we have said, in addition to the very practical and essential exhortation, there is also to be found in them a great wealth of doctrine. So we must now look at the doctrinal statements which we find in this mighty statement. This is something which must engage our attention not only because it is always important to consider doctrine, but also because these two verses have so frequently played a prominent part in many discussions and disputes—not to say quarrels—within the Christian Church herself. All those who have any real love for and interest in Christian doctrine must have known how often various statements found in these verses have been the main bone of contention in particular debates and how frequently they are found to be at the very centre of theological dispute and discussion.

So as we come to consider them, it seems to me that nothing is more important than the spirit in which we do so, or, in other words, nothing is so important as our approach to such theological considerations. There are two main dangers with regard to the approach to the doctrinal teaching of the New Testament. The first is the position of those peo-

ple who say, 'We know that in the past Christian people have spent a lot
of their time in discussing doctrine. Our fathers and grandfathers especially were great experts at this. They read books on theology in a way
in which people do not do so today. You could not enter into the house
of the average Christian without finding certain works on theology; they
were always discussing them and arguing about them; they were very
interested in theology and doctrine. But,' they say, 'it was often at the
expense of more important things.'

So the tendency today is for large numbers to say not only that they
are uninterested in doctrine, but also that doctrine is really quite unnecessary. Theological formulae and truth, they maintain, may be of great
interest to those who take up that kind of study or to those who have
the inclination and time to spend; but what really matters is experience
and the kind of life that people live. 'We are not interested,' they say, 'in
your various ideas and schools of thought with regard to the precise
explanation of how the atonement of Christ works. These things are of
no concern to us. So long as we can say "Whereas I was blind now I
see," so long as we are living a good life and producing good works, that
is the only thing that matters.'

Now what are we to say about that attitude? Well, the reply which
I would suggest is appropriate to such people is something like this:
'Whether you like it or not, to speak like that is, in and of itself, to speak
in a doctrinal manner. To make statements along that line is, in actual
practice, to commit yourself to a particular doctrine. The doctrine of
such people is the doctrine of works and, in a sense, of justification by
works.' 'Ah, but,' they reply, 'we are not interested in such a term as
"justification by works."' But whether they are interested in such terminology or not, that is exactly what they are saying. In other words,
you cannot speak about Christianity and religion without being doctrinal. You may reduce the whole of Christian doctrine to just one term,
but it is your doctrine all the same.

In other words, whether we like it or not, we cannot avoid doctrine.
And we can say the same about religion as we can about doctrine. There
is no such thing as an irreligious person; everyone has his or her religion,
if you mean by religion that ultimate philosophy or view of life by which
people live. Now there are many who say that they do not believe in religion. But not to believe in religion is their religion! You cannot speak
about these things without automatically and inevitably committing

yourself to some particular doctrine or teaching. So there is no way of avoiding the consideration of doctrine; you must be prepared to consider it whether your doctrine is true or false.

But another reason why such people are altogether wrong is that the New Testament everywhere is full of doctrine. So to refuse to consider doctrine is not only to refuse to believe in the Bible as the Word of God, it is insulting to God Himself. If God has chosen to use such terms as righteousness, justification, sanctification, redemption, atonement, reconciliation, propitiation, then it is our duty to face those terms and to consider their meaning; it is dishonouring to God not to do so. Someone may say, for instance, 'I am not interested in all those terms; I believe in God, and I believe in living as good a life as I can in order to please Him.' But how can you please God if you refuse to consider the very terms that He Himself has revealed to the men who wrote the record? This is God's truth, and God has chosen to give us this truth in this particular form, so I must face these terms. My sense of obedience to God compels me to discover as far as I can what He means by them.

Then my third and last reply to such people would be this: The New Testament is never tired of pointing out that to attempt to divorce conduct from belief is always fatal. The Apostle Paul put that in a memorable verse in writing to the church at Corinth when he said, 'Evil communications corrupt good manners' (1 Cor. 15:33). He was dealing there with the doctrine of the resurrection, and he said in effect, 'It is no use your saying, "We are not interested in doctrine; we are concerned about life"; if your doctrine is wrong, your life will be wrong.' And that has surely been the tragedy of the last hundred years or so.

That is the danger on the one hand, but there is also a danger at the other extreme which is equally important, and that is the danger which confronts those who have a very great interest in doctrine. So let me try to paint this type of person as clearly as I have painted the other. There are people who are very concerned about doctrine and theology, but their interest seems to be purely detached, purely theoretical and intellectual. There is nothing they delight in more than arguing about theology; yet they do so the whole time as if they were arguing about some abstract science, something far removed from life, something quite apart from practical living. Very often, of course, they do this in what we may describe as a 'party spirit.' In other words, as they read the New Testament they are not as concerned about arriving at a knowledge of truth as they are about discovering arguments to support their own particular theory or idea.

Now it is at that point that we agree to an extent with the criticism of the modern man against many who lived in the past. Let me be perfectly frank and admit that there is a good deal to be said along that line. Far too often our fathers argued about theology and doctrine, and discussed it and preached it in that detached and theoretical way; indeed oftentimes they lost their tempers, forgetting that by so doing they were denying the very doctrine which they claimed to believe.

So this again is a very real danger, and our tendency is always to be swinging from one of these extremes to the other—either no interest in doctrine or the wrong interest in it. Some of us may have to confess to having wasted precious hours of our life, even perhaps days, in a purely intellectual and theoretical interest in doctrinal truths. There is a certain type of mentality to whom nothing is more fascinating than a theological discussion. Indeed, there is a very good case for the argument that there is certainly no higher intellectual work in which we can ever engage. Theology used to be regarded as 'the queen of the sciences.' If you look back across the history of the Church, and indeed secular history, you will find from the bare standpoint of intellectual interest that there has been nothing that has so stimulated man to effort as a consideration of these particular truths.

But therein lies the danger. Our object always should be the discovery of truth, and to expound and understand the Scriptures. We must always compare Scripture with Scripture; and in arriving at an interpretation of particular texts we must always avoid anything which is going to put us in the position of contradicting some other statement of Scripture. Yet we must strenuously avoid the tendency to come to Scripture merely in search of texts to prove our own particular theories and ideas. Doctrine must never be considered in and of itself. Scripture must never be divorced from life.

I say all this by way of introduction because I want to remind you now of some of the doctrines which people have claimed that they have found in these two particular verses. And as I mention them to you, I think you will agree with me that what I have been trying to show about the place of doctrine in the life of the Christian is really of the greatest importance. Here is a question, for instance, that has often occupied the attention of Christian people—the whole question of our activity in the

Christian life. Does the Christian have to live an active life in this question of sanctification, or is it just a matter of 'letting go and letting God'? Do we believe in passivity, in a doctrine just of relaxation and of doing nothing, believing that the Holy Spirit is going to do everything? Or do we believe in a kind of activism?

Here, you see, is a statement which has often led to that discussion—'My little children, these things write I unto you, that ye sin not.' There are some people who cannot face a text like that without immediately raising that theological question with regard to activity or passivity. So how do we approach that matter? Well, it seems to me that the most important point is that we should always bear in mind what is clearly revealed by the context of any particular statement, because the danger always is to take a statement out of its context. Our first business always is to try to see what the author is trying to show at this point. What was he concerned about? And if you approach this statement in that way, surely you must come to the conclusion that the Apostle here is not telling these people that if they just do nothing and surrender themselves, then the Lord Jesus Christ will see that they do not sin.

No, what he says is this: 'I am appealing to you not to sin'; it is a command, an exhortation and, of course, we find that it is perfectly in accord with what we find throughout the Scriptures—'put off . . . the old man . . . put on the new man' (Eph 4:22, 24); it is something I have to do. 'Work out your own salvation with fear and trembling' (Phil 2:12); I have to do that. God works in me, but having worked in me, now He asks me to 'work out.' 'Mortify, therefore, your members which are upon the earth' (Col 3:5); not just abandon yourself, surrender yourself, become utterly passive and He will, as it were, cleanse your mind and your subconscious of every sin and evil desire. On the contrary, I have to *mortify* my members; I am exhorted to '*fight* the good fight of faith' (1 Tim 6:12); I am told to '*lay hold* on eternal life' (1 Tim 6:12) and to *flee* from certain sins. I am told to '*reckon*' myself 'to be dead unto sin' (Rom 6:11), and so on.

So there, you see, is one of the statements which we find in these two verses which at once raises the question that has often been a subject for discussion. Now the danger is that as we read a verse like that we could immediately be brought into a great debate as between activity and passivity, and as we do so we could be concerned solely with defining our theory; and thereby both parties would be failing to do the very thing for which the Apostle is appealing. No, the thing about which I should be concerned is not my theory with regard to these matters, but that I should not sin.

Then let me come to a second issue which is perhaps still more important and difficult. Do these two verses teach that the Christian must of necessity sin? 'My little children, these things write I unto you, that ye sin not. And if any man sin, we have an advocate with the Father, Jesus Christ the righteous: and he is the propitiation for our sins.' Is sin inevitable? Must the Christian go on sinning in this life and world, or is a state of perfection possible here and now?

How easy it is to argue about that, and how often have these two verses been used as the base from which such a debate has started. I am sure most Christians have, at some time or another, been engaged in this discussion. Is perfection possible, or is it not? This has been debated throughout the centuries, especially since the teaching of John Wesley with regard to perfection about the middle of the eighteenth century. Here again is one of the dangers that confronts us. We come across these words. Do they mean of necessity that we are liable to sin? And immediately we are in the heart of this great dispute. Often, as this matter is discussed, both parties to the discussion are certainly proving that sin is possible whether it is inevitable or not, by forgetting the real purpose of the Scripture and by being concerned about their particular point of view and defending it at all costs.

Of course, it is an extremely difficult matter; take these words: '*And if.*' What exactly do they mean? One commentator, for instance, has written, 'This conditional particle "if" must be regarded as causal, which means this, that we sin.' And that, incidentally, was the exposition of these verses by John Calvin; he said this means that we must sin. He says that the Apostle would not add this immediately—'If you do sin, we have an advocate'—unless he knew for certain that we are open to sin. It is causal, and there you get this one side of the whole debate. And there are those on the other side who would immediately retort that that is dishonouring to the Lord, because He could maintain us in a state of sinless perfection.

So what do we do about this difficulty? It would be utter folly on my part if I were to enter into that discussion as such. Indeed, there is a sense in which I refuse to enter into it, but my reply would be something like this: Our business, surely, is to take the statements of Scripture as they are. All I know is that I am told two things: I am commanded not to sin, but I am given a blessed and glorious assurance that if I do sin, my sin is still covered by the blood of Jesus Christ.

I suggest that this whole discussion with regard to the question of perfectionism is purely theoretical and that in a sense we have no right to sit in our armchairs and argue whether we are perfect or not. Our business is to be striving after perfection, not to sin, and to mortify our members and exert ourselves with all our might to live a life that shall be free from sin. I think the history of the past shows very clearly that if we but theoretically discuss and consider this question of sinless perfection, we shall almost certainly find ourselves falling into sin and at any rate giving practical demonstration that, whether sin is inevitable or not, it is certainly possible, and that it is extremely difficult not to sin. We must hold these two things together, at the same time: 'sin not' and yet 'if any man sin . . .' As Paul says, 'Let a man examine himself' (1 Cor 11:28); let us face ourselves in the light of this word. When we come to the conclusion that we are sinless and perfect by comparing ourselves with some sinner in the gutters of life, let us examine our thoughts and imaginations, let us look at this word and search it. Let us look at the Lord Jesus Christ Himself, and if we discover that we still have the elements of sin within us and that we are still sinful, let us then immediately face it as we are exhorted to do. Let us not view the whole thing in an abstract, theoretical and detached manner.

There, then, is the second question that has often been raised about these two verses; now let me mention still another.

Some people read these two verses and immediately say something like this: 'Are these two verses not inciting us to sin? Was John not doing something very dangerous when he said these words? Doesn't this lead inevitably to what is called *antinomianism*? Doesn't it tend to make a person say, "Well, it doesn't matter what you do. If you do sin, just confess it and apply the blood of Jesus Christ to your sin and you are forgiven, and all is well." Doesn't this therefore inevitably lead to loose living?'

Now there have, it is true, been people who have misinterpreted this statement, and it has often led quite definitely to antinomianism. Yet it seems to me that anyone who looks at it in this way is denying the whole doctrine which John has set out to teach. If I am prepared to excuse my sin because of this blessed doctrine of the atonement, then I am making merchandise of the cross of Christ, I am putting Him to open shame, and I am trading on Calvary. It is a temptation and a very real one, especially to evangelical people—the temptation comes; you hesitate, then a voice says, 'Well, if you do sin, it will be all right; you will be forgiven.' There are people who thus trade upon the cross and the truth.

All that, according to John, is just because they have never really understood the cross. Why did Christ go to the cross? Was it merely to allow us to go on sinning? Was it merely to enable us to sin lightly and loosely and then confess and be forgiven? No. According to the teaching of the New Testament everywhere it was this: He died on the cross that He might separate unto Himself a 'peculiar people, zealous of good works' (Tit 2:14). The whole purpose of the cross is to deliver us from sin, to rid us from it, to put us in such a standing with God that we can receive this new and eternal life which will enable us to overcome sin and to follow in the steps of our Lord and Master Himself. But, you see, if you take this theoretical teaching and doctrine of theology only, you will be in grave danger of falling into the sin of antinomianism.

Then, finally, there is another danger. Do these two verses teach the doctrine of *universalism* or not? What do we mean by that? 'If any man sin,' says John, 'we have an advocate with the Father, Jesus Christ the righteous: and he is the propitiation for our sins: and not for ours only, but also for the sins of the whole world.' Immediately we are involved in a great theological question: did Christ die only for the elect or did He die for all? Is salvation universal or is it only for some? Has Christ died for all; will all be saved? Will even Satan himself be saved? Propitiation has been made for the sins of the whole world; therefore all must be saved. There is no such thing as an ultimately lost person; all will finally arrive in glory, even the sinners.

Now those are the questions, but what does our text say? This is what we face: 'He is the propitiation not only for our sin but also for the sins of the whole world.' But some people leave out the first person. Surely the verses say something like this. It is a clear statement to the effect that the death of Jesus Christ upon the cross is sufficient propitiation for the sins of the whole world. There is no question about that; and, of course, this is of necessity true, because of His perfect nature, because of His perfect work, His atonement. His work upon the cross is sufficient for the sins of the whole world. That is beyond dispute; it is plainly stated. But that does not mean or imply that when He went to the cross He was going to die for all. What it says is that His death was *sufficient* for all.

Let me put it like this: Do you notice the distinction that is made between two groups of people in this statement? 'My little children'—he is not writing to the world, he is writing to Christian people—'if any man sin, we have an advocate with the Father.' He does not say that the whole world has an advocate with the Father. 'We have an advocate with the Father, Jesus Christ the righteous: and he is the propitiation for our sins.' Then comes the further statement, 'and not for ours only, but also for the sins of the whole world.'

You see the distinction? We are not told here that the Lord Jesus Christ is advocating before God on behalf of the whole world. No, *we* have an advocate with the Father, and the 'we' here refers to the people to whom he was writing—the Christian people who have fellowship with the Apostle, the people who have fellowship with God and with His Son, Jesus Christ. So Jesus Christ, he tells us, is only an advocate for such people. At the same time he says that His work upon the cross was so great and perfect that it is actually a propitiation sufficient for the whole world, though efficient only for those who are Christians, for those who are partakers of this fellowship with the Apostle and with God and with His Son, Jesus Christ.

As you interpret it like that you find, of course, at once that you are consistent with the teaching of the Scriptures everywhere. The Bible always divides this world of mankind into two groups: the saved and the lost; the Christians and the non-Christians; those who are going to glory and those who are going to perdition; the sheep and the goats; the wise virgins and the foolish virgins; the good steward and the bad steward.

The whole world of mankind is divided into these two ultimate groups, so that before I begin to say, 'He died for all, therefore all must be saved and all are going to be redeemed,' let me not only face these two verses which in and of themselves divide mankind up into two groups, but let me likewise see that there they bring us into line with the whole teaching of the Word of God from beginning to end, where the redeemed and the lost are eternally separated and divided.

We have, then, glanced at some of the doctrinal issues which are of necessity raised as we read these two verses together. Now my exhortation, to put it in a final word, is this: Let us, Christian people, not waste our time in mere theoretical, intellectual discussions about activity and passivity. We must consider them, but let us not stop at discussion; let us not just end by talking about sinless perfection; let us not just fall into the sin of antinomianism, or debate or wrangle about universalism. Let us rather listen to the plain words of the Apostle himself. 'Sin not' and 'If any man sin, we have an advocate with the Father, Jesus Christ the righteous.' That is the thing on which we must concentrate. I am called not to sin, but thank God I am assured that, should I sin, the blood of Jesus Christ His Son still cleanses me from the guilt of that sin and will deliver me from all unrighteousness. Let us hold on to doctrine, but let us beware of the terrible danger of a mere theoretical position divorced from life.

THE ADVOCATE

My little children, these things write I unto you, that ye sin not. And if any man sin, we have an advocate with the Father, Jesus Christ the righteous: and he is the propitiation for our sins: and not for ours only, but also for the sins of the whole world.

1 JOHN 2:1-2

WE RETURN AGAIN TO these verses because I am anxious that we should do with them what I am quite sure the Apostle originally intended. In the first chapter we saw:[1] the Apostle was laying down some of the basic principles with regard to this whole question of fellowship with God. That was the great thing, that was the thrilling message that he had to pass on to the people. There he was, an old man, knowing that his end was at hand and he was leaving a number of Christian people, many of them very young. So he was anxious to help them in this wondrous fact of communion with God; he wanted them to know exactly how that fellowship is to be arrived at and how it is to be maintained, and he began by laying down principles.

Here, in a sense, he sums it all up, because he is so afraid of being misunderstood. We are all in grave danger of misunderstanding these things; we will clutch at anything to excuse ourselves or to excuse sin. So he has pointed out two things in the first chapter: that 'God is light, and in him is no darkness at all,' and therefore we must walk with Him in the light. Then, secondly, knowing that to be told this makes us feel hopeless, especially when we fall into sin and feel we have no right to go back to God, he has given us this consolation: 'the blood of Jesus Christ his Son cleanseth us from all sin,' and he has gone on repeating this.

So here, summing it all up he says, 'My little children, these things write I unto you, that ye sin not'—do not take advantage of the consolation; do not say, 'Well, because the blood of Jesus Christ cleanses me from all sin, I need not be particular or careful.' No, I am writing to you, not to encourage you in sin and licence, said the Apostle, but in order to keep you from sinning. Yet again, he could not leave it at that. He was the great Apostle; he had written so much about love, and he loved these Christians—the relationship between them was particularly close and tender and affectionate.

So he goes on: 'And if any man sin . . .'—this is a word to those Christian people who are conscious of sin and failure. If there are those who say they are perfect, well, they need not listen to this; it is a word to those who are conscious of sin and failure and who are aware of their own unworthiness. And it is, I venture to say, perhaps the classic statement of this matter. There is nothing certainly which is more beautiful that has ever been written about it. How is my fellowship to be restored with God when I sin? How can I be forgiven? This is the situation which is envisaged here by the Apostle.

We all, surely, know something about this. The devil is constantly present, he is the adversary of our souls, and if we find ourselves having sinned, he comes to us and whispers, 'You have no right to go back to God! You have been walking in the light and you have fallen into sin. Isn't that sinning against the law? How can God forgive you?' Is that not how he speaks to us? And he has spoken to some people like that for long years. He has kept them in a state of utter wretchedness and misery. They wonder if they have ever been a Christian, and they fail to see how they can be restored to that fellowship with God from which they have fallen because of sin. Now here is the great word to such people; it is a wonderful statement on the doctrine of forgiveness, and it is especially about the forgiveness of the sins of Christian people.

The first great principle is that there is no forgiveness except in the Lord Jesus Christ and through Him. So many people seem to think that God could forgive us our sins without the Lord Jesus Christ, and that is why, of course, they never see the necessity for the Lord Jesus Christ. They say that God is love and God can forgive sin, so if we should fall into sin, all we have to do is to ask God to forgive us and He does so at once. And it is because so many believe something like that, that they never believe on the Lord Jesus Christ, because they have never seen how essential He is. But, you notice, that is the introduction to the whole of New Testament doctrine. The moment sin is mentioned in the New Testament, immediately *He* is mentioned. So I put it like that as doctrine: there is no forgiveness of sin apart from the Lord Jesus Christ. John puts it like this: 'If any man sin'—well, what happens, do we just ask God to forgive us? Not at all! 'We have an advocate with the Father, Jesus Christ the righteous.' Immediately He comes in.

And that, in a sense, is the doctrine of the whole of the Bible; everything in the Old Testament looks forward to this person. Take all that you can read in books like Exodus, Leviticus and Numbers, and in other books, about what God told the nation of Israel in that old dispensation—burnt offerings, peace offerings and various meal offerings and all these things. Go through all the great ceremonials and rituals and everything that was connected with the Tabernacle and the Temple, all these minute instructions—they were all but types and shadows of that which was to happen fully and finally in the Lord Jesus Christ. They did not really deal with sin; they were merely a covering for it for the time being. They were all looking forward, suggestions of that which was eventually to take place. Indeed, God gave all these regulations to the ancient people just to impress upon them this great truth, that He cannot forgive sin by just forgiving it.

That is the object of all that teaching. Something must happen before God can forgive sin. God, because He is holy and righteous, cannot just say, 'Well, you have sinned and I forgive you.' That is the danger, always, of transposing what we do as individuals to what God does. Some argue, 'Surely a parent has the right to forgive a child if the child does wrong and then comes and says it is sorry. So if we can do that, why cannot God do the same? He is infinitely greater and has infinitely greater love.' But the fallacy there is to forget that none of us is righteous and our ideas of righteousness are hopeless. God is absolutely holy and just and righteous, and, if I may say it with reverence, God's nature and personality make it impossible for Him to deal with sin in that way. Something has to be done about sin; the shedding of blood is essential, for without the shedding of blood there is no remission of sins (Heb 9:22). All the Old Testament teaches that and points forward to Christ.

Here we have the doctrine, of course, in all its richness and fulness, and when John at this point comes to consider this question of sin and what can be done about it, immediately he has to talk about Christ, and he does so in this particularly impressive and beautiful manner. So let us take a firm hold of this particular doctrine; without the Lord Jesus Christ we can do nothing, from the beginning of the Christian life to the end. The greatest saint dying upon his deathbed needs Him and His atoning work; it is in Him alone that we are rescued, it is in Him alone that we are forgiven. It is He alone and what He has done for us—indeed it is He Himself, as I am going to show you—who covers all our sins and does away with them—forgiveness!

Therefore, once more we ask ourselves that question which we must never cease to ask: 'Is my whole position and all my thinking centred on the Lord Jesus Christ?' The word of John, as it is the word of the New Testament everywhere, is that Christ is the beginning and the end, the start and the finish, the Alpha and the Omega, the all-in-all, and unless we realise always when we go seeking forgiveness that we have no plea but the Lord Jesus Christ, our relationship to Him is essentially false. That is the first postulate.

Now let us consider this statement more in detail. How does Christ thus accomplish or bring to pass our restoration to fellowship with God? John puts it here in these verses in a very beautiful way. He does it, says John, by being our *advocate*. 'If any man sin'—if any of you should happen to fall into sin—then you, we, all of us together, 'have an advocate with the Father, Jesus Christ the righteous.' John uses the same word in his Gospel, in chapter 16 verse 7, where our Lord said that He would send us another *comforter*. So what is an advocate? An advocate is one who represents another; he stands before a court, and he presents the case of someone else; he represents this person and puts forward the pleas. And John tells us that the Lord Jesus Christ is, for all who believe on Him and trust Him, an advocate with the Father.

However, this word merits our closer attention. We must never think of it as if the Lord Jesus Christ were there pleading for us before an unwilling God. You will find that certain hymns do suggest that, and statements have often been made which sound as if God were opposed to us and as if God, who is utter righteousness and absolute perfection, were there insisting on His pound of flesh and insisting upon His right to punish us for our sins. Then they picture the Lord Jesus Christ as pleading desperately and urgently, trying to persuade the Father and at last succeeding in getting Him to change His opinion.

But that is an impossible suggestion, and we must be very careful not to view this idea of advocacy in that way. It is impossible because we are told so plainly and clearly in the Word of God that 'God so loved the world, that he gave his only begotten Son' (John 3:16). It was not that the Son decided to come on His own and then, having done so, is pleading urgently and passionately for our deliverance. No, it was the Father who sent the Son; it was God who 'sent forth his Son, made of a woman, made under the law' (Gal 4:4); 'God was in Christ, reconciling the world unto himself, not imputing their trespasses unto them' (2 Cor 5:19). So as we consider the advocacy, let us get rid of the idea that God is unwilling and that He is one who is not prepared to forgive.

But at the same time we must be very careful not to go to the other extreme and think that what John means by 'advocate' is just that the work of Christ on the cross prevails and continues throughout eternity and is there always in the mind of God, and that therefore, in that sense, Christ and His work are advocates for us. We must not think that, because that makes it something quite passive, and that is an idea we must reject, not only because of this particular text, but also because of those magnificent words in Hebrews 7 where the whole argument is that 'he ever liveth to make intercession' for us (v 25). He is unlike that Levitical priesthood who came and lived and died and then a new person had to be appointed. The whole point about Him, says the author of Hebrews, is that He *lives*. He is without beginning and without end—it is this eternal priesthood—and it is because 'he ever liveth' that He is able to 'save . . . to the uttermost'—and must for ever and ever irrespective of what may happen—those 'that come unto God by him.'

In other words, it does seem to me that once more we are confronted by a conception that baffles our understanding. But of this we can be quite certain: that as the Lord Jesus Christ looked after His disciples and followers while here on earth, as He looked after their interests and did certain things for them, so He is now equally active for us there in Heaven. He is representing His people; He is there looking after us and our interests. We do not understand it; it is not a conflict between Father and Son; but it seems to me that in the economy of the blessed Trinity, the Father has handed this particular work to the Son.

So there we have this great comfort and consolation that the Lord

Jesus Christ is our great high priest, which means not only that He has offered Himself, but more than that, He takes our prayers and transmits and transforms them and passes them on to the throne of God. He adds to our feeble unworthy prayers the incense of His own blessed, glorious, perfect person; so He represents us in that way.

Now the early fathers were very fond of putting it like this, and I think it is very good: They used to say that the Holy Spirit intercedes within us and Christ is interceding for us. The Holy Spirit is within us, building us up in Christ, teaching us and guiding us and showing us what to do and what not to do. And there the Lord Himself is making intercession for us and on our behalf, representing us always to the Father. It is a glorious and sublime conception. Is there anything that can be more comforting and more consoling than to know that at this very moment, and always, the Lord of Glory is concerned about you, is watching over you and is concerned about your interests and is there representing you? We are frail and we are weak and we fall and fail, but we have an advocate with the Father. Therefore, when you begin to feel, at the suggestion of Satan, that you cannot turn back to God and face Him, remember, beloved friend, you are not alone. I agree with you; I know the sensation but too well, the feeling that I have no right to approach God, but remember that you have an advocate and He is there to represent you.

So let us now consider something about the nature of the advocacy. Every word, every sentence, every particular word is in a sense full of consolation. We have an advocate, says John, 'with the Father.' Now that word with is a most important little word; it means face to face with. It does not mean that He now and again enters in and is allowed to represent us, but rather that He is always there. And it means that He is always, as it were, looking into the face of the Father. We have a suggestion here of the great doctrine of the Trinity, the three persons yet one substance. He is face to face with God, not having, as it were, to make an application to God to plead for us to the Father; He is always looking into the eyes of the Father. What a wonderful idea, that the one who represents us is always there in that absolute intimacy with God.

So when you have sinned and are full of a sense of shame and guilt and you feel you have no right to go back to God, remember that God in Christ has become your Father; we have an advocate 'with the Father,' not a God that is opposed to you, a great force or power, but one who loves you with an infinite Father's love. Is there, I ask you again, any greater consolation possible than that?

Let us next go on to ask a second question: Who is this advocate? Look at the description: 'Jesus Christ the righteous.' John did not write these things accidentally. You remember that in the first chapter he talks about 'the blood of Jesus Christ his Son,' and here he says, 'Jesus Christ the righteous.' The words are carefully chosen, inspired; he is controlled as he writes them. The author of Hebrews also writes, 'We have not an high priest which cannot be touched with the feeling of our infirmities; but was in all points tempted like as we are, yet without sin' (Heb 4:15). You see the comfort and consolation? When you are conscious of guilt, when you are conscious of your smallness and frailty and think of God in His utter holiness in the heavens, when you are tempted to ask how God can understand a human being who falls like this, the answer is, 'You have an advocate who understands you perfectly—Jesus.' Read Hebrews 4 and 5 and you will find it worked out at great length and in a most glorious manner. The very Son of God became Jesus, became man, in order that He might understand us. We have a sympathetic high priest; we have one who knows something of our frailty. He knew the frailty of the body; He was tired; He knew what it was to feel weak; so He knows our infirmities. He understands our ignorance, therefore, because He has been a man amongst men. There He is—the Lord of Glory but still Jesus. He has not forgotten what the life of man is in a difficult world like this. Remember that when you are tempted to despair and when you feel God can never take you back. One is representing you who has a feeling and a sympathy for you, an understanding of you and of your infirmities.

He is *Jesus Christ*—and this means of course that He is the anointed one, the appointed one. Therefore, get rid, once and for ever, of the idea that God is against you. It is God who appointed the Son to this particular task of advocacy; it is God Himself who gave Him the office. The high priest was never self-appointed, argues the writer of the epistle to the Hebrews—he was always called of God (Heb 5:4); and God appointed and set apart and anointed the Son to be the Saviour and the representative of those who believe on Him. So, comfort yourselves with this thought: the advocate has been appointed by the judge. The Father, in His everlasting love, has Himself set His Son apart and anointed Him for this particular task. Come to your advocate, therefore, with confidence and with assurance.

But there is still another word—'*the righteous.*' This is, I think, the most wonderful thing of all, and this is the ground of my assurance. John is referring to Christ's character; though He became man, yet He never sinned. No fault was found in Him. He is absolutely perfect, and I need such a representative in the presence of God because of the holiness and the absolute righteousness and justice of God. No one who is himself unworthy can possibly plead for another. Before I can have confidence in my advocate, I must know that He is accepted of God and can stand in the presence of God. No one else could ever have done that; no one but the Son of God is fit to stand in the presence of God and plead. But He is 'Jesus Christ the righteous'!

Thank God, I can rely upon Him never to plead anything that is wrong or unworthy. We can have absolute confidence in this advocate; He will never put forward a plea unless it is right, and this is the righteousness John speaks of. The Lord Jesus Christ does not merely ask God to overlook our sin or forget it; He stands there, and, if I again may use language with reverence in discussing such a high and holy matter, He is there, as it were, to say to God, 'It is but right and just that You should forgive the sins of these people, for I have borne their sins and the punishment of their sins.' The advocate turns to the Father and says, 'I must ask You to put Your law to the side. I am here just to remind You that the law has been fulfilled, that death has died, the punishment has been enacted; they are free because I died for them.' It is He who enables God to be at one and the same time just and the justifier of the ungodly (Rom 3:26). Can you imagine greater comfort and consolation than that? As the result of Jesus Christ and His standing in the presence of God on my behalf, I say this—I say it with trembling and yet I say it with confidence—God would be unjust if He did not forgive my sin. Christ has died for me; it is righteous and just for God to forgive the sins of all who believe on the Lord Jesus Christ—Jesus Christ the righteous!

And lastly, the basis of His advocacy is all put in this one word: '*propitiation.*' To propitiate means to render favourable, to turn one towards another with an eye of favour and of pleasure. And what we are told here is that Jesus Christ Himself is our propitiation; not only what He did, not simply the blood that was shed, but that He Himself is our propitiation. It means that He is the high priest and the offering. In the old dispensation everything the high priest took was outside himself, but Christ is His own offering—He is the sacrifice and the high priest.

Therefore, says John, He is not only the propitiating sacrifice, but the propitiation itself; everything that is necessary to reconcile the sinner with God is in Jesus Christ. He is prophet, He is priest, He is king. He is the sacrifice; it is His blood that has been shed and presented, and He has purified the heavenly tabernacle; it is all in Him. We need nothing else, we need no one else; He Himself is the propitiation. And because it is the Son of God who is the propitiation, we need have no fear about our sin. We can say with John that He is enough, sufficient to cover the sins of the whole world. Therefore when Satan, your adversary, comes and tries to drive you to the depth of despair and dejection because you have fallen into sin, turn upon him and say, 'I have an advocate with the Father, Jesus Christ the righteous, and He is the propitiation not only of my sin but of the sins of the whole world. I am accepted by God, the fellowship is restored, and I continue upon my way.'

That is the New Testament doctrine of reconciliation; that is its doctrine of the forgiveness of sins. That is the way, and the only way, whereby any one of us can ever come into fellowship with God or can ever be maintained in that glorious fellowship. 'We have an advocate with the Father, Jesus Christ the righteous.'

4

KNOWING THAT WE KNOW HIM

And hereby we do know that we know him, if we keep his commandments. He that saith, I know him, and keepeth not his commandments, is a liar, and the truth is not in him. But whoso keepeth his word, in him verily is the love of God perfected: hereby know we that we are in him. He that saith he abideth in him ought himself also so to walk, even as he walked.

1 JOHN 2:3-6

THE APOSTLE HERE, at the beginning of the third verse, proceeds to apply the doctrine which he has been laying down from the beginning of his letter. The great theme, we remember, is that of fellowship with God—fellowship with the Father and with His Son, Jesus Christ; that is the great thing which had prompted the Apostle to write at all. We have seen that fellowship with God is only possible in and through the Lord Jesus Christ and His perfect work. And indeed John has shown us so clearly that as we go forward in this walk with God, even should we fall into sin, that does not make our position hopeless. He shows us that even that is dealt with by the atoning work of our Lord as He presents it to the notice of the Father. He is pleading, an advocate presenting a case, and in the light of that we have this great certainty concerning the whole basis of our standing in the presence of God. That is the fundamental doctrine, and it is because it is fundamental that we have spent so much time with it. It is the foundation on which everything else that he is going to say in the letter is to be built; and you can never be too careful about the foundation. That is the part of the work on which you expend unusual care, and therefore, we have not hurried, in order to make quite sure that we are resting on nothing at all save on Jesus' blood and righteousness, and that it is in Him and in Him alone that we have any hope whatsoever.

So having dealt with that, the Apostle now goes on to state certain other matters which are of great practical importance. The Christian life is a *life;* it is not a matter of intellectual assent to doctrine, and therefore he has to deal with the whole thing in a very practical manner. There are certain things which will interrupt our fellowship with God, and we must be very careful about them. So John, in these verses 3-6, deals with one of these matters, and as we shall emphasise later, it is most important to observe that this is the thing that he puts first.

As he comes to do this, he introduces to us a number of his typical, characteristic words. All these Biblical writers have their favourite words; it is one of the romantic aspects of the whole doctrine of inspiration. Inspiration does not mean mechanical dictation; the personality of these men is here. And as we all have favourite words, as every preacher has words which he tends to repeat, so these men have theirs; Paul had his and so did John and Peter. Well now, John's favourite word appears here, the word *know*—'hereby we know'—and if you read his Gospel and epistles again, you will find that it is there everywhere. He is also very fond of the word *abide*, as we see in John 15, and here it is again—you will find it running through this epistle. Then he also likes to play with the words *keep* and *walking.*

Incidentally, it is a point of interest as you study the problems of authorship—not only the authorship of these epistles, but also that of the Gospels—that these things make it abundantly plain and clear that these men wrote the Gospels as they did the epistles. And it is well to bear that in mind, because it is almost certain that the man who wrote this letter was taking it for granted that the people were already familiar with his Gospel. His primary concern here is not merely to know the gospel but to work it out, as it were, and so he uses the same terminology, and we see this interesting connection between the Gospel and the epistle—the laying down of the doctrine and the working out of the doctrine in life as well.

So we come to more practical matters, and yet we shall still find that it is full of doctrine, again a point which we are never tired of noticing in the New Testament. The New Testament, while in an intellectual sense does divide and separate between doctrine and application, nevertheless never parts them in a radical sense. The application is always the outcome of doctrine; you talk about the source of a river and the river itself; while there is a division, in a sense there is no division. And doctrine is remarkably like that; doctrine and practice and yet both are one in an organic and vital sense.

So let us look at what the Apostle has to say to us, and let us take it in this way. He tells us that the Christian should *know* something; in other words, he introduces the great doctrine of assurance—'hereby we do know that we know.' Now I like that, because it is a perfect way of putting it. Peter tells us, 'make your calling and election sure' (2 Pet 1:10), which is perhaps an equally good way of putting it, but there is something about this verse of John's which surely does fix it once and for ever. Christians are people who know what they know.

I remember once hearing a master describe a pupil, and I think he paid that pupil a very great compliment. He said, 'That boy knows what he knows.' He did not say, That boy knows everything,' but that he was certain of the knowledge he possessed; he had mastered it, he had got it. Now that is what John tells us about the Christian; indeed the whole object of his letter, in a sense, is to give an exposition of this doctrine of assurance. You will find he goes on saying that. He says, as he looks back at the very end, in the last chapter, 'These things have I written unto you that believe on the name of the Son of God; that ye may know that ye have eternal life' (5:13).

This, therefore, is a very vital doctrine. Yet for some remarkable reason there are many people who seem to have a rooted objection to it. I find it very curious that anyone who claims the name of Christian should be capable of objecting to the doctrine of assurance, because it is in many ways the most glorious truth of all. As natural human beings we want assurance; we want to be certain of things in this life and world, and one of our greatest difficulties is that we are uncertain about so many things. Yet when the New Testament comes and offers us this blessed assurance, there is something instinctive in us, as a result of sin, that objects to it.

Now there are some reasons for that. There are some who feel it is presumption; they show a kind of mock modesty. They say, 'Who am I to presume to say that I know Him. He is so utterly and absolutely holy, and I am so aware of my own sinfulness and unworthiness, how can I claim this? What right have I to say, "I know whom I have believed," or "I know that my sins are forgiven?"' And there are others, I know, who are antagonistic to the doctrine because of their reaction to certain people who believe it. They say in effect, 'Well, I don't want to be like those people who say they know—those glib, superficial people who talk in terms of positive assurance and who, as they are doing so, seem to deny the very thing they are saying. There is a loudness about them and a self-satisfaction.'

Now let us be perfectly fair. There is a sense in which we can understand people reacting against such an attitude, and that is why we must be so careful that our personality and actions and everything that is true of us should be in conformity with the claims which we make. But while there is a sense in which one can understand the people who are antagonised in that way, it is always a very poor argument to refuse a doctrine simply because of other people. Indeed, I think I can prove that to you quite logically and conclusively. If you are going to judge everything in terms of liking certain people, then you will end by believing nothing. You cannot belong to a political party, or any other party, without finding that there are always people you do not like, and so you will find that you have to come out of everything!

But the final answer is that whatever certain people may do, the New Testament is full of this doctrine; indeed, it is, finally, the only solution that the New Testament offers to people in a world like this. You see, the New Testament's picture of life in this world is a very dark and gloomy one. It talks about 'wars and rumors of wars' (Matt 24:6), and it prepares people for persecution and trials and tribulations. But this is the way to come through it—that we know that we know Him; that we have this blessed assurance that 'neither death, nor life, nor angels, nor principalities, nor powers, nor things present, nor things to come, nor height, nor depth nor any other creature shall be able to separate us from the love of God, which is in Christ Jesus our Lord' (Rom 8:38-39).

That was Paul's comfort and consolation. There he was, an old man, a prisoner at the end of his life. So how did he keep going? 'I know whom I have believed, and am persuaded that he is able to keep that which I have committed unto him against that day' (2 Tim 1:12). The New Testament is full of it, so that apart from anything else, not to believe this doctrine is really to deny one of the most central of the New Testament doctrines.

Here, then, the Apostle John puts it quite plainly to us: what are we to know? And he tells us that there are two main things. Firstly, we are to know the Lord Jesus Christ. Let us be quite clear about this. 'Hereby we do know that we know him'; he does not say we are to know certain things *about* Him. No, rather, he says, we are to know Him. He has just been telling us about Him. He is our 'advocate with the Father, Jesus Christ the righteous'; He is 'the propitiation for our sins: and not for ours only, but also for the sins of the whole world.' And what John says here is that we are to know that we know Him.

There are certain matters which I always feel should truly be put in the form of a question, and this is one. Do we know Him? I am not asking whether we know certain things about Him. We know about His birth as a baby in Bethlehem; we know about Him as a boy in the Temple; we know He was a carpenter; we have read the Gospels; we know about the miracles. We are full of knowledge of these things. But that is not what John has in mind. It is something personal, direct, immediate, this word *know*.

Now the Bible is always very strong. It does not mean a general, superficial acquaintance; there is an intimacy about it, a knowledge in a special sense; it is a *personal* acquaintance, an intimacy and an interest. It is nothing less than that, and John says that we should know the Lord Jesus Christ in that way. Our fellowship is to be with the Father and with His Son; and in this verse the 'him' is undoubtedly a reference to the Son about whom he has been speaking, but it includes a knowledge of the Father also. So we are back again with this fundamental question, this question which we should really ask ourselves every time we pray: Do I know God? Am I simply going to offer up a prayer of hopes and fears and aspirations, or do I know that God is there; is the Lord Jesus Christ real to me?

That, the New Testament tells us, is the Christian position, not to believe things about Him but to know Him. So let us examine ourselves by this test. Are you able to hold conversations with the Lord Jesus Christ and to have fellowship and communion with Him?

The second thing we are to know, John tells us, is that we are in Him. Let me remind you of our text: 'And hereby we do know that we know him, if we keep his commandments. He that saith, I know him, and keepeth not his commandments, is a liar, and the truth is not in him. But whoso keepeth his word, in him verily is the love of God perfected: hereby know we that we are in him. He that saith he abideth in him ought himself also so to walk, even as he walked.'

Here is the other doctrine which John is constantly teaching, that we are not even to stop at a knowledge of Him in a sense of a personal, intimate acquaintance. We are to be aware of a union with Him, this mystical union of the believer with Christ. It is one of the great New Testament phrases—'in Christ.' In Romans 16, in the list which Paul gives of those to whom he sends his regards, he, referring to certain people, says they were 'in Christ before me.' You can find this everywhere in the New Testament; we are incorporated into Christ, we are in Him in the sense that any one member of my body is in the body—'Ye are the body of Christ,' says Paul, 'and members in particular' (1 Cor 12:27).

So the Christian is in Christ. That analogy which is used in John 15 puts this perfectly, the reference to the branch and the vine. It is a vital, organic relationship—not a mechanical attachment, but a live one; it is sharing the life of the vine itself. And that is the relationship of Christians to their Lord. John tells us we ought to know that we are in that vital, organic relationship; we should know that we are a part of Christ, that we are in Him and He is in us and we have received of His life.

And here we see again the great New Testament doctrine of regeneration. Christians are not just people who hold a number of opinions, though they do hold opinions. They are not only men and women who are aware of forgiveness; they are people who can say, 'I live; yet not I, but Christ liveth in me' (Gal 2:20). They are aware of another quality of life; they are aware of the life of the Son of God Himself in their lives; they are in Christ, and the life of Christ has come into them and through them. Now what John tells us is that we must know these things—'We know that we know.' Do you know that you are in Him in that way? Do you know for certain that His life is in you? This is the great principle which John emphasises.

How does the Christian know these things? That is the second point; or, to put it another way, let us consider the basis of this knowledge. How do we test the validity of our experience? It is a most important subject. There can be very little doubt but that John as he wrote these words had certain people very definitely in his mind. We have already referred, in dealing with the first chapter in my book *Fellowship with God*, to the Gnostics of this early century. There were, you remember, certain people who laid claim to some special knowledge. The mystery religions had already started, these strange amalgams of the Christian faith and eastern religions which were sometimes an admixture of philosophy and mysticism.

Now this is something that was not confined to the ancient world. I think you will find that there are quite a number at the present time. Philosophers tend to become mystics. It is a curious thing; it sounds contradictory at first, and yet in the end it is not contradictory at all. These men of ability and understanding have set out as philosophers, and they claim that by thinking and reasoning, they can discover the whole meaning of life. They set out to do so, and then, after a while, in utter honesty, they have to admit they have not succeeded. So they say, 'What is to be done?' and their tendency is to pass by, as it were, the gospel of Jesus Christ, which is here in the centre, and to swing from philosophy right over to mysticism. Having tried reason, they in a sense abandon it and submit themselves to some strange mystical experience.

There were people like that in the ancient world, and I have no doubt John had this in mind. They had been initiated—that was the word—into some mystic truth. They met together, and there things were revealed to them. They were always thinking about their experiences, and they said that they had this unusual knowledge as a result. Read the epistle to the Colossians with that in your mind as a background and you will find it most illuminating.

So John deals with the question in this way. 'It is very important,' he says, 'that you should test your experience; every experience is not a true one, for there are false experiences. So prove the spirits, test them, examine them. Do not believe every spirit; there are antichrists and false spirits. The devil transforms himself into an angel of light. He can counterfeit most of the Christian experiences—I do not say all, but most—so if you have an experience, you must test and examine it. Now,' says John, 'there are people who claim they have an unusual knowledge of Christ and they are claiming a mystic experience, so how do you test it?'

And here he leads us to his great first test. This is of vital importance, because I find in my experience as a minister that there are large numbers of people who are unhappy about themselves and their Christian life simply because they have not had the same unusual experience which somebody else has had. They have not, for example, had the experience of seeing a ball of fire and feeling that the whole room has been illuminated, and because of that they do not feel that they are Christians at all. They say that they have not had this special vision and thereby they are robbed of the wonderful experience that the New Testament has to give.

How may I know that I know Him? Well, observe how John puts it, and I must say there is to me almost an element of divine humour at this point. People are fond of describing John as a mystic. You will find there are certain people who do not like the Apostle Paul, but they like John. They say that Paul argues too much and that there is too much logic and reason about him, whereas John is full of love and mysticism.

So how interesting it is that John, who is described as the mystic, is the man who tells us that the way to test ourselves is not to seek for some mystical experience, but to examine our conduct and our lives! 'Hereby we know that we are in him'; not by the strange, the mystical, far from it; it is as prosaic as this: 'If we keep his commandments'; nothing less than that. It is not experience that enables us to say that we know Him; it is not feelings, not sensations, not vision, not amazing answers to prayer, not thrills, nor the unusual. We are all familiar with this kind of thing. There are so many who seem to think that the only way in which you can be absolutely sure is that you have one of these things and that you should always be talking about them. But no, says John, that is not what comes first, that is not the safe thing.

Now God forbid that anyone should misunderstand me! There *are* experiences in the Christian life, and I thank God for them, rare experiences that come, certain things like those which the Apostle Paul experienced and which he is almost afraid to mention. He says, 'I do not talk of that man taken up into the third heaven some fourteen years ago, but rather thank God that these things are possible' (see 2 Cor 12). However, these are not the things that John puts first. Here is the first test: What is your life like; how do you live? The test whereby we know we are His is this: are you keeping His commandments?

Keeping His commandments does not mean I just put on the wall a list of specific injunctions and do my best to keep them. Rather, it means that I am always concerned to be living the Christian life as fully as I can; that my great object is to be well-pleasing in His sight. I know what He wants me to do; I find it in the Old and in the New Testaments. I have the Ten Commandments and the Sermon on the Mount which apply to me, and I have the whole moral, ethical teaching of the New Testament.

Those are His commandments and I have to keep them. 'And if you can say quite honestly,' says John, 'that you are very concerned about doing that; if you can say you are striving to do that and that that is your ambition in life, you can know that you are in Him, for to know Him is to walk as He walked.' 'He that saith he abideth in him ought himself also so to walk, even as he walked.' That puts it perfectly once and for ever.

The Bible often describes our life as a walk. 'Enoch *walked* with God' (Gen 5:24); 'Noah *walked* with God' (Gen 6:9). Then read what God said to Abraham in Genesis 17:1—'*Walk* before me, and be thou perfect.' 'I,' said Jesus Christ, 'am the light of the world: he that followeth me shall not *walk* in darkness, but shall have the light of life' (John 8:12). Then, listen to Paul saying the same kind of thing: 'For ye were sometimes darkness, but now are ye light in the Lord: *walk* as children of light' (Eph 5:8).

It is a wonderful picture of the Christian life; it is a journey; we walk along, and what John says here quite simply and without any explanation is this: 'If you say you are in Him, then you ought to walk as He walked. Look at His walk, look at His demeanour, see how He lived His life in the world. If you say that you are in Him, if you say His life is in your life, if you say you are like the branch to the vine, then you will bear the character of the tree—that is inevitable. That which takes of the life of something represents and manifests that self-same life. If you, therefore, say you are in Him, you ought also to walk as He walked.'

See how our Lord walks through the pages of the four Gospels. The first thing you see is a humble, lowly and meek person. 'A bruised reed shall he not break, and the smoking flax shall he not quench' (Isa 42:3). 'Come unto me . . . ,' He says, 'learn of me; for I am meek and lowly in heart' (Matt 11:28-29). It is as we look at Him, as we begin to examine ourselves, that we feel we have no right to be here at all. There is so often a hardness about our testimony; we think we are in Him; we imagine we are testifying to the power of the Christian life. But the great thing we know about Him is that He was meek and lowly. The world does not encourage modesty, and I am afraid that at times the Church today does not do so either. We try to imitate the world, and we become self-assertive. We are so afraid of being called weaklings by the world that we develop into a boisterous kind of Christian. But I do not see that in the New Testament—meek and lowly.

The Corinthians in their folly said of the great Apostle Paul that his presence was 'weak, and his speech contemptible' (2 Cor 10:10), though he was introducing the meekness and the lowliness of his Lord. We are anxious to impress, and it is as true of the Church as it is of the world. The Church would turn the preacher into a man of great and dominating personality. How different that is from what we find here; we ought to walk as Christ walked. His great concern was to do the will of God, to please Him and not to please men. He was a man of sorrows and acquainted with grief. He mourned because of the sin of this world; it hurt, it pained Him. Do we share something of His godly sorrow because of the state of the world? Paul puts it like this in 2 Corinthians 5:4: We 'do groan, being burdened.' Do we groan? Do we give the impression of being burdened because of the sin and iniquity that is rampant around and about us? That is how He walked, and that is how we ought to walk.

And above all we see in Him love to God and love towards men and women—His compassion, His sympathy, His patience, His lovingkindness.

Well, according to the Apostle John, that is the test we are to apply to ourselves. Not the thrills and the visions, but that within me I feel a great desire to be like Him, to follow in His steps, to walk as He walked, to keep His commandments and to fulfil His word.

This is an inevitable test. Now John does not say, 'If you live that life you are making yourself a Christian,' but rather, 'If you are a Christian this is how you live.' If you have the life, it is bound to show itself, and if it does not, then you have not the life. That is logical; it is absolutely inevitable. These things are not matters to be argued about; we just face the facts. You cannot be receiving the life of Christ without becoming like Him. You cannot walk with God without keeping His commandments. You cannot know God without immediately, automatically loving Him. Love always manifests itself by doing what the object of its love desires.

There, then, is the first great test, the safest test; not the strange mystical initiation into some new knowledge, but keeping His commandments, keeping His word, walking even as He walked.

So again, do you know that you know Him? Does your life prove to you that you do? If these are the things you are most concerned about, it is because you know Him. God grant that we all may be able to say together, 'I know that I know Him.'

5

LOVING THE
BRETHREN

*Brethren, I write no new commandments unto you, but an
old commandment which ye had from the beginning. The
old commandment is the word which ye have heard from
the beginning. Again, a new commandment I write unto
you, which thing is true in him and in you: because the
darkness is past, and the true light now shineth. He that
saith he is in the light, and hateth his brother, is in darkness even until now. He that loveth his brother abideth in
the light, and there is none occasion of stumbling in him.
But he that hateth his brother is in darkness, and walketh
in darkness, and knoweth not whither he goeth, because
that darkness hath blinded his eyes.*

1 JOHN 2:7-11

THESE FIVE VERSES must obviously be taken as a whole because they
contain one particular, great message. So before we consider them in
detail, let us observe first of all the connections between them and what
has gone before. John has just said that the final proof any man can have
of the fact that he is a Christian is that he keeps, and delights in keeping, and goes on keeping, the commandments of the Lord. There, he
says, is something which is really safe as a test, much safer than any
experience that one may have had, certainly much safer than any feel-

ings or sensations that one may be conscious of within. Here is an objective test, and yet, obviously, a proof of life itself.

Then, having laid that down, John, as we have been considering, very naturally and almost inevitably brings it down to the realm of the particular. And so he now brings us to this vital and all-important New Testament doctrine of the *love of the brethren*.

Here again we are face to face with something which is absolutely vital to the Christian position. John is concerned about our fellowship with God, so he has been telling us there are certain things that hinder it, and here is another and one of the most important of them. To fail to love the brethren will interrupt our fellowship with the Father and therefore rob us of many of the blessings of the Christian life.

But we can also put it in a different way, and this is true of every one of these items that John singles out. It also provides us with a very wonderful test of our whole position. You see, we can go on looking at this epistle constantly in a two-fold manner. We can look at the various things that John enumerates as the things that hinder the fellowship, and we can also see them all as tests of our Christian position, and so you will find that when people have studied this epistle, they have generally looked at it from one of those two standpoints. But both are true, and it would be well for us always to bear the two in mind.

John starts off by putting it like this: 'Brethren, I write no new commandment unto you, but an old commandment which ye had from the beginning. The old commandment is the word which ye have heard from the beginning. Again, a new commandment I write unto you, which thing is true in him and in you: because the darkness is past, and the true light now shineth.'

Now, people are sometimes puzzled as to the meaning of this 'old' and 'new,' and the answer is really to be obtained by considering John 13:34 where our Lord Himself used this expression: 'A new commandment I give unto you, That ye love one another. . . .' There is a sense in which this exhortation to love one another, to love the brethren, is at one and the same time old and new.

It is old in this sense: 'I am now going to tell you something you already know,' says John in effect. 'In other words, from the moment you first heard the gospel, you heard this particular doctrine emphasised. I shall not add to the gospel which you have already believed and received. I am simply reminding you of what you already know.' So it is an old commandment, and an essential part of the Christian position. Integral to the gospel of Jesus Christ is the whole conception of a new family with the members loving one another; so in that sense it is not new. You will also find it in the Old Testament. It is there in the Old Testament law: 'Thou shalt love thy neighbour as thyself' (Lev 19:18), so that even when our Lord talked about a new commandment He was in a sense simply emphasising that old commandment that had been given to the children of Israel long ago. They had been separated as God's people, and God had told them that they must have this love one to another.

But though it is in that sense an old commandment, it is also a new one in that it is possible now in a way that it was never possible before. The Lord Jesus Christ, by coming into this world and by doing what He has done, has made this old commandment in a sense a new commandment because there is a new possibility connected with it. John puts it like this: 'Again a new commandment write I unto you, which thing is true in him and in you.' 'This thing,' says John, 'which I am now emphasising has been realised in Him and in you. Look at the people in the old dispensation. They had this command to love, and yet they found it very difficult. But in the Lord Jesus Christ we see it fulfilled and carried out. The Lord Jesus Christ has fulfilled the law of God. He loved men and women in the sense that the Old Testament meant; it has been realised in Him, and it is true in Him.'

'But not only that,' says John, 'it is also realised in you, it is true in you.' In other words, the Lord Jesus Christ has made it possible for us to keep this commandment in an entirely new manner. John is here reminding them that they are left without excuse; it is possible now for Christians, as the result of receiving new life from Christ, as the result of the power of the Holy Spirit, to love their fellow men and women, to love their brethren in the way that God originally intended. As we, as Christians, consider this commandment, there is a sense in which it is absolutely new.

It is idle to ask the world to love the brethren because it is incapable of it, as I am going to show you. That is why it seems to me that it is quite a heresy to approach the world, which does not believe on the Lord Jesus Christ, with the gospel of the New Testament and say, 'Practise that.' That is why it seems to me to be an utter illusion for anyone to think that you have only to preach Christian ethics to the world and then you can banish wars and disturbances, because the world is incapable of it. But to Christians there is a new possibility. They have received a new life; they have the life of Christ in them, and as Christ loved, so Christians can love. But nobody else can, so that in this setting it is a new commandment. It has been realised in Christ and in all who have received life from Him. So having laid down that background, John now goes on to make this appeal, this exhortation to these Christian people, to love one another.

Let me put it to you in the form of some two or three propositions. The first thing we have to see is that Christ has brought into this world a new order of life which has changed everything; the difference that He has made is, in a sense, the difference between light and darkness. Notice again—'because the darkness is past, and the true light now shineth.'

This is, of course, absolutely vital to the whole New Testament position. The Apostle Paul likes to put it in this way: 'Therefore if any man be in Christ, he is a new creature: old things are passed away; behold, all things are become new' (2 Cor 5:17). Or he puts it like this: 'Wherefore know we no man after the flesh: yea, though we have known Christ after the flesh, yet now henceforth know we him no more' (2 Cor 5:16). Being a Christian has changed everything; we are like new people in a new world; nothing is the same as it was before.

And John is saying exactly the same thing here. He has said that this world is a realm of darkness; we have already seen him emphasising that in the first chapter where he talks about 'walking in the light' and 'walking in darkness.' And here he comes back to this same conception. Again the Apostle Paul uses exactly the same language in writing to the church at Colosse; he talks about our being 'delivered . . . from the power of darkness, and . . . translated . . . into the kingdom of his dear Son' (Col 1:13). The Apostle Peter has the same idea when he says, '. . . which in time past were not a people, but are now the people of God . . . who hath called you out of darkness into his marvellous light' (1 Pet 2:10-9). Indeed the New Testament is full of this. Our Lord Himself said, 'I am the light of the world: he that followeth me shall not walk in darkness, but shall have the light of life' (John 8:12). That is the essential part of the New Testament picture of the Christian and of the Christian position.

But in order to show you fully the way in which the New Testament puts this, we must consider verse 11: 'But he that hateth his brother is in darkness, and walketh in darkness, and knoweth not whither he goeth, because that darkness hath blinded his eyes.' The metaphor is rather involved, but to put it simply John is saying that people who are not Christians are walking in the dark; yes, but not only that, there is a darkness within them also. The trouble with sinners and unbelievers is not simply that they have darkness around and about them and cannot see where they are going; the darkness has blinded their own eyes—they are blind as well as being in the dark. It is of real and vital importance that we should bear those two concepts in mind. Unbelievers are in the realm of darkness, and they themselves are in a state of darkness, so that, in a sense, even if you put them into the light they would not be able to see. So when people become Christians, two things happen to them: their own eyes are opened, and they are enabled to see; and they are also in an entirely new realm.

Now both these conceptions, as we have seen, are to be found constantly in the New Testament. Those who become Christians are those who are translated from the kingdom of darkness into the kingdom of light, or into the 'kingdom of his dear Son.' Their position has been changed, yes, but they themselves are also changed. The god of this world had blinded their eyes, so that they could not see the gospel; but now their eyes have been opened, they have been enlightened, and let me emphasise again the importance of bearing those two aspects in mind. I am changed, and I am in a new realm; I am a different person, and I am a citizen of a different kingdom. Both things are true. I am not simply the man I was in a new kingdom. I am a new man in a new kingdom, and the two things come out here in the language employed by the Apostle.

So the thing we have to hold on to is that if we are truly Christian people, we are left without an excuse in this matter of brotherly love. The darkness is passing away, the light has come, and we are a new people. There is no excuse for us whatsoever, if we are not fulfilling the commandment.

But, secondly, therefore, whether or not we belong to this new order is proved by our behaviour in the matter of love. The test of whether we are truly in this new realm of light, which Christ has brought into this world, is our response to this commandment to love one another, to love the brethren.

Now John does not put it loosely. Notice his customary blunt language: 'He that saith he is in the light, and hateth his brother, is in darkness even until now. He that loveth his brother abideth in the light, and there is none occasion of stumbling in him.' You see what he means; there is no need of argument about this, it is an absolute test. 'There is no explaining it away on the basis of one's particular disposition,' says John; 'you proclaim and portray exactly what you are by your conduct and behaviour in this respect. If you are not loving your brother, you are still in darkness, and the darkness is within you, whatever you may say. But if you are loving your brother, it is a proof you are truly a Christian in the realm of light, whatever defects you may happen to have.'

Let me put it like this; it is not our intellectual opinion that proclaims truly what we are. You know, it is possible for us to be perfectly orthodox but to be unloving. But your orthodoxy is of no value to you if you do not love your brother; you can talk about this doctrine intellectually, you can be a defender of the faith, and yet the spirit in which you are defending it may be denying the very doctrine you are defending.

This is a terrible test! Orthodoxy is essential, but it is not enough. 'If you are not loving your brother,' says John in effect, 'you are in darkness, you have not the love of Christ.' To love your brother is much more important than orthodoxy; yes, it is more important than mere mechanical correctness in your conduct and behaviour in an ethical sense. There are people who, like the rich young ruler, can say, 'All these things . . .' They are not guilty of the gross sins which they have seen in others, and yet their spirit as they criticise is a portrayal that they do not love their brother. Harshness, the criticizing spirit—all that is a negation of this spirit of love. It is something that rises up in my heart and nature and it is, therefore, the proof positive of whether I belong to Him or not. 'If ye know these things,' said the Lord Jesus Christ, 'happy are ye if ye do them' (John 13:17). 'If I,' He also said in effect, in the same passage, 'whom you call Lord and Master, have washed your feet, how much more in a sense ought you to wash one another's feet and be loving towards one another and be anxious to serve one another.' This thing is inevitable—if we belong to Him, we must be manifesting this spirit and type of life.

But let us put it finally in the form of a comparison. Let us just glance at the characteristics of the Christian and the non-Christian in the light of this pronouncement. John puts it very plainly. Let us look at the man who does not love his brother, this unloving kind of person, the man who claims, as these people has claimed, that he is truly Christian.

You see, John still has the Gnostics in mind, those people who claimed an unusual knowledge and advancement in the realm of the kingdom of God, but who were denying it by their very attitude towards their brethren whom they despised. 'It is no good boasting of your mystical experiences,' says John; 'what shows whether you are a Christian or not is your attitude towards the brethren. If you love them, you are a Christian.'

Now, what are the things John tells us about unloving people? The first thing is that they are in darkness; that means they belong to the order or realm of the kingdom of darkness. I can do nothing better at this point than to quote the Apostle Paul in Titus 3:3, where he gives this perfect yet terrifying description of the life of the world which is not Christian. This is how he puts it: 'For we ourselves also were sometimes'—that is to say once upon a time—'foolish, disobedient, deceived, serving divers lusts and pleasures, living in malice and envy, hateful, and hating one another.' That is what it means to be in darkness. That, according to the New Testament, is the state of the world outside Christ.

Now you may say that it is not a true description of the world, of men and women who are not Christians, but I suggest to you that it is a simple and correct account. The world hides itself; there is a superficial charm and manner, there is a superficial culture and chivalry that would conceal this. Yet look at people's faces and listen to what they say about one another, what they say about a person to whom they have recently been so charming and polite. Look at the sneer on their faces—the world is full of this, in spite of all the superficiality. 'Hateful, and hating one another,' selfishness, greed, jealousy, envy, malice, self-centredness—those are the characteristics of the life of the world, the state of being in darkness. And according to John, anyone who is not a Christian is in that position; he is in darkness.

But notice, he puts it like this also: '. . . he that hateth his brother is in darkness, and walketh in darkness, and knoweth not whither he goeth.' This person is not only in that realm of darkness where that is the kind of life and outlook—he is also altogether controlled by that outlook. In other words, the tragedy about the non-Christian is that he is not master of himself or in control of himself; he is governed by his surroundings and circumstances.

Is that not absolutely true? This kind of person is always governed by what is taking place. If things go right, he is happy; he may meet a person whom he likes, and he is happy, but if someone else comes along, he is aroused and angry. It all depends on a sort of accident and chance—whom he meets, what happens to him, what his state and condition is. He has no idea where he is going, no standard, no control; there is no steady policy in his life. He is the victim of the darkness, and thus his life is always uncertain and unreliable.

But let me mention the third thing: '. . . [he] knoweth not whither he goeth, because that darkness hath blinded his eyes.' In other words, because all his trouble is just that he really is blind as to the true nature of life, he has not understood the gospel, he does not realise what is happening to him in this world. He does not realise that he is going on to the next world; he does not know that he has to face God in the judgment; he has not awakened to the whole, real meaning of life. He does not realise that God will ask him about his attitude towards his brother; he is blind to his eternal destiny.

Then the final thing about such a person is that he is a stumblingblock. This is how John puts it: 'He that loveth his brother abideth in the light, and there is none occasion of stumbling in him.' Let me put it like this: The man who is in darkness and who is walking in the darkness and whose mind is dark is an occasion of stumbling both to himself and to everybody else. Because he has this unloving spirit within himself, everything he comes into contact with is going to cause him to stumble, and because he is an unloving person he causes other people to stumble also.

Is this not perfectly true? These people with this unloving nature are always finding problems and troubles. They always see insults where they do not exist; there is always something upsetting them; they are always being put out; they are constantly stumbling because of their unloving spirit. But, says John, they cause other people to stumble also, because as they are in this state and condition no one knows what to do with them. They are always so touchy and sensitive, and they constantly run other people into trouble.

So there is the Apostle's description of the person who does not love his brother; there is this horrible picture of the unloving nature. John gives it in detail, and I have repeated it in detail, trusting that having seen this picture we shall hate it and ask God to forgive us if we have seen anything of ourselves in it.

But let me conclude with a word on the other side. What are

Christians, the loving people? They are just the exact opposite of all I have been describing. They are in a different realm—in the light and not in the darkness. They have a purpose governing their lives; they are not dependent upon circumstances and accident and chance; they have a central gospel and a central doctrine. Their eyes have been opened; they have understood the gospel of Jesus Christ, and the result is that there is no occasion of stumbling in them. They do not trip and stumble constantly as they go about the world and meet people, and so other people do not stumble because of them. There is something about them that draws the best out of others.

This is how it works: They are always in the light, they have been enlightened, and they have come to see certain things. Christians have come to see the nature of sin; with the Apostle Paul they have come to see that they were hateful and that they were dwelling in the darkness. They have come to see that the devil had introduced principles into their lives which made them hateful; they were alienated from God. But they realised their danger, and they heard the gospel that offered forgiveness because of the love of God in the Lord Jesus Christ. They saw themselves as hell-deserving sinners who are only saved because of the love of God, and they realise now that this must govern their attitude towards the whole of life.

So they look at their fellow men and women; they see people exactly like themselves before their eyes were opened, and now they are sorry for them. They see that poor person behaving like that because he is a victim of sin; they must be sorry for him and pray that he may see himself and know the love of God in Christ and be delivered out of his sin. They begin to love the hateful person instead of hating him; they say, 'We are all in the same position,' and they begin to have an eye of compassion for them. Their knowledge of the love of God in Christ makes them love other people even as they have been loved themselves. They are new men and women with a new outlook; they are in a new realm. They feel the love of God in their heart, and they want to love Him and glorify Him, and they know they can glorify God most of all by being new men and women, by living as Christ lived and thereby showing and proving that they are indeed true disciples.

Christ our Lord put this perfectly once in a parable of the man who was a servant and was in trouble. He went to his lord and pleaded for forgiveness, and that lord forgave him. But there was another man who was a servant under the first servant who came to him and made exactly the same plea, but he took him by the throat and said, 'No, I won't let you off—you have to pay to the last farthing.' Well, said our Lord (Matt 18:23-35), that man must not think he has been forgiven, for the man who does not forgive will not be forgiven.

What this means is that you and I can only be happy about the fact that we are Christians if we find this loving, forgiving spirit within ourselves. It is idle for us to say that we know that God has forgiven us if we are not loving and forgiving ourselves. People who say they are in the light but who hate and do not forgive their brother are in darkness even now. Men and women who have seen the truth, those who are in the light, have seen themselves and others all under the law of the love of God. And having realised this love which has pardoned them in spite of their unworthiness, they are prepared to do the same to others and to love them and rejoice with them in the same common salvation, in the same common love for the wondrous Lord who 'loved his own . . . unto the end' (John 13:1), even to the Cross and its shame and agony.

'He that abideth in the light loveth his brother, and there is none occasion of stumbling in him.' God grant that as we have examined ourselves in the light of these great pictures we may be able to say with assurance and confidence that we are abiding in the light and loving the brethren.

6

CHILDREN, YOUNG MEN, AND FATHERS

I write unto you, little children, because your sins are for-
given you for his name's sake. I write unto you, fathers,
because ye have known him that is from the beginning. I
write unto you, young men, because ye have overcome the
wicked one. I write unto you, little children, because ye
have known the Father. I have written unto you, fathers,
because ye have known him that is from the beginning. I
have written unto you, young men, because ye are strong,
and the word of God abideth in you, and ye have over-
come the wicked one.

1 JOHN 2:12-14

THESE THREE VERSES come as a kind of parenthesis in the series of appeals and exhortations which the Apostle makes at this particular point in his letter to these early Christians. We have considered the verses in which he tells them that they must keep that commandment of love to the brethren which is so essential to fellowship with God, and he is now proposing to go on to make another great and striking, and to many perhaps, a startling exhortation—'Love not the world, neither the things that are in the world. If any man love the world, the love of the Father is not in him.' But before he does that, he introduces this break, and therefore it is important to discover exactly why the Apostle does this, why he suddenly interrupts his series of exhortations and at the end of verse 11 pauses and says, 'I write unto you, little children, because your sins are forgiven you for his name's sake,' and so on.

Now this is very interesting. The Apostle, as it were, puts it like this: 'I have been showing you,' he says in effect, 'some of the basic principles. I have been reminding you of some of the demands which the Christian life makes upon you; I have been showing you what are the very conditions of blessing.' Why, then, the pause and the break? Well, the answer, it seems to me, is this: it is because the Apostle was a pastor, an understanding and loving pastor. His object after all, as we have seen, was not simply to lay down Christian doctrine; he had a very practical object, which was to help these people. So he has to appeal to them; he wants to make sure that he is carrying them with him; so here, in his typical, practical manner, he just stops for a moment and says, 'Now are you quite clear about all this? You see the line of argument; let me once more just remind you of the thing on which I am basing my whole appeal and exhortation.'

Now that is the way to understand this particular parenthesis. John, at this point, was anxious to do three main things. Firstly, he was anxious to comfort these people; he has been holding forth a very strong and stern doctrine before them—keeping the commandments and loving the brethren—and it is as if he said to himself, 'Now I wonder if these people will be discouraged. Will they feel I am holding the standard so high that they cannot attain to it? Will it make them feel they are condemned sinners and that there is no hope for them at all? Very well, I will just stop and give them a word of comfort.'

The second thing he is anxious to do is to encourage them, and he does so in this way: He, in effect, says to these people, 'Now do not think of this commandment and exhortation of mine as something quite separate or disconnected from anything else. Let me remind you,' says John, 'that all I am saying to you is based upon the fundamental doctrine which I have already outlined to you.' If we were presented with the Christian standard of life and morality and ethics without first of all being shown clearly how this is possible in the light of the Christian doctrine, there would be nothing more discouraging in the world than the New Testament. But, thank God, the New Testament never appeals to us to do anything at all until it has told us certain vital things which are essential to the carrying out of the Christian life; so John writes this to encourage them.

I think he has a third object also, and that is to show them that there is no excuse at all for failure in this life in view of the provision that has been made. In other words, we can look at it like this: Someone may say to me, 'That is all very well! It is an easy thing to tell us to love our brothers; it is a very simple thing to say we are to keep God's commandments; but if you look at them, surely no one can be expected to do these things.' 'But,' says John, 'in the light of my doctrine there is no excuse for failure.' So he introduces this parenthesis in that way; comfort for those who feel condemned, encouragement for those who feel this is some exalted task, and, before he goes any further, taking away every excuse that we may tend to put forward, any attempt to excuse ourselves from this high calling, this great vocation into which we have been called in the Lord Jesus Christ.

John here, as it were, stops and says, 'Do you think this is all hopelessly impossible? Do you think that what I am really asking of you is so heroic as to be entirely outside the reach of the average Christian? It may be possible, you think, for those who go off into monasteries and who spend their whole life in doing nothing but cultivating their religious life, but surely not for the average Christian in business and other affairs. Now,' says John, 'if that is your feeling, it is quite clear to me that you have not grasped the original doctrine. You are approaching the whole thing in the wrong way. Indeed it seems to me that you must be uncertain somewhere as to the basic elements of the Christian faith. So,' he says, 'I am not going to take any risks; I am not going a step further; I shall not make another exhortation until I am perfectly satisfied that we really are agreed about the bases, the fundamentals. It is no use going on with the building if there is something wrong with the foundation.'

And this is the way in which he proceeds to do that: He tells them that he is writing these things to them on a certain assumption: 'I write unto you, little children, *because* your sins are forgiven you for his name's sake. I write unto you, fathers, *because*'—in the light of the fact that—'ye have known him that is from the beginning. I write unto you, young men, *because* ye have overcome the wicked one.' 'That is my basic assumption,' says John, 'and if you are uncertain about that, then obviously these appeals and exhortations of mine will be utterly useless. I shall be wasting my time,' he says, 'if I go on to tell you not to love the world and the things of the world, because unless you are in the basic Christian position you obviously will not understand it and you will feel that the whole thing is a sheer impossibility. So let us go back and just make sure we are agreed about the vital things.' In other words, we have, in these three verses, what I am again describing as the very fundamentals, the bare essentials, the irreducible minimum of the whole Christian position.

Now I shall not go into a detailed discussion as to the mechanics of the way in which John puts this great conspectus of Christian doctrine. You will find that the commentators spend most of their time in doing that—debating as to what exactly John means by 'little children,' 'fathers,' and 'young men' and why he repeats himself as he does. Such discussion is all quite interesting as far as it goes, but it seems to me that it is not very important and not very profitable. Different writers have different views about it, and you will find that it is almost impossible to find two who will agree about this matter. Does 'little children' in verse 1 mean all Christians, or does it literally mean little children—and similarly with 'fathers' and young men'? Then in verse 13 it is not the same word in the Greek, and there is a discussion as to whether it means his little children or whether it does not.

We cannot decide all this, and it does not matter. There are two ways of looking at it. You can say that 'little children' means all Christians; he says at the beginning of the chapter, 'My little children, these things write I unto you,' so he is including them all—it is a term of affection from an old man to disciples and followers; that view may well be right. Then there are others who say that there you have all Christians, and then there are two subdivisions—fathers and young men. Again in verses 12 and 13 he talks about children and once more he divides it into fathers and young men, so the possibility is that he has three divisions. Well, they ask, if that is what he has in mind, why does he put fathers immediately after little children and then young men after that? Would it not be more natural to say, children, young men, fathers?

But I repeat, it does not matter, because what really matters is that clearly the Apostle is telling us that these truths of the Christian life and of the Christian faith must be understood by all of us. At the same time, there are particular emphases that are more important at particular ages and stages. In other words, we must realise that not only the little children are to know that their sins are forgiven—all Christians must know that. It is not only the fathers who know that from the beginning, all Christians should know it. It is not only the young men who overcome the wicked one; that is to be true of all Christians. So he writes for all, but at the same time there are steps and stages in this Christian life, and at these stages we need one emphasis more than another and then we go on to need another one.

That, to me, is the glory of this Christian faith. The whole is meant for everybody, and yet there are particular applications at particular points, and that, I think, is exactly what John is doing. He is reminding them of the whole position, and as a wise pastor he just has this particular word of emphasis for people in particular ages or stages.

So let us look at it from the particular like this: It is essential that we should be clear about the basic Christian position; there are certain fundamental postulates and assumptions without which it is a sheer waste of time to appeal to people to live the Christian life. That is the New Testament doctrine from beginning to end; it has nothing to say by way of appeal for conduct to anyone who is not a Christian. It is no part of the Christian Church's business to be exhorting the world to practise Christian ethics, for it cannot do it. It is difficult for the Christian, it is impossible for the world, so there is no single ethical exhortation in the Bible to a person who is not standing on the Christian position. Christians do not turn to people of the world and say, 'Love not the world, neither the things that are in the world'; they know they cannot understand the language, still less can they practise it. No, we must be absolutely clear about these fundamental, basic things.

That is why, I think, John repeats these things twice, for repetition is the very art of teaching. Wise teachers always repeat themselves. There are certain things that can never be repeated too often, and although John is an old man, he is a teacher.

So what is it that every Christian should know? What are these basic postulates and assumptions behind the Christian appeal for keeping the commandments, loving the brethren, hating the world, and all the other exhortations? Well, there are just three. First, we must be perfectly clear in our knowledge with regard to the whole question of the forgiveness of sins. 'I write unto you, little children, *because your sins are forgiven you for his name's sake*'—a fundamental postulate.

What does this mean? Let me divide it like this: The first thing that Christians should know is that their sins are forgiven. That can perhaps best be put by a series of negatives. The Christian is not a person who is seeking forgiveness, or who is hoping to be forgiven. The Christian is not a person who is uncertain about forgiveness or who prays for it or tries to merit it. No, Christians are people who *know* that they are forgiven.

Now this is absolutely vital and fundamental. So many people, when you ask them if they know that their sins are forgiven, say, 'I am hoping that they are; I am seeking forgiveness; I am praying for it; I am very uncertain about the whole thing, but I am hoping that my sins will be forgiven me.' 'No!' says John. 'That is not the Christian position—that is a typical non-Christian statement. The Christian is one whose sins are already forgiven.'

Let me emphasise that still more. The Christian's certainty and assurance of forgiveness of sins is based upon his knowledge of the *way* in which his sins are forgiven—'I write unto you, little children, because your sins are forgiven you for *his name's sake*.' What a glorious statement! You know, the whole of the Christian doctrine in its fundamentals is there. He is everything. This is the basis of our certainty and assurance; we are forgiven because of the perfect, the finished, the full work of the Lord Jesus Christ on our behalf. Christians know that their sins are forgiven, not because they bank loosely and vaguely upon the love of God, still less because they rest upon the hope of their own good lives and merits or their own good works.

Again, this is absolutely central. Let us ask ourselves the question, Have I believed my sins are forgiven; and if so, on what grounds do I believe? Now you put that question and you will find that people say, 'I believe my sins are forgiven because God is love.' Yes, but if those are your grounds for believing, then I ask again, where does the Lord Jesus Christ come in? Is He central? He is central with John because 'your sins are forgiven you for his name's sake.'

John has already put that like this in verses 1 and 2: 'If any man sin, we have an advocate with the Father, Jesus Christ the righteous: and he is the propitiation for our sins: and not for ours only, but also for the sins of the whole world.' Christians have certain objective grounds for their assurance of forgiveness of sin. Let me summarise them again. It is 'for his name's sake.' What makes me know my sins are forgiven is that the Lord Jesus Christ is standing there as my representative with God; it is for His sake, for His name's sake, that I am forgiven. My sin has been dealt with in Him—'The Lord hath laid on him the iniquity of us all,' and 'with his stripes we are healed' (Isa 53:6-5). Our sins have been taken and laid upon the Lord Jesus Christ by God Himself; and because

He has borne the punishment of my sins, I shall not bear the punishment for them because my sins are forgiven in Him, for His name's sake. As we saw in our consideration of Chapter 1, 'If we confess our sins, he is faithful and just to forgive us our sins,' because the very justice of God insists upon my being forgiven, because Christ has been punished for me. These are the grounds of my certainty and assurance.[1]

But let me rather put it in this practical form—and I do not hesitate to put it like this: if you are uncertain about the forgiveness of your sins, that in itself is sin. I want to be ruthless about this because there are people who feel that an assurance of forgiveness of sins is presumption, and they rather give the impression that they are being humble and modest. They say, 'I would not like to say my sins are forgiven, I do not feel good enough to say that, I am so conscious of my own unworthiness.' They give the impression that they have unusual lowliness and humility.

The simple reply to that is that if you speak in that way there is only one explanation of it, and that is lack of faith, that is unbelief; it is no mark of saintliness to be uncertain that your sins are forgiven; it is to deny and doubt the Word of God. The certainty of the New Testament is that your sins are forgiven you; you have been forgiven for His name's sake. If you, therefore, do not know that, it is because you are not clear about the doctrine, because you are still relying upon yourself, because you are not relying upon the finished, complete work of the Son of God for you upon the cross. It is because you do not realise the merit and the power of His blessed name. That name pleaded before God immediately assures pardon—the name that is above every other name, the name in whom all fulness dwells, the name that gives an entry to the courts of heaven and to the very presence of God.

So let us be quite clear about this. It is absolutely essential to living the Christian life, because while you are unhappy or disturbed about this question of forgiveness of sins, you cannot be going forward; in a sense there is no point in going forward. What is the point of my saying to myself, 'Well, from now on, I am going to live the Christian life, I am going to try to keep the commandments,' if I am uncertain about my past sins? Though I may live a good life from now on, the past guilt remains. How can I go on until that has been dealt with? And the only way to deal with it is to believe on the Lord Jesus Christ. You cannot undo what you have done, you cannot go back and erase your past—it is impossible. But it has been done in Christ, and I say once more with

John that there is no point appealing to people to go forward until they are clear about the past.

Are you clear about it? Do you know that the Lord Jesus Christ has borne your sins and has died your death and risen again to justify you, and are you relying utterly and absolutely upon Him and upon Him alone? If so, you can say that you know your sins are forgiven you. That is the first thing that every Christian should know.

The second is that every Christian should know the way in which sin can be overcome. 'I write unto you, young men, because ye have overcome the wicked one' (v 13), and 'I have written unto you, young men, because ye are strong, and the word of God abideth in you, and ye have overcome the wicked one' (v 14). Again I would call attention to the way in which John puts it. 'I write unto you, young men, because *ye have overcome*'—not because you are going to, but because you have.

Now what does this mean? Well, it can be put very briefly like this: There is an immediate victory of which one becomes conscious the moment one believes on the Lord Jesus Christ. Let no one misunderstand me. I spend a good deal of time denouncing the gospel of perfection, and I am as far from preaching it as I have ever been, but I say this: the moment we believe on the Lord Jesus Christ, we are conscious of a victory over the wicked one—not complete, absolute victory, but victory. We may still be conscious of great weakness, yes, but the moment we believe on Christ we have an immediate consciousness that we are somehow or other no longer under the dominion of sin. Yes, the wicked one is very great; he is very powerful and we may be afraid of him in our weakness, and yet we know that there is something about us, there is an immediate victory. Though we have not finished with sin, we are no longer under the dominion of sin and Satan. We may be conscious of great weakness, and yet we know that he is a defeated enemy and that we are fools if we listen to him.

But to put it still more simply, we can say that those who believe on the Lord Jesus Christ know that they are in Christ; they know that Christ has already defeated the wicked one. It is a great thing when you are confronted by an enemy to know that that enemy is defeated. That is the position of Christian men and women; they cannot be beaten by the enemy in combat because there is Someone standing by them who has done it. You are a little child in the victorious army, and you can leave the enemy to Him.

That is the way to understand this victory over sin. John divides it like this: we know we have been made strong. 'I have written unto you, young men, because ye are strong'—it does not mean that they are strong in and of themselves, or that they have developed some strange, mystic strength. Rather it must be that they know they have been made strong. Every Christian should know that, and we know it like this: We receive new life and power; the moment we believe on the Lord Jesus Christ and become Christians, we are aware of a change and of a difference. We know that something has come into us, something has happened to us, there has been a kind of infusion of new life, we are aware of a power that we never knew before. There is strength, though it may be small, which we never had in the past. So we can see why John has this parenthesis. What is the point of telling us to keep the commandments and to love the brethren and to hate the world unless we have been given strength?

Furthermore, *'the word of God abideth in you.'* The word of God is the word which brings new life to us. 'Being born again,' says Peter, 'not of corruptible seed, but of incorruptible, by the word of God, which liveth and abideth for ever' (1 Pet 1:23). James talks about this life being *engrafted* into us by the word (Jas 1:21). The word of God comes into us and gives us life, and it abides and the life grows. We can think of this word also as the 'sword of the Spirit.' Paul, when he tells the Ephesians to put on the whole armour of God, gives a list, and he refers to the 'sword of the Spirit' with which we are to fight the enemy—'the sword of the Spirit, which is the word of God' (Eph 6:17).

How is it that this word of God makes us strong to fight sin? I think it does it in this way: it shows me the horrible nature of sin; and while the word of God abides in me, I am made to see sin in all its ugliness and selfishness and perversion and I hate it. It also teaches men and women about the destiny of those who are the slaves of sin. It shows them that they are going to hell and destruction outside the life of God for all eternity. It also shows them, thank God, the power of Christ and how Christ has defeated the enemy already and how Christ comes into them and makes them strong and enables them to become more than conquerors against all these things that assail them.

Let me sum it up again like this: If we feel that the demands of this Christian life are too high or impossible, it is nothing but sheer ignorance, a sheer lack of faith. If we feel that we would rather be talking about our own weakness and about our own failures, then let me emphasise once more that that is not humility, nor Christian modesty; it is lack of faith and lack of knowledge. There is a sense in which we have no right to be weak, no business to be failures when all this is offered to us. 'So then,' says John, 'I am writing to you because you know these things and because you know that these things are facts.' So the Christian must have this certain knowledge of the power of Christ and the ability to overcome sin.

And that brings me to the third and last point, which is that we must all have a knowledge of the Father and of the Son. This, as we have seen, is the basic truth in the whole epistle. 'I write unto you, fathers, because ye have known him that is from the beginning'—that is, the Lord Jesus Christ: 'That which was from the beginning, which we have heard, which we have seen with our eyes, which we have looked upon, and our hands have handled, of the Word of life' (1:1). Then: 'I write unto you, little children, because ye have known the Father.' This is the blessed knowledge that every Christian must have, a knowledge of God—not God as some great power, not as some great force, not someone who is opposed to us and hates us, imposing these commandments upon us— but God as Father, God who has loved us with an everlasting love, the God and Father of our Lord Jesus Christ.

This is the God who so loves us that He counts the very hairs of our head, the God who causes the sun to rise upon this world, this amazing Father God. 'We know Him,' says John. 'I write to you because you know Him, and if you know Him you will not feel that His commandments are a sacrifice; you will know that they are all destined for your good; you will know He has brought them in because He wants to bless you and because He wants you to be conformed to the image of His own dear Son.' So it is a knowledge of the Father and likewise a knowledge of the Lord Jesus Christ; to know Him in person, to know His work for us, to know Him in His offices as the sin-bearer, as the sacrifice, as the prophet, priest, and King. It is to know the New Testament doctrine concerning Him, and above all to know Him and to feel that He is near in the hour of need and in temptation so that we can rise above it; to know perfect peace in Him and through Him; to know the Father and to know the Son.

There, then, are the three basic things which every Christian must know: sins forgiven for His name's sake, power to overcome the sin, and to know God the Father and God the Son through God the Holy Spirit.

This is the knowledge that John also applies in particular to the different age groups. While we are young in this Christian faith and feel so weak and small, the one thing we really want to know is that God is our Father, that God loves us and that our sins are forgiven; so he emphasises that in writing to the 'little children.' You see, in that first stage all we really want to know is that we can, as it were, recline in safety in the loving arms of God. That is what the child wants; he depends upon the parent; he wants to receive everything, but he does not give anything, and God is like that with us, in the early stages. At the beginning of the Christian life we do not understand much, so God gives us everything.

I have often said in passing, and I am sure every minister and preacher will confirm what I say, that as a man goes on preaching this gospel, he finds he has to work more and more. In the early days of my Christian ministry I was given sermons, but now I have to work harder, and it is like that in the Christian life. God is the Father, and the child is given everything. Little children, you know your sins are forgiven you.

Yes, but go on a little bit and you become a young man; you find now there is a fight involved, and 'young men' in the Christian life are conscious of that fight, and the enemy is attacking them. In the beginning the Christian life was easy; now there is a conflict and difficulties. 'You are quite right,' says John, 'and what I would emphasise for you is this: He can make you strong, and you can overcome the wicked one, and the word of God will abide in you, so that when you are in this middle stage of the Christian life you have to remember this—the young man, the middle age group, must especially hold on to this—that you are not left to yourself. The word of God abides in you, and Christ who has defeated the enemy can enable you to overcome. And, fathers, you who are old in age, some old in the Christian life, what should be true of you is this: you no longer as children must expect everything to come automatically. You are not in the stage to fight combats and conflicts. No, you have gone beyond that, you should have gone beyond it, you no longer are interested in the gifts, no longer interested in the fight, though you are still fighting. What matters to you is the knowledge of the giver Himself. You are old, and you know you have not much longer in this world, and what should be occupying your mind and attention is that the day will soon come when you will see Him face to face. You know Him that is from the beginning. Do you dwell more and more on Him? As a child you thought of gifts; you now are thinking more of the giver. You have gone through the struggles, and you have overcome; you know all about that; now what you are thinking about is the consummation, the ultimate reward, of standing and seeing Him face to face. So you dwell more and more upon the person, and you say, "Oh, what I long for is to know Him better; to know my Saviour as a person and to know God better." And you look wistfully to the day when with Paul you will be able to say, "To me to live is Christ, and to die is gain" (Phil 1:21), for it means "to be with Christ; which is far better"' (Phil 1:23).

There are steps and stages like that in the Christian life, and whatever stage we are in, there is an aspect of the truth that speaks specifically and especially to us, some basic doctrine for us all and a special word of encouragement according to our several positions. Let us thank God that He caused His servant, the Apostle, to pause at this point to introduce this glorious, magnificent parenthesis. Let us thank God that we stand on such solid ground: a knowledge of sin forgiven, a knowledge of how to overcome sin, and above all the knowledge of Himself, God the Father, God the Son, and God the Holy Ghost.

7

THE LOVE OF THE WORLD

Love not the world, neither the things that are in the world. If any man love the world, the love of the Father is not in him. For all that is in the world, the lust of the flesh, and the lust of the eyes, and the pride of life, is not of the Father, but is of the world. And the world passeth away, and the lust thereof: but he that doeth the will of God abideth for ever.

1 JOHN 2:15-17

WE FIND HERE THE Apostle resuming the list of practical injunctions and exhortations which he was giving to these people, after having interrupted this list in order to remind them of their resources. He is anxious that they should understand clearly that he is not asking the impossible, nor is he raising the standard too high. Their sins are already forgiven them; they have the strength and the power whereby they can overcome; and they know God and have fellowship with Him and the Lord Jesus Christ. So it is in the light of these things that he exhorts them in this way to put certain principles into practice.

Now here in these verses we have a great negative exhortation. Having told them what they are to do, he here reminds them of something that they are to avoid—'Love not the world.' As we are to love God and keep His commandments, as we are to love the brethren, so, equally definitely, we are not to love the world, neither the things that are in the world. And this is something that follows quite logically and inevitably from what he has already been saying. This negative is vitally important; it is quite as important as the positive, and I think we can agree in saying that there are no more solemn words addressed to Christian people anywhere in the Scriptures than these.

It behooves us, therefore, to approach them carefully lest we misunderstand them, because I believe it is equally true to say that there are perhaps no words which have been so frequently misunderstood and misinterpreted as these. I think the explanation of that is that we all have a tendency to engage in self-defence, and the danger is to approach these words and to interpret them in such a way as to make me all right and probably condemn other people. We are all experts at rationalising our sins and explaining away what we do, and it is interesting to hear how people often quote these verses, fondly imagining that they are perfectly all right themselves with regard to these words and yet who often display in their lives that they have certainly completely misunderstood one of the main emphases of this particular injunction. We must approach it, therefore, with an open mind, and we must take the words as they stand.

There have been two main misinterpretations of this injunction. The first is what I would call the *ascetic* interpretation, which says that these words mean that Christians literally have to go out of the world and segregate themselves from society. This is the misinterpretation which led to monasticism and to the whole tendency to go out of the world and to live what is called the 'religious life'—people divide Christians up into the 'religious' and the 'lay,' or the 'religious' and the 'secular,' as if living within the confines of some kind of institution or order were a guarantee that one would no longer love the world or the things that are in it.

The second misinterpretation is the one I would describe as the *incomplete* or *partial* interpretation of these words. Instead of taking John's words as they are, people say, 'We must not be guilty of worldliness' and then they proceed to define worldliness as they think of it and not as John thinks of it. Their conception of worldliness is a small one, and they fail to face John's full exposition of it here.

There are two main subdivisions of this incomplete or partial interpretation. The first says, 'We will not go to dances or to cinemas. We will give up smoking, we will not go to theatres, we will give up gambling and a few other things like that.' The moment these people talk about worldliness, that is all they think about; they are not guilty of the charge of worldliness.

Secondly, there are those who really seem to think that worldliness just means being interested in politics and social activities. They say, 'No Christian should ever be concerned about political matters because that is of the world, and the Christian is not to love such things.' So as long as they take no interest in political and social questions, they feel they are not guilty of worldliness. But they ignore completely, as I hope to show you, the Apostle's interpretation of what exactly is meant by loving the world and the things that are in the world.

Now I feel that this is of very great importance. One often hears people talking eloquently, and with much feeling, about worldliness and denouncing it, and one realises at once that they have only taken one little section and have completely ignored the remainder. I say again that the cause of that—and we are all subject to it—is this instinct of self-defence; we introduce our definition to guarantee that we are all right and others may be wrong, but that is not the Scriptural definition of what is meant by worldliness. So we must face these words with unusual interest; we must come before them as they are; we must allow them to search and examine us in order that we may know truly and exactly what worldliness really is. As we do so, of course, we shall discover exactly where we are and where we stand. It is a searching and very serious word as I have said; there is no word that so examines us down to the very depths of our being as a word like this.

Not only that, it is a word that again reminds us of something that is absolutely essential to the enjoyment of the fellowship of the Father and of the Son. There are so many people within the Christian world who are unhappy in their Christian life and who are not getting the benefits and enjoyment simply because they have not faced a text like this; they have not allowed it to search them and influence their whole life. So let us approach it in this way.

First of all, let us ask what John means by this injunction. Well, the first thing to ask, obviously, is this: what is '*the world*' in this case? Now I think it is important that we should agree that he is not referring here to creation as such; he is not thinking of the mountains and the valleys and the rivers, the streams and the sun and the moon and the stars; he does not mean the physical world in that sense. There are people who have even thought that to 'love not the world, neither the things that are in the world' means to shut one's eyes to the glory and the beauty of nature.

But it does not mean that; neither does it mean the life of the world in general. It does not mean family relationships, though there are people who have misinterpreted it like that; they have often regarded marriage as sinful. Not once but very often in my ministerial life have I had to deal with nice, sincere Christian people who have solemnly believed, through misinterpreting a text like this, that Christian people should not marry. Their reason is that marriage involves certain relationships which they regard as sinful; they would regard the very gift of sex as being sinful in and of itself.

So the 'world' does not mean creation; it does not mean family relationships; it is not the state; it does not mean engaging in business or a profession or all these things which are essential to life; it does not mean government and authorities and powers, for all these have been ordained by God Himself. So there is nothing so grievous as to misinterpret 'the world' in some such terms as that.

What, then, does it mean? Clearly the very text and the whole teaching of the Bible shows that it must mean the organisation and the mind and the outlook of mankind as it ignores God and does not recognise Him and as it lives a life independent of Him, a life that is based upon this world and this life only. It means the outlook that has rebelled against God and turned its back upon Him. It means, in other words, the typical kind of life that is being lived by the average person today, who has no thought of God, but thinks only of this world and life, who thinks in terms of time and is governed by certain instincts and desires. It is the whole outlook upon life that is exclusive of God.

What, secondly, are the characteristics of that kind of life? Well, fortunately John answers that question in verse 16. First, verse 15 says, 'Love not the world, neither the things that are in the world. If any man love the world, the love of the Father is not in him. For'—there it is—'all that is in the world, the lust of the flesh, and the lust of the eyes, and the pride of life, is not of the Father, but is of the world.' Now *lust* means an inordinate affection or desire; lust means the abuse of something which is naturally and perfectly right and legitimate in and of itself. Paul, I think, puts this perfectly in his first letter to the Corinthians when he tells us to use this world and not abuse it (1 Cor 7:31), and to abuse it means we are guilty of lust. Lust, in other words, means that instead of controlling our desires and using them as we ought to, we are controlled by them; they master us and they control us. There are certain desires in us that are perfectly legitimate, they have been given by God. Yes, but if we are governed and controlled by them and our whole outlook upon life is circumscribed by these things, then we are guilty of lust; that is the meaning of the word.

The Apostle mentions 'the lust of *the flesh*.' What does this tell us? Well, here John is talking about lust in the sense that it arises from and appertains to nature, belonging as such to our physical bodies. Now we are living in an age when people say they believe in plain speaking; therefore let us put it quite plainly. This is his definition of sensuality; he is talking about the kind of person who lives only for sensual gratification. That includes the kind of man or woman who lives to eat; the lust for food, people whose whole outlook seems to be just that—their interest in food and drink—the expert knowledge they have on drink! How they delight to talk about it and call themselves connoisseurs and experts in tastes and flavours, living for eating and drinking. Now the hunger instinct is perfectly legitimate; we have to eat in order to live; but if you live to eat, you are guilty of the lust of the flesh, and it is exactly the same with drinking. If it is your controlling and main interest in life, it is a lust.

The same applies to sex. I need not labour these things; you have only to look at the newspapers and journals and you see the whole thing shouting and blaring at you; the world seems to be full of it. These clever, subtle businessmen who produce the newspapers and magazines know exactly what appeals to the public palate, so they put these things always in the forefront, and they all belong to this lust of the flesh—the abuse of certain natural instincts and desires that are a part of human nature and life. Do not love that, says John, do not be guilty of that, do not be controlled by that sort of thing; that has nothing to do with this godly life, it is the very antithesis of it.

But let us go on; not only 'the lust of the flesh,' but also 'the lust of *the eye*.' The best way of defining this is to say that it is the kind of man or woman who lives according to false values. They judge by appearances and by outward show. This, of course, often leads to the one we have already dealt with. It is through the eyes that so often sin arises; it is what we see and what the world makes us see that so often makes us sin. That is a large subject, and I can only just touch upon it in passing, but it no doubt includes sin when it is in the intellectual stage. Our Lord put it in this way: 'Whosoever looketh on a woman . . .' (Matt 5:28). The lust of the eyes includes that; it is a kind of invidious looking, sin in the intellect, the toying and playing with it in the imagination and thought. But it does not stop at that; the lust of the eyes means also a kind of vanity which delights in pomp and mighty splendour, in an appearance, in anything that appeals to the eyes. How full the world is of this kind of thing—mighty pomp and show, merely the appearance, giving an impression.

This pleases also the people whose main interest in life is their personal appearance. I am trying to speak of these things dispassionately, but it seems to me that there is nothing which is sadder in the world than people who just live for their own personal appearance and the impression that it makes. Clothing—oh, the time and the energy and the enthusiasm that goes into this! The talking and the writing; again you see it shouting at you everywhere. But you get it equally with certain people in the matter of their house and home. The lust of the eyes—how pathetic it is that human beings, endowed with the faculties that God has given, can live for things like that, this outlook of pomp and appearance and show. It is sad, too, to think how this often enters into the realm of the Church; you find people are dressing up in vestments all for processions and appearances—the lust of the eyes, the outward show.

The next step that John introduces is what he calls 'the pride of life.' The best way to define this is to call it self-glorification, a very subtle thing. This is something that perhaps we can divide into two sections; it includes ambition, and it includes contempt of others; 'the pride of life' means a pride in oneself generally at the expense of someone else, glorifying in something that is true of oneself in this life and world, something, in a sense, that has nothing to do with the soul and spirit of man. Let me analyse it a little: pride of birth, pride in your family, pride in your industry, proud that you have a particular name or that there is particular blood in you, so-called pride in social status. How men brag about this! Pride in influence, the people we know, our acquaintances! People love all this sort of thing; they are anxious to get into certain circles, anxious to belong to a certain club; but it has nothing to do with the soul, nothing to do with the spirit, nothing to do with God and His honour and glory! How men and women give their thought to this kind of thing; and oh, the money they spend on it, the time and the energy, the way they suffer, the jealousy and envy which arises—the pride of life!

Then there is the question of wealth, the way people pride themselves on their wealth and their material possessions. The pride of life as it shows itself in the school to which you went—a little better than somebody else's school—the college you attend, the university you belong to—how this influences life! There is a sense of superiority and a despising of others, feeling rather sorry for others. 'Where do they come from?' people ask.

Now I go into these things in detail because this kind of thing creeps into the life of the Christian Church. This is the sort of thing one often hears in Christian circles; these are the standards of judgement rather than spirituality—pride in knowledge and learning, ability and culture and erudition. Man boasts of his brain, his knowledge and his understanding; it is just a part of this pride. It is a striving for worldly honours, and, let me be quite honest again, not only worldly honours, but often ecclesiastical honours also. It is part of the pride of life, this ambition to get on and succeed, to be greater than someone else, this idea of self-glorification in some shape or form. And that, according to the Apostle John, is what is meant by 'Love not the world, neither the things that are in the world.'

Now I do not know whether he intended to give a comprehensive definition, but it does seem to me that in his third statement John really does cover the entire field. But let me emphasise this. There is an order in the three steps—the lust of the flesh, the lust of the eyes, the pride of life—the body, the soul and the spirit—and I am putting it like this in order to bring out this particular emphasis, that there may be no question whatsoever that the most serious and the most terrible of the three is the third, the pride of life. It is not for us to make comparisons in these things, but I think the Bible does teach us that the sins of the spirit are always worse than the sins of the flesh. There is something more or less natural about the sins of the flesh in one sense, but the sin of the spirit is the thing that is most opposed of all to the life of Christ and that which was manifested in Him. Let us be careful, therefore, that in denouncing the sins of the flesh we are not at the same time guilty of the pride of life, which is worse. Let us be careful, when we say we are not guilty because we do not do certain things, that we are not proud and despise others because of birth or position or university or one of these other things. It is as you go up in the scale from the body to the spirit that the sin becomes more and more subtle and more and more harmful to the true Christian life.

Next, why should we not love the world and the things that are in the world? Why is it of vital importance that we keep this injunction? John puts it like this: not to obey this commandment means a denial of our love to God and of our knowledge of Him. 'If any man love the world, the love of the Father is not in him,' says John; 'if you love these other things, they are incompatible; you cannot serve God and mammon; you cannot love God and the world at the same time.' 'Whosoever therefore will be a friend of the world is the enemy of God,' says the Apostle James (4:4). It is an utter denial of what we claim to believe.

Consider, then, the second reason: Love of the world and the things of the world is a denial of the life that is in us. 'For all that is in the world, the lust of the flesh, and the lust of the eyes, and the pride of life, is not of the Father, but is of the world,' and the word 'of' there means that it is not derived from, it does not originate in the Father. Christians, according to the Apostle's definition, as we have seen, are people who have in them the life of Christ—Christ dwelling and living in them. Therefore, says John, if you claim that Christ is dwelling within you, you cannot be guilty of loving the things that arise from the lust of the flesh and the lust of the eyes and the pride of life. Look at Him; He was never guilty of those sins of the flesh. He did not believe in outward pomp and show and appearance. No, He was meek and lowly; He was someone who was the very antithesis of all the loudness and vulgarity of the world and its delight in appearance and mere show. And when you come to this question of the pride of life, why, you see it still more definitely. He lived with very poor parents; He was born in a stable, and His cradle was nothing but a manger. He worked with His hands as a carpenter, a manual labourer, and that is the Lord of glory, the Saviour of our soul! That is the life which we claim is in us.

And what was His teaching? 'Blessed are the meek'; the very opposite of the so-called worldly type of person. 'Blessed are the poor in spirit'; not those who are proud and arrogant and ambitious and who look down upon others because of certain things. No, 'poor in spirit,' feeling that they are unworthy and that they have nothing at all. 'Blessed are they which do hunger and thirst after righteousness'—that is His teaching (Matt 5:5, 3, 6). 'The Son of Man came not to be ministered unto, but to minister, and to give his life a ransom for many' (Matt 20:28). In the world the great lord it over others; it is not so in His kingdom: '. . . he that is greatest among you shall be your servant,' said our

Lord (Matt 23:11). He was the friend of publicans and sinners, and He was much misunderstood because of that. In other words, the great characteristic of our Lord was that He was interested in people's souls. He did not look at their clothing, or at their birth or ancestry or possessions. He valued the soul that was there, and that is true of all His followers. Paul puts it like this: 'Henceforth know we no man after the flesh; yea, though we have known Christ after the flesh, yet now henceforth know we him no more' (2 Cor 5:16). Or again, he said, 'There is neither Jew nor Greek, there is neither bond nor free, there is neither male nor female: for ye are all one in Christ Jesus' (Gal 3:28). All these things are demolished; the soul is what matters, not these other things.

In other words, Christians have an entirely different conception of all these things from the man of the world; the birth that Christians know is the rebirth, not natural birth; the wealth they are interested in is the wealth of the riches of glory; the knowledge they aspire after is not human knowledge, but the knowledge of God. The associations of which they are proud are not those which you find in noble circles; it is the people of God, it is the Christian Church, the saints, however humble and lowly they may chance to be. The honour that they crave for is not the honour of a great name amongst men, but the honour of being known by God and of anticipating the day when they shall hear the blessed words, 'Well done, thou good and faithful servant . . . enter thou into the joy of thy Lord' (Matt 25:21).

All that is the very opposite, the antithesis, of that which is so true of the world. Christians can say with the Apostle Paul, 'God forbid that I should glory, save in the cross of our Lord Jesus Christ' (Gal 6:14). God forbid that I should boast of anything but that; not my birth, not my appearance, not my knowledge, not my understanding, not my wealth, not my social status, nothing! 'God forbid that I should glory, save in the cross of our Lord Jesus Christ by whom the world is crucified unto me, and I unto the world.'

But the last reason given by John for not loving the world is that if we love the world, it means we do not truly understand this great gospel of salvation. 'The world passeth away,' says John, 'and the lust thereof: but he that doeth the will of God abideth for ever.' What he means is this: if you still love the world and the things that are in it, then it is clear that you have never understood the principles of sin. Cannot you see that all that belongs to the world is passing away? All these things, says John, are disappearing, they are dying. You may be proud of your personal appearance, but you will soon be old and haggard. You will be dying, and then you will have nothing to boast of, it is all passing. Oh fool, to glory in something that is so transient! Wealth, riches, learning, knowledge, social status and all these things, they are vanishing, they have the seeds of death in them. Christian people, how can we glory in things like that? It means we are blind to our own gospel which starts by telling us that all that is under the wrath of God and will be destroyed. It is all going to perdition and eternal destruction; so those who live for these things, therefore, are utterly inconsistent and show that they have never understood that if they belong to that realm they will be destroyed to all eternity. They must come out of and escape from it, and they should glory in the fact that there is a new life and realm, a new kingdom, and if they belong to this, they will abide for ever.

'So,' says the Apostle, 'that is my injunction to you; realise these truths; do the will of God; do not be concerned about your own desires. Do the will of God, and if you do that, you will abide for ever. You will be building up a firm foundation, a building which will be tried and tested as by fire, but because it consists of gold and precious metals and not of wood, hay and stubble, it will last and it will stand the test. And when you arrive in glory, your works will follow you and you will rest in eternal joy from your labours.'

8

THE ANTICHRIST

*Little children, it is the last time: and as ye have heard that
antichrist shall come, even now are there many antichrists;
whereby we know that it is the last time. They went out
from us, but they were not of us; for if they had been of
us, they would no doubt have continued with us: but they
went out, that they might be made manifest that they were
not all of us. . . . Who is a liar but he that denieth that Jesus
is the Christ? He is antichrist, that denieth the Father and
the Son. Whosoever denieth the Son, the same hath not
the Father: but he that acknowledgeth the Son hath the
Father also.*

1 JOHN 2:18-19, 22-23

IT IS IMPORTANT FOR us to realise that these verses must be taken in
the context of the whole section which runs from verse 18 to verse 28.
Furthermore, even before we come to analyse the section, it is also
important that we should realise the connection between it and what has
gone before. The Apostle's theme is that we must always bear in mind
that, placed as we are in this difficult and trying world, the great thing
which is offered us by the Christian gospel is fellowship and communion
with God, God the Father and God the Son through the Holy Spirit. So
having laid down the basis of the fellowship, he has then gone on to tell
them of certain things that may rob them of that fellowship, and we have
looked at these.

Then having said all that he now goes on to this further statement, but how do we fit it into the scheme? Well, so far the Apostle has been dealing with certain things within ourselves that tend to interrupt the fellowship—my failure to keep the commandments or to love my brethren; my failure to observe this injunction of not loving the world and living according to its mentality and outlook—all that, in a sense, is addressed to certain possibilities of failure resident within the Christian believer. 'But,' says John, 'unfortunately we cannot stop at that point; the dangers besetting us not only arise from within, there are certain dangers also outside us.' And what he deals with in this particular section is the great danger that ever confronts us as Christian people, arising, as it were, in the very atmosphere in which we live. Indeed, the danger which he emphasises here is the danger that arises in and from the life of the Church herself.

In other words, we have not only certain things to watch as individual Christians; but also collectively, as Christian people, we have to be very wary of certain common, general dangers to which we are subject as members of the Church; and that is the theme with which he deals here. There is a great enemy outside us who, as he tells us later on in this section, is trying to seduce us, and he says in verse 26, 'These things have I written unto you concerning them that seduce you'—those who would lead you astray, those who would entice you away from the real truth itself to something which is not actually the truth although it looks like it. It is the danger of being led astray by the great power that is amongst us and which is out for our destruction and for the destruction of the entire Christian Church. That is the theme of this section from verses 18 to 28. You can see it follows very logically from the previous exhortations; he goes from us, ourselves, to the whole atmosphere in which we live.

Now for the sake of clarity of thought and understanding let me suggest to you the way in which this section should be divided up. There are three great points in this whole exhortation; the first is the importance of realising the nature or the character of the spiritual conflict in which we find ourselves. This is the theme of verses 18 and 19 and partly also of verses 22 and 23.

The second theme is the way whereby we may realise this danger; that is the special message of verses 20 and 21 and 27, where you find this: 'But ye have an unction from the Holy One, and ye know all things. I have not written unto you because ye know not the truth, but because ye know it, and that no lie is of the truth. . . . But the anointing which ye have received of him abideth in you, and ye need not that any man teach you: but as the same anointing teacheth you of all things, and is truth, and is no lie, and even as it hath taught you, ye shall abide in him.' This is the great doctrine of the anointing and the unction which is possessed by every true Christian believer.

And then the third theme is the way to avoid the dangers that arise from this mighty spiritual conflict in which we find ourselves, and that is the theme of the remaining verses of the section. These then are the three great matters: realising the danger; the faculty and the power that are given unto us by God to enable us to realise it; and the way to fight against it, to avoid it, and to be delivered from all its terrible consequences.

This, you will see at once, is a theme that one meets with quite frequently in the New Testament. There are many other instances of it; you will find it for instance in 2 Peter 2, where Peter deals with exactly the same thing. But a classic example of this is Ephesians 6, where Paul talks about putting on 'the whole armor of God'—and why?—because 'we wrestle not against flesh and blood, but against principalities, against powers . . . against spiritual wickedness in high places' (Eph 6:11-12). And, of course, the book of Revelation is in a sense a book which is entirely devoted to this particular matter. In other words, the New Testament is full of this great question of the spiritual conflict in which we find ourselves as Christian people.

Now at this point I want to consider only the first section—the importance of realising the nature of this conflict in which we find ourselves. 'Little children, it is the last time: and as ye have heard that antichrist shall come, even now are there many antichrists; whereby we know that it is the last time. They went out from us, but they were not of us; for if they had been of us, they would no doubt have continued with us: but they went out, that they might be made manifest that they were not all of us.'

It seems to me that we have two things to do in order to understand what John means here. First, we have to try to understand these terms. What is he warning us about? Secondly, we must relate this danger with which we are confronted to our present experience. How are we going to react to it; what are we going to do about it? Obviously the Apostle deals with it because it was something that was discouraging to these first Christians, and it is a matter that still tends to discourage people. So it is vitally important that we should not only understand the problem, but also that we should be quite clear that we are relating ourselves correctly to it.

So let us first of all look at the very terms which the Apostle uses. He starts by saying that this is '*the last time*,' or *a* last time. Here again is a phrase that you will find in many places in the New Testament. For instance, the Apostle Paul, in writing to Timothy, says, 'In the last days perilous times shall come' (2 Tim 3:1). Or again, 'God, who . . . spake in time past,' says the author of the epistle to the Hebrews, 'unto the fathers by the prophets, hath in these last days spoken unto us by his Son' (Heb 1:1). These are the terms which are characteristic of the New Testament and its teaching; so it is all-important that we should understand exactly what they mean.

Of course there are some who think that this is no problem at all. They say that it is just part of the general error of which the Apostle and those first Christians were all guilty. They thought that the Lord was going to return in their time and generation; they all fell into the same trap, and John here really was just saying, 'You have only a few years left in this world, because it is soon coming to an end—it is the last time.' 'All of them,' say these people, 'fell into that particular error, but looked at from the twentieth century with all its enlightenment and especially in view of the higher criticism of the last century which has thrown such light upon these problems, there is no difficulty.'

But that is much too simple an explanation; the New Testament teaching itself prohibits us from explaining it in that way. Take, for instance, 2 Thessalonians 2, where Paul goes out of his way to teach the Thessalonians that quite obviously we are not to expect the return of the Lord at any moment. He says that certain things have to take place before the day of the Lord will come. He warns them that there may be a great interval, that there is going to be a great apostasy. 'It is not coming as quickly as you think,' he says; so he immediately counteracts that tendency, and there are many other passages in the New Testament that do exactly the same thing. Indeed, the book of Revelation alone, the Apocalypse, is sufficient in and of itself to show this cannot be dismissed as just that common error of imagining that the Lord's return was at hand.

No, it seems to me that when we put together all the New Testament uses of these phrases, we are driven to some such conclusion as this: The whole period from the coming of our Lord, and especially from His death and resurrection and ascension and the descent of the Holy Spirit on the day of Pentecost—the whole of the period from that until His final return is 'the last time.' You will find that sort of distinction in the Old Testament; they talk about the present age and the age to come; the age of the Messiah; the present time and the last times. And here in the New Testament, these different apostles tell us that now they were already in the last time. John, you notice, says that at the end of the eighteenth verse—'it is the last time'—so that whatever else we may say, it must include that. 'The last time' is sometimes used to cover the whole era, the whole epoch, that lies from the finished work of Christ until His ultimate return in glory.

But it is equally clear that it is not confined to that. Sometimes this phrase 'the last time' is used about certain special epochs. There are times of particular crises and of special judgment, and those times are in a special manner 'the last time.' In other words, as you see in the Old Testament many judgments upon the world, and upon Israel in particular, that prophesy the final judgment, so you see these times that indicate the final last time. So the whole age is the last time; but also peculiar eras and epochs when sin and evil are being unusually severe and fierce, and then the time just before the final return of our Lord and Saviour Jesus Christ into this world, is, as it were, the ultimate last time.

So there have been intervening periods and epochs in the history of the Church, like the terrible persecution of the first Christians, first by the Jews and then by the Roman power and empire. Then there was the terrible period of the dark Middle Ages, and there have been other equally bad times. And the right way, it seems to me, to look at this whole matter is to realise that from the very institution of the Christian Church there has always been this conflict, this mystery of evil, this 'mystery of iniquity' as Paul called it in 2 Thessalonians 2:7, that has been going on right through. There are times when it is unusually fierce and unusually severe and the Church is subjected to particularly terrible trial, but it will all head up to a final conflict of almost staggering dimensions, which will be the immediate prelude to the actual visible return in glory of our Lord and Saviour.

So that, I think, is what John means here by 'the last time,' and that, in turn, brings us to the next term he employs and that is *the antichrist*, which is a term that is actually only used by the Apostle John. It is very clear that the other writers in different places are concerned about exactly the same thing. Second Thessalonians 2, again, is clearly a description of the same person, the same power, and the same condition. Then in Daniel 7—11 you will find clear descriptions of the same thing, and of course there is another classic passage in Revelation 13 where you get an account of the two beasts, the one arising out of the sea and the other arising out of the earth. All these are clearly references to the same power, and you get, as it were, incidental references also in 1 Timothy 4 and in 2 Peter 2 and 3.

Now what exactly does John mean by this? He talks about 'antichrist' and says that there are many antichrists who are already in the world at his time. Yet these other teachings lead us very clearly to see that there is something which is also future about the antichrist of which these writers speak. This is a notoriously difficult matter; the literature on the subject is almost endless, and it is extremely difficult to find any consensus of opinion or any general agreement as to what exactly is meant.

These matters of prophecy are very difficult, and people who speak dogmatically about them are just displaying their own ignorance. It is a matter with which the greatest men in the Christian Church have wrestled from the very beginning, and yet we all know that there are certain pamphlets which seem to be able to explain it quite simply. They only know one view, they have obviously never heard of another, and the whole thing is simple and plain! Well, we know that history has often proved the ignorance and also the error of this oversimplification, and we must approach a matter like this with humility, with caution, and with reverence, knowing that when saintly, godly, able men have confessed the difficulty, it is clearly not something upon which we can easily and glibly pronounce a final judgment.

So let us just look very briefly at some of the views that have been held on this matter.

In the period that followed the Apostle, the view was held by the Church that this was a reference to a Jew who was to arise; that the Temple of Jerusalem would be rebuilt and that this Jew, possessing extraordinary powers and making extraordinary claims, would therefore manifest himself in Jerusalem and would harass and persecute the Christian Church and mislead many Christian people.

That was followed by a phase which can be described more or less as the common teaching of the Roman Catholic Church in the Middle Ages. According to this teaching the antichrist was finally to be a great worldly power—not a Jew of necessity, but a great earthly power and potentate who would establish himself with great claims and who with his great material power would tyrannise the Church, but would finally be destroyed at the coming of Christ. This was the view of the Middle Ages, and it is still more or less the Roman Catholic view.

Then we come to the view of the Protestant Reformation. Speaking in general, the Protestant Reformers were perfectly convinced in their minds that the antichrist was none other than the Roman Catholic Church herself, and especially the Pope. They said that it is clear that this power arises from within the body of the church, hence the term *anti*christ—not so much opposed to Christ as trying to take the place of Christ and opposing Him in that subtle manner. Paul says that this will happen in the Temple and that he will reveal great signs and wonders. There is all this evidence, they said, that the antichrist comes out of the true Church; so they believed that the Antichrist is the Roman Catholic Church, and particularly the pope and the whole power of the papacy.

These have been the leading views that have been held throughout the centuries. Now what is it that we can find about this antichrist in order that we may look at these views and try to evaluate them? We can say this much: the antichrist is one who, in one sense, stands instead of Christ, taking the Christian name and yet opposing the very kingdom of truth which the name implies. John says, 'As ye have heard that antichrist shall come, even now are there many antichrists. . . . They went out from us, but they were not of us; for if they had been of us, they would no doubt have continued with us: but they went out, that they might be made manifest that they were not all of us.' So that when we think of the antichrist, we have to bear that in mind. 'These antichrists who have arisen,' says John, 'belonged to us, but they were not of us.' In other words, they took up the Christian position, they claimed they were Christian, they professed to be teachers of the Christian Church, and yet they have been separated from the Christians in order that it would be clear to all that they were not of them. In other words, they claimed to delight in the true religion and yet they destroyed it.

At the same time it is clear there were many theories of the ultimate mystery which is going to be revealed, the mystery of iniquity. Already they appear, says the Apostle Paul, and yet this man is to come. Now all these things we can put perfectly clearly. The antichrist, or the antichrists, are the various teachers of the gospel who, while they profess to believe the gospel, pervert its teaching in such a way as finally to destroy it. Again you see why the Reformers thought of that aspect of the papal power which called itself the 'representative of Christ,' the great one who really could forgive sins. That is the kind of argument the Reformers used, and you remember how Paul in Acts 20 warned the people of Ephesus that these various teachers would arise amongst them and would, in this very subtle way and manner, mislead and entice many away from the truth.

So to summarise the teaching with regard to this subject, it seems to me that there are things of which we can be certain, though a great deal remains uncertain. The antichrist was already at work in the days of Paul and of John. Secondly, it is abundantly clear that although there have been many imitations of him, he will reach his maximum power just before the end of this age. It is equally clear that Daniel pictures the political aspect of this power, whereas Paul emphasises the ecclesiastical aspect, and in Revelation 13 you get both—the beast from the sea (the political), the beast from the earth (the ecclesiastical). Indeed we cannot be certain but that these two aspects might very well follow one another instead of coming together. First a terrible political power and then a terrible ecclesiastical power—a great deal can be said for that view. And the last point, I think, of which we can be certain is that this power will ultimately be concentrated in one particular person. John says there were many antichrists, and yet the teaching is clear that there is going to be an ultimate antichrist, one person, a person having terrible power, able to work miracles and do such wonders that he almost deceives the elect themselves.

Now this, it seems to me, is the very essence of this teaching, and what we have to realise is that in this present age in which we live we are confronted by such a power. Now, of course, the danger at this stage is to be guilty of oversimplification, but what we can be sure of is that from the commencement of the Church until today and from today until the very end there is an evil power at work in the Church. 'We wrestle not against flesh and blood, but against principalities, against powers . . . against spiritual wickedness in high places' (Eph 6:12). John says here that these people have already been warned—'*As ye have heard* that antichrist shall come . . .' Not one of these apostles seems to have preached without warning the people against this danger, and yet how ignorant we often are of it.

So the Church is always confronted by this subtle power, a seducing power, a power that represents itself in the name of Christ and yet is denying Christ, for that, you observe, is the very essence of this false teaching. He is 'a liar,' says John 'that denieth that Jesus is the Christ. He is antichrist, that denieth the Father and the Son.'

So the particular characteristic teaching of this antichrist who opposes us, not always openly but often in a very subtle manner, is that he denies that Jesus is the Christ.

Now I reminded you, when we began to deal with this epistle,[1] that no doubt John had in his mind in a very special way these denials of Jesus as Christ. There were two main manifestations of that. There were those who said that Jesus was only a man and that was the end of it, He was just a great teacher and nothing more. But as we have considered, there was also that subtle Gnostic error which said that the eternal Christ had come upon Jesus at His baptism and had left Him on the cross. So that Jesus the Son of God never died; it was the man Jesus who died—Christ had left him before death. They talked about Jesus, but they denied that He is the Christ.

But the Christian teaching is that Jesus Christ is God-man, and the God-man died and did the work, and any denial of that is a manifestation of this antichrist. So a denial of the deity of Christ is a manifestation of the antichrist. Yes, but a denial of the humanity is equally a manifestation of antichrist! There were some who taught that Christ had a phantom body, which was why John said in his Gospel, 'The Word was made flesh, and dwelt among us' (John 1:14); that is why he tells us we have 'seen' and 'handled' Him (1 John 1:1)—the reality of the Incarnation. It was not a phantom body but a true body; the Son of God died literally and actually, and He rose again.

Now this is not only a subtle but also a difficult subject. The great thing for us to realise is that this tendency thus to deny that Jesus is the Christ has been running through the whole long history of the Church; and what light this casts upon the history of the Church! If you read the accounts of the Christian Church in those first centuries, you will find that they talked about the nature of Christ—the two natures but one person. The Greek philosophers came into the Church and said, 'Yes, we believe Jesus Christ but not that explanation of His person.' So the Christian Church had to fight for her life on this very doctrine in those first centuries.

Then you find it in the dark Middle Ages in the domination of the Roman Catholic Church with its priesthood—those intermediaries between man and God; all that is a denial that Jesus is the Christ. And then look back across the Protestant story, especially of the last hundred years, with the subtle denial by the Church herself that Jesus is the Christ, the denial of the miraculous and the supernatural, the idea that Jesus is a great teacher perhaps, a political teacher or a great moral example, but not the Christ. All these are but manifestations of these antichrists, of the ultimate great antichrist who is to come; and our business is to relate all these to our own day and time and to our own generation.

We are living in the last time in that general sense. We may be living in a last time also in a more particular sense. Not only Christians, but also many secular writers and historians at the present time are teaching us that we are living in what they call an 'age of transition,' in one of the great turning-points of history and there can be no doubt but that this is perfectly true. We are living in a time when essential changes are taking place in the history of mankind; there has been no such period at any rate since the Renaissance or the Protestant Reformation.

It is one of those turning-points when things which appeared to be stable are being shaken; there can be no doubt at all but that Western civilisation is coming to an end. It is certainly one of the last times, and there are those who tell us it is *the* last time. I am not prepared to argue with them; my own personal position is that I am not convinced. I would not like to say whether they are right or wrong. I know that many times before, people have said that it was the last time, but it was not so. Every age is liable to think that it is the last time; every period of trial and of difficulty and turmoil in the Church and world tends to make people say, 'This is the end.' So let us be careful.

But what we can be certain of is that the power of iniquity is working. He was working in the time of Paul, and he is working in a very special manner today. It is a time of judgment; it is the time when God's people must be very careful and very circumspect, when they must be doubly certain of the truth and their position. They must beware of this subtle power that would lead them astray, and they must learn to stand, as John exhorts, valiantly for the truth.

May God give us grace to consider, to read about, and to think about these things again, that we may be forewarned and therefore forearmed.

9

OF THE CHURCH

Little children, it is the last time: and as ye have heard that antichrist shall come, even now are there many antichrists; whereby we know that it is the last time. They went out from us, but they were not of us; for if they had been of us, they would no doubt have continued with us: but they went out, that they might be made manifest that they were not all of us.

1 JOHN 2:18-19

JOHN, LET ME REMIND YOU, introduces us here to the whole question of the spiritual conflict, this great theme of the entire New Testament. As Christian people, as soon as we come into the Christian life we become part of this mighty conflict between the forces of God and the forces of hell, and we are involved in it whether we like it or not. So what he does here is to try to enlighten these people with regard to that; he warns and prepares them to meet and withstand it. We saw that we can divide this section up into three parts: first of all, the importance of realising not only that we are in the conflict but also the nature of that conflict; secondly, the equipment that has been given us to enable us to meet and combat it; and thirdly, the appeal and the exhortation, or, if you like, the reasons which John adduces and gives us for our resistance to this malign power, and for our maintaining the good fight of faith.

Now we have begun our consideration of the first. We have looked at the doctrine of the antichrist and at what is meant by 'the last time,' and I have drawn some general lessons from that. But we cannot leave it at that. The very words of these two phrases tell us to go on and apply it still further. John here puts this particular doctrine of the 'antichrist' and 'the last time' in terms of the Christian Church herself, and we must consider what he has to say about that because that, in a sense, is the most urgent matter which confronts us as individual Christians and as members of the Christian Church at this present hour.

Let me put it like this: We are all aware of the fact that we are living in a very difficult and critical period; there has been a great falling away in the Christian Church. Compare churches and attendances at churches today with what it was earlier in this century. Then it was the thing to do and the custom to go to God's house on Sunday; the Church was popular, and the Church counted. But now it is almost an exception to be a member of a Christian church, and because of that, certain things are tending to happen. Because of this dwindling in the Christian Church, because also of the attacks that are being made on the Church from the outside—the attack on civilisation, the materialistic politics and all these other things—because of this present grave situation, certain things tend to happen to many who are within the Church.

It seems to me, further, that it is essential that we should face together what the Apostle has to say, because at this point his words are as relevant to us now as they were in the first century when he wrote them. There are very many whose faith is being shaken because of the present position. There is a kind of encouragement, after all, in proving that we are only natural and human, and there are many people who look at the dwindling Church and the dwindling attendance and are liable and tempted to ask, 'I wonder if this is right after all? Are we, who are but a handful of people, the only ones who are right, and are the masses, the great majority of people, wrong?' The time of falling away is always a time when people's faith is under attack. We all tend to conform to 'the thing to do.' We follow the majority, and there are many who are filled with a sense of foreboding and who find that their faith is being seriously shaken. In other words, there is a good deal of despondency and pessimism.

Indeed, if I were asked to name the peculiar temptation that confronts us as Christians in these days, I would say it is the tendency to despair, the tendency to become profoundly pessimistic. As we look at the situation, we are tempted to say, 'What of the future? How can the Church possibly go on?' Now that is the kind of condition with which

John deals, because of course such despondency leads to confusion. A time of difficulty not only leads to despair—it is also a time in which there is a tendency to panic. People become frantic and desperate and say, 'We must do something to save the Christian Church.' They look at the numbers; they emphasise statistics; they say, 'We must be up and doing—we must organise something to stop the rot.' And so they rush into a busy activity.

So it behooves us to consider the message that the Apostle has for people in that precise situation—what has he to say? Let me try to summarise the message by putting it in the form of some three or four propositions.

The first thing John tells us is that we must not be surprised or alarmed at such a situation. 'Little children,' he says, 'it is the last time: and as ye have heard that antichrist shall come, even now are there many antichrists.' 'You have heard that it is coming,' says John, and that is the first point which we must emphasise. It seems to me that there is nothing, in a sense, which so thoroughly tests our knowledge of the New Testament Scripture, indeed of the whole Bible, there is nothing which so certainly tests our faith as our reaction to the situation in which we find ourselves. If we are given to panic or a sense of despair, it is because we have not read our Scriptures truly, for the Bible is literally full of warnings of the very kind of thing which we are experiencing. Those who know their Bible should not be surprised at the state of the world as it is, nor at the state of the Church. There is nothing at all which is so false and so far removed from the New Testament picture of the Church as the idea that the Church of God, from the beginning, should go on to develop and increase, so that every century should see the Church stronger than she was before, and that this should go on until you arrive at a state when the whole world has become Christian. There is no passage anywhere in the Scriptures to support such a view.

Indeed, I have tried to show that it is the exact opposite. Read the epistles in the New Testament, go back even before that to the book of the Acts of the Apostles, and you will find that the first preachers of the gospel warned the first believers. They said, 'You are going into a fight, a conflict. There is a mighty, subtle adversary opposed to us, and he will fight to ruin and destroy the Church.' All the prophecies—about the man of sin, the antichrist and so on—are here before us. Indeed, you remember, our blessed Lord Himself asked this question: 'When the Son of

Man cometh, shall he find faith on the earth?' (Luke 18:8). No, this idea that the Church was going to be an institution which would increase and ever go onwards and upwards is not based upon Scripture but upon a false philosophy, a false teaching.

Now I do not hesitate to assert that the very state of the Church and of the world is one of the most striking and amazing confirmations of Scriptural teaching that one can ever find. We must, therefore, not be surprised; we must not be amazed or shaken. There is a sense, though it may sound paradoxical, in which the weakness of the Church today should confirm our faith and be an assurance to us of the truth of the Word of God. So, far from being cast down, we should, in a sense, be able to say as we confront the present situation, 'The very wrath of man shall praise Thee, and is praising Thee.' Man, in spite of himself, is confirming the word of God.

The second principle is this: the Church's first consideration at a time like this should be the purity of her doctrine. I think that follows obviously. You remember what John says. 'Little children, this is the last time: and as ye have heard that antichrist shall come, even now are there many antichrists, whereby we know that it is the last time. They went out from us, but they were not of us; for if they had been of us, they would no doubt have continued with us: but they went out, that they might be made manifest that they were not all of us.'

In other words, John's great concern in this whole section is not at all about the numbers in the Church, about the fact that so many had left, but rather about the purity of the doctrine of the Church. These antichrists were the people who denied that Jesus is the Christ; they denied the Son and the Father; they denied the Trinity. So as you read these words, indeed this entire section of the whole epistle, you will find the one thing that John is concerned about is the true doctrine.

Let me emphasise this because, surely, it is a point that needs to be emphasised at the present time. John, I say, is not interested in numbers, nor is he interested in organisation. Is this not one of the subtle temptations that comes to us today? So much of our talk and interest centres upon numbers and the organisation. This is very natural, very human; we like facts and figures and statistics. We, because we are the inheritors of certain traditions, tend to think of the Christian Church in a building and as a gathering of people, a denomination, or an interdenominational organisation. We were brought up to think of the Church in some such terms, and our whole thinking tends to be controlled by such mechanical statistics.

But my point is that as you read the New Testament you will find that idea to be false to the very atmosphere of the New Testament. The great thing that is emphasised here is the purity of the Church and not her size. I wonder whether we are prepared to face the fact that the Church of God in this age and generation may in a sense have to go back to the catacombs. We may have to face that; there are people who are facing that, and it is the position in many countries today. The Church is 'in the home of so and so,' as it was in the New Testament, and we must realise that the Church is quite as much the Church if she is a handful of people as if she is a great crowd; the thing that matters in the Church is not numbers, not organisation, it is the purity of the doctrine.

We can see the relevance of this to the present position. You read constantly in the religious books and journals, and even in the newspapers, an argument which works itself out like this: They say that the Christian Church today is fighting for her life; there are forces and factors in the world inimical to her and opposed to the doctrine of the gospel. We see these mighty forces, organised and amalgamated, and there they are facing the Church. We see our own dwindling numbers and congregations, and the statistics are telling their tale from year to year. So what are we to do? They say, 'There is only one thing to do; we must all get together. This is no time for arguing about what people may believe; if they believe in God and use the name Christian they are one with us. So let's all get together and form a union to face this common enemy.'

Now obviously there is a sense in which we are all in a kind of general sympathy with such talk, and yet it seems to me that unless we are careful we shall be denying one of the essential New Testament doctrines. I say that whatever the feeling may be, whatever the departure from the Church, the one thing we should be concerned about is the purity of the doctrine. Better a handful of people who believe that Jesus is the Christ than a crowd who are uncertain as to whether He is or not and who falsely use the word 'Christian.' 'These people,' says John, 'have gone out from you in a sense; but,' he goes on to say, 'that does not matter; the question is, are you who remain all right?' The purity of doctrine is paramount: *Jesus is the Christ.*

In other words, we must realise that true unity can only be obtained in terms of truth. Yes, you can have your unions, you can have your amalgamations, you can have your coalitions apart from truth; but it is impossible to have the unity of the Spirit except in terms of truth. The Holy Spirit binds people together who are agreed about the doctrine—people who say, 'Jesus is the Lord' and who recognise Him as the unique Son of God—people who believe in the Incarnation, in the atoning sacrifice, in the Resurrection, and in the person of the Holy Spirit—that is the doctrine without which there can be no real union.

Now that is the doctrine of the whole Bible. Have you not noticed how in a most ironical manner and almost with an element, if one may use the word, of divine humour the Bible pours its sarcasm upon great numbers? Is there any doctrine in the Bible from beginning to end like the doctrine of the remnant? Is there anything that stands out so much as that God has done everything through one man who stood in the breach alone? Go through the Scriptures and see how God often deliberately reduced the numbers. Read the story of Gideon and see how he gets rid of a great crowd until he has only a handful left. Yes, they are the people who come to realise that their doctrine is pure and that this God can vanquish the mighty enemy. This is the doctrine of the Scriptures. It is the power of the Spirit that matters. We have a power behind us and in us which is mightier than the enemy and which must prevail, but He only honours those who honour Him; He only recognises those who profess and confess the pure doctrine.

The Apostle Paul said exactly the same as John says here. There were many leaving the Church at the time, and poor Timothy had become depressed. He could see the people going away and following false teaching, believing those who said that the resurrection was past already. He had been sending his mournful notes to Paul, and Paul's reply was, 'The foundation of God standeth sure' (2 Tim 2:19). God knows those who are His; it is the purity of the faith and of the doctrine that matters.

But that in turn, I think, brings us to the next point. Having thus seen that the present position must not depress us, having seen that it is the purity of doctrine that matters, the next thing to do is to examine ourselves. 'Little children, it is the last time . . . they went out from us,' and the question is, what about us? John here plainly teaches us something like this: The mere fact that we claim we are Christians and that we belong to the Church does not prove that we are Christians. 'They went out from us, they were amongst us,' these antichrists whom he is denouncing and the people who believed they were within the Christian Church. 'These people had joined the Church, they had claimed to be Christians, yet,' says John, 'they have gone out from us, proving they were not of us though they had been amongst us.'

Now, it seems to me that this is a serious and important thing for us. That may sound a rather surprising and startling thing to say, and there are people who would say that you should not be pressing an examination like that at the present time. 'The churches are small enough as it is,' they say; 'are you going to tell people to examine themselves and cause a still greater drift? Surely, you should rather encourage the people to come in!' But the New Testament does not do that; it has never done so. Rather it says that it is possible for people to be in the Christian Church and yet not be of her.

Let me put it like this—and I do so by way of encouragement and comfort. We may think, as we look at the modern Church, and as we compare and contrast it with what appertained earlier this century, that we have fallen upon evil days and that the Church is no longer the Church of God. But look at it like this: at one time everybody went to church, and the churches were packed and crowded. But are we to assume from that that everybody who went to church was a true Christian? There were people who went to church for very strange and curious reasons; it was a habit or a custom; it was a social thing; it paid for people to go to church. No, we must not assume that because the churches were packed they were packed with Christians; here were people who were in the Church, and yet they were all wrong. So it behooves us to examine ourselves and to make certain that we are truly of the faith and truly in Christ.

The ultimate test is that we are *of* the Church. That is how John puts it—'they went out from us, but they were not of us; for if they had been of us, they would no doubt have continued with us.' What does this mean exactly; how may I know whether I am really of the Church or not? Well, it surely means this: True Christians are those who are in vital union with the Church. They are not loosely attached to it; they have not just got their names on the roll. They do not merely recognise a general sort of allegiance once a day or on some special Sunday. No, they are bound by vital bonds of union. In other words, they have life in them; they do not have to force themselves, but rather, they cannot help themselves. It is the difference between a member of the family and a great friend of the family; there is something within that tells them, 'This is my life; I am bound to them; these are my people.' For them it is the big thing; they are bound by bonds of life itself; it is an organic and vital union, and the result is that they are in true fellowship with other Christians. They feel bound to them in a sense that they are not bound to anybody else. They feel that they understand them in a way that they do not understand anybody else; they feel that the Church is their home in a sense that nothing else is their home—'of us.'

There, it seems to me, is the vital distinction. So we ask ourselves a simple question: where do these things come in my daily life? What exactly is the place and value of these things in my experience? What is my attitude towards the whole thing? Is it central and vital, or is it something on the periphery of which I constantly have to remind myself? The people who are not 'of us' are the people who are on the fringe, and when anything goes wrong they are always the first to go away.

And that brings me to the last principle: We must, according to John, try to see the place and purpose of a time like this in the plan of God; how do we relate it all to God's great purpose? And John answers that question like this:

God, according to John, had in a sense thrust these people out of the Church in order that a distinction might be made, in order that He might show the false and reveal and manifest the true. Now I interpret that in this way: A time like this is one of great value to the Christian Church; it is a time that tests us. So we take courage, then, Christian friends, as we remind ourselves of this. The 'thing to do' in the modern world is not to worship God, is not to go to a place of worship; indeed, there seems to be every reason and excuse for not doing so, and the fact that we are concerned about these things in and of itself proclaims a great deal concerning us. A time like this tests people, and those who hold on to these things at such a time have got something. The majority are not interested, and how easy it is to go with them!

There is a sense in which we should glory in the fact that we are here today and not in the later Victorian era. Then everybody would have been going to church, so we would not have been tested. But now we are being tested; we are being sifted and examined; we are reading literature that is opposed to us; we see the crowd going the other way, and still we stand. Paul was saying that same thing in his letter to Timothy. John the Baptist said the same thing about our Lord: 'whose fan is in his hand, and he will thoroughly purge his floor, and gather his wheat into the garner; but he will burn up the chaff with unquenchable fire' (Matt 3:12). It is a time of sifting the wheat and the chaff. A time like this obviously gets rid of that which is wrong and false and thereby cleanses the Church. The loose adherents leave, the people with the doubtful doctrine go, and thereby the dead branches are being removed and the Church is being cleansed and purged and purified.

Here again is a doctrine running right through Scripture. You find it at all times of revival; indeed, to me one of the most striking things during the period of revival is the idea of discipline. We read in the *Journals* of John Wesley about how he insisted on church discipline. They made a fair show of numbers and then he proceeded to examine the church. He invited the members one by one, and he adds a kind of laconic note at the end of his account in which he says that when he had finished they were below three hundred! It is this idea of sifting, pruning, getting rid of the dead leaves and branches so that the Church may be purified and cleansed. And the very time in which we are living is doing that. People with false doctrine are disturbed, so many have turned their backs upon them because they have gone astray in their doctrine; and that is helping to purify and cleanse the Church.

But, lastly, a time like this, it seems to me, provides us with a very great ground of assurance, and it does so like this: 'They went out from us,' says John, 'but they were not of us; for if they had been of us, they would no doubt have continued with us.' The Authorised Translation here puts in the words 'no doubt,' and in a sense it does help us to understand the meaning—'for if they had been of us, they would no doubt have continued with us'—they have not continued with us, yet we are continuing. Why is that? And there is only one answer finally, and that is that we continue because we must be of the faith.

This, in a sense, is the doctrine of the final perseverance of the saints: 'If they had been of us, they would no doubt have continued with us,' whereas they have been removed. When the false has been taken away, the true remains; those who belong to the Church and are of the Church remain steadfast and continue—'the foundation of God standeth sure. . . . The Lord knoweth them that are his' (2 Tim 2:19). And 'neither shall any man pluck them out of my Father's hand' (John 10:28). They will be true, they will be sifted and tested, but if they are of Him they can never be removed.

So we should look at a time like this in that way. It is a time of apostasy, of falling away; it is a time when the faith of many is failing. But we are not seeing the end of the Christian Church. No, the end of the Church will be going to glory; the Church is indestructible. The Church belongs to Him, and all that belong to Him truly are members of His glorious, glorified Body. Therefore, in this remarkable and amazing way there is a sense in which we should glory in the fact that we are in the world at this hour and in the Church at this present difficult time.

Do not misunderstand me. We all mourn the fact that so many are outside Christ; we mourn the fact that the Christian Church is apparently so weak and helpless. Yet we must not covet crowds and numbers; we must be concerned about the purity of the doctrine, the purity of the Church herself in life as well as in her doctrine. We should glory in the fact that at a time of apostasy and falling away we belong to the remnant, and we should look with the eye of faith to the crowning day that is coming, to the day of the return of the Lord with all the hosts of His people, when, though now few in number, we shall belong to that great multitude which no man can number—

> *Ten thousand times ten thousand*
> *In sparkling raiment bright*
> *The armies of the ransomed saints*
> *Throng up the steeps of light.*
>
> HENRY ALFORD

We shall be with them. Though small and despised perhaps today, if we are of Him we shall certainly share in the glory that is to come.

10

THE ANOINTING OF
THE HOLY SPIRIT

*But ye have an unction from the Holy One, and ye know
all things. I have not written unto you because ye know
not the truth, but because ye know it, and that no lie is of
the truth. . . . But the anointing which ye have received of
him abideth in you, and ye need not that any man teach
you: but as the same anointing teacheth you of all things,
and is truth, and is no lie, and even as it hath taught you,
ye shall abide in him.*

1 JOHN 2:20-21, 27

IN ORDER TO HAVE the right setting for these three verses let me briefly
remind you again of what the Apostle is doing in this particular section.
He is dealing especially in this chapter with the hindrances to a true fellowship with God. There are certain things, in other words, which we
must always bear in mind very clearly if we are to continue to enjoy this
fellowship with the Father and with His Son, Jesus Christ. This is the
greatest blessing of all that the Christian gospel has to offer; greater than
forgiveness, greater than peace and joy and all the various sensations
which we may know from time to time, is this wonderful fact of fellowship with God the Father and God the Son through the Holy Spirit.
Now we have been considering the things that we have to bear in mind
which might hinder the fellowship, and so far the Apostle has dealt with

what we may describe as the peculiar difficulties that arise as it were within the Christian life itself.

But here in this section, you remember, from verses 18 to 28 he deals with the difficulty which is a little more external, the difficulty that tends to come to Christian people from outside themselves, but well within the realm of the Christian Church. It is the danger of apostasy, the danger of false doctrine, and that is the great theme of this section: these antichrists who have already come, as John says; and the fact that we are in the last time and that there is a great conflict between mighty spiritual forces going on around and about us. It is the danger of being sidetracked from the truth, the danger of being seduced, as he puts it, into a false view of the Lord Jesus Christ. So that is the theme, and I have suggested that the best way of dividing it is to divide it into three sections—the first of which is to realise the importance of the fact that there is this spiritual conflict going on, because if we do not realise that, then inevitably we shall succumb to it, and we have considered that in its various aspects.

So now we move on to the second section, in which John tells us that provision has been made for us to prevent our going wrong and going astray in that way. And that is the matter which we shall now consider in terms of these three verses. John is writing to people who are still in the Church. As we have seen, some had left though they had been a part of the Church. 'Now,' says John in effect to the others, 'you remain, you are all right, you have not been seduced by these antichrists. So why do you stay, what is the difference, what is it that has enabled you to reject that false teaching and to stand firm?' And in these three verses he provides us with the answer to those questions.

This is a most important statement, a very vital part of Christian doctrine and one of the most glorious aspects of Christian truth. What is it that enables us to stand and to remain and to avoid the seduction of false teaching which would separate us from God and Christ and eventually take us out and lead to our condemnation? Well, John says here that it is all due to the work of the Holy Spirit. Christians are who they are because of the Holy Spirit. Christians, he says, are those who have received unction, or *the anointing*—that is his way of describing the Holy Spirit. It is because of Him that they are able to discern and understand and avoid these subtle dangers that threaten them within the realm even of the Christian Church itself. John says in verses 20 and 21,

'But ye have an unction from the Holy One, and ye know all things. I have not written unto you because ye know not the truth, but because ye know it, and that no lie is of the truth.' Then he adds in verse 27, 'But the anointing which ye have received of him abideth in you.' Now let us, before we go any further, try to get these terms clear. John's words 'unction' or 'anointing' are just a very graphic way of describing the influence and the effect of the Holy Spirit upon the believer. It is the wording of the Old Testament where we are frequently told that prophets, priests and kings, when they were inducted, as it were, were anointed with oil; that was the mechanism, the ceremonial, that was used to set them apart for their office. Samuel anointed first Saul and then David as king; the same anointing was given to the priests and prophets, and the results of that pouring of the oil upon them was that in that way they were regarded as consecrated; they had become anointed ones who were now enabled to do their duty.

Very often you find that the Holy Spirit is compared to oil. The oil that went into the golden candlesticks in the Temple was an illustration of the same thing—the oil that provides the life or the power for the light. Those are the symbols that are used constantly in Scripture for the influence and the power of the Holy Spirit, so that what John is really saying is that every Christian in that sense is one who has been anointed, set apart, by God, and enabled by God to do certain things. If you go through the New Testament you will find that Christians are described as prophets, priests and kings. We are 'a royal priesthood, a holy nation,' says Peter (1 Pet 2:9); and in Revelation we read that we are 'kings and priests unto God' (Rev 1:6); those are the terms that are used. So there is a sense in which it is true to say that as the Lord Jesus Christ is prophet, priest and King as the result of His anointing, so all of us who are Christ's are prophets, priests and kings.

Again, just to complete this picture, we are told that our Lord was, as it were, anointed and set apart for His Messianic and saving work when the Holy Spirit came upon Him in Jordan when He was baptised by John the Baptist; and in that kind of sense, the same thing is true of the individual Christian. 'Ye have an unction from the Holy One,' says John. Who is that? The context makes it quite plain—He is none other than our Lord Himself; and in verse 27 the reference is still to the Lord Jesus Christ.

This is an interesting point which can be looked at in two ways.

We are told by the Apostle Paul in Ephesians 4:8 that 'when he ascended up on high he . . . gave gifts unto men.' It was the Lord Jesus Christ who sent the Holy Spirit upon the infant Christian Church. The Holy Spirit did not come until Christ had ascended up into heaven; then He came. He comes from the Father and the Son, or from the Father through the Son; it is as a result of the perfect work of the Son that the Father gives the Holy Spirit to all who belong to Him. That is one way of looking at it.

But there is another way of looking at it. Because we are incorporated into Christ, and into the life of Christ, we partake of what is true of Him. Therefore, as He has been anointed and has received the Holy Spirit without measure, all of us who are in Him receive the gift of the Holy Spirit because we are in Him. That is why any kind of teaching which would ever suggest to us that you can be a Christian without receiving the Holy Spirit is unscriptural. It is impossible for one to be a Christian and then later on receive the Holy Spirit. To be in Christ means that you are receiving the Spirit; no one can be a Christian in any sense without having already received this unction, this anointing, the gift of the Holy Spirit.

That, then, is what you may like to term the mechanics of the terminology which is employed by the Apostle. But what I want us to consider is the result of all this. There are these people who have remained true in the Church, and they have remained true because they have this unction. So what does this gift of the Spirit lead to? John says here that these Christians 'know all things'—'Ye have an unction from the Holy One, and ye know all things.' Now it is true that another translation is possible at that point; we might read it like this: 'Ye have an unction from the Holy One, and ye all know'—as if to say, 'These people who had come out did not know, but you know because you have an unction.' You can take it either way; both are perfectly legitimate translations.

And then in verse 27 he says, 'But the anointing which ye have received of him abideth in you and ye need not that any man teach you.' These are the main results, according to the Apostle, of receiving this anointing of the Holy Spirit, and the question at once arises, What does this mean? I need scarcely remind you that this is a very important and vital doctrine. These two verses have been the debating ground of people within the Christian Church from the very beginning, so let me just give you a few historical details about these verses and the doctrine contained in them.

They were in a very special manner the great theme of the dispute in the seventeenth century between the Puritans and the Quakers. It is a most fascinating study just to read something of the history of that century and of the church in this country [England] at that time. In the Puritan movement you find the gradual development of an extreme radical wing which eventually became the Quakers. There are a number of books on this subject, one of which is called *The Holy Spirit in Puritan Thought and Practice* by Nuttall. I strongly recommend it to those who are interested in this matter. The great point at issue was this: what exactly is the relationship between the Holy Spirit in the Christian and the Word of God?

That was the dispute between the Puritans and the Quakers. The Quakers tended to emphasise what they called the 'inner light'—this unction, and they tended to say that that was sufficient, that they received a direct revelation, that the Word of God was unnecessary and that in a sense they were inspired as were the first apostles. That was not true of all Quakers, but it was certainly true of some of them. 'We are told by John,' they said, 'that we have an unction from the Holy One; we know all things, and we need not that any man should teach us. We have this inner light, this inner monitor, this enlightening, and we do not need any instruction; we do not need to be guided by the Word of God.'

But this is not only something that emerges in the history of the Puritans and the Quakers; it is a question that is always raised by the whole teaching of mysticism. Mystics tend to look inwards; they believe that God is resident within them and that really the way to be blessed of God and to live the spiritual life in the full sense is to look within, to dwell within, and to be sensitive to the vision that speaks to you and the light that is given you and the leading and the guidance. It is the inward process, the turning inward on oneself, the belief that God is in the depths of one's being. So the idea of mysticism always has likewise raised, in a very acute form, the very doctrine that John mentions here; so the mystics are generally fond of these verses which we are considering together.

But the matter also tends to arise in a third way. Whenever a special emphasis is placed upon the Holy Spirit, this problem invariably arises. There are today, as there were very commonly and generally in the history of the Church, certain groups of Christian people who seem to put more emphasis on the teaching concerning the work of the Holy Spirit than anything else. They believe the other doctrines, yes, it is true; but their great emphasis is upon the Holy Spirit, and the moment you tend to do that you tend again to raise in an acute form the doctrine which the Apostle is dealing with in these verses.

So let me try to sum up what I would call the tendencies that almost invariably follow whenever you get this special emphasis upon the Holy Spirit and the subjective aspect of the Christian life. These are the things that tend to follow: The first is that there is almost invariably a claim to direct revelations; such friends always tell us something has 'come to them' or it 'has been shown to' them. In other words, they do not hesitate to claim that as the Holy Spirit taught the Apostle Paul and these other apostles and revealed the truth to them, they too, in a sense, are receiving truth directly and immediately from the Holy Spirit. The seventeenth-century Quakers did not hesitate to claim that, and there are people today who would claim the same thing. They say, 'Because I have the Holy Spirit, I am as inspired as if I were an apostle'—a claim to direct revelation.

The second tendency is to judge everything by means of their subjective state and condition. You will find that certain people use a phrase like this: they say that the way to judge truth is to judge whether or not it produces the 'rising of Christ within'; if it does produce this, then it is true—if it does not, it is false. Truth becomes subjective, the effect it has on me.

Another tendency is this, and it follows, I think, of necessity the tendency to depreciate the place and the importance, the value and the position of the Holy Scriptures in the Christian life and in our own experience. The more you emphasise this subjective state and condition, the less need is there for the objective Word, and that is why you always find the tendency amongst such people to say, 'Ah, these others are mechanical; they are tying it down to "the Word." They haven't had this subjective experience, and they are always talking about something external.' You find that most mystics are not famous for reading the Scriptures regularly; indeed you often find something like this: They say that one verse is enough for them; 'one verse sets me thinking, so I begin to think and then things happen to me'; and they get this 'revelation.' They do not read their Scriptures systematically and that obviously must tend to depreciate it.

And the last tendency is always towards a claim of infallibility. Go back to the history of the Quakers and you find it there. They tended to claim a kind of infallibility for themselves, and if you read the history or study any movement which emphasises the mystical, the inner light, or this principle of inner guidance, you will, I think, without a single exception always find that somewhere or another in such a movement there is either a pope or a number of popes. There is always somebody whose guidance is infallible and who cannot go wrong, and so you find this principle of infallibility reasserting itself.

Those, then, are some of the dangers and tendencies that arise from a misinterpretation of these three verses. So that leads us to the positive question: what then does the Apostle really teach? Well, once more perhaps we must put it negatively before we come to the positive. To start with, before we go any further, let us be quite clear that the Apostle is not dealing with the question of guidance; these verses have nothing at all to do with that. They are not concerned to teach me with regard to this whole difficult question of how I am to know what God wants me to do with regard to particular decisions. John is discussing here a knowledge of truth, a knowledge of doctrine; this concern is the truth of the doctrine that Jesus is the Christ. That is the context, so we must exclude everything else.

Secondly, he does not teach here that every Christian receives fresh truth directly and immediately even as the apostles did, for his whole case, in a sense, is that he has already told these people that he writes to them in order that they may have fellowship with him and with the other apostles. They have received the truth which they have believed through the apostolic witness and teaching and preaching; they are, as it were, the second generation of believers. These people had not received the truth directly by divine illumination. No, the apostles had gone around preaching the Word to them, so that is how they had entered into that fellowship, and the fellowship which the apostles had was fellowship with the Father and with His Son Jesus Christ.

Or let us look at the way in which the Apostle Paul puts this. Paul, describing the Church in Ephesians 2:20, says that it is established 'upon the foundation of apostles and prophets.' So they are the foundation, and you cannot repeat the foundation—there is only one. You can build upon it and put stones and bricks upon it, but you cannot repeat it; the building is not a succession of foundations. So the claim of the New

Testament everywhere is that the apostles and prophets are a separate and unique body of people. It was to them that the Holy Spirit specially revealed this truth that they recorded in these Scriptures and on which we build and by which we must walk and on which our whole faith must rest. The apostles and prophets are a class apart, and therefore for people to claim that they are as uniquely and directly and divinely inspired as the apostles and prophets is to contradict the plain teaching of Scripture. We, as Christians, are not supposed to receive fresh truth. The truth, the faith, has been once and for ever delivered to the saints and to the apostles. We cannot go into this in detail, but you will find that the Roman Catholic Church does not believe that; the Roman Catholic Church says she is as divinely inspired today as were the apostles and prophets. She claims to have received fresh truth since the end of the New Testament canon. The Quakers make the same sort of claim—God has revealed something to them. They all claim this special revelation. But it is a denial of the plain teaching of the Scriptures.

Thirdly, John does not teach here that a Christian knows everything. 'But surely,' says someone, 'when it says "ye know all things" doesn't "all things" mean just that?' But if you think that, then you must mean that every Christian knows everything—astronomy, geometry, the classics and everything else that is in the realm of knowledge—which is patently and obviously ridiculous! No, we must take these statements within their context—John obviously does not mean secular knowledge.

Does he then mean spiritual knowledge? No, he does not mean spiritual knowledge either, in every sense, for this good reason. If John is here saying that every man or woman who receives the Holy Spirit automatically knows the whole of spiritual truth, how can you apply the New Testament teaching about growing in grace and in knowledge? How can there be any development in our knowledge and understanding? Not only that, I think we can say that if that were true, then there would be no need for the New Testament epistles. Clearly that is not the case. John's reference to 'all things' here is a reference to the particular subject with which he is dealing; it is not an all-inclusive, all-comprehensive statement.

Let us go back again to this question of infallibility. John does not teach here that because of this knowledge every Christian is infallible. We can prove that in this way: If the unction of the Holy Spirit means that every Christian knows everything and is therefore infallible, it would follow of necessity that every Christian would have to agree with every other Christian about every aspect of Christian doctrine. But that is not the case. There are divergences and differences amongst Christians who manifest the Holy Spirit in their lives—about the question of baptism, about the prophetic teaching, about church order and many other subjects. So that automatically, it seems to me, rules out this whole possibility of infallibility. Not only that, Christians—good Christians—have from time to time fallen into error. They have gone astray in their doctrine and have subsequently acknowledged it; so there is no such thing as infallibility here.

And lastly, I would point out that negatively this does not teach that the Christian needs no instruction. 'But surely,' says someone, 'that must be wrong. Does not your text say, "and the anointing which ye have received of him abideth in you, and ye need not that any man teach you"? Surely you are playing with words; you are not being true and honest in your interpretation. John says, we do not need any man to teach us and yet you say that the Christian Church still needs instruction. How do you reconcile this?'

It seems to me that the answer is as simple as this: the very fact that John is writing to them proves that they need instruction. If they do not then John need have no concern about them at all. If the Christian needs no instruction, then the apostles' claim to be divinely inspired when they wrote their epistles was a sheer waste of time. These epistles are full of instruction. We are told that the Christian is to 'grow in grace, and in the knowledge of our Lord and Saviour Jesus Christ' (2 Pet 3:18); there is milk provided for him, and then there is strong meat. That is impossible if you take this statement literally and maintain that John is saying the Christian never needs any teaching. No, clearly that is not what he means.

So let us put it in this positive form: Surely the context here determines the interpretation. What John is really saying is what the Apostle Paul says in 1 Corinthians 2:13, 14. He is saying that the Christian has spiritual understanding which the natural man has not. These things are only understood in a spiritual manner, and what John is here saying is that the Christian, having received the Holy Spirit, has a spiritual understanding. 'The natural man receiveth not the things of the Spirit of God: for they are foolishness unto him: neither can he know them because they are spiritually discerned,' says Paul, and John says the same thing here. 'You,' says John, 'are holding fast to this truth because the Holy Spirit has given you this enlightenment and understanding.'

What is this truth about? Well, John is dealing here with the particular doctrine of the birth of our Lord—'I have not written unto you because ye know not the truth, but because ye know it, and that no lie is of the truth. Who is a liar but he that denieth that Jesus is the Christ?' (vv 21-22). That is what John means. These people, because they had the Holy Spirit and His enlightenment, understood the doctrine concerning the person of the Lord Jesus Christ and the work that He had come to perform. If they had not received the Spirit, they could not have done that, but they did understand these things. They understood the doctrine of the two natures in one person. They understood the doctrine of the death of Christ upon the Cross; they understood the doctrine of justification by faith; they had an unction which enabled them to explain these things—'we have the mind of Christ,' says Paul (1 Cor 2:16).

This is the wonderful thing that is true of Christians. They may not have much natural ability, but if they have the Holy Spirit they can understand this truth, and that is why the Christian faith is not only a faith for philosophers—it is a faith for anybody. It is not something that depends upon the natural man's ability; it is an enlightenment, an unction. The Holy Spirit enables men and women to see and to understand something of the glorious nature of salvation. Though they may be simple, though they may be ignorant, though the world may dub them as being unintelligent, if they have this enlightenment they understand things that the greatest natural philosopher cannot understand.

That is what John says: 'You understand these things; the other man does not.' Or we can put it like this: because they have this anointing, Christians understand error and are able to save themselves from deviations from the truth. I can put this in historical form. It has often been the case in the Christian Church that when the learned and all the professors have gone astray and became wrong in their doctrine, certain simple people have remained steadfast and solid in the truth. You often find that in the past. When the whole Roman Catholic Church seemed to have gone wrong in its doctrine in so many vital respects, there were those in various parts of the continent of Europe who held to the simplicity of the faith.

That is what John is saying, and there is a sense in which something like this has been happening in the last hundred years. Simple people have heard and recognised the centralities of the faith when the more learned have all become confused and have tended to go astray; it is because of this unction and it is in that sense that the Christian needs no instruction. There is no need to instruct Christians about the person of Christ, for they know it if they are Christians at all. That is why John says, 'I write unto you because you know the truth—you would not be a Christian if you did not know these things. How can you be a Christian if you are not right about the person of the Lord and about His death and about the Resurrection and so on? I am writing to you because you know them, and I am writing especially to you to point out the kind of subtle seduction that is threatening you.'

The writer of the epistle to the Hebrews put it like this: 'Let us go on unto perfection' (Heb 6:1). 'I do not want,' he says in effect, 'to lay again the foundation, the first principles; you know all these things, because if you do not you are not a Christian at all. I am going on now to deal with these higher principles. You need teaching there because you have only been babes so far; now I am going on to higher doctrine.' Did Paul not say the same thing in writing to the Corinthians: 'We speak wisdom among them that are perfect' (1 Cor 2:6). The Christian does not need instruction about first principles; he already knows them; that is why he is a Christian—that is what John is saying here.

And lastly, he says that if we have this unction and anointing of the Holy Spirit in us, it will keep us in the truth and in the faith. Is there not something wonderful about the history of the Christian Church? The Holy Spirit came upon her on the day of Pentecost, and He has remained in the Church ever since. Yes, there have been times of terrible apostasy, there have been times of falling away, there have been times when the leaders of the Church all seem to have gone wrong, and yet the remnant has always remained. Why? Because the unction of the Holy Spirit abides, keeping them in the faith, keeping them in the truth.

And, thank God, while this unction and anointing abides in us we cannot go wrong. I do not hesitate to make that assertion. Those who are truly God's people cannot go wrong in their doctrine on particular aspects. About the person of Christ and about the way of salvation, on these two vital fundamental things, they cannot go astray—the unction keeps them. They may listen to false teaching about certain other matters which are not vital and central; but about these things which determine whether people are Christians or not, the unction and the anointing of the Holy Spirit will keep them and hold them and sustain them. And while others go out and leave and fall away, these will remain because they see it, and having seen it, they cannot possibly believe anything else.

That is the doctrine. We have been anointed and been set apart; we have received this unction, and it has given us this understanding of truth which enables us to say that 'we have the mind of Christ' (1 Cor 2:16).

11

THE TRUTH AND THE LIE

Who is a liar but he that denieth that Jesus is the Christ? He is antichrist, that denieth the Father and the Son. Whosoever denieth the Son, the same hath not the Father: but he that acknowledgeth the Son hath the Father also. . . . And this is the promise that he hath promised us, even eternal life. . . . And now, little children, abide in him; that, when he shall appear, we may have confidence, and not be ashamed before him at his coming.

1 JOHN 2:22-23, 25, 28

I TAKE THOSE FOUR VERSES together because they are the four verses with which we have not already dealt in our consideration of this section which runs from verses 18-28. We have seen that the themes of this section are: the character of the enemy who is opposed to us; the understanding that is given us with respect to him; and then the way in which to fight him, or the arguments which we use in order to stimulate ourselves for the fight in order that we may defeat him. It is that third matter which we are concerned with now in these verses. They, again, are full of interest; indeed, it would be good if we could take the time to deal in detail with each verse separately. Take verse 22: 'Who is a liar but he that denieth that Jesus is the Christ?' The language which is used there by the Apostle is very strong; he does not hesitate to refer to these antichists as *liars*.

Now that is not only strong language, but it is also, in a sense, somewhat surprising. It comes as a real shock to some people, especially as John has just been previously appealing to us to love the brethren. 'How do you reconcile these two things?' some say. 'Here is the man who appears as the great Apostle of love and who talks so much about love in this particular epistle—so how is it that he should thus describe these people who had gone out, and those who had seduced them, as liars?' This comes as something very strange to many people, especially at the present time, for the great word today is the word *tolerance*. We claim that we are the most tolerant generation that the world has ever known. We do not like strong language and controversy; we rather pride ourselves on having advanced beyond all that in every realm and department. The great thing today is to be getting together and understanding one another's point of view; we should not denounce a point of view as John does here.

There are many instances of this. You have doubtless listened to discussions between Christians and unbelievers on the radio and heard how they often congratulate themselves on being such nice men! They spend so much time in trying to understand one another's point of view. One Christian said recently that we must not hold these views too fiercely and strongly. So certainly we must not call a man who is an unbeliever, and who denies Jesus as the Christ, a liar!

That is, as you will agree, the characteristic of the present mentality and outlook. It is a time for getting together, we are told, and, in view of the common enemy and the unbelief that is facing the Church, we must not be over-punctilious; and if people want to call themselves Christian, then let us welcome it and be glad that they do so, though they may say that Jesus is only a man and not the Son of God. If they are in any way interested in Him and anxious to practise His ethics, let us all get together, even perhaps with those who are just theists and merely believe in the being of God.

That is the modern attitude, and it makes a word like this sound very harsh to our ears. But what we have here is in many ways very characteristic of the New Testament. John is not the exception; John did not use language like this because he was Boanerges, one of 'the sons of thunder' (Mark 3:17)—you find others doing the same thing. Listen to the Apostle Paul using language like that to the Galatians: 'Though we, or an angel from heaven, preach any other gospel unto you than that which we have preached unto you, let him be accursed' (Gal 1:8). You cannot imagine anything stronger than that. Or listen to him as he writes to the Corinthians: 'If any man love not the Lord Jesus Christ, let him be Anathema' (1 Cor 16:22). Again it is very strong language.

Remember, too, the preaching of John the Baptist when he looked at his congregation, which consisted of Pharisees and others, and said, 'O generation of vipers, who hath warned you to flee from the wrath to come?' (Luke 3:7). Think also of the words of our blessed Lord Himself as He addressed the Pharisees, towards the end of His life; He referred to them as 'whited sepulchres' (Matt 23:27). Now I emphasise all this merely because surely we must be rather careful lest we put ourselves into a position in which we claim that we are more Christian than the Lord Jesus Christ Himself and His blessed apostles. There is a danger that we may confuse sentimentality and a doctrinal laxity and looseness for a true spirit of charity. The New Testament uses the language of which I have just been reminding you, and here it is in its essence—*liars*.

So then, how do we reconcile these things? Well, there is a very real distinction drawn in the New Testament between what we are to endure for ourselves and our response when the truth is attacked. The Sermon on the Mount tells us to 'turn the other cheek'; quite right, there is no inconsistency between what John says here with that teaching. With regard to ourselves and our own personal feelings we are to endure any-thing and everything; we are not to stand up for ourselves; we are not to call people liars who attack us in person. But where the truth is con-cerned, where doctrine is involved, where the whole essence of the gospel comes in, and especially the person of the Lord Jesus Christ, we are to stand and be strong and we are not to hesitate to use language like this. As regards ourselves, tolerance and charity; let the world despise us and malign and persecute us and say what it will concerning us—we are to go steadily forward, expecting such things to happen. But when it becomes a question of truth which is absolutely vital to salvation and to the glory of God, there must be no compromise and there must be no attempt just to accommodate ourselves to the other person's point of view. We are rather to take the position of John and to say, 'Who is a liar but he that denieth that Jesus is the Christ?'

Now this is a very dangerous statement to make. It is very easy to persuade ourselves that we are just manifesting righteous indignation and 'being angry and sinning not' when really we are just contending for some particular *shibboleth* of our own. We are only to stand like this about great, vital, central matters of doctrine. There are matters about which Christian people have never agreed. We must not, for example, use this kind of language for odd points of prophecy or if a man does not take our particular prophetic view; the New Testament does not make this stand on matters like that. No, but on central doctrine, this is where we have to walk carefully and circumspectly. So we are not only to draw the distinction between ourselves and the truth, but also between truth which is central and of which we must be certain, and matters about which there may be what we can describe as a legitimate difference of opinion. So the point here is that John does regard this particular matter clearly as of central and vital importance. That is why he not only uses this language but makes such a strong appeal.

Let us, then, consider it like this: Why is John so concerned about this matter? Why does he call these antichrists liars? Why does he say that these people who are teaching that the eternal Son of God came upon the man Jesus at the baptism and left Him on the Cross—why does he say that such people are liars—why does he denounce them so vehemently? There are a number of answers to that question. The first is that what the antichrists are saying is a lie, and John goes on to elaborate: 'Who is a liar but he that denieth that Jesus is the Christ? He is antichrist, that denieth the Father and the Son.' John has already said, 'I have not written unto you because ye know not the truth, but because ye know it, and that no lie is of the truth' (v 21). And that is his first reason—that what these people were teaching does not correspond to the facts.

We can put it like this: John has already said that the essence of his preaching is based upon what he has seen with his eyes—'which we have looked upon, and our hands have handled, of the Word of life' (1:1). He says, 'For the life was manifested . . . that which was from the beginning' (vv 1-2). 'Now,' says John in effect, 'these people are denying certain facts of which I am a witness and about which I can testify—they are liars.' He has been reminding us, in other words, that he and the other apostles had been with the Lord on the Mount of Transfiguration. Peter, James and John were there, and they saw and heard the conversation and the testimony; they even heard the voice from heaven which said, 'This is my beloved Son, in whom I am well pleased; hear ye him' (Matt 17:5). 'So what these people teach,' says John, 'is a contradiction of what the voice of God has said; it is a lie, and what else can you say about it?'

'To say that the eternal Christ left the man Jesus on the cross and that it was only the man Jesus who died is a lie,' says John, 'I was there— I saw the Son of God die. I was in the upper room when He said to Thomas, "Reach hither thy finger, and behold my hands" and when He said to all of us, "A spirit hath not flesh and bones as ye see me have; a spirit cannot eat as you see me eating." I am a witness of these things. I am here to testify that it was the Son of God who died, and we saw Him ascending into heaven after His resurrection.' So there is a sense in which we say that there is nothing else to be said about such teaching except to brand it as a lie. It is not true; it is a denial of the facts; it is a denial of God's own testimony to His only begotten Son who came here on earth.

Now to put that in its modern form, take all these attempts, so-called, during the last hundred years to reconstruct 'the Jesus of history'—attempts to get rid of the miracles and the supernatural element. It seems to me that there is only one thing to say about all this—it is not true, it is a lie, it is a monstrosity. Look at these attempts of the liberals to reconstruct Jesus—that is not the person I see in the New Testament, that is not the Saviour of my soul. What they have produced is something unreal; it does not correspond to the facts. You cannot explain the New Testament in that way; you cannot explain the history of the Church like that; so John denounces it, because it is nothing but a simple departure from the truth.

Furthermore, I wonder whether we will not all agree that it would have been a better thing not only for the Christian Church but also for the world perhaps if our fathers and our grandfathers had faced this false teaching which came from Germany, this subtle attempt to reconstruct Jesus. Would it not have been better if they had faced it and branded it as a lie instead of trying to accommodate to it and to fit it in—instead of all this false spirit of toleration which is such a striking departure from that which we see characterised the apostles, and even the Lord Himself in His teaching. That is the first thing the Apostle has to say.

Then secondly, John warns these people against this subtle danger and urges them to avoid it because of certain consequences which follow from believing it. It is not only untrue in and of itself, but consider these consequences: 'He is antichrist, that denieth the Father and the Son. Whosoever denieth the Son, the same hath not the Father; but he that acknowledgeth the Son hath the Father also.' Let me split that up a certain way. Here are the consequences of accepting this false teaching.

It first of all involves a denial of the real nature of the person of the Lord Jesus Christ. It denies the Son, says John; in other words, it denies the very doctrine of the Incarnation. If this false teaching which John is denouncing is true, then everything that is described in Philippians 2 is not true either—that great passage where Paul speaks of Him who was 'in the form of God' and 'thought it not robbery to be equal with God.' The divesting Himself of the insignia of His glory and being here in this world in the fashion of a man, taking the form of a servant and so on—all that is then not true. The Incarnation is no longer a fact; the glory and the marvel and the mystery of the birth and death is just a fairy tale. Jesus as a babe in the manger is just a human being and no more; there is no such thing as the virgin birth or the miraculous. He was just an ordinary child like every other child. And then, it is said, upon that child grown man at the baptism by John in the Jordan, there descended the eternal Christ who came for a while and influenced Him, raised Him up above Himself and then left Him upon the cross!

No! This is a denial of the whole doctrine of the Incarnation, which is most central in the New Testament. You no longer have the God-man, all these things are not true and one of the central glories of the gospel is lost.

But not only that—you see, of course, that at the same time it also makes some of the other most essential parts of the gospel history quite untrue; the agony in the Garden becomes very unreal if this teaching is right, and the Son of God no longer died upon the cross; the most amazing thing that the world has ever seen really did not happen. Well, we need not delay with this; you see immediately that it is a denial of the doctrine of the two natures in one person, that amazing truth which is central and vital in this New Testament teaching.

But let me go on to point out that it not only denies the person—it also denies the work of Christ, and it does so in this way. 'Who is a liar but he that denieth that Jesus is the Christ?' What or who is '*the Christ*'? He is the Anointed One, who has been set apart by God to do a certain work. And what the New Testament teaches is that Jesus, the Son of God, was set apart by his Father and anointed with the Holy Spirit without measure in order to do that work. What was that work? It was the work of saving mankind; it was the work of taking the sins of the world upon Him, of suffering and bearing our punishment to make reconciliation for us; and then rising again to be our representative and advocate and to stand in heaven on our behalf.

So it is obviously a denial of that if the Son of God left the man Jesus. Where is the atonement? The only one who could make atonement must be the Eternal Himself. No man could do it; it is only the Son of God who can bear the sins of the whole world. So if He left the man Jesus upon the cross, there is no atonement; you and I are still in our sins; we are still under the law; we are still under the wrath of God; there is no forgiveness for us, and we are truly undone and lost.

Are you surprised now that John called these people 'liars'? Is it surprising that he brands that teaching as a lie? Anything that robs me of my salvation and my standing with God is a lie, and I must denounce it with all my being. It is a denial of the person and of the work of the Lord Jesus Christ.

But John does not stop at that; he goes on to say that anyone who denies the doctrine concerning God the Father is a liar: 'Who is a liar but he that denieth that Jesus is the Christ? He is antichrist, that denieth the Father and the Son. Whosoever denieth the Son, the same hath not the Father: but he that acknowledgeth the Son hath the Father also.'

Now this is very high doctrine, but you remember that our Lord Himself has already indicated the same truth in the fifth chapter of John's Gospel. What it really amounts to is this: there is no real doctrine of the Father, and of God, except in terms of the Lord Jesus Christ. Our Lord also said, 'I am the way, the truth, and the life: no man cometh unto the Father, but by me' (John 14:6). So if we deny the person of Jesus Christ, we do not know the Father—we have lost Him. We may be living with some vague belief in God as a power or force or someone who can help us in a moment of need, but the teaching of our Lord Himself, as it is the teaching of all the New Testament apostles, is that there is no such thing as a true knowledge of God apart from the Lord Jesus Christ.

You can believe in a creator, you can believe in some unseen influence, but you will never know the Father except in the Son. 'He that hath seen me,' said our Lord, 'hath seen the Father' (John 14:9). So to deny the Son is to deny the Father; we do not know God as Father except in and through the Lord Jesus Christ. That is why John calls this other teaching a lie; that is why he brands these people as liars. They are not only robbing me of the Son, they are robbing me of the Father also, and I am left in the old position of vaguely groping in the dark trying to find God.

Let me put this in another way. I not only lose the Father from the doctrinal standpoint, I lose one of the greatest comforts that the gospel has to offer me. Do you remember those tender words which our Lord spoke to His disciples and the Pharisees when He taught them how to pray? He said, 'Your heavenly Father knoweth that ye have need of all these things' (Matt 6:32), and He told them that the very hairs of their head were all numbered (Matt 10:30), and that God is our Father in that sense. But if this other teaching is right, then God is not my Father, and I am left to myself with a God whom I fear in the distance, some almighty terrible power. To deny the Son is also to deny the Father, whom I can only know truly through the Son; and therefore the great comfort that John offers these Christians—that of fellowship with the Father and with His Son, Jesus Christ—is not true. And if that is not true, what have I as a Christian in a world like this? Where is my joy to come from; how can I withstand the forces that are set against me? The very basis of his epistle has gone, and hence his strong language.

But there is one further step. This false teaching not only denies the person of the Son and of the Father, it therefore of necessity denies the doctrine of the Trinity. It is only as we believe the truth concerning Jesus of Nazareth as the Son of God that we really arrive at our doctrine of the Trinity at all. It is He who opens the door to an understanding of this ultimate doctrine of the Christian faith. I do not know about the Father until I know the Son; and it is when I know the Father and the Son that I begin to understand the doctrine of the Holy Spirit who is sent by the Father and the Son and who, as it were, is there with the Father and the Son and explains the intimate relationship between them.

I lose everything if I deny the doctrine of the Son. It is the eternal Father who has planned salvation; it is the Son who came and worked out that plan; and it is God the Holy Spirit who opens our eyes to it and who makes it real and actual in us all. So you see why John is concerned about all these matters, because to deny this central aspect is to rob us of all the glorious doctrine of our Christian faith. To deny the Son is to deny the Father, and to deny the Father and the Son is to deny the Holy Spirit; so we are left to ourselves with our human wisdom and understanding and philosophy and our own vain efforts and endeavours to try to find God. No, says John, this is a lie, and it leads to such consequences.

But lastly, just a word on John's third ground of appeal, which is the consequences of believing the truth. We have just been looking at the consequences of believing the lie, but, says John, 'I would not stop at that. Let me show you the consequences of believing the truth.' 'And this is the promise that he hath promised us, even eternal life.' 'Beloved people,' says John in effect, 'don't believe the lie. It not only robs you of the doctrine, it robs you of life; it is that which robs you of God's greatest gift which has been made possible by the incarnation of His Son. If the eternal Son had not come from God and been made flesh, if there is no union between human nature and the Son of God, how can I have a new nature? I cannot be born again, because to be born again means to receive the nature of Christ and if the nature of Christ is unreal, if there is only the coming of the Son of God upon the man Jesus and then His leaving him, there is no union, and therefore the rebirth is impossible. But that is the wondrous thing that is offered and is possible to me. It is the very thing that God does promise us, even eternal life.'

And then the final thing is that which John emphasises in verse 28: 'And now, little children, abide in him; that, when he shall appear, we may have confidence, and not be ashamed before him, at his coming.' 'Don't believe that lie,' says John in effect, 'because if you do, you will find yourself face to face with it as a fact. These people have denied the truth,' says John, 'they think they are being clever. They have this mixture of philosophy and mysticism, and they have been trying to make us believe in a kind of phantom body and that the eternal God came upon a man and then left him. It is unreal,' says John, 'don't believe it. The day is coming when you will face the fact—the God-man is coming into this world. He will come again, and then you will see Him; and if you believe that lie, you will be ashamed when you see Him.'

Writing in the Apocalypse, John says, 'Every eye shall see him, and they also which pierced him' (Rev 1:7). And when they see Him they will cry out 'to the mountains and rocks, Fall on us, and hide us . . . from the wrath of the Lamb' (Rev 6:16). This is a fact; this is not fancy. The God-man will come again, and if you want to rejoice in that day, if you want to have confidence when you look at Him, and if you want to say, 'Even so come, Lord Jesus,' then avoid this lie, beware of these seducers, these liars who deny that Jesus is the Christ, and hold on to the truth.

Let the truth abide in you, for if it does, that great day of His appearing will not come to you as a surprise. It will not come as a shock or as a condemnation; you will not be offended or ashamed; no, you will rejoice in it, you will glory in it, and you will stand with confidence and look into His holy face.

That is the argument of the Apostle. The false teaching is a lie; it leads to those terrible consequences, and it robs us of the blessed consequences of believing the truth of the rebirth and regeneration, of new life from God and that blessed hope of His appearing, the truth of the new heaven and the new earth in which dwells righteousness, in which we shall be with Him for ever.

NOTES

CHAPTER ONE: SIN

1   This sermon was preached on Sunday, January 2nd, 1949.

2   Cf. *Fellowship with God,* Vol. 1 of this series (Crossway, 1992).

CHAPTER THREE: THE ADVOCATE

1   Cf. *Fellowship with God,* Vol. 1 of this series (Crossway, 1992).

CHAPTER SIX: CHILDREN, YOUNG MEN, AND FATHERS

1   For a detailed discussion of these verses, see *Fellowship with God,* Vol. 1 of this series (Crossway, 1992).

CHAPTER EIGHT: THE ANTICHRIST

1   Cf. *Fellowship with God,* Vol. 1 of this series (Crossway, 1992).

VOLUME THREE

Children
of
God

ACKNOWLEDGMENTS

THESE SERMONS WERE first preached in Westminster Chapel. The basic editing of these sermons was carried out by Christopher Catherwood, the Doctor's eldest grandson and Editorial Director at Crossway Books in England. However, as usual, an enormous amount of work on these manuscripts has also been done by Elizabeth Catherwood, the Doctor's elder daughter and literary executrix, and to her go special thanks. (She has also done much unsung on many of his other books, so it is fitting that she should be given her due honour here.) As before, Alison Walley has not only copy edited the manuscript, but typed it onto disk for the publishers, and so full thanks are due to her as well.

Lastly, much of the vision for this series comes from the enthusiasm shown by J. I. Packer, who with his wife heard many of them preached back in the 1940's, and also to Lane Dennis, the publisher for Crossway, whose commitment to the cause of Christian truth has made their publication possible.

1

CHILDREN OF GOD

If ye know that he is righteous, ye know that every one that doeth righteousness is born of him. Behold, what manner of love the Father hath bestowed upon us, that we should be called the sons of God: therefore the world knoweth us not, because it knew him not.

1 JOHN 2:29—3:1

IN THESE TWO VERSES we come to a new section in this letter of the Apostle John, a section which starts at Chapter 2, verse 29. It is a new movement in the argument which John presents to the Christians to whom he was writing, and I think we may say, if such comparisons are at all possible and legitimate in such matters, that in a sense the Apostle moves here to a deeper argument, something still more profound. Let us, before we go any further, try to get the connection clear in our minds by once more standing back for a moment and looking at the general scheme, which is, I would remind you, something like this:

The Apostle's great object in writing is that these people might have a full joy; that is the theme as announced in the fourth verse of the first chapter—'these things write we unto you, that your joy may be full.' There is possible for the Christian, in this life and in this world, such as it is and with all its troubles and its trials, a fulness of joy. And the desire of this old man, as the Apostle was when he wrote his letter, is that these Christians might enjoy it to the very full. So he is concerned to give them some instruction as to how that is possible, and the first big thing he tells them in this letter is that they must always bear in mind that they can have fellowship with the Father and with the Son through the Holy Spirit. Though we are here on earth, we can and do enjoy fellowship with God.

Then he goes on to show that if that is the first thing we must realise, then we must at once also realise that there are certain conditions which are absolutely vital and essential to the maintenance of that fellowship and that walk with God. And we have been considering[1] these conditions as they are outlined in the first chapter and in the whole of the second chapter down to the end of verse 28. We have taken them in detail one by one, these conditions controlling fellowship and communion with God.

They can all be summed up, in a sense, in one word, and that is the word *righteousness*. That is what John has been saying in different ways: 'God is light, and in him is no darkness at all' (1:5), therefore we must 'walk in the light' (v 7); that is to be righteous. And in the same way we must 'keep his commandments' (2:3); that is righteousness. Again, we must love the brethren; that, too, is a manifestation of righteousness. He tells us, 'Love not the world, neither the things that are in the world' (2:15); that is a negative manifestation of righteousness; and of course we must avoid all these subtle, seducing temptations to go wrong in our central belief because, apart from the Lord Jesus Christ, there is no righteousness at all.

Righteousness, then, is the thing that is essential to fellowship with God; in other words, the great stress of this epistle from beginning to end is the ethical stress. John is anxious that they see that these conditions must be observed. The great blessings come to us freely in Christ, but if we want to enjoy and to continue enjoying them, then we must walk in this righteous manner. That is the argument until the end of verse 28 of the second chapter.

But here in verse 29 we come to one of those points of transition. You see the connection; John takes it up like this: 'If ye know that he is righteous, ye know that every one that doeth righteousness is born of him.' Now that is a new key. 'In other words,' says John, 'I would have you realise that as the result of the work of the Lord Jesus Christ you are not only in fellowship with God, you have also become children of God; you are born of God. You are not only in a new relationship in an external manner, there is a vital internal relationship. It is not merely that you are having communion and association with God, but that you are in a vital union with Him. You are in Christ, and Christ is in you, and this vital thing has happened to you.' Now that is the theme that occupies our attention in this epistle until we reach the first verse of the fourth chapter. That is the whole theme, especially of this third chapter and leading on into the fourth—the fact that we are thus born of God and in this organic, internal relationship to Him.

And here, of course, John is again producing another argument to show us the all-importance of righteousness. If righteousness is essential to an external relationship and walk with God, how much more so is it obviously essential because of the relationship that obtains between us and God in this vital organic sense. If as a companion of God I must live a righteous life, how much more so must I as a child of God live a righteous life! You see, that is why I suggest that the argument does go here to a deeper level. Comparisons, as I have suggested, are almost ridiculous at this point, because to be in communion and in fellowship with God is such a high privilege that one can regard nothing as being greater and higher. Yet we are here reminded that we are born of God, and therefore the argument for righteousness is greatly reinforced. And as we shall see, the Apostle again works out this argument of relationship to God, or being born of God, in exactly the same terms as he has worked out the argument of fellowship. We must keep the commandments; we must love the brethren; we must avoid the things of the world and those seducing spirits that would take us away from the central doctrine. It is another argument for righteous walking and living based upon this internal relationship with God, rather than on external fellowship with Him.

So that is the theme, and John announces it bluntly in his typical manner. It is the point of the twenty-ninth verse of the second chapter, and he puts it in a very interesting way. He says, 'If ye know that he is righteous, ye know [or perceive, or understand] that every one that doeth righteousness is born of him.' Now he does not say, 'Ye know that every one that is born of him doeth righteousness'; he puts it the other way round. By which he means that if you see men and women who are living a truly righteous life in the sense of the New Testament term 'righteousness,' you can be quite sure, says John, that they are born of God.

Now righteousness obviously does not just mean morality, nor does it just mean living a good life. There are plenty of people who are outside the Christian church today who deny the elements of the Christian faith, but who are quite moral and decent. They are quite good people, using the term 'good' in its moral or philosophical connotation, but they do not conform to what the New Testament means by *righteous*. *Righteous* means the quality, the kind of life that was lived by the Lord Jesus Christ Himself.

So John puts it like this: 'Every one that doeth righteousness . . .' If you see people who are living the kind and quality of life that was lived by the Lord Jesus Christ, you can know for certain, says John, that they are born of God—they could not do it otherwise. No one can really live the Sermon on the Mount until they are born again; the Sermon on the Mount is impossible to the natural man or woman. Indeed, the Christian life as a whole is impossible to them, and it does not matter how good people are, they cannot live the Christian life. They can live a moral, ethical life up to a point, but they cannot live the Christian life, and the New Testament does not even ask them to. The New Testament standard of living for the Christian condemns the natural man or woman, and it should drive them to see the absolute necessity of the rebirth.

Now that is John's theme in a sense, that is his great argument. And then he takes it up like this: 'If, then, we are born of God, does it not follow of necessity that we must be living a certain quality and kind of life?' That is the argument that he works out from verse 3 in chapter 3 to the end of the chapter. 'It is inconsistent if we are not,' he says; he ridicules it. He says, in effect, 'If you are breaking the commandments and are living in sin, you cannot claim you are a child of God. If you live that sort of life, you are not a child of God, you are a child of the devil. The child of God must be living a different type of life.' And he continues in the same way with the love of the brethren and these other matters.

However, before he goes on to work out the argument which is inevitable because we are children of God, he pauses for a moment in the first three verses of chapter 3 just to contemplate what exactly it means when we are told that we are the children of God. He has mentioned being 'born of him,' but it is as if he says to himself, 'I cannot just leave it like that as a closing, passing phrase. The whole thing is so wonderful and amazing that we must stop for a moment to worship and adore as we realise what we are talking about. Before I work out the argument, let me remind you again of what you are and who you are.'

Now those who are interested in what we may describe as the mechanics of Scripture, or the form of the composition as distinct from the message, will recall that this is very typical of John. Do you remember how we had to pause halfway through the second chapter and look together at verses 12, 13 and 14 where John said, 'I write unto you, little children, because your sins are forgiven you. . . .' You remember how we pointed out that he interrupted his argument in order to remind them who and what they were, and then he made his argument inevitable. And he is doing the same thing again here; so this is, as it were, the pause: 'Behold, what manner of love the Father hath bestowed upon us, that we should be called the sons [or children] of God: therefore the world knoweth us not, because it knew him not. Beloved, now are we the sons of God, and it doth not yet appear what we shall be: but we know that, when he shall appear, we shall be like him; for we shall see him as he is. And every man that hath this hope in him purifieth himself, even as he is pure.' And then he goes on with the argument, but before he does so, he asks us to pause for a little to contemplate this amazing, wonderful thing that is true of us as Christian people. And now I want us to look at it only in terms of the first verse; the three verses are perhaps the three most moving verses in the entire epistle, and they do merit our detailed consideration.

Before we go on to do this, we must just refer to the fact that in the Revised and other versions there is an additional phrase in verse 1: 'Behold, what manner of love the Father hath bestowed upon us, that we should be called the sons of God *and such we are. . . .*' This phrase is to be found in some of the best manuscripts, and probably, therefore, it was in the original document. It is not, of course, a material point, because he says the same thing in verse 2: 'Beloved, now are we the sons of God'; so it is, therefore, just a matter of interest from the standpoint of textual criticism. So now, having dealt with that, let us look at this first verse. First of all, let us look for a moment at what we are, we who are Christians. According to John, we are 'the sons of God,' or, better perhaps, 'the children of God.' What does this mean exactly? Well, we can analyse it, I think, quite simply and legitimately by putting it like this: As children we stand in a certain position; a child is in a certain relationship to the parents—it has a certain station and is therefore entitled to certain privileges. The word *child* or *son*, especially at this point, carries with it a kind of legal statement which defines the relationship and position and status. A child is one who is related to a given parent in a way that no one else is; so you can look at it in that external manner, from the pure standpoint of legal relationship.

And here John asks us to pause and contemplate this wonderful thing, that you and I, such as we are, here in this world of time, are in that position, in that relationship to God. We are 'children of God'; we stand in this unique and separate relationship to Him. 'But surely,' says someone, 'are not all people children of God? Don't you believe in the universal Fatherhood of God and the universal brotherhood of man; isn't that something which is taught in Scripture?' The reply is, of course, that there is a sense in which all men and women are children of God, in the sense of being the offspring of God; by which we mean that they have been created by God and derived from Him. But at the same time, Scripture is very careful to differentiate that from those who come into this special relationship of sonship to God as the result of the work of the Lord Jesus Christ.

John is going on in this chapter to differentiate between the children of God and the children of the devil, and our Lord Himself did the same, as we read in John's Gospel where He turned to certain people and said, 'Ye are of your father the devil.' You are not the children of God, he tells them, you are the children of the devil, and 'the lusts of your father ye will do' (John 8:44). So that this idea of the universal Fatherhood of God and the universal brotherhood of man is not a Scriptural statement at all. Indeed it violates, if we stop at it, that which is the plain and clear teaching of the New Testament. It is only those who are born again, who are in Christ and who are truly the children of God, who have 'the Spirit of adoption' and cry out, 'Abba, Father' (Rom 8:15); it is they who are in this intimate relationship to God. The other is something that belongs to creation, not to the realm of salvation, and the Bible says that those who are not in this new relationship are outside the life of God. 'This is life eternal,' says Jesus Christ, 'that they might know thee, the only true God, and Jesus Christ, whom thou hast sent' (John 17:3). Apart from that, we are outside the life of God; we remain dead in trespasses and sins and have none of the privileges of sonship. 'But,' says John, 'we are called the children of God,' and 'called' does not merely mean an external application or appellation—it means that we are, we have become, the children of God.

But it does not only mean that, of course; it means also that we share the very nature of God, and that is why the authorities are all careful to point out that the right translation here is 'children of God' and not 'sons of God.' Is there a difference between a child and a son? Well, there is in this sense, that the word *son* emphasises a legal, external relationship, whereas the word *child* always puts the emphasis upon the common nature, that the child is derived from the parent and shares the nature and the blood of the parent. It emphasises this internal, vital, organic aspect of the relationship rather than the legal position. And what John, therefore, is reminding us of here is that we who are truly Christians are sharers of the very life of God.

Peter expresses this by saying that we have become 'partakers of the divine nature' (2 Pet 1:4). It is difficult to put this into words, and yet it is something that is taught everywhere in the New Testament. The figure of the vine and the branches in John 15 puts it perfectly; the branch is in the vine, and so the life of the vine, the sap, the vitality passes into the branches—there is that organic relationship; and that is what John is emphasising here, so that we share the nature of God.

Or we can put it like this: As children we are members of the family of God. The Apostle Paul makes that point in writing to the Ephesians, where he tells them, 'At one time ye were without Christ, being aliens from the commonwealth of Israel.' But 'now,' he goes on, they have been made 'fellow citizens with the saints, and of the household of God' (Eph 2:12, 19). We have become members of God's family; we really are in that relationship to Him because we have His nature. Because we have received of His life, we, as children, belong to His family, we belong to his household, and we are therefore in this unique relationship to Him. And that, of course, in turn means that we are heirs of God; as Paul says in Romans 8:17: 'If children, then heirs; heirs of God, and joint-heirs with Christ.'

Now these are some of the things that are immediately conjured up as we just ask the question raised by the first verse—What are we? The answer is that we are 'called the children of God,' and there is a sense in which this is so staggering and so overwhelming that we find it almost impossible to accept it, and to retain the idea in our minds. Yet that is what is said about Christians everywhere in the New Testament. Let us never again think of the Christian as just someone who is trying to live a good life, trying to be a little bit better than somebody else, a person with a belief in doing certain things, going through certain forms and ceremonials and keeping certain regulations dictated by the church. Christians do all that, but before all that is this vital fact that they are children of God. They have been born again, born from above, born of the Spirit; they have received something of the very nature and life of God Himself. They are transformed people, they are a new creation, and they are thus absolutely, essentially different from those who have not experienced that. That is the very basic thing which the New Testament everywhere emphasises concerning the Christian.

Then the second question is, How have we become this—how have we become children of God? John answers that in this way: 'Behold, what manner of love the Father hath bestowed upon us.' This is a very interesting way of putting it. John does not merely say that God has shown His love to us, nor that He has revealed it or manifested it or indicated it. He does not merely say that God loves us, though He does love us and He has shown and displayed His love to us. 'Yes,' says John, 'but He has gone further—He has *bestowed* His love upon us.' Now that means there is a sense in which God has put His love into us, implanted Himself if you like, infused or injected His love within us, and we must emphasise that, because what really matters is the word *that*, which should be translated *in order that*. 'Behold, what manner of love the Father hath bestowed upon us in order that we may become, be made, the children of God'; that is what John actually says.

In other words, what really makes us children of God is that God has put His own life into us. God's nature is love, and he has put His nature into us so that we have the love of God. We cannot be children of God if we are not like God; the child is like the parent, the offspring proclaims the parentage, and God in that way makes us His children. He puts His own nature into us, and we become His children, and that nature which is in God is in us, and it is acting and manifesting and expressing itself. Paul says that 'the love of God is shed abroad in our hearts by the Holy Ghost' (Rom 5:5). Here again, I say, is something that is so wonderful and surpassingly strange that it is almost impossible for us to receive and to hold on to it, and yet nothing less than that is true of the Christian. John will make use of this argument later on in this chapter, where he says that if you have the love of God in you, you are bound to love one another. Even though your brother may be unworthy, you must love him. Is that not the whole message of Christ's death upon the cross? He is in you, and He has made you children of God.

Let us now look at the third aspect of this matter; let me emphasise the mystery of all this. '. . . therefore the world knoweth us not, because it knew him not.' This is a mystery. This condition in which we find ourselves as Christians, this being a child of God, is a great mystery. The world does not understand it; it does not know what we are talking about. The world ridicules it 'because it knew him not'; the world does not understand this sort of thing; it says, 'You Christians claim that you are children of God, that something of the divine nature is in you and that you are different, separated from other people. Away with your suggestion!' Says the world, 'Do you mean that you people, as I see you to be, are children of God, sharers and partakers of His divine nature? No; you are just ordinary people like everybody else.'

'It is all right,' says John; 'don't be upset if the world says that to you—"it knew him not." The world said, "This fellow, this son of Joseph and Mary, this carpenter of Galilee, that talks and says, 'I and the Father are one,' who is He?" The world did not know Him; it saw nothing else; it did not see the Godhead; it did not see the Trinity that was there, and it does not see it in you,' says John. 'So don't be surprised if you are misunderstood or if you are laughed at. The world may say that you have religious mania and count you soft or say that you have suddenly developed a psychological complex, but don't be surprised,' continues John. 'It did not know Him, and it won't know you. This thing of which I am speaking is only discerned spiritually. It is something hidden, something within, in exactly the same way as the Godhead was veiled by the flesh of Christ, hidden and revealed at the same time—and so it is true of the Christian; we have the divine nature within us, and yet it is veiled, and the world does not see through that. But it is all right,' says John; 'this is a mystery, this is something internal.'

You will find exactly the same idea in Revelation 2:17 where we are told that a secret name is given to Christians, to the children of God who receive a sign and a name, and no one understands this hidden name but the Christians themselves; that is the same idea exactly. It is a great mystery; in a sense it is one of the most glorious aspects of the Christian life. The world does not know us, but we know Christ, and we know one another, and that is proof of life. We are aware that something is happening to us; we are aware that God has dealt with us and has done something to us; we know that we are new creatures. We are aware that we cannot explain ourselves to ourselves except in terms of Christ, and we know when we see it in another; nobody else does, but we know one another.

This is one of the most mysterious aspects of Christian life and experience. Those who have the life of God always know one another, and they feel an affinity and an attraction which no one else can understand.

Other people may mix with them, they may know people very well, and yet there is something those others have not got. There is a barrier; ours is a life which does not show itself in external affairs, it does not show itself even in the mode and manner of living, but it is a life which recognises itself in the other, and this is a great mystery. But it is a great reality at the same time. 'The world knoweth us not'; it does not understand us; it says, 'What have you people got—what is this something you are always speaking about?' It looks on from the outside but cannot discern it. If you want a perfect commentary on what I am trying to say, read 1 Corinthians 2, especially towards the end: 'He that is spiritual judgeth all things, yet he himself is judged of no man' (1 Cor 2:15). That is it; we know one another, but no one else knows. We understand, they do not, and 'the world knoweth us not, because it knew him not'; this is the mystery of this gift of life and of the life that is within us.

But lastly, there is the marvel of it all. 'Behold, what manner of love'! Words, of course, become meaningless at this point; there is nothing to do but to gaze upon it and to wonder at it all, to stand in amazement and in astonishment. Oh, the quality of this love! Just realise what it means, the freeness of it all, that you and I should be called and become children of God! The freeness of this love that has looked upon us in spite of our sin, in spite of our recalcitrance, in spite of our unworthiness, in spite of our foulness as a result of the Fall and our own actions. Oh, the love that has not merely forgiven us but has given itself to us, that has entered into us and shared its own nature with us; stand in awe at the greatness of it all! Think of what it cost Him, our Lord Jesus Christ, to come into the world, to live in the world, suffering its treatment, staggering up Golgotha with that cross upon His shoulders and being nailed to the tree. Think of Him dying, suffering the agony and the shame of it all in order that you and I might become children of God.

'Behold, what manner of love'—you cannot understand it, you cannot explain it. The only thing we can say is that it is the eternal love, it is the love of God and is self-generated, produced by nothing but itself, so that in spite of us and all that is true of us He came and died and suffered so much. The Son of God became the Son of Man that we, the sons of men, might become the children of God. It is true, we are that; we have been made that. Amazing, incredible, yet true!

2

DESTINED FOR GLORY

*Beloved, now are we the sons of God, and it doth not yet
appear what we shall be: but we know that, when he shall
appear, we shall be like him; for we shall see him as he is.*

1 JOHN 3:2

I SUPPOSE WE MUST agree that nothing more sublime than this has ever
been written, and any man who has to preach upon such a text or upon
such a word must be unusually conscious of his own smallness and inadequacy and unworthiness. One's tendency with a statement like this
always is just to stand in wonder and amazement at it. I have never chosen, in and of myself, to preach upon this text. I have often felt that I would
like to, but there are certain great words like this in Scripture of which
frankly I am, in a sense, frightened; frightened as a preacher, lest anything
that I say may detract from them or may rob anyone of their greatness and
their glory. That may be wrong, but this is how it always affects me.

However, here we are, working through this first epistle of John and
we come to this magnificent and glorious statement. So we must look at
it, for it is to do violence to Scripture not to consider and examine it,
and we must not be content with some mere general effect as we read
these words. They are moving, and yet we must not let ourselves merely
be moved in an emotional, and still less in a sentimental, sense; so it
behooves us to examine the statement and to see something of its richness and its wonder.

Furthermore, it is when one confronts a text like this that one
realises what a privilege it is to be a Christian minister. I am rather sorry

for anyone who has not had to spend a week with a verse like this! I assure you it is a very enriching experience, a humbling one and an uplifting one. There is nothing surely in life that can be more wonderful or more glorious than to have to spend a week or so with a word like this, looking at it, listening to it, and considering what others have said about it. It is indeed something for which one humbly thanks God.

What we have here is one of those great New Testament descriptions of the Christian and of the Christian's life in this world. A number of things inevitably must strike us on the very surface before we come to any detailed analysis. The first thing is how utterly inadequate are our ordinary, customary ideas of ourselves as Christian people. When you read this, and then when you think of yourself and what you generally see and observe about yourself and about your life as a Christian in this world, oh, how inadequate are all our ideas! Or take it as it was put in that hymn of the great Richard Baxter:

> Lord, it belongs not to my care
> Whether I die or live;
> To love and serve Thee is my share,
> And this Thy grace must give.
>
> If life be long, I will be glad
> That I may long obey;
> If short, yet why should I be sad
> To soar to endless day?
>
> Christ leads me through no darker rooms
> Than He went through before;
> He that into God's kingdom comes
> Must enter by this door.
>
> Come, Lord, when grace hath made me meet
> Thy blessed face to see;
> For if Thy work on earth be sweet,
> What will Thy glory be?
>
> Then shall I end my sad complaints
> And weary sinful days,
> And join with the triumphant saints
> Who sing Jehovah's praise.

My knowledge of that life is small;
The eye of faith is dim:
But 'tis enough that Christ knows all,
And I shall be with Him.

Can we really say those words from the heart? Is that our view of ourselves and of our life as Christian people in this world? Is that our view of the possibility of our life being short or of being long? Is that our view of life and of death and of eternity? Well, according to this text we are looking at in this chapter, that is the Christian view. 'Beloved, now are we the sons of God, and it doth not yet appear what we shall be; but we know that, when he shall appear, we shall be like him; for we shall see him as he is.'

I do feel that this is perhaps the greatest weakness of all in the Christian church, that we fail to realise what we are, or who we are. We spend our time in arguing about the implications of the Christian truth or the application of this, that and the other. But the central thing is to realise what the Christian *is*. We grumble and complain, and it is all due to the fact that we have not really seen ourselves in terms of this picture. Surely, as we read these words, we must of necessity be humbled, indeed in a sense humiliated, as we realise the inadequacy of our ideas and the unworthiness of our view of ourselves as Christian people.

Or let me put it to you like this: is it not the honest truth that most of the unhappiness that we experience in this life is due to our failure to realise this truth? We are full of complaints and unhappiness. They arise partly from our own faults, partly from what others do to us or from what the world as a whole does to us. But all our unhappiness is ultimately to be traced back to this, that we are looking at the things that are happening to us, instead of looking at this vision that is held there before us. It is because we do not see ourselves as the children of God and going through this life and world in the way that this text indicates; that is why our unhappiness tends to get us down. We do not relate it to the whole; we do not put it in its context; we live too much with the things that are immediately in front of us instead of putting everything into the context of our standing and of our destiny.

In the same way we must at once realise, I think, that most of our failure to live the Christian life as we should live it is also due to the same cause. If only we realised who we are, then the problem of conduct would almost automatically be solved. This is how parents often deal with this problem in instructing their children. They say to them, 'Now remember who you are.' In other words it is our failure to realise who we are that causes us to stumble on this whole question of moral conduct and behaviour. This objection to the stringent demands of the gospel is due to one thing only, namely that we do not realise who we are. If once we saw ourselves as we are depicted here, there would be no need to persuade us to live the Christian life. As the next verse tells us, we would feel that we have to, it is inevitable, it is logical. The whole trouble is to be traced to a failure to realise our true greatness and position and standing.

In other words, the more I read the New Testament, the more I am impressed by the fact that every appeal for conduct and good living and behaviour is always made in terms of our *position*. The Bible never asks us to do anything without reminding us first of all who we are; you always get doctrine before practical exhortation. Look at any epistle you like and you will always find it; these men, under the inspiration of the Holy Spirit, first of all tell us, 'This is what you are as the result of the work of Christ—therefore . . .' It is never the other way round. To put it bluntly, the New Testament is not interested in the conduct of people who are not Christians. It has nothing to tell them except that they are destined for hell and for perdition. That is its only statement. They must repent, and until they repent and believe on the Lord Jesus Christ it is not interested in their behaviour—that is its one message to them. But the moment they become Christians, it is vitally interested in their conduct; it appeals to them because of what has happened.

Or we can put it like this: there is no comfort or encouragement offered in the Bible to anybody except those who are the children of God. When things go wrong in the world, people tend to turn to religion. In times of difficulty there is always a sort of turning to God; people pray to Him and think of the gospel. But in the first instance, the one message of the gospel to them is still the message of condemnation; it warns them to flee from the wrath to come. The gospel is not some psychological agency just to tide people over little troubles, nor is it meant to make us feel happy for the moment. No, this consolation and comfort which is absolute and eternal is always solidly based upon our understanding and realisation of who we are and what we are. The key to the understanding of everything in the New Testament is that we should realise what Christ has done for us and what we are in Him as the result of His work.

Now that is the very thing that John is concerned about in this epistle. His appeal at this point is based upon what we are. We have seen that John is out to comfort these people, and he shows them that it is vitally important, if they are really to reap the full benefits of the Christian gospel, that they should be living the Christian life. This is a great appeal for righteousness, keeping the commandments of God, loving the brethren, hating the world. Someone says, 'Why should I do these things?' John replies, 'Beloved, realise what you are and who you are, and if you do, you will see that these things follow automatically.' That is what he does in this second verse; so let us look at it together.

The first thing we must do with this word is to be careful we do not misinterpret it. The very form of the words which are to be found, especially in the Authorised Version, almost tend to make us misinterpret or misunderstand them. There is a kind of suggested contrast in the text which in reality is not there at all. The danger as you read this statement is that you will contrast the 'now' and 'not yet appear what we shall be.' Furthermore this word 'but' which you find in various versions is not in the best manuscripts, and it should not be there.

So there is no contrast between 'now' and 'shall be,' and this word 'but' should be omitted—all these statements are positive. We must never read this verse in such a way as to regard it as a kind of alternating series of certainties and uncertainties. They are all a series of positive statements; the Apostle in each case is telling us what he does know. Also this word 'appear' which is used is not the best translation; it ought to be 'manifested,' so that we read our text like this: 'Beloved, now are we the sons [or, better, children] of God, and what we shall be has not yet been manifested; we know that when he shall appear, we shall be like him, for we shall see him as he is.' We are the children of God; we know what we are going to be, but it has not been manifested; we know that when He shall be manifested Himself, we shall be like Him, for we shall see Him as He is.

In other words, the text is a great series of positive statements. John says, in effect, 'Here we are—Christian people in this world, and the world does not understand us. It may perhaps hate us; it may be unkind and cruel to us. Very well,' says John, 'don't be disturbed or upset by that; don't think of yourselves or estimate yourselves in terms of what the world says about Christians because the world can know nothing at all about it. It did not know Christ when He came; it has never known God; so the world, when it laughs at you, is giving you a great confirmation of your faith.'

The Bible is very fond of saying something like that; it suggests that we are in a very bad condition if all men speak well of us. 'Yea,' says Paul to Timothy, 'and all that will live godly in Christ Jesus shall suffer persecution' (2 Tim 3:12); we ought rather to be concerned about ourselves if the world thinks highly of us and seems to think it does understand us. No, the world knows us not because it knew Him not. 'The one thing that matters,' says John, 'is that you should know yourself, that you should know what you are as a Christian, that you should know these things and that you should know Him.'

Let me, therefore, divide up the verse like this: There are three main statements made here by the Apostle. The first is that we know that we are the children of God. The second is that we know we are destined for glory. And the third thing we know is something concerning that glory. Those are the three positive statements in the verse.

The first thing, then, is that we know that we are the children of God. 'Beloved, now are we the sons of God.' You notice that he does not say, 'we shall be,' but rather 'we are.' We have already dealt with this in a sense in dealing with the first verse. I am just emphasising it once more. The Christian is meant to know exactly where he is and where he stands. He is not left groping in the dark, neither is he just meant to be hoping. The Christian is someone who should be able to say, 'I know, I am persuaded, I am certain.' These things are facts.

Let me put it strongly like this: we shall never be more the children of God than we are now. I do not hesitate to make that statement. I am as certainly a child of God now as I shall be in glory; I shall be a much better man then, but I shall be no more a child of God. The human analogy puts that perfectly; conduct does not determine relationship; relationship is something vital, organic, internal. The prodigal son was as much the son of his father as was the elder brother. Behaviour, conduct and appearance—all these things do not determine relationship, thank God! Therefore we are children of God now as much as we shall be throughout the countless ages of eternity in glory. You are either a child of God or you are not, and once you are a child of God you are His child for ever and ever in that divine and eternal relationship. You cannot be a Christian one day and not the next day. Once you are born of the Spirit and born of God, you are a child of God. You may vary a lot in your conduct and behaviour, but we must never hold the view of holiness or backsliding or any one of these doctrines which gives the impression you can be in and out of the relationship. You cannot! Relationship is something that is fixed and remains. Other things are variable and come and go, but, 'Beloved, now are we the sons of God.' So again I ask the question, do we know this, are we quite certain about it? I am not asking at the moment, 'How do you live?' I am not asking you your views on various matters. No, my question is, do you know you are a child of God?

But how does one know this—how is this knowledge obtainable and possible? What indications do I have that I am a child of God? Well, here are just some of the answers. Men and women who are children of God are aware of a new life, a new nature within them. They can say, 'I live; yet not I' (Gal 2:20). They are aware that there is another factor, another person, another presence. In a real sense, in a true sense, they are aware of a kind of dualism—they themselves, and yet somebody else. And they can only explain themselves to themselves in terms of this other life and this other person—I, yet not I, but Christ. One like that is aware of a new nature, another life, a different order of being from that which is merely natural.

Or let me put it like this: we know that we are children of God when we are deeply aware of sin within. I emphasise that deliberately. It is only the children of God who realise that they have a sinful nature. The unregenerate, the natural men and women, are not aware of a sinful nature. They may admit that they do certain things which they should not do, but begin to tell them that they have a sinful nature, that they are dead in trespasses and sins, and they will hate you and begin to defend themselves; they hate preaching that condemns them.

No, it is only the children of God who realise that they have an utterly sinful nature. It is only a saint like Charles Wesley who says, 'Vile and full of sin I am.' It was Saint Paul who said, 'For I know that in me (that is, in my flesh), dwelleth no good thing' (Rom 7:18). It is the Christian who cries out and says, 'O wretched man that I am! who shall deliver me from the body of this death?' (Rom 7:24). An unregenerate believer has never uttered such words and never can—it is impossible. It is the indwelling of the Holy Spirit that exposes our sinful nature and the depths of sin and iniquity that reside in our hearts. 'The heart is deceitful above all things, and desperately wicked: who can know it?' says Jeremiah (Jer 17:9). 'I dare not trust my sweetest frame,' says the hymn-writer. All these things are indications of the new nature—an awareness of sin and above all a desire to be rid of it. If you are hating the sin within you and longing to be delivered and emancipated from it, I assure you, you are a child of God—it is one of the best signs.

Next there is a desire for God and a desire for the things of God and a desire to walk in the ways of God. Do you know what it is to long to know God better, to long to know Him truly? Do you feel that you wish you really could say those words of Richard Baxter from the depth of your being? Have you felt that you are a child of God? Have you wished that you could say this? Well, I can honestly tell you, that is never an unregenerate person's desire. His mind is enmity against God; he wants certain blessings from God when it suits him. The people who delight in the things of God and like to read the Bible and want to pray and are grieved that they do not pray more—all these are indications of being children of God.

Then there is what the Apostle Paul calls 'the Spirit of adoption, whereby we cry, Abba, Father' (Rom 8:15), the feeling that God is not just some great potentate far away in some distant eternity, but that somehow or another we do know that He loves us. We are aware of a filial feeling with respect to Him, and there is something within us that cries out, 'Father!' We are aware that God is coming nearer to us and that we are related to Him.

And then there is one other thing which I have already mentioned, the love of the brethren. I say again, a very good and a very subtle test of whether we are children of God is whether we really love and like God's people and whether we like to be amongst them. Do not misunderstand me—that does not mean that there are not certain things in Christian people which you may find objectionable! But do you feel instinctively drawn to a good person? Do you feel an affinity with people who like to talk about these things, and with those who are the children of God? Or are you still fascinated by the glamour of the world? Which do you *really* like; which do you prefer? The children of God love to realise that they are in the family; they love the brethren; they feel, 'These are my people—these are the people with whom I want to spend eternity.'

These are just some of the tests which we apply to ourselves to prove whether we are indeed the children of God.

Now let us go on to the second principle, which is that we know that we are destined for glory. 'Beloved, now are we the sons of God, and it doth not yet appear what we shall be.' What we are going to be has not yet been revealed to us, but we know that we are destined for it. That is obviously what John means. He is not here in a sort of uncertain state which says, 'Well, we are the children of God. At the present time I do not quite know what is going to happen to us, but no doubt it is going to be all right.' Not at all! John has seen something of the glory, and he says, it has not yet been revealed to this world which does not understand it, but it will be revealed.

We can put it like this: Here we are in a state of humiliation, but we are going to be in a state of glorification. Do you not see that as Christian people we, in a sense, have to retrace the steps trodden before us by our Lord? You remember how Richard Baxter puts that—we have to enter into the room which He has already been through here on earth in a state of humiliation—born in Bethlehem, working as a carpenter, people not recognising Him—it was humiliation. While He was on the earth that was His condition, and the world did not know Him. 'He came unto his own, and his own received him not' (John 1:11); the world, His own world, rejected Him; His own people rejected Him. Yes, but He is no longer in the state of humiliation; He has passed on to glory, and He is in a state of glorification. The Apostle Paul had a vision of Him there on the road to Damascus; John had a vision on the island of Patmos; there He is in glory, and you and I are to retrace those very steps. Here we are in a state of humiliation, yes, but as certainly as He has gone before, we also shall go on to glory.

'Let not your heart be troubled,' said our Lord, 'ye believe in God, believe also in me. In my Father's house are many mansions: if it were not so, I would have told you. I go to prepare a place for you. And if I go and prepare a place for you, I will come again, and receive you unto myself' (John 14:1-2). That is it! It is the same thing exactly.

Christians, therefore, know that they are destined for that state of glory; it is part of their essential belief. It is as much a part of their belief as their forgiveness of sins by the work of Christ upon the cross. So what the Christian says is, 'I am destined for glory. It has not come yet, but it is coming, and I am going on to it.' It will be manifested for certain, and so they are full of confidence and assurance. Paul in that great eighth chapter of the epistle to the Romans is in reality saying the same thing.

This verse is John's way of saying, 'For I am persuaded that neither death, nor life, nor angels, nor principalities, nor powers, nor things present, nor things to come, nor height, nor depth, nor any other creature, shall be able to separate us from the love of God, which is in Christ Jesus our Lord' (Rom 8:38-39). Your glorification and mine is an absolute certainty. As certainly as our Lord has entered into His glory, you and I who are children of God shall enter into it also.

It does not look like it now—John agrees entirely—it 'doth not yet appear,' and the world is against us—it does not understand it. That is exactly how it was with Him, but the thing is certain.

On what grounds can I be sure of this? Here is my answer: the purposes of God. Consider Paul again: 'For whom he did foreknow, he also did predestinate to be conformed to the image of his Son, that he [Christ] might be the firstborn among many brethren' (Rom 8:29). That is a perfect statement of the whole thing. Your glorification and mine is a part of the purpose of God in salvation, and when God has purposed and planned a thing, it is certain and nothing can prevent it. Read again that mighty logic of Romans 8 and you will see it put perfectly. I can therefore rest my confidence of glorification upon the promises of God, and the promises of God are based upon the character of God. God cannot, because He is God, break His promises, and He has also given an oath, so we have a double assurance. The promises are there with His purposes and His character at the back of them.

If you are still uncertain, add the power of God. 'For thy sake we are killed all the day long; we are accounted as sheep for the slaughter,' but what does it matter? 'In all these things we are more than conquerors through him that loved us' (Rom 8:36-37). 'Who shall separate us from the love of Christ?' (Rom 8:35). It is impossible; there is nothing that can do so. We talk about the power of God, the One who made the world and the One who could end it in a second. All the almighty, illimitable and absolute power of God guarantees my glorification.

Indeed, I have an even further argument than that. What we are now is a guarantee, in a sense, of what we are going to be. Our sonship is in itself a guarantee of our glorification because God never starts a work and then gives it up. 'He which hath begun a good work in you will perform it until the day of Jesus Christ' (Phil 1:6). You and I start things and drop them; that is typical of mankind as a result of sin. But whatever God begins, God continues, and God will end it in absolute perfection. If therefore I am but a child, insignificant, unworthy, immature, the fact that I am alive is proof that I am going on to ultimate maturity; Christ is 'the firstborn among many brethren,' and He is preparing and leading others, a great crowd of brethren, until eventually we arrive in eternal glory. Do you know that you are destined for glory, my friend; do you know within yourself that that is something that is awaiting you, that you are being led and taken on to that glory which awaits you? John says, 'We *know*' this.

But that brings me to my last point. What do we know concerning this glory? These are the things that are indicated. We know that this glory is to be ushered in by the appearing, or the manifestation, of the Lord Jesus Christ Himself. 'We know that, when he shall appear, we shall be like him.' This is the great New Testament doctrine of the Second Coming, but God forbid that we should immediately begin to think of our several theories of this, that, or the other, of how it is going to happen. All I know is this, that the Lord Jesus Christ will come again. Let us take the Scripture in its broad statement, and let us beware of robbing ourselves, I say, of the life-giving glorious doctrine by thus particularising these mere theories and philosophies rather than accepting this true exposition of Scripture.

The Second Coming is a fact. The Lord Jesus Christ is coming again, and there will be a judgment, and all that is sinful and evil will be consigned to the lake of fire and destroyed throughout all eternity; and there is to be 'new heavens and a new earth, wherein dwelleth righteousness' (2 Pet 3:13). When He comes, these things will take place; that is the way the glory will be ushered in. The world is to be rid of everything that is impure, foul and unworthy; 'the elements shall melt with fervent heat' (2 Pet 3:10); there is to be a renovation and a regeneration; there will be a new world, and all evil will be banished. That is how the glory is to be ushered in, and I know that whatever the appearances may be in this world, as certainly as the Lord Jesus Christ came into the world the first time as a babe in Bethlehem, He will come again as the King of kings and Lord of lords, and He will wind up the affairs of this universe of time. I know that it is certain.

Furthermore, 'we shall see him as he is.' 'Now we see through a glass, darkly, but then face to face: now I know in part; but then shall I know even as also I am known' (1 Cor 13:12). Do you know that you are destined for that? We shall see Him as He is—blessed, glorious vision to see the Son of God in all His glory, as He is, face to face—you standing and looking at Him and enjoying Him for all eternity. It is only then that we will begin to understand what He did for us, the price He paid, the cost of our salvation. Oh, let us hold on to this! Shame on us for ever grumbling or complaining; shame on us for ever saying that the lot of the Christian is hard; shame on us for ever objecting to the demands of this glorious gospel; shame on us for ever half-heartedly worshipping, praising and loving His honour and His glory. You and I are destined for that vision glorious; we shall see Him as He is, face to face.

But consider something still more amazing and incredible. We shall be like Him. 'We know that, when he shall appear, we shall be like him; for we shall see him as he is.' This is John's way of putting the whole doctrine of the resurrection of our very bodies, the ultimate final resurrection, the ultimate glorification of God's people. What John is telling us, in other words, is that when that great day comes we shall not only see Him, we shall be made like Him. Paul says that God's purpose is that we shall be 'conformed to the image of his Son' (Rom 8:29). That is the argument, and that is the doctrine.

In other words, while we are here on earth, the Holy Spirit is working in us, doing His work of holiness in us and ridding us of sin so that eventually we shall be faultless, blameless, without spot and without rebuke. We shall have been delivered from every sin and vestige and appearance of sin within us, and in addition to that, our very bodies shall be changed and shall be glorified. Paul says that we expect Christ to come from heaven for this reason—that He shall change the body of our humiliation 'that it may be fashioned like unto his glorious body' (Phil 3:21). There will be an amazing change then in those who love Him when He appears. Again, read 1 Corinthians 15 where Paul tells us that 'we shall all be changed, in a moment' (vv 51-52). Our bodies will be glorified; there will be something of the radiance of His own glory in your body and mine, so that in this new heaven and new earth we shall have bodies made fit for our glorified spirits. We shall be like Him.

The New Testament does not tell us much more than that, because we could not stand it; our language is inadequate, and if it were adequate, the description would be so baffling we could not tolerate it, the thing is so glorious and wonderful. When the three disciples were with our Lord on the Mount of Transfiguration, they could not stand it; the magnificence of the glory, the brightness of the appearance was too great. Consider too what happened to Paul when he had one glimpse of that vision on the road to Damascus—he was blinded. No, I could not stand it as I am as the result of sin; but when I am delivered from sin and the bondage of corruption, and when I have a new, glorified body, I will be able to stand it. I will look at Him, I will see Him face to face, I will see Him as He is, I will be like Him. If I were not like Him I could not stand it—that is John's argument.

I believe there is another thing here, and that is that as we look at Him, we become like Him; and as we continually look at Him, we shall be perfected.

> *Changed from glory into glory*
> *Till in heaven we take our place*
> *Till we cast our crowns before Him,*
> *Lost in wonder, love and praise.*
>
> CHARLES WESLEY

We are changed into this same image, from glory into glory, as we look at Him and contemplate Him; and when we see Him perfectly, it will be an absolute change.

Those, then, are some of the things of which the Christian is sure, according to the Apostle John. We know that we are the children of God, we know that we are destined for glory, and we know that glory is to be ushered in by His manifestation. We know that then we shall see Him as He is, and, wonder of wonders, we shall be like Him! What blessed vision, what glorious hope, that I, small, insignificant, fallible, sinful, unworthy, shall be like Him, 'the firstborn among many brethren,' and made conformable to His glorious nature. Beloved people, let us lay hold on this hope and look upon it and meditate upon it day by day.

HOLINESS

And every man that hath this hope in him purifieth himself, even as he is pure.

1 JOHN 3:3

THIS VERSE, AS THE very first word 'and' reminds us, is one that is intimately connected with the previous verse. Now these two verses in their relationship to one another remind me very forcibly of those incidents in the life and ministry of our Lord which we find recorded in the Gospels, in which we have two scenes, the one immediately following the other. The first is the scene on the Mount of Transfiguration where our Lord went up onto the Mount with Peter and James and John and was transfigured before them. Then, after the amazing and extraordinary things that happened there, they went down again onto the plain, where they were confronted by the case of that poor lunatic boy who had been brought by his father to the disciples in order that they might heal him. It is a familiar and well-known contrast between the glory and the wonder of the Transfiguration and the heavenly scene upon the Mount, and the scene of the problem and the unhappiness and the misery which was found down on the plain; and the interesting thing, of course, about the two incidents is how the one immediately follows upon the other (Luke 9:28-43).

And there is a sense in which one is constrained to remember those two incidents as one reads these two verses. We have been on the mountain of God, and we were shown things unseen. We were given that glimpse of glory, of the glory that awaits us and the astounding and amazing things to which we are heirs. But here we are now, as it were, back to earth again. We are reminded that before we enter into that glory and enjoy it in all its fulness, certain things remain and abound. We are still men and women in the flesh, in this world which, John has already told us, does not know us. It does not understand us and, indeed, it is opposed to us and inimical to our highest and best interests. Yet though we do feel that, we must be very careful—and that is the point I want to emphasise most of all here—we must be very careful lest we regard this third verse as some sort of anticlimax after the second. It is not an anticlimax, and to regard it as such is simply a manifestation of our sinful nature.

Indeed, not only is this verse not an anticlimax, it is not even a contrast to the second verse; the very word *and* which connects the two verses reminds us that these two things are indissolubly bound together and that verse 3 follows verse 2 very directly and immediately and, indeed, of necessity. There is a sense in which we can say that the whole object of verse 2 is to lead to verse 3, and if we fail to regard the second verse in that light, if we fail to see that its real object and purpose is to prepare the way for this third verse, then we have abused the second verse entirely, and we have failed to appreciate its true message to us.

I emphasise all this because knowing myself I think that such a warning is very essential. We all of us, because of the effect that sin has upon us, rather like reading verses like the second verse. People always like a sermon or an address on a verse like that, and yet, if we do not realise that John wrote the second verse in order to prepare the way for what he says in this third verse, then we have not been using it aright. We have been using it for the time being to forget our trials and problems; we have been enjoying ourselves and having a spiritual feast. Like Peter on the Mount of Transfiguration, we have been rather tending to say, 'Let us make three tabernacles' and spend the rest of our lives here in the wonder and enjoyment of the feast of the glory. But we must not do that; we are not meant to; we were taken up by John to the top of the mountain in order that we might descend onto the plain and do this essential work that is waiting there for us—in exactly the same way as our Lord came down from the mountain to deal with the problem which had baffled and defeated his poor disciples. You and I, having had a vision of glory, have to come down and translate it into practise and put it into daily operation, and if it does not lead to that, then we are abusing the Scripture.

Now there is a logical connection between these two verses. John does not argue about it, he just states it—'every man that hath this hope in him purifieth himself, even as he is pure.' There is no need to discuss it; the one thing follows the other as the night follows the day. Therefore this third verse is one which comes to us as a very real and a very sure test; the extent to which I have really grasped the teaching of verse 2 is proved by the extent to which I implement verse 3. We can put it this way: it is what we are and what we do that really proclaims our belief and our profession.

That is the great theme in the epistle of James which has been so misunderstood—'faith without works is dead' (Jas 2:20)—and no one must dispute it. There is no disputation between James and John; both are saying the same thing—namely, that the profession of faith is of no avail unless it leads to this particular practise. Therefore we can put it the other way round with James and say that the real test of our profession is not so much what we are as what we do. Whatever I may have felt as I contemplated that second verse, if it does not lead me inevitably to the position which is described in the third verse, then it has been a false view because, according to John, this is pure logic. There is no discussion about it—'every man that hath . . .' He does not say, he *ought* to purify himself, he says that he *does*, and therefore it becomes a very thorough test of what we truly are.

In other words, is it not the case once more that our failure, most of us, is in the realm of belief, because this belief, says John, leads inevitably to that practise. Why do we therefore fail so much in practise? The answer, it seems to me, is that our belief is defective; if only we really did see ourselves as we are depicted in the New Testament, the problem of conduct would immediately be solved. So the real trouble with most Christian people is not so much in the realm of their conduct and practise as in the realm of their belief, and that is why the Church, whenever she puts too much emphasis upon conduct and behaviour and ethics, always leads eventually to a state and condition in which Christian people fail most of all in that respect.

This is a very subtle matter. Of course the tendency is for people to argue like this: 'Ah,' they say, 'there is not much point in talking to us about doctrine; you have to remind people of their practical duty.' So holiness teaching not infrequently becomes a constant repetition of certain duties which we are to carry out. I agree that we do have to do these things, but I say that the ultimate way of carrying out these duties, and really practising these things, is to have such a grasp and understanding of the doctrine that the practise becomes inevitable. And that is, of course, precisely what the New Testament always does. In other words, we cannot very well look at this verse without observing the way in which the New Testament always presents its teaching with regard to this whole question of holiness.

Here, I think, is a great corrective to what has so often taken place, and still does take place, in connection with this matter. Holiness, according to the New Testament, is an inevitable deduction from doctrine; it must never be regarded as something in and of itself. In other words, we must never approach the holy life simply in terms of living the holy life. And that, I think, is where the whole idea of monasticism and asceticism went astray. But the monastic conception of holiness is not, of course, confined to Roman Catholicism by any means. There are large numbers of evangelical people who clearly have a false idea of holiness; it is regarded as something in and of itself, something one has to go in for because of its nature, because it is a particular kind of life.

But that is never the teaching of the New Testament. Holiness is something that follows and is an inevitable deduction from doctrine, from an understanding of our position as Christian people. And especially, I think, we must admit that the New Testament presents its teaching and doctrine of holiness in terms of this great truth concerning the blessed hope. It is after it has told us what we are and who we are and of the hope that lies before us that the New Testament brings in this doctrine of holiness and sanctification and Christian behaviour. I must therefore never talk about this idea of living the holy life because it is a good life in and of itself. Rather, my only reason for being holy is that I am a child of God and that I am destined for glory, and if I do not practise holiness in those terms I will sooner or later inevitably go astray.

That is, of course, what has happened with this other teaching of holiness. When you make holiness a thing of itself, you then produce your rules and regulations. You begin to pay too much attention to little details; you become legalistic without realising it; you become self-righteous because you have carried out your duties, and you forget the real objective for which you have originally set out.

Secondly, holiness is not something we are called upon to do in order that we may become something; it is something we are to do because of what we already are. Take this whole question of Lent.[1] There is a great deal of teaching on this subject which really amounts to this: that we are to be holy and live the holy life in order that we may become truly Christian. Every phase or aspect of the doctrine of justification by works really teaches that; so any suggestion we may have in ourselves that we are to deny ourselves certain things, that we are not to do certain things, and that we are to discipline ourselves in order that we may become Christian is a denial of the doctrine of justification by faith. But I am not to live a good and holy life in order that I may become a Christian; I am to live the holy life *because* I am a Christian. I am not to live this holy life in order that I may enter heaven; it is because I know I am going to enter heaven that I must live this holy life.

That is the emphasis here—'Every man that hath this hope in him purifieth himself, even as he is pure.' I am not to strive and sweat and pray in order that at the end I may enter into heaven. No; I start rather from the standpoint that I have been made a child of God by the grace of God in the Lord Jesus Christ. I am destined for heaven; I have an assurance that I have been called to go there and that God is going to take me there, and it is because I know this that I am preparing now. I must never regard that as contingent and uncertain in order that I may make it certain. It is exactly the other way round: it is because I know I am going to meet God that I must prepare to meet Him.

Thirdly, I must never conceive of holiness or sanctification as a kind of higher or happier or holier life which we are meant to enjoy as Christians and into which I ought to be entering. I must regard it rather as a life to which all Christians are inevitably called and which every Christian ought therefore automatically to be living. Now far too often the subject of holiness is handled like this: We are told that there is a wonderful life which you can live—a life with a capital *L*—a life of happiness and joy and peace. 'Why don't you enter into this life?' we are asked. Indeed, we are told that there are two types of Christians, the ordinary Christian and then the Christian who has had some kind of double blessing. You can be a Christian without that, but how foolish you are not to take this higher something which is there for you. I say there is no such definition in the New Testament at all. Holiness is something that is applicable to every Christian, not something which is some kind of extra. It is the norm of the Christian life, the life that everyone who has truly seen the doctrine is doing his or her utmost to live and to practise, with none of this division or dichotomy. All Christians, if they understand the doctrine truly, may be, and are, living this kind of life. It is not something in a separate category and department; it is something that flows out of the life that is in them; it is an inevitable expression of what they have received.

Or, lastly, let me put it like this: The holiness of which the New Testament speaks and the holy life, the life of sanctification which John talks of, is not so much something which we receive as a gift—it is rather something which we work out. Now here again I think this correction is needed. How often is the holiness doctrine presented in that form. We are told that as you have received your justification by faith as a gift, so you must now receive this gift of sanctification and holiness as a gift. So people get the idea that this life of holiness is something which comes to you perhaps in a meeting or a convention. You suddenly get it; you went to the meeting without it and then suddenly you got it.

But surely this is a denial of this very teaching which John is holding before us. No; the position is rather this—not that it suddenly comes to me and I receive some special or exceptional blessing; the position, rather, is that I am reminded of the doctrine, I am reminded that I am a child of God, I am told of the inheritance that awaits me. I have been given a glimpse of the vision of the glory that awaits me beyond death and the grave, and having seen it I am told, 'Now then, in the light of that, proceed to work this out, purify yourselves even as he is pure.' It is not a gift received but something which I must work out and put into practise. Consider how the Apostle Paul puts the same thing in Philippians 2:12-13: 'Work out your own salvation with fear and trembling: for it is God which worketh in you both to will and to do. . . .' And because of that you work it out. It is not some mystical experience that suddenly comes to us, but the outworking of the doctrine and the truth which we claim to believe.

Now all that is surely something of which we are reminded as we take a superficial glance at this third verse in its connection with the second verse, and we can put the teaching like this: If I really believe what that second verse has told me, if I really know that I am a child of God, with all that that means, if I believe and know that I am destined for eternal glory in the presence of God the Father, if I really believe that the Lord Jesus Christ is going to return again, to be 'manifested,' as John puts it, in this world as the King of kings and Lord of lords, if I believe He is coming to judge the world and to destroy everything that is evil and vile out of the universe as a whole, if I believe that I am going to be with Him in that glory, if furthermore I believe that I am going to see Him as he is, if I really believe that I am going to be like Him, that my very body shall be glorified, and that I shall be faultless and blameless and spend my eternity in His holy presence, if I really believe all that, says John, then of necessity this must follow.

What is it, then, that follows? The first thing that John tells us is that anyone who really believes that and has 'this hope in him *purifieth himself*.' Now it is very important that we should realise that 'him' does not refer to the man himself, but to Christ. John does not say, 'Every man that hath this hope within himself,' but 'Every man that hath this hope *in him*,' in the Christ of whom he has just been speaking in verse 2, in the Second Coming and in the power of our Lord to change our vile body so that it may be fashioned like unto His glorious body. It is the hope that is in Christ, in all that He is going to bring into the world and in all that He will do.

So, then, men and women who have this hope purify themselves, and this is a very interesting and a most important word. It is a very positive word; we must never think of it as negative. There is a difference between purifying and cleansing. We have considered 1 John 1:9,[2] 'If we confess our sins, he is faithful and just to forgive us our sins, and *to cleanse* us from all unrighteousness,' and the main difference between the two words is that between an external action and an internal action. To *cleanse* is to deliver, on the surface, from evil and pollution and all that is unworthy; *purification* is something that happens within, in the spirit and in the mind and in the essential nature. Therefore to purify means, in a sense, not only to get rid of the tarnishing effect of sin upon me, but also to avoid sin in my whole nature and in my whole being; so what I am told is that, as a Christian, I inevitably purify myself.

This means not only that I try to separate myself from the sins which I have committed in the past; it includes that, but it goes well beyond it. It means that with the whole of my being I shun sin, I avoid it. I have a desire within me to be like Christ; I am striving to be like the Lord Himself. It is not just that I do not sin, but that I am positively and actively pure even as He was pure. That is the whole idea of this word;

it is a deeper and more profound word than just the idea of cleansing and of getting rid of the effects of sin upon the surface.

It is indeed perfectly expressed in just one phrase; people who are concerned about purifying themselves are those who want to be like the Lord Jesus Christ. They do not any longer merely think of just being a little bit better than obvious sinners in the world, nor a little bit better than they once were. Their whole idea is intensely positive and active. They say, 'I want my nature to be such that I shall love the light and hate the darkness instead of loving the darkness and hating the light. I want my whole being to be a positive desire to be like Christ and to be well-pleasing in His sight.' That, according to John, is the feeling of the men and women who truly understand this promise of the glory that yet awaits them.

Secondly, how do I do this? And here again we have to put it in the form perhaps of a criticism of a particular teaching. How am I to purify myself? Well, according to John, it is an active process, not a passive one; 'Every man that hath this hope in him *purifieth himself.*' He does not submit to purification; he purifies himself. The whole emphasis is upon the activity. In other words, the New Testament teaching about holiness is not one which tells me that all I have to do is to let myself go and to surrender myself, to give up effort and striving. It is not just telling me that all I have to do is to die and get rid of myself and forget myself and then life will come in. No! It is active, and I am told to purify myself 'even as he is pure.'

Now that is a doctrine which is not confined to John; you will find it everywhere in the New Testament. Take, for instance, the Apostle Paul in 2 Corinthians 7:1: 'Having these promises, let us cleanse ourselves from all filthiness of the flesh and spirit, perfecting holiness in the fear of God.' That is an identical statement with the verse that we are considering here. Let us *'cleanse ourselves,'* not submit passively to some process which will cleanse us. Take also Hebrews 6:11-12 where we are exhorted to show some diligence in this matter of 'the full assurance of hope unto the end'; we are not to be slothful, but, like those who have gone before us, we must be diligent and press on and strive to perfect ourselves because of the hope that is set before us.

There are many other terms in the New Testament which suggest the same thing. Take those words which are used by the Apostle Paul in various places: 'Mortify therefore your members which are upon the earth' (Col 3:5). I have to do that; these members will not agree to be mortified; *I* have to take them, and I have to punish my body. I am enabled to do that by the Holy Spirit who has been given to me; yes, and that is included in the fact that I am a child of God. I have been born again, I have received a new nature, and the Holy Spirit is in me. Therefore, because of that, I must do this, I must purify myself even as He is pure.

But, still more in detail, how am I to do this? Well, this is the way in which the New Testament indicates that the process must be followed up: I purify myself by considering Him, by looking at Him and His perfect life; that is the pattern I am to follow. We are reminded of that by the Apostle Paul. God has called us that we may be 'conformed to the image of his Son' (Rom 8:29). So if that is God's plan and purpose for me, then the first thing I must do is to look at the Lord Jesus Christ, to look at the way He conducted Himself in this life and world. I am to be like Him, so I consider Him. I realise that is what I am destined for, so I begin to put it into practise.

The other way in which it is put is this: we are told to 'set your affection on things above, not on things on the earth' (Col 3:2). Again observe the activity—*set* your affections on things above. Read your Bible every day; meditate upon eternity and the glory that awaits you; think about these things; reflect upon the glory. Do not let your mind be set upon things that are on the earth; deliberately refuse to do so.

Or consider again: 'for our light affliction, which is but for a moment, worketh for us a far more exceeding and eternal weight of glory; while we look not at the things which are seen, but at the things which are not seen: for the things which are seen are temporal; but the things which are not seen are eternal' (2 Cor 4:17-18). We must look at the things that are not seen, so we meditate upon them; and having looked at Him and having followed Him, and while we are looking and setting our affection on the things which are above, we must do our utmost to see that vision of glory more and more clearly. We must not love the world. We must mortify our members that are upon the earth. We must crucify the flesh. And as we do all these things we shall be purifying ourselves even as He is pure. That is how it is to be done.

Then, lastly, what are the encouragements and the motives for Christians to purify themselves in this way? I think they are quite self-evident. Is it not a matter of what we might call Christian common sense? If I believe that I am a child of God and that I am really going to heaven and to glory, if I believe that this uncertain life of mine may suddenly come to an end at any moment and then I shall be with the Lord in all the glory and perfection, is it surely not common sense that I ought to be preparing myself for that? Is it not hopelessly illogical and unreasonable to go on living in antithesis to that to which I am called? It is not a matter to be argued; there is a sense in which we should never have to appeal to Christian people to live a holy life. What John does is what we all ought to do. If we believe this, if we claim this, then it is consistent, it is a matter of common sense, it is a matter of logic, it is a matter of being reasonable that we should do so.

But there are further inducements given us in the Bible. Because of our frailty, another great reason for purifying ourselves is that we may not find ourselves feeling ashamed when we arrive in glory. John has told us that in the previous chapter and the twenty-eighth verse: 'And now, little children, abide in him; that when he shall appear, we may have confidence, and not be ashamed before him at his coming.' This means that if you are a child of God, you are going to see Him when he comes; you will see Him as He is, for the first time. You will really understand what your salvation meant to Him and what it cost Him when you look into His face and into His blessed eyes. 'And if you do not want to feel ashamed,' says John, 'if you do not want to feel you are a cad and that you have been a fool because you have kept your gaze fixed upon the little things of earth with their foulness and their unworthiness, then prepare for the vision now; be ready for its coming, and avoid that sense of shame.'

But that is negative. An even stronger reason for purifying ourselves is that we all ought to have a positive desire to be like Him. We ought to be filled with a yearning and a longing to live this glorious, wondrous life that Christ has made possible for us by His death and resurrection. Should not we all be animated by a desire to please Him if we really believe He came from heaven to earth? If we really believe that He suffered the agony of the cross and shed His holy blood that we might be redeemed and rescued, if we really believe that and love Him, should not our greatest desire be to please Him?

That is the reason for holy living, that is the New Testament appeal for holiness; it is an appeal to our sense of honour, to our sense of love and gratitude. But if you want a final appeal, let me appeal to you in terms of the time element. 'He that hath this hope in him,' those who believe they are going to see Him and be like Him and be with Him, purify themselves even as He is pure, and they feel there is not a moment to be lost. Oh, the unworthiness that is in me! Not only the sins I have committed and still commit, but the evil nature, the unworthiness in me, all these things which I have to mortify. There is so much to be done, and time is uncertain. We do not have a moment to spare or to waste. We may find ourselves with Him, facing Him, at any moment.

That is the spirit of the New Testament—people pressing on towards the mark, straining at the leash, looking forward, going forward with all their might. And because they are looking at the vision of glory for which they are destined, they are pressing on towards it and towards Him, forgetting the things that are behind, redeeming the time, buying up the opportunity, using every second because of the certainty that they will see Him as He is and that they will be like Him. God grant that this inevitable logic may be plain and clear to each and every one.

4

The Sinless Saviour

And ye know that he was manifested to take away our sins; and in him is no sin.

1 JOHN 3:5

WE SHOULD READ VERSES 4 to 10 to get this verse in context, because it is essential that we should bear all this in mind as we come to look together at the message and at the statement of this particular fifth verse. We see that here in this verse, and in this entire section, the Apostle is continuing the discussion of what he had begun to deal with in the third verse. In the first two chapters he has written about our fulness of joy as Christians, about our fellowship with God and how that fellowship is to be maintained. That is his first great theme. Then, you remember, here in this chapter he is dealing with the whole position of the Christian as a child of God, and this is his second great appeal. He has shown us that another great secret of living this Christian life thoroughly in this world is to realise this whole standing and position of ours.

But here he goes on to his other theme, and the first thing he wants to emphasise again is that this whole question of righteousness and of holy living is an essential and vital part of this whole position and of our understanding of the position, and he feels that he must make this so abundantly plain and clear that we can never go astray about it. He again warns them: 'Little children, let no man deceive you' (v 7). As there are heresies that would lead us astray about the person of our Lord and His work, so there are heresies with regard to sin, and that is the subject with which he deals in this great and familiar passage.

Now it is again interesting to observe in passing that his method of handling this whole question of holiness and righteousness is so typical, not only of him, but also of all the New Testament writers. The appeal for holiness, as we have seen, is always made in terms of doctrine. Holiness must never be isolated; it is always deduced from something that has gone before. It is an inevitable consequence of a true understanding of our position in Christ Jesus. And John goes on to show us once more that that is his method. Holiness is a matter of working out what we claim to believe; therefore failure in practise does suggest a failure truly to understand the doctrine, and is an indication that there is something essentially and fundamentally wrong with one's view of the Christian life.

Now the particular failure with which he is concerned here is the failure really to understand the nature of sin. There are many tendencies with regard to this; John has already dealt with one of them in chapter 1,[1] where he showed us the danger of the false perfectionist ideas. People have such an inadequate view of sin that they think they are already perfect; they regard sin in terms of particular actions and so fail to realise its pollution as well as its power within them.

Now here he seems to be pointing out quite a different danger and heresy with regard to sin—that of regarding it lightly, dismissing it in some inadequate way as if it were something that really does not matter very much so long as one is a Christian. But John is careful to guard very strongly against that. He says, 'Whosoever committeth sin transgresseth also the law: for sin is the transgression of the law' (v 4). 'You must be right, therefore,' says the Apostle, 'about this whole question of the real nature of sin, because if you are wrong there, you must be wrong on your doctrine of salvation, and then you are wrong everywhere.' And so his great emphasis at this point is that sin is lawlessness, the breaking of God's law, rebellion against God, disobedience, a failure to live our lives as God would have us live them.

That is the very essence of sin. It must not be thought of as just a sort of weakness or failure on our part; it must not be regarded as some sort of bestial past which we have not yet sloughed off. No, John says, sin is not negative, it is positive. It is the transgression of the law; it is disobedience to God and His holy will with respect to us. 'So if you fail to realise this,' says the Apostle in effect, 'then it does just show that you are muddled and confused in your thinking about the whole principle of the coming of the Lord Jesus Christ into this world. And it seems clear that your whole conception of salvation must be entirely false and erroneous'—and then he proceeds to deal with that.

'Man's essential trouble,' says the Apostle, 'is that he is guilty and condemned by the law of God. Sin was introduced into this world by the devil; the devil came at the very beginning and tempted man to disobey God. That is *lawlessness*: he tempted him to break God's holy law, and man in his folly listened to him and did so. That is a part of the work of the devil, and its effect has been to make us break the law of God and to render us guilty in the sight of God and His holy law. There we are, under the wrath of God, meriting and awaiting punishment. That is the position,' says John, 'so that if you do not view your sin in that way, then it is quite obvious that you cannot understand anything else because the Lord Jesus Christ was manifested, or appeared, in this world because of that.'

John, you notice, makes two separate statements with regard to the object of the coming of our Lord Jesus Christ: 'Ye know that he was manifested to take away our sins' (v 5), and 'For this purpose the Son of God was manifested, that he might destroy the works of the devil' (v 8). That is the whole purpose, and we must view His coming in the light of those two great statements.

So let us consider now this first statement in verse 5. Let us pause and ask this most vital question: why did the Son of God ever come into this world? We know that He was 'manifested,' and we have reminded ourselves how John likes to put it in this way. He says, 'That which was from the beginning, which we have heard, which we have seen with our eyes, which we have looked upon, and our hands have handled, of the Word of life; (for the life was *manifested*, and we have seen it . . .)' (1:1-2), and here he says it again. So why was this?

When we think about the Lord Jesus Christ and especially about His death on that cross on Calvary's hill, what is its purpose?[2] Is it just something about which we sentimentalise? What does it represent to us? We have to ask, Why was the Son of God born into this world as a baby in Bethlehem? What is the meaning of the Incarnation? Why did He ever leave the courts of heaven and come in that way into this world? Then, why did He spend His life as He did those first thirty years? What is the meaning of His preaching and His teaching and His miracles? What is the purpose of His life here on earth, and above all, why that cross? Why this manifestation and demonstration; why the burial and the rising again and the appearance and the Ascension? What is the explanation of it all?

That is the question that John answers here, and let me first put the answer in its negative form. Our Lord did not only come to give us a revelation of God, though that is a part of the purpose. He said, 'He that hath seen me hath seen the Father' (John 14:9), and we also read, 'No man hath seen God at any time; the only begotten Son, which is in the bosom of the Father, he hath declared him' (John 1:18). But that is not all, though He has indeed revealed the Father and has come to do that. In the same way, He has not only come to teach us about God. There *is* incomparable teaching there, such as the world has never known before and has not known since, but He did not come only to do that. There is also, of course, the example of His life, a matchless one, but He has not come only to give us an example of how we should live in this world. He is not just a teacher or a moral exemplar; he has not come to give us some kind of picture as to the nature and being of God. All that is there, but that is not the real reason, says John.

He has really come, he says, because of our sins, because of the predicament and the position of men and women, because of this whole question of law. He has not come only to instruct us and to give us encouragement in our endeavour and a great example. No, there is a fundamental problem at the back of it all, and that is our relationship to God in the light of God's holy law. We are under the law, and He has really come because of that. 'Ye know that he was manifested to take away our sins; and in him is no sin.' So it is only as we understand this whole question of sin in terms of law that we can possibly understand why He came and especially why He ever went to that cruel death upon the cross. He came, as the New Testament tells us everywhere, because in a sense He had to come if we were to be delivered. He came because there was no other way whereby we could be redeemed and rescued. He came 'to seek and to save that which was lost' (Luke 19:10). He came because of this whole question of what sin has done to us and the position in which it has landed us with respect to God and His holy law. And here John puts all that to us in this particularly striking manner.

So let us see what God has done with regard to this predicament in which we find ourselves. The first thing John tells us is that we do not understand the Lord Jesus Christ properly apart from ourselves and our sinful condition, apart from this whole question of the law. So the first statement that John makes is that He Himself is without sin. There was no sin in the Lord Jesus Christ; He was perfect, spotless, blameless; He was born without sin. So, you see, it is looking at Him in terms of law that really shows us that we must not only accept the biblical statement with regard to the virgin birth of our Lord, but also why this is essential. The Holy Ghost came upon Mary, and He was born. He became man; He took unto Himself this human nature, yes, but He was without sin. In the miracle that took place there He received the perfect human nature.

'In him is no sin.' We have to start with that for the reasons which will emerge as we continue, but that is always the starting point. There can be no true view of salvation and of the redemption that is possible for us in the Lord Jesus Christ unless we are right about the person. That is why John, you remember, used such strong and striking language in chapter 2[3] when he talked about those people who were leading them astray by denying the person of our Lord. 'Those antichrists,' he said, 'are liars, and they must be called such because they are robbing us of the whole of our salvation.' If we are wrong about the person, we shall be wrong everywhere. So as we look at this person we are reminded again in this verse that here is one who has been in this world of ours with all its sin and its shame, but who was without sin. He 'was in all points tempted like as we are, yet without sin' (Heb 4:15). He remains there unique and separate. He is the Son of God, and none other. He is not just a great moral teacher, nor just a great religious genius. He is not one who has gone a little bit further than all others in this quest for God and for truth. No, He is the Son of God incarnate—'in him is no sin.'

But not only was there no sin in Him and in His birth—He committed no act of sin. He always honoured God's holy law; He obeyed it fully and carried it out perfectly. God gave His law to man. He intended that that law should be carried out, that it should be honoured and obeyed. Let me go further and say this: no one can ever be with God and spend eternity with Him unless they have honoured the law. God's law must be kept, and without fulfilling it there is no fellowship with Him and no hope of spending eternity with Him. And here is One who has kept the law, who lived in this world exactly as you and I have to live in it. He worked as a carpenter. He had been a child, yet no one was ever able to convict Him of sin. He defied them to do so; He rendered a perfect obedience to God and to His holy law. What God has demanded from man and man has failed to do, here is One who does it. He fulfils it. 'In him is no sin'; He has satisfied the law of God. He has actively and positively obeyed it and rendered it fully.

This, I say again, is something which is absolutely essential to our salvation, for the problem of man with respect to God is not only the problem of the guilt of sin. Merely to be forgiven is not enough; we have to keep the law of God. Notice how Paul puts that in Romans 8, where he says that in Christ Jesus God has 'condemned sin in the flesh: that the righteousness of the law might be fulfilled in us' (vv 3-4). We have to keep that law, but we have not kept it; we cannot do so, and we can only keep it in Him. He has kept the law for us; He has rendered this obedience and satisfied this demand of the law of God.

But let us go on another step. In addition to that He has dealt with the problem of the guilt of our sin, because He has provided a perfect sacrifice and offering for our sin. In the Old Testament we read of all the burnt offerings and sacrifices, those types and shadows which God gave the ancient people of Israel in order to show them how sacrifice must be made for sin. 'Without shedding of blood is no remission' of sin (Heb 9:22), and the sacrifice and offering had to be perfect. It had to be 'without blemish'—that was all a type and a shadow of the perfect offering. It must be human, it must be a man, and here is the perfect sacrifice for sin, for 'in him is no sin.'

You see, it is all in terms of the law. While the law demands perfection, it cannot admit any blemish; you cannot offer a perfect sacrifice for sin if there is any defect. If the Lord Jesus Christ had sinned once, He could no longer have been that perfect offering for our sins; but 'in him is no sin,' and therefore He is the sacrifice. 'There was no other good enough to pay the price of sin.'[4] He has come in the flesh, He has been born as a man, and yet He is without sin; therefore He can offer Himself, and it is a perfect offering.

And that leads us to the next step. By doing that, says John, He has taken away our sins—'Ye know he was manifested to take away our sins.' We are reminded of the words of John the Baptist when he looked at Jesus at the beginning and said, 'Behold the Lamb of God, which taketh away the sin of the world' (John 1:29). That is the meaning of Good Friday, that is the explanation of the Cross—our sins have been laid upon Him, and they have been dealt with there in Him; He has taken them away. Your sins and mine do not any longer belong to us;

they have been taken from us; He has made Himself responsible for them. The ideas here are those of the lamb that was slain, and also of the scapegoat, on whom was placed the sin of the people and then he was sent away into the wilderness (Lev 16). That is what the Lord Jesus Christ has done for us. That is why He came, that is the whole purpose of His Incarnation, that is why He staggered up Golgotha, that is why He was nailed to the tree. He is bearing away my sins and yours.

But it was the law that demanded that; it would never have happened were it not for the law, and that is why we must never regard sin as something light and trivial. That is why we must never refer to it as some sort of weakness and say, 'It does not matter very much now that I am a Christian.' Sin is a transgression of the law. It is such a terrible thing that it led to the death of Christ, and one sin is enough to demand that. 'Let no man deceive you,' says John. Do you not see that if you are wrong in your outlook upon sin, then it just means that you have never seen its enormity, you have never seen the problem it has created for man and, in a sense, I say it with reverence, for God Himself. This holy law, this expression of God's being and character, condemns sin utterly. The condemnation is death, and without the sacrificial atonement there is no forgiveness. But, wonder of wonders, God has provided and found the way there on the cross. My sins are no longer imputed to me, they are no longer on record against me, and as my sinful story is there revealed in the Book of Life, it is all cancelled by Christ.

So those who believe that cannot regard sin lightly. They cannot say that a righteous life is a matter of indifference. Those who really believe this and are governed by it and who are truly holy in the New Testament sense are not holy just because they believe it is a 'good life.' They see it all in the light of the law of God and of the cross and of the Christ who came as the Lamb of God; the argument and the logic are inescapable. So the New Testament does not just appeal to us to be holy for the sake of being holy—it puts it into this context.

But lastly, there is one further step. It is obvious that in this context and setting, when John says that 'he was manifested to take away our sins,' he is not stopping at the guilt of our sins, for salvation goes beyond that. We are delivered from the guilt—it is the first thing that is essential—but, thank God, the process does not stop there. He delivers us also from the power and from the pollution of sin. His work is such that he takes away our sin in a more vital sense. We are growing in grace and in the knowledge of the Lord; we are increasingly being made to conform to the image of His Son. We are being delivered—we have been, we are, and we shall be ultimately. The glorification is coming when He will take away our sin altogether, so that we shall be blameless and faultless and spotless and perfect in His holy presence.

That hymn which tells us, 'There was no other good enough to pay the price of sin' also tells us this: 'He died that we might be forgiven'; yes, but 'He died to make us good' is equally true. The Apostle Paul, writing to Titus, says: '[He] gave himself for us, that he might redeem us from all iniquity, and purify unto himself a peculiar [separate] people, zealous of good works' (Titus 2:14).

So we must never separate sanctification from justification; we must never separate holiness and forgiveness; we must never talk about a kind of series of separate blessings; all is one—it all belongs together. And it is all a matter of this law that condemns us and from which he delivers us through the cross and by the gift of new life. He went to that cruel death on the cross not only that you and I might have pardon. Thank God, that does come out of it, that is the first thing. But He did it really to separate, to put aside, a people for Himself as an especial treasure and possession, who, as Paul puts it, should be 'zealous of good works,' who would live a righteous, holy life, a people who would be a demonstration and manifestation to the whole world, and, yes, to the principalities and powers in heavenly places, of this wondrous Christ of God who has been able to do so much and to make so much of sinful, fallen men and women.

That, then, is what we know. 'Ye know that he was manifested to take away our sins; and in him is no sin.' I do hope that you know that you are forgiven, that the guilt of your sin has been taken away. I trust you know also that He is delivering you increasingly from the power of sin and from its pollution and that you look forward to 'that blessed hope, and the glorious appearing of the great God and our Saviour Jesus Christ' (Titus 2:13), when He shall finally come back and wind up the affairs of earth and of time and destroy evil in its every manifestation and usher in that eternal glory in which we, as the children of God, shall share.

God grant that that may be our position and our experience.

5

VICTORY OVER THE DEVIL

For this purpose the Son of God was manifested, that he might destroy the works of the devil.

1 JOHN 3:8

THIS IS THE SECOND OF the two great statements which John makes in this first section of chapter 3 with regard to the whole object and purpose of the coming of the Son of God into this world of time. We have been considering the first statement in verse 5: 'And ye know that he was manifested to take away our sins; and in him is no sin.'

These two statements together remind us of what the Fathers were very fond of describing as the 'Drama of Redemption.' This is a very good phrase, a phrase which helps us to look at the gospel in the right way and manner and which reminds us immediately of the very essence of the gospel message. It is astounding that in spite of the records which we have in the New Testament, our tendency always is to turn the gospel into a point of view, into an idea and a teaching, and to forget that it was first and foremost a series of events and of facts which actually took place.

That, it seems to me, is the inevitable result of sin. The Apostle Paul tells us in his letters to the Corinthians and to the Colossians that he was aware of that very subtle danger. He was always afraid of somehow or another nullifying the whole message of the Cross by turning it into a philosophy. For the very essence of the gospel message is that it is not first and foremost a teaching, but a proclamation, an announcement of certain things that have happened. When you read the book of Acts you will find that the first preachers travelled around and were heralds of the message. They told that ancient world of certain things which had happened; they talked about a person, and they reported what had happened to Him. And with a very special emphasis, they told people of the amazing fact of the Resurrection; how this person, Jesus of Nazareth—who had been completely misunderstood, not only by the common people, but by the rulers and elders of the people—how He had been put to death. But, they said, God had raised Him from the dead, and He had manifested Himself to them, His chosen witnesses, and to certain other people. And they told how, after He had spent forty days on the earth, they had seen Him rising into the heavens; and now they were preaching in the power of the amazing gift He had sent to them, a person they called the Holy Spirit.

And we are reminded of all that by these words that we are now considering. We see that our Lord did not come into the world only to teach. He did do that, and He gave incomparable teaching, but before we ever come to consider His teaching—at any rate before it can be of any value to us at all in any practical sense—we must first realise what He came primarily to do. 'For this purpose the Son of God was manifested,' not that He might teach us, not that He might give us a glorious example to follow, not that He might give us some transcendent idea which would illumine our minds and thrill us—not at all!

He came, He was manifested, He appeared that He might 'destroy the works of the devil.' He came to do something, and our salvation is dependent upon what He Himself has done. He does not just come and call upon us to do something. The first and the most essential message of the gospel is to ask us to recognise and then to receive what He has done. That is why salvation is a gift, and that is why the business of preaching is to offer men and women this gift of salvation and to hold it before them.

And that is what John here emphasises in these two striking statements. Now you observe that in both instances he puts it in terms of sin. Whether we like it or not, that is always the context and the background to this presentation of the truth. Our Lord really came, says John, and had to come, because of sin, and that is what he is outlining in this whole section.

First of all he looks at sin as it brings us under the condemnation of God's holy law, and secondly he looks at sin as it puts us under the dominion and under the government of Satan and makes us become a part of Satan's work. 'He that committeth sin is of the devil; for the devil sinneth from the beginning . . .,' but 'Whosoever is born of God doth not commit sin. . . . In this the children of God are manifest, and the children of the devil' (vv 8–10). So there are two ways of looking at sin and at the effects of sin on us.

The first way is to see that sin is unrighteous, that it is a transgression of the law, and that *sin* means we are violating God's holy will for us and God's holy purpose with respect to us. But this is the other way: 'To continue in a life of sin and evil,' says John, 'is just to identify yourself at once with the devil and his ways and with everything that belongs to him,' and it is that which is emphasised in this eighth verse.

Now two things stand out very clearly in the particular way in which John puts it. The first is that our Lord came into this world to wage a great fight; He entered into a mighty battle. The second is the way in which he was victorious in the fight, the way in which He overcame for us the adversary and his approaches. That is the thing that is celebrated especially on Easter Day;[1] this is the day that reminds us of Christ's victory, of a fact. It is not a day that reminds us of certain principles in life. You often hear people thank God for this whole 'principle of resurrection,' how the flowers begin to appear, and how the trees and life come into being in the Spring. Now, that has nothing to do with this blessed message of the Resurrection. We are concerned about a fact, not a principle of nature, and the fact is that there, in the Resurrection, our Lord ultimately established His conquest over the devil.

So realising this, realising, as John says, that Christ came that He might destroy the works of the devil, let us begin by considering this 'adversary,' as he is described, the devil. The Son of God came because there was a certain state and condition in this world that had been produced by the devil. Now whether we like it or not, the fact is that the whole drama of redemption, as it is outlined in the Bible, simply cannot be understood at all unless you accept the Biblical doctrine with regard to the devil. It is an essential part of this message; it is here from the very beginning and right through to the end.

And this is the Biblical teaching. The explanation of the problem of mankind and the whole state of our world is to be traced back to this fact about the devil. According to the Bible, God made the world perfect; so what has gone wrong with it? And here is the answer. Someone, who is described in various terms and to whom various names are given in the Bible, came and spoke to the man and the woman whom God had placed in that perfect world. He is called 'Lucifer,' 'the son of the morning' and 'the god of this world.' He is called 'the serpent,' 'the prince of the power of the air,' and 'the strong man armed.' There are various names given in the Scriptures, but they all describe the same person. And according to this teaching, this is the explanation of evil and of sin and of all our miseries in this world. The devil came and spoke to man, and he enticed him to sin; so man went against God; and the result of all that is the state of the world as it has been from the moment that man fell.

Summing it up we can put it like this: This world has become the kingdom of Satan; Satan has produced certain results which we shall consider together—these 'works of the devil' about which our text speaks. And our Lord and Saviour Jesus Christ came into this world because of that fact. Men and women need to be delivered from the law of God that condemns them; and thereby they need to be delivered from the punishment of their sin. But they also need to be delivered out of this kingdom of the devil, out of the kingdom of Satan; and they need to be translated into the kingdom of God. And the Son of God came, according to this whole biblical teaching, because of that kingdom which Satan had established. Christ came into this world in order to conquer Satan and his kingdom and in order to introduce His own kingdom. So what you have in the Bible, in a sense, is the story of the conflict of the two kingdoms—the kingdom of God and the kingdom of the devil, the kingdom of Christ and the kingdom of Satan, the kingdom of light and the kingdom of darkness, the kingdom of the Son of God and the kingdom of this world. It is the conflict between heaven and hell and between light and darkness—that is the Biblical terminology.

Now that being the statement in general, let us look at it a little more in particular. Evil has come in through the devil, this great adversary of God and of man. So what are the works of the devil; what has he been trying to do? Well, his great endeavour is to separate men and women from God; that is what he is really concerned to bring about. He was jealous of man's obedience and allegiance to God, and in his very hatred of God his one desire is to ruin, to mar and to destroy the glorious works of God in this world.

Now he has proceeded to do that work, according to the Scriptures, in a very deceptive manner. He is often described as 'subtle,' and he is also described as a 'liar.' You will find that our Lord Himself in speaking of him says of him that he is 'a liar, and the father of it' (John 8:44), and all his works have just been, in some shape or form, the repetition of some kind of a lie. He has persuaded men and women to believe and to accept these various lies, and all our unhappiness in this world is the result of our folly in believing the subtlety and the lies of Satan. That is the essence of the biblical explanation of our predicament. There would be no unhappiness in the world but for this. Evil and sin, according to the Bible, would not be here. There would be no drunkenness, no quarrelling; there would be no infidelity and divorce, there would be no threats of war, and no confusion and disturbances, were it not that people in their folly have believed the lie of Satan.

There are various forms which that lie has taken. The essence of the lie which Satan has persuaded man to believe is the lie about God Himself; it is the old lie about God's attitude towards man. God made man and woman perfect and gave them a perfect world to live in; and God gave them the supreme privilege of holding communion with Him. He gave them everything that they needed. They did not have to work to make a living at the beginning; there was the fruit, and they had but to take it and enjoy it. God showered His blessings upon them, but the devil came and said, 'Are you foolish enough to believe that God really loves you? Can't you see He is making slaves of you? This one thing He is prohibiting you is just a mark of His hostility with respect to you.' So the lie of Satan is the lie against God at the beginning. And is that not true of all of us? Have we not known in our hearts that when things go wrong, our first hatred is a feeling of hatred against God? This enmity against God is the work of Satan, who lies to us about God, about His attitude towards us, about His love to us, and about His concern for our happiness and well-being.

And that in turn leads to the second lie which is, as we have just seen, the lie about God's holy will. God gives laws to man, and He gives us these laws for our good and for our benefit. It is because God made men and women that He knows what is good for them, and when He gave them conditions at the beginning it was for their good. But they did not see it, and they believed the lie of Satan that the laws of God were against them. How fond people are of saying that the gospel is narrow, and how many reject it for that reason—as if to live a life like the Lord Jesus Christ is to be so small and petty and narrow! No, that is the lie about God's law, God's way of life, God's holiness. By nature we all instinctively dislike the holy life because we believe the lie of sin.

Then, of course, the next lie was the lie about the consequences of sin and of disobedience. 'God has told you,' said Satan to the first man and woman, 'that if you disobey and break His law, then certain consequences will come upon you and you will die. Don't believe Him,' said Satan. 'If you do this which is prohibited, your eyes will be opened and you will become like gods. God doesn't want you to be like Him, so He is holding you down and repressing you. But do this thing and I tell you, you will be greater than you are now.' So he lied to them about the consequences of sin and disobedience, and that produced all the terrible consequences of the Fall.

And Satan still does this self-same thing. He whispers to us all and tells us to disobey God and to break His holy law; and he assures us that we can do that with impunity and nothing will go wrong. And in our folly we all tend to believe him. But later we come to understand that the way of the transgressor is hard and that though for a moment we may go against God and imagine we have wonderful freedom, sooner or later we begin to discover that 'whatsoever a man soweth, that shall he also reap' and 'he that soweth to his flesh shall of the flesh reap corruption' (Gal 6:7-8). The devil lies about the consequences, and men and women in their folly believe the lie.

So the question arises, Why does Satan do all this? Why did he do it at the beginning, and why has he continued to do so? The answer is that he was anxious to get the man and woman under his own power and dominion. His motive and desire was to make them sin and to live a sinful life, and he succeeded. They did sin, and they began to live that sinful life. Not only that, Satan is also anxious to prevent us from living the godly and good life. He is anxious to rob us of all the benefits that God has for us, and the result of all this is that, having listened to the lie of Satan, we have put ourselves under his domination.

Our Lord put that in a very memorable picture when he said, 'When a strong man armed keepeth his palace, his goods are in peace' (Luke 11:21). 'That is the result of sin,' says our Lord. 'You have made yourselves the slaves and the serfs of Satan. You are in the stronghold, the castle, of Satan, and he won't let you get out; nor will he let you live the godly, holy life. If you try, he will strike you down; you are under his power and dominion.' And that, according to the Bible, is the whole state of the world today. The results of the activity and the works of Satan are that men and women are under the rule of Satan. They have disobeyed

God and offended Him. They have broken God's holy law and have been condemned. They had been told what not to do, but they deliberately did it; so they are left with no excuse and are under the wrath of God.

Not only that, their very nature is sinful—they prefer evil to good. There is an instinct in them that takes them astray; there is that within them which lusts and gives way to passion. Their very nature has become twisted and perverted, and as a result of this, they experience misery and unhappiness. Indeed their world has become a place of woe and trouble. It is no use pretending otherwise; it is a fact, and we in this century have experienced it in an exceptional manner—wars and confusion and despair and unhappiness. All this is the result of the work of Satan.

And standing at the end of it all is the fact of death itself. By listening to the lie of Satan, men and women have put themselves under the power of death. As the Scripture is so fond of teaching us, whether we explain it away to our own satisfaction or not, we all in this world by nature live under the tyranny and the fear of death. It is ever present, always advancing towards us, spoiling our greatest and best pleasures. It is the last enemy, it is inevitable, and it is tyrannising the whole of life.

Finally, and perhaps the greatest of all the results of the works of the devil, is the state of the world apart from Christ. That is the sort of world into which Christ came, in which the Son of God was manifested. He appeared in a world that was under the dominion of Satan, a world miserable, unhappy, sinful, perverted, alienated from God, under the wrath of God and with death ever facing it. So why did He ever leave the courts of heaven and the glory which He shared with his Father from the beginning; why did He come?

Here is the answer: 'For this purpose the Son of God was manifested, that he might destroy the works of the devil.' Thank God for this message! By doing all that He has come to do, the Son of God has fulfilled the ancient promise which was given to man and woman immediately after the Fall. Into the chaos that resulted from evil and sin the promise came: The seed of the woman shall bruise the serpent's head. 'Satan has got you down, the serpent has misled you in his subtlety,' said God to Adam and Eve, 'but it is all right—I will send someone who will bruise his head, the seed of the woman' (Gen 3:15)—and that is the Lord Jesus Christ. So we must view His coming into this world in terms of all that Satan had done and had produced. Christ has come to fight it; He has come with a mighty sword. 'Think not,' he said, 'that I am come to send peace on earth: I came not to send peace, but a sword' (Matt 10:34). He has come to destroy and to undo the works of the devil.

And He has done it like this: His very incarnation undoes the lie of Satan, for if the Incarnation tells us one thing more than anything else, it is that God is love and that God has loved us with an everlasting love. 'God is against you,' says the devil. 'God hates you, and He delights to keep you down. He wants to rob you of everything that is yours by right.' 'No,' says the Incarnation, 'God is love.' Here is a world that has rebelled against God. It spat into His holy face; in arrogance it lifted itself up against Him; it said, 'I have a right to be equal with God.' Now, a world like that deserves nothing but punishment; it deserves perdition. Yet into that very world that I have been describing God sent His Son— 'God so loved the world, that he gave his only begotten Son' (John 3:16). The babe in Bethlehem is a denial of the lie of Satan. He says, 'I am here because God loves you.' He has come to undo the works of the devil; He has come to contradict the lies of Satan, and His very appearing and coming, let me emphasise it again, is in itself an undoing of the original lie—it is proof that God loves us.

But look at His life, look at His way of living. Think of Him as He stands before us in the Gospels; look at that perfect, spotless life. Can you still say the holy life is a small, narrow one? Do you believe He was just an apology of a man because He did not drink and curse and swear and gamble and do the various things that men claim are 'life' in a real sense today? Look at Him; look at Him in all His virtue and all His utter sinlessness. He has established there, once and for ever, that the only life worthy to be called life is one which is lived in utter, absolute conformity to the commands of the holy God; in His life He denies the lie of the devil.

Listen, then, to His teaching as He exposes in its utter depths the evil nature of sin and of wrongdoing. Listen to His interpretation and exposition of the law of Moses. In the Sermon on the Mount, for instance, He says, 'You do not have to *commit* sin; just to look with lust in your eyes is sufficient' (Matt 5:28); that is the exposure of sin. He gets down to the depth and says that 'out of the heart proceed evil thoughts, murders, adulteries' and other evils (Matt 15:19). He exposes the perversion and the twistedness of evil—the foulness and ugliness of sin. In His teaching He is undoing the lie, the works of Satan.

But watch Him as He works His miracles and His mighty deeds; what is He doing there? Well, He is just doing this great work of destroying or undoing the works of Satan. Take the occasion when He healed a poor woman who was not only a cripple but was utterly doubled up and indeed had been like that for eighteen years. He spoke to her, and immediately she stood erect. What has He done here? This in effect is what He says: 'Satan has bound this woman for eighteen years, and I am undoing the chains which Satan has forged around her; I am setting her free.' (Luke 13:10-13). 'When a strong man armed keepeth his palace, his goods are in peace: But when a stronger than he shall come upon him, and overcome him, he taketh from him all his armor wherein he trusted, and divideth his spoils' (Luke 11:21-22). He sets the captive free. That is what He is doing in His miracles; He is undoing the works of Satan. He is breaking the chains that had been forged in various ways; He is setting the captive at liberty.

Look thus right through His life and then come to His death. What is He doing on that cross on Calvary's hill? He is dealing there with the guilt; He is undoing there the condemnation of the lie. He is wiping away the guilt; He is setting us right with God; He is reconciling us to God. He has undone the condemnation of sin that results from listening to the lie of Satan.

Let us come to the Resurrection. There He is giving us the final proof that God is pleased with His work; He is proclaiming to us that we can be sure of our salvation. There He says, 'Now is the judgment of this world: now shall the prince of this world be cast out' (John 12:31). He is showing there that He has conquered even death itself, the very 'last enemy' as Paul described it (1 Cor 15:26). There, by rising from the dead, He has established that He has conquered every single enemy. On His cross He has exposed Satan himself and all the principalities and powers. He has shown that He has conquered the ultimate consequence of death itself. All the works of Satan have finally been undone by the Lord Jesus Christ. If we believe in Him, we have been raised with Him. He has 'made us sit together in the heavenly places' with Him (Eph 2:6). We have been raised, we have risen again, we are in Him, we have conquered death and the grave, and we know we shall rise incorruptible and be with Him for all eternity.

In addition to all this, in the light of the Resurrection we know that we can have life anew. He has not only brought life and immortality to light through His Resurrection, He gives us His own life. He took upon Him our human need, He died for our sins, He has taken the guilt away.

But more, He has engrafted us into Himself, and He has given unto us—we have received—the divine nature. We have risen with Him as new men and women, a new creation. The works of the devil have thus been destroyed and undone.

But there is more. This work is still being carried on; that is His method. He takes hold of us one by one; He rescues and delivers us out of this world and from Satan one by one. As we believe the message of this gospel, we are translated from the kingdom of darkness into the kingdom of light—the kingdom of God's dear Son. He is building up His own kingdom; he is drawing men and women unto Himself out of the world; He is going on with the work. He is in glory seated at the right hand of God, and He must reign until His enemies shall be made His footstool; He is going on until the number of the elect shall have been gathered in. And when that has happened, He will come again. He will return into this world as King and Lord, and He will finally finish the work. He will come with a mighty sword, and not only evil and sin but Satan himself and all his cohorts shall be cast into the lake of fire and will finally be banished from the sight of God for all eternity. And our guarantee of all this is the glorious fact of the Resurrection: He 'was manifested, that he might destroy the works of the devil.'

Remember then what He has already destroyed, and look forward in anticipation; the blessed hope that faces us as Christian people is that He will destroy these works of the devil utterly, completely and finally; evil and sin will be finally destroyed out of existence, burnt, destroyed for ever. God shall be all and in all, and if we are in the army of the mighty Victor who has already risen from the grave and thereby conquered death, if we belong to Him, we shall behold that final judgment of Satan, and we shall dwell for all eternity in a perfect state with no sin and no sorrow, with no sighing and no tears. There will be no need even for the sun itself, for the light of the glory will be the face of this self-same Lord who was born as a babe in Bethlehem, and we shall bask in that glorious sunshine entirely free from sin for ever and ever. 'The Son of God was manifested'—appeared, came into this world—'that he might destroy the works of the devil.' Thank God for the Victor who came who could conquer even the last enemy, death itself, and give us life which is life indeed.

6

GROWING IN GRACE

Whosoever abideth in him sinneth not: whosoever sinneth hath not seen him, neither known him. Little children, let no man deceive you: he that doeth righteousness is righteous, even as he is righteous. He that committeth sin is of the devil; for the devil sinneth from the beginning. For this purpose the Son of God was manifested, that he might destroy the works of the devil. Whosoever is born of God doth not commit sin; for his seed remaineth in him: and he cannot sin, because he is born of God. In this the children of God are manifest, and the children of the devil: whosoever doeth not righteousness is not of God, neither he that loveth not his brother.

1 JOHN 3:6–10

WE HAVE SEEN THAT from the end of the second chapter and right through this third chapter, John is showing us that the second great thing we must realise as Christians in this world is that we are children of God. 'Beloved, now are we the sons of God'—not, we are going to be, but we *are*. Now you must hold on to that, says John. You must always retain a firm grasp of it if you want to rejoice while in this world. You are the children of God, and you have a glorious destiny awaiting you.

But, obviously, if you really believe that, you must see that certain things follow of necessity; you cannot claim to be a child of God and still go on living as if you had not been born again. In other words, one of the first implications of this realisation of our sonship is the realisation of the absolute necessity of living a holy life, and that is the theme of this section from verse 4 to verse 10. We have already looked at this section twice, and I have picked out those two striking statements which are to be found in the fifth and eighth verses. But now we come back to it again, and we shall look in particular at verses 6 and 7, the first part of verse 8 and then verses 9 and 10.

This is notoriously one of the most controversial passages in the New Testament. Of course, no passage in and of itself is controversial, but there has certainly been great controversy over these verses. Anybody who is at all interested in Christian theology, or who has even the faintest interest in doctrine, or indeed anyone who is concerned about living the Christian life, must at some time or another have confronted these statements. The great question which is asked is: do they teach sinless perfection? Do they mean that the Christian in this life can be perfect, delivered altogether from sin not only in act, but also in thought, in desire, in mind, and in every other respect? Anyone who has ever read anything at all on this question of sanctification has at some point come across people who have used these various statements on one side or on the other. So, bearing all that in mind, there are, surely, certain warnings which should be uttered before we attempt to expound a statement such as this one.

First of all, as we look at statements like these, we must try to rid our minds of prejudice. We are all creatures of prejudice; we are born like that as the result of sin, and we tend to start with minds which are biased. One of the most difficult things in life in any realm is to get rid of such prejudice, but surely if we would understand the message of Scripture, we must try to rid our minds of it. Or, to put it another way, we must avoid theories, especially those with respect to sanctification. Again, this is a very difficult thing to do because we all rather like theories; we like to have truth in tabloid form. It seems much easier, it avoids a lot of trouble and mental effort; our natural laziness as the result of sin rather makes us hunger after such easy tabloid thinking, and it is the particular danger in this day and age in which we happen to live. But we must try to avoid theories, and we must try as far as we can to come and look at the Word itself as it is; and above all we must avoid a controversial spirit.

By that I mean that when we come across some of these statements, immediately they become battle cries! Immediately we hear these words, we take sides; we are either going to be for or against sanctification or sinless perfection, and so we become impervious to the message of the Scripture itself. So whenever we come to a passage like this that has so often been discussed in the past, we must make an unusual effort to rid our minds of a mere controversial spirit or a desire to prove that we are right and that somebody else is wrong. Rather, we should have a desire to discover the truth in order that we may apply it in our lives.

If you read the history of the Church you will find that oftentimes, in contending about a passage of Scripture like this, people on both sides have denied the real teaching of the passage. In their desire to prove that they were right they have been guilty of bitterness. Sometimes those who argued for sinless perfection contended in such a way that they proved they were not sinless and indeed not perfect! The spirit of controversy was such that they forgot the truth about which they were arguing and debating. Therefore it is necessary that we should bear this in mind. I suppose the classic discussion of this matter is really to be found in the eighteenth century. I do not want to discuss it historically here, but those who are familiar with the great story of the Evangelical Awakening of that century will remember how there was a very striking cleavage between John Wesley and his followers on the one hand, and the followers of Whitefield and others on the other. There was a great discussion which went on for many decades on this whole question of sinless perfection, and these words which we are considering here were to be found prominently at the heart and centre of the discussions.

Now the great question for us to face is this: Do these statements, which are made here about the Christian, refer to individual, particular acts of sin, or is the Apostle referring to something else? Let me remind you again of some of these statements: 'Whosoever abideth in him sinneth not'—does that mean *particular* acts of sin or does it not? 'Whosoever sinneth hath not seen him, neither known him'—again we must ask the same question. 'He that doeth righteousness is righteous, even as he is righteous,' 'He that committeth sin is of the devil,' 'Whosoever is born of God doth not commit sin'—do those mean individual acts of sin? 'For his seed remaineth in him: and he cannot sin.' Does that mean that a person cannot perform or do individual acts of sin because he or she is born of God? 'In this the children of God are manifest, and the children of the devil; whosoever doeth not righteousness is not of God, neither he that loveth not his brother.' So that is the question we have to face. Are these statements referring to separate, particular acts of sin? If they do, then I think it is perfectly clear that the Apostle is teaching sinless perfection, but the question is, do they mean that?

Let us look at it in this way: First of all, I think we must understand the grammar, and although we are approaching a passage of Scripture, surely the first and the obvious thing to do is to make certain of the exact statement which is before us. We believe that the Word of God is definitely inspired, but that does not mean that every translation is definitely inspired. We must be sure we have understood the true meaning of the Word. So what does the grammar tell us? Well, I think that all the authorities are agreed that all the verbs which are used in this section are present and continuous. In other words, they describe character and prevailing habit rather than particular acts.

Now that applies to all the verbs from verse 4 to verse 10. Verse 4 reads like this: 'Whosoever committeth sin transgresseth also the law: for sin is the transgression of the law.' But a better way of translating that would be: 'Every one who *keeps on doing sin* keeps on breaking the law, or doing lawlessness.' These verbs all carry that meaning of keeping on, so that we render the sixth verse like this: 'Whosoever keeps on doing sin hath not seen him, neither known him.' Therefore when we come to the ninth verse we read: 'The one begotten of God does not *keep on sinning* because God's seed abides in him and he is not able to *keep on sinning*.' So John is talking about those who keep on doing sin, who keep on being guilty of lawlessness, and therefore, on the other side, he says that, 'Whosoever is born of God does not keep on doing sin.' That is the first consideration.

But let me also put this consideration to you: Take, for instance, the full implication of the statement made in verses 6 and 9. We must take the statement as a whole and observe exactly what is stated; and we must also bear in mind the other passages of Scripture and make sure that our exposition of one section of Scripture will never contradict another section.

So take the whole of verse 6 and see the position into which it lands you if you regard John as speaking about individual acts of sin. 'Whosoever abideth in him sinneth not; whosoever sinneth hath not seen him, neither known him.' Now if that means particular acts of sin, then John is saying, 'Whosoever abides in Him does not commit acts of sin;

whosoever commits acts of sin has not seen Him nor known Him.' And that means that a person who is guilty of individual acts of sin is not a Christian: 'he hath not seen him, neither known him.' So if you are conscious of having committed acts of sin, then according to this statement, you are not a Christian at all! That is the implication if we say that John here is referring to individual acts of sin.

But consider his words in the ninth verse: 'Whosoever is born of God doth not commit sin; for his seed remaineth in him: and he cannot sin, because he is born of God.' Now if John is referring to individual acts of sin, then he is saying that the man who is born of God, the man who is truly a Christian, does not commit any acts of sin at all; so that, again, if you do commit acts of sin you are not a Christian.

So it is important that we should take the whole statement. What happens generally in discussions about this matter is that people only want one half of the verse. They say, 'Doesn't John say, "Whosoever abideth in him sinneth not"? As long as you abide in Him, you don't commit acts of sin.' But they forget the second part, 'Whosoever sinneth hath not seen him, neither known him.' Then again, they quote the first part of verse 9: 'Whosoever is born of God does not commit sin.' 'There,' they say, 'it is quite plain,' but they forget the statement, 'for his seed remaineth in him: and he cannot sin, because he is born of God.' It seems to me that there, again, is a powerful consideration which must force us to the conclusion that John is not talking about individual acts of sin. He is talking about a state or habit, about people who keep on doing sin.

Or we can put it another way, like this: Take the positive statements of verses 7 and 8—'Little children, let no man deceive you: he that doeth righteousness is righteous, even as he is righteous. He that committeth sin is of the devil; for the devil sinneth from the beginning'; and then the tenth verse, 'In this the children of God are manifest, and the children of the devil: whosoever doeth not righteousness is not of God, neither he that loveth not his brother.' Now I think that the positive statements in those verses are again of vital importance, and we must observe very carefully the way in which the Apostle makes them. You would have imagined that he would have put the statement the other way round—'He that is righteous doeth righteousness,' but John does not put it like that. He says, 'He that doeth righteousness is righteous,' and I think his object is to impress upon our minds the point that what he really is con-

cerned about is our state or condition. He is really comparing people
who are righteous with those who are unrighteous, and obviously he
does that because he has started the chapter by talking about our being
children, referring to our sonship.

So what he is saying is that what really matters is what we *are*. The
man or woman who is righteous will show that by living a righteous life;
the one who is not righteous shows it by not living a righteous life. That
is where his reference to the devil is so significant—'He that committeth
sin is of the devil; for the devil sinneth from the beginning.' That is his
characteristic, his nature, his habit; that is his way of living. That is the
thing that is so true of the devil: he sins from the beginning; he *goes on
sinning*. 'And the man,' John says, 'who goes on sinning is, therefore,
the man who is proclaiming that he has the kind of nature that the devil
has. He does not have the new nature that the Christian has.'

I suggest to you, therefore, that those considerations taken together
surely should persuade us that the Apostle is not here considering individual acts of sin at all, because that would be a doctrine of sinless perfection. It would also prove that there was no such thing as a Christian
at all, because we have this clear statement that the Christian cannot
sin—if he means that. So what the Apostle is dealing with is the general
state and prevailing condition.

But perhaps we can reinforce this conclusion by putting certain
other considerations also before us. We must remember that the Apostle
here is speaking about *all* Christians. Now some of the people who
believe in sinless perfection tell us that the Apostle here is only talking
about *some* Christians. But at this point they become inconsistent,
because they forget the message of verse 6; they say he is only speaking
about some, but John is speaking about all Christians: 'Whosoever
abideth in him sinneth not.' If a man does not abide in Christ, he is not
a Christian at all; to be a Christian means to be abiding in Christ. Now
there are some who would have us believe that you can be a Christian
without abiding in Christ, but surely that denies the whole doctrine of
the rebirth. We are either in Christ or we are not, and if we are not in
Christ we are not Christians at all. 'If any man hath not the Spirit of
Christ, he is none of his' (Rom 8:9); if we have not been born of the Spirit
we are not Christians. You cannot be in Christ one day and out the next;
every Christian is in Christ and abides in Him. No, John is not only
speaking to certain Christians—he is speaking to all Christians.

Neither is he speaking of some ideal which is set before us or of some object to which we might attain; nor is he speaking only of the new nature that is in us. Let me remind you, there are some who would interpret this statement in that way; they say, 'Whosoever is born of God doth not commit sin,' and when you ask them what that means, they reply that John is talking about the new nature. They say that he is saying that the 'new man' in the Christian cannot sin. But John is not talking about the new man only—he is talking of Christians as they were and as they are; he is talking about us just as we are, as human personalities. He does not say that the new nature of the Christian cannot sin; he says, '*Whosoever is born of God*' cannot sin, and it is I, as a believer, who am born of God; it is the individual who is born again. My new nature is not born again. I have a new nature because I am born again, and the statement is about me and not the new nature. Indeed, there is nothing more dangerous than this, to divide up the personality like that, and it is also a very false piece of psychology just to say that these statements have reference only to the new nature.

So let me try to sum all this up. The Apostle is referring to the general tenor of life of Christian people, and in effect this is what he teaches: If you are truly born of God, if you are a child of God, if the seed of God has entered into you, if you are truly a partaker of the divine nature, then it is bound to affect your life in a profound sense. You will be unlike the man or woman who has not been born again. The characteristic of men and women in their natural state is that they are like the devil; and the characteristic of the evil nature is that they go on sinning, they dwell in sin. The whole atmosphere of that life is one of sin continuing.

But that is not any longer the case with those who have been born again and who have received the divine seed in their nature. They have been made different; they have been lifted out of the realm of sin and have been put into a new realm. They have been taken out of the kingdom of darkness and are now citizens of the kingdom of light; they are people who are walking in the light. That does not mean that they are sinless or perfect; no, but they are walking in the light and not in the darkness. The general condition and appointment of their life, the whole level of their existence, is one of righteousness; they are righteous people, holy people, not perfect people. They are saved, but the fact that they are saved does not mean that they are sinless and absolutely perfect. Yet they are essentially different from the men and women who are still sinners.

That, surely, is the teaching of the apostle at this point. It is the only way in which it can be interpreted which can avoid these contradictions and those false claims that inevitably result if we teach that the Apostle is referring to individual acts of sin. What he says is that he who 'abideth in him' does not keep on committing sin. He tells us that those who abide in Christ do righteousness; they do not go on being guilty of doing that which is wrong. The whole tone and level and attitude of their life has become entirely different, and it is in that sense that it is true to say of them that they literally cannot go on doing sin. Is that not true to experience? The seed of God abides in these people; the new nature that is in them makes it quite impossible.

Let me put it like this: It is the whole question of levels. Those who are not Christians, though they may be morally able to raise their heads, are essentially on a low level. What is the position of Christians? We can put it like this: Their lives are on a different level; they are up on that high level. Alas, they fall into sin occasionally, but they do not stay on the ground—they get back to the high level. They know that they have sinned; they hate sin and repent and confess their sin, and the blood of Jesus Christ again covers them, and back they go walking in the light. It does not mean that they are in a state of sinless perfection, but, thank God, it does mean they know that they are new men and women; they know there is a seed of righteousness in them; they cannot live as they lived before; they have been translated into the kingdom of God's dear Son.

But now when I say something like that, I am quite sure that there are those who want to raise certain objections. 'Are you not implying,' they ask, 'that there is imperfection in God's great plan of salvation? Aren't you there suggesting that God does not deliver us entirely from sin? Aren't you putting a limit on the power of the Lord? Surely,' they say, 'you cannot teach that, because it implies this imperfection!'

Well, my way of answering these objections is to ask some further questions. Why was it that God did not destroy Satan entirely and completely when our Lord was here on the earth? He could have done so; why didn't He? Why is Satan allowed to live and persist and continue? What is the answer to that question? Or let me ask another. Why is it that the moment any person believes on the Lord Jesus Christ as his or her personal Saviour and Redeemer he is not from then onwards entirely delivered from sin and made perfect? God could do it. There is no limit to His power; all things are possible with Him. I put it like that to show that merely to ask such questions is surely an irrelevance, and it is not for us to ask why God does not do this and that. What we must do is to face the facts of experience and the plain teaching of Scripture.

Is it not perfectly clear, therefore, that God in His own wisdom and eternal will has chosen that the plan of salvation shall work out in this way? Satan has been left. The power of sin is not immediately destroyed in us. God has chosen to do this work gradually. This word '*seed*' (v 9) is rather significant. Does that not simply mean God's method and plan in every realm? In the realm of nature you sow the seed, but it may be weeks and months and perhaps years before you get the full bloom. Why does God do it like that? My answer is, I do not know, but that is God's method; it is His way, and it seems to me that is what we are taught in the Scriptures. We are taught about being 'babes in Christ,' we are taught about growing and developing, we are taught about 'growing in grace.' John has already dealt with that when he said, 'Every man that hath this hope in him purifieth himself, even as he is pure' (v 3). It is a process, a development, and surely if we do not interpret a section like this in that way, then it means that we are denying what he has already told us in the first chapter—'If we say we have no sin, we deceive ourselves, and the truth is not in us' (v 8).

John's object in writing is 'that ye sin not. And if any man sin, we have an advocate with the Father . . .' (2:1). But why is that, if the Christian is immediately delivered and made perfect? No, this is a great mystery. It is not for us to understand, but we must face the facts. Is there anyone who would like to claim that he or she is perfect? Well, if you interpret this passage as referring to individual acts of sin, then if you are not perfect, you are not a Christian. No, we must avoid that; we must realise that experience, the experience of the greatest saints, denies this teaching of sinless perfection, and we see that that is not in accordance with the teaching of Scripture.

Lastly, this exhorts us to strive to purify and cleanse ourselves and to interpret Scripture in our daily lives. No, we do not just have to submit and resign ourselves in order to be made perfect; we are to understand the Scriptures and their doctrine. We are to see their implication and to implement them in our daily lives. Is this discouraging? To me it is the height of encouragement, for what I am told is that if I am a Christian at all, if I am a child of God and the divine seed is in me, then

God has started to work in me. He will go on, and He will bring it to perfection. But He does so by opening my mind and understanding; He reveals sin to me; He tells me to put these things into practise, to press on and to strive; and He gives the final assurance that if I confess my sin He is faithful and just to forgive my sins and to cleanse me from all unrighteousness (1:9). And experience confirms that. I cannot continue in sin. I cannot live that life of sin; my very new nature objects to it, and I rise out of it. I confess, I acknowledge my sin, I go back, and I strive to walk in the light.

Let us all examine ourselves. Do you find it possible to continue in sin, to keep doing sin? If you do not, it is because you have been born again; the seed of God remains in you, and you cannot go on doing sin because you are a child of God and an heir of eternal bliss. If, therefore, we say that we are the children of God, let us go on to prove it; let us demonstrate it by living that righteous life, even as the Son of God Himself lived it and exemplified it when he was here on earth. 'Every man that hath this hope in him purifieth himself, even as he is pure.'

7

FROM DEATH TO LIFE

In this the children of God are manifest, and the children of the devil: whosoever doeth not righteousness is not of God, neither he that loveth not his brother. For this is the message that ye heard from the beginning, that we should love one another. Not as Cain, who was of that wicked one, and slew his brother. And wherefore slew he him? Because his own works were evil, and his brother's righteous. Marvel not, my brethren, if the world hate you. We know that we have passed from death unto life, because we love the brethren. He that loveth not his brother abideth in death. Whosoever hateth his brother is a murderer: and ye know that no murderer hath eternal life abiding in him.

1 JOHN 3:10–15

IN THESE VERSES AND in those that follow, we find ourselves facing the next great appeal and exhortation which this Apostle addresses to these first Christians in terms of their wonderful position as children of God. The first point we saw was that if we are truly the children of God, then we must live a righteous life, and now here, starting at the end of the tenth verse, John takes up the second argument under this question of sonship. It is that as children of God we are not only to obey God's laws and live the righteous life, we are also to love one another. The very fact that we are children in and of itself presupposes this, but because we are so slow to realise that in practise, the Apostle provides us with certain arguments, and again his logic is surely quite irresistible. Reading these words we are left in the position that this is not a matter to be debated. It is quite inevitable; certain things lead inevitably to certain conclusions, and John is showing us how this question of loving one another as brothers and sisters in Christ is inevitably the outcome of our being children of God.

So we must consider carefully the argument which the apostle provides us. It is not enough merely to *say* that we are children of God; we must give proof of that fact, and John therefore puts it in this manner which is so characteristic of him. We have already seen, as we have worked our way through this epistle, that he almost invariably puts his truth in a double form. It is first and foremost an exhortation, and yet his exhortation is at the same time a test.

Take, for instance, this eleventh verse: 'This is the message that ye heard from the beginning, that we should love one another'; that is the exhortation, and yet he puts it in such a way that it becomes quite plain to us that this question of loving one another is not only a duty, it is also a test, for as he goes on to say, if we do not love one another, we are not children of God. He has already said this in verse 10: 'Whosoever doeth not righteousness is not of God, neither he that loveth not his brother.' The man who does not love his brother is not a child of God; it puts him out of court in exactly the same way as his failure to do righteousness puts him out. Here, then, once more we have this great principle which John goes on repeating chapter after chapter; what we are inevitably expresses itself in our lives. The great thing, therefore, that Christians have to concentrate upon is a full realisation of what they are.

Now we can never be tired of repeating this; the New Testament never calls upon us to do anything without first of all reminding us of who we are. That is its invariable method: doctrine—practise; the whole doctrinal position—the inevitable practical outlook. And John does exactly the same thing here. In other words, he does not ask people to love one another before he has reminded them of the fact that they are children of God. He is right, and therefore he can make his appeal, and that is the New Testament method. It comes to us and says, in effect, 'If you claim to be this, don't you see that it inevitably follows that you ought to behave like that.' There is a kind of inevitable logic in the argument as it is always presented. Mere claims, then, are of no value; it is, rather, our practise that ultimately proclaims what we are.

Now there can be no doubt at all but that John originally wrote this because of certain people in the early church—and there have been people like them ever since—who took the kind of position that nothing matters but our understanding of the truth. This is a position that very often leads to carelessness in practise. It is possible for people to be highly orthodox and yet to be loose in their living. That is what is called *antinomianism*—I am saved, and therefore what I do does not matter at all. And it is the same with this question of brotherly love. There are people who are sometimes so intent upon the cultivation of their own spiritual state that they are lacking in love. They are unconcerned about their brethren; they are so absorbed in their own moods and condition that they forget the practical, obvious duty of the Christian life.

Now John is here showing that that is something which is a self-contradiction; true Christians, being what they are, are people who of necessity must 'love one another.' 'This,' says John, 'is the message—you have heard it from the beginning: we are to love one another'; and you cannot read the New Testament, even in a cursory and superficial manner, without seeing that this is one of the great messages that is impressed upon us and repeated everywhere. If you read especially those tender passages in John's Gospel, from chapters 13 to 17, where our Lord addresses His followers just under the shadow of the cross and gives them His last message, you will find that this is His final appeal. This is the message that He keeps on repeating—'A new commandment I give unto you, that ye love one another' (John 13:34); 'By this shall all men know that ye are my disciples, if ye have love one to another' (v 35). John therefore has a right to say, 'This is the message that ye heard from the beginning,' because our Lord repeated and emphasised it.

Then if you read the various New Testament epistles you will find that it is everywhere. It does not matter who the writer is—they all repeat this message. They never forget the impression that was made upon their minds by those statements of our Lord, so they go on appealing for love. Think of 1 Corinthians 13 and various other notable passages. You must not be jealous and envious of one another, 'rendering evil for evil' (1 Pet 3:9). 'That is the old life,' they say, 'but you are in a new life; so you must love one another.' And this kind of exhortation goes on even beyond the New Testament canon. We know as a literal fact of history that there was nothing that so impressed the ancient world as the way in which Christians loved one another—this great process of demolishing 'the middle wall of partition' (Eph 2:14), the way in which Jews and Gentiles were one in Christ. They showed it in practise, in the way in which they were ready to sacrifice for one another, in the way they shared their goods with one another, and in the way they prayed for one another. These were the things that amazed the ancient world, and they were perhaps more productive in turning people to Christ than anything else. It was said, you remember, 'Behold, how these Christians love one another.' So we are entitled to say that in many ways this is the one great differentiating characteristic of Christian people.

Now we are concerned about this not from a theoretical standpoint, but from an intensely practical one. The argument works in two ways. If we are to experience the full blessing of this Christian salvation, we must love one another; we cannot experience this life without doing it. But I call attention to it not merely from the standpoint of our own personal enjoyment. There is another and greater reason for repeating this exhortation, which is that it is still the way in which the Christian church is going to affect and influence the world. The world in its darkness and blindness still expects something different from the Christian. It expects to see something in the Christian community which no one else can show; so to the extent that we fail to practise and exemplify this great virtue, the whole testimony and witness of the church will be correspondingly weak.

So I want to put this whole question to you in exactly the same way as John does in this section. First of all, he says that if we realise what we are as Christians we will do this. Then, secondly, he says that the proof that we are truly Christians is that we love one another. So let us consider now his first argument. The first thing that is of vital importance, says John, is that we should realise what it means to be a Christian. What is a Christian? What is happening to the Christian? What is it that makes Christians what they are? What is the ground or the basis on which this great superstructure of brotherly love can be erected?

Well, here John tells us three things about the Christian, and I pause at them because they are so wonderful. It does seem to me more and more that what accounts for most of our failures in Christian living is our failure to realise what we are. It is our failure to realise what God has done to us, what has happened to us. Our whole tendency always is to rush to practical applications before we have truly grasped what we are. I have already reminded you that the whole emphasis of the New Testament is put in that way. We must think less and less of doing and more and more of being. If we only are what we ought to be, then the doing will more or less look after itself; and John here reminds us in these wonderful verses of what we are as Christians and what has happened to us.

Let me note these three things. The first we find in verse 14—'We know that we have passed from death unto life, because we love the brethren.' What then is the Christian? The first thing we are told is that the Christian is someone who has passed from death unto life. What is it that makes Christians primarily different from those who are not Christians? Christians are not just those who go to a place of worship on a Sunday. No, according to the New Testament they are essentially different; they have 'passed from death unto life.'

Now, what does this great conception have to give us? Let me put it like this: According to the teaching of the New Testament everywhere, we all by nature are in a state of spiritual death. I am not only referring to those who are guilty of gross and violent and obvious sins. No, this is true of everybody born into this world. We are born in sin and 'shapen in iniquity'; by nature, by birth we are all 'the children of wrath.' We are born into the realm of death, and we exist in that realm as we are by nature. This is, of course, the result of the Fall; that is the result of man's sin at the beginning. When God made man He said to him, 'If you obey these laws of Mine, you will go on living; if you break them, then you will die.' Man broke God's law and sinned against Him, and he died; and the result, as Paul puts it in Romans 5, is that death reigns. The world has become a world of death, and we are born into a condition in which we are dead—dead spiritually—dead in trespasses and in sins. We are born into the realm of death, and we live in that atmosphere and condition of death.

'From death unto life'—what does this state of death mean? Let me summarise for you what the Bible tells us in various places about this state in which we are by nature. The first thing it means is that we do not know God, that we are outside the life of God and of His Son, Jesus Christ. At the end of His life our Lord said, 'This is life eternal, that they may know thee, the only true God, and Jesus Christ, whom thou hast sent' (John 17:3). So if that is life, then death is the exact opposite. It means not to know God, to be outside the life of God, to have no fellowship with Him, to receive nothing from Him, to be living a life entirely apart from Him.

And that is what the New Testament, and indeed the Bible everywhere, tells us about the state of men and women as they are by nature—they are without life, in death. They do not know God, they have no trafficking or business with Him, and their life is not centred upon Him. To them, God is just some terrible force or power or some philosophical category, or someone to be hated. They are living altogether apart from God. God does not enter into their calculations, and they do not experience anything of the joy that comes from an intimate knowledge of Him. They are, as Paul puts it, 'without God in the world' (Eph 2:12). That is the first thing that characterises this state of death.

But another characteristic, and one which follows of necessity from the first one, is that such people are entirely dead to spiritual things. 'We,' says John, 'have passed from death unto life.' 'You hath he quickened, who were dead in trespasses and sins,' said Paul in writing to the Ephesians (2:1). Those who are dead are dead to the value of their soul; they are quite oblivious of the importance of life in this world and its relationship to their eternal destiny. They do not know why God has given them the gift of life; they are unconcerned about these things. Their interest lies in eating and drinking and enjoying themselves, living for this life and world; and they do not realise that there is within them something which is imperishable. They do not realise that God has made them body, soul, and spirit. They forget the highest category of all; they are living only in the lower realm, utterly dead to spiritual things.

Furthermore, they are not aware of the nature of sin and of evil. They do not realise the terrible spiritual conflict that is going on in this life and world between God and Satan, the powers of heaven and of hell. When you talk to them about sin they laugh at you. They say, 'Surely nobody nowadays believes in sin! That is the old thing that people burdened themselves with a hundred years ago; it is just some kind of imagination that people conjure up out of the past.' They do not understand the nature of the spiritual conflict and the whole position in this world, through which they are rapidly moving to an ultimate end which they cannot avoid. They are spiritually dead; they live to the material and physical, to the seen and temporal, and the unseen and eternal are outside their ken and interest.

Of course the inevitable result of that is that they live a certain type of life, and the type of life that is lived by the person who is thus spiritually dead is perfectly described in Ephesians 2. They walk, says the Apostle there, according to 'the prince of the power of the air'; they are subject to 'the lusts of our flesh, fulfilling the desires of the flesh and of the mind' (vv 2-3). That is it. And is it not obvious in the world in which we find ourselves? Being dead to God and the life and the things of God, men and women live according to these lusts and desires, and it leads to all the miserable, wretched kind of life that you see depicted in the morning newspapers, in the proceedings in the courts, and in all the loudness and clamour and ugliness of life at this moment.

And the last thing we see about such a life is that it is a life which becomes more and more dead as you go on in it. 'The wages of sin is death' (Rom 6:23) and in that life of death, men and women go on dying. That is one of the most terrible things about it. Trace the life stories of those who never become Christians, and you will find a gradual degeneration and decline. In their earlier years, perhaps, they were interested in ideals and idealism, proposing to do certain things. But watch them as they go on. They gradually shed one thing after another; a kind of cirrhosis enters into the soul and imagination, and they go down and down and lose everything that is uplifting and ennobling. There is a kind of hardening process, dying in death, putrefying in a state of sin.

Now that, according to this description which is given here and everywhere else in the Bible, is the state of everybody born into the world by nature, a state of death. 'Thank God,' says the Apostle here, 'that is no longer our position.' To be a Christian means that you pass from death unto life and nothing less than that. Though we were dead in trespasses and in sins, we have been quickened. God in His mercy has looked upon us and by His Spirit has begun to deal with us. He has awakened and aroused us; He has put into us the principles of life, and we are passed from death into another realm altogether. That is what it means to be a Christian—not just deciding to live a better life than you lived before, not just establishing certain moral maxims and principles and making a great effort to keep them. No; it is a change in nature, a *translation*. These are the terms of the New Testament: we have been translated from the kingdom of darkness into the kingdom of His dear Son. Or, as Peter puts it, 'which in time past were not a people, but are now the people of God . . . who hath called you out of darkness into his marvelous light' (1 Pet 2:10-9). It is the same idea, and it is everywhere in the New Testament.

How, then, do we know that we are in this realm of light, the realm of life? Well, this means the exact opposite of everything I have been describing. The people who have passed from death unto life are those who can say that they know God. 'This is life eternal, that they may know thee, the only true God, and Jesus Christ whom thou hast sent' (John 17:3). Do you know God, my friend? This is life eternal; have you life? I am not asking whether you believe certain things; that is possible intellectually. Rather, I am asking, have you life, are you in the realm of life, do you know God, do you know the Lord Jesus Christ? Those who have life do know this, for this is life eternal. When you pray, do you know that you are speaking to God? Is it just a question of dropping on your knees and offering up a number of pious hopes and aspirations, or do you know that God is there? Is there something happening between you and God; are you in real communion with Him?

The only people who know that are those who have life within them. They are no longer dead in trespasses and sins; they have been quickened, born again. They have been given a new life, and they are aware of this life within them. They can say, 'I live; yet not I, but Christ liveth in me' (Gal 2:20). They are aware of certain things in which they were not interested before and to which they paid no attention. They are aware of their own spiritual being and nature; they begin to take an interest in spiritual things. Paul says that those who are Christians are those who '*mind* . . . the things of the Spirit' (Rom 8:5). They take an interest in them; whereas before they were interested only in this world and its affairs, they now become interested in the spiritual kingdom of God. They are concerned about the propagation of the gospel; they pray for the world and its people; they mind spiritual things.

Not only that; they are aware of the fact that there is indeed this principle of life in them. We saw that the others were dying and sinking in death; but these men and women who have been brought from death unto life are aware of growth and development. Life cannot remain static. Look at the flowers; look at the trees during the Spring. Do you not see everything growing and developing? Life must go on; it must develop if you have passed from death unto life. Are you growing in grace; are you developing in the Christian life? Are you further forward than you were a year ago? This life principle must manifest itself.

And perhaps the greatest test of all is that such people desire holiness; they delight in God and in His holy law, and their supreme ambition is to be living this new life with its wondrous principles. They know that God has come to them in His infinite love. I am loath to leave this verse, but we must, so I repeat its message once again: You, beloved Christians, have passed from death unto life; you have been taken out of that grave into which you were born. You are in a new realm; you are new men and women with new principles within you, and you are in a new realm altogether, and you are growing into the likeness of Christ. Do you think of yourself like that? When you think of yourself as a Christian, do you do it in that way? Or is it as just a member of a particular church or denomination, or that you are just a little bit better than somebody else who is a profligate sinner living in the gutters of this world? Do you think of yourself like this: I have passed from death unto life! What a glorious, wonderful thing it is to be a Christian!

But let me just mention the other two things which John tells us here. We have, in a sense, already dealt with the one in the tenth verse. 'In this the children of God are manifest, and the children of the devil: whosoever doeth not righteousness is not of God.' That is it—the second thing that is true of the Christians—that they are *of God*; they are children of God. Christians not only know God, they have received something of God's own nature; they have become 'partakers of the divine nature.' They are born again of the Spirit—that is to say, of God Himself. He has become kin to us, says Paul to the Ephesians; we are members of 'the household of God' (Eph 2:19). So Christians belong to the family of God, and of course they are bound to manifest something of the traits and characteristics of that family life.

Once again, can you fail to be impressed by the fact that you can never make yourself a Christian? You cannot produce the characteristics of God and His family; but if you are a Christian, you do so—you are of God, children of God. Our Lord put this clearly in a verse in the Sermon on the Mount: 'Be ye therefore perfect, even as your Father which is in heaven is perfect' (Matt 5:48). He was talking about the very theme that John is handling in this section: loving people, loving your enemies, doing good to them that hate you, blessing them that use you despitefully and malign you. Do not only love those who love you—anybody can do that; the whole test of your position is that you love your enemies. You who are of God, you who are children of God, you are to reproduce God in your lives.

That is what the Christian is. Christians are new men and women, not just people who are better than anybody else. They are essentially different, they are made on a new pattern, they have a new nature within them, they are of God. Therefore you can turn to them and say, 'Be like God; "Be ye therefore perfect, even as your Father which is in heaven is perfect."'

But let me just mention the third thing which John tells us in this section about the Christian. It is in verse 15: 'Whosoever hateth his brother is a murderer: and ye know that no murderer hath eternal life abiding in him.' But I want to put that in a positive form. The third characteristic of Christian men and women is that they have eternal life abiding in them. I am amazed at times at the fact that I, or anybody else who is a Christian, can remain so silent, can live such a poor, unworthy life. Was I not right when I said at the beginning that the whole trouble with us all is that we do not realise what we are? We insist on thinking about this Christian life as some great height which we have to climb. But before we are asked to do anything, we have been made something; we have eternal life abiding in us, otherwise we are not Christians at all.

John has given us the same idea in verse 9: 'Whosoever is born of God doth not commit sin; for his seed remaineth in him.' The life of the Christian is one which is mastered, governed, controlled by a new principle of life. God is working in the Christian. 'Work out your own salvation,' says Paul, 'for it is God which worketh in you both to will and to do of his good pleasure' (Phil 2:13). That is it—eternal life abiding in us. He has implanted it in us, He has put it into us; it is like a ferment working and developing and influencing, and it is irresistible. Ultimately it is producing a new man or woman, forming us according to the image and pattern of life; this principle of life abides in us and goes on. It is the kind of thing that one sees in the Spring. You notice this about the leaves that were on the trees in the winter. What is it that takes them away? People do not pull them off! No; the new leaf comes and pushes the old leaf off. It is the same here. It is what Thomas Chalmers called 'the expulsive power of the new affection'—eternal life abiding in us.

I cannot do better than put it in verses of Scripture: 'Now unto him that is able to do exceeding abundantly above all that we ask or think, *according to the power that worketh in us* . . .' (Eph 3:20). Or again:

'whom we preach, warning every man, and teaching every man in all wisdom; that we may present every man perfect in Christ Jesus; whereunto I also labour, striving according to his working, which worketh in me mightily' (Col 1:28-29).

So I put it in the form of a question again: are you aware of a mighty power working within you? Do you know there is a new life principle in you? Are you aware of a ferment in your own nature, something pushing you on, urging you forward, making you desire holiness, making you desire to be able to pray in a more worthy manner, longing to know Christ better? Are you aware of something disturbing you; has something been put into you that will not let you remain in that existence of death? We are not Christians unless we know something of that disturbance and turmoil and working within—eternal life abiding in us, going on, moving us and leading us on to other and greater things.

8

THE MARKS OF A CHRISTIAN

For this is the message that ye heard from the beginning, that we should love one another. Not as Cain, who was of that wicked one, and slew his brother. And wherefore slew he him? Because his own works were evil, and his brother's righteous. Marvel not, my brethren, if the world hate you. We know that we have passed from death unto life, because we love the brethren. He that loveth not his brother abideth in death. Whosoever hateth his brother is a murderer: and ye know that no murderer hath eternal life abiding in him.

1 JOHN 3:11–15

WE HAVE BEGUN OUR consideration of these verses, and we have seen that if we are to experience sonship and its benefit to the full, we must obey God's commandments, we must live as children of God. In a sense, John's argument is that as we are children of God we are therefore like the Lord Jesus Christ; and being like Him, we must live as He lived. He went through this world, which was so cruel to Him, without faltering and without failing because of 'the joy that was set before him' (Heb 12:2). It was that communion and that knowledge which enabled Him, and therefore He always obeyed God. His life was a life full of perfect obedience; as a son He rendered perfect obedience of God's holy will and law. And, secondly, the great characteristic which we see in Him is this quality of love. So John says, 'As you are like Him, you are to display and manifest these things in your daily lives; you are to keep the commandments.' That is the argument up to the middle of the tenth verse, and at the end of that verse he says, 'Whosoever doeth not righteousness is not of God, neither he that loveth not his brother.' He introduces there the theme that is now occupying our attention, and he proceeds to deal with it from verse 11 well on towards the end of this particular chapter.

Now the Apostle's method is one which is full of interest. It is his statement that if we are children of God and realise what that means, then we must of necessity be like the Lord Jesus Christ in our conduct. And the point that I want to make is that this is not so much an argument which John deduces, as a statement of something which is absolutely inevitable. John is not asking us here to deduce certain things from our position of sonship. He says, 'If you are God's children, then you must do so-and-so, and if you do not, you are not His children.' It is the inevitability that I wish to emphasise. This is his argument with regard to this question of loving one another, exactly as it was with regard to conduct. He says, 'Whosoever is born of God doth not commit sin; for his seed remaineth in him: and he cannot sin, because he is born of God' (v 9). We have already looked at that, and it is just the same with this question of sonship.

In other words, we must again point out that John puts his whole exhortation to us, that we should love one another, in terms of our position. It cannot be said too frequently that the New Testament never asks us to do anything without first of all reminding us of who we are. It does so because its doctrine is that we cannot do the things we are asked to do unless we are children of God. Therefore, let me remind you that the New Testament has no general indication to the world as to how it shall live. Its only message to the world is to repent and believe on the Lord Jesus Christ. But it has a great deal to say to the believer. It starts with our position and then it says, 'Because you are what you are, does it not inevitably follow that you must produce these works?'

We have considered the description that is given of us. There are three things: Christians are those who have 'passed from death unto life'; secondly, they are 'of God'; and lastly, they have eternal life abiding in them. 'Therefore,' says John, 'the vital question you have to ask yourself is this: are you such a person? Can you say that you have passed from death unto life? Do you know that you are of God? Do you know that there is eternal life abiding in you; is that your claim? That should be the claim of every Christian and nothing less. Now,' says John, 'there is, in a sense, no need for you to make a statement about it. What you are will demonstrate very clearly whether there is any substance in your claim or not. Your life will prove and demonstrate whether you really are a child of God or whether you are not.'

There is something glorious and yet terrible about the Christian position. We are all the time proclaiming what we are; the world in a sense is right when it tells us that it is more interested in our life than in our statements. Let us never forget that as Christian people, we are the whole time proclaiming what we are. We are bound to. It is inevitable—that is the whole argument at this point. Life and nature simply cannot be hidden. What we are, we are bound to express. It does not matter what our clothing or our disguise may be. Life or nature will show; or as it is sometimes put, 'breeding will out.' The blood that is in us will show itself; we cannot help it. We may even try to conceal it, but it will be there.

Our Lord Himself put this perfectly in the Sermon on the Mount when he said, 'Ye shall know them by their fruits. Do men gather grapes of thorns, or figs of thistles? Even so every good tree bringeth forth good fruit; but a corrupt tree bringeth forth evil fruit. A good tree cannot bring forth evil fruit, neither can a corrupt tree bring forth good fruit' (Matt 7:16-19). It is not a matter to be argued about; people may try to talk as Christians, but they show very clearly in their lives whether they are Christians or not. These are absolutes, and this is precisely the argument of the Apostle at this particular point.

Let us be quite clear about this—the doctrine is not that we make ourselves Christian by loving the brethren and so on. No, rather it is the other way round—that we prove we are Christians by loving the brethren. That is why it seems to me always to be so utterly fatuous and ridiculous to say that there is conflict between the doctrine of James and that of the Apostle Paul. That is the very thing that James said: 'Show me thy faith without thy works, and I will show thee my faith by my works . . . faith without works is dead' (Jas 2:18, 20). It is this very doctrine, the doctrine of this chapter, the doctrine, as we have seen, of the Sermon on the Mount, the doctrine to be found everywhere throughout the New Testament.

Let me put it like this: We have said that what we are and what we claim to be can be checked and proved by our conduct and by our behaviour. 'Very well,' says someone, 'if it is as inevitable as that, what is the point of John's exhorting these people to love the brethren?' There are many answers to that question. One is that while John wants to remind us of our nature and of the life within us, he also wants to encourage us to live life in conformity with that nature, and he also wants to increase our joy by stimulating us to produce still more fruit.

It is, if you like, similar to this: You see a tree bearing fruit, but if you dig round the roots and feed it, you will help to bring forth more fruit. John is just aiding and assisting and stimulating these people. It is exactly the same as when we exhort the child to behave himself and remind him that the whole dignity of the family is in his hands; it is a good thing to remind him what he is in order that he may represent the family in a still better manner.

As Christian people, we should make the claim that we have 'passed from death unto life' and that we are 'of God' and that we have 'eternal life abiding' in us. 'Now,' says John, 'there are absolute proofs of whether this claim of ours is true or not. Here is the first: if we want to know for certain that we are children of God, and therefore Christians, then here is the first test—we have become unlike the world.' That is the first argument in verse 12: 'Not as Cain.' John always starts with the negative—'Not as Cain, who was of that wicked one, and slew his brother. And wherefore slew he him? Because his own works were evil, and his brother's righteous.' Cain stands once and for ever in the Bible as the type of the worldly person, the person who is not of God, the unspiritual person; therefore everything that is true of the world, in contradistinction to the Christian, is to be seen in Cain.

What are the characteristics of this worldly type? The answer is that such people are the exact opposite of the Christian. The Christian, as we have seen, is of God, and what we are told about the worldly man here is that he is of the devil—'of that wicked one.'

The second thing we are told about him in verse 14 is that he 'abideth in death,' while the Christian has 'passed from death unto life' and has 'eternal life abiding in him.'

And the third thing, going along with the second, about this worldly man is that he does not have 'eternal life abiding in him'; that is the statement of verse 15. So there is a general description of the worldly person.

He is of the wicked one; he belongs to the devil, Satan. He is of the kingdom of darkness, under the tyranny and dominion and thraldom of the god of this world. That is the realm in which he lives; that is the person to whom he belongs. As we have seen, Christ said to such people, 'Ye are of your father the devil' (John 8:44). That is it. And they abide in death. They have not been quickened; the Holy Spirit has not given them life. They are still dead in trespasses and sins, and the awful thing is that they have no principle of eternal life abiding in them.

But let us work this out a little more in particular, for that is only a general description. What in particular do we find to be the characteristics of this life? They are seen clearly in the devil himself and in the kind of life that belongs to him. The great characteristic of such a life is that it is self-centred, a life of self-will and of selfishness. That is what produced the original fall of Satan. He was a perfect being created by God, so why did he fall? It was because he became self-centred. He was not content with spending his eternity in worshipping and glorifying God. He began to think of himself, and he began to feel that he was worthy of more attention. He wanted to live life in his own way and in selfishness, and that is the characteristic of this kind of life. It is an ugly, foul, hateful thing, but you see how it is the great thing in life today—the sheer selfishness of it all, people living for themselves.

And of course the other characteristic is that it is a life of hatred of God and a hatred of good. 'Wherefore,' asks John, referring to Cain and Abel, 'slew he him? Because his own works were evil, and his brother's righteous.' And that, also, is the second great characteristic of the devil. He hated God, he hated the power and the glory of God, and he turned against all that; and everyone who belongs to the devil does the same thing. The Apostle Paul says, 'The carnal mind is enmity against God: for it is not subject to the law of God, neither indeed can be' (Rom 8:7). 'Ah, but,' we say, 'surely that is not true of good people who are not Christians; there are so many nice people.' But however nice they may be, the carnal mind is enmity against God, it is of the devil, it is of the wicked one, and it manifests itself in some shape or form.

The results of these wrong attitudes are seen clearly in the case of Cain. This evil life of hatred of God and of His holy law, this self-centred, self-willed, selfish life, always is a perverted and an unnatural life, and you see what it did in Cain. Here are two brothers, Cain and Abel, and you see what sin does to a man. A brother should love a brother, but Cain became jealous of his brother, and he hated him to such an extent that he killed him. What made him do it? The two brothers took offerings to God, and God praised the offering of Abel, but He did not praise the offering of Cain, and that made Cain so angry with his brother that he killed him. This is the self-centred life. 'I am so desirous of praise—what is my brother when I am being hated!'

And that is the spirit that rules the world today. That is what produces the horrors of the law courts; that is what produces wars between nations. It is men and women in their self-centredness hating anyone who seems to have something that they have not. Murder is but the logical conclusion of all this. But this is the principle that is in all who are not Christians. Paul has given us a terrible description of this in writing to Titus, 'For we ourselves also were sometime [that is, before we became Christians] foolish, disobedient, deceived, serving divers lusts and pleasures, living in malice and envy, hateful, and hating one another' (3:3).

That is the life of the world. I need not press it; is it not true? Listen to people's conversations. You do not know them, but listen to them as they are talking about somebody else. Listen to the spite and the malice and the envy. Look at their eyes; there is murder in them. They may not actually commit murder, but the principle is there. I am not condemning such poor people; I am sorry for them. Look at the faces of the people who are always criticising somebody else. Look at them; they cannot see themselves. That is the tragedy. If only they saw the ugliness and the venom! Pray for them; have pity on them; they are of the devil, and they are living in malice, hating and hateful. What a terrible, horrible life that is.

Are we like that? It does not need any argument. It is impossible that we have the divine nature abiding in us if we are like that. What we are is proclaimed by what we do and how we behave, and the thing that is essentially and obviously true of Christians is that they are not like the world, 'not as Cain.' They do not have this hateful, horrid spirit in them of jealousy and envy and malice, hating and criticising. Oh, the ugliness! Thank God for the passing from death unto life, from such a world into the kingdom of light, the kingdom of love, the kingdom of God!

The second proof that we are Christians is that the world hates us. Verse 13 says, 'Marvel not, my brethren, if the world hate you.' Again, we do not need any proof; this is absolutely inevitable in view of the first proposition—it is bound to happen. As John puts it here, do not be surprised if the world hates you. It is not surprising in view of what we have been saying.

Let me put this as an historical fact. This is one of the great principles which we find in the Bible from the beginning. There are many people who are in difficulty about this verse. If this is true of you, then you have somehow failed to understand the first great essential divisions of the Bible. The difference between Cain and Abel was in Cain, not Abel. Cain (the world) hates Abel (the Christian). Look at Joseph and his brethren. Look at David and Saul; read the story of how King Saul treated David and tried to get rid of him—the jealousy, envy and malice. Look at the treatment that was meted out to the prophets, those men of God who were trying to save the nation. It is there everywhere.

Look at the supreme example of our Lord Himself. Here is the Son of God incarnate; here is the eternal life in the flesh. Look at the world sneering at Him, how they picked up stones to cast at Him, how they shouted, 'Crucify Him, away with Him!' The world crucified the very Son of God who had come to save it! 'Marvel not, my friends, if the world hate you.' The world does not hate you because you are hateful people; the case of Cain and Abel proves that. Cain did not hate his brother because there was something hateful about him. There was nothing to be hated in Abel, but Cain hated him in spite of that.

Neither does the world hate us because we are good. Let us be quite clear about that. The world does not hate *good* people; the world only hates *Christian* people; that is the subtle, vital distinction. If you are just a good person, the world, far from hating you, will admire you; it will cheer you. And what is true of the individual is true of the whole Church. The psychological explanation is quite simple. The world likes good people because it feels that they are a compliment to itself. So the world applauds them. But the world, we are told, hates Christians, not because they are hateful, not because they are good, not because they do good, but specifically because they are Christians, because they are of God, because they have Christ within them.

I think this does not need any demonstration. If anyone did good in this world, it was the Lord Jesus Christ; but as I have shown you, the world hated Him. It is not goodness—it is this specific thing that makes us Christian that does it. Now I believe that this is one of the most profound and thorough proofs of the new life within us that we can ever have. Our Lord put it like this: 'Think not that I am come to bring peace on earth: I came not to send peace, but a sword. For I am come to set a man at variance against his father, and the daughter against her mother, and the daughter-in-law against her mother-in-law. And a man's foes shall be they of his own household' (Matt 10:34-36). Our Lord has prophesied and predicted this very thing.

Now being good does not divide families. Here is something, and the only thing, that should upset the family relationship. The family will not hate you if you are good and do good. The family will not even hate you if you do wrong; it will forgive things in you that it would not forgive in anybody else—it always has a soft spot for the prodigal son. But become a Christian and live like the Lord Jesus Christ and 'a man's foes shall be they of his own household.' This is an amazing thing, but this is where the true perversion of sin begins to emerge.

What is the explanation? Well, I think it is quite simple if you read your Bible. To be born again means that you become essentially different from what you were, and you no longer belong to the family as you did before. I can best put this to you by way of an illustration. I knew a man and his wife, indeed I had the pleasure of taking the service when they got married—two highly respectable, moral people. At first they lived a happy married life together. Then the husband was converted and became a Christian. His entire life became different, especially when he began to know this great fondness for the things of God. He attended all the meetings of the church, weeknights as well as Sundays, and he lived for these. On one occasion when he went home from a meeting in the church, his wife (I repeat, a very good, respectable, nice woman, even a member of the church) received him with this greeting: 'I had sooner see you carried helplessly drunk into the house than see you perpetually coming home from these prayer meetings!' She would sooner see him helplessly drunk! Why? Because she had the feeling that he now belonged to someone else; Christ came even before her.[1]

Christ demands that. He said, 'If any man come to me, and hate not his father, and mother, and wife, and children, and brethren, and sisters, yea, and his own life also, he cannot be my disciple' (Luke 14:26). And, you see, the world thus pays tribute to the fact that we are born again and have become children of God. It realises that we have been taken out of the realm of the world and we are in a new family. We cannot enjoy the things it enjoys, and it is offended by this. It says, 'This thing has taken him from me, and I hate it.' Sin does not divide in that sense. The only thing that divides in the very depths is the gospel of Jesus Christ, the new life. But this divides absolutely, and soon a Cain murders even his own brother.

The world hates us because it does not understand us or the life we have. It does not share this life with us, and it feels we are condemning it, even though we may not say a word. But because we are so different, it feels condemned. It feels lost, and it hates the feeling of condemnation, so it hates us. That was why the world hated our Lord. He never did any wrong, He was without sin, He preached that perfect message, He went about doing good, and yet they snarled at Him, the Pharisees especially. This was because by just being what He was, He condemned them. He showed them that He belonged to a different order, a different realm. He was God in the flesh, and everyone who reproduces this will get the same response and reaction from the world. Make sure, my friends, that you are not just good. Make sure you are Christians.

The final proof of the fact that we are Christians is positive—we love the brethren. We are unlike the world, we are hated by it, but verse 14 tells us, 'We know that we have passed from death unto life, because we love the brethren.' It is the final proof, the glorious proof, the positive proof, something again which is quite inevitable; and what John is saying is that we now love Christians as Christians and because they are Christians. Is this not inevitable? Our new nature is one of love; that is what we have been given by the Holy Spirit—the fruit of the Spirit is love. So, having this new nature, there is the principle of life in us which was never there before. It is natural to love members of the family; the world has become unnatural in sin and does not do that, but this is natural, to love members of the family, to love those that are in it as we are.

But the real explanation is that we love the brethren because they are 'of God.' We see God in them, Christ in them; it is the expression of our love to God. As our Lord put it, they share the life of God, which being interpreted is this: if you love God like that, you are bound to love your neighbour as yourself; it is an expression of your love for God.

Let me put it practically, like this: Christians rejoice in the work of God in themselves, and they rejoice to see the same thing in others. So when we see people who have been born again, we want to praise God. We love them because they are in the hands of God, because they are God's workmanship, because we detect this principle of Christlikeness in them. We love them; we rejoice with them in that they also have what we ourselves have got.

But not only that—we love the brethren because we share the same interests; we have been brought out of darkness into light, separated from the world into this new kingdom. We are sharing and are interested in the same thing, in this glorious Word, in this praise of God. We have the same enjoyments as we go through this world of time. And back and beyond it all, we are facing the same destination. We are making for the same glory, we are travellers together through this weary pilgrimage, and we look forward to the glorious day that is coming. We know that our eternity is to be spent together there, beyond time, beyond death. There in the everlasting and eternal glory we are going to bask together in the sunshine of His wondrous peace and all His glory and His grace.

Is it not inevitable that we love one another? We are marching together to Zion; we are going together to the Promised Land. 'Brother clasps the hand of brother,' through being the same in nature, the same in outlook, the same in desires, the same in interests, having the same blessed hope, and seeing the same work in us all. It is not a matter of argument or of deduction; it is something that is absolutely inevitable—'We know that we have passed from death unto life, because we love the brethren.' There are certain people we now love whom we would not love if we were not Christians; as natural people we would not love them, but we now see them in a different way, and we love that in them—we love the brethren.

God grant that as we examine ourselves in the light of these things, we may be able to say together and individually, 'I know that I have passed from death unto life.'

9

LOVE IN ACTION

*Hereby perceive we the love of God, because he laid
down his life for us: and we ought to lay down our lives
for the brethren. But whoso hath this world's good, and
seeth his brother have need, and shutteth up his bowels of
compassion from him, how dwelleth the love of God in
him? My little children, let us not love in word, neither in
tongue; but in deed and in truth.*

1 JOHN 3:16–18

WE COME HERE, OBVIOUSLY, to the practical side and to the application of what John has already been telling us about 'lov[ing] the brethren.'
He has been talking about this love, but, wise teacher and pastor as he is,
now an old man who has had a long experience, he realises that you cannot just live these things as general statements, so he comes right down to
the practical level. He gives us illustrations in order that we may be perfectly clear in our minds as to what he means, and in order that we may
not be deceiving ourselves, because, as he goes on to tell us from verse 19
onwards, this is a matter which is of the most vital importance from the
standpoint of Christian experience. It affects our whole condition as we
go to God in prayer and our whole thought about ultimately meeting God
in the judgment. So it is intensely important from our own personal standpoint and well-being, as well as from the greater standpoint of the testimony and the witness of Christian people in a gainsaying world.

So John comes down to practicalities, and of course in doing this he
is doing something that is very characteristic of the New Testament,

indeed of the whole Bible. It always becomes practical, it never leaves us a loophole, and that is why we are always without excuse if we do not live this Christian life as we ought. It comes down to details, details which we feel at times to be almost ridiculous, but the Bible knows us so well and it recognises that nothing can be taken for granted. You have to come down to the smallest detail, and John gives us a perfect example of that in these three verses. It takes us from the heights where we have considered the death of Christ on the cross, to humdrum details—the matter of either giving or not giving to a brother in need. We are brought right down to that practical level, and John tells us why he does so.

Now as we address ourselves to the practical aspect of loving the brethren, there is one preliminary point which I feel constrained to make because I believe that there is often a good deal of confusion in people's minds with regard to this question of loving, and I think the confusion can be put most conveniently like this: There are many people who are troubled about this matter and who rather feel in the light of that great statement in verse 14—'we know that we have passed from death unto life, because we love the brethren'—that they are not Christians at all. They confess that they cannot honestly say that they like certain Christian people, and therefore they ask in the light of that text, 'Am I a Christian at all? If I am quite honest, I have to admit that I do not like certain people, and yet I am told that if I do not love the brethren, then I am not a Christian.'

Now I think that the point here is that we have to be careful to draw the distinction between loving and liking, and this is by no means an artificial distinction. It is a very vital one which I could illustrate at great length from the Bible itself. So let me put it at once like this: we are not called to *like* the brethren, but we are called and commanded to *love* them. Furthermore, I would assert that loving and liking are not degrees of the same thing but are essentially different. What is liking? What is it to like a person? Well, I would say that liking is something natural, something instinctive or elemental, something that is not the result of effort; you find yourself liking or not liking. In other words, liking is something physical and unintelligible.

Now do not misunderstand that. When I say that something is unintelligible, I mean that it does not happen as the result of the operation and the use of the intelligence. Liking is something that belongs to the animal part of life and nature. You find it in the animal world itself; there is something instinctive, something that is just an expression of nature, and it is not intelligent in the sense that it can give reasons for its like or dislike. Or, to put it further, the state of liking is one in which we are naturally interested in the person as such. It is certain qualities of that person, certain things about them which we like or dislike. In other words, liking does not penetrate to the central height of personality; it is an interest in superficial things, appearance, colour, temperament, behaviour or certain mannerisms. Indeed it is something still more physical—almost, we might say, some kind of physical emanation that goes from one to another. If you think of it in terms of the animal kingdom, I think you will see very clearly what I am trying to convey.

But loving is something entirely different. Loving is something which we must think of in terms of God. Now when I talk about love, I obviously do so in the way in which the Bible talks about it, and not in the way in which modern books and articles think about it, which is generally infatuation or some intense form of liking rather than true loving. We will agree, I am sure, that one of the real tragedies of the age in which we live is that this great word has become so debased and misused. I am talking about love, not about infatuation. Love is that which we must always think of in terms of God, because we are told that 'God is love' (1 John 4:8), and that is the thing about love, as John proceeds to tell us in these three verses.

Therefore, we can give this kind of preliminary definition: love is always highly intelligent; nature is not the greatest thing in love; the intellectual and intelligent aspects are indeed the most prominent. Love is never elemental or instinctive, because love is something that penetrates to the person; it goes beyond the superficial and the visible, the carnal and physical attraction, to something bigger and deeper. Indeed, it is an essential part of love that it goes out of its way to do that. Love overcomes obstacles and excuses; it sees beyond what it does not like and minimises it, in order to see the person who is at the back of it.

Now all this inevitably becomes a part of our definition of love, otherwise it would be impossible for God to love the sinner. We draw a distinction often, and we say God loves the sinner in spite of his sin. Love penetrates beyond the ugliness and the unattractiveness; it seeks out something. It is highly intelligent, it is thoughtful, and it is understanding. It is discriminating, and that is why I thus emphasised and stressed the intelligent aspect of love.

Therefore, we can arrive at a further definition: To love those whom we do not like means that we treat them as if we did like them—to choose to act kindly toward them even though we do not like them. Now I trust that will help those who are in difficulty about this matter. The Bible does not ask us to like the brethren, it asks us to love them, and that means, therefore, something like this: From the animal standpoint—and men and women have an animal part of their nature, let us never forget it—we may not like certain Christians. I mean by that, there is none of this instinctive, elemental attraction; they are not the people whom we naturally like; yet what we are told is that to love them means that we treat them exactly as if we did like them.

Now the men and women of the world do not do that; if they do not like people, they treat them accordingly and have nothing to do with them. But Christian love means that we look beyond that. We see the Christian in them, the brother or sister, and we even go beyond what we do not like, and we help that person. Love your brethren—that is the exhortation with which we are concerned.

Having dealt with that preliminary, practical point, let me now go on to call attention more directly to the points which John himself emphasises and stresses in these three verses. But before we consider them in detail, I must point out that it is generally agreed that in verse 16 the words 'of God' should not be there; so the verse should run: 'Hereby perceive we love' or 'Hereby know we love, because he laid down his life for us. . . .'

So then as we come to consider the verses, I shall vary the order in which John puts them, and my only reason for that is that I think it will enable us to end with the grand appeal. John's exhortation, in a sense, is that which is found in verse 18: 'My little children, let us not love in word, neither in tongue; but in deed and in truth.'

Now here we have first of all the danger of being theoretical only. I do not think we need stay long with this; we must all surely know this dangerous possibility in our own lives and experience. What an easy thing it is, not only in this matter of love, but in the whole question of practising and living the Christian life, how easy it is to be content only with thoughts and with feelings and with expressions of what we believe and feel, and to fail utterly and entirely to put it into practise. How easy it is to fall in love with loving instead of actually loving! How easy it is, when we are alone in our room, perhaps reading a wonderful book about love and about the actions of some great saint, how we seem to be thrilled and captivated and lifted up as it were into the heaven of heavens. We say,

'Thank God for this,' and then the next minute we go out and we are annoyed or bad-tempered or we fail in some simple elementary duty.

We all know about this. How easy it is to be in love with love; how easy it is to be content with elevating thoughts, to feel on Sunday, in church, that having contemplated the love of God in Christ, we can go back into the world and be absolutely different. Then something annoys us in the church porch or on the street and, almost before we have left the place, suddenly we go down and fail. Now that is what John is concerned about. 'My little children, let us not love in word, neither in tongue; but in deed and in truth.'

John is very concerned about this because, as he goes on to show, misbehavior here is a denial of God. There is a sense in which you cannot love in word and in thought only, as I am going to show you. So this is the danger which we must constantly keep in mind, and I wonder whether it would not be true to say that this is perhaps a greater danger with regard to the whole matter of love and love for one another than it is with regard to any other aspect of the Christian life and practise.

I suppose that this is so because 'the greatest of these is charity [love]' (1 Cor 13:13); love is, as it were, the ultimate, because of its very nature and delicacy. I do not know whether my experience has been yours, but I do find that this is one of the more difficult things—and not only for myself; I am referring especially to my experience with others. I think it is the simple, honest truth for me to say that the two most difficult men with whom I have ever had to cooperate were two men who were concerned about the question of pacifism. I remember one of these two brethren making a most impassioned statement with regard to it; he was one of those people who would die for their pacifist principles, and he was delivering an address on loving our enemies. After I had listened to him, I was constrained to point out in the discussion later on that some of us might have to remember that before we talk about loving our enemies, we may have to start with loving our brethren! It is possible for us to say and to talk a great deal about these things and yet to be jealous and envious of one another and to be harsh and critical of one another.

This is one of the paradoxes of love. I would say that people who emphasise love for others in their teaching are those who of all others must watch that they are not bitter in their spirit. They may be more bitter in their spirit than those who are not pacifists, because that is the central thing on which they concentrate. Now that is the point which John is making; the more we consider this question of love, the more careful have we to be that we are not just in love with an idea and utterly fail to put it into practise. I think that the ultimate explanation is probably that if we set ourselves up, especially as exemplars of this question of loving the brethren, then we can be sure that the devil will make a special target of us. It is in the greatest meeting that we have to be most careful; it is when we have been unusually drawn out in prayer, whether in private or in public, that we have to watch ourselves. It is when we talk about our faith to others, it is when we are nearest to God ourselves, that the devil will be most active. It was after the baptism and when the Holy Ghost descended upon Him in the Jordan in the form of a dove that our Lord was led into the wilderness to be tempted of the devil.

Let us, therefore, bear that general point in mind; but we must enforce it by some of the solemn warnings about it which are to be found in the New Testament. Let me mention some of them. Take, for instance, what our Lord says towards the end of the Sermon on the Mount. He talks about those people who will say, 'Lord, Lord, haven't we done this, that and the other because of our love for You?,' and He will say to them, 'I never knew you: depart from me, ye that work iniquity' (Matt 7:23). He goes on to say that there is no point in saying, 'Lord, Lord,' unless you do His commandments, and then He ends it all with the terrible picture of the two houses—the house built on the rock and the house built upon the sand. He portrays the man who hears our Lord's sayings and does them as being controlled by them and lifted up by them; he is the man who builds his house upon a rock, a house which stands in the storm and in the flood. But the other man, hearing these sayings of our Lord, says, 'It is marvellous, it is wonderful!' He is moved, but he does not do them; he is like the man who builds his house upon the sand. This is no good, and it does not stand in the storm. No; the doing, says our Lord, is absolutely vital and essential.

And then think of the same point as He makes it in the three pictures in Matthew 25. The first is that of the ten virgins, five of whom were wise and five foolish, the latter being the people who did not make sure and who did not take a supply of oil. Then take the parable of the talents and the man who hid his talent in the ground. He did not use it, he did not do what he was told to do. And then lastly comes the picture at the end—the great judgment of the sheep and the goats. Those who are compared to the goats are condemned—what was the matter with them? The trouble with them was that they had not put this supposed love of theirs into practise in the matter of helping one of the 'least of these my brethren.' 'I was in trouble and in prison,' said our Lord, 'and you did nothing for Me.' 'But,' they said, 'Master, when did we either see You in prison or without food or naked, and when did we fail to do these things?' Our Lord's reply is, 'Inasmuch as ye did it not to one of the least of these, ye did it not to me' (Matt 25:45). There, you see, is this same solemn warning about being content only with some vague, general feeling of love and with some precepts which we do not put into practise. Here, surely, is one of the greatest dangers concerning ourselves.

Now perhaps there are those who are in difficulty at this point because of a misunderstanding of the New Testament teaching with regard to this whole matter. The very Scriptures which I have been quoting seem to some to suggest an apparent contradiction. They say, 'We read our New Testament, and we really are confused, because it seems at one time to emphasise the spirit only, then the next time it is pressing the actions only. Which is it?' And they spend their whole time in oscillating between one and the other.

Let me illustrate what I mean. Take for instance 1 Corinthians 13. There the great emphasis is all the time upon the spirit—'Though I speak with the tongues of men and of angels, and have not charity, I am become as sounding brass, or a tinkling cymbal.' Here is the man who may give his body to be burned, and yet if he has not love, it is of no avail whatsoever. Here is a man constantly doing things, putting it into practise, giving his goods to the poor, a wonderful man in action, and yet we are told that this is utterly useless because his spirit and motive are wrong.

But then there is another side to this that seems to put all its emphasis upon the action. We saw in Matthew 7 that our Lord, in talking about the response to His sayings, spoke about the man who '*doeth them not*'; and that is the thing that condemns; it is the doing that matters. Consider also His parable about the two sons in Matthew 21, how the father went to one of his sons and said, 'Son, go work today in my vineyard. He answered and said, I will not; but afterward he repented, and went. And he came to the second, and said likewise. And he answered and said, I go, sir; and went not. Whether of them twain,' asks our Lord, 'did the will of his father? They say unto him, The first' (vv 28-31), and that is absolutely right. There again the emphasis is not on saying to your father, 'Yes, father, I will go and work in the vineyard.'

'The question is,' says our Lord, 'will you go *and work* in the vineyard'; the whole emphasis is on the doing.

And you remember, too, our Lord's solemn words just before the end as they are recorded in John 14:21-24. Let me pick out the salient words: 'He that hath my commandments, *and keepeth them*, he it is that loveth me; . . . if a man love me, he will keep my words. . . . He that loveth me not keepeth not my sayings.' 'That is the test,' says our Lord. It is not the people who spend hours before the cross or before a picture or who spend their time in some mystical state. Love must not be thought of in that way: 'He that keepeth my commandments, he it is that loveth me'—that is the way.

Well, what is the explanation of the apparent contradiction? It is to be found in the nature of love. I feel that all our troubles arise because of our loose and sentimental thoughts about love. The nature of love is surely shown us perfectly in Luke 7, in the story of what happened in the house of the Pharisee who invited our Lord in for a meal. When our Lord was seated at the table, an immoral woman came in and fell at his feet; weeping, she washed his feet with tears and wiped them with the hairs of her head and anointed them with ointment. And then you remember what the Pharisee thought, and the surprise of the other people. And what our Lord said to them all in effect was this: 'Simon, love is something which by its nature always expresses itself. Love is something which by its very nature has got to go into action. This woman loves Me, and she shows it by washing My feet and drying them and anointing them with ointment.' Love is always active; if there is no expression, there is no love.

There is another illustration of the same thing in our Lord's teaching in Matthew 18, where He talks about that servant who had been forgiven by his lord and then refused to forgive one of his own servants. Our Lord said, 'Unless you forgive, you will not be forgiven' (Matt 18:23-35).

'Well, doesn't that teach that we merit salvation?' asks someone. 'Doesn't that say that if I can forgive I shall be forgiven?' Nothing of the sort! What it teaches is that the men and women who truly believe and know that they are forgiven by God as the result of God's infinite grace are the people who have the love of God in their hearts, and that love is bound to show itself. Unforgiving people have not been forgiven themselves; those who are forgiven are so broken by it that they cannot but forgive others. They are children of God, and they act like God. In other words the New Testament does not merely exhort us to do things; it does not merely tell us to obey the rules. Rather, what the New Testament does is to ask us a question: 'Are you sure that the love of God is in you?' Or, as an exhortation it says, 'Make sure that the love of God is in you; and the way to know whether it is in you or not is this: if it is in you, you will love your brethren.'

Now this is the very nature of love. It must express itself; it is always active; and if our love does not do that, I say it is not true love. You see, the real trouble with the person who is seated there in his study reading beautiful poems or books about love and who feels that he is controlled by it and that he is a fine Christian is this: What is really happening to that person is that he is simply in love with himself, because he appreciates these elevating thoughts. He is loving himself because he thinks he is in love. He has turned in upon himself, and that is the very antithesis to love; love does not look at itself—it is absorbed in the object of its love.

However, we need not remain in mere theory. John brings us right down to the practical level. He gives us an abundant illustration in the case of this man who shuts up his 'bowels of compassion'—who has no pity. Here is a man who has received this world's goods; then he sees a brother in Christ who is in need, and he has no pity on him. He does not do anything about it, and he goes on as if he had not seen it. Now there is no need to argue; there is no love of God in that man, because he is thinking only of himself. 'He may be thinking beautiful thoughts about the love of God, but it is valueless,' says John. 'If he had the love of God in him, he would have to do something about it.'

But finally John puts it in the positive form of the royal pattern, the royal example: 'Hereby we know the love of God, *because he laid down his life for us.*' The great commentary on this is to be found in the second chapter of Paul's epistle to the Philippians. What was the characteristic of that perfect life? Here are headings. He saw our predicament, and He had compassion. There in the bosom of God, in eternity, from eternity to eternity, He looked down upon us, and He saw our tragedy, our predicament, our trouble, our sin and condemnation under the wrath of God. He saw it all, and He had compassion—that is the first thing.

Secondly, He did not think of Himself; He did not think of His rights. He did not say to Himself, 'I am the eternal Son of God, co-equal with the Father, co-eternal, sharing in all this splendour and absolute eternal glory.' 'He did not clutch at that,' said Paul—that is the meaning of He 'thought it not robbery to be equal.' He did not insist upon His rights;

He did not think of Himself because He was so concerned about us. He thought of us; He was interested in our good. He was concerned about our being delivered and our being saved, and because of that He laid aside the insignia and the signs of His eternal glory. He placed that limitation upon Himself. He was born and laid in a manger as a baby; He was misunderstood; He worked as a carpenter—the One by whom the whole world was made making simple little things; and He endured the contradiction of sinners. 'Yet,' said Paul, 'He went on humbling Himself, down, down. He went even to the death and the shame of the cross. He was not thinking about Himself, nor about His rights and His possessions. He thought of nothing but us and our need. He pitied our position, the hopelessness and the despair, so He laid down His life for us.'

That is the essence of love. It acts, it gives, it expresses itself; it cannot help itself—it *must*. May I suggest, in reverence, that it was because God is love that He created the world, something to love, in order to express this love because love must express itself. I may be wrong, I do not know, but it seems to me to be a necessity. True love is always active, and there we see it to perfection: God giving Himself for the evil, the perfect for the vile and the condemned.

'Let this mind be in you,' says the Apostle Paul (Phil 2:5). John puts it like this: 'Hereby we perceive the love of God, because he laid down his life for us: and we ought to lay down our lives for the brethren.' If the need should ever arise, there will be no hesitation if there is real love. If we love God, we will be ready to die for Him. The first Christians died by the thousands; they counted not their lives dear unto them, even unto death. They died for Him gladly, and they died for one another. If He did that for us and we say His love is in us, we shall do that for the brethren. And obviously if we are prepared to die for the brethren, we surely cannot refuse them when there is some little temporal, physical need. If we are called to the greater, surely the lesser, the smaller, the infinitesimal must be something that we do automatically.

'Herein we know love,' and this is how you get the whole of the doctrine of the Atonement in these few words: He laid down His life for us. Beloved friends, let us meditate upon these things; let us look at them; let us realise the nature of love and the implication of claiming that the love of God is in us. And then let us proceed to prove that we have it by loving one another, not in word, not in tongue, but in deed and in truth.

10

CONDEMNATION, CONFIDENCE AND ASSURANCE

And hereby we know that we are of the truth, and shall assure our hearts before him. For if our heart condemn us, God is greater than our heart, and knoweth all things. Beloved, if our heart condemn us not, then have we confidence toward God. And whatsoever we ask, we receive of him, because we keep his commandments, and do those things that are pleasing in his sight. And this is his commandment, That we should believe on the name of his Son Jesus Christ, and love one another, as he gave us commandment.

1 JOHN 3:19–23

THE WORD 'HEREBY' at the beginning of the nineteenth verse reminds us that the Apostle is here continuing the subject, the theme, with which he has been dealing in the preceding verses; he has not finished with the subject yet. He presses the vital importance of really loving the brethren wholly, and he does it in this particular way in these verses that we are now considering.

First of all, he reminds us again that the subject under consideration—loving the brethren—is the proof that we are 'of the truth.'

'Hereby,' he says, 'we know that we are of the truth,' so that once more we just hold on to that. It is a final proof of the fact that the truth of God is really in us and is abiding in us. But, and this is his main theme in this verse, this actual loving of the brethren is also, he says, of tremendous importance in a very practical sense, and that is from the standpoint of our own experience, and especially our experience of communion with God in prayer. John now comes right down and says something like this: 'If for no other reason, love the brethren were it merely for your own sake, for the sake of your own experience and especially for your experience in this matter of prayer.'

Here again we are reminded of something that is always, it seems to me, so plain in the Bible from beginning to end if we look at it with a spiritual eye. There are certain laws in the spiritual life, and they must be observed; sooner or later the truth will insist upon having its place in us. Sooner or later, as the Bible puts it, our sins will 'find us out,' however long we may go on apparently living a kind of double life, subscribing intellectually to a body of doctrine but failing in practise; sooner or later it will come home to us. We cannot play fast and loose, according to John's argument here, because a position will arise, and especially in this matter of prayer, when we shall find ourselves denied perhaps the greatest thing of all in our Christian experience.

That is the theme with which he deals in these verses—the place of prayer in the life of the Christian in this world. Nothing is more important than this in our worldly pilgrimage. Our Lord Himself put that once and forever in a memorable verse. He said that 'Men ought always to pray, and not to faint' (Luke 18:1); in other words, if you do not pray, you will faint. The thing that keeps one going in the Christian life is prayer—communion and fellowship with God; it is something which is absolutely essential. I would go further and say that the Christian life is really impossible without it. Read the Bible again with this in mind, and you will find that everywhere this is the thing that is emphasised. Look at the Psalms, for instance. How often does the psalmist tell us that his friends had let him down, his enemies were attacking him, and the people he had relied upon most of all had forsaken him, but he thanks God that the gate is still open. 'When my father and my mother forsake me, then the Lord will take me up' (Ps 27:10). As you listen to the men of God in their trouble, you hear that the one thing that keeps them going is their access to God in prayer. You find it in the Old Testament, and in the same way you see it in the New Testament. You see it in our Lord Himself; in the agony in the Garden of Gethsemane, He was praying to God, and Hebrews 5:7 is a comment on that. Read the biographies of God's people throughout the centuries, and you will find that this is something that stands out in an unmistakable manner. They were conscious of their dependence upon God, and they relied upon this access which they had to Him in prayer.

Now that is the matter with which John is dealing here, and his point is that we must be perfectly certain in our minds as to the conditions which control this whole question of prayer and access to God. So here he puts it in terms of this question of our loving the brethren, loving one another.

Let us take the matter in this way. The first question that John seems to raise is this: what is prayer? I wonder how often we stop to consider that, and yet it seems to me that it is a question which should always be uppermost in our minds. What exactly am I doing when I pray? Is it not our tendency to rush into prayer without considering what we are doing? Is it not our tendency to regard it as something automatic? Are we not always in danger of talking too easily about 'saying our prayers'?

There are many things which tend to encourage us to do that. Those who are more liturgical in their outlook have a habit of talking about 'saying a prayer,' and it seems to me that that is very different from the New Testament teaching on this whole subject. We do not 'say a prayer.' There is nothing automatic in it; indeed, I think a case should be made for saying that the most difficult thing of all is to pray. Prayer is not just a repetition of certain phrases, nor is it merely emitting certain desires or giving expression to certain beautiful thoughts. Prayer is not some process of auto-suggestion or of treating oneself by means of psychology, nor is it something that ought to make us feel better. It is not something, as I once remember hearing a man describe it, you do five minutes a day for your health's sake, so that you always feel better when you utter these beautiful thoughts. That is not the New Testament idea of prayer, nor that of the Old Testament.

What is prayer? Well, I cannot think of a better way of describing it than these two words which we have at the end of verse 19: 'Hereby we know that we are of the truth, and shall assure our hearts *before him.*' That is prayer; prayer is coming before Him. Now, we are always in the presence of God—'in him we live, and move, and have our being'

(Acts 17:28)—and we are always under His eye. But prayer is something still more special. Prayer is having a special audience and going immediately and directly to Him—'before him.' Prayer is something in which we turn our backs upon everything else, excluding everything else, while, for the time being, we find ourselves face to face with God alone. There is a sense in which one cannot expound it further; it is just that.

The first thing, then, that we have to realise always in this matter of prayer is that that is exactly and precisely what we do when we pray. Obviously, therefore, in a sense the most vital thing in prayer is just that realisation that we are before Him. And you will find that the saints have always talked a great deal about this. That is the difficulty; thoughts will keep on obtruding themselves, and our imaginations will wander all over the world, and certain ideas and proposals and wants and needs will intrude, but all that must be dismissed, and we must just start by realising that we are actually and literally in the presence of the living God. 'Before him'!

Now, says John, this whole question of brotherly love is of importance because of that. It is when you come there, when you are before Him, that you begin to realise the importance of what you are doing with the rest of your life and with the rest of your time. It is when you come there that you begin to see the relevance of this.

That is the very essence of prayer, so that always and at all times, whether alone or together in the house of God, that is the thing that should be uppermost and predominant. I think we would say less at times if we realised that. There would certainly be no room whatever for any cleverness or mere effort to try to utter beautiful thoughts and phrases; we would not be concerned about things like that. Realising His presence, we would be lost to all such things; we would be intent upon this communion and this fellowship with Him.

That, then, is the general idea, but let us come right down to the particular as John here expounds it. If that is what is meant by prayer, what are the conditions of true prayer, or what is essential to it? The matters that John expounds here are of vital importance. The first thing that is absolutely vital and essential to true prayer is freedom from a sense of condemnation. 'Hereby we know that we are of the truth, and shall assure our hearts'—or reassure, or persuade, our hearts—'before him. For if our heart condemn us . . .'—that is it! If your heart is condemning you, or if your heart is against you, there will be no true prayer. The first thing that is essential is a deliverance, a freedom, from a sense of condemnation.

I suppose there is nothing which really tests us so much as being in the position or the attitude of prayer. It is when we are truly praying before Him that we actually realise what we are. This is a much more thorough test than a talk or a discussion. We can be tested by talking to people about spiritual things, or as we discuss them together; even preaching an address or a sermon should be a means of testing. It is meant that all these things should test us, but I suggest they do not test us in the same way that prayer does. I suggest that prayer is a more thorough test also than thought or meditation. These too should test us, and we should spend time in thinking and meditating. Indeed, we go on to self-examination, but I say that prayer tests us in a way that even self-examination does not test us. Self-examination can be a very painful process as we look at the New Testament description of the Christian and examine ourselves in the light of this Word. But, I suggest, nothing makes us so see ourselves as we are as being there in prayer before Him.

This is so for this reason, that when we are in this attitude of prayer, we are no longer in control. The very fact that I get on my knees in prayer (and that is the value of kneeling), that very fact in and of itself is a submission. I am there submitting myself, I am abandoning myself. Now while I am talking, I am in control, and while I am discussing I am in control. Someone may be examining me, but I am still able to defend myself. When I am engaged in thought and meditation, I am still in control. But when I get on my knees in prayer, then, in a sense, I am doing nothing, I am submitting myself, I am abandoning myself before Him. It is He who is in control, it is He who is doing everything, and that is why prayer tests us in a way which nothing else can possibly do.

Now this is not theory. I am sure I am speaking to the experience of many. Is this not what happens when you truly pray? I do not mean when you repeat the Lord's Prayer or some mechanical prayer you have made for yourself. Nor do I mean when you rush and offer a number of petitions when you need something very desperately. I mean when you shut the door and are alone in your room, or wherever it is, and you kneel down and you realise that you are before Him.

Is this not what happens? Something within you begins to speak; it is what John here calls the 'heart.' It is the conscience, but it is something more than the conscience. The conscience begins to act and to speak, and this is what happens: We remember certain things we have done and said. We had forgotten them, we would never have reminded ourselves of them, but back they come. The angry expression, the unworthy thought, the unkind deed—as you are there alone with God, these things—the things you failed to do, the broken vows and pledges and so on—come back, and they condemn. We remember how when, perhaps, the last time we were like that alone with God we protested our love and we promised Him we would go out to serve Him, but we have not. We have forgotten our promise, and a voice within us says, 'You are a cad; you have no right to pray to God. Who are you to come into the presence of God?' We are made conscious of our utter unworthiness and our failure and our smallness and our foulness; our hearts condemn us. They bring up all these things against us, and there they say, 'Look at yourself—compare yourself to the saints—what right have you to ask God anything—what right have you to submit your petitions to God?' Do we not know about this?

But that is not all. There is something further, and that brings me to the twentieth verse: 'For if our heart condemn us, God is greater than our heart, and knoweth all things.' Now I suppose that there has been more controversy over the exact meaning of this verse than over many verses in the Bible. I am seriously tempted to give you a list of the great commentators of the centuries and to show you how they have taken different sides with regard to the interpretation of this verse; all equally good Christians, and yet they have taken different views. There are two main views which have been advocated. One view says that this is a great verse of comfort, and that what John is really saying is that if, there in the presence of God—before Him—your heart does condemn you, do not be downcast. It is all right, for God is greater than our heart. He knows our desires in spite of our failure in practise; all things are open unto Him; He knows everything, and with Him there is mercy and grace and compassion. Though your heart condemns you, God beholds and forgives you; be confident in your prayer. That is one view.

The other view is the exact opposite. 'If our heart condemn us,' if my own heart makes me feel and know I am a sinner and that I am a cad, if my own heart does that, how much more shall God, for God is greater than my heart and 'knoweth all things.' I do not know everything about myself; at that point there before Him, I know enough. Alas, I know more than I like to know, and I know that even then I do not know half the truth about myself and my sinful nature. There are secret faults of which I am unaware. God sees me in a way I do not see myself; He sees into the innermost recesses. If my heart condemns me, what must be my position in the sight of God?

Now I am not going to give a list of the great names, but let it suffice to say that two great Reformers took different sides; Luther took one side and John Calvin the other, and other men have been divided through the centuries. Bengel agreed with Luther, and Charles Simeon agreed with Calvin; so the division has been manifested from the beginning. Obviously, then, we cannot hope to decide this matter conclusively, and it seems to me that we must all decide this for ourselves, but for myself I cannot but take the view that this verse is not meant to comfort us, and my reasons for that will be given in the paragraphs to follow.

It seems to me that to interpret this verse as one of comfort is to contradict the whole purpose of the passage, which is to warn us, to exhort us. Read the whole passage on brotherly love again, and you will find that its whole purpose is to search us and to make us examine ourselves and to warn us against assuming glibly that all is well when it is not. It is to warn; and not only that, it seems to me that if we regard this as comfort, we are doing something which is very dangerous. We are silencing the voice of conscience and of the heart by talking about 'the love of God.' We are all very ready to do that; we are all very ready to avoid the point of conviction by saying, 'God loves me, and all is well.' To me that is a dangerous thing to do. Indeed, does it not lead directly to antinomianism? Is not the argument for antinomianism just that? The love of God covers me; therefore I can do anything I like. I say I am forgiven and all is well and I become slack about my conduct. To me that is surely the height of danger, and I argue that the ultimate proof is to be found again in the beginning of the nineteenth verse: 'Hereby we know that we are of the truth.' That is John's argument, which is a reference to what he has been saying. The way I am to reassure my heart when it does condemn me is not to say, 'God knows everything, and God therefore loves me.' No, it is something that I myself have been doing—'hereby,' by loving my brethren in deed and in truth and not merely in word and in thought. If you do that, says John, you will be able to reassure your heart.

So I put the argument like this: Here we are on our knees in prayer; we are 'before him,' and we are conscious of the presence of God. Our lives are being searched and examined as by some invisible searchlight, some X-ray; the eye of God is upon us, all these things are brought to the surface, and our hearts are condemning us. Well, while we are in that state we cannot pray, we are condemned; we do not know what to do with ourselves. Now we have to talk to ourselves; we must reassure these hearts of ours; we must persuade them that we have this access and that all is well.

So how do we do it? 'You do it like this,' says John; 'your heart is there reminding you of all these things, condemning you. You say to your heart, "It is all right; I admit that all that is absolutely true of me, and I bemoan and regret it. Yes, but I do find that I love the brethren. I find myself drawn out to them. I love their society and their company; I cannot look and see my brother or sister suffer without helping them. I find myself loving them, thus, in practise, and because I do that, I must be a child of God—I would not do it otherwise. The fact that I am thus loving the brethren is a proof that I have passed from death unto life. It means that I no longer belong to the world; it means I am a child of God. By nature I would not love such people, I would not be interested in them, I would not be concerned to help them, but I find the desire in me to do so and I am doing it; and though what you say against me is true, I say that this is a proof that I am a child of God. So I can reassure my heart, and that is why I do it."' Have you not known yourself having to do that kind of thing? Have you not known this argument with yourself there in the presence of God, and have you not had to find this confidence in terms of Scripture and to prove to yourself that you are a child of God and therefore can pray to Him?

The interesting point to me here is that John puts the argument in that particular way. Why does he not tell us, I wonder, that the way to reassure our hearts before Him is to think of the Cross and to remind ourselves of the death of our Lord for us? Now here, I think, we see the very depth and profundity of John's teaching. You see, he is concerned about people who are much too ready to fly to the Cross. John knows that the human heart is desperately wicked, and he knows the danger of men and women referring everything to the Cross, in order that they may have ease and peace of mind and conscience and then go on with their sin. We find the same thing exactly in Hebrews chapter 10, but this test of John's—I say it with reverence—is even stronger than the other. I have known a drunken man tell me that he is relying upon the Cross;

I have known people speak of the Cross with tears and then continue in their drunken, unworthy life. There is a terrible danger here; men and women may make intellectual assent to truth and then fail, but John's test makes that impossible.

If I am truly loving the brethren, that is not something intellectual; people who really do love and prove it in practise are not those who are merely giving intellectual assent; their lives are proof of the fact that they are born again. And if they are born again, they must be forgiven, and the Cross is covering them. John puts a more thoroughgoing test, the test not only of experience but of experience proving itself in practise— 'Hereby we know that we are of the truth because we love the brethren.' That is the first thing—we must be utterly and entirely free from a sense of condemnation.

Let me say a word on the second condition, which is *confidence* (v 21): 'Beloved, if our heart condemn us not, then have we confidence toward God.' Now that first stage of which we have been speaking is not enough in and of itself. It is negative because, as I have emphasised, we have to get rid of the sense of condemnation, because while we are unhappy about ourselves and our whole position we cannot pray with confidence; the sense of condemnation holds us down, and we cannot bring our petitions and our requests to God.

Again I put that to you in terms of your own experience. Have you not known what it is to have an experience like this? You suddenly find yourself in a crisis—perhaps you are ill, perhaps someone dear to you is ill, or you may be confronted by some critical position owing to something that has happened to you, and you are at the end of your tether. So you say, 'I will pray to God,' and you get on your knees, and the moment you do so comes this thought: 'But you have no right to pray; you are a cad, you have forgotten God, you only turn to God when you are in trouble.' So you somehow have no confidence in your prayer; you are uncertain. 'Now,' says John, 'you cannot pray truly and you cannot have fellowship unless you have confidence.' So you settle that first thing; you must get rid of the sense of condemnation, but then, having done that, you go on to this second step.

Now this matter of confidence is absolutely vital to true prevailing prayer. Let me remind you how the Scripture puts it. Have you noticed that word 'boldness' that is used in connection with prayer in the Scriptures? You often find it in the epistle to the Hebrews: 'Let us come boldly unto the throne of grace, that we may obtain mercy, and find grace to help in time of need' (Heb 4:16), or again, 'Having therefore, brethren, boldness to enter into the holiest by the blood of Jesus' (Heb 10:19), or, 'let us draw near with a true heart in full assurance of faith' (Heb 10:22). Or consider what Paul says in Ephesians 3: 'In whom we have boldness and access with confidence by the faith of him' (v 12). That is the way to pray; if our petitions are to be of any value, we must have boldness and assurance and confidence in our access.

How is this to be obtained? Well, it seems to me that we are here dealing with the answer, and it is still this question of sonship. The consciousness of our sonship and the assurance of our sonship is again something to be determined by our love of the brethren. It works like this: if I am truly loving the brethren, then I remember that I am a child of God. Therefore, when I am before God in prayer I argue like this: I must think of God now not as my Judge but as my Father. John goes on to remind us of that in the next chapter. I do not come to God, therefore, in a spirit of fear, because 'fear hath torment' (4:18). But I go rather in the spirit of love, and 'perfect love casteth out fear' (4:18). So, assured of my sonship, I know that God delights in me, that God indeed is much more ready to bless me than I am to ask to be blessed. I know He is ready and willing and waiting to grant me everything that is for my good; assured of my sonship, I know that 'all things work together for good to them that love God, to them who are the called according to his purpose' (Rom 8:28). In other words, the only thing that really can give me confidence in prayer before God is this utter, absolute assurance that I am a child of God, and I go as a child to my Father—that is the basis of confidence. So you see the same thing gives me confidence as has already, negatively, delivered me from a sense of condemnation.

But that brings me to the third and last condition, and that is what we must call *assurance*. 'Beloved, if our heart condemn us not, then have we confidence toward God. And whatsoever we ask, we receive of him, because we keep his commandments, and do those things that are pleasing in his sight.' He has already put it in terms of assuring our hearts before Him. Now this is the final statement. Over and above my confidence is my right of access; I must have assurance with regard to my petitions.

James puts it like this: 'If any of you lack wisdom, let him ask of God . . .' But notice this: 'But let him ask in faith, nothing wavering: for he that wavereth is like a wave of the sea driven with the wind and tossed. For let not that man think that he shall receive any thing of the Lord' (Jas 1:5–7). If you are uncertain, doubtful or hesitant and lacking assurance in your petition, you will not get your request, says James. Listen to the psalmist in Psalm 66:18: 'If I regard iniquity in my heart, the Lord will not hear me.' If I go to God with a double mind, holding on to my sin and knowing that I am living a wrong life, I will have no confidence in my prayer. 'God is greater than my heart and knoweth all things'; yes, if I am condemning myself and know I am wrong, how much more so must God.

Now I think that our Lord Himself has answered this question in certain teaching which you will find recorded in the Gospel according to St. John. He put it like this: 'If ye abide in me, and my words abide in you, ye shall ask what ye will, and it shall be done unto you' (John 15:7). Or again: 'I have chosen you, and ordained you, that ye should go forth and bear fruit, and that your fruit should remain; that whatsoever ye shall ask of the Father in my name, he may give it you' (John 15:16). Now John puts that like this: 'Whatsoever we ask, we receive of Him, because we go on keeping His commandments and we go on doing those things that are pleasing in His sight.'

'Does he mean,' asks someone, 'that as long as I live a good life, anything I may ask God in prayer I am certain and guaranteed to receive?' Oh, no! What it means is this: if I am keeping His commandments, if I am really doing His will, if I love God and my neighbour as myself, if I really am living the Christian life in that way, then I can be certain that my life is a life which is being controlled by the Holy Spirit, and therefore I know that any petitions and desires I may have, have been created within me by the Holy Spirit. And because my petitions and my desires are produced by the Holy Spirit, I can be certain that they will be answered. 'We know not what we should pray for as we ought: but the Spirit itself maketh intercession for us with groanings which cannot be uttered' (Rom 8:26). We do not always understand what we are saying, but 'He that searcheth the hearts knoweth what is the mind of the Spirit, because he maketh intercession for the saints according to the will of God' (Rom 8:27)—that is it.

In other words, if I live the life, keeping the commandments and loving my brethren, that is proof that I am being controlled by the Holy Spirit, and in that state the Holy Spirit is dictating my prayer to me, and that prayer will be answered. But if I am not living the life, then my petitions are probably arising from the flesh, from my own carnal nature, and I must not be surprised and disappointed if my requests are not answered and granted to me.

We see prayer perfectly again in the case of the Lord Jesus Christ Himself. Look at Him. He obeyed God's commandments perfectly, and He received the Holy Spirit without measure. He was led and guided of the Spirit. He had put aside His own eternal glory, and He came to live as man. Then He received the Spirit and was guided and led by the Spirit and thus He lived this life of prayer. Remember how He prayed, 'Father, if thou be willing, remove this cup from me: nevertheless, not my will, but thine, be done' (Luke 22:42).

His supreme object and desire was to do the will of His Father, and as long as that is our supreme will and desire, as long as we are concerned about that and are submitting to the leading of the Spirit, our requests will be granted as His requests were granted. God answered Him and granted His requests, and the nearer we approximate to Him, in the same way we can be certain that our requests will be granted. 'Whatsoever we ask, we receive of him, because we keep his commandments, and do those things that are pleasing in his sight. And this is his commandment, that we should believe on the name of his Son Jesus Christ, and love one another, as he gave us commandment' (v 23).

So there you are 'before him.' Have you confidence in your prayer? Do your prayers avail; have you assurance about them? These are the things that are necessary; you reassure your heart, you get rid of condemnation, you are confident as a child of God, and above it all you have the assurance which is given alone by the Holy Spirit, by His indwelling within you and by His life in your life and in your very petitions. What a glorious, wondrous thing this is—we come before Him, we have audience with the King, we speak to the living God.

11

THE HOLY SPIRIT

*And he that keepeth his commandments dwelleth in him,
and he in him. And hereby we know that he abideth in us,
by the Spirit which he hath given us.*

1 JOHN 3:24

IN THIS VERSE WE HAVE the first specific and explicit mention of the Holy Spirit in this particular passage. We have had in the second chapter an indirect reference to Him, where the Apostle has reminded us of the unction which we have from the Holy One and the anointing which we have received of Him. But here is the actual expression, the Spirit with a capital *S*. It is not a reference to some vague spirit that is in man, in the sense in which we often use the word when we speak of man's nature or temperament or character. It is a reference to the gift of the Holy Spirit, and here John is introducing a further proof of our sonship. The theme which has been occupying him right through this third chapter has been that we are the children of God. That, he says, is one of the most vital things which we can ever grasp in this life and in this world.

Now John, you remember, is writing to Christian people in the first century who were having a very difficult time, knowing persecution and suffering and misunderstanding. The world then was remarkably like the world today, and John sums it all up in this phrase: 'We know that we are of God, and the whole world lieth in wickedness' (5:19). That is his object—to help, to comfort and to encourage these Christian people who were living their Christian lives in such a difficult and gainsaying world. There are certain things, he says, which they must hold in their minds. The first is that they are in fellowship with God and are walking with Him. Then the second great theme is that of sonship, that we are the children of God. The Christian is nothing less than that—you cannot be a Christian without being a child of God. John holds up this glorious concept, you remember, in those three noble verses at the beginning of this chapter, with their almost incomparable statement of the Christian position.

But John, with his practical pastoral mind and intent, was most concerned that these people should show it. It is no use talking about being children of God unless we really are giving practical proof of that fact now. Unless we give that practical proof, we will not have the assurance—that is his theme. And let me remind you, he says, that there are certain things that we must never lose sight of in that connection. The first is, we must keep the commandments: 'He that doeth righteousness is righteous, even as he is righteous' (3:7). Then he comes on to the second great proof of our sonship—that is, our love for one another, love of the brethren: 'We know that we have passed from death unto life, because we love the brethren' (v 14).

And now here he tells us that there is still an additional proof of our sonship, and that is the reception of the Holy Spirit: 'Hereby we know that he abideth in us.' If we are children, it means that He is in us and we are in Him; and if you want proof of that fact, says John, here it is—'by the Spirit which he hath given us.' So, we are face to face with this great doctrine and truth concerning the Holy Spirit. It is to be found everywhere in the New Testament, and it is absolutely vital and essential to the true Christian position and to Christian experience. And here, in this one verse, John presents the doctrine to us in what seems to me to be a most interesting manner. He combines what we may call the objective and the subjective in one verse. He reminds us of the great fact, and yet he reminds us at the same time of the complement of the fact in personal experience.

It is to this that I am anxious to call your attention now, and I think that the best division of our subject is this: First of all we must consider the gift or the place of the Holy Spirit in the plan of salvation, and we look at that in this way: First, we must look at the fact, about which we can read in Acts 2. We are confronted there with a fact of which we must never lose sight. That is history, and if we do not realise that it is history, quite as much as the various other facts that are recorded in the Bible, then our whole position is wrong.

There in Jerusalem on that Day of Pentecost so long ago, this astounding and amazing thing happened. There that group of people met together in the upper room, and suddenly this tremendous thing happened. The Holy Ghost descended upon them as 'cloven tongues like as of fire' (Acts 2:3); the whole place was shaken, and these people were transformed. This wonderful thing happened to them, and they began to speak; they had the gift of speaking in other languages, so that the people, who had come together at Jerusalem for the feast of Pentecost from the various parts of the then inhabited and civilised world, all heard these men speaking in their own languages and telling about the wonderful works of God. That is just literal, actual history, and this day on which I am preaching to you[1] does insist upon our emphasising that fact. Of course, we do have to deal with it subjectively, but the big thing we must start with is this objective fact, this historical event that there in Jerusalem, literally and actually, the Holy Ghost came down upon the early church—the gift was given.

Now many authorities believe that this verse is a reference to that and that only, that it is a direct pointer to the Day of Pentecost at Jerusalem. Well, to say the very least, that is included, and that must always come first. We realise that from that moment onwards the Christian Church was constituted in a new sense and began to function as the Christian Church in a way which it had never done before, and we realise too that we today are just a continuation of that which began there so long ago. It is, I say, a fact—a mighty fact, one of the great turning points of history, one of the most significant events in the whole story of the human race.

That, then, is the fact, but let us also consider something of the meaning of this fact. We are still discussing the place of the Holy Spirit in the plan of salvation. What was the significance and the meaning of that which happened there on the Day of Pentecost? Here are some of the things.

That was the last step in the series of great acts or enactments in connection with the plan of salvation. Now, the glory of our position as Christians is that we do not so much believe a teaching as that we believe truths which result from events and happenings. Christianity is not a philosophy; it includes philosophy, but it is not just that. You are not a Christian in the sense that you may be a Platonist or an Aristotelian. It must not be thought of like that. We are saved not by believing a truth; we are saved because of what God has done for us.

Therefore this event on the Day of Pentecost at Jerusalem is an event that you must put into a certain series. You start way back in the Garden of Eden when man fell and when God spoke and gave a promise. Then you come on to all the history that is recorded in the Old Testament. The Flood, the call of Abraham, the isolation of that man and the turning of him into a nation—that is all God doing something, it is God acting. Then you go on right through the Old Testament history; the going down into Egypt, the going out of Egypt, the crossing of the Red Sea—all these are events, part of the great plan of salvation.

And when you turn to the New Testament, there are crucial facts which we must always hold on to. Consider the birth of Jesus Christ in Bethlehem—that fact is absolutely essential. He, the Son of God, was there born as a babe and placed in a manger; this is the Incarnation, that shattering, cataclysmic event when God came on earth in the form and in the likeness of human flesh. Then you go on and you see certain other crucial facts and events. They are all of vital importance, but some we obviously must single out.

You come especially to the Crucifixion. There is something which is basic to our salvation. In other words, as Christians we do not just speak about the love of God which forgives us. We say God's love forgives us because He did something there on the cross of Calvary. Without Calvary there is no forgiveness—an event, a fact, that which took place literally upon that hill, upon that tree—the Crucifixion. Then the next great fact is the Resurrection. He rose from the grave—He could not be held by it, and He literally came out of that tomb on the morning of the third day; it is a fact, it is history. Then the Ascension; He actually rose from amongst those disciples and went into Heaven. Again it is an event, a fact. And here, at Pentecost, we have what we may well call the last great step in the series of acts or enactments or events which made our salvation possible.

That is the way in which we must understand what happened there at Jerusalem on that day. It was God again doing something; it was an event; it was essential to our receiving this great salvation. That is the series into which it must go and to which it belongs.

The second thing is that the sending of the Holy Ghost thus upon the early church on the Day of Pentecost is the final proof of our Lord's claim for Himself. It is this because it proves that Jesus of Nazareth is in reality the only begotten Son of God. That was Peter's argument in the sermon which he preached to the people on that day; that is what he set out to prove. He said, 'You crucified Jesus of Nazareth. You did not realise who He was; you felt Him to be an imposter and a blasphemer, and that is why you put Him away. But there are certain things which prove that He is what He claimed to be, the Son of God. The Resurrection proved it. But,' says Peter, 'here is something further. You have looked at me and at my brethren and you have said, "These men are drunk and full of new wine. They are talking in languages we can understand, and they seem to be possessed." No, no,' says Peter, 'I will tell you what this is. This means that Jesus, whom you rejected, is, as He claimed to be, the Son of God. And when He died and arose from the grave and ascended into Heaven, God, according to His ancient promise, gave Him the gift of the Holy Ghost to give to His people; and He has given that gift, and that is what has happened to us. God has fulfilled His promise; He has given to Him the gift of the Holy Spirit, and He, Christ, has sent the Holy Spirit. And that proves that He must be the Son of God, the Christ, the Saviour of the world.'

So this event, this fact, is of crucial importance in this whole matter of salvation. That is—let me emphasise this again—the final, ultimate proof of the unique Deity and Sonship of the Lord Jesus Christ. It is there we have this final statement of the fact that He is the Son of the eternal Father. The Father gives Him the gift, and He passes it on to us; so the gift comes from the Father and the Son.

But let us also look at it like this: The gift of the Holy Ghost to the Church is also, then, the absolute proof of the sufficiency of the work of Christ and of its acceptance with God. The crucial question in a sense is whether that work of Christ on the cross is indeed sufficient. The problem is, how can God forgive sinful men? How can this Holy God conceivably or possibly forgive sin? The answer is, the death of Jesus Christ upon the cross; but is that sufficient? How can we know that God has accepted that work? How do we know that God has accepted the offer of Christ when He went into heaven and offered Himself and His own blood and said, 'Here is the sacrifice that I offer for sin'? What proof have we of the acceptance of it?

Again the Resurrection is partly the answer, but the New Testament constantly tells us that, in a sense, the ultimate proof of that action is the coming and the sending of the Holy Spirit, for that means that God the Father said to the Son, 'I accept Your work, it is sufficient; You have died for the redeemed, they are Your people. So I will give you My Spirit to give to them, and then they will know that they are Your people and My people. I forgive them freely, and here I will give proof of it.' Therefore, the event that took place on the Day of Pentecost at Jerusalem is of tremendous and vital importance in giving us this assurance of the acceptance and the sufficiency of the work of Jesus Christ for us.

I can put it still further like this: The coming of the Holy Spirit is the means whereby salvation is mediated to us. Do you remember what our Lord said to His disciples just before His death? They were crestfallen and unhappy as He was talking to them increasingly of His departure and about His going away. He said to them, 'It is expedient for you that I go away'—it is a good thing, it is beneficial to you that I go away—'for if I go not away, the Comforter will not come unto you; but if I depart, I will send him unto you' (John 16:7).

Now that means this, and I say it with reverence—do we always realise, Christian people, that you and I who have never seen the Lord Jesus Christ with the eye of flesh are in a much more advantageous position than were His own disciples who looked into His face? Are we not often guilty, in our folly and misunderstanding of the Scriptures, of saying, 'Oh, if only I had been alive when He was here, if only I could have seen Him with my eyes, then I would have believed in a way that I do not now.' But that is utterly unscriptural. He said, 'It is expedient for you that I go away'—by which he meant that it is only because He has gone away, because He has done His work and has sent the Holy Spirit to dwell within us, that the result of His work really becomes part of our life and experience. It is through the work of the Holy Spirit that the perfect, finished work of Christ upon the cross and His mediation is transmitted to us and enters our lives; so it means that.

And then the last thing I would say about it in this connection is that, of course, the sending of the Holy Spirit upon the Church on the Day of Pentecost was the ultimate fulfilment of the promise of God. Can you not hear the thrill in the voice of Peter as he speaks those words: 'This is that which was spoken by the prophet Joel'? It is one of God's ancient promises, one of the most glorious of all. God has said that He is going to pour out His Spirit; the young men shall dream dreams, and even the unenlightened will understand truth. It will no longer be only a certain few, select people who will know the truth. The common people shall understand. 'I will pour out my Spirit,' and the great salvation will come to all and sundry. And here God has fulfilled the old promises; He has sent and has given the gift of the Holy Spirit.

We have, then, looked briefly at the gift of the Holy Spirit in the plan of salvation. That is its place, and that is the real way to look at it, so that as Christian people we must never be guilty of stopping either at Calvary or at the Resurrection. I put it like that because I often fear that we do that. We give a place to the cross, and to the Resurrection, but we do not always come to the Day of Pentecost, and that shows that we have not known the relevance of this. This is the ultimate step, the last step in the great series and one which is essential and vital to our salvation.

So, having looked at it objectively, let us become a little more subjective. My second principle is that the Christian is one who has received the gift of the Holy Ghost. 'Hereby we know that he abideth in us, by the Spirit which he hath given us.' What is a Christian? I am never tired of putting forward that question, because I think that of all the things that are misunderstood in the world today this is the one that is most misunderstood. What is a Christian—a good person, a moral person, a formal member of a church, one who pays an occasional visit to God's house? Is that a Christian? Shame upon us if ever we have given that impression! No, a Christian is pneumatic, spiritual. Is that not the statement of the New Testament everywhere—a *spiritual* man or woman?

A spiritual person is one who has received the Holy Spirit—that is New Testament terminology. Christians are people who are altogether different from those who are not Christians. They are not just a little bit better, or people who do certain things. No, they themselves are different; they are spiritual. 'We have received,' says Paul, 'not the spirit of the world, but the Spirit which is of God; that we may know the things that are freely given to us of God. . . . He that is spiritual judgeth all things' (1 Cor 2:12, 15); but not the natural man—that is the difference, naturally and spiritually.

Now, there are some people who say that you become a Christian and then later you receive the gift of the Holy Spirit. But you cannot be a Christian unless you have received the gift of the Holy Spirit. It is that, in a sense, that makes you a Christian. It means this new birth; it means being born again; it means, to use the language of Peter, to be 'partakers of the divine nature' (2 Pet 1:4). It means, to use the language of our blessed Lord Himself, that God is *abiding* in us. 'He that keepeth his commandments,' says John, 'dwelleth in him, and he in him.' And if you want the best commentary on that, read for yourselves John 14, those great words of our Lord: 'I will not leave you comfortless: I will come to you' (v 18); or, as some would translate it, 'I will not leave you orphans, I will come again.' 'I will come through the gift of the Holy Spirit; I will send another Comforter, and the result of His coming will be that He will dwell in you—I and the Father will dwell in you.'

These are the amazing words describing the mystical union of the believer and Christ and God, and here it all is in a phrase in 1 John 3. Surely if all of us who claim the name of Christian only realised that and what it means to be a Christian, not only would the whole church on earth be transformed, but I think the world would be shaken. If we but realised that this is the Christian, the spiritual man or woman with the Holy Spirit, with God dwelling in us, if we but realised that, I think our world would rather look at us and say, 'What is the matter with these people—what is this?' And we would be able to give the same answer as Peter gave way back so long ago in Jerusalem: 'This is that which was spoken by the prophet Joel.' We have received the Holy Spirit, and we are therefore what we are. That is the Christian.

Let me come to my last principle. How may we know that we have the Spirit? That is obviously the vital question. That is the basis of my assurance; that is how I know that He dwells in me; that is the practical question. How do we know that the Holy Spirit has come to us, that we have received the gift of the Holy Ghost? I shall simply suggest a number of headings by way of an answer.

Here are the things that are taught by the New Testament. Those who have received the Holy Spirit are aware of a power dealing with them and working in them. 'Work out your own salvation with fear and trembling: for it is God which worketh in you both to will and to do of his good pleasure' (Phil 2:12-13). A disturbance, something, someone interfering in our lives. We are going along, and suddenly we are arrested and pulled up, and we find ourselves different. That is the beginning; that is what always happens when the Holy Ghost begins to work in a human being. There is a disturbance, an interruption to the normal ordinary tenor of life. There is something different, an awareness of being dealt with—I cannot put it better; that is the essence of the Holy Spirit dealing with us.

Then it leads to this, that we find ourselves beginning to take an interest in these things, in a spiritual sense. Paul says that they who are carnal 'mind the things of the flesh,' but the Christian, he says, is the one who minds 'the things of the Spirit' (Rom 8:5)—he is interested in them. Non-Christians say that the Bible is a terribly boring book, and when you talk about spiritual things, they do not know what you are talking about. I am not criticising them; I rather pity them. They just do not understand, and the whole thing is boring and has no relevance to life.

If you feel like that about these things, you have not received the Spirit, because when people receive the Spirit, they find themselves curiously interested in these things. They are amazed at the fact that they could ever have lived without them. This, they say, is the most wonderful thing of all. They are no longer interested in the mechanics of religion. You can be interested in that, in the work of the church or in your work in the church, without being interested in the Spirit. That is not what I am talking about; those who have received the Spirit are spiritually interested in truth.

And that leads to the next thing, which is the conviction of sin. They are men and women who see themselves unworthy and guilty before God. They begin to see that their nature is wrong, and they hate it. That is the Spirit—He leads them to believe on the Lord Jesus Christ and to understand the truth. John has already told us: 'This is the commandment, that we should believe on the name of his Son Jesus Christ' (v 23). Only the Holy Spirit can enable us to see Jesus Christ as the Son of God and the Saviour of our souls. You will dismiss Him entirely until the Spirit enlightens you; but once He works, you begin to see and understand the truth. Then you are aware of a new life within you; you are conscious of a new being, and a new nature. 'I live; yet not I, but Christ liveth in me' (Gal 2:20). I cannot understand myself; there is 'the old man' still—the man that I do understand, but there is someone else, because I have become a new creature.

And then there are the fruits of the Spirit. The fruit of the Spirit is love, joy, peace, love of the brethren. Once the Spirit comes in, the fruits of the Spirit begin to show themselves—hatred of sin, desires for holiness. We love God's commandments, as John says in chapter 5: 'His commandments are not grievous.' Christians begin to love them, and they want to show the fruit of the Spirit in that way.

This is that 'Spirit of adoption, whereby we cry, Abba, Father' (Rom 8:15), and we know what the Scripture means when it says, 'the Spirit itself beareth witness with our spirit, that we are the children of God'

(Rom 8:16). Those are some of the things that you recognise. It means holiness is in you. Do you recognise all of these things? These are the proofs of the indwelling of the Holy Spirit. There were also those gifts which God gave on the Day of Pentecost; they may still be given. Yes, I may, in His sovereign will, still get these. The gifts of the Spirit also are a proof of the indwelling of the Spirit.

Take, then, all those things together and there are the proofs of the fact that we have received the Holy Ghost. Oh, the marvel and the wonder of such a gift, the free gift. In spite of our sin and shame, in spite of our unworthiness and all that is so true of us, this amazing God has given us His own Spirit, and with the Spirit He comes to dwell and to abide in us. What a wondrous gift! What an amazing gift that God, the eternal, should come and dwell in us and enable us to dwell in Him. 'Hereby we know that he abideth in us, by the Spirit which he hath given us.'

NOTES

CHAPTER ONE: CHILDREN OF GOD

1 Cf. the earlier Vols. 1, 2 in this series, *Fellowship with God* and *Walking with God* (Crossway Books, 1992, 1993).

CHAPTER THREE: HOLINESS

1 This sermon was preached in the season of Lent, on 3rd April, 1949.

2 Cf. *Fellowship with God,* Vol. 1 of this series (Crossway Books, 1992).

CHAPTER FOUR: THE SINLESS SAVIOUR

1 Cf. *Fellowship with God,* Vol. 1 of this series (Crossway Books, 1992).

2 This sermon was preached on Palm Sunday, 1949.

3 See *Walking with God,* Vol. 2 of this series (Crossway Books, 1993).

4 "There Is a Green Hill Far Away," by Cecil Frances Alexander.

CHAPTER FIVE: VICTORY OVER THE DEVIL

1 This sermon was preached on Easter Sunday, 1949.

CHAPTER EIGHT: THE MARKS OF A CHRISTIAN

1 Readers will be glad to know that the wife herself became a Christian soon afterwards. Ed.

CHAPTER ELEVEN: THE HOLY SPIRIT

1 This sermon was preached on Whit Sunday, 1949.

VOLUME FOUR

The Love
of
God

ACKNOWLEDGMENTS

AS WITH PREVIOUS BOOKS in this series, the editing work on these sermons has been carried out by Christopher Catherwood, the Doctor's eldest grandchild and Editorial Director of Crossway Books in England. Elizabeth Catherwood, the Doctor's elder daughter, has gone through them carefully, to make sure that all the editing has been faithful to the Doctor himself. To her, as always, go the very warmest thanks for all the work that she has done. Full thanks are also due to Alison Walley, for preparing the transcript for publication, and not least because of her wonderful ability to read the handwriting of the Doctor's descendants, the editor's not being dissimilar in legibility to the Doctor's own . . .

Renewed thanks must go to the team at Crossway USA. Once again, prime thanks are due to Lane Dennis for his commitment to the Doctor's work. Some have spoken of a renaissance of interest in the books of Martyn Lloyd-Jones in recent years, and there is no doubt that the work of Crossway Books, under the leadership of Lane Dennis, has been a major factor in that growth. Warm thanks are also due to Fred Rudy, Len Goss, and Ted Griffin. Backroom editors like Ted do not always get the credit they deserve, and so it is a pleasure to give it here. Crossway USA shares the love for God's Word that the Doctor had, and it shows.

NOTE TO READERS

WHEN WE CAME TO editing this volume, we discovered that one of the transcripts early on in the series on 1 John 4 was missing, and a search among the duplicate set in Scotland confirmed this. However, we decided that the Doctor's sermons on this chapter remain so powerful that we should go ahead and publish them anyway. Dr. Lloyd-Jones often recapitulated his previous sermon at the beginning of the next, and so the reader can in fact partly discover what he said in the missing sermon in this way.

As readers of volume 2 of Iain Murray's biography of Dr. Lloyd-Jones will remember, the Doctor had some major spiritual experiences during 1949. One can get a flavour of this by the sermons in this book, preached mainly just after the events which Iain Murray describes. It is easy to see why Jim Packer felt that the Doctor at this time was on a 'plateau of supreme excellence.' As all the sermons were faithfully transcribed at the time, we can enjoy them now, and can be as challenged and encouraged to hear of the love of God for His people as were those in the congregation of Westminster Chapel to whom they were preached.

1

Test the Spirits

Beloved, believe not every spirit, but try the spirits whether they are of God: because many false prophets are gone out into the world.

1 JOHN 4:1

AS WE BEGIN OUR consideration of the fourth chapter of this first epistle of John, perhaps it would be helpful if I would remind you very briefly of our understanding in general of the teaching of this epistle. When we began to consider it,[1] I reminded you that many have analysed this epistle, and that it is almost impossible to find any two who agree in their analysis. So we decided that we had as good a right as anybody else to offer our own analysis of the epistle, and we have been looking at it in this way.

The great theme of the Apostle is the possibility of having joy in this world, a joy that comes from God, in spite of circumstances and conditions. John has made that perfectly plain, it seems to me, in the fourth verse of the first chapter: 'And these things write we unto you, that your joy may be full.' That is what he is concerned about, and that is the extraordinary thing which he unfolds to these people. They were Christians in a very difficult and gainsaying world, and yet John, now an old man, writes to them to say that although 'the whole world lieth in wickedness,' nevertheless it is possible for them to have a joy, a fullness of joy, in spite of it all.

And we have been suggesting that he says that there are two great and main things which as Christians we have to remember and hold on to, come what may. The first is that we have fellowship with God; that the main effect of the coming of the Lord Jesus Christ into this world, and of His work, is that we who believe on Him and belong to Him and are in Him have fellowship with God; we are walking with God. The second great thing is that we, as children of God, not only have fellowship with Him, but we are in that relationship which makes us children.

Now this question of fellowship is the one which is dealt with in chapters 1, 2 and 3 and until verse 6 of the fourth chapter. John has been dealing with the condition and position of being children—that we are sons of God. 'Those two things,' says John in effect, and he keeps on repeating it, 'you must never lose hold of: first, you are walking with God, and your fellowship is with the Father and with His Son Jesus Christ, and, second, you are the children of God.' But, you will remember that he, as a very practical and wise teacher, is not content merely to make general statements like that. He has his own experience, and he knows perfectly well from that, leave alone from his handling of other Christian people, that there are certain things in this life and world which always tend to militate against our enjoyment of this joy. There are things which would always try to break our fellowship with God, and there are things which will tend at any rate to make us less conscious of the fact that we are the children of God. So he has been dealing at length with these things.

Now it is interesting to observe that these things which militate against fellowship are exactly the same things which militate against sonship, and we have been dealing with them.[2] There are three main things which we have to watch. The first is that we must keep the commandments; if we want to enjoy fellowship with God we must obey Him, we must keep His commandments. You will find that John deals with that at the beginning of the second chapter. The second thing is that we must love one another; we must 'love the brethren.' And the third thing is that we must beware of false teaching. There are antichrists, there are enemies of the faith, and we must be absolutely clear and certain as to what we believe, and especially about our belief about the Lord Jesus Christ himself.

Then at the beginning of chapter 3, John comes to the second great point, that we are children of God. 'Behold, what manner of love the Father hath bestowed upon us, that we should be called the sons of

God'; and he tells us about that. He then goes on to say in effect, 'If you want to live in full enjoyment of that sonship, there are certain things you must beware of. You must obey the law—"whosoever committeth sin transgresseth also the law"'—and the first verses of chapter 3 emphasise the all-importance of obeying the commandments.

Having done that, he goes on to remind them of brotherly love: 'In this the children of God are manifest, and the children of the devil: whosoever doeth not righteousness is not of God, neither he that loveth not his brother. For this is the message that ye heard from the beginning, that we should love one another.'

Then here in the first verse of chapter 4, we come to a continuation of the theme on which John had started at the end of the previous chapter: 'Hereby we know that he abideth in us, by the Spirit which he hath given us.'[3] And we have seen that we are undoubtedly face to face with one of the most important matters in the whole realm of our Christian faith and profession. Not only that, we are also confronted by one of the most difficult subjects in connection with our Christian faith and one which has consequently led often to much discussion and dispute, not to say controversy and bitterness.

The way in which the Apostle deals with it seems to me to be thoroughly typical and characteristic of the Scripture. Indeed, I always feel that one of the most glorious things about Scripture is this extraordinary balance, and that is what always strikes one at once as one comes across a statement like this. 'Hereby we know that he abideth in us, by the Spirit which he hath given us. Beloved, believe not every spirit, but try the spirits whether they are of God.'

Now this is very characteristic of the scriptural method; indeed, had the Church, and had Christian people, always been careful to observe this perfection of balanced statements, then much of the controversy to which I have referred, and certainly much of the bitterness, would have been entirely avoided. But the trouble with us as the result of sin is that we always seem to delight in extremes, and we tend to go from one extreme to the other instead of maintaining the position of scriptural balance. That seems to be the tendency of mankind, and perhaps it has never manifested itself more, and more often, than concerning this very subject which faces us as we look at this verse. The subject is the whole problem of the place of the Holy Spirit in Christian experience. Or if you prefer, there is a more particular problem here, and that is the problem of the respective places of experience and doctrine in the Christian life: experience, doctrine, and the Holy Spirit.

Now the trouble has generally been due to the fact that people have emphasised either experience or doctrine at the expense of the other, and indeed they have often been guilty, and still are, of putting up as contrasts things which clearly are meant to be complementary. This is something which has been happening in the Church almost from the very beginning. There was a great deal of this in the early years of this present century. Many books were published then, nearly all of them dealing with this subject; one of the books was called *Religions of Theology and Religions of the Spirit*, and that was the vogue at the time, to compare these things which were put up as contrasts. It was said that your religion must either be a religion based upon some authoritative doctrinal, dogmatic teaching, or else it was one of those 'free religions of the Spirit,' and the one was generally put up against the other.

This is something which could be dealt with very easily from the historical standpoint, though we shall not do this at any length. But the whole difficulty is this tendency to oscillate between two extreme positions instead of combining the two. These are those who tend to emphasise the work and influence of the Spirit. They emphasise experience at the expense of doctrine and of truth. They say, 'But doesn't the Scripture say, "We know he abideth in us, by the Spirit which he hath given us"? It is not your authorities, not your creeds and definitions, but something alive and living—the religion of the Spirit!' But then you have people on the other side who have said, 'Yes, that is all right, but what the Scripture really says is this: "Believe not every spirit, but try the spirits whether they be of God."'

And thus when the whole emphasis is placed upon one or the other, you have either a tendency to fanaticism and excesses or a tendency toward a barren intellectualism and a mechanical and a dead kind of orthodoxy. That is the position put more or less in general. It is all the result of putting the whole emphasis on one or the other instead of seeing that the two are essential. It is the thing about which the Apostle Paul was contending with the church at Corinth, the whole idea of identifying the complete body; they were tending to think of the separate parts instead of realising this balance which is always a great characteristic of life.

This is a problem which can be illustrated perfectly at particular points of history. It was in a sense the problem with which the early church herself had to contend. There was a grave danger that the whole of the Christian faith, the balance of the truth and of the gospel and of the faith, might have been entirely upset as the result of the activity of certain people. It was exactly what John was writing about in this epistle. There were certain people who claimed unusual authority from God, who claimed to have the Spirit in an unusual and marked manner and were impatient of teaching and definition and doctrine. And the great fight for the faith which was fought in this early century was against this tendency, *for* the apostolic teaching and authority and *against* those who talked more in terms of the special authority which they had received and of the Spirit's guidance of which they said they were the recipients.

We see, of course, exactly the same thing at the time of the Reformation. Luther and Calvin and others as the result of their wonderful experience, as the result of what the Spirit of God had done to them, renounced the teaching of the medieval Church. They began to preach a living gospel and faith, but almost immediately after they had started doing so they were confronted by a new and fresh problem. The Reformation immediately led to a whole host of new sects, led by people who were claiming some immediate revelation, those who spoke, as they claimed, by the inspiration of the Spirit and were guilty of all kinds of excesses. As you read the stories of Luther and Calvin and other Reformation Fathers, you will find that they began to fight this war on two fronts. They were fighting a dead, mechanical intellectualism on one hand, and they had to fight these other people who were running to excess and riot on the other.

Then in the seventeenth century you find the same kind of thing in connection with the Puritan movement. It is one of the most fascinating bits of history to read the story of the fight that went on within the ranks of Puritanism itself. There were three main sections. There were those who eventually became the Quakers, who exhorted the doctrine of the 'Inner Light' and immediate experience, and who were rather negligent of the Word itself and all examining and testing. That was one extreme. Then on the other hand you had those who became guilty of a kind of intellectualism, who discounted the Spirit altogether, who were concerned about the more or less legalistic statements of the truth. Then in the middle you had people like the great Dr. John Owen, and Thomas Goodwin in London, who constantly emphasised what they regarded as the only true scriptural position—namely, the one we have here, the position which emphasises Spirit and doctrine, experience and definition. You must not say it is either/or; it is both. These, too, had to wage a warfare constantly on the two fronts; they had to fight the dead, barren intellectualism of many in Anglicanism and in the ranks of Puritanism, and the wild excesses of the early Quakers and various others who troubled them not a little.

That is a brief history survey. 'But,' someone may say, 'that is all right, and no doubt if we were living in the sixteenth or seventeenth centuries, or in the early centuries, this may have been very important for us. But surely by now this has become quite remote. It is just academic. No doubt some of you rejoice in reading about things like that, it is your particular hobby, but what has it to do with us?'

I suggest that in many ways it is one of the most acute problems confronting the Church at the present time. So let us look at it like this: I maintain that in those who take their Christian faith and religion at all seriously, there are still these two tendencies manifested at the present time. Alas, I am sure it is true to say of the vast majority that they are utterly indifferent to true doctrine—they are concerned only about supporting the mechanism of the Church. They seem to be quite unconcerned about these things, and because of their lack of interest in doctrine, their one idea is to establish a great world Church without any doctrine whatsoever. But amongst those who really are alive and alert, these two ancient tendencies are still manifesting themselves.

There is what I would call a movement to a kind of new orthodoxy; I am anxious to avoid mentioning names, and yet it is more or less essential that I should do so. There is that movement which is known as Barthianism, which is merely concerned about doctrine and spends most of its time in teaching doctrine. There we see the tendency to pure intellectualism, a concern about truth in the abstract, about definitions and ideas, and to stop at that. But then there is another movement, and there is always this opposite movement. There is a great tendency on the part of many to stress only the experimental side—the experiencing side, and to talk only about the gifts of the Spirit and the various manifestations of life and religion, as they call it.

My point is that those who really are concerned about these matters are still tending to take up one or the other of these positions. As I understand it, the position of those of us who claim to be Evangelical is nothing but a repetition of that of the Protestant Fathers and that of certain of the leaders of the Puritan Movement in the seventeenth century. As Evangelicals we find ourselves fighting on two fronts. We are obviously critical of a pure intellectualism and of a dead mechanical Church which lacks any life. We are here to say that 'Hereby we know that he abideth in us, by the Spirit which he hath given us.' We say, 'It is not enough for people to be church members.' We ask, 'Are they born again? Have they evidence within them of the life of God in their soul?' We say we are not concerned about a mere theoretical belief; the gospel of Jesus Christ is a life-giving gospel. That is one side; but on the other side we see certain tendencies and we see certain excesses and we say, 'Believe not every spirit, but try the spirits whether they are of God.' And thus we seem to be opposing everything, and so we receive criticisms from all sides.

Now we are not concerned merely about our own position; we are concerned primarily about the truth. But let me say this. It seems to me that we have a right to be fairly happy about ourselves as long as we have criticism from both sides; but if the criticism should ever stop on one side, then is the time to be careful. For myself, as long as I am charged by certain people with being nothing but a Pentecostalist and on the other hand charged by others with being an intellectual, a man who is always preaching doctrine, as long as the two criticisms come, I am very happy. But if one or the other of the two criticisms should ever cease, then, I say, is the time to be careful and to begin to examine the very foundations.

The position of the Scripture, as I am trying to show you, is one which is facing two extremes; the Spirit is essential, and experience is vital; however, truth and definition and doctrine and dogma are equally vital and essential. And our whole position is one which proclaims that experience which is not based solidly upon truth and doctrine is dangerous. That, then, is a comprehensive general statement, but now let us look at it in detail as it is presented to us here by the Apostle. Let me divide it up in this way:

First of all, there is the necessity for testing and trying the spirits. 'Beloved, believe not every spirit, but try the spirits whether they are of God.' Now there are some people who object root and branch to this process of testing. There are many reasons for that, of course. In the case of some people it is nothing but slackness, indolence, and laziness—a desire for ease. Religion? 'Ah,' they say, 'you must not always be arriving at your definitions and examining and testing.' They dislike the whole thing; they just want to go on as they have always done. I do not think we need to discuss them further—there is no excuse for such an attitude.

Then there are others who seem to object to this process of testing because they are what we may call 'anti-theological.' It is amazing how many people who claim the name *Christian* are actively opposed to theology; they dislike it and say, 'I am not interested in theology. All I believe is that a man should do this, that, and the other'; they look askance upon definition and dogmas. Well, all I can say to such people is that their first duty is to read the history of the Christian Church and the lives of the saints. Indeed, they can start by reading the New Testament itself, and they will find that it is essentially theological; it is our duty to understand the truth we claim to believe, in order that we may state and express it in such a manner that God can use it for the salvation of others.

But there are those who feel that this whole process of testing and trying the spirits is something unscriptural. I am not anxious to caricature such people, but they do take up that position. The scriptural person, according to their idea, is one who, as it were, lives with his head in the clouds and must never come down to earth on matters of definition; and the moment you begin to discuss and consider and debate and define, you cease to be a purely spiritual person. A spiritual person, according to such ideas, is some ethereal being who really must not be bothering with these mechanical and mundane matters of definition.

And then there are those who object to such testing because they say that surely the only thing that matters is that people should be honest and sincere; and if people are absolutely sincere about these things, then their doctrine will look after itself.

Now there is a great deal of this spirit abroad—an objection to testing and trying the spirits. I remember a man saying to me on one occasion, after I had made a brief reference to this matter, 'I am not interested in what you are saying. The great question is, are you being used?' In other words, it does not matter what I say in terms of truth so long as I feel something and experience something—that is the attitude. But my reply to this is that we must test and try the spirits because Scripture commands and exhorts us to do so, and for me that is enough. 'Beloved, believe not every spirit, but try the spirits.' This is a commandment, and I have no right to put it aside.

Not only that, but Scripture tells us why we ought to do so—'because many false prophets are gone out into the world.' The Scripture tells us that 'We wrestle not against flesh and blood, but against principalities, against powers, against the rulers of the darkness of this world, against spiritual wickedness in high places' (Eph 6:12). Alas, there are false prophets; there are evil spirits; there is a devil who is so clever and subtle that he can transform himself into an angel of light. If we were confronted with the Holy Spirit only, there would be no need to test the spirits, but the very name '*Holy* Spirit' suggests other spirits, devilish spirits—and there are such powers.

The third reason for testing and trying is the evidence provided by the long history of the church of the havoc that has often been wrought in the Church because people would not try and test the spirits—because they said, 'I have received such a wonderful experience, and therefore I must be right.' But for the reasons I have given for definition and dogma and examination, the whole history of the church presses us and urges us to test and to try and to follow the scriptural injunction. In other words, what we are concerned about is not a matter only of sincerity and honesty—we are concerned about truth and error, and truth and error is something which has to be defined.

But let me ask a second question: Is this something only for theologians and professors of theology or perhaps for ministers and leaders? Is it only for certain people? And the answer is that it is for *all*. 'Beloved'—he is writing to the average church member—'believe not every spirit, but try the spirits.' Later on he says, 'Ye are of God, little children' (v 4), and I think he used the expression 'little children' deliberately— 'you, the ordinary church members, little children—you hear us because you are of the truth.'

It is the duty and the business of everyone claiming the name *Christian* to be in a position to try and examine and test the spirits. Indeed, we are given the power to do so—'greater is he that is in you, than he that is in the world' (v 4). We have been given this capacity by God, through the Holy Spirit; the Spirit dwells in us, and therefore we have this power of discrimination and understanding. The Apostle Paul tells us that at great length in 1 Corinthians. For example, 'We have received, not the spirit of the world, but the Spirit which is of God; that we might know the things that are freely given to us of God' (2:12). That is it!

Then I come to the last and vital question: How is this testing to be done? How are we to know whether certain spirits are true or false? Let me mention, first of all, tests which are dangerous if we rely upon them only, and let me first put it in general.

There are those who claim that the gifts of the Spirit are absolutely essential, and that unless men and women are able to manifest certain gifts of the Spirit, they have not received the Spirit. They say, for example, 'You have not received the Holy Spirit unless you are able to speak in tongues, or have done this or that.' They refer to a particular gift, and they say that if you have not experienced that, you have not received the Spirit, in spite of the fact that the Apostle Paul asks the question, 'Do all speak with tongues?' (1 Cor 12:30). The whole of that chapter is designed to show that the gifts are distributed by the Lord Himself. He may or may not give these gifts, and the manifestation of gifts is not an essential proof of the possession of the Spirit.[4]

But let me go on to particular matters. A very dangerous way of testing or examining the claim to having the Spirit is to judge in terms of phenomena, as in the gift of healing, or the particular result of a ministry. These are the tests that are put up. People say, 'Surely this man must be right. Haven't you heard what he has been doing? Haven't you heard of the cures he is able to bring about. Look at the results he has had.' The test of phenomena, taken alone, is an extremely dangerous one because evil spirits can work miracles; our Lord warned His followers that these spirits would be able to do such marvelous works.

Let me give you a piece of historical evidence. A man by the name of John Brown, who was a surgeon to King Charles II, published a book in 1684 bearing the title *Scrofula treated by the touch of Kings*, and these extraordinary facts are therein revealed: From 1660-1662 Charles II laid his hands upon 90,000 people suffering from scrofula—a tubercular disease of the glands of the neck. The man who writes the book was a surgeon, and he says he has evidence to prove that in at least fifty of the cases the cures were miraculous. Charles II had the gift of healing! I pass that on as a piece of evidence which is well worth our consideration.

The same applies to fervour; the fact that people are full of fervour does not imply that they have the Holy Spirit. Evil spirits are often very fervent. Great excitement is not a proof of the Spirit; great energy is not a proof of the Spirit; much assurance or confidence is not a proof of the Spirit. How often the only tests and the true tests taken are that a man speaks with confidence and assurance and that he is energetic. I would to God that energy in a man's preaching was proof of the power of the Spirit, but, alas, I know it is not; the flesh can evidence false feelings, and to put that up as a test is dangerous.

It is likewise with the test of experience. People may come and say they have had visions; they have had most extraordinary dreams. They say that strange things have happened to them; they have had unusual guidance, astonishing answers to prayer. 'I prayed,' says a man, 'and this happened,' and we tend to say this man must be full of the Spirit. Experience! But believe me, such experiences can be counterfeited by the enemy and often have been; experiences have come and do come to us, but let us not rest on them, and let us not put up the test of experience as the sole test.

So, if we reject those tests, then what are the true tests? Let me first just note them.

The first and the most important test is conformity to scriptural teaching. Try the spirits; test the spirits. 'Hereby know ye the Spirit of God: Every spirit that confesseth that Jesus Christ is come in the flesh is of God' (v 2). How do I know that this is a spiritual test? All I know about Him I put up to the test of Scripture. Indeed, you get exactly the same thing in the sixth verse where John says, speaking of himself and the other Apostles, 'We are of God: he that knoweth God heareth us; he that is not of God heareth not us. Hereby know we the spirit of truth, and the spirit of error.' The first thing to ask about a man who claims to be filled with the Spirit and to be an unusual teacher is, does his teaching conform to Scripture? Is it in conformity with the apostolic message? Does he base it all upon this Word? Is he willing to submit to it? That is the great test.

But I want to emphasise this next one: A readiness to listen to scriptural teaching and to abide by it is always a characteristic of the true prophet. You will find that the other man rather tends to dismiss it. 'Ah yes,' he says, 'but you are legalistic, you are just a theologian; I have experienced, I have felt, and I have produced this and that.' The tendency is not to abide by the teaching of Scripture but to be almost contemptuous of it; that has always been the characteristic of those who have tended to go astray. Read the history of the Quakers, and you find that such an attitude became a prominent feature—the inner light rather than the objective teaching of Scripture itself.

But, of course, and this is the greatest test, the true Spirit always glorifies Christ; He is always in the centre; He is always given the pre-eminence. And the true prophet is not the man who talks about experiences and visions and what he has done and seen, but about Christ. And when you have heard him you do not say, 'What a wonderful man'; you say, 'What a wonderful Saviour!' You do not say, 'What a wonderful experience this man has had'; you say, 'Who is the Man of whom he is speaking?' The attraction is to Christ; he glorifies Christ.

The last thing I would mention is that with which I started—the perfect balance. 'God,' said Paul to Timothy 'hath not given us the spirit of fear; but of power, and of love, and of a sound mind' (2 Tim 1:7). This is discipline, balance. The man who has the Holy Spirit is the man who always manifests balance and proportion. 'Be not drunk with wine, wherein is excess; but be filled with the Spirit' (Eph 5:18); there is power and balance, but no excess. Speak one at a time, says Paul to the people of Corinth. 'But,' they say, 'we cannot. Isn't that quenching the Spirit?' 'No,' says Paul, 'let all things be done . . . in order' (see 1 Cor 14:33, 40). The Holy Spirit is the Spirit of order, not of disorder. Doctrine and love are required; experience and power, intellect and mind—the whole person is involved and functions as this perfectly balanced body with no schism, with no rivalry and competition, but with the whole manifesting and ministering unto the glory of the Lord and Saviour, Jesus Christ.

We have only been able to deal briefly with this subject which, as I have said, is a great one. 'Beloved, believe not every spirit, but try the spirits.' I say, make sure you have the Spirit. It is 'hereby we know that he abideth in us, by the Spirit which he hath given us.' Make sure the Spirit of God is in you, and then make sure that it is the Spirit of God and not some false, evil spirit to whom you are listening.

2

THE ALL-SUFFICIENCY
OF CHRIST

Hereby know ye the Spirit of God: Every spirit that con-
fesseth that Jesus Christ is come in the flesh is of God: and
every spirit that confesseth not that Jesus Christ is come
in the flesh is not of God: and this is that spirit of
antichrist, whereof ye have heard that it should come; and
even now already is it in the world.

1 JOHN 4:2-3

HERE IN THESE TWO VERSES John emphasises what is, after all, the
ultimate test in this matter of trying and testing the spirits. We have considered a number of general tests, and, in an attempt to give a fairly comprehensive list, I mentioned in passing that one of the most valuable and
thorough tests always is whether such a teaching or such a person glorifies the Lord Jesus Christ.

Now in these two verses we have to return to that, and John appeals
to us to do so. It is not enough just to say in general that a teaching
should glorify the Lord Jesus Christ; we must know what we mean by
that. And, indeed, the whole epistle, in a sense, is nothing but one great
repetition of the Apostle concerning this central and vital matter.

So let me try to summarise this by putting it in the form of a number of principles, and let me say in passing that this is the note on which
Christian preaching should always begin and should always end. Let us

look at it like this: The ultimate test of all who profess or teach Christianity is their attitude towards the Lord Jesus Christ. 'Hereby know ye the Spirit of God: Every spirit that confesseth that Jesus Christ is come in the flesh is of God: and every spirit that confesseth not that Jesus Christ is come in the flesh is not of God'; whatever their gifts may be and however wonderful they may be, they are not of God; 'and this is that spirit of antichrist, whereof ye have heard that it should come; and even now already is it in the world.'

So this is the infallible test. John goes on repeating it, and we must continue to do so. The Lord Jesus Christ is absolutely vital, central, and essential to the Christian position, and I do not hesitate, therefore, to aver that any teaching in which the Lord Jesus Christ is not in that position is not true Christian teaching, whatever else it may be. Now let me try to enforce that by putting it in terms of a number of negative statements.

Christianity is not a mystical feeling or experience only. I put it like that because there is a good deal of interest in that kind of experience at the present time. I think you always tend to get a return to mysticism at a time of crisis or of difficulty in the history of the world. When men and women see all other powers fail on all hands, when they see that all the optimistic prophets and teachers and politicians and poets have been entirely wrong, when they are troubled and bewildered and perplexed, there is always some kind of innate tendency in men and women to turn to mysticism. People nowadays talk about 'getting in tune with the heart of the universe'; they talk about 'getting in touch with the Unseen.' There is also a considerable revival of Buddhism at the present time. Certain popular well-known novelists, people like Mr. Aldous Huxley[1] and others, who once claimed to be pure intellectuals, are now saying, one after another, that the only hope for this world is mysticism, and the mysticism that they are interested in is Buddhism.

There is, indeed, a revival of interest in these so-called 'Eastern religions.' People, in a kind of desperation, are anxious to get back into something that is eternal and unseen, and there are many people who think that anybody who is at all interested in these things is automatically a Christian. 'Ah,' they say, 'I used to be quite materialistic, and I was only interested in the things I could see, but I have developed a great interest in the unseen and in the spiritual'; and so they have become interested in experiences and feelings along the mystical line.

Now there *is* a mystical element in the gospel of Jesus Christ, and it is very practical and experimental. But here I would emphasise that a mere vague, general interest in the unseen and the spiritual does not make one a Christian. Spiritism can do that, and so can Buddhism and most of the other religions. But that is not the Christian position.

Or let me put it to you like this: Merely to claim that one has a new sense of power in one's life does not prove that one is a Christian. There is also a great deal of interest in these days in this sense of power. People say, 'My life had gone to pieces. I became conscious that I lacked power. But now I believe that there is a new power in my life; I am able to do what I could not do before.' And many people believe that to say such a thing is proof positive that one has become a Christian. But the simple answer is that there are many agencies that can do that; Christian Science does it, psychology does it—it is a part of such religion.

I once read a book by a man in which he stated this whole position. He was an author, a playwright, and he pointed out that the big mistake he had been making in his professional life was that he has used the higher part of his brain too much. There he was with his mind as it were sweating and straining, and then he said, 'I made this marvelous discovery,' and it happened to him as the result of some experience that he had. 'I found,' he said, 'that the great thing to do was not to use the active part of my brain, but to use the lower part of my brain.' He went on to describe the ease with which he now wrote. He allowed the lower part of the brain to rule his life for him, and he was conscious of some strange, extraordinary power. There are many who are interested in power in life. There *is* a great and glorious power in the Christian faith, but merely to be able to claim we have a new power in our life does not prove we are Christians.

Let me even say that the Christian position is not just one in which we subscribe to a number of exalted teachings and ideas. Here again you will find that this idea is very frequent. People say, 'I have gone on for years, and I have never been interested in these elevated thoughts and ideas of life, but now I *am* interested in them'; and having subscribed to this elevated conception of life, they think they have become Christians. But there are many elevated teachings. You can find them in Greek pagan philosophy or in many modern philosophies; but these thoughts and ideas alone are not Christianity.

Indeed, I do not hesitate to go as far as this: Even to accept the teaching of the Lord Jesus Christ, just as teaching, does not make one a

Christian. The whole emphasis of this epistle, as of the whole of the New Testament, is on the person Himself. It is possible for people to take up certain parts of the teaching of Christ and to praise it. A man like Mahatma Gandhi did that. He was not a Christian, but he praised the teaching of Christ and told people they ought to try to practise it. Merely to praise the teaching of Christ does not make one a Christian. No; the emphasis is upon the person Himself, and upon our relationship to Him. 'Hereby know ye the Spirit of God: Every spirit that confesseth that Jesus Christ is come in the flesh is of God.'

But now this leads to a further careful definition, and that, of course, is because of these antichrists about whom John is speaking. It is not enough even for people to say they believe on the Lord Jesus Christ; we must know something of what they mean by that. After all, John is here reminding these people that there were those in the early church who said that they believed in the Lord Jesus Christ and yet were false prophets, antichrists, false teachers.

Definition is absolutely essential. That is why any people who say that they are not interested in theology and doctrine are not only unscriptural, they are ignorant; they are denying the Scriptures. So it is very important that we should be clear about these things, because of the teaching of antichrists. Perhaps the best way to put that clearly is to remind ourselves of what we saw when we considered this question of the antichrists in the second chapter.[2] The antichrists did not completely deny the Lord Jesus Christ. That was not the trouble with them. A teaching which denies the whole of the teaching of the Lord Jesus Christ is self-evident and is to that extent not a danger. That is why I never agree with people that the main danger confronting the church is something like communism. No, the greatest danger is always something within, and these antichrists were within the church.

What is the teaching of the antichrist? It is not a denial of Christ; it is a misrepresentation of Christ; it is a teaching that either does something to Him or detracts something from Him. You remember how John put it; he said these people 'went out from us, but they were not of us: for if they had been of us, they would no doubt have continued with us; but they went out, that they might be manifest that they were not all of us' (2:19). They were in the church. The antichrists had arisen *within* the Christian church; they said they believed in Christ, and yet, says John, their teaching is such that we can prove that they do not truly believe in Him.

Now this is a very important principle to grasp. Merely for people to say, 'Yes, I believe in the Lord Jesus Christ; I always have believed in Him,' is not enough, until we have tested them further. The Apostle Paul says that these people preach 'another Jesus.' Ah, yes, they were preaching Jesus, but it was *another* Jesus; it was not the Jesus that Paul preached (2 Cor 11:4). They preached Christ, yes, but what sort of a Christ, what kind of a Jesus? That is the question.

Therefore we ask this question: How can we decide whether the teaching concerning Jesus Christ is true or false? And here the one answer is given perfectly clearly. Our ultimate authority, our only authority, is the apostolic teaching. Now that is the whole point of this first epistle of John. In a sense this is what he is saying from beginning to end. 'Go on believing,' says John, 'what I and my fellow Apostles have taught you and have told you.' There were these other people who claimed wonderful gifts, they seemed to be doing extraordinary things, they had some sort of spirit in them, and they were claiming authoritative teaching. But John's whole purpose in writing was to say to these early Christians, 'Hold on to what I and the other Apostles have told you.'

You remember how he began? 'That which was from the beginning, which we have heard, which we have seen with our eyes, which we have looked upon, and our hands have handled, of the Word of life.' He is referring to the Apostles, and he says that he writes these things that these Christians 'may have fellowship with *us*.' Who are they? They are still the Apostles.

Now this is something which is absolutely primary and fundamental. The claim of the New Testament is that it alone is authoritative in these matters. It teaches us that the Apostles and Prophets were the people to whom God, through the Holy Spirit, had revealed spiritual truth, and He meant them to teach it in word and to write it. The Apostle Paul tells us in Ephesians 2:20 that the Christian Church is 'built upon the foundation of the apostles and prophets.' All teaching must derive from them, and so you have this extraordinary claim in the New Testament. These men claimed a unique authority.

Listen to the Apostle Paul putting it again in writing to the Galatians; he uses strong language like this: 'But though we, or an angel from heaven, preach any other gospel unto you than that which we have preached unto you, let him be accursed' (Gal 1:8). 'What egotism!' says someone. No, it is not egotism; it is the claim of a man who has been commissioned by God. God has set him apart; God has given him the revelation. And he goes on to argue in so many of his letters that what he preached was also the message that was preached by the other Apostles. This Apostle and all the other Apostles do not hesitate to say that they exhorted these people to test every teaching by their teaching. In other words, you and I are still committed to the same position. We are to judge teaching not by the experience it gives, not by anything flashy or spectacular that may characterize it. It is not enough, John says, to name Christ. The question is, does the teaching conform to the teaching of the New Testament concerning the person of our Lord and Saviour Jesus Christ or does it not? That is the test.

That leads to the next question. What is this apostolic teaching concerning Him? Now in a phrase in our text John gives us the perfect answer. John does not use words like this haphazardly. Listen to the way in which he puts it: 'Hereby know ye the Spirit of God: Every spirit that confesseth that Jesus Christ is come in the flesh is of God: and every spirit that confesseth not that Jesus Christ is come in the flesh is not of God.' Now here is the statement: *'Jesus Christ is come in the flesh'*; Jesus Christ arrived in the world 'in the flesh.' What does this mean? Let me try to show you how John in putting it like that was countering and answering some of those grievous heresies that had already arisen even in his day in the church, before the end of the first century.

Take the expression 'Jesus Christ.' Why does John say *'Jesus Christ is come in the flesh'*? Why did he not say that Jesus or that Christ has come in the flesh? Ah, that is most important; that is his way of emphasising the unity of the blessed person. The Lord Jesus Christ is one person, but He has two natures—the divine and the human; and yet there is only one person. Now as we have seen in the earlier chapters of 1 John,[3] there were false prophets, the antichrists in the early church, and some of them said something like this: Jesus of Nazareth was just a man like every other man, but when He was baptised by John in the Jordan, the eternal Christ came upon Him and began to use Him; and the eternal Christ continued with the man Jesus until He came to the cross. But on the cross the eternal Christ went away, back to heaven, and it was only the man Jesus who died. There were two persons—the man Jesus and the eternal Christ. No! says John; *'Jesus Christ,'* one person but two natures—the two natures in one person.

The history of the church shows very clearly the vital importance of emphasising this. All the subsequent heresies with regard to the person of our Lord arose in the first few centuries. Someone put this very well when they said, 'The canon of infidelity was closed about exactly the same time as the canon of Scripture was closed.' That is a very interesting statement. There is no modern heresy. All the clever people who propound their apparently new ideas about Christ are simply repeating what has already been said; there have literally been no new heresies since the first centuries. But, you see, men have constantly fallen into that error; some have seen God only, and others have seen man only, and others have tried to see the two. That is why we must never say Jesus is God, Jesus is man; no, Jesus Christ is the God-man. In the Incarnation, the eternal Son of God took our nature unto Himself deliberately; He is the God-man, Jesus Christ.

Let me hold another phrase before you: 'Jesus Christ *is come*.' What a significant statement! Do you see what it implies? It suggests that He was before; He has come from somewhere. It could be said of no one else that he has come into this world and into this life. You and I are born, but He *came*. John, as I have already reminded you, has already said at the commencement of the epistle, 'That which was from the beginning'; that is it! This eternal life has been manifested. He is still talking about the eternal Son of God who has come into this world; he is describing the whole miracle and marvel and wonder of the Incarnation. That is the theme; He is come.

You get this in so many places in Scripture: 'This is the condemnation, that the light *is come* into the world' (John 3:19); 'Unto you that fear my name shall the Sun of righteousness arise with healing in his wings' (Mal 4:2). All these phrases are pointing in the same direction, so that as we look at the person of the Lord Jesus Christ we must be absolutely confident and sure that we do verily believe that that person, that babe in the manger, is the one who has come from the realms of glory—no one else, none other. 'Jesus Christ is come'; He has entered into the world. He is a visitor from another realm; He has erupted into history. That is the idea. So you see John was not using a casual phrase when he said, 'Jesus Christ is come.' There were people already denying His Godhead, His unique Deity, His eternal Sonship, and here John is emphasising it.

Even further, he says, 'Jesus Christ is come *in the flesh*.' In other words, the eternal Son did not have a mere phantom body. People had taught that. Some of those antichrists, those first heretics, said, 'Yes, the person described as Jesus is the eternal Christ, the eternal Son of God, but you must not talk about the Incarnation. You must not say, "the Word was made flesh," you must not say He has come in the flesh. What happened,' they said, 'was that He took upon Himself a kind of phantom, ethereal body. What happened was something similar to those theophanies when the Angel of the Covenant suddenly appeared to Abraham or somebody else, a temporary appearance of the eternal Son, not a real incarnation.'

'Avoid that heresy,' says John, 'as you value your souls and as you value the faith. Jesus Christ is come *in the flesh*.' 'The Word was made flesh, and dwelt among us' (John 1:14). He was born as a baby in Bethlehem. He grew 'in wisdom and stature, and in favor with God and man' (Luke 2:52). His humanity is absolutely real; may we never lose hold of that. 'Jesus Christ is come in the flesh'—this is the actuality of the Incarnation.

Why is John so concerned about all this? Why is he so careful to define what he believes about the Lord Jesus Christ in such detail and in such minute accuracy? It was all because of the false teachings that were then current and have been current ever since. What was the matter with them? All these false teachings were somehow or other detracting from Christ. Some were detracting from the glory of His person. Some said He was only a man, a wonderful man, the greatest religious genius of all time, one who was given the Holy Spirit in an exceptional degree and was therefore able to teach. Indeed as one has put it, 'Jesus achieved divinity.' Man only, but so wonderful that He, as it were, reached up and therefore will encourage us to follow His effort. Some therefore detract from Him by regarding Him as man only. Others detract from Him equally by regarding Him as God only. They would have us believe He is nothing but God appearing in a kind of cloak of flesh. Now each of these teachings detracts from Him because, let me emphasise again, He is not only man and not only God, but the astounding thing that has happened is that He is the God-man; He has taken humanity unto Himself.

But these false teachings detract also from the wonders of His works. And that is why John was so careful to emphasise that He is God 'in the flesh.' You see what it involves? If the Incarnation is not an actual fact, if He really has not been made flesh and dwelt among us, then there was no real humiliation involved in His coming into this world. He really did not limit Himself, as it were, to the position of a man dependent upon God; there is no real meaning in the laying aside of the insignia of the eternal glory; there is no true humiliation.

Furthermore, if He has not actually come in the flesh, there was no real suffering. If the eternal Christ left Him on the cross, the eternal Son of God did not suffer for the sins of mankind. There was no suffering at all in a sense; it was all appearance, it was all play-acting as it were. But I must go further. If it is not true to say that the eternal Son of God, having taken human nature unto Himself, has become the Lord Jesus Christ, if that glorious person in the unity of His person did not die upon that cross, then there is no atonement for sin, there is no expiation, and it is not true to say that He has tasted death for every man.

Yet that is what the New Testament claims for Him. It tells us that He was made for us 'a little lower than the angels . . . that he . . . should taste death for every man' (Heb 2:9). I say that if you are not clear about the Incarnation, you cannot believe that He has tasted death for you. How vital is this doctrine of the person of Jesus Christ! No man could die for my sins, and I say, with reverence, weighing my words, that God alone could not die for my sins. The Incarnation was essential, because we who need redemption are of the seed of Abraham. He has taken upon Himself this same nature, that as man He might die for our sins; and because He is the God-man, His dying is of eternal worth; thereby I am redeemed.

Do you see how important it is to contest and fight for these things? You cannot be a true Christian if you are unconcerned about the person of Jesus Christ and say, 'I do not understand these two natures in one person; I am not interested; I am not a theologian.' If you are not clear about this, you cannot be clear about your salvation. The Incarnation was essential because His death was essential. He came to die, and 'He died that we might be forgiven, he died to make us good'; He died to reconcile us to God.

In other words, the last point I am emphasising is that this false teaching detracts from the self-sufficiency of His work. You will find that so many of these false teachings talk about receiving power without mentioning Him at all. They claim wonderful power as the result of an experience, but they are detracting from the sufficiency of His work.

They say, 'You must have an extra-special experience.' No, the teaching of the Scripture is that He alone is enough.

This teaching is as essential today as it was in the first century. Look, for example, at the place that some give to the Virgin Mary. I object to such teaching because it detracts from the all-sufficiency of my Lord. I do not need the assistance of the Virgin Mary. I speak with reverence: He and He alone is enough. I do not need to pray to the saints, because I have 'one mediator between God and men, the man Christ Jesus' (1 Tim 2:5). He needs no assistance. I am not dependent upon the sacraments for my salvation. I object to such teachings, for they detract from His unique and absolute all-sufficiency and comprehensiveness. The sacraments are of value, but they are not essential.

Let no one misunderstand me at this point. I am afraid I even object to teaching which emphasises the Holy Spirit at the expense of the person of the Son. The Holy Spirit was given in order that He might reveal the Son to me; the function of the Holy Spirit is not to call attention to Himself, but to direct attention to Christ, to present Him, to cause Him to dwell within us. Let us be careful that we do not emphasise even the Holy Spirit at the expense of the Son. The Son is alone, and He alone is enough.

What you and I are called upon to do as Christians I can put like this: We are to be ready to confess Him, and we are to do so gladly. Our confession is that He came into this world in order to save, that He alone can save me, and that He has done everything that is essential to my salvation. I need no other, and I will tolerate no other. He is central, He is enough, He is all and in all. 'Of him are ye in Christ Jesus, who of God is made unto us wisdom, and righteousness, and sanctification, and redemption' (1 Cor 1:30). Is there anything else you need? It is all in Him. In Him we are complete. Let us therefore give Him all the glory. 'Jesus Christ is come in the flesh'; He is enough. Let us therefore declare His death and His all-sufficiency until He comes again.

3

Born of God

*Beloved, let us love one another: for love is of God; and
every one that loveth is born of God, and knoweth God.
He that loveth not, knoweth not God; for God is love.*

1 JOHN 4:7-8

BEFORE WE START on our consideration of these verses, I suggest to
you that in my opinion John has really finished his active teaching at the
end of verse 6 in this chapter, and that what we find after that is but a
kind of reemphasis of what he has already been saying. There is no fresh
doctrine from here on; he has laid down the two vital things—*fellowship* and *sonship*, and if we have these nothing can harm us.

But the man was such a wise teacher that, having said all that, he
now ends with a *practical exhortation*; and the passage from the seventh
verse in the fourth chapter to the end of verse 12 in the fifth chapter is
just a repetition of these three things. And he starts with this particular
matter of loving one another. He says, 'Beloved, let us love one another,'
and he goes on with that theme until the first verse of the fifth chapter.
Then from the second verse he goes back again to the all-importance of
keeping the commandments; and from verse 5 to the end of verse 12 in
the fifth chapter he returns to the correctness of belief, and especially to
a correct belief concerning the person and work of the Lord Jesus Christ.
Then from verse 13 to the end you have a kind of summary of the whole
teaching.

Now I remind you of the scheme because it does help us to understand exactly what the Apostle has to say. So then, having done that, let

us go back to this particular section, which begins with verse 7 in chapter 4 and goes to the end of verse 1 in chapter 5. John comes back once more to insist upon the vital importance of this demonstration of brotherly love. He has done it twice over, and he has been careful to go into details in his exposition of it, but still he comes back to it, and therefore I deduce that as the Apostle thus focuses upon this subject and dwells upon it and repeats it, it must be something which is of vital and paramount importance to him. It is interesting to observe that when he has finished his doctrine and direct exhortation, he puts this question of loving one another first.

This is characteristic of John. John is sometimes described as the Apostle of love. People say that Paul is the Apostle of faith, John the Apostle of love, and Peter the Apostle of hope; but I dislike these comparisons, because nothing on the subject of love has ever been written to compare with Paul's 1 Corinthians 13. Yet I suppose there is a sense in which there is something in such a distinction. However, it is very clear that this question of love is of vital importance, and John constantly emphasises it; and it is in connection with this that he says some of the most glorious and elevating things that can be found in the whole of Scripture. We have, for example, the great statement, 'God is love'; but it is the whole question of brotherly love that led him to say it. It was as he thought about this that he arrived at that great statement.

This, then, I would suggest, is indeed one of the things that is emphasised more than anything else in the whole of the New Testament. Our blessed Lord Himself at the very end of His ministry kept on repeating this same thing—'love one another.' He constantly told them that the world would be against them and that they would have tribulation. 'But,' he kept on saying, 'you love one another, and that is how the world will know that you are my disciples; this is the way in which you can demonstrate more clearly than anything else that you are my true followers and that you are children of God.' You will find this standing out in a most exceptional way if you read John 13—17.[1] But it is indeed a great theme running right through the entire New Testament—the Gospels and the Epistles.

I do not hesitate, therefore, to say that the ultimate test of our profession of the Christian faith is, I believe, this whole question of our loving one another. Indeed, I do not hesitate to aver that it is a more vital test than our orthodoxy. I am the last man in the world to say anything against orthodoxy, but I am here to say that it is not the final test. Orthodoxy is absolutely essential; this epistle has shown us that repeatedly, and it will show it to us again. We must believe the right things, for apart from that we have nothing at all and we have no standing whatsoever; so the correctness of belief is absolutely essential. And yet I say that when we come to the realm of experience and self-examination, the test of orthodoxy is not the ultimate test.

Alas, let us admit it, it is possible for a person to be absolutely correct and yet not to be a Christian. It is possible for men and women to give perfect intellectual assent to the propositions that are to be found in the Bible; it is possible for them to be interested in theology and to say that one theology is superior to another and to accept and defend and argue about it, and yet to be utterly devoid of the grace of the Lord Jesus Christ and of the love of God in their hearts. It is a terrible thought, it is a terrible possibility, but it is a fact. There have been men, also, who have clearly been perfectly orthodox—champions of the faith, and yet they have denied that very faith in the bitterness with which they have sometimes defended it. I repeat, the test of orthodoxy, while it is so vital and essential, is not enough.

There is something, as John shows us in these two verses without going any further, that goes very much more deeply and is a more certain guarantee of where we really are. I suggest that it is even a more thorough test than the exercise of faith as a principle. I need not emphasise that. Paul has done this once and for ever in 1 Corinthians 13 (here paraphrased): 'Though I have faith that I can remove mountains, and have not love, I am nothing. Though I speak with the tongues of men and of angels, though I have knowledge and understanding and wisdom, if it is without love, it is no good; it is like sounding brass or a tinkling cymbal—no use at all.' Faith is a most glorious and valuable thing, and yet there is something deeper than that. Indeed, there is a more thoroughgoing test, and it is this test of brotherly love—love for one another.

Likewise, this is a more thorough test than conduct and behaviour. John has a great deal to say about that; conduct and behaviour and deportment are of the most vital importance. 'Be not deceived,' says Paul. 'God is not mocked: for whatsoever a man soweth, that shall he also reap' (Gal 6:7). And remember what he tells the Corinthians: 'Be not deceived: neither fornicators, nor idolaters, nor adulterers, nor effeminate, nor abusers of themselves with mankind, nor thieves, nor covetous, nor drunkards, nor revilers, nor extortioners, shall inherit the kingdom of God' (1 Cor 6:9-10). Conduct is essential and all-important, and yet the fact that men and women live good, moral, and highly ethical lives does not prove that they are Christians. The ultimate test of our whole position is this question of love. Do we possess the love of which the Apostle is here speaking?

So let us approach it more directly. What is this love? Well, it is generally agreed that it has reference to Christian people. John is not talking about people who are not Christians; he is here emphasising this one thing to those who claim to be Christians, to those within the faith. And this, evidently, is an exhortation which is necessary. What does he mean when he exhorts and pleads with us to 'love one another'? I cannot think of a better way of putting it than simply to say that we are to be manifesting in our lives with one another, and in our attitude towards one another, everything that we read about love in 1 Corinthians 13. We are not to be puffed up; we are not to be easily provoked; we are not to think evil; we are not to rejoice in evil about others; we are to hope for all things and to hope for the best in other people.

I am afraid that as we read those words together, we all feel condemned. Loving one another is to love like that, and not only those whom we happen to like, but even those whom we dislike. That is the test of the Christian. You remember how our Lord put it in the Sermon on the Mount. He said, 'If ye love them which love you, what reward have ye?' (Matt 5:46). That is not difficult—anybody can do that—natural love does that. But the whole test of the Christian is to love the difficult person and to manifest 1 Corinthians 13 with the trying person.

'But I thought you said,' says someone, 'that this is only applicable to Christian brethren?' Yes, it is; but, alas, we all know that though we are Christians we are not perfect; there are things about all of us that irritate others. *God, forgive us for it.* There are things that should not belong to us, but they are there, and this calls for patience in others, it calls for sympathy, it calls for understanding; and that is what John is pleading for at this point. He is asking these people to do all they can to help one another, to bear with one another, not to be antagonistic, not to become irritated. If you see your brother at fault, be patient with him, pray for him, try to help him, be sorry for him, instead of feeling it is something that is hurting you. See it as something that is hurting him terribly and doing him great harm and robbing him of so much joy in his Christian life.

That is what love means—that you somehow detach yourself from the problem and do not think of it in terms of that which is hurting you, but look upon it as Christ did, and have compassion for that person, take hold of him, love him out of it. I do not want to go into this in detail because I am anxious rather to emphasise the great appeal which John makes and the terms in which he puts that appeal, trusting that as we do so we shall all not only feel condemned for our failure, but also that we shall feel a great sense of longing to live this Christian life in all its glory and in all its fullness.

Now John not only puts this as an appeal, he lifts it to a higher level. He goes further than that, and he puts it in such a way that it becomes something very solemn, and it becomes a warning. That, again, is something that is so typical and characteristic of the New Testament method of teaching holiness. It does not consist of a mere denunciation of sins or the doing of certain little things. It is so easy to stand and condemn people who do certain things; but that is not the teaching of holiness. *This* is holiness—loving one another—and this is to be seen in terms of our whole relationship to God. It is a great doctrinal matter, and the New Testament always puts the teaching about holiness in terms of ultimate doctrine. Let us see how John does this here.

He does it in a very characteristic way. John, as we have had occasion to see in our study of this epistle, had an interesting type of mind. There was a great deal of the poet and the mystic in him. His method is not logical like that of Paul. As someone has said, John thinks in circles; he generally starts on a practical point, then he philosophises about it in a Christian way, and then he arrives at some glorious statement of doctrine. And this is a perfect illustration of his method.

In my opinion, John ends with what Paul would have said at the start. John says, 'Beloved, let us love one another . . . every one that loveth is born of God.' Then comes the negative which he is so fond of: 'He that loveth not, knoweth not God,' and then he says, 'for God is love.' Now that is the poet's way of arriving at truth, but I think it will perhaps be more helpful to us, especially those of us who are not poetic and those of us who are more logically minded, if we put it the other way round. The fundamental statement is, 'God is love'; and because God is love, certain things must be true of us. That is the logical approach.

So, let us start like this, and more than ever do I feel my utter and complete inadequacy as I try to handle words like these. Indeed, who is sufficient for these things? What right has a pigmy man to make such statements as these? And yet it is true—'God is love.' No one can answer that; one trembles even to handle it; it cannot be analysed. I simply want to point out that John does not say merely that God loves us or that God is loving. He goes beyond that. He says, '"God is love"; God essentially is love; God's nature is love; you cannot think of God without love.'

Of course he has already told us that God is light in exactly the same way—that was the first pronouncement. 'This then is the message . . . God is light' (1:5), and in exactly the same way 'God is love' and God is spirit. This baffles the imagination; it is something that is altogether beyond our comprehension, and yet we start with it.

St. Augustine and others deduce from this the doctrine of the Trinity. I think there may be a great deal in that; this very fact that God is love declares the Trinity—God the Father loves the Son, and the link is the person of the Holy Spirit. Ah! this is high doctrine; it is beyond us. All I know is that God, in the very essence of His nature and being, is love, and you cannot think of God and must not think of Him except in terms of love. Everything that God is and does is coloured by this; all God's actions have this aspect of love in them and the aspect of light in the same way. That is how God always manifests Himself—light and love.

'Therefore, because that is the fundamental postulate, because that is so true of God,' John is saying, 'that works itself out for us like this: Because God is love, we ought to love one another, for three reasons.' The first is that 'love is of God'; in other words, love is from God, love flows from God. It is as if John were turning to these people and saying, 'You know, we ought to love one another. We ought more and more to clutch at the great privilege we have of being like God. God loves, and this love I am talking about,' says John, 'is something that only comes from God—it is derived from Him.'

John is not talking about natural love at all—let us get rid of that idea. The Greek scholars know that this is a word that really belongs to the New Testament. The pagans did not understand it; it was a new conception altogether. Indeed, there was a sense in which the Jews themselves did not understand it; it was something new that God gave to the world through Jesus Christ. Our whole idea of love is so debased, it is so carnal; it is the thing you read about in the newspapers or see in the cinema. But that is not the thing that John is speaking about. He is speaking about this love that comes from God, something that God Himself is doing. 'Beloved,' says John, 'love one another. Cannot you see that as you are doing this you are proving that you are of God? You are doing something that God Himself is doing.' How foolish we are not to rise to the great height of our calling; let us manifest the fact that we have received this from God. That is the first reason for brotherly love.

The second reason for loving one another is that it is the evidence of our new birth. 'Beloved, let us love one another: for love is of God; and every one that loveth is born of God.' Now that is why I said at the beginning that this is the most thorough test of whether we are true Christians or not. You see, what finally makes us Christians is that we are born again, we are born of God. It is not a certain intellectual proposition; it is not that we are defenders of the faith and so are concerned about being strictly orthodox; it is not that we are highly moral and ethical; it is not that we do a lot of good and are benevolent. The one thing that makes us Christians is that we are born of God, that we are partakers of the divine nature—nothing less than that, nothing short of that.

'Here is the thing that proves you are born of God,' says John in effect; and this works out in two ways. Only those who are born of God can love like this; nobody else can. The natural man cannot exercise this love; it is obvious that he cannot. Look at the life of the world and you see the breakdown; the natural man cannot love in this sense. The only people who can love as God loves are those who have received the nature of God. It is no use asking the world to 'love one another.' It is impossible; they are incapable of doing it. We need the divine nature within us before we can truly love one another. If within the church you have failure on the part of men and women to love one another, what hope is there for the world to do this? It is utterly impossible.

Let me put it like this: According to this argument, and this is the argument of the New Testament everywhere, those who are born of God must love one another—they cannot help it. If something of the divine nature is in me, and the divine nature is love—'God is love'—then there must be this principle of love within me. It must be here, it must be manifesting itself; and if I am not conscious of this life within me, and if I am not manifesting this life somehow or other, however feebly, then I am not a Christian.

As we have said, John does not put this merely as an exhortation.

He puts it in such a way that it becomes a desperately serious matter, and I almost tremble as I proclaim this doctrine. There are people who are unloving, unkind, always criticising, whispering, backbiting, pleased when they hear something against another Christian. Oh, my heart grieves and bleeds for them as I think of them; they are pronouncing and proclaiming that they are not born of God. They are outside the life of God; and I repeat, there is no hope for such people unless they repent and turn to Him. They belong to the world; the murderous spirit of Cain is in them. God is love, and if I say I am born of God and the nature of God is in me, then there must be some of this love in me. 'Every one that loveth is born of God,' and everyone who is born of God loves—the two statements mean the same thing, so that this is proof positive, final evidence, of my new birth and that I am born of God.

Do you feel any love within you towards that person you naturally dislike, that person who is so irritating and can be in certain respects so hurtful to you? Do you know a sense of compassion and pity? Do you pray for that person? Can you truly say you are sorry? That is what love does. Do you feel that with regard to these people? If you are born of God, you must, however feebly.

And, lastly, John says that to love one another is evidence of spiritual knowledge. 'Beloved, let us love one another: for love is of God; and every one that loveth is born of God, and knoweth God.' He puts this negatively also: 'He that loveth not, knoweth not God.' In other words, it is by manifesting this life to one another that we give proof of the fact that we have a truly spiritual knowledge, that we really know God. Now this is the logical development of spiritual knowledge; it is to know God. God is love, and therefore the more I know God, the more will I know that God is love, and the more will I know about love.

We go through stages in this matter. Let us use Paul's analogy in 1 Corinthians 13. 'When I was a child, I spake as a child, I understood as a child.' Yes, but we are growing, says Paul in effect; '"now I know in part," but when I see Him face to face, I will know everything. I do not know everything now. I start with a little knowledge, but it is growing and developing as I walk in fellowship with God.' We start with knowing certain things about God: God is great, God is limitless in power, God is someone who is love and is prepared to forgive us for our sins. 'I know a whole series of things about God, and, you know,' says John in effect, 'as I go on and grow in Christ, I pay less and less attention to the things I know about God; now my interest is to know God Himself. I was interested in gifts, but I now want to know the Giver. My knowledge has become the knowledge of the person; and as my knowledge of the person increases, I know more and more that God is love. At the beginning there were times when I was tempted to doubt whether God loved me. Things went against me, and I felt I was not receiving a fair deal; but as I go on, I cease to think things like that. I know that God is love, and when I am tempted to question, I still say God is love. I know that more and more; and as I know more and more that God is love, I see that nothing matters but love. And the more I see this in God, the more I want to look at Him, and the more I love my brethren; and the more I love my brethren, the more I prove that God is love.'

This is a wonderful argument. I think that all writers on the spiritual life are agreed that the ultimate stage is this stage of loving. Knowledge and love become one at a certain point; knowing God means, I repeat, not knowing things *about* God but really knowing Him. The same word is used about God's knowledge of us. God said of the children of Israel through Amos, 'You only have I *known* of all the families of the earth' (Amos 3:2). He did not mean that He knew nothing about the others; He meant He knew them in this intimacy of love. Do we know that God is love, and are we giving proof of this by loving one another? It is not surprising that John exhorted us all to that. These are the reasons for loving one another.

But there is another point in exhorting men and women to love one another. You cannot command natural love, but you can command Christian love. This means that as I live with others, and as I am in this world of time, suddenly I may come across something that tempts me to act like the old, natural man. But as a Christian I am not to do that. Before I act, I am to say to myself, 'I am a Christian. I am born of God. I am unlike the natural man. I have no right to live like that. I must live as a new man. I will put off the old and put on the new. I will claim that God is in me, and the Holy Spirit, and that Christ dwells with me, and therefore I will not act like that; I must be like Him.'

In other words, you bring the Apostle's great argument to bear; you look upon that other person, and you see him with the eyes of God as it were. You have pity; you have compassion; you feel sorry for the other person; you remember that you have been commanded to love one another as Christians. You just remind yourself of the three mighty arguments—love is of God, it belongs to us who receive the divine nature, it is the inevitable corollary of knowing God. It means being like God Himself.

What a privilege and what a glorious honour that God calls upon us to be like Himself! 'Be ye therefore perfect, even as your Father which is in heaven is perfect' (Matt 5:48); and that was said in the context of loving one another.

'Beloved, let us love one another: for love is of God; and every one that loveth is born of God, and knoweth God. He that loveth not, knoweth not God; for God is love.'

4

THE MANIFEST LOVE OF GOD

In this was manifested the love of God toward us, because that God sent his only begotten Son into the world, that we might live through him. Herein is love, not that we loved God, but that he loved us, and sent his Son to be the propitiation for our sins.

1 JOHN 4:9-10

IN THESE TWO VERSES the Apostle continues with the theme of the vital importance of brotherly love. We have seen that he considers this theme in terms of his great proposition that 'God is love'; it is from that base that his whole appeal to us to love one another arises. Now here he continues with this same subject, this vital importance of our loving one another, we who claim to be Christians; and John proceeds to deal with this by elaborating that fundamental postulate of his that 'God is love.' He has told us that God is essentially love—not only that God loves us and that God is loving, but that God's very nature is love. As God is light, so God is love; and His holy love is something that covers the whole of His life and His every activity.

But now the Apostle is anxious to remind us that God is actually manifesting that essential nature of His. He is love, but mercifully for us He has *'manifested'* that love, He has made it unmistakably plain and clear. So we can put John's immediate argument like this: 'If only you really understood this love, if only you knew something about it, then most of your problems and difficulties would immediately vanish.' So he proceeds to tell us something further about this great and wondrous and glorious love of God.

Surely we all must agree that this is something that is equally true of us. The more I study the New Testament and live the Christian life, the more convinced I am that our fundamental difficulty, our fundamental lack, is the lack of seeing the love of God. It is not so much our knowledge that is defective but our vision of the love of God. Thus our greatest object and endeavour should be to know Him better, and thus we will love Him more truly. Now John's object is to help these first Christians to whom he writes in just this way, because he is quite sure that once they love God, they will love one another.

That is something we find running right through the Bible; the second commandment follows the first. The first commandment is, 'Thou shalt love the Lord thy God with all thy heart, and with all thy soul, and with all thy mind. . . . And the second is like unto it, Thou shalt love thy neighbor as thyself' (Matt 22:37, 39). But you will never do the second until you have done the first; so we must start with the love of God.

Now in these two verses we have a sublime statement of this. You notice how reminiscent this is of John 3:16: 'God so loved the world, that he gave his only begotten Son, that whosoever believeth in him should not perish, but have everlasting life.' It is just a variation of that. It is a wonderful statement concerning the love of God, but at the same time it is a perfect summary of the gospel. Indeed, I want to go further and suggest to you that these two verses together are a perfect and complete synopsis of Christian theology. And I am particularly anxious to emphasise that last statement. You notice that John does not content himself with just saying that God is love; he does not leave it at that. John says that the love of God can only be understood in the light of certain vital truths, and those truths are highly theological.

Let me explain what I mean by that and give my reasons for putting it in that particular form. I think this is a statement that needs to be repeated and emphasised at the present time, because the great tendency in this present century has been to put up as antitheses the idea of God as a God of love on the one side, and theology or dogma or doctrine on the other. Now the average person has generally taken up such a position as follows: 'You know, I am not interested in your doctrine. Surely the great mistake the Church has made throughout the centuries is all this talk about dogma, all this doctrine of sin, and the doctrine of the Atonement, and this idea of justification and sanctification. Of course there are some people who may be interested in that kind of thing; they may enjoy reading and arguing about it, but as for myself,' says this man, 'there does not seem to be any truth in it; all I say is that God is love.' So he puts up this idea of God as love over and against all these doctrines which the Church has taught throughout the centuries.

Now that is something which must be faced and faced very frankly. Indeed, is it not true to say that men have not only put up this idea of God as love over the doctrines I have mentioned, but they have gone so far as to say that they are not interested in the doctrine of the person of Christ? 'The one thing that matters,' they say, 'is that God is love. Jesus of Nazareth was a great teacher, but when you talk about the doctrine of the Incarnation and the Virgin Birth—I am not interested in these refinements. All I know is that Jesus was a wonderful man, and He taught us that God is love.' So this idea of God as a God of love has been used as the argument of all arguments for denouncing doctrine and theology.

But all that, according to these two verses which we are considering here, and according to the whole of the New Testament, is an utter travesty of the Christian truth and position. According to these two verses, people who thus put up as opposites the idea of God as love and these basic, fundamental doctrines can, in the last analysis, know nothing whatsoever about the love of God. Is it not interesting to observe that it is John, whom people like to call the Apostle of love, who is the one who outlines the love of God in this particular way and manner? It is as typical of his Gospel as it is of this first epistle; it is John who explains the love of God in this highly doctrinal and theological form.

The vital question which we must ask ourselves is this: How do we know that God is a God of love? What is the basis of our knowledge? What is my ultimate sanction for saying I believe that God is a God of love? 'All I am interested in,' says the average man, 'is that God is a God of love and that He will forgive my sins.' But how do you know that He will forgive your sins? What right have you to say that you believe that God will do that? Oh, how easy it is to use these expressions; but let us stop and ask the question quite simply: What is my authority, and how do I know?

I suggest to you that there are only two ultimate answers to that: You are either basing it upon your own or somebody else's philosophical conception of God, or you are accepting in simplicity, and as they are, the very statements that are made in the Bible concerning God and His love. I do not think that it is at all difficult to prove that the average person, and especially the kind of person of whom I have been speaking, bases his whole idea of a God of love solely upon his own thoughts. He has no proof if he denies these facts and doctrines. He says that he believes what he says he believes, but he cannot prove it—he has nothing to substantiate it. He believes it, and he says that others have said it, and therefore it must be the case; but as to any final, ultimate proof, he has none.

Now the Bible itself actually does teach us that God has manifested Himself and His love in different ways. God has manifested His love in creation; the very act of creating the world at all must have been a manifestation of it, and this is seen in the order and arrangement which we see in the world. In the same way you can deduce the love of God from Providence. Certain things that happen are indications of it. Indeed, our Lord and Saviour Jesus Christ once put it like this: '[God] maketh his sun to rise on the evil and on the good, and sendeth rain on the just and on the unjust' (Matt 5:45). The love of God, then, is something which is manifested in God's providential care for and dealings with mankind.

But the great statement of the Bible from beginning to end, and especially the great statement of the New Testament, is that the love of God is only to be seen finally, and to be known truly, when you look at what God has done for us and in us in and through the Lord Jesus Christ. That is the great theme of the Bible. The Old Testament is a book that looks forward to the coming of Someone. It is God's gracious promise that a deliverer, the Messiah, is going to come; and in the New Testament you have an account of how He came and what He did.

This is something which is absolutely essential. The love of God can only be finally understood and appreciated in the Lord Jesus Christ. It is what God has done in Him and through Him that ultimately reveals it all. 'In this was manifested the love of God toward us, because that God sent his only begotten Son into the world, that we might live through him. Herein is love, not that we loved God, but that he loved us, and sent his Son to be the propitiation for our sins.' That is the manifestation of the love of God, says John, and here again is a compendium of theology, a synopsis of doctrine. There is no greater theological statement in the whole Bible than these two wonderful verses.

John does not say, 'God is love' and then pass on to something else. He says, 'If you want to know anything about love, you must realise these truths, because it is in this way that God has manifested His wondrous love to us. Apart from these things, you know nothing about love.' But let me go further. The love of God, I maintain, is only understood and felt in terms of theology, and to reject the theology is to reject the love of God and to be bemusing ourselves with some hypothetical and imaginary love. 'In this was manifested the love of God,' and here we have John's exposition of it.

Having, therefore, emphasised that fundamental attitude, let me attempt with reverence to look at this glorious and sublime statement. Would you like to join 'with all the saints,' as Paul puts it, in trying to measure and estimate 'the breadth, and length, and depth, and height; and to know the love of Christ, which passeth knowledge' (Eph 3:18-19)? This is how John proceeds. We are, of course, attempting the impossible. We are going to measure the immeasurable; we shall try to plumb the depths that no man can ever reach; we shall ascend the height which no man can ever aspire unto; and yet, says Paul, let us do it. And as we attempt to do so now, let us be guided by the Apostle John.

His general proposition is this: God's love has been manifested in what He has done for us or in us in the Lord Jesus Christ. So let us start in the depths; let us start to look at the love of God and attempt to measure it by looking at ourselves. You will never know the love of God until you know yourself. We will never appreciate the love of God until we know the startling truth about ourselves apart from Him and about His wondrous grace. God, we are told, has loved us. Why? Has God loved us because we are lovable? Has He loved us because we are such kind and wonderful people, so deserving of His favour?

Consider the answer of the Apostle John in these two verses: the love of God, let me emphasise it again, is only to be understood theologically. Here is what we are told: God sent His only begotten Son that we might live through Him; from which I deduce that apart from Him we are dead, and that is the fundamental statement about man as the result of sin which runs right through the Bible. 'You hath he quickened,' says Paul writing to the Ephesians, 'who were dead in trespasses and sins' (Eph 2:1). All of us, apart from Jesus Christ, are in a state of spiritual death. We not only lack a knowledge of God, we lack an understanding of spiritual things; the great spiritual faculty that God gave man at the beginning is lying dormant. As a result of sin we have no life in us; we do not *live*, we *exist*. Read the first three verses of Ephesians 2, and there you have it: 'And you hath he quickened, who were dead in trespasses and sins; wherein in time past ye walked according to the course of this world, according to the prince of the power of the air, the spirit that now worketh in the children of disobedience: among whom also we all had our conversation in times past in the lusts of our flesh, fulfilling the desires of the flesh and of the mind; and were by nature the children of wrath, even as others.' Dead—dead to God and to His spiritual qualities—dead to everything that is truly uplifting and ennobling—living according to the course of this life and of this age—an existence in a state of death. This is what John says—namely, that Christ came that we might live through Him; without Him we are dead.

But not only that. According to the Bible, far from being lovable and loving, men and women by nature hate God. 'Herein is love, not that we loved God'; that is, it is not the case that we in our natural state loved God and He responded to our love. The picture of the Bible is not that people are ever seeking for God because they love Him. That is the popular theology—that men and women are seeking God and that God responds to their request. Not at all! 'Not that we loved God, *but that he loved us.*' People, by nature, do not love God. According to the Bible, by nature and as the result of sin and the Fall, they are enemies of God. 'The carnal mind'—the natural man—'is enmity against God,' says Paul; 'it is not subject to the law of God, neither indeed can be' (Rom 8:7).

Is all that not the simple truth, and must we not all confess that by nature and apart from the light we have had in the gospel of Jesus Christ, when things go wrong the feeling is one of enmity? We are enemies, aliens, strangers, at enmity against God. 'God commendeth his love toward us, in that, while we were yet sinners. . . . For if when we were enemies, we were reconciled to God by the death of his Son . . .' (Rom 5:8, 10). That is the picture that is given of man; dead and hating God; far from loving him, but rather feeling opposed to Him; and because of all that, man by nature is under the wrath of God and deserves the punishment of God for his sins. That is Paul's statement, and it is the statement of the Bible everywhere.

We are, let me remind you, trying to measure this amazing love of

God, and that is the first measurement: men and women down in the dregs and depths of sin, deserving nothing but wrath, and with nothing to be said for them. And the whole argument of the New Testament is that until we see that that is the simple truth about us, we do not begin to know anything about the love of God. That is the first step in measuring it.

But let us go on to the second. Let us proceed immediately from the depths right up to the heights. We have seen man. Now let us look at God and see what He has done, and the astounding thing we are told is that God has 'sent *His only begotten Son* into the world.' That is the central message of the New Testament, and indeed of the whole Bible; it is about a person called Jesus Christ of Nazareth. Who is He? John has been talking about Him; his whole message is about this person, and this is what he tells us about Him: He is God's 'only begotten Son.' The original reads like this: 'In this was manifested the love of God toward us, because that God sent his only begotten Son into the world, that we might live through him.' His Son—His only begotten Son. That statement means that this person has a unique kinship with God. It is John's way of saying that Jesus Christ is none other than the eternal Son of God, co-eternal, equal with God, dwelling in the bosom of God, the effulgence of God, one with God, the second person of the blessed Trinity.

But, you see, John puts this in another form: God '*sent*' His Son. So if Jesus Christ is someone who has been 'sent' into the world, he must have existed before. None of us have been sent into the world. We are born into this world, but here is someone who was sent from somewhere else. He existed before, in eternity. His birth at Bethlehem was not the beginning for Him. He began His earthly course, He came, He was sent from heaven. That is another way of estimating the love of God. God has manifested His love towards us in that He, there in glory, has sent from heaven, with its eternal bliss and absolute perfection, into this world His only begotten Son. We cannot fathom this—it escapes us. But can we try to imagine something of what this means. God, we are told, 'sent' His Son; He asked Him, His only begotten Son, to come into this world, consisting of men and women such as I have already been describing. 'In this was manifested the love of God,' that out of heaven He 'sent His only begotten Son,' the one who is in His own bosom.

Fathers and mothers, does this mean anything to you? Think of your own love to your children and multiply it by infinity, and that is God's Father-love to God the Son; and yet He sent Him into the world. So you know nothing about the love of God unless you believe the doctrine of the Incarnation. Believe me, you cannot talk of the love of God dwelling in you unless you know that Jesus of Nazareth is the unique and only begotten Son of God. If you are uncertain about the person of Christ, you have no love of God in you—you are fooling yourself. You must not put the love of God as an opposite to the doctrine of the person of Christ. He is the God-man; all the miracles and the supernatural power, all the fullness of the Godhead dwells in Him bodily. Understanding the person of Christ is absolutely essential to understanding the doctrine of the love of God.

But let us pause there. From the heights let us come down again to the depths, and let us glance for a moment at what the Lord Jesus Christ has done. We have said that God has 'sent His only begotten Son' from heaven; but He sent Him, John says, '*into the world*.' O blessed be His holy name! The Son, the only begotten Son, came into this world. We are measuring the love of God—and this is the way to measure it. Look at the world into which He came. You remember His birth and what we are told about it. This is the sort of world that the eternal Son of God, who had come from heaven, came into: There was no room for Him and for Mary and Joseph in the inn. The selfishness of mankind was such that even a woman in this condition did not get a room and had to go into a stable; so the Lord of glory was placed in a manger in a stable. That is the sort of world He came into; a selfish, grasping, self-centred world in which every man is out for himself.

You also remember the story of Herod and the massacre of the innocents—all the malice, envy, hatred, and bloodshed. And, oh, the poverty into which He came! They could not afford to give the price of the highest offering for Him; they had to offer the two turtledoves—they could not afford any more. He was born into a very poor home; he knew something of the squalor and the need that accompanies poverty. And for thirty years He lived a very ordinary life as a carpenter, mixing with ordinary people. Can you imagine what it must have meant to Him, the Lord of glory, the eternal Son of God who came out of God's eternal bosom, to see sin firsthand? To look at the ugliness of evil and sin and see it face to face? The shame of it all and the foulness of it all! We are measuring the love of God, and that is the measure of it. How could He in all His purity and holiness ever come from heaven and live for thirty years in the kind of world in which you and I are living? How could He have done it? How could He stand or bear it?

Then watch Him in His ministry, teaching His pure, loving, holy doctrine, seeing the opposition that arose. Look at the people looking at one another, asking their questions, trying to trip Him—the cleverness they display in trying to pull Him down. Look at the scheming; look at the treachery even among His own friends; look at Him deserted by all His disciples; look at Him on trial; look at the crown of thorns they put upon His holy brow—that is the world into which He came. 'In this was manifested the love of God . . . that God sent his only begotten Son into the world.'

But more, he sent Him, we are told, to be '*the propitiation for our sins.*' What does this mean? Here, of course, is the great classic doctrine of the atonement, and it means that he sent Him into this world in order that He might become the sin offering for us. It means that God 'hath made him to be sin for us, who knew no sin; that we might be made the righteousness of God in him' (2 Cor 5:21). It means that Jesus Christ is not only the priest, but He is also the offering, the propitiation, the sacrifice offered. God sent Him into the world in order that God might punish our sins in Him. He has made His Son the sacrifice; it is a substitutionary offering for your sins and mine. That was why He was there in the Garden sweating drops of blood, because He knew what it involved—it involved a separation from the face of His Father. And that is why He cried out on the Cross, 'My God, my God, why hast thou forsaken me?' There we see the love of God not only in the world He came into, but in the propitiation, the sacrifice, the substitutionary death, so that you and I might be delivered. Herein was manifested the love of God, that God sent His only begotten Son to death, to the cruel shame and agony and suffering of the cross, to be made sin for us who Himself knew no sin and so was innocent.

But thank God, it did not stop at that. He raised Him again from the dead and thereby proclaimed that the sacrifice was enough, that the law was satisfied, and that everything was complete. I say again, you do not begin to know anything about the love of God until you see that if Christ had not died on the cross in that way, God could not forgive sin. I say it with reverence: that is God's way of making forgiveness, for without the doctrine of the atonement you do not understand the love of

God. Let me beseech you, never again put the love of God and doctrine as opposites. It is only in this way you understand the love of God. There is the depth again.

But let us once more rise from the depths to the heights; let us rise with Him in resurrection, and let us look at what He has meant to us as the result of that. Christ died—that is what we are told; He has been made 'the propitiation for our sins.' In other words, as the result of what He has done, God forgives us for our sins; by His death we are reconciled to God in Him; we have redemption through His blood. The blood is essential; never speak about it as if it were something that is legalistic. 'In [Him] we have redemption through his blood, even the forgiveness of sins' (Col 1:14). In Him we are reconciled to God, pardoned, forgiven, and restored. Yes, and even more, God sent His Son into the world, that we might live through Him. We receive the gift of life; we begin to live, because He came. We are given His nature; we are given His power. He becomes One who resides in us; we live in Him, and He is in us; we live through Him. There we again rise to the height.

That is what God has done for us in His love through Christ—pardon, forgiveness, peace, reconciliation, life anew. We begin to live in a new world, and we see new possibilities. We know something of His mighty working in us and the power which operates in us. That is how the love of God is manifested, that He sent His Son, and the Son has taken hold of us and, as Paul puts it, has 'raised us up together, and made us sit together in heavenly places in Christ Jesus' (Eph 2:6). But shall we dare to venture to rise still higher and to the highest height of all?

Finally, why has God done all this? Why has God had anything to do with such creatures as men and women, dead in trespasses and sins, rebels—hating Him, being against Him, turning His world into a living hell? Why did God ever even look on them, let alone send His only begotten Son to them, and even to the cruel death and shame of the cross, making Him a sin offering? Why has God done this? What led Him to do it? What is this love of God, and wherein does it consist? 'Not that we loved God, *but that he loved us*,' moved by nothing but His own self-generated love. Though we are what we are, 'God is love,' and His great heart of love, in spite of all that is in us, unmoved by anything save itself, has done it all.

I do not know what your feeling is at this moment, but I will tell you what mine is. I cannot understand the hardness of my own heart.

How could any of us look at all this and believe it and not be lost in love to God? How can we contemplate these things and not be utterly broken down? How can any hatred remain in us? How can we do anything but love one another as we contemplate such amazing love? How can we look at these things and believe them and not feel utterly unworthy and ashamed of ourselves and feel that we owe all and everything to Him and that our whole lives must be given to express our gratitude, our praise, and our thanksgiving? Oh, let us resolve together to meditate more and more every day upon this amazing love. Look at it in terms of yourself, in terms of God, what God has done, what Christ has done. Go over these things; study them; read the Bible about them; examine them. Go on looking at them; contemplate them until your heart is broken and you feel the love of God possessing you wholly. 'Love so amazing, so divine, demands my soul, my life, my all.'

5

WE OUGHT ALSO . . .

Beloved, if God so loved us, we ought also to love one another.

1 JOHN 4:11

THESE ARE THE WORDS that follow in exalted magnificence the ones we were considering in verses 9 and 10, and this word 'so' in our text refers us back to those two great verses. Nothing sublimer than that can be found anywhere, and we have looked at those verses and tried through them to measure the breadth and the height and the depth of the love of God in Jesus Christ. We have considered that glorious revelation of the love of God, and now these are the words that follow. 'Beloved, if God so loved us, we ought also to love one another.'

I wonder how you felt as you read these words. I wonder whether there is anybody who feels that it is a bit of an anti-climax, after that magnificent contemplation of God's revelation of His love, to have an exhortation, an appeal, to love one another. I always feel myself that when we come to a verse like this, after verses like 9 and 10, we place ourselves in one of the most thorough and profound tests of our spiritual perception and understanding that we can ever face. I do not hesitate to say that it is a verse like this that really tests where we stand spiritually. Verses 9 and 10 are, of course, the essential doctrine; I described them as a synopsis of Christian theology because in them we see the doctrines of man, of sin, of the person of Christ, of the Trinity, of the Incarnation, of the atonement, the resurrection and the ascension. It is all there, and it is absolutely essential; but our test in this verse is equally essential, equally a part of the truth. It tests our spirituality in this sense: it shows whether we are deeply and vitally concerned about these things or whether we just look at truth in general.

This is another characteristic of the gospel—the New Testament message. Have you not noticed how often it does this sort of thing? It takes you to the heights and then suddenly brings you down to the plain. And that is the way, I think, in which we should approach this statement—with, first of all, a bit of self-examination. Is our first feeling as we hear it, 'Ah, well, there is not going to be anything very wonderful to consider here? We are really again just facing an exhortation and an appeal to love one another. It was marvelous to look at the manifestation of the love of God and to contemplate all those great doctrines. How glorious all that was, but, "You ought also to love one another"— this is going to be unpleasant!' I trust nobody is reacting like that, but a verse like this does test us; it finds out exactly where we are and places us in our spiritual condition.

There are two obvious answers to such an attitude which stand out on the surface of this statement. Let me put them like this: First and foremost, Christianity, the Christian gospel, is not merely truth to be contemplated. It is that, but it is also a life which is given and a life which is to be lived. Let me put that in terms of a comparison like this: Those two verses which we considered earlier and this verse which follows make me think instinctively of the records we have in the Gospels of what happened on the Mount of Transfiguration. Our Lord took Peter and James and John aside; they went up into the mountain together, and He was transfigured before them. Moses and Elijah appeared and began to speak, and the three disciples were lost in a sense of wonder and rapture. Peter, the spokesman, jumped in as usual and said, 'Let us make three tabernacles; one for thee, and one for Moses, and one for Elijah' (Mark 9:5), by which he meant, 'Let us stay here; this is magnificent, this is glorious, this is wonderful.' But in effect our Lord said, 'No, Peter, there are great and terrible problems at the foot of this mountain. There is a man coming even now with a lunatic boy who is helpless, and my disciples whom we left behind cannot deal with him. We have to go down; we cannot stay here and contemplate the glory; we must go down and do something in the plains.'

That is the sort of thing we have in our text here, and we had a similar feeling when we dealt with those verses at the beginning of Chapter 3.[1] We were certainly on the Mount in verses 9 and 10, beholding glorious things; but we must not stay there. Christianity, let me emphasise this again, is not merely a truth to be contemplated—it is a life which is given and a life which must be lived. Unless our contemplation of truth leads us to do something about our own lives and about other people, that contemplation is useless.

We are here, of course, face to face with the whole error of what is called mysticism; that, I think, is its carnal error. The mystic is very concerned about the love of God. He is right when he says that the *summum bonum*, the highest good, is the contemplation of the love of God and sets out upon the mystic way. He puts himself under very rigid discipline; he will deny himself many things which the world affords him, quite legitimate things in themselves, because he is hoping to arrive at this knowledge of love. But the tragedy of the mystic is that he does all that in a more or less philosophical manner. He is concerned simply to *contemplate* love, and the result is that he is far remote from love. He is a wonderful man himself, but he does not know anything about the problems of life and human existence. He does not help other men and women.

How different from the Lord Himself, the friend of publicans and sinners, the one who said to Peter, 'No, we must not build a tabernacle here and stay here; we must go down and do something about those problems which are down there.' Mysticism is, in a sense, the very antithesis of the New Testament teaching. Thank God that, according to the New Testament, love is not a feeling only. It is not something even that you contemplate philosophically. Love is the most active and practical thing in the world, and it shows and manifests itself in action. 'In this was manifested the love of God toward us.' 'Beloved, if God so loved us, we ought also to love one another.' Never separate these two things; they belong together.

Then my second general remark, which is obvious on the very surface of the text, is that this statement is the characteristic New Testament method of teaching holiness. I suggest you will never find a more typical New Testament expression of the teaching of sanctification and holiness than you have in these verses. Let me put that negatively. I am prepared to prove the contention that the New Testament nowhere comes to us and says something like this: 'Wouldn't you like to have a further blessing—wouldn't you like to have an abundant life—wouldn't you like to be living life with a capital *L*—wouldn't you like to be living the victorious life? Now it is all here, and you only have to receive it.'

The New Testament never does that. Rather, it teaches holiness in the way it does it here. It does not say, 'You are missing a great deal; there is a wonderful, higher life possible to you.' No! It says, 'My friend, you are living a low type of Christian life, and you have no right to be doing so. You ought to be ashamed of yourself for doing so; you are denying the gospel you believe. "Beloved . . . you ought."' The New Testament pronounces this as a kind of divine logic. It says, 'You have no right to be living any other kind of life if you call yourself a Christian, if you say you believe all that.' That is the New Testament method.

Let me put it like this: The living of the Christian life, according to the New Testament, is not primarily dependent upon some experience or some blessing which we have received. It is, rather, the outworking of the truth which we claim to believe. Now I suggest that that can never be repeated too frequently. Go through these New Testament epistles, and I think you will always find that that is their invariable method. The first half of most of these epistles is pure doctrine, a reminder to the people of what God has done to them and the exalted position in which they have been placed. And then the writer says, 'Therefore . . .'

I can never understand people's objection to logic. The New Testament is full of it. It is here—'If God so loved us . . . then you ought.' We talk about divine imperatives. Well, here, if you like, is one. If you believe, then it must follow on; you have no right to be in any other position. Everything in the New Testament is in terms of truth. You are not exhorted by the New Testament not to sin and to live a good life in order that you may live life with a capital *L*. Not at all! The New Testament tells you, 'Ye are not your own. For ye are bought with a price' (1 Cor 6:19-20); so you have no right to use the body for fornication.

I wonder why we object to the truth being put like that. Why do we prefer it to be put in some sentimental form? Why avoid this tremendous logic? This is the New Testament method. If I say I believe *this*, then I must live like *that*. There is no use in my saying I believe *this* unless I behave like *that*, and there are terrible warnings against not doing this. The New Testament teaching of holiness is always in terms of truth. It is something that is to be applied; so let us proceed to do so, let us work this out together. I grant you that this is not a pleasant procedure; I grant you that it is much nicer to look at verses 9 and 10. It is even easier for the preacher!

John writes this epistle in order that these people may conquer the world in which they are living. He says, 'I write unto you, that your joy may be full'; and he goes on to say, in effect, 'If you want your joy to be full, you must put the Christian belief into practice.' We are engaged in Christian warfare; we believe in the fight of faith; and here is the way to learn how to fight it. Let us now get down to practicalities.

I am a Christian in this world, and there are other Christians. We are members of churches together, and I find some of these people to be rather difficult. I find that there are Christians whom I do not like by nature and instinctively. That was the position in the early church, and it is still the same; that is why John is making this great appeal. 'Beloved, let us love one another: for love is of God.' The whole of this section, from verse 7 right on to the first verse of the next chapter, is all about the question of brotherly love, and here he tells us how to do this. Now the question is, what do you do about it when you come up against these other people who seem to irritate you and are a problem to you and who really are making things rather difficult?

Here is John's answer: 'If God so loved us, we ought also to love one another.' This means something like this: Instead of giving way to that instinctive feeling that I have, instead of speaking or acting or react-ing at once, I stop and I talk to myself. I remind myself of the Christian truth which I believe, and I apply it to the whole situation. Now that is something which you and I have to do. This life of which the New Testament speaks, as I am never tired of pointing out, is full of the intel-lectual aspect. It is not a feeling. You do not wait until you feel like lov-ing other people—you make yourself love other people (*'we ought'*). According to the New Testament, Christians can make themselves love other Christians, and they are failing sadly if they do not do so.

How do they do it? They remind themselves of this truth: 'If God so loved us.' In other words, this is the procedure. The first thing I do when I feel irritated and disturbed and bewildered and perhaps antagonistic is to look at myself. Now that is half the battle. We all know perfectly well from experience that in this kind of problem the whole difficulty is that we are always looking at the other person and never at ourselves. But if I start with myself—if God so loved *me*—what do I find?

But usually I instinctively feel that I am being wronged, that I am not being dealt with fairly. I feel it is the other person who is difficult, and if only this other person could somehow change, there would be no diffi-culty, and all would be well and we should live happily together. 'One minute!' says the gospel; 'stop for a moment and look at yourself and remind yourself of exactly what you are.' The gospel brings us immediately face to face with this self that is in us which is the cause of all these troubles. 'In this was manifested the love of God toward us, because that God sent his only begotten Son into the world, that we might live through him . . . he loved us, and sent his Son to be the propitiation for our sins.'

In other words, let me remind you again of the truth we have been considering, that by nature we are dead in trespasses and sin, and that as Christians the old man and the old nature are still there. And the old man and the old nature can be described in a word: *self*. Self causes all these troubles. Self-will, self-love, self-trust, self-exaltation—these are the troubles. When we are honest with ourselves and examine ourselves, I think we will find that most of our troubles and difficulties arise from these causes. Let me give you a list which I have read in a book of the manifestation of this self-love. This is how it manifests itself: self-centredness, self-assertion, self-conceit, self-indulgence, self-pleasing, self-seeking, self-pity, self-sensitiveness, self-defence, self-sufficiency, self-consciousness, self-righteousness, self-glorying.

Is there anyone who would like to say that this is not a true description of himself or herself? That is the sort of persons we—all of us—are. It is no use denying it; that is the effect of the fall and of sin; that is what it has made of us. Self-centredness—looking at myself, watching myself, examining myself, always regarding myself. Self-assertion—asserting myself; I desire things, and I must have them. Self-conceit—how ready I am to defend myself and to condemn the same things in others! Self-indulgence—I am very indulgent with myself; I prohibit things in the other person, but it does not matter if I do the same thing myself. Self-pleasing—always doing things that please *me*. Self-seeking—always out for self. Self-pity—why should people treat me like this?—I have done no harm; I am not in the wrong at all—why should people be so difficult?—I am having a hard time and it really isn't fair. Self-sensitiveness—how touchy I am, how easily wounded, imagining difficulties and attacks, seeing them when they are not there, an abominable sensitivity. Self-defence—always on the defensive, waiting for people to be unpleasant, and because we are like that, we almost make them unpleasant—we are on the defensive.

Self-sufficiency, self-consciousness—oh, to get away from self! 'O wretched man that I am! who shall deliver me from the body of this death?' (Rom 7:24). How can I get away from this wretched, ugly self I am always thinking about? Isn't that the cry of every man and woman convicted of sin by the Holy Ghost? Now the effect of verses 9 and 10 is to expose all that, and I really am not prepared to listen to people who tell me that they glory in the revelation of God's love unless they have dealt with themselves. There is no value in any such striving to keep the tenets of the Christian faith unless they have made you see yourself in the world, unless it has flashed upon you in such a way as to make you see this manifestation of self; that is what the love of God always does. 'Herein is love, not that we loved God, but that he loved us'; incredible, that God could love such a person as I have been describing. That is the amazing thing! That is love, says John.

Therefore, if you believe and know all that, it makes you see yourself as you are, and do you see what happens at once? The moment you see yourself like that, you cry with John Bunyan when he says:

> He that is down need fear no fall,
> He that is low no pride.

John Bunyan meant that when I see myself as I really am, nobody can insult me. It is impossible, because they can never say anything that is bad enough about me. Whatever the world may say about me, when I know myself, I know that they do not know the truth about me—it is much worse than they think. When we really see ourselves in the light of this glorious gospel, no one can hurt us, no one can offend us. We see ourselves in the dust, and we are so low that no one can send us lower. 'Beloved,' says John, '*if God so loved us . . .*' You must start with yourself. Before you begin to defend yourself against that other person who you think is offensive or who has acted in an offensive manner, look at yourself and see yourself, and when you have seen yourself, you will be 75 percent of the way towards solving the problem.

But we do not stop there. Having seen ourselves, of course, we then go on to look at others. 'If God so loved us, we ought also to love one another.' Now you are looking at the other person, but of course you are doing so having first of all seen yourself. What a difference that makes! When you are lifted above another person, you look down upon them; but when you are groveling in the dust, you of necessity have to look up at that other person, and the condition is different at once, the perspective is different.

Let me summarise this. When the love of God is operating in our hearts, when we believe this gospel and reason out the meaning of this love, what happens is that we see the person rather than the thing that the person is doing. And is that not half the trouble in these human relationships? We see what people are *doing*—we do not see *them*. Now the gospel makes us see them as souls, objectively, and not only in terms of actions or in terms of what they are doing to us.

Still more specifically, let us put it as follows: When I look at these matters in the light of the glorious revelation of God's love, I see myself. Then I look at this other person who is making things difficult for me— as I thought at first—and this is what I see: I do not really see the offensive action of the person; I see a victim of sin, a victim of Satan. The gospel enables me to differentiate between the actions of that person and the person behind them.

That is exactly what God did with us when He loved us in Christ. God looked down from heaven and saw us on earth and saw our miserable actions. How could God ever love a sinner? Well, the answer, of course, is that God differentiates between the sinner and the sin. God loves the person and the soul in spite of the action. God draws that vital distinction, and He has pity upon us. He is sorry for us; He does not stop merely to look at what we do. He says, 'There is a soul I want to save.' He draws that distinction, and when you and I are animated by the love of God, we do exactly the same thing. This love of God enables us to look at the people who may be offensive to us and to feel sorry for them. We will say about them, 'Poor things; they are just victims of sin and Satan, and they do not know it. It is the god of this world who has them in his grip; it is this foul canker that is in them—*that* is the trouble.'

Think of a man with terrible sores. You love that person. Now, because he has these terrible sores, do you hate him? No; you love the person in spite of the offensive sores on his skin. And we must do the same thing about the sinner. We must see the soul at the back of it all; we must see men and women conforming to sin and Satan like ourselves, and when we do that we begin to feel sorry for them. As God has had pity upon us, we find ourselves praying for them. We say, 'God, have mercy upon them. We know it is Satan and sin in them; manifest Thyself to them, and make them glorious children of God.' That is how it works. 'If God so loved us, we ought also to love one another.'

And the third step is that we now see ourselves and the other person as joint-sharers in salvation, as joint-heirs of the same glory awaiting us, and what a wonderful thing that is! Instead of looking at them as possible enemies, I see them as men and women who were one with me in sin, but who are now one with me in the great salvation that God has sent in the person of His Son. We see one another as pilgrims traveling together towards the same country, and by the eye of faith we look into it and we say, 'I am going to heaven, and so is that person; we are going to be there together.' How can we then look at the face of God and remember we hated one another on earth? We cannot do it; we are fellow-pilgrims, joint-heirs with Christ, children of the same Father, going to the same Home. How ridiculous it is to be at variance; we must become one—we must love that person. We see ourselves, thus, in the light of the glorious gospel.

And then, lastly, the contemplation of this truth makes us realise what we owe to the love of God ourselves, and that therefore we must be the same towards others.

In the parable in Matthew 18 (vv 23-35), our blessed Lord Himself put this truth perfectly. He said that there was once a king who took a reckoning with his servants, and he found one who owed him the great sum of ten thousand talents. The poor man had nothing wherewith to pay this debt, so the lord commanded that he should be put into prison with his wife and children. But the servant went on his knees and begged the lord to have mercy upon him. He said in effect, 'Give me time, and I will pay you everything.' So the lord forgave him everything, and the man went out. But then he found a man who owed him one hundred pence, and he said to him, 'Pay me what you owe me.' The poor man replied, 'I cannot, but have patience with me and I will pay you all.' The man said to him, 'You must pay it all now,' and he had him cast into prison. But when the lord was informed of this, he condemned this unrighteous servant and cast him into prison. Do you remember our Lord's words at the end? He said, 'Likewise shall my heavenly Father do also unto you, if ye from your hearts forgive not every one his brother their trespasses.' These are our Lord's own words; our Lord Himself makes the truth perfectly plain.

In a sense we say the same thing every time we say the Lord's Prayer together: 'Forgive us our debts, as we forgive our debtors.' But I wonder whether we catch the full meaning of the parable. The first servant owed his lord ten thousand talents, which comes to two million pounds. The first servant owed his lord all that money, and he was forgiven it all; but he refused to forgive his fellow servant for a much lesser amount. His debt was about four hundred thousand times more than the debt of the man whom he refused to forgive. That is our Lord's own picture, which being interpreted is this: My debt to God is infinite. If He forgives me the two million, how can I possibly refuse to forgive someone else for so much less?

Indeed, our Lord goes further and says that men and women who know they have been forgiven for so much must forgive others. They cannot help themselves. Those who know they are debtors to mercy alone, those who realise what God's love has done for them, cannot help forgiving. The love of God has so broken them that they feel they must; God has done so much for them, they must do the same for others. 'Beloved, if God so loved us, we ought also to love one another.'

You see, the love of God is active. God did not merely look in love upon us—He did something about it. He sent His only begotten Son. 'God so loved' that He sent Christ to the cross; He sent Him to the grave. This is not love in contemplation, but love in mighty action. God did something about it and thereby saved us. We ought so to love one another. I must do something about that difficult person. I must pray for him and help him; I must do my utmost to enable him to overcome his sin. I do not just condemn such people and say they are impossible—I must do my utmost to help them. God did that for me. He spared not His only Son, His only begotten Son. That is love; it means going out myself to do something as God did it. And if the love of God is in us, this 'ought' will come into operation. This is a divine imperative; we will love one another even as, and because, God has so loved us.

Beloved friend, I ask you again, have you seen yourself? Well, if you have, you see yourself as utterly undeserving of the least of God's mercies. All your self-righteousness has vanished and gone. And as you see yourself like that, you see that others are also victims of the same horrible thing which we call sin. So you are sorry for them and have pity upon them, and you do everything you can to help emancipate them, so that they may become sharers with you of the love of God. You do that so that you may march together through Emmanuel's land to the glory that remains, where there will be no sin, no sorrow, no sighing, no weeping, no tears—nothing at all to mar the perfection and the glory of this life of love. Let us then be up and doing. 'If God so loved us, we ought also to love one another.'

6

GOD DWELLS IN US

No man hath seen God at any time. If we love one another,
God dwelleth in us, and his love is perfected in us.

1 JOHN 4:12

AS WE COME TO A consideration of this particular verse, I do not hesitate to say that in many respects it is, from the standpoint of exposition, one of the most interesting and, I would say, the most difficult of all the verses which we have hitherto considered in this epistle. Not that the truth which it contains is inherently more difficult or obtuse than many which we have already encountered, but from the standpoint of precise interpretation, it does present us with a problem. Those who are familiar with the commentaries on this epistle will know how this has always been so, the problem being, of course, exactly where to fit it in, and how to fit it in with its own context and to discover exactly what it was that the Apostle was anxious to convey on this particular point. That, perhaps, may very well lead us to say something which will be of interest and value to those who are students of the Bible. There is surely no interest and no occupation which can be more interesting and fascinating than to deal with a situation like this which confronts us as we come to expound such a statement, and for myself I feel that the only thing to do with a verse like this is to ask it questions.

And there we come upon a general principle that is always of great value in the exposition of Scripture. I feel that oftentimes we fail to expound correctly and we misinterpret Scripture because we do not talk to it and ask it questions. It is a very good and a very rewarding thing to do that with Scripture. Let me put it as simply as this: You get a verse like this, and you say to it, 'Well, why do you say that? Why do you say it in this way, and why do you say it just here?' In other words, no statement in Scripture is made in a haphazard manner, and we must never allow ourselves just to pass over a statement which seems to us to be suddenly interpolated without any connection or sense or meaning. That is never true of Scripture; if we can but arrive at its meaning, there is always some reason for what is being said, there is some link, there was some process in the mind of the writer, under the influence of the Holy Spirit, that led him at that particular point to say that particular thing. So I am suggesting that the way to arrive at that is to ask these questions—to put up possibilities and to consider them and to reject them one by one until you are left with an explanation which seems to you to be satisfactory, or the most satisfactory in the given situation. And that, inevitably, has to be done with this verse that we are now considering.

So why does John suddenly, in the midst of this argument, say, 'No man hath seen God at any time'? What is the connection? What does he mean? What was it that suddenly, at this point, made him burst out, as it were, with this extraordinary statement? Several answers have been put forward to those particular questions. There are those who would say that what John was really saying was something like this: Following on from verse 11, 'Beloved, if God so loved us, we ought also to love one another,' he then said, 'No man hath seen God at any time.' 'In other words,' John said in effect, 'the only way in which we can love God is by loving one another. We cannot see God, but we do see one another, and therefore the only way to love God is to love one another.' That is a possible and, in a sense, a plausible answer. It is as if John were saying to them, 'Get right out of your minds all this mystical conception of love. Finish with any such thought, and realise that there is no value in your saying that you love God unless you love your brother. You do not see God, but you do see your brother; so love your brother, and you are thereby loving God.'

There are others who would say that we ought to interpret it in this way: our love ought to be like the love of God itself, and the love of God, as John has just reminded us, is something which manifests itself in the realm of the concrete and the actual. 'God is love,' said John in effect, 'and God has manifested this love in that He has sent His only begotten Son into the world, that we might live through Him.' In other words, to love is not something sentimental or mystical, because love manifests itself by loving persons in the concrete. And John is saying to us, 'You must do something. No man has seen God at any time, and therefore if you want to claim that you are loving God, then love as God loves—love the people you see—love the brethren. This is the only real way in which you can love.'

Now those are the two most common explanations that are put forward as an attempt to expound to us why John suddenly introduced this idea of the invisibility of God, and yet it seems to me that we must reject both these suggestions at once. And I would argue that verses 19-21 in this very chapter we are considering make it imperative that we should reject them, because John says there that we love Him—namely, God—because He first loved us. 'If a man say, I love God, and hateth his brother, he is a liar: for he that loveth not his brother whom he hath seen, how can he love God whom he hath not seen?' (v 20). We shall give a detailed exposition of that later, but for the time being it is enough to establish this point. John does not say that we cannot love God except through loving our brethren; that is not his argument. Nor does he say that we can only love God by means of loving our brethren. Rather, he tells us that we are to love God—that we *can* love God and that we *should* love Him.

Take again our Lord's exposition of the great commandment: 'Thou shalt love the Lord thy God with all thy heart, and with all thy soul, and with all thy mind. . . . And the second is like unto it, Thou shalt love thy neighbor as thyself' (Matt 22:37, 39). So we must be very careful always not to put the second before the first, as these expositors would do. The first is to love God and then secondly to love our neighbour; we must never put the love of our neighbour before the love of God Himself.

But if we reject these two possible explanations, what is our explanation of the sudden introduction of this statement at this point? It seems to me that the explanation must be something like this: John is here introducing a new theme, a new subsidiary, a new idea, into his great discussion of this question of loving the brethren. And this new theme I would describe as the theme of the assurance of salvation; it is the whole question of our knowledge of God and of the way in which we can know God. In other words, I am suggesting that John here is linking up with that with which he left off at the end of verse 8. Let me reconstruct it to you in this way: 'Beloved,' he says, 'let us love one another: for love is of God; and every one that loveth is born of God, and knoweth God. He that loveth not, knoweth not God; for God is love. . . . No man hath seen God at any time. If we love one another, God dwelleth in us, and his love is perfected in us.'

Now I am not suggesting by putting it like that that verses 9-11 are a digression. They are not, but they are, as it were, an amplification of that statement that 'God is love.' So we can put the argument in this way: The central theme of this whole section is the importance of loving the brethren. Why is that important? Here are John's arguments: The first is that 'love is of God,' it is a very wonderful thing, and therefore it is something we can covet, something that links us up with God and makes us God-like. Not only that, it is proof of the fact that we are born of God, and there again is something of vital importance. Every person who is born of God must love, for surely it is the only way we can demonstrate that we do appreciate the love of God to us. That was the argument of verse 11—'If God so loved us, we ought also to love one another.'

'But,' says John in effect, 'it is not only that, but it is important that you love the brethren from the standpoint of your own assurance of salvation and from the standpoint of your fellowship with God.' Now, verses 9-11 are just an amplification of the statement that 'God is love.' John says, 'In this was manifested the love of God toward us'; one of the ways in which we know that 'God is love' is what He has done in and through our Lord and Saviour, Jesus Christ. But having said that, having implied that, he goes back again to the main argument, which goes on from verse 12 to the end of the first verse of the next chapter. So the theme at this point is assurance of salvation and the importance of the love of the brethren in this matter of assurance, in this whole question of our knowledge of God and especially our knowledge of God as a God of love.

I think we have been dealing with what I would call the mechanics of this particular chapter, and it is of vital importance that we should do so. Though John has this peculiar style on which we have previously commented, though he thinks more like a poet than a logician, though he tends to arrive at his position in circles instead of straight lines, though there is something of the mystic in his thinking, nevertheless there is firm logic at the back of it; there is a definite line of reason. He does not throw out thoughts suddenly—there is an intimate connection between them all; and I suggest that if you bear this in mind, it will be helpful in understanding the remainder of the chapter.

So we look at it as follows: Let me use the comparison, if I may venture to do so, of a symphony. You have in these epistles movements, in exactly the same way as you have them in a symphony. We have often underlined and emphasised the various major movements of this epistle, but as you realise, within every movement in a symphony there is a further analysis, a sub-division. There are subsidiary themes even in the movement, and I suggest that that is what we are dealing with at this particular point. The particular movement here is *loving the brethren*; that is the ultimate idea, and John deals with it in an analytical manner. As I have reminded you, he says that this is very important for us because it is of God—there is the subsidiary idea in the movement. He says it is important also because we are born of God, and *those who are born of God must love*—there is another little theme. And then he says that this is tremendously important from the standpoint of knowing God.

Those who are interested in music—in Beethoven's music, for example—will realise how typical that is of a composer like Beethoven. Beethoven produces his movement; then a thought comes and he mentions it; and then he springs something else on us and says, 'This is what I am going to explain.' But all the time it is subsidiary to the main idea of the movement. I am suggesting that is what we have here. The main movement is concerned with the importance of loving the brethren, but then there are the subsidiary ideas, and the one he is going to explain and elaborate is this whole question of the knowledge of God, fellowship with Him, the assurance of salvation. That is what John really is ultimately concerned about in the whole epistle, as we saw at the beginning.[1] That is the astounding thing. 'Our fellowship is with the Father, and with his Son Jesus Christ' (1:3), and 'I am writing to you,' he says in effect, 'that you may enter into this fellowship. And now,' he says, 'if you really want to do that and to know how it can be done, there is nothing more important than that you should love one another, that you should love the brethren. This is vital in this whole question of knowing and having fellowship with Him.' So if we just bear that analysis in mind, I think it will help us to understand the whole situation.

Let us see, then, how John proceeds to handle this question: How can we arrive at this knowledge of God? That, surely, ought to be the great question in all our minds. 'Every one that loveth,' we are told, 'is born of God, and knoweth God. He that loveth not, knoweth not God; for God is love.' So how can we know God? How can we be sure of it? Do we not all understand the feelings in the mind and heart of Thomas and Philip as they are recorded in John 14: 'We know not whither thou goest; and how can we know the way?' 'You are telling us,' says Thomas in effect, 'that You are going to the Father. You talk about another world and about great mansions, and You tell us that you are going to prepare places for us. But You know, we do not understand this. Don't You realise that You are essentially different? We are of the earth, earthy; it is all vague, and we cannot grasp it. What is all this—how can we know?' And then Philip put the same question again: 'Seeing You are talking to us about the Father,' he said in effect, 'if only we could see the Father, it would be enough for us' (vv 5, 8).

That is the kind of craving and longing that is in the hearts and minds of all who are concerned about these things, this longing to know God for certain. You see it in the hymns:

> *Tell me Thou art mine, O Saviour,*
> *Grant me an assurance clear.*
>
> WILLIAM WILLIAMS
> (TRANS. R. LEWIS)

There is in the human heart undoubtedly a craving for certainty. We need not delay over this; the explanation of it is perfectly obvious. Our world is so uncertain—'Change and decay in all around I see.' Nothing is durable, nothing is steadfast; the things that can be shaken are being shaken. The whole world and the whole of life is so uncertain that there is nothing, in a sense, so deep in the human heart as a longing for stability, a certainty, an assurance, and this is something that has always manifested itself in the realm of religion. I use the term *religion* advisedly, for in every religion there is this craving for certainty, and it comes into practise even in the Christian faith, this longing for assurance. And the great question is, how is this to be obtained?

Indeed, another great theme is this: What is the nature of religious certainty? What is the character of religious knowledge? What is to happen to us as Christian people? On what, ultimately, is our assurance established? And John, in the verses that follow this twelfth verse, takes up that theme and gives us some answers to the question.

Let us look now at the answer given in this particular verse. First he makes a negative statement: our assurance or knowledge is not based upon external events. 'No man hath seen God at any time.' The first thing we must get rid of is any idea that there can be an immediacy of knowledge; we must once and for ever get rid of everything which would encourage us to think that through various stages we come to a literal vision of God.

This is a wonderful statement of Scripture which you find repeated on many occasions. You get the same words in John's Gospel: 'No man hath seen God at any time' (John 1:18). Then the Apostle Paul, in writing to Timothy, makes a very similar statement: '[God] only hath immortality . . . whom no man hath seen, nor can see' (1 Tim 6:16). This is a very important theme from the standpoint of a true understanding of our relationship with God.

There is a sense, perhaps, in which the Old Testament throws an almost clearer light upon this matter than the New Testament itself does, because in it we have a number of instances which are described as *theophanies*. A theophany means an appearance of God which was given to certain people. Consider, for example, the appearance that was given to Abraham, and also to Lot, and there are other examples of the same thing. These people saw and yet they did not see God, and they talk and write about 'the angel of the Lord.' Now there can be very little doubt that all those incidents were concerned with appearances of our Lord Jesus Christ before the Incarnation. He appeared temporarily in human form for certain specific purposes, and so we can still say that no man has seen God at any time.

But perhaps the most interesting example of all is what happened in the case of Moses. God said to Moses on one very special occasion, in effect, 'I will pass before you, I will appear unto you.' Yet observe what he also said. He said that Moses would be allowed to see His back, as it were. We are not told that Moses saw the face of God; but there was an appearance, God passing by, and Moses looked at His back (Exod 33:19-23). That is one of the most extraordinary scenes in the whole of the Bible, and yet obviously it is a situation which we must look at very carefully because it maintains this Biblical statement that 'no man hath seen God at any time.'

Of course, those very words that were used by our Lord in reply to Philip's question were the same thing in a different way. 'Show us the

Father, and it sufficeth us,' said Philip; in effect he was saying, 'Give us a clear vision of the Father, and we will be content to go on even though you are leaving us.' 'Have I been so long time with you, and yet hast thou not known me, Philip? he that hath seen me hath seen the Father,' replied our Lord (John 14:8-9). 'It is not,' he said in effect, 'that you have seen the Father directly, with the naked eye; but look at Me and you will get your only conception of what the Father is like.' Is that the Father? No, that is the Son; but the Father is in the Son, and the Son is in the Father; and the only way in which we can see the Father, so far, is to see the Son. In other words, we must still hold to this basic idea that no man has seen God at any time.

Now we cannot go into this matter in as great detail as we should like, but let me sum it all up by putting it like this: We must turn our back very resolutely upon every teaching which would ever lead us to try to obtain a direct vision of God. We should never covet visions; we should never try to come into that immediate vision of God. There is an ultimate promise given to us, thank God: 'Blessed are the pure in heart: for they shall see God' (Matt 5:8); that is the ultimate. There is a time coming, a day coming, when we shall see Him, but not yet; and while we are here on earth and in this earthly pilgrimage, we must not even desire it. We must not desire ever to hear audible voices or to have such visions as will give us a kind of mechanical, material security. There were many mystics who went in for that kind of thing and who claimed to have visions, and it seems to me that if we do set our minds upon things like that, we probably shall be seeing things. But the whole question that arises is, what do we see? You enter into the realm of hallucinations and the realm of psychology, not to say the realm of the psychic, and that is something that John was anxious to warn people against.

In those early centuries there were mysteries of religions—a peculiar mixture of mystery religions, great philosophies, and so on. Some people did not like the idea of faith; they did not like the life in which, as Paul describes it, 'We walk by faith, not by sight' (2 Cor 5:7). They wanted to see and hear, they wanted something tangible; and so they fasted, and they passed through certain rites. They had the appropriate music, and they brought in the artistic; everything was being done to get this vision, this immediacy, this directness. And the result was that they became victims of aberrations, of heresies, and of hallucinations. In addition to that, they thus lost this fundamental understanding of the utter inscrutability of God because of His utter holiness. Their moral life degenerated, and you have all the manifestations which invariably accompany this craving for the immediate. You see this today in connection with spiritism, those people who claim to see and hear—I am speaking generally; and John's great concern was to warn these people against that. Your assurance, he says, will not be based on visions or audible voices; it has to be based on something deeper and stronger.

On what, then, is it based? How can I know God? Well, in verses 9-11 John has partly answered that question. I know that God is love, in that He has manifested this in everything that has happened in the Lord Jesus Christ. I do not need a vision. God in His grace may give me a vision, but I do not seek and covet one. Why? I have the facts of the Lord Jesus Christ; I have something concrete and tangible in the realm of history; God is there manifesting Himself as love.

But that is not all. I have something further, and it is this: God dwells in us. That is the second ground of my assurance, my certainty. 'No man hath seen God at any time.' Very well, then, do we go on in doubt and almost in despair wondering whether there is a God? 'No!' says John; 'if we love one another "God dwelleth in us, and his love is perfected in us."' Now, I confess very readily that I approach a theme like this with fear and with a sense of awe. Consider the great statement in John 14 of this intimate union between the believer and God the Father and God the Son, of their abiding in us and dwelling in us. We are familiar with chapters 14, 15, 16 and 17 of John's Gospel,[2] and here we have the same thing again. 'God dwelleth in us, and his love is perfected in us.' And John goes on to say (v 13), 'Hereby we know we that we dwell in him, and he in us, because he hath given us of his Spirit'; and in verse 15, 'Whosoever shall confess that Jesus is the Son of God, God dwelleth in him, and he in God.'

At this point, like Moses, we take off our shoes! We are concerned with something that is glorious and magnificent, and so we have to be very careful as we handle it. We are not discussing some people who lived in the first century; we are talking about ourselves. The statement is that if we love one another, God—God who is love, God the Almighty, God the eternal—*dwells in us*. What does this mean? Well, I think that the great thing at this point is to realise that we must not materialise that conception; that is always the danger here, to think of it in material terms. We can avoid that if we remember that other fundamental postulate of the Bible that God is spirit. We are using words that in a sense elude us, and yet that is the nearest we can get to this exalted conception. We must not think of God in material terms; God is spirit. It is God, who is spirit, who dwells in us.

Perhaps an illustration will help us here. In all of us there is what we call the soul, but what is the soul? A famous doctor once said that having dissected many human bodies he had never come across an organ described as 'the soul'—thereby, of course, betraying a pathetic ignorance of the spiritual definition of the soul. The soul is immaterial; it is not a substance, nor is it an organ; and no man dissecting the human frame should ever seek for it. The soul is a spiritual entity and quality. But I say that my soul is in me and that my soul will go out of my body.

I cannot get nearer to this conception than that, and as this which we call 'soul' is in our bodies, so we are told in Scripture that God who is spirit dwells in us; He takes up His abode in us and lives in us. It is not that the eternal God is resident in me in a peculiar sense. No; but in some strange manner God, the eternal God who is spirit, enters into my life, moves in my life, deals with my life, organises my life, and manifests Himself in my life. This is something we will never understand truly while we are in the body and in this world and life. It is in a sense comparable to the whole mystery of the Incarnation; the fact that there, in that one person, Jesus Christ of Nazareth is God, the eternal Son, and yet there at the same time is the man Jesus, the carpenter. You cannot *understand* a thing like that, and yet there is the statement of Scripture. The eternal Son came out of the bosom of the Father and was incarnate as Jesus of Nazareth. The eternal Son came in the likeness of sinful flesh and dwelt in a human frame, and in some such way as that God dwells in us and we in Him.

We will have to go on dealing with this—I am simply giving an outline here—but that is the astounding and amazing thing that the Apostle tells us. Here is the practical import of it all: Do not seek for visions; do not covet audible voices; do not enter into anything where you anticipate something eerie. 'Beloved people,' said John; 'you have something infinitely greater than that. God, who is love, dwells in you! If you love the brethren, here is a certainty, here is an assurance.'

Let me put it like this: If I love the brethren, I have an assurance of God in this way: the very fact that I do love the brethren and that I am capable of loving them is in itself proof to me that God is and that God is love, because apart from the love of God in me I could not love the brethren. Man by nature does not love. You remember how John elaborates on that in the previous chapter,[3] where he has told us that 'this is the message that ye heard from the beginning, that we should love one another. Not as Cain, who was of that wicked one, and slew his brother.' That is the world; if the world hates you, that is the kind of thing the world does, and that is how we all are by nature.

If I find myself loving a person who is not lovable, if I find myself ever praying for someone who has been persecuting me and has been dealing with me despitefully, if I find myself helping someone who has done his or her best to harm me, if I find myself doing that, I know that God is love and that He is within me, because if He were not in me I would never do it. I do not want to do this by nature; so if I love the brethren, I have a certainty that God is love. 'No man hath seen God.' How may I know that God is and that God loves me and that God is love? Here is the answer: If we love one another, God dwells in us. I do not have visions, I do not hear audible voices, I do not seek some material substantiation of what I claim; but I have it within me. So God must be in me; otherwise I could never do what I am doing.

But, indeed, John goes one step further. He says, 'God dwelleth in us, and his love is perfected in us.' What a glorious statement that is, and it means this: The ultimate objective of God in sending His Son into this world to be the propitiation for our sins and to do all that He did—the ultimate objective was that God might make of us such people that we should love the brethren and love one another even as He has loved us.

Now that is glorious! God sent His Son into the world to die on the cross of Calvary not simply that He might make a way whereby you and I could be forgiven—thank God that is there, and it is the first thing, for without that we are altogether lost; but that was not the end. The end was this: God was anxious to perfect His love, and He perfects His love in us not so much by what it does externally as by what it does within us. In other words, show me a Christian man or woman who is loving the brethren in spite of everything that is so true of them, and *there* is a demonstration of the love of God in a human soul. God has so dealt with them that He has made of them people like Himself.

All this was put so perfectly by our Lord Himself in the Sermon on the Mount: 'Love your enemies, bless them that curse you, do good to them that hate you, and pray for them which despitefully use you, and persecute you.' 'What credit, what merit have you if you love those who love you? The heathen do that. You know the sort of love I am talking about,' said our Lord in effect. 'Be ye therefore perfect, even as your Father which is in heaven is perfect.' That is the way you are to love. You are to love as God loves. He sends the rain upon the just and the unjust and causes His sun to shine upon the evil and the good (Matt 5:43-48). That is what we are to do. God's love is perfected in us, and therefore we must be perfect, even as our Father in heaven is perfect— and that context is solely about loving one another. So, as we love the brethren we are manifesting and demonstrating God's ultimate objective in all that He did in the Lord Jesus Christ. He is producing a race, a humanity like Himself, a people set apart, men and women who can rise to this height and to this level, men and women who love even as God loves.

There, it seems to me, is what the Apostle is telling us in this particular twelfth verse. We have started this new theme of assurance of salvation, this certainty of our fellowship and our relationship to God; and the first way to make sure of it and to know it is to love one another, to love the brethren. If I am loving the brethren, then I know that God must be in me, for otherwise I could not do it, and I am demonstrating God's ultimate eternal objective in sending His only begotten Son into the world to make Him the propitiation for my sins.

What a glorious doctrine! Let us cease to ask for visible tangible signs; let us cease from maligning this glorious truth; and let us accept this simple yet profound teaching which tells us to our amazement that God dwells in us.

7

The Gift of God's Spirit

*Hereby know we that we dwell in him, and he in us,
because he hath given us of his Spirit.*

1 JOHN 4:13

IN THIS VERSE John continues the theme which has really been occupying him from the beginning of verse 7—the importance of loving one another. The reason, he says, for stressing this is that it is only as we love one another that we truly come to know God, and that is the most important thing of all. And the great basis of a true knowledge of God in this world and life is to know in that way that God is dwelling in us and we in God. John, therefore, is now suggesting to us various tests by which we may know this. And John in the twelfth verse gives us the first test: Are we loving one another? If we find that we are loving our Christian brothers and sisters, then we can be certain that God is in us, because apart from God dwelling in us there is no love in us.

Then here, in this thirteenth verse, John comes to the second great proof which we have of the fact that God is dwelling in us and we in God, and here it is: 'Hereby know we that we dwell in him, and he in us, because he hath given us of his Spirit.'

Now it is very interesting to observe the way in which John probably arrived at this statement. I think he must have done so like this: He has been talking about this love which we should have for one another, and then he asks himself, 'But where does this love come from?' And he is at once reminded that it comes from the Holy Spirit. As Paul says, 'The love of God is shed abroad in our hearts by the Holy Ghost which is given to us' (Rom 5:5). John has been talking about this love; well, the possession of this love means the possession of the Spirit. And that is the second test.

It seems to me that there are three main things stated in this verse. Firstly, we are reminded of the nature of the Christian life. I start with this because I am increasingly convinced that most of our troubles arise from the fact that our whole conception of the Christian life tends to be inadequate. I am not referring to people outside the church at the moment, but to Christian people. I speak for myself when I say that there is nothing of which I have to remind myself more constantly than the very nature of the Christian life. We are all the same; the first Christians were the same as well, and that is why the epistles were written. It was because of this constant tendency to think and conceive of the Christian life in an inadequate manner that the Apostles were led and moved by God to write their letters with their wonderful instruction.

We always tend to narrow down the Christian life. There are so many people who still seem to think of it as if it were a question of giving up two or three particularly gross and obvious sins and attending a place of worship; but how unworthy and inadequate a view that is! So let us start by means of a negative. What is the Christian life? What does it mean to be a Christian? What is the essential nature of this life to which we are called? Let me remind you again of certain things which are hopelessly inadequate. Living as a Christian does not just mean moral living, nor just being good and decent. Of course it includes those things, but that is not the whole of the Christian life.

I start with that because is it not obvious that there are large numbers of people who think seriously that that constitutes the Christian life? There are many people attending morning services in church who say that just because they are not guilty of certain things, they are true Christians. To which I reply, 'Hereby know we that we dwell in him, and he in us, because he hath given us of his Spirit'; then their little morality shrivels into nothing. Morality is essential, but God forbid that we should reduce this glorious thing and this glorious life to just a little decency and morality!

Or there are those who think of it in terms of high ideals. There is a great deal of this being noised abroad at the present time. There are various movements which I regard as nothing but an equating of the Christian life with the holding of certain high ideals. And people think that by preaching them, every workman will be prepared to work twenty-four hours a day because he is animated by these noble ideals, all in the name of Christianity. As if that were the total of Christianity! There are thoughts associated with Christianity, the highest and noblest thoughts that have ever come to man; but if we equate them with what we are told here, then we are merely in possession of certain high ideals and are insulting the work of our blessed Lord and Saviour Jesus Christ.

Then there are those who think of Christianity just as a matter of religious conformity. They actually believe that they are Christians and others are not simply because they conform to certain habits and practices. They attend a morning service, and then they may do anything they like for the rest of the day; that morning service has made them Christian. They are conforming to a certain conduct and behaviour, and that, to them, is the Christian life. And because other people do not do all this, they look at them and say, 'We are different; we are doing something they are not'—religious conformity. Of course, again it is obvious that this is part of the Christian life, but to regard that as the whole of it is to miss the splendour and the glory and the wonder of this great thing that is expounded in the new Testament.

Or let me go one step further and say that a general belief in the Christian message does not make one a Christian. Obviously this again is essential, but merely to subscribe to certain tenets of the faith does not make us Christians; that is one of the preliminary conditions, but it is not the thing itself. To believe certain things about God and Christ in and of itself does not make one a Christian; there is something higher than that, and here it is: '*Hereby* know we that we dwell in him, and he in us'—that is the nature of the Christian life. We saw this in verse 12 where John says, 'If we love one another, God dwelleth in us.' We saw that this is something that eludes definition and understanding in a sense, and yet it is something very definite, and John amplifies it here. Not only does He dwell in us, but we dwell in Him. This is an amazing, mystical relationship with God into which we have been brought by the Lord Jesus Christ and His perfect work. What does this mean? It means that we are in a living relationship with God; that is why I have contrasted it with believing certain things *about* God. There is all the difference in the world between these two things.

Have we not known this experience? There is a stage in which we believe certain things about God and Christ, but we do not know Him. When we went on our knees to pray, we felt there was a distance, a strangeness, an uncertainty. How different that is from knowing that we are in a vital relationship with God, being aware of the fact that somehow we are participating in the life of God and that God is in our life. There is a change in us—we are not merely ourselves; there is this other factor. We know that this is not merely a question of intellectual acceptance; it is not a question of our just doing duties or merely in a mechanical way saying our prayers or something like that. No. We are aware of being in a living relationship to God; there is something vital about our whole position, and we are aware of the fact that in some astounding manner we are, in reality, sharing the life of God Himself. As Peter puts it, we are made 'partakers of'—we are sharing in—'the divine nature.'

Now we must be careful not to materialise this, and we must not reduce it. So I am anxious to emphasise again that when we consider these other conceptions of the Christian life—that morality, those high ideals, that noble conception of life and the high sense of duty and religious conformity and even an intellectual belief—we should see how inadequate are all those put together when we come to this. Here we are taken up into the life of God! Because, you see, in those discourses of His just before the end, our Lord talked about the Father and Himself abiding in us—God dwelling in us; 'Abide in me and I in you.' That is the Christian life; nothing less than that must ever satisfy us, and we must never conceive of it in any terms that are lower than that.

That brings me to my second proposition, which is that we may know, and should know, that we are in that relationship to God and that we possess that life. That is the nature of the Christian life. 'Hereby,' says John, '*know we*'—we know it, and we are certain of it. I have often, in dealing with this epistle, pointed out that this is, for John, one of the greatest things of all. He has told us several times, and he will tell us again before we have finished, that his whole business in writing this letter is that we may have this knowledge: 'These things have I written unto you that believe on the name of the Son of God; that ye may know that ye have eternal life, and that ye may believe on the name of the Son of God' (5:13).

Now we all possess this knowledge, and we must never be satisfied with anything less than that. I put it like that because I know a number of friends who really are opposed to such teaching. I remember once saying something along this line in a different connection and afterwards having a conversation with a good man who had been present at the service.

He said, 'Don't you think you were a little bit hard on us this afternoon?'

'Why?' I asked.

'Well,' he said, 'you said that *all* of us ought to have this knowledge of God.'

'Certainly,' I replied. 'Wasn't I explaining my text?'

'Ah, yes,' he said. 'I believe Peter and John and Paul should have had this knowledge, but surely not all of us ordinary Christians.'

And then he proceeded really to defend his own ignorance and regarded my saying that every Christian should have this knowledge as a hard statement.

But this knowledge is to me the very essence of the New Testament teaching. What the Bible offers us is nothing less than this knowledge that God is in us and we in Him, and we should not rest for a moment until we have it. We have no right to be uncertain—'that ye may *know.*' Christians who are uncertain of where they are, are doing dishonour to the gospel of Jesus Christ, to the work of Christ upon the cross, and to His glorious resurrection. We must not rest until we have full and certain assurance, confidence, and jubilation. The whole of the New Testament has been written in order that we may have it, and I argue that this is something that really must be inevitable. I cannot understand anyone who not only lacks this certainty, but who would even be prepared to argue against such a certainty. I cannot understand such a person, even on the grounds of logic.

Let me put it in this way: As unbelievers we were dead; we had no spiritual life. A Christian must be born again, by faith, in order to have the life of God in his soul. So, is it possible that we can have such life in us and not know it? I say that is impossible! The presence of the life of God in our soul is so different from the life without God that we cannot but know it; and therefore if you are uncertain, you must examine the foundation of your life. For this is what is offered: nothing less than that God will come to dwell in us and will take us into Himself; so we must know this, we may know it, and we can thank God we can know it.

This brings me to my last proposition, which is the way in which we may have this knowledge. 'Hereby know we that we dwell in him, and he in us.' How? The answer is, *'because he hath given us of his Spirit.'* So it all comes down to that in the last analysis. How do I know that I have received God's Spirit? How may I know for certain that I have been given and receive something of the Holy Spirit of God? Now this is a great subject, and I can only touch on it briefly. Let me say as a word of warning that there is a great danger of confining this whole teaching concerning the Holy Spirit to particular aspects only or to particular results of the gift of the Holy Spirit. Let me just suggest to you certain tests which we all should apply to ourselves in order that we may know that we have received the Holy Spirit—this gift of God.

Here are some of them. I shall start at the lowest and rise to the highest, and I do that for the good reason that if you can say 'Yes' to my first test, then you can be happy that you have received the Holy Spirit. So I start with this: Are you concerned about these things, and have you a desire to have them? Are these things of great concern to you—are they the things that interest you? I often notice when traveling by train that there are large numbers of people who seem to be first of all interested, and tremendously interested, in the latest murder or something like that. They rush for the paper, and they want to read all the latest news. Is that the limit of your interest, or are you interested in other things? Are you concerned about the life of your soul? Are you concerned about knowing God? Are you interested in eternity? Are these the things that interest you? I assure you that if they are, the Holy Spirit is in you, for people apart from God 'mind earthly things' (Phil 3:19)—carnal, fleshly things. It may not always be murder; it may be the Royal Family; it may be in what is happening in so-called high society and all the pomp and show of life. It is the same thing—it is the same interest in the last analysis. Is that the limit of your interest, or is your interest spiritual? Are you concerned about immortality and the things invisible and eternal? If you are 'minding' these things, that is a proof that the Holy Spirit is in you.

Or let me hurry on to another test: a sense of sin. By this I mean that you are aware that there is an evil principle within you—not simply that you do certain things you should not do and feel annoyed with yourself because of it. No; rather, I mean that you are aware that you have an evil nature, that there is a principle of sin and wrong in your heart, that there is a fountain emitting unworthy, ugly, and foul things, and in a sense you hate yourself. Our Lord said that the man who loves himself is in a very dangerous condition. The Apostle Paul was a man who could say about himself, 'In me (that is, in my flesh,) dwelleth no good thing. . . . O wretched man that I am!' (Rom 7:18, 24). Have you ever felt like that about yourself? If you have, you can take it from me that the Holy Spirit is in you; no man or woman has said this until God the Holy Spirit has come into them. So if you have ever felt yourself a sinner, and if you have hated this thing in you that gets you down, that is a proof that you have received the gift of the Holy Spirit.

What else? A belief on the Lord Jesus Christ. I need not stay with that here because we will come to it in verses 14-15. But I just mention it now as something essential. Paul says in writing to the Corinthians that the princes of this world did not recognise Him when He came (1 Cor 2:8). Why? Because they did not have the Holy Spirit. But we do believe, because we have received the Spirit, and 'the Spirit searcheth all things, yea, the deep things of God' (1 Cor 2:10). Anyone who believes truly on the Lord Jesus Christ has received the gift of the Spirit.

But I must hurry on to another test. Are you aware within yourself of a struggle and a conflict between the flesh and the Spirit? Paul deals with that in Galatians 5: 'The flesh lusteth against the Spirit, and the Spirit against the flesh' (v 17). He means this: Are you aware of two opposing natures within you? It is not merely that occasionally you want to do things that are wrong and have to struggle in your mind; no, it is deeper than that. Are you aware of the fact that really in a sense you are two people? There is a new kind of person in you who wants these heavenly, spiritual things; but there is another who wants to get you down, and there is a struggle and conflict one against the other. According to the Scriptures, that is one of the best tests of whether the Holy Spirit is in you. If you are in a state of conflict with these opposing forces, you can be quite sure the Holy Spirit is in you, because without the Holy Spirit there is no such conflict—it is all the 'old man.' But if you are having a conflict between the new and the old, then you know the Holy Spirit is indeed within you.

Let me take it a step further. Are you aware of the fact that God is working in you? 'Work out your own salvation with fear and trembling,' says Paul, 'for it is God which worketh in you both to will and to do' (Phil 2:12-13). This is a marvelous, wonderful thing. It is one of the great tests of the possession of the Holy Spirit. It means something like this: We are aware of the fact that we are being dealt with; it is not that we decide to do things. You see, moralists and religious conformists are doing it all themselves, and that is why they are so proud of themselves. They get up on Sunday mornings instead of spending the morning in bed, and they go to church. They do it because *they* have decided to do it, not because they have been moved. No, they are in control the whole time; and having done it, they preen themselves with their wonderful, ennobling ideals. How marvelous they are!

But that is not what the Bible talks about. 'It is God which worketh in you both to will and to do.' In other words, you are aware of the power of God dealing with you, surging and rising within you, and you are amazed and astonished at yourself. Far from being proud you say, 'It is not I. This is not the sort of person I am. It is God doing something; it is Christ dwelling within me; it is the Holy Spirit that is in me. I am taken up beyond myself, and I thank God for it.' Is God working in you? Are you aware of a disturbance in your life? Are you aware of a wonder-working power active in you, moving, disturbing, leading, persuading, drawing you ever onwards? If you are, it is because you have received from God the gift of His own Spirit. God is resident within you, and He is working out His own grand purpose in you in that way.

And that brings me to the next great test, which is again to be found in Galatians 5—that which Paul describes as 'the fruit of the Spirit.' The Spirit is life, and life always manifests itself in some shape or form as fruit; a live tree bears fruit, a dead tree does not. These are scriptural analogies, and I have nothing to do at this point but to remind you of what Paul tells us about the fruit of the Spirit. 'The fruit of the Spirit is love, joy, peace, long-suffering, gentleness, goodness, faith, meekness, temperance' (Gal 5:22-23). The way to test whether the Holy Spirit is in you is to examine yourself, your own life, and to discover whether there is any evidence or manifestation of such fruit.

Do you know that the Holy Spirit cannot be in you without that fruit appearing? I know there is a great variation in the fruit. In the Parable of the Sower we read that there is some thirty, some sixty, some a hundredfold; but thank God, even the thirty proves that the Holy Spirit is there. Even ten would prove it; even one. Thank God for that! Not that I am to rest with the tenfold, but thank God for the assurance that any fruit at all proves that He is there. 'Love, joy, peace, long-suffering, gentleness, goodness, faith, meekness, temperance'—are these things in us? Are they being evidenced in our lives? If they are, the Holy Spirit is in us, and we are becoming more and more like the Lord Jesus Christ. In a sense, that is the most perfect description of Him that you will find anywhere—that ninefold fruit, the three groups of three. This is the description of Jesus Christ. Love—there it was to be seen in His life; the love of God incarnate. Joy—that holy joy in spite of everything. That peace that never forsook Him. Gentleness, goodness, meekness . . . And as the Holy Spirit is resident in us and produces this fruit, we become more and more like Christ. This is the fruit of the Spirit.

Then the next thing I would mention is the Spirit of adoption. You remember how Paul works that out in Romans 8. Because we have received the Spirit, we 'have received the Spirit of adoption, whereby we cry, Abba, Father' (v 15). God is no longer some distant potentate in eternity. He has become a Father to us; and when we come to Him, we feel we come to our Father, the Father of the prodigal, and we come without fear. John elaborates that toward the end of this chapter when he says that there is 'no fear in love'; we will come to that. But to know God and to see 'Abba, Father' in the Lord Jesus Christ and to know ourselves to be His child—do you know Him like that?

And lastly I would mention the various gifts of the Spirit, the various powers the Spirit may give us. You can read the list in 1 Corinthians 12. You may have some of them—you may have one of them, or you may have more. That chapter does not say that every Christian has them all. Paul goes out of his way to say that. Not all have the gift of prophecy; all cannot speak and preach; there is variation; and they are dispensed according to His sovereignty. He may give us the gifts, or He may not. 'And yet,' says Paul, 'show I unto you a more excellent way' (1 Cor 12:31). The gifts of the Spirit—what are they? They are all summed up in one word: *love*. The fruit of the Spirit is love pre-eminently; and if we have that, then we have that final and ultimate proof: 'Hereby know we that we dwell in him, and he in us, because he hath given us of his Spirit.' Do you know this? Have you received this gift of God's Spirit? I have reminded you of the tests; if you have them, God bless you. Now go on to covet the best gifts more and more; long increasingly for the fruit of the Spirit; and ask God to work more and more in you.

If, having listened to all this, you have come to the conclusion that you have not received the gift of God's Spirit, then all I say to you is what our Lord Jesus Christ said: 'If ye then, being evil, know how to give good gifts unto your children; how much more shall your heavenly Father give the Holy Spirit to them that ask him?' (Luke 11:13). If you feel you have not got this gift, and if you long to possess this priceless possession, go to God without delay. Acknowledge your bankruptcy, confess your emptiness, ask Him to have mercy upon you, plead His own promise, and go on asking until you receive it. For the promises of God are ever sure, and we have His gracious, blessed word: 'Him that cometh to me I will in no wise cast out' (John 6:37). Ask Him, and if you ask and seek and knock, you shall receive a great and glorious abundance. 'Blessed are they which do hunger and thirst after righteousness: for they shall be filled' (Matt 5:6); they shall be filled with the fullness of God Himself.

8

THE FULLNESS OF BLESSING

Hereby know we that we dwell in him, and he in us,
because he hath given us of his Spirit.

1 JOHN 4:13

THIS WAS WRITTEN BY AN Apostle of Jesus Christ to men and women in a very troubled and perplexing world, towards the end of the first century. The world then was a difficult place, just as it is today—full of troubles and contradictions, full of confusion. It has always been like that. There have been periods of comparative peace, but the world has always been a hard, trying place, and in a sense we can never truly understand the message of the Bible unless we realise that the various books of the Bible were written in a world like that. Our danger in every generation is to think of our immediate perplexities as being quite exceptional; yet any reading of biography or of history should clear our minds of any such idea, for we find that men and women have always regarded their particular era as an unusual and particularly difficult one. Thus we must always bear that in mind as a kind of background to our consideration.

So here, as we have seen, is an old man writing just before he leaves this world, and he gives his final words of advice to men and women who will go on living after his departure. He is concerned about them, he is vitally interested, he wants to help them, and yet what does he write to them? Well, he does not attempt any evaluation of the political situation, nor does he deliver a number of pompous generalities and vague and pious hopes and aspirations. There is, in a sense, no reference to the political or international situation. Rather, he writes to them individually and directly. He does say something about the world, but what he says about it is, 'We know that we are of God, and the whole world lieth in wickedness' (5:19). So according to this man the question is, what are we doing in such a world? What can be done for us? What is most important for us?

Now, it seems to me that we are in precisely that situation. We are all aware of the world in which we live and its condition and its trouble, but the question is, what has the Christian Church to say in the midst of all this? What is the message to Christian people at this point? And if we want to be true to the New Testament we must do exactly what it does. We all have our opinions, and I suppose we are ready to argue for our opinion, and yet surely this century should have taught us that we waste a good deal of time in our prophecies and forebodings concerning the future. We know so little, and our prognostications are almost invariably wrong. Surely, therefore, the great thing for us is rather to view all these things in the light of the teaching of the Scriptures themselves; and as I understand the teaching of the Bible it comes to this, that whatever people may say and whatever may be held out as hopes before us, this world is a place of sin.

This has been so throughout the centuries—look at the long history that is recorded in the Bible. The world has been a place of woe and a place of warfare, misery, unhappiness, and wretchedness, and in spite of all that we were told in the last century as to how different the world was going to be in the twentieth century, we have lived to see that the world is still the same. Therefore, it seems to me to be utterly unchristian and completely contradictory to the message of Scripture to attempt to put forward solutions which are somehow or another going to put this world right, because the whole message of the Bible is to show that this cannot happen. The essence of wisdom, according to Scripture, is that we should make certain that we are not involved in the perdition of this world which is coming, but that rather we should be saved out of it and should be reconciled to God.

That is the message of this Book from beginning to end. The people in whom the Bible glories are men and women who set their gaze upon another world. That was the great secret of Abraham. He did not become immersed and involved in the political situation of the cities of the plain; he was a man who 'looked for a city which hath foundations, whose builder and maker is God' (Heb 11:10). Such people, we are told, are strangers on the earth; they are men and women who are set apart in life and who have learned that the vital thing is their relationship to God. They make sure that in spite of the world that is around and about them they are not involved finally in the catastrophe that is to overwhelm it because of sin.

And thus it seems to me that the whole principle of Christian preaching is not to express vague, general, contradictory ideas as to what should happen. Let us, rather, come to something of which we are certain, and what we are certain of is that the whole world is to be judged by God, that no one can escape Him, and that there is but one way to be reconciled to God, and that is in and through our Lord Jesus Christ. We know that we need to be delivered out of this world; we know the whole world is passing away. It is not for me to try to predict what the next year will hold for all of us—we do not know; but what I do know is that if I am right with God in Christ, I can face whatever happens, and I can say with the great Apostle that 'I am persuaded, that neither death, nor life, nor angels, nor principalities, nor powers, nor things present, nor things to come, nor height, nor depth, nor any other creature, shall be able to separate us from the love of God, which is in Christ Jesus our Lord' (Rom 8:38-39).

Can *we* say that? Are *we* in that position? That is the question! That is the theme, as we have seen, of this particular section of 1 John 4. The knowledge of God—that is the thing, says John, that we may know that we dwell in Him and He in us. How do we arrive at that knowledge?

I have pointed out that there are certain tests that we can apply to ourselves in order that we may know whether we have received the Spirit of God, the Holy Spirit. That is the most important question for anyone in this world today. It is infinitely more important than the question of whether there will be another war or not. Infinitely more important than the atomic bomb and its possible use is this question, have I received the Holy Spirit of God? For whether there is to be a war or not, I have got to meet God, and therefore the urgent question for me is, have I received His Spirit? Am I dwelling in God, and is God dwelling in me?

Now there are certain general tests that one can apply to oneself, and we have seen some already. A sense of sin, a sense of unworthiness, a realisation of who Jesus Christ is and what He has done, and an increasing longing to be more like Him—an awareness of a conflict between the flesh and the Spirit, this internal warfare—the fruit of the Spirit, and the possession, perhaps, of certain of the special gifts which the Holy Spirit in His sovereignty dispenses to certain people at certain times—these are the general tests. They are of vital importance, and we tried to look at them in their ascending order.

But I come back to this subject because it is such a vital one, and I return to it also because it does seem to be the subject which leads a great many people into confusion. It is a question which is frequently discussed among Christian people, this whole question of whether I have received the Holy Spirit. How can one receive the Holy Spirit, what does one do to receive the Spirit, and what are the manifestations of the Spirit in one's life and experience?

First of all, let us remind ourselves of what is possible for us as Christian people. Now, there is no question as to this when you read the pages of the New Testament itself. The picture there of the Christian is something that is perfectly clear and definite. The New Testament Christian is always someone who seems to know what he has; there is a clear division between the Christian and the non-Christian. The New Testament talks about those who belong to the world. It also talks about those who are in Christ, and you notice the assumptions which are constantly made by the writers of the various New Testament epistles. For example: 'Whom having not seen, ye love; in whom, though now ye see him not, yet believing, ye rejoice with joy unspeakable and full of glory' (1 Pet 1:8). That is the assumption that is made about Christians in the New Testament; they are people who glory in Christ—they love Him. The people described in this Book are people whom you can describe, if you like, as being 'pneumatic'; they are spiritual people. There is a new order, a new quality in their lives; they are not just ordinary people striving to be good. A life has been given to them; something has happened to them. They have received this gift of the Spirit of God; they are a changed and a different people.

Look at the first possessors of the Holy Spirit on the day of Pentecost. The people said, 'These men are drunk'; they were like men possessed. You cannot read the New Testament without gaining that impression. There was a power about them, a radiance, a newness, a love, a warmth and enthusiasm about them which was quite unmistakable, and that is why I say that as these letters were written to them, these great assumptions were so constantly made. The Christian is one set apart: a 'new man,' a 'new creation,' a 'new life.' Christians are people who give the impression that they have received something from above, and therefore they are so different.

Now this is something which is confirmed by the subsequent history of the church. You read about that history during any period of revival and reawakening and you will find exactly the same thing. There is this same quality of life and exuberance, this joy, this sense of exhilaration; in other words, the fruit of the Spirit, in all its aspects, is being manifested in the lives of Christian people at such times. In other words, when the Spirit of God comes into people's lives, that will of necessity make a difference; and thus we find it in the New Testament and in the history of the church at every period of revival and true life. The thing I am anxious to emphasise here is that the New Testament makes it very clear that that order and quality of life is possible for *all* Christians; it is not only for some. I defy anyone to give any statement in the New Testament which says that this particular order and quality of life is only meant for certain people.

Now there are many who hold that idea. They say, 'Yes, that is all right for certain exceptional people whom you may categorise as religious geniuses.' But the New Testament never says that. It is all-inclusive in its description. The Apostle Paul, for example, never said that he had something which no one else possessed. Indeed, he went out of his way to say the opposite in writing to the Roman Christians. He was anxious to visit them so that he could 'impart . . . some spiritual gift . . . that is, that I may be comforted together with you by the mutual faith both of you and me' (Rom 1:11-12). This is for all who are sinners saved by grace, all who respond to the same Holy Spirit.

In other words, the great message of the New Testament is that natural divisions and distinctions become comparatively unimportant. Because we all can possess and be filled by the Spirit of God, we share the same life and the same experience. Therefore, we must start with the proposition that this is something that is possible for all of us. So this comes back to us again as a very urgent question: Have I received the Holy Spirit? 'Hereby know we that we dwell in him, and he in us, because he hath given us of his Spirit.' Has God given me His Spirit? That is the question. Do I know that I am in God and God in me because I have received God's gift of His own Spirit?

Now, I say there are difficulties which confront certain people as they face that question. There are many who are perplexed about this whole subject, and I suggest to you that there are three main causes of difficulty.

The first cause of difficulty I would describe as wrong teaching, and there are various kinds of false teaching with respect to this matter. There is, for instance, the idea that this receiving of the Holy Spirit is something that always happens suddenly. There are those who think that the Holy Ghost can only be received suddenly; further, because they never receive any sudden experience, they say that they have never received the Holy Spirit. Now there are instances in the Bible where people did receive the Holy Spirit suddenly, but there are also instances where people did not, and in the history of the church you find exactly the same thing. Attention always tends to be focused upon that which is most dramatic, and thus as you read books on this subject, you will find that they generally give a list of the people who received the sudden gift. But it is equally clear in the Bible and in the history of the church that the gift does not always come to individuals in a sudden and dramatic manner.

Or let me put it like this: There is a teaching which would have us believe that the Holy Spirit is always received with great emotional upheaval. Once more I think the reason is exactly the same. In some instances there was a remarkable, dramatic, and emotional experience; but it does not always happen in that way. I was reading recently what I regard as a most sane illustration of that point. It was an essay about that great man of God who was used so much in China, Jonathan Goforth. He tells us about his own experience. He thought that this gift of the Holy Spirit would come upon him as it did to men like Finney and D. L. Moody, who received the gift suddenly and with great emotional upheaval. Goforth thought that he would receive it in the same way. And yet he tells us that when he received this fullness of the Spirit there was no dramatic intensity, and he thanks God for that because, he says, 'If I had received this gift in the same way as Finney and Moody, then I would have been another wonder added to the list of those who had got it like that. But let me place on record that I have received the same gift and it came quite quietly to me and almost unconsciously. I became aware of the fact that God's Holy Spirit was resident in me and was filling me with power.' He was then led to take part in a great revival movement in China and various other parts of the Far East. That, I think, is a very salutary reminder of this great fact—it is not always a great emotional upheaval. What is important is not *how* but *whether* I receive it.

Then there are others who say we have nothing to do in the matter, and we receive the gift of the Holy Ghost passively. They say you must cease from striving; you become utterly passive, and in that passive condition you receive the gift of the Holy Ghost.

And lastly, I would say that the other wrong teaching is a failure to differentiate between the gift and the grace of the Holy Spirit. Once more it is very natural that we should look at that which is most dramatic, and some of the gifts of the Spirit are very dramatic: for example, the gifts of healing, the gifts of tongues, and the gifts of interpretation. We tend to concentrate upon these, but we must be clear in our minds that the Holy Spirit can come to us not only in outstanding gifts, but still more in what are called the graces of the Spirit. Paul gave us a list of the graces in 1 Corinthians 13. Let us realise that the Holy Spirit produces this wonderful fruit, the grace of the Lord Jesus Christ Himself, in the life of men and women.

Those, then, are some aspects of false teaching. But secondly, I suggest that there are others who are in difficulty about this matter because of wrong desires or wrong motives. Take, for example, the case that is cited in Acts 8, that of the man called Simon. He had listened to the preaching of Philip and of Peter and John, and he had seen how Peter and John prayed that the gift of the Holy Ghost might descend upon the believers. And when Simon saw that through the laying of the Apostles' hands upon them they received the Holy Spirit, he coveted that power for himself, and he wanted to buy the power and so be able to give that wonderful blessing to others. His motive was wrong; his desire was wrong. And many of us have to plead guilty of that very thing. So often we desire particular feelings or particular experiences; so often we desire particular gifts.

That is one of the dangers in reading Christian literature, as I have already been indicating. We read about Finney or about Moody, and we say, 'Wouldn't it be wonderful to have an experience like that!' But we must not covet experiences; we must not covet gifts. Rather, we are to covet and desire righteousness; we are to covet holiness. What we should desire is not that we may have some great flashing experience, or that we may have some great miracle-working gift, or the gift of speech, or any other gift; we should desire earnestly that gift that would most make us like the Lord Jesus Christ. We should desire to be the kind of person that is described in Romans 12. That is what we should covet; we must hunger and thirst after righteousness, not after blessing. And if we do so, we shall obtain the blessing, we shall be blessed, we shall be filled, we shall receive this gift of the Holy Spirit. Therefore, we must be careful to examine our motives and desires, and we must be perfectly certain that we do not just desire to be like somebody else who was known to be a remarkable Christian, so that our names will go down in church history, and people will point to us and say what remarkable and wonderful persons we were. All that, of course, would quench the Spirit; the motive is wrong, and the desire is false.

My third heading would be wrong practice, and wrong practice is summarised in the New Testament in this way: We are perhaps not aware of the Holy Spirit within us because we are guilty of quenching the Spirit. That may mean not obeying the prompting of the Holy Spirit within us. The Holy Spirit may have come into our lives quite quietly and unobtrusively, and He is resident within us and moving us and prompting us; not to obey His prompting, not to yield to it, is to quench the Holy Spirit. And if we are quenching the Spirit, we will not be aware of the power and the life and activity of the Spirit in our lives.

Perhaps one of the ways of doing this today is by what I would call intellectualism, and this is something about which some of us have to be very careful. There are those perhaps who have enough discrimination to see that what so often is claimed to be a gift of the Holy Spirit is nothing but a riot of the emotions. There are those who having read and studied can say of certain people who claim to be filled with the Holy Spirit that their fleshly character is obvious. It is quite clear that they are suffering from some emotional complex. But the danger to such critics is that they could be so afraid of having something like that that they actually quench the Holy Spirit within them. They can be so afraid of the false that they even miss the true, and therefore I would say to all who are intellectual and who are concerned about these things that we must beware of quenching the Spirit and of reducing the gospel of Jesus Christ to a mere intellectual proposition. This is *life*; it moves, it disturbs, it fills with love and joy and makes people enthusiastic. Those New Testament Christians, and the history of revivals, prove that. Let us be careful that in our fear of emotionalism we do not fall into the same error as the church of the eighteenth century which condemned Whitefield and others as mere enthusiasts and failed to recognise them as men who had been filled with the Spirit of God. This is quenching the Spirit!

The other way in which we engage in wrong practise is to grieve the Spirit. 'Grieve not the Holy Spirit,' says the Scripture (Eph 4:30). We grieve the Spirit by committing sin, by being disobedient to God's holy law. So if you want to know that the Spirit of God is in you, you must not sin. Sin grieves the Spirit; to do deliberately that which you know to be wrong is to be in the position in which you cannot know that the Holy Spirit is in you. So if there is anything doubtful in your life, you must get rid of it, for while there is any doubt, the Holy Spirit will not manifest Himself.

These, then, are some of the causes of difficulty, but let me hurry to a positive point. If those are the causes of difficulty, how does one obtain a fullness of the Spirit? How can we be sure that the Holy Spirit dwells in us? Well, you do not remain passive—you do certain things. First of all, you read the Bible. I put that first because I regard it of first importance. It is only as we fill ourselves with the Word of God that we shall really know what is possible to us; it is as I read this New Testament day by day that I see more and more the possibilities for every Christian. It is only as I read this Word that I shall be guarded against error. It is those who do not read it who are misled by the false. If we keep to the Word, there are tests that can be applied, there are proofs that can be given. The reading of the Bible must come first. Go again through the lives of the people throughout the centuries, and you will find that they always did that. They read the Word of God, and they saw what was possible to them as they read it, and they said, 'Oh, that I had that gift!' Read it, and you will see the difference between the true and the false.

Then secondly, I would mention obedience; we must avoid grieving the Spirit, and we must avoid quenching the Spirit. We must humble ourselves, as the Scriptures exhort us to. Scripture has told us that we must not think more highly of ourselves than we ought to think (Rom 12:3); this is a danger confronting us all. The Bible tells us to humble ourselves and not to overestimate ourselves. It tells us to 'mortify' the flesh, to wage a warfare, to battle against everything that tends to drag us down. 'Mortify therefore your members which are upon the earth,' says Scripture (Col 3:5), and we ought to do that actively. We are also to obey every prompting and leading of the Spirit and every holy desire and aspiration and every urge to prayer; all these things must be immediately obeyed—that is the instruction of Scripture.

And then next I cite that which in a sense makes these first two really possible—namely, prayer, an earnest desire for this, petitioning and pleading before God for it. And we must go on with this; we must continue, and we must persist. Nothing comes out more clearly in Christian biographies than that. Take note of these men and women who received the gift; they tell you that they became dissatisfied; they saw that they were lacking in the centre of their being. They not only read the Scriptures, but they began to pray, and they prayed day by day. They pleaded with God; they asked for this fuller blessing of the Holy Spirit, and they went on and on and on until they received the answer that they desired—prayer, pleading, continuously imploring God to grant them this great blessing.

And I close with another practical word: How does this blessing come? Well, I do not see any evidence in the New Testament to support what used to be called a 'tarrying meeting.' Some people had that idea. God had certain blessings to give, and they thought they had to wait until they received them. But the gift is given by God in His own way and time; this gift does not come of necessity at once. It is God's gift, and He knows when to give it and when to withhold it.

Here once more it seems to me that history is very helpful. Do you remember the case of Moody? This was his story. He became conscious of his lack and need, and he began to pray to God about it. He gave obedience to the Word of God as well as he could, and he went on praying for months. Nothing happened to him, but still he went on praying. Yes, he waited for it, but it did not come, and the story is that one day, walking down a street in New York, not in a tarrying meeting, not even in a prayer meeting, suddenly God overwhelmed him with this mighty blessing. It was so mighty that Moody felt he must be killed by it, and he held up his hand and said, 'Stop, God!'

God has His own time. Thank God that He knows us better than we know ourselves! Some of us have asked for great gifts and, thank God, He has not given them to us; we would have spent them upon our own lusts. I think that every Christian, looking back, must thank God that certain things were withheld in his or her life and experience. If God gave certain gifts to some of us, we would consume them in our own self-glorification; but thank God, He withholds them. Some of us perhaps need to be humbled; some of us need to be brought to the very dust. God knows when to give the gift, and we must never imagine that by going to a meeting or following a certain procedure it is bound to come. No; the Holy Spirit is sovereign, and He gives in His own way. It may be dramatically or suddenly or quietly; that is irrelevant, because what really matters is that we receive the gift.

The essence of it all, I think, can be put very simply: 'Trust and obey.' If we realise that there is this difference between us and those New Testament Christians, and if we long to be like them, we shall persist in reading this Word and in giving obedience to everything we discover in it; and we shall pray to God to shed His love abroad in our hearts and to give us His own gracious, glorious fullness. We shall go on and on, and as we do so God will answer us; of that we can be certain. This is God's will, even our sanctification. He is anxious to bless us and to give us this gift more than any human father is anxious for the well-being of his own child. God desires that we be filled with His own fullness; so let us ask Him, and let us leave the time and manner to Him and to Him alone. 'Blessed are they which do hunger and thirst after righteousness: for they shall be filled' (Matt 5:6). If I truly desire to be holy, if I desire to be like Christ and to do my utmost to be that and to look to God for the enabling for that, God will give me this fullness, this gift of the Holy Ghost, and I shall be filled. And then I shall know for certain that I dwell in Him and He in me because He has given me of His Spirit.

I say again, the most important thing in the world at this moment is to know we possess this gift. Has God given you His Holy Spirit? Oh, that we may come in simplicity to this Christian way and follow the simple steps that will certainly lead us to the fullness of blessing.

9

THE APOSTOLIC WITNESS
AND TESTIMONY

And we have seen and do testify that the Father sent the
Son to be the Saviour of the world. Whosoever shall con-
fess that Jesus is the Son of God, God dwelleth in him, and
he in God. And we have known and believed the love that
God hath to us. God is love; and he that dwelleth in love
dwelleth in God, and God in him.

1 JOHN 4:14–16

WE COME HERE TO another of those great and magnificent statements
which are such a characteristic feature of this first epistle of John. We
have noticed as we have gone through the letter that ever and again these
mighty statements of the gospel apparently suddenly appear and lift us
to the heights. I constantly feel as I read and study this particular epistle that it is remarkably like a mountain range. You know how, when
looking at a great range of mountains, you observe that while the total
elevation is high, there are occasional peaks that stand out above the
others and suddenly tower out in their magnificence. I feel that this letter is remarkably like that. The whole letter—every statement—is at that
elevation, that great spiritual height, and ever and again as we look at
it we suddenly observe these particular statements that seem to stand out
with exceptional glory and wonder. We have already found several such
in this very chapter.

Yet nothing is more important than that we should remember that this statement is in intimate association and connection with everything that is around it, and that is why a systematic study of Scripture is always ultimately the only true and fair and legitimate way of approaching it. We could take a verse like this and deal with it and preach on it in and of itself, and of course there would be a purpose in doing so; but if we want to understand its true significance, we must take it in its context, and that is why I feel the comparison of the great mountain range is very helpful. These verses must be taken together; verse 14 must be taken with verse 15, and 15 with 14, and verses 14 and 15 must be taken with the preceding verses and with the following verses, because they are all part of an argument in the Apostle's great statement.

John does not merely throw out statements like this at random; this is not something that suddenly juts out without any explanation or without any apparent rhyme or reason. He is working out an argument, as we have seen, and this is an essential part of his whole argument and position. The theme that engages us here is this whole theme of the assurance of salvation. He arrived at it by talking again about the importance of loving the brethren, and he says that if we do not love the brethren, that means we do not know God. That in turn leads him to talk about this subsidiary theme of knowing God; and that, according to John, is the most important thing in this world, that I should know that God is in me and I am in God.

Now here in verses 14 and 15 he goes to his next test as to how I can know this, and the main text as such is in verse 15: 'Whosoever shall confess that Jesus is the Son of God, God dwelleth in him, and he in God.' That is the third way in which I may know that I am in Him: loving the brethren, possessing the Holy Spirit, and confessing that Jesus is the Son of God. What he is concerned about is to show us and to explain to us how one can arrive in the position in which one can make this great confession.

So the test we must consider here is this one: Do I confess that Jesus is the Son of God? If I do, then I know that God is dwelling in me and I in God. That seems a simple statement, and yet I think we shall find it is a very profound one. I suggest, therefore, that we approach verses 14-15 in the light of these propositions.

First of all, I would state that a correct belief is proof of the possession of the Holy Spirit. John is really dealing here in essence with the doctrine of the Holy Spirit, and what the Holy Spirit in us enables us to do. His argument, in a sense, is that if we confess that Jesus is the Son of God, we do so because the Holy Spirit is enabling us to do so, and that means that the Holy Spirit must be in us; and as he has proved, if the Holy Spirit is in me, then I am in God and God is in me. That is the argument, but I think at this point that it is important that we should perhaps put it like this—namely, that a correct belief is impossible apart from the Holy Spirit.

I think John is anxious to put it as strongly as that, and here again we see how John by proceeding in this order corrects some of the false teachings that are current with regard to this whole doctrine of the Holy Spirit. There are people who do not hesitate to teach that you can be in a position in which you believe that Jesus is the Son of God and then later on you receive the Holy Spirit—that it is possible to be a believer without having received the Holy Spirit. Clearly by this particular passage that is an utter impossibility. John's whole case is that you cannot believe that Jesus is the Son of God unless God dwells in you and you in God; that is his argument. 'Whosoever shall confess that Jesus is the Son of God, God dwelleth in him, and he in God.' And the way in which God dwells in us is by the Holy Spirit. So we can say that the people who do confess that Jesus is the Son of God have the Holy Spirit already within them. Or to put it another way, they cannot believe that Jesus is the Son of God without possessing the Holy Spirit.

Now this is a doctrine which is common to the whole of the New Testament. The Apostle Paul puts it like this: 'We speak the wisdom of God in a mystery, even the hidden wisdom, which God ordained before the world unto our glory: which none of the princes of this world knew: for had they known it, they would not have crucified the Lord of glory. . . . But God hath revealed them unto us by his Spirit: for the Spirit searcheth all things, yea, the deep things of God' (1 Cor 2:7-8, 10).

You see, the whole case can be put like this: Even the princes of this world, the great men of the world, the mighty and the noble and the wise, looked at Jesus of Nazareth and saw nothing but a man, a carpenter, an artisan. They may have regarded Him as a kind of unusual religious genius, but they did not know He was the Lord of glory. Why not? Well, says Paul, because they had not received the Holy Spirit. But you and I, he says to the Corinthians, we understand these things, we believe them. Why? Because God has revealed them to us by His Spirit, the Spirit who searches all things, 'yea, the deep things of God.'

And then in 1 Corinthians 12:3 he again puts it in a very categorical statement. 'No man,' he says, 'can say that Jesus is the Lord, but by the Holy Ghost.' He cannot do it otherwise; it is impossible. So the way in which John puts it comes to this, that if a man does say that Jesus is the Lord, it must mean that the Holy Spirit is already resident within him. Thus I lay down this first proposition, that a correct belief, a true belief, is proof of the fact that we do, in entirety, possess the Holy Spirit; it is the Holy Spirit alone who can enable us to believe truly, and without the Holy Spirit we cannot believe.

Now this, of course, is something that can be seen very clearly in the history of the church, as it can in the Bible. It is seen in church history as a message preached to men and women, and there are those who believe it and those who do not. Here is a message which has been presented to men and women of intellect and understanding and great wisdom and knowledge, people who have been famous for their sanity and balance. They have heard it, and they have seen nothing in it. But on the other hand, you have some of the humblest and most ignorant and untutored and unlettered people who have heard it and rejoiced in it and who have been transformed by it and have become saints in the Church of God. To what is the difference due? What is the explanation? The explanation, says Scripture, is that the Holy Spirit has enabled these people to see and believe.

This teaching that you can believe first and then go on to receive the Spirit is utterly unscriptural. Of course, probably what such friends mean is that one can go on to have deeper and greater experiences of the Holy Spirit, but if that is what they mean, then let them say so; there is no such thing as belief apart from receiving the Holy Ghost. We can go on to receive a greater fullness. We can do that many times in our lives—we *should* be doing so; but what is fundamental is that the mere statement, in a true sense, that Jesus is the Son of God is proof positive that God dwells in us in His Holy Spirit and that we dwell in God.

There, surely, is something that ought to be of great comfort. There may be those who are very conscious of their imperfections, very conscious of their unworthiness, their faults and failures and sins. Now I am not anxious to administer false comfort, but I do say that whatever you may feel about yourself and however much you may be disposed to condemn yourself, if you really believe from your heart that Jesus is the Son of God, I assure you that God dwells in you and that God has given you

His Holy Spirit, because you cannot believe it apart from that power which you have received.

Let us put that another way. A correct belief means an acceptance of the apostolic witness and testimony. That is what we mean by a correct belief. Now it is there that we see the importance of taking verses 14-15 together. 'And we . . .' says John, referring to himself and to his fellow Apostles and to those who are already Christians. He is referring to those of whom he speaks in the very introduction of the letter, where he says, 'That which we have seen and heard declare we unto you, that ye also may have fellowship with us: and truly our fellowship is with the Father, and with his Son Jesus Christ' (1:3). 'We,' says John here, 'have seen and do testify that the Father sent the Son to be the Saviour of the world.' Then he goes on to say, 'Whosoever therefore shall confess that Jesus is the Son of God, God dwelleth in him, and he in God.' So a correct belief comes to that; it is an acceptance of the apostolic witness and testimony.

This word 'confess' in verse 15 really means assenting unto, expressing my agreement, saying my 'Amen' to that which is said to me. I receive the statement, and I believe and accept it; that is what he means by confessing. Now here again surely is a vitally important statement. What makes men and women Christians is that they accept and subscribe to a certain body of teaching and doctrine concerning our Lord Jesus Christ. But how can they do that? What is it that enables them to make this confession that Jesus is the Son of God? On what ground do they make that statement?

Here it seems to me that there is only one answer given in the New Testament itself, and it is the one which I have already put to you. I can only confess in a true sense by accepting and believing the apostolic witness and testimony. I have not seen the Lord Jesus Christ with the eyes of flesh. I was not on the earth when He was here. So what do I know about Him? How can I believe in Him? Here we come back to this vital doctrine of the ultimate and final authority of the Scriptures themselves in all matters of faith. And that is why we must ever insist upon that vital matter. There are those who say that they do not accept the authority of the Scriptures but that they believe in the Lord Jesus Christ. The question I ask is, how do they know Him? What do they know about the Lord Jesus Christ except what they find in the New Testament?

It is there, it seems to me, that this whole so-called higher critical approach to the Scriptures is, in the last analysis, not merely an error but utter folly. How can I sit in judgment on the New Testament? How can I say *this* is true of Christ, but *that* is not? What do I know about Christ apart from the New Testament? I am shut up to this Book; anything that I may say that I believe apart from the Bible will be sheer imagination. That is why this talk about going directly to Christ (without reference to the Scriptures) is, according to the New Testament, the most dangerous position one can be in. That is why the New Testament epistles were written, to correct error and heresy. 'Believe,' says John in this chapter, 'not every spirit, but try the spirits whether they are of God: because many false prophets are gone out into the world. Hereby know ye the Spirit of God: every spirit that confesseth that Jesus Christ is come in the flesh is of God' (vv. 1-2).

In those first years there were all sorts of apocryphal gospels. There were men drawing on their imagination, and, perhaps inspired by the devil himself, they were spreading stories about the teachings of Jesus of Nazareth and were making havoc in the life of the early church. So God raised up the Apostles to write these authoritative accounts, in order that we might know what is true and what is false; that is the whole purpose of our belief in the canon of Scripture. The promise of Jesus Christ to the disciples when He said the Holy Spirit would guide them into all truth was fulfilled in the writing of the New Testament Scriptures; and the wisdom given to the Church to deliver the canon of Scripture is that which can be traced back to the Apostles and which therefore can be regarded as the Word of God. And John, in a sense, is just saying at this particular point that if we do make this confession that Jesus is the Son of God, then God dwells in us and we in God; we can only make that statement because of those people who have seen and testified that 'the Father has sent the Son to be the Saviour of the world.'

Let me again, therefore, stress and emphasise that the second great principle is that a correct belief means the acceptance of and agreement with the apostolic witness and testimony. I know no Christ apart from the Christ I find in the New Testament. I have no immediacy or directness of approach. I do not believe in visions, and I cannot find Christ directly; I find Him in the Scriptures. That was the great emphasis of the Protestant Reformation, and we must come back to it. A lot of mystical talk is made in an attempt to avoid the authority of Scripture because of its miraculous and supernatural element. People have been reconstructing a Jesus of their own, but he is not the Jesus of the New Testament. Which Jesus can I know apart from *this* Jesus? I am, therefore, shut up to the Bible, and I either accept the apostolic witness and teaching or I reject it. I ask again, how can people living in the twentieth century sit in judgment upon the Gospels? What do they know? By what canon do they describe and define this Jesus they depict? I know nothing about Him apart from what I am told concerning Him in the Bible, which is the record and the account of the apostolic witness and the apostolic testimony.

Ah, let us be careful of these subtle temptations of Satan which would try to persuade us that we are in a superior spiritual condition! I once read an article in which a man claimed that those of us who believe in the ultimate authority of Scripture and who bank our all upon it are guilty of what he calls seeing the Book rather than the Saviour. He claims he is in a superior spiritual condition, and this is the position taken up at the present time by those who claim that their authority is Christ. 'We do not see the Book,' they say; 'Christ himself is the authority.' To which again I ask my question: What do you know about Christ apart from the Book? Who is your Christ unless He conforms to this? Who is the Christ who gives you the authority? The Bible—that is my authority. I am dependent upon the record and witness of John the Baptist—of Peter, James, and John and the other disciples and Apostles who preached and bore testimony to these first Christians.

And that brings me to my third great principle: What is this correct belief? Now here we are outside the realm of controversy if we accept the apostolic witness and testimony and we remind ourselves of the very centralities of our faith. We have been looking at the mountain range; now let us centre on this glorious peak that stretches up to heaven and beyond them all. What is it? 'We have seen and do testify that the Father sent the Son to be the Saviour of the world.'

I see the importance of the apostolic witness. What is it? John, in effect, is putting it like this: 'The important thing is to know God. But how can I know God? "No man hath seen God at any time." But we have seen and do testify that Jesus is the Son of God.' That is the statement. Notice how he puts it. He had not had a vision. What then? Thank God, 'we *have seen*.' He said it all in the introduction: 'That which . . . we have seen with our eyes, which we have looked upon, and our hands have handled, of the Word of life . . . that which we have seen and heard we declare unto you,' said John. 'No man hath seen God, but we have seen Jesus, and Jesus said, "He that hath seen me hath seen the Father"' (see John 14:9).

In other words, the apostolic vision on which my faith is grounded is this: It is a belief in that which the Apostles tell us they saw, and the explanation of their understanding of what they saw is found in the four Gospels. The statements in the Gospels are not simply objective statements; they are statements plus interpretation, and at long last modern man has come back to see that. They used to contrast John with Matthew, Mark, and Luke. They said that John preached, but that Matthew, Mark, and Luke just gave the facts. But they now have to admit that what they wrote was facts plus interpretation. Like John, the men who wrote the first three Gospels believed and understood that Jesus is the Son of God and the Saviour of the world. They saw and they testified; in other words, they saw and they expounded.

What, then, did they see, and what did they expound? There were two elements, a double emphasis. The first statement is that Jesus is the Son of God. 'We have seen,' says John. This word 'seen' is a strong word; it means 'gazed upon.' He used that same word in the prologue of his Gospel—'and we beheld his glory' (John 1:14). To behold is not merely to give a cursory glance; it is not a passing glimpse of something. No; we have looked upon, we have beheld, we have sat in amazement, we have contemplated, we have seen, 'and we beheld his glory, the glory as of the only begotten of the Father, full of grace and truth.' That is it!

What John is saying is something like this: 'We looked at His person, and I remember the enigma that was presented to us. We looked at Him. He was a man like every other man apparently, and He had worked as a carpenter. He was quite ordinary, and yet He was always surprising us. There was something—a radiance—a glory that kept on peeping out. There was something unearthly, and we said one to another, "What is it?" He frightened us at times, this ordinary person who became extraordinary suddenly—there was something about Him. "We beheld His glory." And then there were His teachings. He had never been to the schools; He had never had any learning in a formal sense, and yet He taught as one having authority, and not as the Scribes. And there was the way in which He handled the Doctors of the Law. There was the sermon He preached one day on a mountain with those extraordinary Beatitudes of His. There was a glory that came out in His words; gracious words came streaming forth from His lips.

'And then there were His works—the things which we saw Him do. We were in a boat with Him one day, and He was asleep in the stern of the vessel when suddenly a storm arose, and the water was gradually filling up our little boat, and we were trying to get rid of it, but we could do nothing. We felt we would be drowned at any moment, and we awoke Him and said, "Master, we perish," and what did He do but rebuke the waves and they were still, and we were afraid. And on another occasion we saw Him even raise a man who was dead. A poor widow came out of a town called Nain mourning her dead son. We were going into the town, and we met, and He spoke a word, and the dead arose. And we remember, too, what happened in Jairus' house. He mastered the elements; He controlled everything—life, death, all things seemed subservient to His supernatural power—His works, His miracles. We beheld the glory streaming and shining out of it all. He did signs and wonders, and they proclaimed to us that He was the Son of God.

'But we also saw things happening to Him. I remember,' says John, 'how one day he told Peter and James and myself to come aside with Him. He said, "I want to take you three to the top of that mountain; we will leave the others for a time. I want you three alone to be with Me." So we went to the top of the mountain, and there we saw His whole body transformed and transfigured. It became shining and exceedingly white, and we saw two men appearing. They were Elijah and Moses, and they talked; and then we heard a voice from heaven—we beheld His glory—and the voice said, "This is my beloved Son, in whom I am well pleased; hear Him." It was the transfiguration!

'And I remember seeing Him in the Garden, sweating drops of blood. And I remember looking at Him upon the cross, and the words He spoke to me there—and we beheld His glory. We saw Him buried, yes, but He appeared to us afterwards. We saw Him resurrected, and He came and spoke to us. He came into the room with the door shut, and on another occasion He sat down and ate some broiled fish with us. We have seen, and we testify—we beheld His glory. Indeed, we were with Him one day, and suddenly we saw Him rising and ascending into the clouds and into heaven, and He disappeared out of our sight. We believe, we have seen, and we do testify. And then we remember that amazing day at Pentecost at Jerusalem when He promised that the Holy Ghost would come upon us, and we began to speak with strange, new tongues, and we were filled with power and radiance ourselves—we have seen and we do testify.'

That is the record. So, I say, what makes men and women Christians is that they confess that. They do not merely accept it intellectually. They say, 'This is the thing that matters; this is the thing by which I live; this is the thing which means life to me.' They confess that Jesus is the Son of God.

Ah yes, but they also confess that He is 'the Saviour of the world.' In other words, these men taught and reminded people of what Jesus Himself had been saying. They reminded the people of how He once said, 'The Son of Man came not to be ministered unto, but to minister, and to give his life a ransom for many' (Matt 20:28). They remembered the word of John the Baptist: 'Behold the Lamb of God, which taketh away the sin of the world!' (John 1:29). They remembered that He said, 'I must go to Jerusalem' and that He set His face steadfastly to go there—there was this compulsion, this constraint. They remembered how He himself had said, 'For this cause came I unto this hour. . . . And I, if I be lifted up from the earth, will draw all men unto me' (John 12:27, 32). They remembered all this, and they taught it.

That was the apostolic teaching and witness and testimony. They did not go around preaching moral uplift or talking about the international situation. They gave these facts about this extraordinary person that they had seen. They said, 'This is the Son of God; this is what happened to Him, and the meaning of it all is that He has been sent by God to be the Saviour of the world.' That was their preaching! They said in effect, 'We did not understand Him fully until after the resurrection. There seemed to us to be a strange contradiction in Him; He made these exalted claims, and yet He appeared to be so weak. He said He could do everything. He could raise the dead, but He could not save Himself on the cross. So we were very dejected when He was buried in the grave; but then He rose again, and He came back and spoke to us. He opened the Scriptures to us; He took us through the Old Testament, and He showed us that the Christ had to suffer. He expounded the doctrine of the atonement to us. He said, "I am the Lamb of God. My Father has placed the sins of the world upon Me. I have died to set you free." He opened our understanding of the Scriptures.'

That was the Apostles' preaching that was the apostolic witness and testimony. Jesus—who He is, what He means, the explanation of His extraordinary life and death, His rising again and ascension, and ultimately what it all means to us—can be put in this form. Whoever confesses that Jesus is the Son of God is one who has come to understand God's great love to us, which is the theme of John's next statement in verse 16. The Apostles really were teaching the love of God, that 'God so loved the world, that he gave his only begotten Son, that whosoever believeth in him should not perish, but have everlasting life' (John 3:16). They perish apart from Him; but believing on Him, they do not perish but have everlasting life. 'Whosoever shall confess,' therefore, that 'Jesus is the Son of God' has accepted the Apostles' teaching.

You see, that includes it all—not only the doctrine of the Incarnation, not merely the teaching, not only the miracles, but the death, the meaning of the death, the whole idea of the atonement; that He is 'the Saviour of the world'—God's way of salvation. Those who believe that, says John, can be quite certain that God dwells in them and they in God, for apart from this indwelling of the Holy Spirit, Jesus of Nazareth is but a man—a political agitator to some, a moral exemplar to others, just a philosopher to others, the pale Galilean to another. People do not understand that the princes of the world look at Him, but they never behold His glory. But these men, the Apostles, 'beheld His glory, the glory as of the only begotten of the Father,' and we have their record and witness and testimony; and if I accept and see it and give my assent to it from my heart, there is only one reason why I do so, and that is that the Holy Spirit has opened my eyes. I can thus say, 'I know that God dwells in me and I in God.' It is the Spirit who 'searcheth all things, yea, the deep things of God' (1 Cor 2:10). God opens blind eyes; however poor and weak and ignorant we may be, He can enable us to behold Him with the eye of faith.

And so I accept the record, I subscribe to the testimony, and through their eyes, as it were, I behold His glory, 'the glory as of the only begotten of the Father, full of grace and truth.' I therefore say that 'the Father sent the Son to be the Saviour of the world' and to be *my* Saviour.

10

THE SAVIOUR

And we have seen and do testify that the Father sent the Son to be the Saviour of the world.

1 JOHN 4:14

WE RETURN ONCE MORE to this great statement which I have compared to a great mountain peak. I feel, with this fourteenth verse, very much as Peter, I imagine, must have felt when on the Mountain of Transfiguration with James and John. They had been taken up by our Lord, and when Moses and Elijah appeared, Peter said, 'Let us make here three tabernacles; one for thee, and one for Moses, and one for Elijah' (Matt 17:4). In other words, the glory had so gripped him that he said, 'Let us stay here.' This glory was so very different from the world down in the plain, and as I read this verse, I think I understand him.

We are concerned about the whole argument of the Apostle, and the argument is vital if our Christian experience is to be a triumphant and victorious one. Yet, though we are concerned about the argument, I find it difficult to leave this peak, this glorious height represented in this verse. Indeed, I can justify our return to it in this way: If we are not perfectly happy about the statement of this verse, then the argument completely collapses, because it is based upon this statement. So there is a sense in which we must stay on this mountain a little longer. All the argument that is deduced by the Apostle is deduced from this fundamental postulate, so that if there is any suspicion of doubt, or even the faintest query in our minds about it, we cannot work out the Christian faith, and we have no grounds of assurance and confidence. Therefore, we come back and look at it again.

This is the statement: 'We have seen and do testify that the Father sent the Son to be the Saviour of the world.' The whole of the gospel in a phrase! This is the only time in which John uses the expression 'Saviour' in the entire epistle. He gives the same teaching, of course, in other places. We have already had it back at the beginning, in the second chapter,[1] where he says that our Lord is 'the propitiation for our sins: and not for ours only, but also for the sins of the whole world' (v 2). There is a sense in which he repeats the saying here, but he does not use this precise phrase and describe Him as 'the Saviour of the world' except at this point. To those who are interested in these matters, which are more or less mechanical and yet have their place, it is interesting to observe that John only twice in the whole of his writings uses this phrase. You find it again in John 4 in connection with the woman of Samaria, but it is not a characteristic of his writings. Paul, however, is fond of it, and if you examine his epistles, you will find that he often makes use of this particular expression.

Another important thing is to be certain that we grasp the meaning. Earlier we looked at it in this way: We looked at the person of our Lord—we considered the apostolic witness and testimony with regard to the person, the emphasis being that Jesus is the Son of God; and that, of course, is logically the statement which must come first. The essential doctrine concerning Jesus of Nazareth is always this two-fold doctrine: His person and His work; and there is a sense in which we simply cannot understand the work and the nature of the work until we are perfectly clear in our minds with regard to the person Himself. And so, having looked at the person, we now go forward and are proposing to look at the work which is done by the person—'We have seen and do testify that the Father sent the Son to be the Saviour of the world.'

All I want to do here is to underline some of the essential things which are conveyed by this magnificent and glorious statement of the gospel. In other words, we must look at this word 'Saviour.' What does it mean exactly? It is very important that one should ask a question like that, because one of the great difficulties in connection with theology and Christian thought, especially in this present century, has been that men and women have persisted in using Christian terminology, but have emptied it of the real meaning and have imposed their own. There are people who talk of Christ as Saviour, but they certainly do not mean by that what the New Testament means.

Let me illustrate this. The word 'Saviour' does not merely mean a helper. We are not told that the Father sent the Son to help mankind; it does not mean that He is just someone who assists. Nor does it mean that He is just one who teaches or indicates to us what we ought to do; He is not merely an instructor. Indeed, I would go further and say that the term 'Saviour' and its connotation must not be thought of in terms of an example or pattern or encourager. I use these various terms because so often people speak about our Lord as 'Saviour,' and yet if you ask them to define what they mean by it, they will tell you something of that kind. Their conception of Christ as Saviour can be put like this: He saves us by preaching the Sermon on the Mount and by describing a certain kind of life. He does this by setting before us a great example—as one who lived that high and exalted teaching; and He is constantly calling us to rise to the same height. They say that Christ as Saviour is one who is marching ahead of us and who is leading the way, turning around occasionally to appeal to us and to inspire us to follow in His footsteps, so that ultimately we shall succeed in scaling the heights with Him and will arrive in the presence of God.

Now the element that is seen in all those ideas is this: that ultimately it is you and I who have to save ourselves, and what the Lord does is to aid and assist us—to give us encouragement and make it somewhat easier for us to do so. Now that, of course, is clearly a complete denial not only of the Biblical teaching, but also of the historic faith and creeds of the Christian Church. To use the term *Saviour* with regard to our Lord and mean something like that is dishonest, for it takes the original meaning right out and substitutes for it something that is utterly foreign to the New Testament.

Perhaps the best way to put that is this: If that is all that is meant by 'Saviour,' then Jesus of Nazareth is no Saviour at all. That is something that had already been tried, and it had failed before He ever came into this world. God confronted the children of Israel and gave them the Ten Commandments and the moral law. He said to them, 'Ye shall therefore keep my statutes, and my judgements: which if a man do, he shall live in them' (Lev 18:5). That was God's challenge, as it were, in the giving of the law to the children of Israel, and the whole story of the Old Testament shows us that men and women failed, and failed entirely.

'There is none righteous, no, not one'; 'all have sinned, and come short of the glory of God'; '. . . that every mouth may be stopped, and all the world may become guilty before God' (Rom. 3:10, 23, 19). That describes the world as the result of trying to save itself by keeping the law and the commandments of God. That is a complete failure. There was not a character in the Old Testament who did not fail. The greatest prophets failed and were conscious of sin; the greatest saints were all defeated by sin and by Satan.

I repeat, therefore, that if our Lord and Saviour is to be the Saviour on some such terms, then all He does is really to make things quite impossible for us. For if I cannot keep the Ten Commandments and the moral law, what is the point in confronting me with the Sermon on the Mount? If I cannot even satisfy my own demands, if I cannot come up to the standard of the saints, what is the point of putting before me Jesus of Nazareth? He makes it utterly impossible for me! I, for myself, have never been able to understand the mentality of people who can glibly talk about 'the imitation of Christ' and who believe that they are meant to save themselves and that our Lord just helps them in this external way by giving them a kind of general encouragement. I know of nothing more discouraging than the life of Jesus Christ, taken in that way! If I am left to myself I am entirely undone, I am damned before I move, I am utterly hopeless.

But that is a complete misinterpretation and misrepresentation of what is meant by the phrase 'the Saviour of the world.' Surely the whole Biblical meaning of this particular term should rather be put like this: Christ is the Saviour as the result of something that He has done. We must get rid once and for ever of this idea that we are the actors and receive encouragement from Him. Not at all! The Biblical representation is that God sent Him into the world to do something, and that we are saved as the result of something He has done quite apart from ourselves and our own action. He has acted, and it is His action that produces salvation and the way of escape for us.

Now here is something that is utterly fundamental and primary, and unless we are agreed with this statement there is really no point or purpose in our proceeding any further. Salvation, according to the New Testament—take, for instance, Colossians 1 where you have a perfect illustration of salvation—is something that is entirely worked out by the Lord Jesus Christ. It is something that has come to men and women as a free gift to them, and they have nothing to do but to receive this gift. It is something provided; it is the righteousness of God which is given.

That is something which is surely basic, and of course there is no phrase, perhaps, that puts all this more perfectly than that great and glorious phrase which was uttered by our Lord Himself upon the cross when He cried out, 'It is finished' (John 19:30). He had already talked about having to finish the work which the Father had sent Him to do. He spoke as one who had been given a particular task, and He set out upon it, and there, with His last breath as it were, He cried out, 'I have done it! I have completed the work which Thou gavest Me to do.' Christ is the Saviour; we do not save ourselves. It is He who saves, and our salvation arises from Him and is derived from something He has done once and for ever on our behalf. 'The Father sent the Son to be the Saviour of the world.'

Of course, if you read the Book of Acts you will find that the Apostles and the first preachers went around the world, and this is exactly what they preached. They said that they had great, good news to offer to the people; they were making an announcement, as the angels had already made the announcement to the shepherds. They went from place to place, and they said in effect, 'We are bearers of glad tidings; we have something to tell you, and what we tell you is that God in His Son has done something which means salvation and deliverance for the world.' So that is the first thing we have to realise, that He is 'the Saviour' and that salvation is something that is worked out by Him.

Having said that, having seen that He Himself, by what He does, is the Saviour, let us briefly consider the second principle: how the Lord Jesus Christ saves us. We have already seen that He is the Son of God, that He is the one who has come, who has been sent into the world. He is not an ordinary man born like others; He has been sent from heaven, He has come into the world. So how does He save? I can merely give you a summary of what the Bible teaches in this respect.

First of all, we are told that He saves us by His life of perfect obedience to God's holy law. So the life of Jesus Christ has its importance in that way and in that respect. When we talk about salvation, we have to realise our predicament and our position, and here it is: God has given the law to mankind, and He has told all people that they must keep the law. God has said that if they do not do so, they will be punished, and the punishment is death. God's law stands, and it can never be uprooted.

It is eternal; it is an expression of the character of God Himself, and before anyone can be saved, that law of God has to be fulfilled—it has to be honoured and satisfied. That was, therefore, the first task confronting our Lord Jesus Christ. No one had ever succeeded or could ever succeed in keeping the law, and that law must be kept; so the first thing He did was to live a life of absolute obedience to it. In all things He fulfilled righteousness; every demand of the law positively was answered and was satisfied by His blameless, spotless life.

But, of course, that is not the end. For the law not only makes its positive demands on us—it pronounces its judgment upon us, and it has already pronounced that judgment: 'the wages of sin is death' (Rom 6:23). Those who fail to keep the law know that they are under the wrath of God, and the punishment meted out by God for this failure is death; so they are confronted with that positive enactment. Therefore the second thing that our Lord has to do is to deal with this problem of the guilt of man face-to-face with the law of God, and according to the Scriptures He has done so once and for ever by going to His cruel death upon the cross on Calvary's hill.

We are always confronted by the cross; we cannot get away from it. It is central in the New Testament. Look at all the wealth of detail we are told about it in the four Gospels; look at the emphasis placed upon it in the Acts and in the epistles. It is there always—for example, 'in whom we have redemption through his blood' (Eph 1:7). You cannot get away from this blood in the New Testament. It is central; without it there is no salvation. The law of God demands sin's punishment, and the punishment is death; so our Lord came face-to-face with that demand likewise. Before He could be 'the Saviour of the world,' He had to satisfy the demands that the law makes upon guilty sinners in the sight of God. The message is that He went to the Cross; He set His face steadfastly to go to Jerusalem; He would not be delivered. He told His servants in effect, 'I could command twelve legions of angels; but if I did, how could I fulfill all righteousness? I must meet the demands of the law.' He gave Himself as an offering and a sacrifice; He died passively there upon the cross, and God poured upon Him His wrath against the sin of man. He is our Saviour by His atoning death as well as by His perfect, blameless, spotless life of obedience.

But even that does not exhaust this idea of Christ as our Saviour, for you will find that the author of the Epistle to the Hebrews takes us beyond that. He tells us that our Lord has become the great High Priest. There on the cross He was the sacrifice and the offering, and He is also the High Priest. The writer says that He entered into heaven by His own blood. 'Neither by the blood of goats and calves, but by his own blood he entered in once into the holy place, having obtained eternal redemption for us' (Heb 9:12). By His own precious blood which was shed upon the cross He there demanded, as it were, the release of the captives, the setting free of the guilty, the absolution of the sins of man. And because of the work that He has done there upon the cross, He has entered into heaven.

But He does not stop at that either, for we are told that He is seated at the right hand of God and that He is there interceding on our behalf, and that is why He is able to save to the uttermost those that come unto God by Him (Heb 7:25). He is there, and His very presence is pleading the merit of His blood. John has already put that like this: 'If any man sin, we have an advocate with the Father, Jesus Christ the righteous' (2:1). He is there advocating our cause by His presence, interceding on our behalf with God. He is not trying to persuade an unwilling God to look upon us and to forgive us and have mercy upon us, for as John tells us, it was the Father Himself who 'sent the Son to be the Saviour of the world.' He there, by His very presence, guarantees that we are forgiven, and He there, as it were, is offering His blood, and it is in this way that God forgives us.

But there is even more! We are told that it is only thus, in a sense, that we can pray to God. Our prayers are taken by our Lord, and He offers them up to the Father. He adds the incense of His own holiness; He takes our unworthy prayers and petitions, and He transmutes them with His own perfection and presents them to the Father, so that in all these actions He is the Saviour, He is acting as our Saviour, He is representing us before God. And thus, in Him God looks upon us and absolves us from all our guilt.

But according to the New Testament, this idea of *Saviour* is even richer than that. For He not only saves us by the objective work which He does in the way I have been trying to describe, but He saves us also by coming to dwell in us by His Holy Spirit. Here, of course, we are again directly looking at these magnificent statements that are made by John in this section of the epistle. God dwells in us, and we in him. He has already said that He has given us His Holy Spirit; and by entering into our lives by the Holy Spirit, our Lord is carrying on this work of saving our souls, for not only do we need thus to be represented in the presence of God and to be justified by the law before we can stand in the presence of God and dwell with God for all eternity, but we also need to be perfected, to be cleansed and purified. So our Lord Jesus Christ, we are told, enters within us and dwells within us and works within us 'both to will and to do of his good pleasure' (Phil 2:13).

And then the last step in this mighty work which our Lord does as our Saviour is the work that yet remains for Him to do. While on earth He kept the law and died for us; then He ascended into heaven and presented His offering. He is seated there, and He intercedes and acts as an advocate for us. He enters into us and works within us, and yet even there the work is not finished. There is still something final that remains to be done, and Paul in writing to the Philippians puts it like this: 'Our conversation [our citizenship],' he says, 'is in heaven,' and then he adds, 'from whence also we look for the Saviour, the Lord Jesus Christ: who shall change our vile body [our body of humiliation], that it may be fashioned like unto his glorious body, according to the working whereby he is able even to subdue all things unto himself' (Phil 3:20-21).

What he means by that, of course, is that before our salvation is complete, our very bodies have to be redeemed and glorified and changed and saved. And the announcement of the New Testament is that Christ as Saviour will again come into this world; and when He does so, in that great regeneration He will take us and our very bodies and will then form and fashion them according to His mighty working, in order that we may be perfect and complete, saved in body, soul, and spirit, and we shall be faultless and blameless in the presence of God.

We have thus hurried through these great aspects of the work of our Lord and Saviour Jesus Christ—the Saviour of our souls. But perhaps the best way to look at it is for me to give you a summary of what it is that He saves us from. For this idea of salvation of necessity carries this need of being saved *from* something, and that can be put like this:

Our Lord and Saviour Jesus Christ clearly saves us, in the first instance, from the guilt and the penalty of sin. We are all, as we have seen, guilty before God and before His holy law. We are guilty in His presence; so the first thing I need is to be saved from the guilt of my sin. I need a Saviour in that respect apart from anything else. I have broken the law of God, and I am under the condemnation of that holy law; so before I can talk about salvation or about being saved, I must be perfectly clear that I am delivered from the guilt of my sin. That is the glorious message that the New Testament Gospel brings to me. In Christ my guilt is removed. It is no use my facing the future and proposing to live a better life; I am confronted by my own past—I cannot avoid it, I cannot escape it. I have broken the law—I must deal with the problem of my guilt—and I cannot do so. I cannot undo my past; I cannot make atonement for my misdeeds and for everything I have done against God. I must be delivered from the guilt of my sin, and Christ—and Christ alone—can so deliver me.

But having thus had the assurance that the guilt of my sin has been dealt with, I am still confronted by the power of sin. The world in which I live is against me; it does not encourage me to live a Christian life. I battle the world and the flesh and the devil; forces and factors outside me are trying to drag me down, and I am aware of their terrible power. The man or woman who has not realised the power of sin all around him or her is a novice in these matters. The whole outlook of the world, the whole of its pleasures and organisations—the whole mentality of the modern world—is something that is opposed to my highest interest. If you consult the Bible, you will find that no man can deliver himself from this power. As I have already reminded you, the prophets and the patriarchs and the greatest saints have all failed. God's people throughout the centuries have testified to this terrible malign power that is opposing them in the world, and they cannot conquer it. There is only one who has conquered Satan, there is only one who has conquered and defeated the world, and that is this Son whom the Father sent into the world to be its Saviour. Jesus Christ can deliver me from the *power* of sin as well as from the *guilt* of sin.

The third and last thing He delivers me from is what the Fathers used to call the 'pollution' of sin. I am not only confronted by sin all around me, but there is sin within me. The Apostle Paul said he had discovered that 'in me (that is, in my flesh,) dwelleth no good thing' (Rom 7:18). My very nature is polluted; there is a desire for and an inclination towards evil. Apart from my actions, my *nature* is sinful, and that is where all the sinless perfectionists who think of sin only in terms of actions go so sadly and hopelessly astray. Before I do anything, my nature is polluted; there is a sinful propensity in me, and I need to be delivered from that. I need to be saved from it; and, blessed be the name of God, according to the Scriptures the Lord Jesus Christ as Saviour deals with that problem also! He not only saves from the guilt of sin and the power of sin but also from this terrible pollution of sin, and that is the special work of the Holy Spirit within us. He deals with us; He reveals sin to us; He creates a hatred of sin. He shows the enormity of sin; He gives a desire for holiness; He encourages us to engage in good works. He is working within us, for He has been sent by the Son, the Saviour, thus to perfect, to purify, and to cleanse us, and to rid us of this foul pollution of sin. And the result of this work ultimately will be that He will present us faultless and blameless without spot and without rebuke, without any vestige of pollution in the presence of God in glory.

That, in its essence, is what the New Testament would teach us concerning the Lord Jesus Christ as the Saviour of our souls. You can see that He is not a helper, nor is He an assistant. He is not merely one who encourages us; He is not only an example to follow. How can I follow? He is so glorious, so holy and divine, that I cannot. And thank God that I am not called upon to do so, in that way! Primarily, this is the message: He is the Saviour, He has kept the law, He has satisfied its demands, and He offers me His righteousness. He is working in me mightily, as Paul puts it, in order to deliver me from sin in all its aspects, and eventually He will take me by the hand and will present me to His Father, and I shall be received into everlasting glory.

'We have seen and do testify that the Father sent the Son' in order that He might be 'the Saviour of the world.'

So the question we ask ourselves is this: Do I realise that Christ is my Saviour in that way? Do I believe that He is the Son of God and the Saviour of my soul? On what am I relying as I think of facing God? Do I look to my own life and actions, or do I look entirely to Christ—Christ as 'Saviour'? I either depend upon Him or I depend upon myself; but He and He alone is the Saviour of my soul.

11

KNOWING THE LOVE OF GOD

And we have known and believed the love that God hath to us. God is love; and he that dwelleth in love dwelleth in God, and God in him.

1 JOHN 4:16

IN THIS VERSE, the Apostle sums up what he has been saying and arguing. First of all, this is the summing up of what he has just been saying in the immediately preceding context; he both sums it up and carries it a stage further. He has been reminding us that he and the other Apostles 'have seen and do testify that the Father sent the Son to be the Saviour of the world'; then he says, 'Whosoever shall confess that Jesus is the Son of God . . .' In other words, he puts his signature to what he has testified. 'Whosoever,' he says in effect, 'says, "amen" to what we have testified and witnessed can be sure that God dwells in him and he in God. So then,' John says, 'we [no longer merely himself and the Apostles, but all Christians] have known and believed the love—of which I have been speaking—the love that God has for us.' This is a summing up of the immediate context; he takes it beyond the state of belief to that of knowledge.

In a sense, John is dealing here partly with the relationship between belief and experience, and it seems to me that there are two main suggestions at this point. The first is the vital importance of our understanding something of the connection between the objective and the subjective in the realm of our Christian life. This is the special glory of our Christian position—that it is at one and the same time objective and subjective. It is outside us, and it is inside us; it is something which is believed as a body of truth, of doctrine, or of dogma; and yet it is experimental. It is life, it is actual, it is living.

Now here is a very vital and important subject. The history of the church and the history of God's people throughout the centuries in every country shows forcibly that much harm and trouble is often caused by a failure to regard the relationship between the objective and the subjective in the way in which the New Testament itself does. There seems to be this fatal tendency in all of us as a result of sin and the Fall to concentrate exclusively on either the one or the other. There are those who are interested in theology and doctrine in a purely intellectual sense. It is full of great beauty and truth, which they are interested in, but they are not always concerned with practise. They will sometimes lose their tempers with one another as they talk about the love of God, thereby showing that it is purely theoretical, something entirely in the mind which has never been applied and translated into life and has never been experienced.

On the other hand, there are those to whom the Christian life is purely subjective, and they dismiss dogma. They are not interested; they are not concerned about definitions; they say the only thing that matters is that we should be able to say, 'Whereas once I was like that, now I am like this.' 'Don't talk to me about your doctrine,' they say, 'I have had an experience—I have felt something.' The tragedy is that we should ever be guilty of one or the other; furthermore, it seems to me that one is as bad as the other, for the glory of the gospel is that it always takes up the whole man—not only the mind, not only the heart, not only the will, but mind, heart, and will. Paul puts this in a resounding statement when he says, 'But ye have obeyed from the heart that form of doctrine which was delivered you' (Rom 6:17). They obeyed with their will, they obeyed from the heart—there is the emotion. And what had they obeyed?—the form of sound words of doctrine that was delivered to them; there is an objective statement of the truth that comes to the mind.

Here in this particular section John puts this all very plainly and clearly to us. You see, he does not talk about what we know and believe until he has first of all put it in the objective form. He says, 'We, the apostles, have seen and do testify'; there is the message. But what am I to believe, what am I to know, what am I to experience? That which has already been testified by the Apostles. In other words, we must always be sure and certain that we follow the order as it is laid here and everywhere else in Scripture. The love of God is only known and felt adequately and completely in and through our Lord and Saviour Jesus Christ.

John has gone on repeating this, and you notice how he never tires of doing so. 'In this was manifested the love of God toward us, because that God sent his only begotten Son into the world, that we might live through him' (v 9); and, 'We have seen and do testify that the Father sent the Son' (v 14). He repeats it again. This is because he knew that in his own day and age there were all those so-called mystery religions or curious cults which talked about the love of God; and they all tried to teach that you can know the love of God directly. That is always the characteristic of mysticism; what finally condemns mysticism is that it bypasses the Lord Jesus Christ. Anything that bypasses Christ is not Christian. I do not care what it is, however good, however uplifting or noble; it is Christ who is the manifestation of the love of God, says John.

I do not hesitate, therefore, to aver and to add as strongly as follows: I must distrust any emotion that I may have within me with respect to God unless it is based solidly upon the Lord Jesus Christ. In Him God has manifested His love. 'God commendeth his love toward us, in that, while we were yet sinners, Christ died for us' (Rom 5:8). Therefore, I say that I must never attempt by any means or method to get to know God or to to try to make myself love God except in and through my Lord and Saviour Jesus Christ. I must avoid every other direct approach to God, every direct dealing with God. There is but 'one mediator between God and men, the man Christ Jesus' (1 Tim 2:5), and without Him I have no knowledge of God. So any love which is not based upon this is to be distrusted. And in the same way I would argue that a belief which does not lead to such a love is in and of itself useless.

Let us, then, leave it at that. But let us always remember the objective and the subjective; the objective is the doctrine concerning the Lord Jesus Christ, and if I truly believe that, then I will love. Let me put it again in a phrase from the Apostle Peter: 'Unto you therefore which believe he is precious' (1 Pet 2:7). There is little value in confession unless He becomes precious to us. 'We have known and believed the love that God hath to us'; I have not only believed, I *know* it.

That takes me to my second point—the relationship between

knowledge and faith. It is a great subject, and let me first just make one or two remarks in passing.

The first is that there is a sense in which knowledge and belief always go together and must go together. There is a sense in which we can argue that you cannot believe a thing unless you know it. It is an old and a great question as to which comes first: belief or knowledge. Indeed, there is a sense in which it is a foolish question. You must have a certain amount of knowledge of what you believe. You believe something, and if you do, then you know what you believe, and that is knowledge. So there is a sense in which a person who believes, knows. You do not believe in a vacuum; nor do you believe something vague and nebulous. You believe something, and that defines it and makes it concrete.

But, of course, there is another sense, looking at it from the experimental standpoint, in which knowledge is something that always follows. As Browning put it, 'A man's reach should always be greater than his grasp.' So in that sense I think the New Testament does teach very clearly that our knowledge always follows our belief. It is like a horse drawing a carriage; they are bound together, and they are never separated, but the horse is always in front, and the carriage is being drawn by him. Belief, then knowledge—that is the position. The Apostle Paul states the whole thing in Philippians 3. He thanks God for the knowledge that he has in Christ Jesus his Lord, and yet he goes on to say, 'that I may know him' (Phil 3:10). He forgets the things that are behind and presses forward towards the mark. Nevertheless, 'whereto we have already attained . . . let us mind the same thing' (v 16). We know certain things, and yet we want to know more; knowledge follows belief and is always being led onwards by it.

In other words, we may put it like this perhaps, that knowledge is but a more sure form of belief. Knowledge is that state in which I really have grasped what I have believed. I possess it perfectly; in a sense I knew it at the beginning, but what I believed, I have now really got. John is here emphasising the certainty of belief. He says in effect, 'We know and have believed the love that God has towards us.' It is as if he were saying, 'Thank God, you and I who are Christians—we know this love of God; and yet we do not know it all yet. It is too big—it is so high—it is so broad and deep. We will join all the saints in investigating it. Thank God, we know, and yet we do not know! We will go on to know; we will go on increasing in knowledge.'

That is why John puts knowledge before belief: I do not know, and yet I know much more than I have actually experienced. I have experienced, yes, but my belief is greater than my experience, and I am stretching forward unto that which I have not yet attained. So there is nothing odd about putting knowledge before belief. I think it is a very good way of putting it. I have, and yet I want; I possess, and yet there is more to be possessed. The love of God is like a mighty ocean; I am swimming in it, and yet how much remains! We know, and we have believed, and we ever go on, therefore, to know more perfectly that which we believe by faith.

Therefore, it seems to me that the great thing here is that we come to the practical application of all this. John is summing up. He has finished with arguments and propositions, and now he comes back to this experimental aspect. So the great question is whether we can join John and the first Christians in saying that we know this love of God to us. After all, there is little value in our profession unless it lead to some practical result in our lives. John was writing to men and women in a difficult world, even as we are in a difficult world; and the thrilling thing, he tells them, is that although the whole world lies under the power of the evil one, it is possible for our joy to abound.

How can my joy abound? How can I walk through this world with my head erect? How can I come through triumphantly? Well, here is the main thing: I should know this love which God has towards me. If I have that, I can say that 'neither death, nor life . . . nor height, nor depth, nor any other creature, shall be able to separate us from the love of God, which is in Christ Jesus our Lord' (Rom 8:38-39). Therefore, the questions come to us one by one: Do I know this love? Can I make this statement? It is made everywhere in the New Testament. Paul is fond of stating it generally, and yet you find that he also delights in stating it particularly: '. . . the Son of God, who loved me, and gave himself for me' (Gal 2:20). No man could state the doctrine of the atonement in all its plenitude and glory like the Apostle Paul, and yet here he says, He died for me; He loved me. This is personal knowledge, personal appropriation. You find this everywhere in the New Testament. For example, 'Whom having not seen,' says Peter, 'ye love; in whom, though now ye see him not, yet believing, ye rejoice with joy unspeakable and full of glory' (1 Pet 1:8).

Do we do that? These people did not see Him, and so we cannot argue and say, 'It is all very well for those first Christians; they saw Him.

If only I could see Christ, then I would love Him.' But they did not see Him any more than we see Him. They had the apostolic witness and teaching and accepted this witness and testimony. They loved Him and rejoiced in Him 'with joy unspeakable and full of glory.'

Read your hymnbook. Do you not find that the hymns are full of this sentiment, this expression of love towards God and towards the Saviour, this desire to know Him more and more, this personal, experimental awareness and knowledge of Him? Or read Christian biographies, and you will find that this is a theme that runs right through them all. The Christian position, thank God, is not merely that I accept theoretically certain ideas about the love of God. It is something that I experience, that I know. Look at that great statement of Paul's: 'I know whom I have believed, and am persuaded that he is able to keep that which I have committed unto him against that day' (2 Tim 1:12). 'We do know,' said John in effect, 'the love that God has for us'; Christian people must know it. Do *we* know it?

I keep on repeating my question because it is to me the most vital question that we can ever face in this life and world. Let me put it like this: I do not know what the future holds for me; nobody does. Our whole life and world is uncertain, and I say that in a world like this the supreme matter is to know that God loves me—to know that I am in that relationship and that whatever happens around me, God will always be with me. Whatever may or may not come, God loves me, and I am a child of God. If I know that, then there is a sense in which anything else does not matter very much and cannot vitally and essentially affect me.

So the question remains: How may we know this—how do we know that God loves us? I will, first of all, give a general answer to the question. First, I have an increasing awareness and an increasing realisation that I owe all and everything to the Lord Jesus Christ; I am utterly dependent upon Him and the perfect work that He has done for me in His life and death and resurrection. I am bound to put that first because John puts it first. How do I know that God loves me? Is it because of some sensations or feelings? No! Rather, in the first instance, the first thing is Christ, what I feel about Christ, what Christ is to me. 'In this was manifested the love of God toward us, because that God sent his only begotten Son into the world, that we might live through him.' Do you know for certain the love of God to you? Is He central? Is He vital?

Is He essential? Do you know that you are entirely dependent upon the fact that Christ is the Son of God and that He died on the cross on Calvary's hill and bore the punishment for your sins and took your guilt away? Is it all centred in Him?

If it is not, I say, go no further. If Christ is not absolutely essential and central in your position, I am not interested in what you have to tell me about your knowledge of the love of God. For the whole argument of the New Testament is that it is there that God has manifested His love, and if I do not start there, I am ignorant of what God has done. How can I love Him if I ignore that amazing manifestation and demonstration of His eternal love? That is the first test.

But let me come to the particular, and here I am simply going to give you a series of questions or statements. I agree with John that we must be particular, we must have detail. I shall suggest to you ten tests which you can apply to yourself to know for certain that you know the love of God to you.

Here is the first. It is a loss and absence of the sense that God is against us. The natural man always feels that God is against him. He would be very glad if he could wake up and read that some bishop or other had proved that God never existed; he would be ready to believe it. The newspapers give publicity to anything that denies the faith; they know the public palate. That is why the natural man is at enmity against God; he feels God is against him. That is why when anything goes wrong he says, 'Why does God allow this?' And when men and women are in a state of being antagonistic towards God, then, of course, they cannot love God. So one of the first tests, and I am starting with the lowest, is that we have lost that feeling that God is against us.

Secondly, there is a loss of the fear of God, while a sense of awe remains. Let us approach Him 'with reverence and godly fear,' writes the author of the Epistle to the Hebrews (12:28). John is going to elaborate on that; that is the rest of the fourth chapter. We lose that craven fear of God, but oh! what a reverence remains.

Thirdly, there is a feeling and a sense that God is for us and that God loves us. Now I put it like that quite deliberately because it is so very true to experience. I have lost that sense that God is against me, and I begin to have a feeling and sense that God is for me, that God is kind to me, that He is concerned about me, and that He truly loves me.

Fourthly, I have a sense of sins forgiven. I do not understand it, but

I am aware of it. I know that I have sinned; 'my sin is ever before me' (Ps 51:3), as David says. I remember my sins, and yet the moment I pray, I know my sins are forgiven. I cannot understand it, I do not know how God does it, but I know He does it, and that my sins are forgiven.

A sense of sins forgiven in turn leads me to the fifth test: a sense of gratitude and thanksgiving to God. No one can believe that God sent His only begotten Son into the world to die on the cross without feeling a sense of praise and of thanksgiving. It is all pictured in the story of that man of Gadara, the man possessed with a legion of devils. No one could cure him, but Christ drove the demons out, and the man who was cured wanted to go with Jesus. 'He . . . prayed him that he might be with him' (Mark 5:18). I imagine that the man said, 'Let me be Your slave—let me carry Your bag or polish Your sandals—let me do anything I can for You—You have done so much for me.' Or think of Saul of Tarsus there on the road to Damascus. The moment he saw and understood something of what had happened to him, he said, 'Lord, what wilt thou have me to do?' (Acts 9:6). That is, what can I do to repay You—how can I show my gratitude? Do you feel a sense of gratitude? Do you want to praise God? Do you want to thank Him? When you get on your knees in prayer, is it always petitions, or do you start with thanksgiving and praise—do you feel something welling up within you? A sense of gratitude and a desire to praise is a further proof of the knowledge of God.

Then sixthly, there is an increasing hatred of sin. I sometimes think there is no better proof of a knowledge of God and knowledge of the love of God than that. You know, if you hate sin, you are like God, for God hates it and abominates it. We are told that He cannot look upon iniquity (Hab 1:13); therefore, whatever your feelings may be or may not be, if you have an increasing hatred of sin, it is because the love of God is in you—God is in you. No man hates sin apart from God.

Seventh, there is a desire to please God and to live a good life because of what He has done for us. The realisation of His love should make us not only hate sin, but also desire to live a holy, godly life. You may say your heart is cold. You are not aware of any strong emotion. But do you desire to live a better life and to please God more and more? If you are, you love God, because our Lord said, 'He that hath my commandments, and keepeth them, he it is that loveth me' (John 14:21).

Eighth, we have a desire to know Him better and to draw closer to Him. Do you want to know God better? Is it one of the greatest ambitions of your life to draw closer to Him, that your relationship to Him may be more intimate? If you have within you the faintest desire to know God better and are doing something about it, I say you love God.

Ninth, I will put this point negatively, and yet it may be the most important of all. I am referring to a conscious regret that our love to Him is so poor, along with a desire to love Him more. If you are unhappy at the thought that you do not love God as you ought to, that is a wonderful proof that you love Him. Love is never satisfied with itself; it always feels it is insufficient. The men and women who are unhappy because they do not love God more are, in a sense, people who ought to be very happy, because their very unhappiness at their lack of love is proof that they do love. Let me put that in the words of one of my favourite sayings, that great and wonderful and consoling sentence of Pascal's: 'Comfort yourself; you would not seek me if you had not already found me.' Love is dissatisfied, and so if I feel my heart is cold, it is a sure proof that I love Him. The unbeliever is not aware of the fact that his heart is cold, and so the negative becomes gloriously positive.

My last test is that we have a delight in hearing these things and in hearing about Him. That is one of the best tests. There are certain people in the world—alas, there are many—who find all that we have been saying utterly boring; all that we have been saying would be strange to them. Such people are spiritually dead; they know nothing about all this. So whatever the state of your emotions may be, if you can tell me quite honestly that you enjoy listening to these things and hearing about them, if you can say that there is something about them which makes things different, and that you would sooner hear these things than anything else in the whole world, then I say that you know the love that God has for you and that you love Him in return.

These, then, are some tests which seem to me to be the most practical and the most immediate that we can apply. Let me sum them up like this: Jesus Christ, the realisation of who He is, that God sent Him into the world; the realisation of what He has done by coming into the world and going back again, that He is my all and in all; the realisation that He is my Saviour and therefore my Lord, because if He has done that for me, then He has done it so that I might be rescued and redeemed out of this element of sin and that I may live a life pleasing to Him—it is all in Him. The key is my attitude towards Him. Can I say with Paul, 'That I may know him, and the power of his resurrection, and the fellowship of his sufferings, being made conformable unto his death; if by any means I might attain unto the resurrection of the dead' (Phil 3:10-11)? You need not start traveling the mystic way, you need not try to work up feelings; there is only one thing to do: face God, see yourself and your sin, and see Christ as your Saviour. If you have Him, you will have everything else. It is all in Him; without Him there is nothing.

'We have known and have believed the love that God hath to us.' Do you know that God has so loved you that He sent His only begotten Son into the world and to the cross on Calvary to die for you, to rescue you and redeem you from your sin, and to make you a child of God?

May God grant that we may be able to join in this mighty chorus on earth and in heaven which goes on saying, 'I know—yes, I know the love which God has to me'.

12

Dwelling in Love

God is love; and he that dwelleth in love dwelleth in God, and God in him. Herein is our love made perfect, that we may have boldness in the day of judgment: because as he is, so are we in this world.

1 JOHN 4:16–17

As I have reminded you, these verses are a kind of summary of the argument which the Apostle has been developing from verse 7 of this chapter. His theme has been the importance of loving the brethren, and he is developing that argument. He has said that to love the brethren is something we should be concerned about because 'love is of God; and every one that loveth is born of God, and knoweth God.' Then he takes up this question of knowing God, and he tells us that God's great love has been manifested in what He has done for us in and through our Lord and Saviour Jesus Christ. So the great question is, do we know that? Indeed, he goes on to argue, in a subsidiary argument, that that is, in a sense, the only knowledge of God we can have. We cannot see God, but we may know Him in that vital, subjective manner, and he works out the various ways in which we arrive at that knowledge. Knowledge is very largely dependent upon objective facts—the things we have heard from the Apostles and the first Christians which we believe and accept. And having worked that out, he sums it up in the first half of verse 16: 'We have known and believed the love that God hath to us.'

Now in the second half of verse 16 and in verse 17 which we are dealing with now, we have the summing up of the other part of the argu-

ment—namely, the importance of loving one another, and the value of
this in its application to our Christian experience. It is this, of course,
which was John's primary object. He starts with it, and that brings him
to the argument of the love of God and its manifestation. He deals with
that, winds it up, and then winds up the original point with which he
began; and that is what we have here.

Obviously, therefore, it is important for us to remember that these
two things must always go together and be held together. We must never
introduce a kind of artificial dichotomy between them; loving God and
loving the brethren must always be taken together. Let me remind you
again that our Lord, in His answer to the question that was put to Him
when He was here on earth— 'Which is the first commandment of
all?'—replied saying, 'Thou shalt love the Lord thy God with all thy
heart, and with all thy soul, and with all thy mind, and with all thy
strength: this is the first commandment. And the second is like, namely
this, Thou shalt love thy neighbor as thyself' (Mark 12:28-31). They
must always be taken together, and John shows that here, as the New
Testament does everywhere in its teaching.

In other words, John here, though he has had a particular subsidiary
argument, has really been summing up one great thing right through, and
that is the assurance of salvation. And what he says in effect is that there
is no ultimate assurance of God's love to us and of our position and our
standing unless we are living the life of love. That is ultimately the ground
of assurance, and that is what John wanted to leave with these people. As
we have seen, when he wrote he was an old man who knew that his time
on earth was coming to an end, and he wanted to administer comfort to
those people. He knew about their difficulties, about the world in which
they lived; he knew trials were besetting them—those insidious heresies
that were raising their heads, these antichrists and false teachers, quite
apart from the inherent sinfulness of society and the world. He knew all
about that, and he wanted to help them; and his great argument from the
beginning has been that they must be assured of certain things. There is
nothing as vitally important as our certain knowledge that God has loved
us in particular in Christ, and that we therefore should be able to say, 'We
have known and believed the love that God hath to us.'

We can, therefore, add something to the list of ten tests which we
considered earlier. You remember that we ended by saying that if we are
at all uncertain about all this, if there is any hesitancy with regard to our

ability to say, 'I know the love that God has to me,' if I am a little bit afraid of saying that the Son of God 'loved me and gave himself for me,' if we are unhappy about that, then the thing to do is to ask ourselves these questions. Now here we are reminded that we can add yet another, and this perhaps is still more important. The final question we therefore ask ourselves is this very practical one: Do we dwell in love? Are we living and abiding in love? That is the fourth test, you remember, which John applies: 'God is love; and he that dwelleth in love dwelleth in God, and God in him.' Not only that, but 'herein is our love made perfect'— meaning, herein is love made perfect within us—'that we may have boldness in the day of judgment: because as he is, so are we in this world.'

This, therefore, is a very vital matter for our consideration. May I put it to you in the form of two main propositions which I think are obvious and inevitable, and yet they are not only profound—they are testing, and I find them very searching. The first is that as Christians we are to dwell in love. Now what does John mean when he talks about dwelling in love? He takes that for granted about Christians. He does not stop to argue about it—he just states it. Christians are people who dwell in love; this is something vital and fundamental to them. I suggest that at the very minimum John means that Christians are those who are dwelling in an atmosphere of love, that their lives are controlled by the principles of love, that the great difference ultimately between the Christian and the non-Christian is that love is the controlling factor in the life of the Christian, whereas it is not in that of the non-Christian.

John has been elaborating this in the previous chapter,[1] where he says that the non-Christian, the worldling, is typified ultimately by Cain. That is the non-Christian position—Cain, who murdered his brother. Of course, this does not mean that every non-Christian is a murderer, but it does mean that is his mentality, his outlook; that is his spirit. He may murder with his life, as Kipling puts it, or he may murder in thought; he may murder another by the things he does to him in various ways, by things he says about him. His spirit, his outlook, his attitude is ultimately that.

The New Testament gives us many definitions of this. Paul in writing to Titus says of himself and of others before conversion that they were 'hateful, and hating one another' (Titus 3:3); that is it. But the Christian is entirely different; he is a 'new man,' and there is no respect in which he is more different than in this very matter of his spirit, of his outlook and mentality, says John. Christian men and women are characterised above everything else by this spirit of love. They abide, they dwell, they exist in a state of love—obviously so with respect to God and with respect to their fellow men and women. I have already reminded you of our Lord's answer to the question about the great commandment. In other words, as John argues and as I hope to show you, that is, in a sense, the ultimate object of salvation—to bring us into a state in which we love. That is what salvation is for, to enable us to love God and to love our neighbour as ourselves. So that is a rough-and-ready definition of what is meant by dwelling or abiding in love—love to God, love to men.

But let us become a little more particular, and John indeed forces us to do so. He has here a most extraordinary statement, the last statement in verse 17; he says, 'because as he is, so are we in this world.' Christians are people who dwell in love, and that means, says John, that they really are like God; they are like the Lord Jesus Christ. There is a great discussion amongst the authorities as to who 'he' is in the phrase 'as he is.' Some say it is God the Father; some say God the Son. I do not think we can decide which it is, but in a sense it does not matter because the Father and the Son are the same in nature, the same in character. 'He that hath seen me hath seen the Father,' said our Lord when He was here on earth (John 14:9). So we can take it as both, and the astounding and amazing statement which the Apostle makes is that we, in this world, here in this world of time, are the same as He is, there out of time and in heaven and in the eternal world. As He is in His very nature in eternity, in heaven, in glory, so are we in this world before we go to heaven; even here on earth we are like Him.

So Isaac Watts was not romancing or simply giving rein to his imagination when he talked about 'celestial fruits' growing here on earthly ground; he was stating the very thing that John is putting to us in this verse—celestial fruits, the fruit of the Spirit, which is love. That is the first thing. 'As he is'—the Father, the Son—'as he is,' and He is love; 'so are we,' even 'in this world' with all its problems and its difficulties and its trials and its contradictions. So this enables us to underline this tremendous statement a little more in detail; for us to dwell in love, therefore, means that we must have benevolence in our hearts. That is the great characteristic of God, because 'God is love.'

What, then, does this mean? Well, our Lord gave an answer in His statement in the Sermon on the Mount: 'He maketh his sun to rise on the evil and on the good, and sendeth rain on the just and the unjust'

(Matt 5:45). That is God's attitude towards mankind, and 'as he is, so are we in this world.' Therefore, this attitude of benevolence towards mankind and the world at large must be in us.

But let me put it a little more particularly still. Does this not also mean that our attitude towards other people is not determined and controlled by what they are, but by the love that is in us? Now that I think needs no demonstration at all. Is that not the great characteristic of God in His dealings with mankind? God's love is not determined by us; it is in spite of us. Is that not the very essence of the whole gospel? Is that not the meaning of Christ's death upon the cross? Why did God send His Son? Was it because of something He saw in us, in any one Christian? Of course not! God's love to us is not controlled by us—not by what we do or think or say, nor by our attitude towards Him. It is something, if I may use the expression with reverence, that wells up in His eternal heart of love. There is no explanation of salvation except the love of God, caused by nothing save this self-generating love of His— not called forth by us, but emanating from Him. This, then, is the tremendous argument of the Apostle; 'as he is, so are we in this world.'

But let me go a step further and put it like this: The great characteristic of the love of God, therefore, is that God does not consider Himself—God does not consider His own honour and glory. Rather, God considers *us*. God as He looks upon us does not go on saying, 'This is what they have done to Me, this is how they have behaved with respect to Me—they have rebelled against Me; they have become offensive, ugly, and foul as the result of their attitude, and therefore . . .' Not at all! God— I say it again with reverence—in His dealings with us in Christ has not been considering Himself. He has considered us and our lost condition, and it is for that reason that He has done what He has done.

'So if we are Christians,' says John in effect, 'it means that God is in us, and God is love; therefore, we must be like that.' That means our attitude must not be determined and controlled by what other people are like or by what they do. It also does not mean that we are always to save ourselves and to claim the right of justice and honour and credit and all these other things. It means that we are not to look at ourselves and what we are doing; it means that we are to look at others and for- get self in this extraordinary way and manner.

In other words, we can go a step further and put it like this: it means that, like God, we must see others as souls. We must see their need and their sorry plight; we must see them as victims of sin and of Satan. These things need no demonstration; there would not have been a single Christian were this not true of God. God looked upon us and the world, and He did not see us; He saw, rather, our captivity to Satan. He saw us in the bondage of iniquity; He saw that we were being ruined by this evil thing. He looked at us in spite of our sin; and as He is, so must we be if He is in us. 'As he is, so are we in this world'; and that means, of course that, having looked upon others, not just as they are in all their offensiveness and in all their difficulty, we see them rather as lost souls. We see them as the serfs of Satan, as the victims of these evil powers and wickednesses in the heavenly places; and we are sorry for them, and compassion enters into our heart for them.

The result is that as God is in us, so we become ready to forgive and to forget, for that is what God has done with us. God has looked upon us and forgiven us; and even more wonderful, He has forgotten our sins—He has cast our sins into the sea of His forgetfulness. What a loving, wonderful thought that is, that God not only forgives our sin, but He has forgotten all about it! Only Omnipotence can do that. Thank God He can! He does not remember my past sins; He has forgotten them, and they are gone. 'As far as the east is from the west, so far hath he removed our transgressions from us' (Ps 103:12). Blessed be His name! 'As he is, so are we'; because He is in us in this world, we must not only forgive—we must learn to forget. We must not think about our sins; we must not let them come back and dwell with us. We must banish them; we must be like God—forgiving and forgetting.

We must also become positive. We must be ready to leave our sins behind. God did not just passively decide to put our sins aside and forget them; God became active. He did something; He sent His Son, in spite of it all, into the world. Consider that great passage in Philippians 2:5-8. He did not consider Himself, He did not think of His equality with God a thing to be prized or clutched at, but He put it aside, humbled Himself, and became man. God the Father and God the Son spoke together in the eternal council about men and women in their lost state and condition and in their need of salvation. And when the Father laid the problem before the Son and asked Him, 'Are You ready to do it?' He did not say, 'Am I to forsake heaven? Am I to humble myself? Is it fair? I am equal with You!' No! He 'thought it not robbery to be equal with God,' but that did not make Him prize and clutch at the heavenly glories. He gladly put it all on one side; He divested Himself of the insignia of His eternal glory. He humbled Himself, took upon him the form of a servant, and faced the death of the cross, never thinking of Himself.

'Let this mind be in you,' says Paul. 'Yes,' says John, 'as he is, so are we'; we are like that because He is in us. If we are truly His in this world, we are ready to come down and humble ourselves, to be misunderstood, to be laughed at and treated with scorn and derision, in a sense to be crucified—certainly in spirit, perhaps even in body—anything that may help, being always ready to do good, ready to please, not always on the defensive, not always demanding our rights and justice, but coming right down as He came down. 'As he is . . .'

You remember the argument of our Lord? He said, 'For if ye love them which love you, what reward have ye? do not even the publicans the same?' (Matt 5:46). If you do good to those who do good to you, well, what is there in it? That is the natural man, that is the animal in a sense; there is nothing special about that. This is what is special: 'Do good to them that hate you, and pray for them which spitefully use you, and persecute you' (Matt 5:44). But why should I do good to those who hate me? Here is the answer: 'Be ye therefore perfect, even as your Father which is in heaven is perfect' (Matt 5:48). John here is only paraphrasing our Lord. That is what you are to be—'perfect,' says Christ; we are to be like God who is perfect, in this respect, 'even as your Father which is in heaven is perfect.' Jesus is saying, 'Love as the Father has loved you in sending His Son into the world to die for you and to save you. "Be ye therefore perfect." As he is, so are we in this world.' That is what it means to dwell in love.

Now let me go on to emphasise the second principle. The first was that we are to dwell *in love*. Now I want to change the emphasis and say that we are to *dwell* in love; we are to abide in love. In other words, this is not to be something spasmodic in our lives and experience; it is to be the natural attitude, the place in which we dwell. You will find that word used in Scripture. For example, 'He that dwelleth in the secret place of the Most High shall abide under the shadow of the Almighty' (Ps 91:1); that is the same idea. John is particularly fond of this word 'abide.' How often have we met with it in this first epistle—abiding, continuing, going on. The man who is not a Christian does not dwell in love.

So this love is abiding; it is not spasmodic. It is not being kind to other people only when they are kind to you but *always*. God does not change. He is 'the Father of lights, with whom is no variableness, neither shadow of turning' (Jas 1:17). Thank God for that fact! What if God varied with our faults? What if He varied with us and our world, with the sun and the rain? There would never be any crops. But no; He does not change; He abides ever the same. And we are to be like that, not only when we are in the mood, not only when other people are a little bit less intractable, but always—dwelling and abiding.

How is this to be done? Does this not require perfection? Am I making the Christian life utterly impossible? Am I again to be charged with holding the standard too high? I am not complaining of such a charge; there is a sense in which I thank God if that charge is a true one. The preacher who makes the Christian life easy is one who does not know his New Testament, who is not true to his calling and commission. Here is the test: 'As he is, so are we in this world.' Christian people do not meet together to say nice things to one another. This is what we are meant to be! This is what we must be if we would have assurance of salvation and know 'the love that God hath to us.'

So I suggest that these are some of the things we have to do. We must start always by realising the doctrine, always start with truth. Love is not something that can be dealt with directly; it is always something, as it were, produced indirectly; and the way to have this love of God in us is to realise the doctrine. What I mean is this: there is only one way I know to realise the love of God, and that is to realise the truth about myself. We have to be made worse before we can be made better; there are times when we have to be cruel to be kind. We may have to clean that wound before we can put in the oil that will soothe it. We must get rid of certain things, and that is a painful process. Therefore, the highway to realising the love of God is to realise the truth about ourselves.

In other words, there is only one way to realise the love of God, and that is to realise that you are a hopeless, damned sinner, that you can do nothing about yourself. You can never put yourself right; you can never make yourself fit to stand in the presence of God. You must realise that you are altogether lost and undone and heading straight for hell, and that is where you would arrive, were it not that God in His infinite, everlasting love sent His only begotten Son not only into the world, but to the cruel death of the cross, so that you might be forgiven, that you might be saved.

Have you realised that the love of God is already in you? It is when we come to the end of self and are utterly undone and then realise what God has done for us that we begin to realise that the love of God is in us. In other words, mere abstract thoughts upon God as love will never do it. The mystics have tried that way. They have produced psychological statements. But that is not what we find in the New Testament. The way the people John wrote to experienced the love of God was in terms of sin, condemnation, and loss and what God has done about it. It is there they found love, and especially in the statements about our Lord's death upon the cross.

The second thing is meditation upon our Lord. We must recapture the lost art of meditation, and meditation especially upon Him. We must think again about that birth in Bethlehem—what it meant, what it cost, what it really involved. Try to grapple with it; it is baffling—the sacrifice, the humiliation. Look at His life; take it step by step and stage by stage. Look at what He endured and suffered through the thirty hidden years and the three busy years of his earthly ministry. Look at Him; remember what He has done and what He literally and actually suffered. Let us go over these things, let us remind ourselves of them; and then as we begin to realise what He did, we shall realise His love to us, and our love to Him will begin to develop within us and dwell with us, and also our love to others for the same reason.

Thirdly, in practice, having started with great doctrine and especially the doctrine concerning the Son of God, we have to face the situation that confronts us instead of avoiding it and turning our back upon it, excusing ourselves in terms of self-defence. I must relate every single situation that may develop in my life to the doctrines that I have been enumerating, and especially the doctrine of the cross. I am referring to that difficult person, that difficult situation in the business or office, or whatever. I do not care what it is—I repeat, I must take it and put it into the context of the cross. I must think in terms of that person; I must take the whole situation and just face it in the light of that. I must say that if God had treated me as I have treated this situation or this person, what would have happened to me? I must not avoid this; I must bring it into the open. I must flash the light of Calvary upon it, considering the heart of God which is eternal life. Is it not the case that half our troubles, and more, are simply due to the fact that we will not face the situation? We are always avoiding it. We say, 'I believe in the doctrine of the cross and God's love to me, but this situation is extremely difficult.' But we must bring these things together; the whole of my life must be controlled by this principle—the doctrine of love.

In other words, my last general word of advice would be that we must discipline ourselves. We must deal with ourselves actively, and we must deal with everything that is opposed to this life of love. This is a full-time matter. I must realise that every detail in my life counts. I am one; I cannot divide myself up into my spirit part and my other part. I cannot divide myself up into what I do on Sunday and what I do on the other six days in the week. Everything that happens to me is all a part of me. So, my whole life must be disciplined. I must watch myself and observe myself in every detail of my life, and I must mortify everything that is opposed to this love. I must discipline 'my members which are upon the earth' (Col 3:5)—my affections, lusts, passions, pride, self-glory, and all like things. I must keep them down; I must mortify them. I must deal violently with them, in order that I may become more and more like Him.

And perhaps, if I may end with one particularisation, one which is so often emphasised in the New Testament, I must watch my tongue. This 'little member,' as James called it, this unruly member, this little rudder that turns the whole ship of life, is apparently so unimportant, and yet what havoc it makes! You cannot get evil and good to come out of the same fountain; you do not get thorns and grapes from the same tree—these are the words of the New Testament (Jas 3:1-12). Control it, says the Bible. That may sound almost trivial and childish; but you know, there is a distinction between thinking and saying a thing. Do not say it, and if you do not say it you will find that you stop thinking it. Put a watch upon your lips and upon your tongue—that is one of the first things in this life of love. If you cannot control your thoughts, control your speech; and by controlling your speech you will come to use greater control upon your thoughts, and your life of love will grow and develop. This is very practical, but it is of primary and fundamental importance.

Let me give you one more general truth: The ultimate way to develop this life of love is to remind ourselves of the consequences that follow from such a development. 'Herein is our love made perfect, that we may have boldness in the day of judgment.' 'If what I have already said does not influence you,' says the Apostle in effect, 'then remember that a day will come when you will have to stand and give an account; if you want to be able to do that with boldness and with confidence, dwell in love here and now.'

13

THAT GREAT DAY

God is love; and he that dwelleth in love dwelleth in God, and God in him. Herein is our love made perfect, that we may have boldness in the day of judgment: because as he is, so are we in this world.

1 JOHN 4:16B–17

WE HAVE SEEN THE importance of discipline, self-discipline, the importance of facing things, not excusing ourselves for our failures in avoiding the issues, and the importance of controlling what James describes as that 'little member,' that dangerous member, the rudder of a man's life in a sense—the tongue.

But we realise that was not all that could be said. John himself supplies us with other reasons and, in a sense, the profoundest reasons for giving care and attention to this matter of loving the brethren. He takes us to still higher ground and presents us here with three arguments which should always persuade us to give great diligence to this matter of loving one another.

We can summarise the three arguments in one phrase by putting it like this: We must realise the consequence of dwelling in love; and that is perhaps the most powerful argument of all. So often in our Christian lives we go astray because we do not examine the consequences of our actions. Our tendency is to live for the moment—to see things in and of themselves instead of seeing that everything belongs to everything else. Our life is not an automatic kind of life. There is danger in teaching a moment-by-moment existence in any respect, not only from the standpoint of sanctification but from any other standpoint. Our life is a continuous whole, and you cannot isolate things; everything belongs to everything else, and therefore it is true to say that as a river flowing out from its source is already destined for the sea to which it is going, so everyone born into this life is already beginning to die. The whole of our life must always be present in our minds, and we must always be doing everything in the light of its eternal consequences. Cause always produces effect, and we cannot divide these things into compartments and categories. That is the general principle which covers the three particular arguments with which the Apostle here provides us. There are three things which are inevitable consequences of dwelling in love, of abiding in love. Let us look at them.

Here is the first: To dwell in love is the final proof of the fact that God dwells in us and that we are in God. We never could dwell in love and love one another were it not for the fact that we dwell in God and God dwells in us. It is a sheer impossibility to the natural man, who is controlled by hatred and malice. The Bible is full of that teaching; it does not paint a rosy picture of human nature. I have often said, and I often feel, that if I had no other reason for believing the Bible to be the Word of God, this would be sufficient for me: the stark honesty and truthfulness of the Bible which tells the truth about man; it is the only book that does it.

We do not like this, and the world spends most of its time trying to avoid it. We praise one another; we say that if only we were given a chance, how perfect we would be! But the Bible tells us quite bluntly that we would not. The trouble is in our own heart. The truth is that we are quite incapable in and of ourselves; we cannot love as we are by nature. But the Bible shows us this grand and wondrous peace of dwelling in God and God dwelling in us. So if we do dwell in God and He in us, then obviously, and of necessity, we must be living this life of love, for 'God is love.'

Therefore, the Scripture here again causes us to examine ourselves very carefully and closely. There is no point in my saying that I dwell in love, that I dwell in God, and that God dwells in me unless I love the brethren. John works that out in greater detail when we come to the end of this particular chapter, but here is an immediate conclusion at which we arrive: If God is in me, then I must be living a life of love. Whatever I may say in terms of orthodoxy, however correct my statements may be, if I am not living a life of love, there is somewhere a lie in me. There is this artificial division between intellectual belief and assent and having the vital experience of the love of God in my soul.

Here, then, is the great conclusion which we draw. It is the last time in this epistle in which John uses this particular phrase, dwelling in God and God dwelling in us, but it is the fourth time that he has repeated it in these few verses. We have already had occasion to consider this phrase and expression, which we cannot ever understand. It is beyond us; it has eluded the great minds of all the centuries—this whole question of the mystical union between the believer and Christ—this dwelling of the believer in God and God dwelling in him. It is something that cannot be analysed and dissected; it is something you cannot put objectively in front of you and divide into its component parts. And yet it is something that is taught so constantly in the Scriptures.

There are certain, mainly negative things that we can say about this. It does not mean entering in a material sense into the life of God, nor does it mean that there is a material entry of the divine essence into me. But it does mean something like this: God in His own miraculous manner awakens in me something of His own holiness. He plants within me His holy view of life and of being and of existence. God enables me, by His operations upon me through the Holy Spirit, to understand something of His own holy nature and to view life and all its circumstances as He views them Himself.

I think this word 'dwelleth' is a most important and helpful one. 'He that dwelleth in love' means, in a sense, that God is that person's home. My home is the place in which I dwell; I spend my time there. It is where I want to be. I go about my duty, but there I dwell; my heart and mind are there. I come back as much as I can. I like to be there; I live there. They who dwell in love dwell in God. God is their home—God is where they like to be; it is with God they like to spend their time, and they arrange their lives as far as they can so that they spend a maximum amount of time there. In other words, their whole outlook upon life is God. Their thinking and meditation is thus controlled by God; it is all related to Him. They bring their minds back to God—that is what it means. Just as I take my physical body back to the home in which I dwell, so Christians, says John, take their mind and heart back to God.

Now, that is not an artificial phrase. We all know ourselves well enough to know that that is what we have to do. There are other powers and forces that would attract our minds and hearts away from God, and what we have to do is to come back—to come home to God. We are to dwell in God, and God dwells in us, which means that now the presence and the influence of God enters into our consciousness. We are aware of God; we are aware of Him permeating our life and moving and guiding us. Christians are people who dwell in love; and because they are thus dwelling in love, they are aware of the fact that God is dwelling in them. They are aware of a presence in their lives. As a person inhabits a house, so God inhabits and indwells the Christian. You are conscious of His presence and His influence and power, and you are aware of the fact that you are not living to yourself. You stand in amazement; you look at yourself, and you say, 'This is not I myself; it is God—it is God in me. What made me do that? I cannot explain it except by saying it is God who made me do it. He awakened the interest. I felt a movement, a disturbance, and God was there.'

That is what John is saying. He is saying much more than that, but that is the minimum, and what a noble and exalted statement it is concerning the Christian. If I love the brethren, if I am living this life of love, I am dwelling in God and God is dwelling in me, and my life is taken up in that way into the life of God. This is the first conclusion of dwelling in love and loving the brethren.

The second conclusion that we draw is that this is the demonstration of the fact that love has been perfected in us. That is verse 17. The Authorised Version reads, 'Herein is our love made perfect'; but it is generally agreed that the better translation is, 'Herein is love made perfect with us. Here is the perfect proof that God's love is in us.' What does that mean? It means that God's ultimate purpose in salvation and in all that He has done for us in His Son, our Lord Jesus Christ, is that we might become such people. This, says John, is the perfecting of God's love, the perfect carrying out of God's purpose of love.

Now, he has been commenting at great length about this. He says in effect, 'Herein is the love of God manifested, in that he sent His only begotten Son into the world'; and all the doctrine of the atonement came in there. Why did God do that? Why has He set Christ forth as the propitiation for our sins? Here is the answer: that is the ultimate object, the perfecting of His object and purpose—namely, that we may dwell in love, that we may love one another, that we may be in this world even as He is Himself in heaven.

This is something of which we all need to be reminded. Is there not a great danger of our thinking of salvation solely in terms of pardon and forgiveness? Is there not a great danger of our thinking of the cross and

Christ's death on the cross (when we do think of them) as merely designed to enable us to be pardoned and forgiven so that we might go to heaven? But that is not the teaching of the Scriptures. That is only the first step, the grand beginning. God's ultimate object in all that He has done in His Son, the perfecting of it all, is that you and I might become like that Son; Jesus Christ is the firstborn among many brethren. He 'gave himself for us,' says Paul, 'that he might redeem us from all iniquity, and purify unto himself a peculiar people, zealous of good works' (Titus 2:14). He has done this so that you and I might be on earth what He Himself is in heaven.

This, it seems to me, is the right way of viewing our sanctification. Sanctification must always be viewed positively and not negatively. There is nothing I know that is so tragic and unscriptural as the way in which people persist in thinking of sanctification as the mere absence of certain sins. Because they are not guilty of certain sins, they say, 'We are sanctified.' But the biblical way to test your sanctification is to ask, 'Am I like Christ?' Can I say, 'As He is, so am I in this world'? It is a positive, upward view.

In other words, the test of sanctification is our humility. If we are just thinking of sanctification as not doing certain things, then, of course, we shall be pleased, and there will be a self-satisfaction about us. But the men and women who realise that sanctification means being like Him will be those who are conscious of their unworthiness, of the darkness of their own heart. They will see themselves as falling hopelessly short; they will walk with humility because they will see so clearly the difference between the Son of God and themselves. They will be conscious of their harshness, of their bad temper, of their irritability, and of a lack of love and all these other things. And that is the object which God had ultimately in His mind when He sent His Son into the world. It is not a matter of deliverance from certain sins, but of becoming more and more like Him.

Let me sum it up in this way: Not to be concerned about loving the brethren, not to be concerned as to whether I am dwelling in love or not, is to misunderstand the whole purpose of my salvation, and therefore it is to flout God's love. If this is not the greatest concern of my life, then I am a mere beginner in the Christian life. At the beginning, of course, we have a very great concern about forgiveness; we are very concerned about certain particular sins which may have been evident in our lives before our conversion. But we must not stop at that. The hallmark of the saints is their great, increasing concern about the element of love in their lives. They no longer think in terms of action, but in terms of their likeness to God. That is their first ambition—'as He is, so must I be in this world of time'; 'herein is love made perfect with us.' They look back to God in eternity, and they see God planning out the great way and scheme of salvation.

What is man to achieve? That is the grand objective which God had at the back of it all. He is producing a people, a special people, a people for His own possession; and they are all to be, in a sense, like Jesus Christ. There is the model, and He is fashioning and preparing us according to that model. We are not just somehow or another to get into heaven at the end, just being forgiven and no more. No! We are to develop this character, this life of Christ Himself; here and now we are to be like Him.

And that brings me to the third and last conclusion that is put here in this graphic and striking form by the Apostle: 'Herein is our love made perfect, *that we may have boldness in the day of judgment.*' Here, of course, is one of the greatest and mightiest matters that ever confronts us in the Scriptures—the doctrine of judgment, a theme which is taught in the Bible from the beginning to the very end. So what does John mean when he makes that statement? Let me put it like this: The Day of Judgment is not merely a figurative expression of what happens to us when we die. Death, of course, in a sense, is judgment, because once we die our fate is determined; but it is not death that determines our fate. Death just puts us into that place and position in which we can do nothing about it any longer. There is no second chance in the Bible. It is one thing or the other, and our destiny is decided in this life and world of time. So death is a serious matter; but it is not everything. The Day of Judgment is not death; it is rather a great event which, according to Scripture, will take place at the end of the world, at the end of time.

Now while we cannot speak too confidently or too dogmatically about the Day of Judgment, there are certain things which we can say about it. The Day of Judgment will be something formal, it will be public, and it will be final. There are those, in other words—and I put it like this in order to correct that error—who think that the Day of Judgment is just a figurative way of saying that we determine our own fate and that we will reap in eternity what we have sown in time; they say that there is no such thing as an actual Day of Judgment, with God sitting in a formal manner judging all men and the whole world. It is just a question of moral outlook, of what you have been and done. Every action has its consequence. It is just that and nothing more; it is just a way of saying that you will reap beyond death what you have been saying and doing while you are still on earth.

But that is not the Biblical teaching of the Day of Judgment. All the imagery and all the pictures that are used with respect to it in the Bible compel us to say that it is a formal event. It is a visible event, a public event, and a final event. It is something outward, something which will be seen by the whole of mankind and even by the angels themselves. It is legal; that is the picture used in the Bible for God as Judge sitting upon the throne. The books are opened, investigation is made, and sentence is promulgated. This is one of the greatest and mightiest and most extraordinary doctrines taught in the whole of Scripture—the Day of Judgment, the day of the manifestation of the righteousness and the holiness of God. A day when public sentence will be pronounced. And according to the Bible, this is a day which we are all facing and which we are all approaching. It is the teaching which you will find right through the Bible, in the Old and New Testament—and nowhere more prominently than on the lips of our blessed Lord and Saviour Himself.

What other things can we say about this? Let me give you some headings.

First of all, Christ Himself will be the Judge. In John 5:27 we read that God 'hath given him authority to execute judgment also, because he is the Son of Man.' In Matthew 25:31 we read, 'When the Son of Man shall come in his glory, and the holy angels with him, then shall he sit upon the throne of his glory,' and judgment follows. Acts 10:42 reads, 'And he commanded us to preach unto the people, and to testify that it is he which was ordained of God to be the Judge of the quick and dead.' Acts 17:31 adds, 'He hath appointed a day, in the which he will judge the world in righteousness by that man whom he hath ordained; whereof he hath given assurance unto all men, in that he hath raised him from the dead.' So the Judge who will judge all mankind at the end of time and at the end of history is none other than Jesus of Nazareth, the only begotten Son of God.

Let me ask a second question. Who is to be judged? Here the answer seems to be this: First and foremost the fallen angels, the angels who fell from their original state, are to be judged. You find this taught in the epistle of Jude and in 1 Corinthians 6 where Paul says, 'Know ye not that we shall judge angels?' (v 3). So the fallen angels are going to be judged at that great day. But it is not only a judgment of angels—it is a judgment to which every individual human being who has ever lived or ever will live will be subjected. 'We must all appear before the judgment seat of Christ'—not only the ungodly and the unbeliever, but the believer also—'that every one may receive the things done in his body, according to that he hath done, whether it be good or bad' (2 Cor 5:10). Again, Paul says in Romans 14:10, 'For we shall all stand before the judgment seat of Christ.' Revelation 20 says that God's books will be opened and that every man who has ever lived, whether believer or unbeliever, will be there confronted by the Judge.

I know, of course, that there is a difference between believers and unbelievers in this respect: There is a sense in which believers have already passed through judgment. Nevertheless, they will have to appear on the Day of Judgment. There is a difference, a distinction, and there are rewards as well as punishments; but nevertheless we shall all have to appear before His judgment seat. 'Knowing therefore,' says Paul, 'the terror of the Lord, we persuade men' (2 Cor 5:11). We will all have to appear before Him, every single human individual who has ever lived. And the time of the judgment, as I have already stated, is at the end of the world, after the resurrection of the dead.

Now I am familiar with the teaching by people who claim that there are two judgments and things of this kind. But my position is that I cannot find such things for certain in Scripture, and I am trying to say only that of which I am certain. Through the long history of the church there has been disagreement about some matters, but here there is agreement: we shall all rise, and we shall all have to appear at the judgment seat of Christ.

What is the standard of judgment? It is the revealed will of God. We are told in the Scriptures that the Gentiles will be judged according to the light they have—their conscience, says Paul in Romans 2. They will be judged according to that—the law written in their hearts, rather than the law given by Moses. But the Jews will be judged by the Old Testament revelation which they claim to be their Scriptures; they will be judged by the law given to Moses.

Christians will be judged according to the gospel they claim to believe. In other words, the Scripture teaches that there will be degrees of judgment as well as degrees of reward. Our Lord says in Luke 12 that certain people will be beaten with many stripes and some with few stripes (vv 47-48). It is a great mystery—I do not understand it; but I know what Scripture tells us. There will be differences in punishment, as well as differences in reward, according to the deeds we have done in the body.

That in its essence is the teaching of the Bible with regard to this great subject of the Day of Judgment. What John would have us see is that if we want to think of that Day of Judgment without fear, if we want to be able to face it with boldness now, and if we want to stand with boldness and not be ashamed at that great morning, we must give added diligence to loving the brethren. For if I dwell in love, then I know before I face Him on His judgment throne that I may look at Him with boldness at the Day of Judgment, because 'as he is, so are we in this world.' If I know that I have His nature in me here and now, I shall be able to face Him with boldness when I stand before Him. You see how it works: every action in my life while here on earth is important. John has already been teaching this doctrine in the second chapter of this epistle[1]. He reiterates exactly the same thing when he says, 'And now, little children, abide in him; that when he shall appear, we may have confidence, and not be ashamed before him at his coming.'

So we have looked at this third great argument, one which should surely influence each and every one of us in this matter of loving one another and dwelling in love. If I can say I dwell in love, I know that God must be dwelling in me, and I am fulfilling God's ultimate purpose in sending His Son into the world. His love is being perfected in me. And, above all, as I consider not only the nature of my life in this world but also that great day which is coming, the Day of Judgment, as I consider the revelation of God and His righteousness and the ultimate promulgation of God's sentence upon the whole of humanity, separating the good and the bad, the just and the unjust, when I think of that great day in which God will vindicate His own eternal righteousness and justice on not only the whole of humanity but on all the assembled heavenly hosts—if I want to face that without fear and without horror, if I want to face it with confidence, indeed with holy boldness, then the way to do so is to dwell in love—to cultivate this grace and to apply myself by the help of God's Holy Spirit to the perfecting of myself in love.

14

FREE FROM FEAR

There is no fear in love; but perfect love casteth out fear: because fear hath torment. He that feareth is not made perfect in love.

1 JOHN 4:18

JOHN HERE FEELS that this subject which he has been dealing with in the seventeenth verse is so important that he must elaborate upon it. He does not just mention it in passing; further, in the way that is always his custom, not being content with the positive statement only, he uses the negative as well. This is characteristic of all scriptural teaching, and it is perhaps the greatest proof of the profundity of that teaching and especially of its profound knowledge of us as a result of sin. We are so constituted that positives are not enough; we must have the negatives also. We need to be told what *not* to do as well as what to do. It is not enough to be given a positive picture; it must be given in contrast with the negative. Thus the Apostle says here: 'that we may have boldness in the day of judgment: because as he is, so are we in this world. There is no fear in love; but perfect love casteth out fear: because fear hath torment.'

This is concerned with punishment, and that is always something that tends to make us fearful and unhappy. 'He that feareth,' therefore, 'is not made perfect in love.' Love is not perfect in him because if it were, he would have boldness with respect to the Day of Judgment instead of being fearful and full of foreboding. John is dwelling on this ultimate consequence of our dwelling in a state of love. I suggest, therefore, that there is no better test that we can ever apply to ourselves in order to discover the quality of our Christian life and the very nature of our standing in the sight of God than to examine ourselves in the light of this great fact of the Day of Judgment.

Now John is particularly anxious to do that because it serves his ultimate object in writing his letter at all. His object is to encourage these people, to give them comfort and cheer, and to help them; and he believes in various ways and means of doing that. But in a sense, it can all be put like this: The men and women who are most happy to be in this world are those who are most happy about the next world. These things always go together; they are inseparable. So here John puts it in that particular form. The way, he says, to tell whether you are all right at the moment is to test what you feel like when you contemplate yourself at the Day of Judgment. There is, I suggest, no better test in this matter. Indeed, perhaps the supreme test of our love of God and of our love of one another is the way in which we contemplate that great day. In other words, the Apostle, having laid down his doctrine, applies it experimentally.

There again is a great principle in Scripture which we neglect at our cost: *Doctrine and application always go together.* Indeed it is possible, as we have often seen, for people to call themselves Bible students and to be very well versed in the Bible, and yet it does not profit them in the end because they never apply it. They analyse it as if they were analysing a Shakespearean play, and they are just concerned to do that; but Scripture never does that. There must always be an application. There is no value unless I test myself by it, and John does so. These things are not said for the sake of saying them; they are said with great practical interest.

The whole Biblical position, surely, is that this truth is not theoretical truth; it is not merely something to interest the mind. It is supremely interesting, but if I am only interested in it intellectually and as a system of thought, it will finally profit me nothing. This truth is given to me that I may live by it and that I may experience it in my life in all its power and grace and glory. Thank God, it is essentially practical and experimental! Therefore we must always hold these two things together, and so it comes to pass that these great statements of doctrine do become, in practice, a thoroughgoing test of our whole position. Or to put it another way, in connection with the whole subject of the assurance of salvation, there is nothing that is more important than our attitude toward the Day of Judgment.

I wonder how often we contemplate this day; I wonder how frequently we stand before it. You know, it is possible to be so interested in these various theories as to when it is going to take place that you never picture yourself standing there. It often happens that people are interested and argue about it in such a spirit as to make their whole position on that great day shaky and uncertain and unhappy. Much more important than deciding whether there are to be two resurrections, and whether the judgment goes on for a thousand years, and whether it is at the beginning or end or both—much more important than all this is the fact that you and I are facing the judgment; that is the fact that we all have to come to. Now it is that, I suggest, which John is emphasising in this eighteenth verse, and he puts it in this practical and experimental manner. And perhaps the best way we can face it together is for us to deduce some principles which seem to me to be suggested on the very surface of the statement of the Apostle.

The first is that the natural man—all of us by nature—should fear the Day of Judgment. Or let me put it like this: I say that every one of us should have known at some time or another a fear of that day. I deduce that because 'there is no fear in love,' and 'perfect love casteth out fear'; but until perfect love comes, there is fear. Indeed, it should be there, and I say *should* because I am ready to accept the fact that all do not fear. There are many people who say that they do not fear the Day of Judgment and that they never have feared it. They regard it as just a relic of primitive superstition, an aspect of biblical teaching which we ought to have shed long ago, something that is utterly inconsistent with the idea of God as a God of love. Indeed, there is a good deal of ridicule and sarcasm with regard to this Day of Judgment. There are people who are not afraid of it because they deliberately and willfully reject it with their minds and refuse to pay attention to it.

But there are others who are not afraid of the Day of Judgment because they have never thought about it; they are ignorant. The child is often not afraid of things of which it should be afraid. The child is not afraid of sitting in a motor car and attempting to drive it because it is not aware of the dangerous possibilities. Ignorance is often the great cause of a lack of fearfulness; if we are not aware of the dangerous possibilities, we will not fear them. The person who is ignorant of electricity is not as careful as the one who knows all about it. The more people know, the more they see the dangers. So there are large numbers of people in the world who do not fear the Day of Judgment because they do not think about it. They never stop to meditate; they just enjoy life as it comes along, with the latest excitement and craze. They never stop to say, 'What is the meaning of my life? What is to be my ultimate destiny?' They are not afraid of the Day of Judgment just because they have never realised that there is such a day.

But I would suggest that every thinking person knows something about this fear of the Day of Judgment.

> The dread of something after death,
>   The undiscovered country from whose bourn
> No traveller returns.
>
> SHAKESPEARE *(HAMLET)*

Apart from the Gospel of Jesus Christ, that is a terrifying thought. What a tremendous thing life is! We are here—we are gone. But where have we gone?

> *Thus conscience doth make cowards of us all.*
>
> IBID.

There are many people in this world who do not know much about the gospel of Jesus Christ. They are not interested in it. But they are intelligent, and they have a conscience within them. There is something they want to do, and want to do very badly, and they would have done it. So why did they not do it? 'Conscience doth make cowards of us all.' Something said to them at the very moment they were about to do that thing, 'Beware! You may have to pay for this. You do not know but that there is another life.' God and all the Bible say, 'Wait a moment!.' Every intelligent man or woman knows something about this fear of the Day of Judgment. What I am speaking of, in other words, is the fear of death, what Shakespeare called our 'exit.' Shakespeare knew a great deal about this fear of God and of judgment, fear of eternity, fear of the uncertainty of it all.

I suggest that this is all quite right, and that there is nothing so superficial as the popular psychologist who tries to get rid of that, to make us like the boy whistling in the dark to persuade himself that he is afraid of nothing although he is really terrified. That is the foolish attempt of many psychologists to get rid of this fundamental thing that is so deep in the whole of human nature and which is based upon sheer intelligence. The fact is that the very thought of eternity itself surely ought to give one pause for thought and to fill one with a sense of alarm and fear, and even of terror itself, because, putting it at its very lowest, we can say that we really do not know what is coming, and men cannot prove or demonstrate scientifically that death is the end. What if it is not? Can I prove that it is? I say that is an alarming thought; there is something terrifying about the thought of that unknown 'bourn,' that unknown eternity; and I suggest that any intelligent person must of necessity know something of this fear of the Day of Judgment.

But when we get beyond the level of intelligence, there are infinitely more important reasons why we should know something about a fear of the Day of Judgment. It is not merely death, it is not merely the uncertainty of it all. Rather, we are told that 'it is appointed unto men once to die, but after this the judgment' (Heb 9:27). God, the greatness of God, the justice, holiness, and righteousness of God—we are all moving on to that. We shall all have to stand face to face with that, and the further teaching of Scripture everywhere is that my eternal destiny will there be announced—my *eternal destiny*.

I know that some do not like that and would have it explained away. Well, if you are prepared to risk all these other theories, I cannot argue with you! But the plain teaching of the Bible is that our eternal destiny is decided in this world and in this life, and that the Day of Judgment will pronounce it. I confess that I find it very difficult to understand people whose lives are not governed by this thought. There is a sense in which, if I may put it with reverence, I almost admire the courage of people who can do and say certain things—people who say harsh things about one another, people who refuse to forgive one another. I am afraid to do such things; I am afraid, because I know that I myself shall have to answer for them.

I remember once hearing of a man, and I regret to say he was a man in a very prominent position in a Christian church. There had been a quarrel between that man and certain other people in the church. The man had left that church and had been living in another town; he had been a member of another church for years, and he was now on his death-bed. The men with whom he had quarreled heard of his illness, and they met together and said, 'We admit that a great deal of the fault was on our side, and in view of the fact that he is dying, let us go and see him. It may cheer and help him.' So they took the journey, and they arrived at his house. His wife went up into the bedroom and told him they were there, but he refused to see them. I could not do that! How could I go out and face God in eternity and my whole eternal destiny and refuse to forgive a man who came to me with outstretched hand?

This is the teaching of Scripture; our Lord once put it in a parable. He spoke of a man who had sinned against his lord, and his lord told him of the punishment that was his due. But he went to his lord and said, 'Forgive me. I have nothing wherewith to pay.' 'Very well,' said the lord, 'I will forgive you everything,' and the man went out. But there was an underling who owed him something, only trivial compared with the debt he had owed his lord. This man came kneeling to him and asked his forgiveness—'I have nothing to pay you with; have mercy upon me and forgive me.' But the first man took him by the throat and said to him, 'You must pay me to the very last farthing.' Do you remember what the lord said about that man? He went back on his word of absolution, and he said, 'Bind him and cast him into prison.' 'So likewise,' says the Lord Jesus Christ, 'shall my heavenly Father do also unto you, if ye from your hearts forgive not every one his brother their trespasses' (Matt 18:35). 'Forgive us our debts,' says the Lord's Prayer, 'as we forgive our debtors.'

We do well to entertain thoughts of that unknown 'bourn'—and more so, thoughts of God and His justice, His righteousness, His holiness, and above all the love that He has manifested to us. I say once more that I cannot understand people who do not know what it is to be terrified as they contemplate the Day of Judgment. It is the most alarming, awe-inspiring thought in the universe. If you have not trembled at that thought, I beseech you, begin to think and to face it and to remember in your conversations and in your attitude and your comments about others that it is all recorded in the Book of God and may yet confront you. The way in which people can speak of one another astonishes me. I am sorry for these people who have bitterness in their hearts because I know what is happening to them and what is going to happen to them. They will spend their eternity in useless, idle remorse. The natural man should fear the judgment.

But let me come to something which is very different, thank God! This is where the gospel comes in. My second proposition is that the Christian should be free from the fear of judgment. The natural man should fear it; the Christian should be free from such fear. Is there anything that is more glorious about the gospel than just that? But there are people who dispute this. There are poor Christian people who believe that it is their duty to be miserable. There are those who say that it is presumptuous for people in this life and world, who know the darkness of their own heart and who know something of the justice and righteousness and holiness of God which I have been emphasising, to be free from that fear. In the words of Milton, they 'scorn delights and live laborious days,' afraid to say they have the joy of the Lord or the assurance of salvation.

Yet surely it is unscriptural to do so. It is the universal teaching of Scripture that we should be delivered from this fear of the Day of Judgment. Take Hebrews 2:15, where we are told that one of the main purposes of our Lord's coming and one of the main effects of His death upon the cross and of His resurrection is to deliver 'them, who through fear of death were all their lifetime subject to bondage.' It is not death but what comes after it that frightens me; but, says the writer of the Epistle to the Hebrews, that was the whole purpose of Christ's coming, that He might deliver us from this torment of death that holds us captive. Or take 2 Peter 3:12—'looking for and hasting unto the coming of the day of God.' This is the very day of which I am speaking, and this is the teaching which is to be found everywhere.

'Ye,' says the Apostle Paul in Romans, 'have not received the spirit of bondage again to fear; but ye have received the Spirit of adoption, whereby we cry, Abba Father. . . . [We] ourselves also,' he goes on to say, 'which have the first-fruits of the Spirit, even we ourselves groan within ourselves, waiting for'—that is it—'waiting for the adoption, to wit, the redemption of our body. For we are saved by hope' (Rom 8:15, 23-24). This is everywhere in Scripture, so that to assume that this is something to which the Christian is not entitled, and to consider it as a kind of presumption, is to be thoroughly unscriptural.

But the Apostle John has a particular argument to drive this point home. He says that love and fear are utterly incompatible; 'there is no fear in love; but perfect love casteth out fear.'

Now this is something that can be easily elaborated upon. Love and fear are indeed opposites; the spirit of fear is the antithesis to the true spirit of love. Think of the endless illustrations that come rushing into the mind. Think of the mother who nurses the sick child who has an infectious disease. Does she think of the possibility of catching the disease from the child? Not at all! Her love for the child casts out fear. Love and fear are incompatible, and the Apostle in this way drives home his argument.

Take, for instance, the example given by our Lord Himself when He was sending out His disciples to preach and to cast out devils. He warned them they would certainly be in danger. There would be many people who would dislike them, but this was His advice: 'Fear not them which kill the body, but are not able to kill the soul: but fear him which is able to destroy both soul and body in hell' (Matt 10:28). The way to get rid of this fear, says our Lord to these people, is, in a sense, to have this greater fear, which ultimately is the love of God; and the greater drives out the lesser.

That, then, is the first proposition, and John then goes on to say that because Christians are those in whom love has been made perfect, it follows of necessity that they should not dwell in a fearful condition; this is so because of the love of God that is in their hearts. If men and women are fearful, it means they are afraid of punishment and there is something defective in their whole conception of love. They are not loving and abiding in this state of love. So John argues that the Christian must be entirely free. Do you see the steps? Love and fear are incompatible; love drives out fear; love comes into the heart of the Christian and drives out fear; so we have no right to be fearful in this sense.

But what about the argument and the exhortation in the Epistle to the Hebrews about approaching God 'with reverence and godly fear'? What about the statement that 'our God is a consuming fire'? (Heb 12:28-29). What about the statement that 'God is light, and in him is no darkness at all' (1 John 1:5)? How do you reconcile these things? Surely the answer is provided by the quotations themselves. What John is here speaking about is a craven fear which is a very different thing from reverence and holy awe. There is, I suggest, always a sense of reverence in connection with love. You do not love a person unless you respect that person; and if men and women love God, there is a sense of awe, a holiness, about it—there is true reverence in it. 'Reverence and godly fear' is a very different thing from this 'fear [that] hath torment,' a fear that cringes and trembles. That is the thing which perfect love drives out.

So the natural man should have fear of the Day of Judgment, and the Christian should be free from that fear. How then, lastly, does the

Christian become free? There are two main answers to this. The first is that Christians realise the love of God that comes to them in Jesus Christ, and the work of Christ for them. John has been elaborating on that from verse 9 in this particular chapter. To quote it once more: 'In this was manifested the love of God toward us, because that God sent his only begotten Son into the world, that we might live through him.' That is the great thing. The first way to get rid of this fear is to understand the doctrine of justification by faith only. That is why the Protestant Fathers emphasised it, and that is why only an utterly superficial idea of Christianity dislikes this doctrine. The first way for us to get rid of this fear of the Day of Judgment is to realise what God has done for us in the person and the work of our Lord and Saviour Jesus Christ.

Let me put this practically. As I contemplate myself standing before God on the Day of Judgment, I know perfectly well I am a sinner. I have offended God and have broken His law and have forgotten Him. I have not loved Him with all my heart and mind and soul and strength. I have been guilty of sins against His people and against myself. I am a sinner. How can I stand there? There is only one way in which I can stand, and that is to know and believe that He sent forth His Son to bear my sins in His own body on the tree. Hiding in Christ—nothing else can give me peace at that point. I may say that I have done a lot of good, but what is the value of good to counteract the evil I have done? There is only one thing, and it is Christ; I am hiding in Him.

> *Rock of Ages cleft for me,*
> *Let me hide myself in Thee.*
>
> AUGUSTUS TOPLADY

I have no other hope as I contemplate the holiness of God and the holiness of heaven. My only hope is that there is a cloak of righteousness woven by the Son of God Himself which will cover me, which will cover the darkness of my sins and my sinful life, so that I shall stand clothed and robed and perfected in my Lord and Saviour. That is the first thing to realise—the love of God and what He has done for me. Justification by faith only!

The second thing, that which John has been emphasising right through this passage, is to realise that I am a partaker of the divine

nature and that God Himself has come to dwell in me, and that therefore I am like God. This is the very argument which we had at the end
of the previous verse: 'because as he is, so are we in this world.' The second ground of my being able to stand with boldness is that as I contemplate the Day of Judgment I can say to myself, 'Well, as the result of
applying the various tests I find in that first epistle of John, I believe that
in spite of my unworthiness I am a child of God. I want to know God
better; I want to love Him more. This concerns me. I do love the
brethren; I like to be with them. I like reading the Scriptures. I like praying. Those are not things that are true of the natural man; so I must be
a child of God. He has given me His own nature, or I would not be like
that. I know something of this love of the brethren; so as I contemplate
facing Him, I am a child of His! Can the Father reject His child? No! He
has promised He will not do so.'

So, you see, in addition to my justification, my sanctification helps
me. 'Herein is our love made perfect . . . because as he is, so are we in
this world. There is no fear in love; but perfect love casteth out fear:
because fear hath torment.' If we are still fearful, we are not made perfect in love; we must always take those two things together. If I do not
always take justification and sanctification together, I shall be misleading myself. I shall fall into antinomianism. I shall say that if I am justified by Christ, it does not matter what I do. But John does not argue like
that; it is a superficial argument. God knows I have tried it, and I know
what an utter failure it is. No! Divide justification and sanctification at
your peril; they are always together. Christ 'is made unto us wisdom, and
righteousness, and sanctification, and redemption' (1 Cor 1:30).

What is the relationship of these two? It is most important and interesting. I put it like this to you: There is the immediate and the mediate
way of getting rid of the fear of the Day of Judgment; or if you prefer,
there is a direct and an indirect way, and you need both. The immediate or the direct way is to understand the doctrine of justification by faith
only. When I feel utterly condemned and hopeless and sinful, there is
only one thing to do: I can rely upon nothing but the work of Christ for
me. I cannot rely upon my acts; they are the cause of my misery.
'Therefore being justified by faith, we have peace with God . . .' (Rom
5:1). Thank God for that! So if you find yourself on your death-bed with
the memory of an old sin, or if you have done something or thought
something you know to be wrong and you do not have time to start liv-

ing a better life, I say, just hide yourself in Christ; you are all right—you are justified by faith only.

But do remember the other side—the indirect or the mediate method, which works like this: If I am not living the Christian life, and love is not perfected in me, I will have a constant sense of condemnation and of fearfulness. I will spend the whole of my life in this world in condemnation. My whole life will be lived in misery, and I am not meant for that. I am meant to live a life of joy and of peace and happiness; I am meant to have boldness as I contemplate the Day of Judgment.

So how do I do that? Here is the answer: Live a life of love; let love be perfected in you. Love the brethren, and as you do so you will say to yourself, 'In spite of what I am, I find that as He is, so am I in this world.' You will find yourself loving someone who is hateful, and you will draw the correct deduction and will say, 'It must be that Christ is in me.' You will come to the Day of Judgment without fear or trembling. So sanctification indirectly, mediately, will act with the justification that does it directly and immediately, and that is the prescription that is prescribed by the Apostle at this particular point.

Let us be clear as to the position here. We will not be perfect in this world, but as we dwell in Christ and as we manifest this love, we will know that we are in God and God in us. We will realise that we have nothing but Him; that though we are still imperfect, 'He which hath begun a good work in [us] will perform it until the day of Jesus Christ' (Phil 1:6). He will perfect us, and so at the end He will 'present [us] faultless before the presence of his glory with exceeding joy' (Jude 24). The more I am like Christ, the less I will fear the Day of Judgment, and the greater will be my boldness as I think of it and as I contemplate it.

May God give us grace to bear in mind and apply these three steps: The natural man should fear the Day of Judgment; the Christian should not fear the Day of Judgment; and Christians should not fear it because they are justified by Christ and sanctified by Christ and made like Christ and will ultimately be with Christ.

15

MEMBERS OF THE SAME FAMILY

We love him, because he first loved us. If a man say, I love God, and hateth his brother, he is a liar: for he that loveth not his brother whom he hath seen, how can he love God whom he hath not seen? And this commandment have we from him, That he who loveth God love his brother also. Whosoever believeth that Jesus is the Christ is born of God: and every one that loveth him that begat loveth him also that is begotten of him.

1 JOHN 4:19–21; 5:1

I TAKE THESE FOUR VERSES together because it seems to me that in them the Apostle sums up, and therefore brings to a conclusion, everything that he has been saying upon this vital and important theme of loving the brethren, which he began to treat in detail in the seventh verse of this fourth chapter. Fortunately for us, he does so in terms of four propositions, and each one of them is to be found in each of the four verses. But before I touch upon them in detail, I would remind you again that the Apostle's argument is that really this is a matter which needs no demonstration; it is something that ought to be quite inevitable to us, and unless we realise that this is something inevitable in the Christian life, our understanding of the whole position is, to put it at its lowest, seriously defective. Wise man and able pastor as he was, John realised that it was not enough just to say that. He knew that we need to be reminded of the particular argument, and here, therefore, he proceeds to work out these arguments with us in detail.

I shall summarise them here because there is a sense in which we have already worked them out in detail, even as John himself has done. The argument is the one we find in verse 19, which reads in the Authorised Version, 'We love him, because he first loved us'; or perhaps it is better expressed in the Revised Version: 'We love because he first loved us.'

Now that is one of those great and glorious statements in which, again, you have an account and summary of the whole gospel. John has already been saying this in different ways. He said in verse 10, 'Herein is love, not that we loved God, but that he loved us, and sent his Son to be the propitiation for our sins.' We are incapable of love apart from what God does to us. So he concludes that we love because God first loved us. Now there he is saying something like this: Everything, of course, is of God; there would be no such thing as Christianity at all were it not for the love of God. God's love is entirely unmoved by anything in us—by any merit or worthiness in us, or by anything that God has ever seen in us. We must once and for ever get rid of the idea that God has loved us by way of a response either to something that is in us or to something we have done. 'When we were enemies, we were reconciled to God by the death of his Son' (Rom 5:10).

The scriptural teaching is that man is in sin; he is dead and vile, and there is nothing in him to call forth the love of God. Rather, God Himself has been moved by nothing but His own everlasting love. We love because He first loved us. The love of God is self-generated, self-moved, self-created; and it is the very first postulate of the Christian gospel to realise that. But the statement really does not stop at that, because John was concerned about this practical object that he had in mind. So what he is really emphasising is not only that God has loved us in spite of ourselves, but that the effect of God's doing so has been to create love in us. The outcome, as it were, of God loving us is that we should also love God and love one another.

Now here again is something we have seen several times as we have been considering this elaborate statement. 'Herein,' says John, 'is our love made perfect.' In other words, that is the objective of God's love. God has not merely loved us in order that we might be forgiven and saved from hell and thus be rescued from the punishment of sin. God's whole work in us was designed to produce a certain type of person. He has set out to produce a new race, a new generation, and we are all to be modeled on the pattern of our Lord Jesus Christ. He is 'the firstborn among many brethren' (Rom 8:29); we have been 'created in Christ Jesus unto good works, which God hath before ordained that we should walk in them' (Eph 2:10).

So Christians are to be like our Lord Jesus Christ and to reproduce the love of Christ in their lives. Read the Gospels about Him, and you find that He had an eye of compassion; He saw need and suffering. He did not deal with people according to their deserts, but according to His own love. His attitude toward people was not determined by what they were, but by His love to them. And that, says John, is the kind of love that is to be in us; we love, because He first loved us. Thus the inevitable corollary or conclusion which we must draw from realising that God has loved us is that we are to be creatures also who love; and we are to love in the same way as the Lord Jesus Christ Himself loved when He was here on earth, and as He still loves us from His throne in heaven.

Now that is the Apostle's first argument, of which we must never lose sight. An ultimate test, in other words, of our profession of the Christian faith is whether we have within us this quality of love. You cannot read the New Testament without seeing this. It is not our good works or our merit that matters. It is not our zeal, even as preachers of the gospel; we may do that with carnal zeal and with a hard heart. No; the ultimate test is love. It is not something theoretical, nor is it something to which we subscribe on paper. The ultimate test of our conformity to the Lord Jesus Christ is that we manifest this love in our lives and in the whole of our conduct.

The second argument, found in the twentieth verse, is perhaps a little more difficult: 'If a man say, I love God, and hateth his brother, he is a liar: for he that loveth not his brother whom he hath seen, how can he love God whom he hath not seen?' Now the first argument was from the very nature of the gospel, but I would describe this one as an argument from common sense. Here is a man who says, 'I love God,' but it is obvious in practice that he hates his brother. He does not speak to his brother, or he is annoyed with him; he will have nothing to do with him. So his whole attitude towards his brother is one of hatred rather than of love. Well, says John, the only thing to say about that man is that he is a liar. This Apostle is fond of that term. He uses strong language, and he does not apologise for doing so. Such a man is 'a liar'; he does not love God—that is obvious: 'he that loveth not his brother whom he hath seen, how can he love God whom he hath not seen?' The thing is a sheer impossibility.

Now there are two difficulties that present themselves to people as they consider this verse. The first is that we tend to think instinctively that it is easier to love God than to love our brethren, and we think so for this reason: The brother is guilty of sin; he is not perfect, and there are many things about him which we dislike. But as for God, God is perfect; God is without sin. He has no flaws, nothing which is in any way objectionable in His character or in His nature. Therefore, we tend to argue, in human terms only, that it ought surely to be easier for us to love God than it is to love our brother. There are so many hindrances and obstacles to loving our brother which are entirely absent in the case of God. Therefore, we feel at first that John's argument is put the wrong way round and that it is not easier to love the brother whom we have seen than the God whom we have not seen. So it comes to pass that we often delude ourselves into thinking that while we do not love our brother, we really do love and are concerned about our love to God.

The second objection is a more biblical and perhaps a more theoretical one. There are those who feel that this statement here is a contradiction of what we find our Lord saying in the Gospels with regard to the question of the great commandment: 'Thou shalt love the Lord thy God with all thy heart, and with all thy soul, and with all thy mind. This is the first and great commandment,' He said. 'And the second is like unto it, Thou shalt love they neighbor as thyself' (Matt 22:37-39). There the order seems to be, love God first and then love our neighbor. But John seems to reverse the order, some people argue; he says that you must start by loving your brother, and as the result of so doing, you come to love God. People thus feel that John here seems to be supporting an argument which has been so common in this century. It is that of the man who says, 'I don't know much about loving God, but I do know about loving my fellow-man, and if a man loves his fellow-man he must love God.'

These are the difficulties, and we can answer them like this: John does not teach here that we must start by loving our fellow-men and women and then advance from that to loving God; that is an entirely false deduction from this statement. John is not saying, 'If you only love your fellow-man first of all because you see him, that will help you to rise up to the level of God, and you will begin to love Him.' Not at all! Rather, John says that if a man says he loves God and does not love his brother, he must be a liar. Or perhaps we can best explain it by saying that there is no separation between what our Lord called the first and second commandments. Our Lord indeed coupled the two together, and that must be so for this good reason: If the first commandment is that I should love the Lord my God with all my heart and mind and soul and strength, then it must follow of necessity that I am greatly concerned about doing what God asks me to do. And what does God ask me to do? The first thing He asks is that I should love my brother.

So there is a sense in which I cannot love God without loving my fellow-man at the same time; to love God is, of necessity, to love those who are loved by God. Intellectually, of course, we draw distinctions between loving God and loving the brethren, but in actual practise, because of the nature of love and because of the nature of our love to God, it is impossible to love God and to desire to please Him without loving the brethren, because that is what God desires from us.

Thus it seems to me we can put it like this: John here is really getting down to our level and being essentially practical. John is, I imagine, countering some of the heresies and the false teachings that were current in his time, even as they are today. One of the greatest dangers that always confronts us is the danger of what I must again describe as a false kind of mysticism. There is nothing easier in this Christian life than for us to devote our time and attention to the cultivation of our soul. We begin to read manuals on the devout life, and they all exhort us to this pure love of God. They all tend to make us think that it is a matter of feeling and sentiment. We can be outwardly seeking to develop the love of God in our own heart, and yet the whole time in our actual practise, conduct, and behaviour we may be irritable, bad-tempered, and selfish. And what John is concerned to do is to correct that particular danger and tendency.

So he puts it, therefore, in this practical form. He is out to show that to love God is always something practical; he is going to tell us in the next verse that to love God means to keep His commandments. Our Lord elaborated that theme time and time again. He said, 'He that hath my commandments, and keepeth them, he it is that loveth me' (John 14:21). He is not the man who gets himself into ecstasies when he is alone, nor is he someone who is conscious of wonderful feelings. He is the person who keeps our Lord's commandments. If we do not keep them, we are not truly loving God, for the way in which love manifests itself is by keeping the commandments.

This is surely something that is obvious. Is it not evident in our ordinary human relationships? That is where some of the poets are often misleading. They could often say beautiful things about love, but they did not always practise it. Sometimes they were the most difficult men imaginable. It is hard to understand, but the explanation is that love to them was just a sentiment. They were difficult men to live with; their own personal life was often a tragedy, including their married life, because they were unable to see that love is something essentially practical. You really show your love to a person not by just writing letters or thinking beautiful thoughts, but by being practical and doing things which help that person and by showing love in actual conduct and behaviour.

That is the essence, I think, of the argument on this point. Indeed, I can go further. Because we are what we are, actual sight is a great aid to our love. If, of course, we were perfect, then it might be as easy to love someone, whom we do not see as it is to love someone whom we do see. But in our state of imperfection and with sin still clinging to us in this world and life, it is the simple truth to say that sight is a great aid and help to our love.

But I can imagine someone objecting at this point and saying, 'But isn't it true that absence makes the heart grow fonder? How do you explain that in the light of what you have just been enunciating?' My reply to that would be that it is perfectly right in certain senses to say that, but it is a statement that always must be qualified. Because we are what we are, if that absence is prolonged, far from making the heart grow fonder, it may bring an end to love. Is it not true to say of all of us that we tend to forget, and if a certain object is removed out of our sight, then unfortunately, even at our best and at our highest, we may forget that object or person?

For instance, do you see that person suddenly bereft of another, breaking his or her heart, and you say, 'How is that poor person going to live?' It seems to be impossible, but you see that person in five or ten years time and the position seems to be very different. There is a calmness and composure and an almost jovial happiness about them. How do you explain it? 'Well,' you say, 'time is a great healer'; and that is what balances the saying that 'absence makes the heart grow fonder.' It did not make the heart fonder, because the absence was prolonged; the person, being frail and fallible, forgot the other person, and thus the anguish has been removed. Therefore, we must be very careful of these attempts of ours to philosophise concerning life. The fact is, and I think we see how essentially right John is in his argument, because we are what we are, sight and vision and contact are of great help, and that is why John argues as he does.

Let me put it quite directly and bluntly like this: The most difficult thing for each one of us is to love God. How we fool ourselves in much of our talk about loving Him. 'No man hath seen God at any time,' as John has reminded us, and it is because we cannot see Him with the naked eye that it is so difficult to love Him. It is a help to be able to see the object that calls forth our love; we know this from our own human experience. Faith, hope, love—and the greatest of these is love; it is the last thing at which we arrive. We feel a sense of gratitude to God, a sense of dependence upon Him long before we really love Him. To love God is the highest achievement of the Christian in this world and in this life. Therefore, John's argument is perfectly right: It is easier to love the brethren whom we have seen than it is to love God whom we have not seen.

Thus the next step in the argument is that what we see in the brother is nothing but the love of God, and therefore John's conclusions must be right. If we are not doing the easier, how can we do the more difficult? This is not a matter of argument, says John. The only thing to say about the people who say they love God and hate their brother is that they are liars. They are persuading themselves that they are loving God when they are not loving Him at all. For if they know anything about the love of God, they know that those who hate their brother cannot be loving God, because God has loved them even though they were sinners. To know anything about the love of God is to know it means loving the unworthy, loving that which is objectionable.

They know that is the end from which they start; that is the whole basis of their position. And therefore if they do not love that brother whom God has loved in spite of himself, they know nothing at all about love. Christians look at this brother, and as they see him they say, 'Yes, there is a man who like myself has been dealt with by God in His love and grace and compassion. I must learn to look at him as God looks at him and as God looks at me.' The state of the brother should, therefore, stimulate these thoughts of love; and thus by loving the brother whom they have seen, they love the God whom they have not seen. The love of God and the love of our neighbour are indissoluble and indivisible.

There, it seems to me, is that second argument which so often has caused people to stumble because of its apparent contradiction of certain things which we have always believed and certain teachings on the Scripture. It is easier to love the brother whom we have seen than it is to love God whom we have not seen. And here we see the great condescension of God. He does not ask us to face that impossible task of loving Him in that manner. He has told us that the way for us to love Him is to love these brethren who are His. If we love them, we are loving Him, because it is His love shed abroad in our hearts that enables us to do it.

Then John goes on to the third argument, which we find in the twenty-first verse where he says, 'And this commandment have we from him, That he who loveth God love his brother also.' Now the connection can be put like this: 'I have been talking about loving God and about loving one's neighbour,' says John, 'and I have been saying how these things inevitably go together. That reminds me of the actual commandment which God gave us, so that there is no reason whatever for arguing about these matters. If I say I draw these deductions from the nature of the gospel and the nature of the love of God, I am confronted by that commandment, and whether I like it or not, that is God's commandment.'

God has commanded this from the beginning. You find it with Cain who hated his brother Abel, and Cain was dealt with by God. You find it plainly taught in the commandments that God gave to the children of Israel through Moses. Love to God, love of our neighbour—it is put both negatively and positively, so that we are not left in the realm of merely drawing our own conclusions and deductions. God commands us to love one another.

'But surely,' says someone, 'isn't it rather ridiculous to command anyone to love? You cannot command your moods and affections.' There again we are dropping into the error of misunderstanding the true nature of love. What he means by commanding us to love is that I am not governed by my immediate instincts. I do not just obey impulses that come to me; rather, as a Christian I have a new view of life, a new outlook. I do not look at men and women and see them as they are; I see them all in the light and teaching of God's Word. And the moment I begin to think about them like that, my very attitude towards them is changed, because

I realise now that I have to look at them with the eye of God, and thus it is essentially right that we should be commanded to love.

This does not mean that I work up feelings; but, as we have already seen, it does mean that whatever my feelings may be with respect to that brother, I must treat him as a brother. I must act towards him as if he were a lovable character; I must do to him what God has done to me. I must not see the sin, but I must see the heart and soul behind it. I must have compassion upon him, and if I deal with him in that way, such is the alchemy of God's love that I shall face even my feelings with respect to him as a challenge, and I shall begin to experience even the sentiments towards him which I have hitherto regarded as the expression of love. So God commands us to love the brethren, and we do so in that particular way and manner.

And that brings me to the last argument, which is the statement of the first verse of the fifth chapter: 'Whosoever believeth that Jesus is the Christ is born of God; and every one that loveth him that begat loveth him also that is begotten of him.'

'True Christians,' says John in effect, and he is emphasising what he has said many times already, 'are people who have been made partakers of the divine nature. They have been born again; they have been born of God. They have not just decided to become Christians and to do certain things. No; God has worked in their souls, and therefore the Holy Spirit has produced a new nature, a new man, in them, and that new nature is nothing but the nature of God Himself. They are people who have been begotten by God.

'That,' says John, 'is the position and the truth of an individual Christian. But it is also true of that other Christian. These two people are now children of God, and therefore they are brothers. They are members of the same family; they have been begotten by the same Father; they are sharing the same nature; they have the same interests and outlook, the same blessed hope, the same everything.

'Now,' says John, 'this does not need any argument. It follows quite simply and naturally that to love the Father must of necessity mean to love the brethren. It is not unnatural, is it, even on the human plane for members of the same family to love one another? We are more ready to forgive things in those who are related to us than we are in people who are not. I am speaking of the natural man who is very lenient to the faults and failings of his own family, his own children, or parents, or his own brothers or sisters. That is nature; it may be selfish, but it is true to nature; and members of the family, those who share the same blood, love one another.

'Well, that is the principle that operates in the spiritual realm,' says John, 'and as it is unnatural for brothers not to love one another, so it is equally unnatural for those who claim that they are partakers of the divine nature and sharers of God's own nature not to love one another. If you really are in the Christian position,' says John, 'you are members of this self-same great family.'

So you work out the Apostle's argument like this: Consider that other person, that other brother in the church whom you find objectionable in so many respects. I do not hesitate to repeat that, because as I have emphasised several times, we are not told to *like* but to *love* one another. There are certain things about people that we do not like, but we love them in spite of that. So we look at these other people and remind ourselves that they are children of God and are heirs of heaven and eternal bliss, even as we are ourselves. We say, 'Those people are going to be in heaven as certainly as I myself am going to be there. I shall have to spend eternity with them. Is it common sense, therefore, that I should be acting the way I am towards them? I shall not be able to turn away from them in heaven. Everything is open in heaven; everything is light and there is no darkness.'

So I begin to argue like that, and I begin to take myself in hand, and I see that I am absolutely wrong not to love them. I am permitting something in my heart that is a negation of everything I am looking forward to. I then ridicule such an attitude; I see it as a barb of Satan. I draw it out and get rid of it, and, in spite of the things I still dislike, I love the brother. My relationship to him makes me do that; my realisation of the fact that this man and I are heirs of God and joint-heirs with Christ makes me face this essential contradiction. The moment I do this, my difficulty vanishes, and above everything else, I find that my communion with God is again restored, and I enjoy this full fellowship with Him and that abounding joy about which the Apostle is so concerned.

That, therefore, it seems to me, is the essence of the argument that John has developed with regard to this vital and important subject of loving the brethren. Shall I put it in a final statement in this form? Are you enjoying fellowship with God? Do you know that God is your Father? Are you enjoying communion with God? When you get on your knees to pray, do you know God is there? Have you found Him? Do you feel that God is near you when you need Him? Have you confidence when you pray? Are you aware of receiving power from the Lord Jesus Christ to overcome your difficulties?

That is what you are meant to have; that is why John writes his letter: 'that ye also may have fellowship with us: and truly our fellowship is with the Father, and with His Son Jesus Christ' (1:3). 'I want you to enjoy it also,' says John in effect, 'and you can enjoy it.' So, are we enjoying it? If we are not, is this, I wonder, because we are not loving the brethren? Fellowship with God is an utter impossibility if we are not loving the brethren; it is impossible, it cannot happen.

Therefore, if we are not enjoying these full benefits of the Christian life and experience, that is surely the first subject for self-examination. Start with the brother whom you do see; start with the person who is right in front of you. Put yourself right on that, and if you feel you cannot, ask God to help you; confess with shame your failure and sin. Tell him about the hatred that is in your heart, expose it to yourself, and ask God to help you to get rid of it, to take it out of you, and to fill and flood you with His own love. Go to God about it, and keep on going until you have conquered and got rid of it; and the moment you find you are loving your brother, I assure you, in the name and the character of God, that you will find your fellowship and communion with God restored; you will be basking in the sunshine of His face, and your whole life will be flooded with His divine love.

Oh, this is a practical matter! Love is not a sentiment; it ultimately means being in this relationship to God. May God give us grace to be honest with ourselves, to examine and to search ourselves, to not allow the devil to make us delude and fool ourselves—'If a man say, I love God, and hate his brother, he is a liar.' Let us, rather, humbly before God examine ourselves and thus rid ourselves of these hindrances to the full experience of the communion and the fellowship of God and the joy of His salvation.

NOTES

CHAPTER ONE: TEST THE SPIRITS

1 Cf. *Fellowship with God* (Crossway Books, 1992).

2 Cf. the first three volumes in this series.

3 For Dr. Lloyd-Jones' exposition of this verse, see *Children of God* (Crossway Books, 1993).

4 For an extended discussion by Dr. Lloyd-Jones on this point, see *Prove All Things* (Kingsway, 1985); U.S. edition *The Sovereign Spirit* (Harold Shaw, 1985).

CHAPTER TWO: THE ALL-SUFFICIENCY OF CHRIST

1 Editor's note: This was true of men like Aldous Huxley in 1949, but it equally applies in the 1990s with the current interest in New Age thinking, which is strongly influenced by Buddhism.

2 See *Walking with God* (Crossway Books, 1993).

3 Cf. the earlier volumes in the series.

CHAPTER THREE: BORN OF GOD

1 See the four-volume series on John 17 (*Saved in Eternity, Safe in the World, Sanctified Through the Truth,* and *Growing in the Spirit*) by Martyn Lloyd-Jones (Kingsway in the UK, Crossway Books in the USA).

CHAPTER FIVE: WE OUGHT ALSO . . .

1 Cf. *Children of God* (Crossway Books, 1993).

CHAPTER SIX: GOD DWELLS IN US

1 See *Fellowship with God* (Crossway Books, 1992).

2 See the John 17 series by Dr. Lloyd-Jones in four volumes (*Saved in Eternity, Safe in the World, Sanctified Through the Truth,* and *Growing in the Spirit*) (Kingsway in the UK, Crossway Books in the USA).

3 See *Children of God* (Crossway Books, 1993).

CHAPTER TEN: THE SAVIOUR

1 See *Walking with God* (Crossway Books, 1993).

CHAPTER TWELVE: DWELLING IN LOVE

1 Cf. *Children of God* (Crossway Books, 1993).

CHAPTER THIRTEEN: THAT GREAT DAY

1 See *Walking with God* (Crossway Books, 1993).

VOLUME FIVE

Life
in
God

Acknowledgments

As usual, these sermons were edited by Christopher Catherwood, the Doctor's eldest grandson. But as with all the sermons published since the death of Dr. Lloyd-Jones in 1981, a major role was played by the Doctor's eldest daughter, Elizabeth Catherwood, who in her capacity as literary executrix went through all the editing to make sure that it was fully in accord with what the Doctor would have wanted had he been alive to supervise the work. Special thanks are therefore due to her for all her hard work, and also to Alison Walley for copy editing the manuscript and for putting it onto disk ready for the publisher.

1

THE NEW TESTAMENT DEFINITION OF A CHRISTIAN

Whosoever believeth that Jesus is the Christ is born of God: and every one that loveth him that begat loveth him also that is begotten of him.

1 JOHN 5:1

THE PURITANS HAD A very interesting phrase that they often employed when they returned to a verse on which they had already preached. Their way of putting it was that they felt 'there were further gleanings that they could obtain from that particular crop.' I think that is a very good way of referring to the abundant lessons that are to be found so constantly in certain verses we encounter in working through a section or portion of Scripture.

In our study of the previous chapter[1] we took this verse together with the three concluding verses of chapter 4. Indeed, we indicated that in these four verses together the Apostle is winding up his great argument with regard to love for the brethren. And there is no doubt at all that his main purpose in using the words we have there was to provide a very powerful argument that is to be deduced from the family relationship, in support of his contention that as Christians we should love one another.

That was his main reason, but, as I hinted, there is a great deal more in this verse than just that particular argument. And that leads me to make a statement that, I believe, is of great importance whenever we read the Bible. Invariably in Scripture there is not only the immediate argument, but there is also something further suggested. Or let me put it like this: observe the tremendous assumption that John makes in using this particular argument with these people, the basis on which his argument rests. Or, to put it another way, observe what he takes for granted in the understanding of these Christian people.

That is what I want to consider here. He is taking it for granted that they are perfectly familiar with the doctrine of regeneration and rebirth, and it is because he takes this for granted that he is able to draw that deduction. Thus, in arriving at that particular argument by referring to a family relationship, John, incidentally, is stating this profound doctrine of regeneration. This is characteristic of these New Testament Apostles; they assume the acceptance of certain fundamental doctrines on the part of the people, so that there is a sense in which we can say that we simply cannot follow their detailed argument unless we start by accepting the basic doctrine on which everything is founded. So once more we find John apparently repeating himself. He has already dealt with this idea of being born again, being born of God, several times, and yet he returns to it. But in actual practise he is not repeating himself; he always has some particular shade of meaning, something fresh to present, some new aspect of the matter, and as we look at this verse we shall find that he is doing so once more.

Or we can look at this in another way and say that we have here, once again, one of those synopses of Christian doctrine that are such a characteristic feature of this Apostle. John was very fond of stating the whole of the Christian faith in a verse, and this is not only characteristic of John but of the entire New Testament. The Apostle Paul did the same thing; these men realised that nothing was more important than that the people to whom they wrote, and therefore Christians at all times, should always be grasping the entire Christian truth. There is no meaning, no sense in particular arguments unless they are derived from the whole body of doctrine.

I emphasise all this because I believe increasingly that the main difficulty with many people today is that they are so interested in particular matters that they fail to connect them with this whole corpus of doctrine. As a result, they find themselves in trouble and in perplexity. So if we would know something about the relationship of the Christian to politics and worldly affairs, for example, the only way to do so is not to start with a particular question, but to start with the whole truth and then to draw our deduction.

Therefore the Apostle, in elaborating the argument about brotherly love, incidentally reminds us of the whole truth. Now this subject can be best divided into two main sections, since John makes two main statements. The first is this: what makes us Christian is the rebirth; we must be born again. John more or less assumes this. He says, 'Whosoever believeth that Jesus is the Christ is born of God: and every one that loveth him that begat loveth him also that is begotten of him.' 'Now,' says John in effect, 'I am anxious to demonstrate to you this question of the importance of loving the brethren; and, of course, it follows quite inevitably from the doctrine of the rebirth that you know all about.'

However, as I have already suggested, we live in an age when we cannot make any such assumptions, so that we have to lay this down as a proposition. Indeed, as we read words like these, must not we plead guilty in general to the charge that our ideas of the Christian position are totally inadequate and insufficient; must we not admit our failure? Indeed, I believe that most of the difficulties in this connection tend to arise from the fact that we will persist in thinking of it in terms of something that we are, our faith, our belief, our action, our good works, instead of thinking of it in the way in which the New Testament itself puts it.

To test what I am trying to convey, let us ask ourselves some questions. What is my conception of the Christian? What is it that makes one a Christian at all? Upon what do I base my claim of being a Christian? If I am asked by somebody, 'You call yourself a Christian—what are your reasons for doing so?' what would be my reply? Now, I am afraid that far too often we would find that our answers fall very far short of the statement that we have here in this verse, the verse that I want to show you is typical of the whole of the New Testament teaching.

The first thing we must get rid of is this idea that what makes us Christian is anything that we have produced or anything for which we are responsible. The New Testament at once shows us the total inadequacy of the common, current version of what constitutes a Christian. The New Testament terms are *regeneration, a new creation*, being *born again*. Those are its categories, and it is only as we stand face to face with them that we begin to realise what a tremendous thing it is to be a Christian. But let me analyse that a little in the terms John uses here. The first thing, therefore, is that what makes men and women Christians is something that is done to them by God, not something they do themselves—'Whosoever believeth that Jesus is the Christ is born of God.' And then, 'Every one that loveth him that begat.' God, according to John, is the one who begets us; it is God's action, not ours.

Now we need not take time in emphasising the obvious contrast in each of these subdivisions. How ready we are to think of being a Christian as the result of something that we do! I live a good life, therefore I am a Christian; I go to a place of worship, therefore I am a Christian; I do not do certain things, therefore I am a Christian; I believe, therefore I am a Christian. The whole emphasis is upon myself, upon what I do. Whereas here, at the very beginning of the New Testament definition of a Christian, the entire emphasis is not upon man and his activity, but upon God. *He* who begat, *He* who produced, *He* who generates, *He* who gives life and being. Thus we see that we cannot be a Christian at all unless God has done something to us.

But I go beyond that and say in the second place that what makes us a Christian is something that makes us like God. 'Whosoever believeth that Jesus is the Christ is born of God.' That '*of*' is an important word; it means 'out of God'; this is one who has received something of God Himself. Therefore, the action of God in making us Christian is not merely an external one; it does not merely touch us on the outside. And in this respect we must always be very careful in our use of the word 'creation.' When God created the world He did not impart Himself to it—He made it outside Himself. But in the new creation, in the rebirth that makes us Christian, the New Testament teaching is that we do receive something of God's own nature. We have been made 'partakers,' says Peter, 'of the divine nature' (2 Pet 1:4); we are sharers in and participators of it. So the New Testament idea of what makes us Christian is not that we happen to be born in a certain country, nor that our parents happen to be Christians. Not at all! Rather, it is nothing less than that we have been born out of God; we are those who have received something of the divine nature.

Now we have to be very careful with this doctrine; we must not think of it in any material sense. It does not mean that I receive some kind of essence or something tangible and material. But it does mean that I receive the spiritual nature and the spiritual outlook and disposition of God Himself. To be born again means to receive this new disposition; that is what is meant by 'a new nature.' So it is something that is done to us by God that makes us like God. Therefore, I go on to deduce that it is something that makes an essential difference *to* us and something that also makes an essential difference *in* us.

In other words, according to the New Testament, when we become Christian we are entirely unlike what we were before. 'If any man be in Christ,' says Paul, 'he is a new creature: old things are passed away; behold, all things are become new' (2 Cor 5:17). I am transformed—profound language for the change that takes place when a person becomes a Christian. I am showing you how utterly superficial the current notions are; because it is the action of God upon us, it is as profound as that. I am, yet not I; I am something essentially different, and indeed I must be if I have now become a partaker of the divine nature. Therefore, when men and women become Christians they are aware of this great difference in their lives. They can contrast their present self with their former self. Now I am not insisting upon their being able to point to a particular moment. All I am saying is that those who are Christians realise there is that about their lives that was not once the case. There is an awareness of this divine action; they are different from what they once were.

I would also put it like this, that Christians are always aware of the fact that they are essentially different from those who are not Christians. Now the moment one says a thing like that, the response of the men of the world is: 'That is typical of you Christians; it is your spiritual pride. You say, "I thank God I am not like other people."' Well, yes, if I am a Christian at all I must say that; but the way in which I do so is of tremendous importance. The Pharisee said it in that way: 'God, I thank thee, that I am not as other men are.' He was proud of himself, and he despised the publican (Luke 18:9-15).

Christians do not say it like that, but rather with profound humility. They say, 'I thank God that I am not as that other poor man still is and as I once was. I thank God that He has not left me in that state and condition, that He has acted upon me and given me a new birth.' They are not priding themselves. Their pride is in God, in Christ's activity within them. So we must not be guilty of this false and spurious modesty. If I am not thankful to God that I am not like the worldling who is living in sin and vice, I am not a Christian at all. I should rejoice in the fact that God has had mercy upon me and has dealt with me and has made me so different from the men and women of the world who do not know Him and do not see their need of Christ. It follows of necessity that if we are born of God, we must obviously be very different from those who are not, and we should rejoice in the difference.

So the last deduction is that this activity of God upon us is something that makes us like all other Christians. 'Whosoever believeth that Jesus is the Christ is born of God: and every one that loveth him that begat loveth him also that is begotten of him.' All those who are begotten of Him must be alike, because they are all begotten of Him. So, you see, it is a simple deduction. As a Christian I am new and different from what I once was; I am different from the person who is not a Christian. But of necessity I must be like all who are Christians. There is a likeness in the members of a family; those who are begotten of the same father have the marks and the traces of the common parenthood upon them. In the same way, there is a likeness about the people of God, and this is one of the most glorious things about being a Christian. You recognise the others, you see the likeness in them; it is a very good test of whether we are Christians at all that we can recognise a brother or sister. We see the mark, and we understand it.

Now that is where, I think, we have one of those final proofs that being a Christian means to be born again. For by natural birth and temperament we are all so very different; as we were by nature, we would not recognise an affinity with those whom we may heartily dislike and with whom we have nothing in common. But the essential thing about the Christian position is that we recognise something in common with people who by nature and birth are different. So the Church is thus in herself a standing testimony of the doctrine of rebirth. In the Christian Church you have people of every conceivable temperament and psychological makeup, and yet they are all one. Why? Because they recognise this common element. They have all been begotten of the same Father, and they love one another because they recognise this similarity and likeness, this common inheritance that they share together.

There, then, are some of the deductions that we draw from this profound New Testament concept as to what it is that makes us Christians—born of God, begotten of God. Therefore, I ask the obvious question at this point: are we aware of the fact that God has begotten us? Do we know that God has produced a man or woman in us that is not ourselves and not of ourselves? As we examine ourselves have we come to say, 'I am what I am by the grace of God. Not by my activities, nor by my interest; not by my belief, nor by the fact that I do or do not do certain things. I am what I am by the grace of God who has brought me to a rebirth and who has given me His own nature and disposition'?

John assumes that; it is the New Testament assumption everywhere about the Christian. Again I must say it—what a tremendous thing it is to be a Christian! Oh, how we vie with one another in seeking earthly honours; how we try to prove that we are related, however remotely, to somebody who happens to be great—we attach great importance to these things. Yet what the humblest Christian can claim is that he is a child of God, born of God, out of God, generated by God; that is the very essence of what is meant, according to the New Testament, by being a Christian.

The second great principle is the results, or the fruits, of the rebirth. How may we know that we are Christians in this sense? What is the first fruit of being born again? Well, according to John, it is faith, *belief*. Here, again, is a very important and interesting matter. 'Whosoever *believeth* that Jesus is the Christ is born of God.' You can see that He is essential. 'Show me someone,' says John, 'who believes that Jesus is the Christ, and I say there is a person who has been born of God.' John means this. There is no such thing as believing or having faith, in a Christian sense, without the rebirth. Now, all who are in any sense interested in theology must be interested in that question: which comes first—belief or being born again? Well, according to John here, and I think I can show you that it is the same everywhere in the New Testament, it is the rebirth that comes first, and then faith. The first expression of being born again is that one believes.

Let me put it to you like this: our estate by nature, according to the New Testament, is that we are dead in trespasses and in sin. Are the dead capable of any action; can a dead man believe? Surely before you believe you must be alive, and you cannot be alive without being born. Take the way in which the Apostle Paul works it out very plainly and explicitly: 'The natural man receiveth not the things of the Spirit of God: for they are foolishness unto him: neither can he . . .' (1 Cor 2:14). 'But you and I,' says Paul in effect, 'we believe these things.' Why? Because we have received the Spirit, the Spirit who is not of this world, the Spirit who is of God, and 'the Spirit searcheth all things, yea, the deep things of God' (1 Cor 2:10). Indeed, we have received this Spirit 'that we might know the things that are freely given to us of God' (v. 12).

There is a great tragedy before us, says the Apostle to the Corinthians. The very Lord of glory, the Lord Jesus Christ, came into this world, and He stood before men. He spoke to them; He worked miracles in their presence; but the very 'princes' of the world did not believe in Him. They were men of ability; there is no doubt but that 'princes' would refer not only to royal blood, but philosophers, men who are princes in every natural sense. They did not believe on Him. And the reason for this? Because they had not received the Spirit of God; no one can say that Jesus is the Lord but by the Holy Spirit. There is no such thing as faith or belief without rebirth. 'Whosoever believeth that Jesus is the Christ is born of God'; he must be born again—he cannot believe without the new birth. There is nothing, in a sense, that seems to be so contrary to the New Testament teaching as the suggestion that as a natural man I believe and because I believe, I am given the rebirth. The dead cannot believe; the natural man cannot. He is at enmity against God; he is incapable of this. The very fact that a man believes is proof he has been born again; it is the first fruit that is manifested in the life of one who has been born of God.

But let me emphasise also *what* he believes. 'Whosoever believeth that *Jesus is the Christ* is born of God.' Here again is something of great importance to us. Men and women who are Christians are people who have been born again, and the first proof they give that this has happened is that they believe that 'Jesus is the Christ.' You see, John never separates doctrine and experience; they always go together. Christians not only believe in the being and existence of God. There are large numbers of people in the world who believe in God who are not Christians. To believe in God and in the holiness of God and many other things about Him does not make one a Christian. Christian faith is a specific belief—that 'Jesus is the Christ.' In other words, our whole faith must be focused on the Lord Jesus Christ; it is what we believe about Him that makes us Christian.

We must believe that Jesus of Nazareth, that person who belongs to history, that man who worked as a carpenter for all those years and went about preaching and healing, we must believe that He is the Christ, the Messiah, the anointed of God. By this John means that it is in Christ and through Christ alone that salvation is possible to us. The Messiah is the one who is appointed by God to deliver His people. Now, the Jews thought of that in a material, political sense, and because our Lord did not prepare a great army and did not go to Jerusalem to be crowned as King, they said He was not the Messiah. But the whole teaching of the New Testament is to show that He *is* the Messiah, the promised deliverer, a spiritual deliverer. Thus to believe that 'Jesus is the Christ' really means that we say and believe there is no salvation at all possible for us apart from Him.

That is the very essence of the New Testament teaching; yet I am increasingly amazed at the failure of people to understand it. I put this question to people very frequently. I say, 'If you had to die tonight, on what would you rely in the presence of God? What would you say to Him?' And they tell me, 'Well, I would ask Him to forgive me—I believe He is ready to pardon,' and they go on talking, but they never mention the name of the Lord Jesus Christ.

But to be in that position is not to be a Christian at all. The first thing the Christian believes is that 'Jesus is the Christ.' It is to believe, therefore, that He is the Son of God in a unique sense, that He is the eternal Son of God made flesh, that He bore our sins in his own body on the tree (1 Pet 2:24), and that it is only because our sins were punished in Him that God forgives us. It is in that way that He delivers us and sets us free. He rose again to justify us; He is seated at the right hand of God, waiting until His enemies shall be made His footstool. He will return again and destroy evil from the face of the earth and introduce His glorious Kingdom—'Jesus is the Christ.'

Thus the first fruit of the rebirth is that I believe that. And obviously, believing that is not something intellectual or something I only do with my mind. If I believe, I commit my whole life to Him. If I believe, I know I am delivered because Christ has done that for me. I see that apart from Him I am lost and undone and doomed. This is a profound action; it is a commitment; it is a banking of one's everything upon that fact.

The second fruit of the rebirth is *love for God*. John's way of putting it is: 'every one that loveth him that begat . . .' Christians see that they are hell-deserving sinners and that they would have arrived in hell were it not for His great love in sending His Son. They realise the love of God for them, and therefore they love God; they realise they owe everything to Him. It seems to me that this again is one of those fundamental things about Christian men and women. However good a life they may be living now as saints, they still feel that they are hell-deserving sinners in and of themselves, and that they owe everything to the grace of God; that it is God's love alone that has made them what they are. They lose their sense of fear and a sense of enmity against God and are filled with a sense of profound gratitude to Him.

Do we know this gratitude? You see, if we are relying upon ourselves and our good life and our actions and our beliefs, we do not feel much gratitude to God because we have done it all ourselves, and we are grateful to ourselves for being what we are. But if we realise that we are nothing and that God has given us everything, then we shall feel this gratitude; we shall love Him who has begotten us.

And the final thing is, of course, that we *love our brethren*— 'Every one that loveth him that begat loveth him also that is begotten of him.' This needs no demonstration. We look at those others, and we see in them the same disposition as in ourselves. We realise that they owe everything to the grace of God, just as we do. We realise that in spite of their sinfulness God sent His Son to die for them, exactly as He did for us; and we are aware of this bond. Though there may be many things about them we do not like, we say, 'That is my brother, my sister.' So we begin to love them, and we are marching together to that land that God has prepared for us.

There, then, we have the fruits, the results, of rebirth—faith and belief; love for God who has begotten us; and love for those who are, like ourselves, begotten of God by His wondrous grace.

That is the New Testament idea of a Christian. How tawdry do worldly honours and ideas seem to be in the light of this; the things for which people vie and compete, the things about which they get so excited, these glittering prizes after which they run; oh, how small, how unworthy! But we are born of God; we are children of God, heirs of God, joint heirs with Christ. We belong to the royal family of heaven, to the King of kings and Lord of lords, and we are partakers of His divine nature. Let us rise and be worthy of the high calling of God in Christ Jesus our Lord.

2

THE WHOLENESS OF
THE CHRISTIAN LIFE

*By this we know that we love the children of God, when
we love God, and keep his commandments. For this is the
love of God, that we keep his commandments: and his
commandments are not grievous.*

1 JOHN 5:2-3

IN THESE TWO VERSES we come to one of those places of transition in
the movement of the thought of the Apostle. Consequently, these two
verses are really of very great significance in an understanding of the
argument that is being evolved by the writer. Our analysis of the epistle,
let me remind you,[1] is to tell Christian people that even in a world like
this a fulness of joy is possible. The Apostle when he wrote this letter
had become an old man; he was facing the end of his life, and he wanted
to leave this word of comfort and encouragement with these first
Christians, and this is his message. It is a very realistic message; he paints
no rosy picture of a world that is going to get better and better until
everything is going to be perfect. Rather, he puts it in its stark naked-
ness; it is a world that 'lieth in the evil one.' Yet in spite of that—and
this is the essential message of the gospel—there is a joy that, as Peter
says, is 'unspeakable and full of glory' (1 Pet 1:8). And John says that
this is possible because we can, in this world and even as we are, have
fellowship with God; it is fellowship with God that leads to joy.

Then we have been indicating that John, as a wise pastor and teacher, has been warning these people that there are certain things that will rob them of that joy unless they are careful. God's promises are always conditional, and here John tells us that there are very definite conditions that we must observe. You can look at this either negatively or positively; there are things we must avoid, and there are things we have to observe, and here are the three main things that he keeps on emphasising. Firstly, if we want to enjoy that fellowship with God, we must keep His commandments; secondly, if we want to enjoy that fellowship, we must love the brethren—love one another; and, thirdly, we must always be right in our doctrine, and especially the doctrine concerning the absolute centrality and necessity of the Lord Jesus Christ.

Now John constantly illustrates these things, and he puts it in two main ways like this: Firstly, we must always realise in this world that we can have that fellowship with God; and, secondly, we must realise that we are children of God. I have shown that by the end of the sixth verse of the fourth chapter the Apostle has worked out those two main lines. In a sense he has finished his argument at that point, and from there on, I have suggested,[2] he just takes up these major themes again and elaborates them. He was anxious that these people should enjoy the benefits. So, having stated the case, he says, 'now let me sum it up; these are the things you have to watch,' and this is the order in which he puts them: love for the brethren; keeping the commandments; and unswerving loyalty and adherence to the message and the faith concerning the Lord Jesus Christ. And he elaborates these three themes.

We have considered the theme of brotherly love that starts in chapter 4, verse 7,[3] and we finished in the last study [of *The Love of God*] at the end of the first verse in chapter 5. Now, in verses 2 and 3, we come to the point of transition. John is talking about another of his themes, and the way in which he does so is most interesting. John's style sometimes seems to be rather difficult. There is a sense in which he is very much more difficult than the Apostle Paul, and for this reason: the difference between the two writers is that the Apostle Paul always tells you what he is doing before he does it; but John does it without telling you and, as it were, leaves you to find out what he is doing! I suppose in many ways it is the difference between the man who is centrally and primarily logical and who reasons, and the man who is more musical. John's characteristic method is that when he is making a transition from one theme to another, he does not put a full stop and say, 'Now let us look at so and so'—not a bit! Rather he glides from one to another. I believe that perhaps the best way of putting it is to use this musical illustration: you often find in a symphony or something like that, where there are a number of themes, that the composer very often, just as he is finishing one theme, throws out a hint of the one that is coming. Indeed he may do that some time before he really takes up the second theme.

Now that is what John does here. He has been dealing with the theme of love for the brethren, and he says, 'By this we know that we love the children of God'—you can see he is still on the theme of love for the brethren, but he hasn't yet finished the subject—'by this we know that we love the children of God, when we love God, and keep his commandments.' There is a hint of the theme that is coming, and then he takes up that theme: 'For this is the love of God, that we keep his commandments: and his commandments are not grievous. For whatsoever is born of God overcometh the world'; there is the hint of the next theme. That is his method—this gliding from one to the other.

This is a very important point because it really does remind us in a very forcible and striking manner of the whole theme of this first Epistle of John. It is, in a sense, life, life in God, life and its manifestations, so that in many ways there is a great deal to be said for John and for his method. John did not regard the Christian faith so much as a series of propositions; to him it was essentially a matter of life. Now putting it like that may give the impression that Paul did not believe the Christian faith was life, and of course he did. But Paul was speaking of life in terms of his grand propositions, and John never really does that, because his main interest in life is that it is something vital and organic. It is something, in a sense, that you cannot analyse, something that manifests and shows itself and reveals itself in various ways.

So we can very readily say that the theme of his first epistle is this: the life that is given to man by God and the way in which it shows itself, and therefore the importance of examining ourselves to make sure we really have it. That is what he keeps on doing. 'You must test yourself,' he says; 'there are antichrists, false teachers; there is the devil who is suggesting things to you, so you always have to make quite sure—Beloved, believe not every spirit, but try the spirits whether they are of God; because many false prophets are gone out into the world' (4:1). So there it is—life and its manifestations and the importance of making sure we really have it. That is exactly what John does in this interesting way in which he moves from one theme to the other in these two verses; he presents us with the whole philosophy of his method and shows what he is really anxious to impress upon us.

Therefore, bearing all that in mind, let us come a little closer to these verses that are of such vital importance in a true understanding of the whole thesis. Let me put it to you like this: at first sight, when you read this second verse you may very well come to the conclusion that John is contradicting something that he has just been saying. He says, 'By this we know that we love the children of God, when we love God, and keep his commandments.' Surely, says someone, that is the opposite of what he said in 4:20—'If a man say, I love God, and hateth his brother, he is a liar: for he that loveth not his brother whom he hath seen, how can he love God whom he hath not seen?' The way, says John in that verse, in which you may know for certain that you love God is that you love your brother; and yet here he says that the way in which you make certain that you love your brother is that you love God! He is contradicting himself, some would charge.

However, there is no contradiction whatsoever in these two statements. John says that it is all entirely due to the fact that we are concerned with life; it is not a question of starting with one and advancing on to the other, but rather that if you have one you must have the other. I pointed out[4] in dealing with 4:20 that John was not saying you start by loving your brother and thereby come to love God—not at all! He says that these two things always go together.

Let me put all this in the form of a number of propositions. The first thing I find is what we may very well call 'the wholeness of the Christian life.' Life is always something vital and organic. The human body is not a collection of parts, of fingers and arms and forearms all somehow or another attached together. That is not the body at all. The body is organic—vital and essentially whole, and these are but parts of it. Thus in any analysis that we may make, and we must make one, we must always make it in terms of the whole. Take a flower; you can divide it up into petals and stamens and various other parts. But in making your analysis—if you want to do it properly—you must not pull out the petals and the stamens, because if you do you will have no flower at the end. You make your analysis, but you do not destroy anything.

It is exactly the same with life in every realm and department, and it is particularly true of this Christian life with which we are concerned and that John is expounding to us. You cannot understand this epistle without always holding in the centre of your mind the idea that the Christian life is a whole life. What God gives us is *life*. It is not that I believe certain things and do no more; God gives me life, and life manifests itself in certain ways. Furthermore, there are certain things that are absolute essentials to the Christian life, and John's case is that they must all be present in some shape or form before there is such a thing as the Christian life. Or, to put it negatively, the absence of any one of these elements should lead me, at any rate, to doubt very seriously whether there is life at all. Not only must all these things be present—they must all be present at the same time; and if any one of them is not there, then I must examine myself very seriously and query whether any of them is there.

Now this, I think you will see, is really a very important principle. Wherever there is life, certain things will always be there; there will be activity, there will be breathing, and so on. Where there is no breathing or some sort of activity, there is no life; and where there is no development there is no life. There are certain things that are essential before it can be said that a person is alive, and it is exactly like that in the spiritual life. John has already told us what these things are—love for God, keeping His commandments, loving the brethren, holding the faith; and John's argument is that all these are parts of the manifestation of the Christian life.

So we must not think of the Christian life merely as a matter of some external experience of God and certain feelings that I may have. I must not think of it either as merely living a certain type of ethical life or having certain feelings and sensations with regard to other people. Nor must I think of it in terms of holding certain intellectual propositions in my mind with regard to the Christian faith. Rather, the Christian life is a whole life, and there are certain elements that must always be present.

That is the first great proposition, and the second is that the way to test each or any part, therefore, is not so much to concentrate on that particular thing itself, but rather to look for the manifestation of the others. There, I think, we do come to the key to understanding John's particular method. Here I am looking at life, which is a whole thing, complete, organic; and now I want to examine one particular part. I may feel a certain amount of trouble in my mind with regard to one of these manifestations—is it really present in my life? Well, the best way to discover that, says John, is not so much to start with that particular thing, but to look and see if the other things are there. For if they are not, you have no life, and what you think is a manifestation of life is not that at all. And, John suggests, it does not matter much with which of these particular elements you start.

I like to think of this as a kind of circular movement. It does not matter really at which point you start in this circle. If you start at one point, you are bound to go on; and as you go around the circle, you pass these four points. You can think of it in terms of a clock. You set your clock going at the hour or the quarter or the half or the three-quarters, and if your clock is working you will duly pass the quarter and the half and the three quarters until you reach the hour, so that in reality it does not matter where you start.

Now that is the very principle on which John has been working. He sometimes starts with the love of God and goes on to the love of the brethren. At other times he starts with the love of the brethren and arrives at the love of God. And sometimes he starts with the commandments and then goes on to the love of the brethren and the love of God. It is immaterial. Here is a circle, and there are these particular points on it. Now because it is a circle, you must have the four points. If you do not have one, you do not have any; it is no longer a circle. You can start at whatever point you like, and if you want to know whether you are right on that point, make sure the others are also present.

In other words, the great thing to know is that we are on the circle, that we have the life; and we know that if we have life, it will manifest itself in certain ways. If I have one, I must have all; if I am doubtful of one, let me examine the rest. So at one time John says, 'If a man say, I love God, and hateth his brother, he is a liar'; he is testing there my love to God and takes me to the love of the brethren. And here, you see, it is a different method: 'By this we know that we love the children of God, when we love God, and keep his commandments.' So this concept of the Christian life as a whole, as an organic, vital, life-giving, living thing, is really of great importance when we come to this question of self-examination and concern about the parts; and that leads me to my next proposition.

'Why is this testing so important?' says someone. 'Why does John keep on like this? Why didn't he finish his letter at chapter 4, verse 6? Why go on repeating it?' He does it for one reason only, which is that there is a horrible danger of the counterfeit. He has constantly reminded us of that—the antichrists, the false teachers. How easy it is to persuade ourselves that we have life when we do not. How easy to say that the whole of the Christian life is just a mystical feeling, or that it is just an attitude towards other people, being nice and kind and friendly. How easy to say that the whole of Christianity is just a certain moral quality of life and living, or that what makes us Christian is reading books on theology and discussing them, and nothing else.

'No!' says John; 'the devil would have you do that. He would focus your attention on something that appeals to you. I want you to see,' he says, 'that if you do not have this wholeness, this fulness, you are being deluded. You are being misled; the false teachers and antichrists have led you astray.' This life is something that is whole. If you have not got it all, you have not got any. It is not that you have reached maturity when you start; a baby is perfect, and in that newborn baby there is all the promise of the ultimate adult perfection. You can examine life almost in embryo, and it is as whole in the embryo as it is in the fully matured adult.

Testing, therefore, is a very vital and urgent matter because of this terrible possibility of self-delusion, and, of course, the importance of that arises in this way: if I do want to enjoy this fulness of joy that John speaks of, if I want to know fellowship with God and that I am a child of God, then I must be absolutely right about these things. So if you lack assurance of salvation, if you are uncertain as to whether you are a child of God, if you cannot say, 'Yes, I know God, and I have fellowship with God, and I walk with God,' if you are not in that position, I suggest that you have never done what John is pressing upon us in this epistle. We must view it in this way and be certain that we have it. Self-examination is not important theoretically but from this essentially practical standpoint.

The last proposition is simply the working out of the mechanical process of testing, and John does it for us in these two verses. 'Let us start,' he says, 'with this question of loving the brethren. By this we know that we love the children of God . . .' In other words, I must be quite sure that I am really loving the brethren. I may have considered other parts of John's epistle and said, 'That is comforting and consoling. John seems to say that if I love the brethren, then I have the love of God.' But do I love the brethren? 'Well, make sure of it,' says John. There is such a thing as confusing a true Christian love for the brethren with just a liking.

We are all born very differently. Some people are born nice people, some are not. Some people are born with such an easy, almost phlegmatic nature and temperament that they can like almost anybody. They seem to like Christian people; they seem to like being in Christian society. They do not like the noise and bustle of the world. But they are not Christians; they are just born with that temperament. They rather like the atmosphere and society of the Church; they like mixing with people who are quiet. They like singing hymns, they try to live a good life, and they like the whole atmosphere of a place of worship. Such people have to be very careful, when they say they love the brethren, to make sure they are not just manifesting a natural liking. There are some people who instinctively like discussing Christian things. They have always been like that, and they may be right on the vitals of the Christian faith. 'Now there,' says John, 'you must examine yourself.'

And the way to test that is not just to analyse your own feelings and dissect them. Rather, this is the way to do it: 'By this we know that we love the children of God, when we love God.' So if I do not love God, what I have hitherto regarded as love for the brethren is not that at all, but simply this natural liking. In other words, as I go around the circle, can I say, 'I love God'? Because if I truly love Him, then I must be loving the brethren also—it is a part of the circle. So I must be quite sure that my love for the brethren is based upon the love of God and a love for God. I must be able to say quite honestly, 'I like these people not in a natural sense, but because I see in them the grace of God. Love for the brethren means love for the Christian brother or sister, so that what makes me love these people is the grace of the Lord Jesus Christ, the love of God in them, and the love of God working upon them; the thing that is in me I see in them. I am thereby very sure that it is not something elemental, but something that results from having received the life of God into my own soul.'

That is the first test, but it is not enough, because you might say to me, 'You seem to have solved one problem, but you have left me with another. You say I test my love of the brethren by saying, "Do I love God?" and yet some time ago you were telling me the only way to know God is to love the brethren.' 'Wait a minute,' says John, 'I haven't finished—by this we know that we love the children of God, when we love God, and keep his commandments.' So my immediate problem is this: at this point I am halfway around the face of the clock—do I love God?

How can I know whether I love God? Once more John says, 'Don't just sit down and examine your mood and feelings; go on around the circle—when we love God, and keep his commandments.'

Here again, as I think we all must agree, there is nothing about which we can so deceive ourselves as about the fact that we love God. A man may come to me and say he loves God. He says with Browning, 'God's in His heaven,/All's right with the world'; but when something goes against him, he finds he does not love God. He says, 'Why does God . . . ?' Feelings are very deceptive. How do I know I love God? There is the next step—'*when we keep . . . his commandments.*'

Our Lord emphasises that in John 14:21: 'He that hath my commandments, and keepeth them, he it is that loveth me.' You cannot separate these things. Love is not a sentiment; it is the most active, vital thing in the world. If I love, I want to please—I keep the commandments; and what I may regard as the love of God in my soul is a pure delusion unless it leads me to keep God's commandments and to live life as He wants me to live it.

'Again,' says someone, 'you have just shifted the problem; you have got rid of two difficulties, but you have left me with the third. This keeping of the commandments—what is this?' 'Well,' says John in a kind of footnote on which he is going to elaborate in the next verse, 'his commandments are not grievous'—not heavy. In other words, what matters in this whole question of keeping the commandments is my attitude towards them. When I face the commandments of God, do I resent them? Do I feel that God is imposing an impossible load upon me? Do I groan and grumble and say, 'Oh, this hard taskmaster who asks of me the impossible!'?

'If that is your attitude towards the commandments of God,' says John, 'you are not keeping them, and neither are you loving God, and you are not loving your brethren—you are outside the life altogether.' For someone who is truly Christian does not find the commandments of God to go against the grain. He may be acutely aware of his failure—if he is facing them truly he must be—but he does not resent them, he loves them. He knows they are right, and he wants to keep them and to love them. He does not feel they are a heavy load imposed upon him; he says rather, 'This is right; that is how I would like to live. I want to be like Christ Himself—His commandments are not grievous.'

So here is a very thorough and practical test: is my Christian living a task? Is it something that I resent and object to? Do I spend my time trying to get out of it? Am I trying to compromise with the life of the world? Am I just living on the edge of the Christian life, or do I want to get right into the centre and live the life of God and be perfect even as my Father in heaven is perfect? 'His commandments are not grievous' to Christian men and women; they know that is what God asks of them. They love God and therefore they want to keep His commandments.

There, then, it seems to me, are the practical tests as John works them out for us. But let us always remember where we begin; it is the wholeness that matters: loving God, keeping His commandments, loving the brethren, holding the faith.

Thank God for such a life; thank God for its wholeness, its fulness, its completeness, its balance, its perfection of form. Thank God for this perfect thing that He gives us; and as we examine ourselves, let us never forget that the proof of life is that all the parts are always present and always present together.

3

OVERCOMERS

For whatsoever is born of God overcometh the world: and this is the victory that overcometh the world, even our faith. Who is he that overcometh the world, but he that believeth that Jesus is the Son of God?

1 JOHN 5:4-5

IT IS OBVIOUS FROM this word *For* at the beginning of the fourth verse that the Apostle here is continuing something that he has already mentioned; so in order to understand the statement of these two verses, we must remind ourselves of the previous verses. John has just been making the point that to the Christian the commandments of God are 'not grievous.' The way in which we show that we love God is that we keep His commands, and thus if we love God the commandments of necessity cannot be grievous; our very love of Him makes us desire to keep them.

'But that is not all,' says John, 'that is not enough.' John was anxious to help these people, so he does not leave it like that as a general statement; he elaborates it, and he takes it up by using this word *for*. 'By this we know that we love the children of God, when we love God, and keep his commandments. For this is the love of God, that we keep his commandments: and his commandments are not grievous. For [because] whatsoever is born of God overcometh the world.' That is why the commandments are not heavy; that is the connecting link.

Now that is the way in which John here, in these few verses, introduces us to this whole question—indeed, I may say this whole problem—of keeping the commandments of God. It is a problem because it is something at which Christian people very often stumble. The relationship of the Christian to the commandments of God has often been a point of great debate and dispute. There have been those who have emphasised the keeping of the commandments, who have more or less kept them to the letter and, in so pressing the commandments, have become legalistic. It is possible for Christians to become legalistic in their outlook, and they may put themselves under bondage. This had arisen in the early church, and that is why Paul, especially, had to write certain epistles, such as the Epistle to the Galatians, and probably also the one to the Romans. This also seems to be the background to the Epistle to the Hebrews. You find this sometimes put in this way, that people tend to see the end of the ceremonial law as the result of the work of grace, and yet say that the moral law still abides and obtains.

The second danger is what you might call the danger of *antinomianism*, and it has led many Christians into grievous error not only intellectually but often in life and vigour. They say, 'I am free from the law. Because I am now a Christian, I am no longer under the law but under grace, and the commandments have nothing to do with me; I have finished with them.' So they feel that in a sense it does not matter what they do, and they become lax and loose in their living and find themselves in trouble.

But John takes all this in a much more experimental and practical way, and we should thank him for it, because if you stop to think of it seriously, you will see that it is a complete error to say that the Christian has no relationship to the law. The law stands; 'Thou shalt not kill, thou shalt not steal . . .'—those laws have not been annulled. But Christians should be more than conquerors with respect to the law. John takes it for granted—indeed, he has been pursuing that very theme—that we love God by keeping His commandments, and these commandments are not only for the Jews, but for everybody. The Ten Commandments are the commandments of God to men and women at all times and in all places, and they have never been reduced or modified.

But John is much more concerned to be of help to us in a very practical sense, and this is his way of putting it. He tells us that in a sense the difference between the Christian and the non-Christian comes out more clearly, perhaps, with regard to this question of keeping the commandments than anywhere else. People are more likely to proclaim what they really are, whether they are Christians or not, by what they say about the commandments and what they do about them than in any other single respect. To the non-Christian, the commandments are very heavy. The commandments of God to non-Christians are a yoke; they feel they are a task and a burden, and in their heart of hearts they hate God because of this, and they would be very glad to be emancipated out of it all. But not to the Christian; His commandments, says John, are not a task and a terrible duty to the one who really is born again—His commandments are 'not grievous.'

So here is the test that we must all put to ourselves: what is our attitude to the commandments of God? Do I feel that the Christian life is a task, something against the grain, something to which I have to force and press myself? Do I merely attempt to keep the commandments because I am afraid not to; am I just playing for safety, or am I living this life because I enjoy it? Is it my desire to keep the commandments of God; do I recognise that they are essentially right, and do I long to conform to them increasingly? These are the questions, and it is my answer to them that really proclaim whether I am a Christian or not.

Now John, in a sense, helps us to discover all that; so let us summarise his teaching by putting it in the form of a number of propositions. The first, obviously, is this one: that which makes anybody feel that the commandments of God are grievous is the world. John again introduces an argument for saying so: 'And his commandments are not grievous. For whatsoever is born of God overcometh the world.' Now he has already been dealing with the subject of the world, you remember, in the second chapter, where he has put it in the form of a positive injunction: 'Love not the world, neither the things that are in the world. If any man love the world, the love of the Father is not in him. For all that is in the world, the lust of the flesh, and the lust of the eyes, and the pride of life, is not of the Father, but is of the world. And the world passeth away, and the lust thereof: but he that doeth the will of God abideth for ever' (2:15-17).

That is, perhaps, one of the fullest statements in Scripture of what the New Testament means by this term *the world*; here John once more comes back to it. He is always very anxious about it, as is every writer in the New Testament. You cannot read the New Testament truly without seeing the whole of the Christian life as a life of conflict; we are in an atmosphere and in a world where there is a great fight going on.

There are two kingdoms, the kingdom of light and the kingdom of darkness, and you get these constant comparisons and contrasts. Paul says to the Ephesians, 'For we wrestle not against flesh and blood, but against principalities, against powers, against the rulers of the darkness of this world, against spiritual wickedness in high places' (or 'in the heavenlies') (Eph 6:12). 'The world,' says John, 'is there the whole time, and the Christian is fighting against it'; so it is of vital importance that we should know what he means by this.

Perhaps the best way of defining what the New Testament means by 'the world' is that it is everything that is opposed to God and His Spirit. God calls upon men and women to worship Him and to glorify Him; He calls upon them to live for His glory. There is a famous quotation in the Shorter Catechism of the Westminster Confession that says, 'The chief end of man is to glorify God and to enjoy Him for ever.' That is the chief object for which God created us; we are meant to glorify God in every way conceivable. And the world is everything that tries to prevent our doing that.

Now this is a very broad term, as we shall see, and I sometimes think there is nothing that is quite so pathetic as the case of those people who think that 'the world' just means worldly entertainment and nothing else. How pathetic that is in the light of the New Testament teaching! People fondly imagine that they have finished with the world just because they do not do certain things. But you may be as much in the world in the house of God as you are in a cinema or theatre, if you are proud of the fact that you are what you are and not what somebody else is, in that theoretical sense. The world, let me emphasise it again, is everything that stands between us and glorifying God only, utterly and absolutely.

The world, therefore, is something with which we have to reckon outside ourselves. So how do I confront it in that external sense? We cannot attempt to give an exhaustive answer here, so let me just give you some headings. The world does its best to prevent me from glorifying God by its attractions and its temptations. I need not elaborate on these, we are all well aware of them; they are everything that the world holds before us and with which it tries to appeal to us and that is calculated to draw us away from God. As we have seen, that is not the whole of what the world means, but it is a part of it.

But not only that, it is a person's outlook, for there are many people in the world today who would not dream of spending their time reading all the gruesome, detailed stories in the newspapers—they are too intelligent. But still, they may be as much a victim of the world as the other people who do spend their time doing that. The world is opposed to God in its outlook, in its mind, in its mentality, in its own wisdom—worldly wisdom. It is against God in its faith, in its own understanding, in its intellectualism that would banish God and ridicule the Cross and the blood of Christ, especially because it does not seem to be philosophically sound—all that is as much the world as the life of the gutter.

Even further, the world does its utmost to prevent us from glorifying God by persecuting us, and it has many ways of doing that. Sometimes it does it by means of ridicule; it just laughs at us and makes us feel we are not intellectual. How often is this done in the office and in the profession, in the home, in the social contacts, and in various other places. And when ridicule does not succeed, it sometimes becomes isolation; you just find people drifting away. That is a terrible form of persecution, a very subtle and a very vicious one.

Sometimes persecution may even be physical. There are people—hundreds, not to say thousands, of men and women—who are being tempted by the devil, through this world, to deny God and to deny Christ. This is the position in which many find themselves if they go on proclaiming the gospel, or if they go on saying they believe it or continue to practise it. It may be that they will be thrown into prison and their wives and children will suffer; it may be that they will not be put into prison, but something will be done to the wife or the children. In whatever way, the world is trying to prevent their glorifying God. That is what we have to fight—the world outside us that manifests itself in those various ways.

But then there is also the world that is within us, and I put it like that because as we consider this I think we will see at a glance the whole error of monasticism. The world is outside, but, alas, it is also on the inside; the world is within me as well as without, and I have to fight on both fronts. The Apostle Paul says, 'The carnal mind is enmity against God: for it is not subject to the law of God, neither indeed can be' (Rom 8:7); so if I have a carnal mind, I am not glorifying God. A carnal mind is something that is inside me. Or again, he says to the Corinthians, 'We have received, not the spirit of the world, but the Spirit which is of God; that we might know the things that are freely given to us of God' (1 Cor 2:12).

The world, then, may be within me, that 'carnal mind' as the New Testament puts it. But what does that mean? Well, let us examine this foul, horrible thing that is in us as a result of the Fall and as a result of sin. There are two main manifestations of this. The first is *self* and every-thing that is covered by that little word. And what is self? First, it is pride; there is nothing perhaps that is quite so opposed to glorifying God as pride. It does not matter what you are proud of—your physical appearance, your mental ability, your position in life, your success. It does not matter what it is—any feeling of pride you may have is antag-onism to God and makes it more difficult to glorify Him. Pride may take various forms: a desire for praise—we all know this—and a dislike of criticism, which is the negative counterpart. Then there is self-reliance, and this is perhaps one of the respects in which the modern world makes it most difficult for the modern man and woman to glorify God. It has been preaching self-reliance to us for so long: man, the master of his fate, the controller of his destiny; wonderful man, the discoverer of the secrets of the universe, harnessing nature. The popular books and the psycho-logical teaching all suggest self-reliance, and the more you rely upon yourself, the less you trust God and the less you glorify Him and the less you live for Him.

And then, of course, there is ambition, a desire to get on and to suc-ceed, in an unworthy sense; and selfishness, being anxious to have things for myself and for my own, not for somebody else and his own; and self-centredness and self-concern. Then out of that come jealousy and envy and coveting; a hardness in thought and a hardness in speech; unkind-ness; and all these other horrible things that you will find listed in cer-tain passages of the New Testament. Paul has such a terrible list in the fifth chapter of Galatians (vv 17-21); read and examine yourself in the light of it.

Now, all these things are the world within me, and when they are in control and active, I am not glorifying God. When I am living for myself, I am concerned about myself in every shape and form. And then together with that self, there is the flesh; and when I say that, I mean appetites, desires, lusts—these things arise from within. We may be sit-ting by ourselves and suddenly an evil thought comes—it is the flesh, the desire of the flesh and of the mind. That is part of the world, and it is as opposed to glorifying God as are entertainments that are provided by the world outside us.

But it is not only that. One of the most terrible things the Christian has to fight is the flesh as it manifests itself in the form of indolence and a love of ease. There is a sense in which we are all lazy. Have you not often found yourself making excuses for not reading your Bible or praying? You would not think of making an excuse if you were going to read your newspaper; you would not think of ever making an excuse if it was a question of going to an entertainment; but when it is a question of going to a prayer meeting, it is too cold, or you are not feeling well—a thousand and one excuses come. The natural indolence of the flesh is all the time fighting against glorifying God, standing between us and the worship of God. There may be indolence, perhaps, even in the matter of sleep and in the matter of the distribution of our time. All these things come in, and they are a part of the world that is within us. Then there is a fear of softening, a fear of being a fool for Christ's sake; we all know this fear—it is a part of the flesh in us, this desire for ease. It is often, I believe, a lack of trust in God arising from the flesh.

But let me sum up like this: the world—and I think perhaps this is the best way of all to consider it—the world is everything outside me and within me and everywhere else that is doing its utmost to prevent me from conforming to the picture I find of the Christian in the Beatitudes in Matthew.

'Blessed are the poor in spirit'—the world will do its utmost to prevent your being poor in spirit by its praise, by its admiration, by suggesting to you how wonderful you are!

'Blessed are they that mourn'—the world will prevent your mourning because of your sin; it will laugh at you and say, 'Cheer up, all is well!' There is nothing the world hates so much as men and women who are prostrate before God because of their sinfulness and their unregenerate heart.

The Beatitudes are a description of what Christians are meant to be, and the world is doing everything it can to try to stop us, and it does this in the most subtle manner conceivable. It does it, as we have seen, in its suggestions to us. It is all opposed to this poverty of spirit that is the first condition, according to Christ Himself, and that is the high road that leads us to God and to fellowship with Him. The world is everything that is opposed to the message of the Beatitudes.

So the first principle is that it is the world that makes the commandments grievous. It is because we are fighting all that without and within that the commandments seem to be hard and heavy. Now the second principle involves the *relationship of the Christian to the world*, and the truth is that Christians do not conform to it; they have been commanded to be transformed and to be different. Christians not only do not conform to it, but they do not live as near to it as they can. That is the horrible temptation of sin. 'Well,' one might say, 'of course I don't want to be in this world; I want to be a Christian. So I will sit as near as I can to the border.' But that is not the Christian; the Christian does not just manage somehow or another not to go down. No; 'this is the victory that *overcometh* the world.' 'Whatsoever is born of God *overcometh* the world.' John uses that term three times in these two verses.

John means by that that the Christian is one who conquers the world, who masters it. He actually says a most extraordinary thing here, and for once I have to grant that the Revised Version is superior to the Authorised! The Authorised reads like this: 'And this is the victory that overcometh the world, even our faith.' But the Revised has, 'This is the victory that has overcome . . .'; it has already happened. Now John is saying two things here that at first sight, as so often with John, appear to be contradictory. He says that the Christian is one who has overcome the world and also that the Christian is one who overcomes the world. Christian people, John tells us, are men and women who are in an entirely new position with regard to this matter. They are not like the non-Christian, whom we have already been describing; Christians are in this new position because of their faith. They have come to see the real meaning of the world; they have come to see what it is, and they hate it. They know that the world has already been conquered by the Lord Jesus Christ, and they know that they themselves are in Christ; therefore, there is a sense in which the Christian has overcome the world. Christ has overcome it, and I am in Christ, and therefore I have overcome it.

And yet there is a sense in which I am still overcoming it; I am already victorious, but I still have to fight. The New Testament is very fond of saying that. 'But of him are ye in Christ Jesus,' says Paul, 'who of God is made unto us wisdom, and righteousness, and sanctification, and redemption' (1 Cor 1:30-31). He is already that to us; so there is a sense in which I am already sanctified, already glorified. Read the eighth chapter of Romans and you will find that Paul tells us that explicitly (vv 29-30); in Christ Jesus we are already complete, it has all happened. And yet I am also still being sanctified, and I am still on the way to glorification.

I wonder whether an illustration will help at this point. I am trying to say how at one and the same time it can be said that as Christians we have overcome *and* we are overcoming. Think of it in terms of the Battle of Quebec. General Wolfe conquered the French general Montcalm on the Heights of Abraham, and as the result of that battle Canada was conquered. And yet we read in our history books that the fight for possessing Canada went on for some seventy or eighty more years. That is it; the country was captured, and then captured in detail. Now the position of Christian men and women is something like that in this world. They are no longer under the dominion of Satan; they have been taken out of his kingdom, but that does not mean that they have finished with Satan.

Or look at it like this—think of it in terms of two big estates with a road going down between. On one side of the road there is one estate, and on the other side there is another; one of them is the kingdom of Satan, and the other is the kingdom of God. Now, this is what has happened to Christian men and women: they were in the estate under the dominion of Satan, but they have crossed over the road and are now in the kingdom of God. But though they are in this life and world, working in that new estate, the kingdom of God, Satan, their old enemy, is still there in that other kingdom, and he thinks that Christians will be foolish enough to listen to him. He forgets that they have been once and for ever taken out of his dominion; he forgets that they are free. So Christians do not come under his dominion, but they are still subject to his attacks and onslaughts and his suggestions and insinuations. They have overcome, but they are still fighting; they still have to overcome as they go on in this life walking with God and with Christ, walking in fellowship. They are overcoming increasingly; they no longer fall to the temptations that used to get them so easily, and thus they are no longer mastered by them.

But even further, those who are truly Christians are in the position of being able to say quite honestly that they do not want to sin. They do not want to, but still they do it; some things that remain in them from that old life still, as it were, get them down. This is what the Bible calls the flesh, the remains of the old man, and Christians hate it. They have overcome in that sense. They have got the victory, and yet they are not perfect; they have not arrived at sinless perfection. They are still tempted, and they still at times feel discouraged and almost defeated. And yet and yet . . . ! If they are true Christians, they know that they have the victory. They know that the crowning day is coming; they know that the day will dawn when they will be actually, in their walk, faultless and blameless and without spot, without rebuke, when they will be presented by their Lord and Saviour faultless before the presence of God's glory with exceeding joy.

4

FAITH IN CHRIST

For whatsoever is born of God overcometh the world: and this is the victory that overcometh the world, even our faith. Who is he that overcometh the world, but he that believeth that Jesus is the Son of God?

1 JOHN 5:4-5

IN OUR CONSIDERATION OF these verses, we have arrived at this position. There is a worldly mind and outlook and spirit with which we are all afflicted by nature, and as long as we are governed by that, the holy way of God is against us; we are opposed to it, and we find it grievous. But according to John, what makes us Christian is that the whole situation is transformed. Christians are those who overcome the world; they have overcome it in a sense already and are overcoming it, and we have emphasised that. But at the end there still remained this question for us to consider, as to how it is that the Christian is enabled to overcome. Now the Apostle is very careful to tell us this, and here again we find how practical he is in his exhortations and in all his writings. He does not merely tell us that we overcome—he explains to us how we do so, and that makes our victory still more sure.

This is a very great question. There is a sense in which it may be said that the whole long history of the Christian Church is nothing but the story and the history of two great rival views with regard to it. This whole problem of overcoming the world is a theme that has often been handled in the Church throughout the centuries, for anyone who is a Christian in any sense of the term must realise that there is this conflict.

People who have no sense of conflict at all in their lives are patently just not Christians; they are in the sleep of death spiritually. The moment men and women become alive spiritually, they are aware of these forces and powers, and at once they are aware of a conflict. Those who do not realise that they are living in a world that is inimical to everything they hold to be true are not merely novices in these matters—I question whether they are in them at all. 'We wrestle not against flesh and blood,' says the Apostle Paul, and we cannot remind ourselves too often of this verse, 'but against principalities, against powers, against the rulers of the darkness of this world, against spiritual wickedness in high places' (Eph 6:12). That is it!

This, therefore, has been the great question: how is this world to be fought and to be conquered? Now, there have only been two main views with regard to this question, and we can classify them like this: there is what we may call the Catholic, or if you prefer it, the monastic view of this matter, and there is the evangelical view. I think that all the other views can be brought under one or the other of these two main headings. The Church has almost invariably been divided into one of these two groups. Let me say regarding the monastic or Catholic view, before I come to criticise it, that whatever we may say against monasticism, it at any rate has seen very clearly that the world is something that has to be fought. So there is a sense in which I would almost say that I would sooner have a monk or an anchorite who is separating himself from the world and dwelling in a cave or a hilltop because he realises he is in the fight of faith than a smug, glib, self-satisfied individual who has never realised there is a fight to be fought.

So let us look briefly at these two views. We shall favor the evangelical view, as I want to show you in these two verses of the Apostle John; but let us look at it by way of contrast with this other view. The essence of the monastic or Catholic view of fighting the world is this: it believes in withdrawing from the world, but it also emphasises the exercise of willpower and the observance of a number of rules and regulations. The world, they say, is so active, so much with us—it is so insinuating—that the only thing to do is to come out of it, to withdraw from it. That is the essence of monasticism.

There are, therefore, those who have so felt the power of this teaching that they have not hesitated to leave their homes and their various professions and callings and businesses and have gone to places apart from the world. They have deliberately, in a physical sense, tried to go out of the world and have given themselves exclusively to what they call 'the religious life.' They have spent their time in meditation, in prayer, and in thought, and invariably they have prescribed for themselves, or have had prescribed for them, various rules and orders. They have believed in fasting, in the literal sense, twice a week, sometimes more; they have their times and seasons, such as Lent, when they deny themselves and the flesh and the body in various respects. So that is what is meant by this monastic view; you must go out of the world, and by means of rigorous discipline and practices in various respects, you thus attempt to fight and to overcome that world that is doing its utmost to destroy your soul and to stand between you and God.

What, then, have we to say to that view? Well, there are three main things. There has always seemed to me to be one difficulty about it that is more than sufficient to put it out of court, and that is that it is clearly something that all cannot do. There is a sense in which you have to be a very special kind of person before you can practise that kind of life; so it seems to me to fail at that point because it gives the average and ordinary Christian no hope. Now, the way in which they overcome that difficulty is to divide Christians into two groups: those who have to remain in the world, in business or occupation—the ordinary; and the extraordinary, who have taken up the religious life as a vocation and make it a full-time matter. And their teaching, of course, is that those 'religious' people, as they call them, not only acquire sufficient merit for themselves—they also acquire a superabundance of merit. Therefore, they pray to them as saints and ask them for supererogation in order to make up for their own deficiency.

Now I think that by that teaching they are virtually granting that there is something essentially wrong about their whole concept of overcoming the world. It is only for certain select persons, it is not something that the average Christian can practise, and therefore it seems to me it is utterly unscriptural, for there is no such division and distinction between Christians in the New Testament. The Apostles put themselves in with everybody else; these things are preached to all Christians, and not only to a select few.

But there is something else that is equally marked, and here we must see where this view is so superficial. The tragedy with this view, as I see it, is that it forgets entirely that the world is not only outside me, but inside me. We were at pains to emphasise that earlier when we saw that the world is not only outside us with its sin and temptations and attractions, but it is also inside us—the flesh, our own unregenerate nature. So in a sense, it is almost childish to think that I can overcome the world by taking myself out of it, because when I have gone into my cell the world is still within me; so my attempt to escape by physical means is almost doomed to failure. This is something that we all must know from experience. We have all been alone, we have all been isolated at certain times; the world has not been there to tempt us. But was all well with us? Were we perfectly happy; were we free from temptation; was the mind and the outlook and the spirit of the world entirely absent? God knows that such is not the case!

Let me give you a story to illustrate this. I was reading of a saint who lived in Scotland some 250 years ago. He was a farmer, and this man, as the result of a sermon preached one Sunday, had felt very definitely and acutely that he must conquer the self within him. This became such a burden to him that he decided he would spend a whole day alone on the top of a mountain near his house in fasting and prayer in order that once and for ever he might deal with this fiend, this self. So he went up to the top of the mountain, and he spent the day there in struggle, in anguish, and in prayer pleading with God to rid him of this foul thing.

Then towards the afternoon and early evening, at last he felt he had obtained his victory—he felt he had been delivered completely. God seemed to have delivered him from self, and he was filled with a spirit of joy and elation. So he spent some further time in rejoicing and praising God. But then he began to descend the mountain and to go home for the evening, and just as he was coming to the foot of the mountain he saw some of his neighbours just finishing the day's work of carting in the hay. And as he looked at these people who had thus been toiling wearily throughout the day, he found himself saying to himself, 'How much better have I spent the day than they have been doing! While they have been attending to these material, mechanical, earthly things, I have been giving my attention to the soul!' In other words, he found in that moment that the enemy he thought he had finished with once and for ever on the top of the mountain was still inside him.

You can go away and spend your day on the top of a mountain, but you cannot get away from the world; it is in you, so that any retirement to a monastery, or becoming an anchorite or a hermit, is doomed to failure. That is the whole story of Martin Luther; look at that excellent monk in his cell—fasting, sweating, praying; out of the world in a sense, and yet finding that the world was in him and he could get no peace. Therefore, withdrawal from the world and from society does not get rid of the world in the New Testament sense of the term.

In other words, and this is my third objection to it, the monastic view is thoroughly unscriptural; there is no such teaching to be found in the New Testament, and especially when you look at the life of our Lord Himself. Here was one who had overcome the world, and yet, you observe, He did not do so by segregating Himself from the world. He was in the world, and He mixed with the common people; indeed, He was misunderstood because of that. The Pharisees looked at Him and said, 'He cannot be a prophet—He is the friend of publicans and sinners; He does not segregate Himself.' There we see, once and for all, not only in our Lord's teaching and the teaching of the whole of the New Testament, but in His example also, that the way to overcome the world is not just mechanical; it is not a question of withdrawal.

So having glanced briefly at the monastic or Catholic view, let us now contrast it with what I have described as the evangelical view, which, I claim, we are entitled to call the biblical view. How do Christians arrive at the position in which they overcome the world? Well, as I see it here, the Apostle says there are two main things in answer to this question. The first is that they do so because of what has happened to them, because of what is true of them as Christians. And the second is that they do so because of what their faith in Christ enables them to do.

Now let us look at that first principle. Christians, we have seen, are those who overcome; there is a sense in which they have already overcome, and they are still overcoming. But how do they do it? Well, there is nothing here that tells them they have taken up the religious life, so-called, as a vocation; there is nothing about going behind a wall and then putting regulations and rules on the wall and keeping them day by day. Nothing of the kind! First and foremost we are told of certain things that are true of us as Christians; something has happened to us, and it is because of this that we can thus overcome.

What are these things? First, Christians overcome the world because they are born, or begotten, of God: 'Whatsoever is born of God overcometh the world.' Now once more I would call your attention to the order in which the Apostle puts these things. He puts first the new birth; then second, and only second, faith; and thirdly, a particular faith in the Lord Jesus Christ and our relationship to Him. These are points of interest theologically; they are not vital to salvation, but if we want our minds to be clear, we must observe the Apostle's order.

Now, if we are begotten of God this, of course, means that we start with a new disposition, a new outlook, and there you see the fundamental distinction between the Catholic and the evangelical view of this question. Because the Catholic view fails to emphasise this rebirth and regeneration as it should, it has to take us out of the world mechanically and has to impose its list of rules and regulations. But the evangelical view comes and tells us, 'You need not come out of the world; what you need is a new view of it; what you need is new outlook upon it.' It is, in other words, something like this: the whole trouble, says the New Testament, is not so much the world itself as the spirit that is in you and the view you take. I remember once reading a phrase that can be applied to this point: it is not life that matters, but the courage that we bring to it. Now, I am not interested in the courage, but I am interested in the outlook; it is not the world really that accounts for our failure—it is ourselves.

Is this not obvious the moment you begin to think of it? Look at two men walking down the street. One is a saint, the other is a worldling— and what a vital contrast between the two men! There is one sense in which the two men are absolutely different, and yet they are living in exactly the same world, the same surroundings, the same sin, the same temptations, the same everything. So what is the difference? The difference is in the men and not in the world.

> Two men looked out through prison bars.
> The one saw mud and the other stars.

Two men in the same prison look out through the same bars on the same world and see two entirely different things. 'Beauty is in the eye of the beholder'; it is not the world that matters—it is the way in which we look at it.

Now, that is the vital teaching of the New Testament; it is the essence of the evangelical position. It involves being able to look at the world as the Lord Jesus Christ looked at it, and that is the whole meaning of being born again. That is the essence of this doctrine—it is the teaching with regard to the rebirth. We have become, as Peter puts it, 'partakers of the divine nature' (2 Pet 1:4); we have received the disposition of God Himself. We look at things from the Godward angle rather than from the human and carnal and sinful one. What a wonderful doctrine this is, and how it shows the foolishness of that rival view! Where I am, exactly where I am without moving an inch, my whole outlook can be different. Therein I see a hope that puts me right; it puts me right essentially, internally, so that in spite of the world, which remains the same, I am a different person in that world, and I am now in a position to overcome it. That is the first principle.

The second principle is that as a Christian, because of what has happened to me, I am able to exercise faith and to live by faith. Here is the second step. First you see 'Whatsoever is born of God overcometh the world,' and then 'This is the victory that overcometh the world, even our faith.' In other words, my rebirth gives me this faculty of faith and enables me to exercise faith and to live by it. Let me put it in this practical form: the world that I am fighting is very powerful; it is much more powerful than any one of us. The world conquers and masters everyone who is born into it, for indeed we have been born in sin and shapen in iniquity (Psa 51:5); the world is in us the moment we begin to live. Read your Old Testament; look at those great heroes of the faith, the patriarchs, the godly kings and the prophets—they all were conquered by the world, they all failed. 'There is none righteous, no, not one' (Rom 3:10); the whole world is guilty before God (Rom 3:19); and, therefore, if I am to conquer and overcome that world, I need something that will enable me to do so. It is no use trying to fight the world immediately—that cannot be done. Monasticism recognises that and says, 'Run away from it.'

So what do I need? I need emancipation; I need to be lifted to another realm; I need a force and a strength and a power that I have not got myself. That is my need, and here is the answer: I am given a faith—I am given an outlook and understanding—I am introduced to a source of power—I see something that that other person has never seen. I see beyond. I see a might and a power that is even greater than all that is opposed to me. Now that again, you will agree, is the essence of the New Testament teaching. Christians are men and women who have been introduced to another realm. There is another dimension in their lives; there is a power in them and available to them that they had never known before and that no one who is outside of Christ can possibly know. So here are people who have this new nature and outlook, this new disposition and understanding. And that, in turn, is something that enables them to be linked to that other realm.

But let me put it still more specifically, for John goes on to a third step: 'Who is he,' he says, 'that overcometh the world, but he that believeth that Jesus is the Son of God?' That is it—that is everything. The thing, in other words, that makes Christian men and women overcome the world, and enables them to do so, and to do so increasingly, is their relationship to the Lord Jesus Christ, to His work and what He has accomplished and already finished. That is the whole of the evangelical position with regard to this matter. It is not just carrying out a number of rules, nor is it willpower; it is none of these things. We find Paul denouncing this in Colossians 2, where he is dealing with exactly the same idea, this monastic idea. In those New Testament times there were people observing their holy days, and they were doing this, that, and the other. 'It is of no avail,' says Paul, 'it is all of the flesh; it is the old and not the new.'

And in that entire chapter the Apostle's argument is that all that kind of thing is not only wrong but unnecessary; and it is unnecessary because everything we need is in the Lord Jesus Christ—'in him dwelleth all the fulness of the Godhead bodily.' In Him we are 'complete.' 'He is the Head,' says Paul in effect, 'and everything comes out of Him. There is no need for your philosophies or your false asceticisms. There is no need for this mutilation of the body, nor for these mechanical attempts to conquer the world; it is unnecessary. Everything you need is in Christ.' And John is here simply saying exactly that. He puts it in the form of a question: 'Who is he that overcometh the world?' 'Well,' he says, 'he is the man who believes that Jesus is the Son of God; he has seen who Christ is and what He has done, and he is drawing on that perfect, finished work.'

But let me end by putting it again in the memorable phrase of the Apostle Paul. He tells us, 'I live; yet not I, but Christ liveth in me: and the life which I now live in the flesh I live by the faith of the Son of God' (Gal 2:20)—by this faith in the Son of God, by this relationship to Him 'who loved me, and gave himself for me.'

That is the principle that we have to grasp. We shall work out those principles in still further and greater detail, but the vital thing for us is this matter of our relationship to Christ. If I am not in that right relationship, then nothing else can happen; but if I am in the right relationship, then, says the Apostle, everything can happen. Because if I am rightly related to Him, I shall draw from Him; and what makes me rightly related to Him is that I am born again. It is only as I receive this new life, this new birth, that I am able to recognise Him, that I am able to believe in Him, that I am able to exercise faith in Him, that I am able to rest on Him and receive and draw of His fulness. It is this matter of the new birth that relates me to Him, for I am born of Him and I receive of His nature.

So then, that is the principle in which we stand as Evangelicals. I need not try to run out of this world; I need not spend the whole of my life doing things and trying to mortify my flesh. I need not go out of my business or profession, or retire from the world into some cell; I need not conform to mechanical rules that appear to give me temporary satisfaction. No; the essential thing is that my whole outlook upon this world should be different, not only at certain times and seasons, but always; not only on a Sunday, but every day. I, having a new mind and disposition, a new outlook, have seen the world for what is it.

But thank God, I have also seen much more. I have seen the life that is in Christ and the life that is possible to me in Him. I am related to Him; I live by faith in Him and draw from Him the power that is more than sufficient to master and to conquer this world both without and within, everything that is opposed to the highest interest of my soul. Thank God that whether I am in the midst of life, at home or on the street or at work, wherever I am, whatever may be opposed to me with circumstances all against me—in spite of all that, because of what is within me, I can triumph and I can prevail. 'Whatsoever is born of God overcometh the world.'

5

How Faith Overcomes

*For whatsoever is born of God overcometh the world: and
this is the victory that overcometh the world, even our
faith. Who is he that overcometh the world, but he that
believeth that Jesus is the Son of God?*

1 JOHN 5:4-5

WE HAVE SEEN THAT what really makes it possible to overcome the
world is the fact that because we are born again we are vitally and intimately connected to the Lord Jesus Christ. It is our relationship to Him
that enables us to overcome; and we can sum it up by saying that it is
indeed our faith in Christ that makes victory over the world a practical,
actual possibility. So what we must do now is to work out in detail how
this relationship of the Christian to Jesus Christ works out in practice;
how is it that this faith of ours in the Lord Jesus Christ, this belief that
He is the Son of God and all the consequences that follow from that
belief, enables us thus in practice to overcome the world.

Now this is very important in the Christian life. It is the whole secret
of successful living; it is the whole secret of joy.

So we must consider it, and the best way of dividing up this subject
is to divide it into two main headings. This faith of ours that enables us
to overcome the world does so directly and also indirectly—or if you
prefer, in a passive manner and in an active manner. Or to put it in still
another way, we can say that it does so by the exercise of naked faith
and also by meditation upon and working out, even intellectually or in

the understanding, the meaning and the implications of faith. Let us, then, look at these two.

First of all, faith enables us to have a victory over the world and to overcome it directly—passively—by the resting of a naked faith upon the Lord Jesus Christ. I start with that because I am indeed increasingly convinced that it is the greatest lesson that as Christian people we can ever learn in this world. It is the possibility of directly and immediately and passively resting upon the power and the ability of our risen Lord. 'This is the victory that overcometh the world, even our faith'—my faith in Him, my belief in Him, that He is the Son of God. The result of that is that I go to Him and rest upon Him.

This is something that you will find enunciated everywhere in the Bible. Let me give you just one quotation that will illustrate it perfectly and represent all others: 'The name of the Lord is a strong tower; the righteous runneth into it and is safe' (Prov 18:10). That is it! Read the various Psalms, too, and see how those godly men of old were struggling against the world and its temptations and insinuations, and they will all tell you that that was the only thing they could do. They did not attempt to battle. They saw that the forces were too great for them. They might have failed, but they said, 'There is only one thing to do; I will run into the tower, and there in the tower I am safe.'

Or if you like it in New Testament form, it is the doctrine of the vine and the branches, as seen in the statement of our Lord: 'Without me ye can do nothing' (John 15:5). It is put positively by the Apostle Paul: 'I can do all things through Christ which strengtheneth me' (Phil 4:13); and, 'nevertheless I live; yet not I, but Christ liveth in me' (Gal 2:20). All those phrases are merely expressions of this first and all-important way of obtaining the victory that overcomes the world through faith in Christ. It means, in other words, turning to Christ, flying to Him—hiding in Him, looking to Him in a literal sense for protection, defence, and deliverance—relying utterly upon Him.

This is what I would call the simplicity of faith, and yet it is one of the most difficult lessons to learn. Most of our defeats, I think, are due to the fact that we parley with sin, we attempt to fight it. Now there is a sense in which we have to do that, and that will be my second heading when we come to deal with faith indirectly. But what I am concerned to emphasise here is that before you attempt to do the second you must do the first. There are times in our experience when, for reasons often beyond our own control, unless we run to Christ and hide in Him we are certain to be defeated. But thank God, the possibility that is held up before us is that we can go to Him directly, immediately and look to Him. This is what I might call 'the great strategy of faith'; we need to know when to do that and to realise that is something always open and possible to us.

So the rest of faith, in a sense, means just this, that there are times when we do not even attempt to fight this battle against sin and must simply look to Christ. Perhaps an illustration will make my point clear. I once read a little pamphlet that was very simple but that, it seemed to me, shared the whole essence of this particular aspect of the doctrine. It was the story of a Christian in South Africa, travelling out in the country, and he came to an agricultural community. Owing to certain floods in the country, he had to stay where there was a kind of saloon or public house. He was amazed and saddened at the sight of the farmers, many of whom, he noticed, came there and spent in a few days all the money that they had been able to earn and save as the result of their hard work through the year. They had a powerful craving for drink that they could not conquer.

He was especially attracted to one poor man who seemed to be a particular victim to this terrible affliction, and he began to talk to him. First of all he began to reason with him, pointing out the suffering that his wife and children had to endure. The poor man admitted it all and told the story of how he had been almost unconsciously led into it and found himself a helpless slave to drink before realising that anything had happened—how he would give the whole world if he could stop it, but he was now a victim of it. Then this Christian went on to tell him about faith, the possibility of overcoming, and told him about the Lord Jesus Christ who had come into this world to save us. He told him that if only he looked to Christ and relied upon Him, he would be enabled to overcome this thing, and the man was given faith to believe that. He was a simple, illiterate man, and all he was anxious to do was to find the name of this person about whom this Christian was speaking, and he was told the name was Jesus.

The story went on to say how that poor man went away and, having worked again, came back to this same place to sell his grain. There again the tempters came, but he did not go with them, and his own wife and children were amazed. This Christian visitor came back in a year or so to find the man entirely changed. He began talking to him and asked him how it had happened. And the man's simple testimony was this: 'I went back the first time, and my friends came and tempted me, and I felt weak. But suddenly I remembered the name—Jesus. I could do nothing but keep on saying to myself, "Jesus"; I cried to Jesus to do what you told me He would do.' His faith was as simple as that, but it was enough, and he overcame; he did not go back, he was emancipated.

That is what I mean when I talk about this direct faith; it is simply resting upon Christ, and I have to do that. That is 'becoming as a little child,' realising our utter weakness and helplessness and hopelessness. And when the fight is yet strong and the enemy is there and we feel we are on the point of falling, we must simply cry, 'Jesus' and believe and know that He is looking on and that He is there and is ready to deliver us and protect us. 'The name of the Lord is a strong tower, the righteous runneth into it and is safe.'

There are times in Christian experience when that is the only thing to do. You just realise that the Lord is there. You just sing or say the hymn:

> *I need Thee every hour;*
> *Stay thou near by;*
> *Temptations lose their power*
> *When Thou art nigh.*
>
> ANNIE SHERWOOD HAWKS

And then we must just realise by faith that He is there, ever at hand, mighty to save. As little children, we look to Him; we abandon ourselves to Him. We do not look at the enemy; we simply look to Him and rely upon Him. We fly into His almighty arms, and as certainly as we do so, He will protect us, He will save us, He will deliver us with 'the peace of God, which passeth all understanding' (Phil 4:7), He will garrison and hold us.

In a sense that is the great story of every Christian confessor and saint throughout the centuries. What hope, do you think, is there for those to whom the gospel is preached who may never have had any education and who may be victims of subtle temptations of the flesh and of the mind? How are these people to emancipate themselves? What is the use of preaching moral uplift under such conditions? There is only one answer as to the way in which men and women can be changed; it is the power of this risen living Christ to deliver them in their utter hopelessness and helplessness. Whosoever looks to Him will be delivered.

That therefore is the victory that overcomes the world in that passive sense—just simple, utter reliance, in our weakness, upon Him, upon the power of His might. There is a great hymn by Lavacer which expresses it all perfectly. Read something about him, that Swiss Christian man of the last century. He had proved in experience everything he wrote in that hymn, and I urge, in the hour of temptation when the enemy is powerful and strong, that we just repeat it:

> *O Jesus Christ, grow Thou in me*
> *And all things else recede.*
> *Each day let Thy supporting might*
> *My weakness still embrace.*

That is it.

> *Let faith in Thee and in Thy might*
> *My every motive move.*

Victory is only in Him, in His might, and not in myself; this comes with the realisation of my own weakness and the realisation of His almighty power, and simply abandoning myself to Him. Let me say it again: 'the name of the Lord is a strong tower'; the righteous runs into it when the enemy is after him, and he is 'safe.' The enemy cannot enter; the Lord will protect him.

My second division is the indirect or what I have described alternatively as *active*, and which I have also described as the working out of this faith. This is something that is again of tremendous importance, as long as we put it in the second place. It is here I see the glorious nature of our Christian position. In our utter helplessness, when we seem to be incapable of rising or going on, when we see this powerful enemy coming and feel that we are on the point of sinking, we flee. But it is not always like that, thank God! As one goes on in the Christian life, one ought to be working out this indirect method. This is the activity of faith, the thinking out of the Christian gospel and of what faith in Christ really means. It means to understand what we really mean when we say that 'Jesus is the Son of God.' It means working out the implication of that in terms of this fight of ours against the world and the flesh and the devil, and I suggest that this working out means something like this:

First of all, as I look at the Lord Jesus Christ in terms of this fight against the world, I ask this question: why did He ever come into this world? You see I am now working out my faith in Christ. I believe that the person, Jesus of Nazareth, about whom I read in the Gospels, is the Son of God. Very well, I ask immediately, why did the Son of God ever take upon Himself the likeness of sinful flesh and live as man, as He indeed did? What is the meaning of it all? And there is only one answer to that question. It was because of the power of sin, the power of Satan, the power of evil. There is no other explanation. The Son of God came because He was the only way in which we could be delivered from the world.

In other words, it is the doctrine of sin again, the power of Satan and sin and evil. He came into this world because the world was dominated by sin, and it is only as I believe that 'Jesus is the Son of God' that I begin to understand the nature of the fight in which I am engaged. People are optimistic about this world, and they are so because they have never understood the nature of sin. But if you believe that Jesus is the Son of God, you have to believe that the power of sin and evil and Satan is so tremendous that man had failed and the Son of God had to come.

Do you see, then, how this enables us to overcome the world? How can I overcome the world unless I have seen the nature of the problem? But the moment I have faith in Christ, I begin to understand it, for it is only the Christian who can see through this world. Everybody else is dominated by the world—governed by it. Do you not see it around and about you? Look at the newspapers and you will see it. People think that life is wonderful and that the world is a marvellous place. They have never seen through it; they are entirely deluded by its so-called glittering prizes. How they vie with one another in their so-called enjoyments and in their efforts to gain certain positions; oh, the excitement of it all! What is the matter with them? Ah, the tragedy is that they have never seen through it; they are just duped by it. But the moment I become a Christian I see through the world.

This is tremendously significant and is of great practical importance for the Christian. Let me put it in this form to call your attention to it: I would say, for an example, that by definition Christians must never become too excited about politics,[1] and for this reason, that they know perfectly well that there is no solution to the ultimate problem of mankind in politics. So people who believe that, as a result of a win for one party rather than another at an election everything is going to be fundamentally different—those people are either not Christians or else they are very ignorant ones. No; nothing that can happen at an election will touch this problem. The parties are all equally in sin; they are all under the domination of sin.

Now, Christians should be concerned about these things; they have a duty as citizens, and let them exercise it. But if they become excited, if they believe that one rather than the other is going to make the vital difference, they have never seen the truth about the world. Men and women who believe that 'Jesus is the Son of God' have seen through the world; they know that no Acts of Parliament can solve the problem of mankind. They look on, therefore, objectively. There is a detachment about them; they are looking at it from the outside. They do not pin their faith upon it, for they see beyond it. They see the fate of all those who are dominated by the world; they know that all who belong to the world, in this New Testament sense, are going to perdition and damnation. They see through it all, and they know that none but Christ can deliver them from it. That is the first thing.

Secondly, the men and women who believe that 'Jesus is the Son of God' look at the New Testament records, and there they see this Jesus of Nazareth, and they see Him overcoming the world. They see Him tempted by Satan and conquering him; they see Satan giving up; they see one who at last can take the strong man armed and take his goods from him. They look at this perfect life in which there was no blot or blemish; they see Him literally meeting hell at its worst in mortal combat and overcoming it. What a difference this makes! They have read the Old Testament also and have seen that everybody had been defeated by Satan—not a single person had conquered. But at last here is one who conquers Satan, and they see Him conquering in His life, in His death, and in His glorious resurrection. They see in the resurrection that even the last enemy has been conquered; the last thing that Satan could do to bind men and women and hold them has been utterly defeated. So here again is something that enables me to overcome. As I attempt to face the problems of life and to overcome the world, I am aware of my own weakness and all those forces that are against me. But my outlook is immediately changed when I look at Christ and see that He has overcome it.

But the next step is this: by faith I see myself belonging to Christ. I am 'in Christ'—that is the New Testament phrase. As the branch is in the vine, so I am in Christ. I belong; I am a part of Him. I am incorporated in Him. And, of course, if that is true, I am a sharer in everything that belongs to Him; I am already a sharer in His victory. We are told here by John, as we have seen, that the Christian has already overcome, in a sense: 'Whatsoever is born of God *has overcome* the world.' I have done so in Christ. He has overcome, I am in Him, and therefore I have overcome; and at once, again, my whole attitude towards the fight is changed.

But that works out a little more practically in this way, in that it enables me to see that I can literally draw strength and power from Him and from His fulness. John in his Gospel says, 'And of His fulness have all we received, and grace for [or upon] grace' (John 1:16). I have illimitable resources behind me; I have a source of supply that can never fail. 'He that cometh to me shall never hunger; and he that believeth on me shall never thirst' (John 6:35). These are absolutes; there is literally no limit to the power of Christ. In Him are treasured all the resources of the Godhead; 'in him dwelleth all the fulness of the Godhead bodily' (Col 2:9). I am in Him, and I can therefore draw upon Him; I care not what forces are against me when I remember this power that is behind me and within me.

But let me go still another step to show you how practical this is— I am still working out this faith. There are times when I fail because in my folly I do not run into the strong tower, because I try to fight in my own strength, and the enemy defeats me. There are times when I go down. Now this is most important. At that particular point there is nothing that is so liable to happen to me as that the enemy will come and say something like this to me: 'Ah, well, you have failed—you have fallen. You have sinned against the Lord. You have gone back. What is the use of talking about your faith—look at yourself!' And there I am, over-whelmed with a sense of failure and frustration, and I wonder whether I have a right to turn to God and to pray. I have let myself down, I have let God down, I have let Christ down; and I feel utterly hopeless with a sense of despair and futility.

Now there is nothing more precious at that point than to know that Jesus is the Son of God and that He tells me that though I have sinned, though I have failed, as we have already found it in this epistle,[2] 'If we confess our sins, he is faithful and just to forgive us our sins, and to cleanse us from all unrighteousness' (1:9). 'My little children, these things write I unto you, that ye sin not. And if any man sin, we have an advocate with the Father, Jesus Christ the righteous: and he is the propitiation for our sins: and not for yours only, but also for the sins of the whole world' (2:1-2). There is nothing, then, that so enables me to overcome as that deliverance from sins and failure, from that sense of despair that tends to overwhelm me when I feel I have gone down and cannot rise again. The blood of Christ will cleanse me, and I rise up and go forward on my journey.

But, lastly, faith enables me to see the ultimate glory and perfection that await me. The fight in this world often seems long and endless, and we tend to become tired and weary. There is nothing that so encourages me as to realise that the day is certainly coming when I shall be ultimately glorified and perfect, without spot or wrinkle or blemish; when Christ, who has died for me and sustained me, will present me faultless before the presence of the glory of God with exceeding joy. Does that not help you to fight? Does it not help you to know that the victory is secure, that the crowning day is coming, that you shall see Him as He is and be delivered entirely from everything that could hold you down? This is a vision by faith of the ultimate glory that awaits us, the coming again of the Son of God, 'who shall change our vile body, that it may be fashioned like unto his glorious body, according to the working whereby he is able even to subdue all things unto himself' (Phil 3:21).

So let me sum it all up by putting it like this: this is how faith overcomes—I fly to Christ in utter helplessness, but I also work faith out. I reason out the implication of believing that 'Jesus is the Son of God'; and fortified by all these things, I overcome and am enabled to overcome. I triumph, and I find that the commandments of God are no longer 'grievous.'

I end with a simple question: are you overcoming; or are you weary of the fight? The Christian is one, according to the New Testament, who does overcome. If I cannot say, therefore, that I am overcoming the world in these various ways, I had better examine the very foundation of my position once more. 'Whatsoever is born of God overcometh the world: and this is the victory that overcometh the world, even our faith. Who is he that overcometh the world, but he that believeth that Jesus is the Son of God?'

6

THE GOD-MAN

This is he that came by water and blood, even Jesus
Christ; not by water only, but by water and blood. And it
is the Spirit that beareth witness, because the Spirit is
truth. For there are three that bear record in heaven, the
Father, the Word, and the Holy Ghost: and these three are
one. And there are three that bear witness in earth, the
spirit, and the water, and the blood: and these three agree
in one.

1 JOHN 5:6-8

HERE AGAIN WE COME TO one of those points of transition that, as I
have reminded you many times, is one of the characteristic features,
from the standpoint of literary structure and logical order of thought,
that characterised this Apostle. Indeed, we have already arrived at that
point of transition at the end of the fifth verse: 'Who is he that overcometh the world, but he that believeth that Jesus is the Son of God?'
Already you can see in one verse that John is leaving the particular subject of overcoming the world—which was a part of his consideration of
keeping the commandments—and has come to one of his other major
themes, namely, the correctness of doctrine with respect to the person
of our Lord and Saviour Jesus Christ.

Now we have seen that it is an essential part of John's method to
hold certain arguments constantly before us, and you remember we
pointed out how he does this in a kind of circular fashion. There are certain things, he says, that are essential to the Christian position, and we

must hold them and practise them all together and at the same time: love of God, keeping His commandments, love for the brethren, and a correct doctrine about the person of the Lord Jesus Christ. And we have seen how in the epistle, right away from the beginning to the point that we have now reached, he keeps on playing on these four points. Each one leads to the other, so that it does not matter with which one we start, we seem to arrive at all the others. And here is another illustration of that very thing. In dealing with the doctrine of the commandments and the keeping of the commandments, which he puts in terms of overcoming the world, he has arrived at this further doctrine of a correctness of view with regard to the person of Christ.

Obviously, this is something that is of central importance. If the whole basis of my victory and my overcoming the world is that I have faith in Christ and lean upon Him, and if am to I look to Him and rely upon Him, then it is important for me to know that I *can* rely upon Him. If I am going to risk the whole of my life and my whole outlook upon this particular reliance, then I must be absolutely certain about it. You must be sure of your foundation before you begin to erect your building; you must be right about first principles before you can put in the details. And that is how John quite naturally comes to verses 6, 7, and 8. He is talking about Jesus the Son of God; the one who 'came by water and blood, even Jesus Christ.' And now from verse 6 right until the end of verse 12 John is really concerned about this doctrine of the person of Christ. If I am in any doubt at all about Him, then of course there is no prospect whatsoever of my overcoming the world. I must be absolutely certain of this; I must be absolutely right about Him.

The whole of the Christian position rests entirely upon this doctrine. There is no such thing as Christianity apart from Him. To be a Christian does not only mean to believe in God. The orthodox Jew believes in God, and so do Mohammedans; and there are many others who believe in Him. The thing that makes Christians Christian is that they believe that Jesus is the Son of God. In this matter of their knowledge of God and their relationship to Him, they rest entirely upon the Lord Jesus Christ.

That is why we say that there must be absolute certainty at this point, because the New Testament does not offer us anything at all apart from Him. Indeed, I can say that about the whole Bible. The Old Testament saints were all looking forward to Him. Everything points to

Him; everything centres upon Him, so that there must be no querying and questioning. And John, teacher as he was, comes back to it once more. He has already dealt with it several times, but, you see, the man really knows himself and human nature as the result of sin. He knows that you have to go on saying these things because we are so prone to forget them and to slip or slide back into some wrong way of thinking. Heresies and errors came into the early church almost at once; how easy it would be to go astray! And John, knowing that he is an old man, says, 'I cannot take any risk about this. We must be certain as to this question, because without Him there is no hope whatsoever of overcoming the world.'

So this is the theme from verses 6 to 12; and as I understand it, he divides this up into three main divisions. First of all, you have in verses 6, 7 and 8 what I am describing as the testimony of Jesus Christ and His person. In verses 9 and 10 you have reasons given as to why we should accept the testimony. And in verses 11 and 12 we have the consequences of accepting the testimony—what happens to me as the result of so doing.

Let us, then, look at this first section: the testimony or the witness that is borne to the Lord Jesus Christ; how I may know that He really is one on whom I can rely. Now there can be no question at all but that these three verses are not only the most difficult verses in this epistle, but I think I am prepared to say that they are the three most difficult verses, in a sense, in the entire Bible! And anybody who has ever read commentaries and books that deal with this matter will agree with what I am saying, because the moment you look at them you are confronted by an initial difficulty. The sixth verse of the Authorised Version (King James Version) reads, 'This is he that came by water and blood, even Jesus Christ; not by water only, but by water and blood'; then verse 7 reads, 'For there are three that bear record in heaven, the Father, the Word, and the Holy Ghost: and these three are one.' That is not in the other versions. Verse 8 in the Authorised Version reads, 'And there are three that bear witness in earth, the spirit, and the water, and the blood: and these three agree in one.' The Revised and other versions read something like this for verses 7 and 8: 'For there are three that bear record, the Spirit and the water and the blood, and these three agree in one.' There is nothing in the Revised Version about the three that bear record in heaven and the three that bear record on earth; so at once, of course, we are confronted by a problem—why this difference?

In a sense this is just a question of mechanics, and yet in its way it is of some importance, and the answer is that this is purely a question of what is called textual criticism. I do not want to spend time on this, and yet I do believe that if we want to read the Bible intelligently we must know something about this. John wrote this epistle, but we do not actually possess a copy of what John himself wrote; the original manuscripts and documents are not in the possession of the Church. They were written, and then a number of copies were made of these various letters and books; but the original documents somehow or another disappeared. But there are large numbers of manuscripts extant that are copies in various languages of these original documents; you have them in Greek and Latin, in Coptic and in the Abyssinian language.

Those have been current and in existence, of course, for centuries. Now, the Authorised Version is a translation of a Greek text of the New Testament that dates from the twelfth century A.D. It was published by the great Erasmus in the sixteenth century, and it is virtually the text from which this Authorised Version was produced and translated in 1611. The Revised Version is a translation dating from about 1880. That translation was not new. By this time a great deal of research had been going on, and as a result of a lot of drafting, the schools were generally agreed that they now had what might be considered the text that approximated more nearly to the original lost documents. We need not go into this; it is purely a question of textual research. But the result was that a text was produced that is commonly known as the text of Westcott and Hort, and it was from them that the translation was made for the Revised Version. And thus you see there is a difference between the Revised and the Authorised with regard to these particular statements about the witness in heaven and the witness on earth.

But let me go still a step further with regard to that particular seventh verse. It is not to be found in any single Greek text of this epistle before the fourteenth century. It was a verse that gradually began to make its appearance in certain Latin versions, and eventually it got into this Greek text, which was first published by Erasmus. Interestingly enough, it was not in his first published text, but objections were made by certain elements of the Roman Church and they said they could produce it in the Greek text from the Latin translation. Now lest you may think I have become a higher critic, let me just say that there is a unanimity about this and a general consensus of opinion that this statement was put in by somebody and has thus found its way into the text and is indeed a spurious statement.

Now at this point I imagine someone saying, 'Surely by saying that, you have undermined my whole confidence in Scripture. If you take that verse out, isn't that equal to the so-called "higher criticism"?' So what is the difference between that which is called textual criticism and what has been given the name of higher criticism? Textual criticism means just this: it is the endeavour of scholars to find out, as far as is possible, the text that approximates most closely to the original document. So it is something in which we should all believe and something that we should encourage. And as you look at these various Greek, Latin, Syrian, Coptic, and Abyssinian texts and so on, you will find a slight variation here and there. But, and this is the point, the variations affect not a single doctrine. They are quite irrelevant. They make no difference to Christian truth; they are more a matter of detail—merely technical. Take, for instance, this particular verse that is verse 7 in the Authorised Version. It makes no difference whatsoever to Christian doctrine if that verse is omitted. The variations are not only slight—they are quite unimportant; and we are entitled to go further and say that the text, so-called, of Westcott and Hort we can undoubtedly take with confidence as being the original manuscripts and documents.

But higher criticism is something very different. The object with which the higher critic sets out is not to find what he can describe as that which approximates clearly to the original. He wants to know certain other things; he want to know what the book contains in a later edition, whether it is a composite work, whether the reputed author is the real author, when the book was first written, and so on. In other words, higher critics approach the Bible as if it were any other book. The man who is concerned about textual criticism starts by saying that it is the inspired Word of God; he is not concerned about pulling it to pieces. But the higher critics begin with certain ideas and propensities, and they make a criticism of this Book in terms of their idea; they place their literary and historical criticism over against the idea of divine inspiration. They do this with regard to the New and the Old Testaments. They say the books of Moses could not possibly have been written by Moses. Deuteronomy, they say, was written not many centuries before Christ came into the world. They say that we know about the history of the world, and they put up their theory of evolution—that men started by worshipping spirits in trees, and since then have gradually evolved from a belief in many gods to a belief in one God. They come to the Scriptures and analyse them in terms of their historical postulate. They believe their so-called historical canon and their literary and scientific canons and therefore they dismiss the miracles; they dismiss the history of the Old Testament, and they likewise dismiss the history of the New Testament.

Now can you see the difference between the two things? Textual criticism leaves the great doctrines exactly where they were; higher criticism is an attack ultimately not only upon the unique inspiration of the Bible but upon the cardinal doctrines and tenets of the Christian faith. It is men setting up their own ideas over and against this revelation. But textual criticism does nothing of the sort. Textual criticism is not concerned to analyse the books of the Bible; it is simply concerned to compare and contrast and collate various documents and manuscripts in order to try to arrive at the right text. It does not start with its ideas and impose this upon the Bible.

I have been led to emphasise all this in order that we may have clearly in our minds this whole question of the statement of the seventh verse. But now, having disposed of that, let us consider the claim that is made here. It is: 'This is he that came by water and blood, even Jesus Christ; not by water only, but by water and blood. And it is the Spirit that beareth witness, because the Spirit is truth. For there are three that bear record . . . the spirit, and the water, and the blood: and these three agree in one.'

Now I think that John means this: he is concerned about the person of the Lord, and he wants to give his readers evidence; he wants to produce witnesses who will not only confirm and substantiate their faith, but will also give them real confidence. The claim is, of course, the claim that he puts into words, and those words are, '*Jesus Christ.*' He has already said, 'He that believeth that Jesus is the Son of God'; here he says 'Jesus Christ.' On whom am I going to rely; on whom am I going to rest my faith? And the answer is: Jesus Christ—the God-Man.

In other words, this is another interesting way of stating the doctrine of the incarnation, and that is something which John has been doing from the very beginning. 'That which was from the beginning, which we have heard, which we have seen with our eyes, which we have looked upon, and our hands have handled, of the Word of life'—you remember that he started on that; everything depended upon Jesus

Christ, and here he comes back to it again. The whole doctrine rests, in a sense, upon this vital doctrine of the incarnation.

Who is Jesus of Nazareth? And the answer is, He is 'Jesus Christ.' He is Jesus; He is a man; He was born as a baby and laid in a manger. He was a boy, and He argued with the Doctors in the Temple. He worked as a carpenter; He was a man who suffered hunger and thirst. He said that there were certain things He did not know—Jesus. Yes, but 'Jesus Christ'—He is the Anointed of God; He is the Messiah long expected, the one whom God has set apart in order that this mighty work of redemption and salvation might be brought about. It is very difficult, in a sense, to put this because while it is right in a way to say that He is man and He is also God, there is another sense in which one should never say that, because He is only one person—two natures in the one person, and yet only one person. He is not so much man and God—He is God-Man, two in one, not intermingled—'Jesus Christ.'

Now that is the great thing that John is here anxious to assert; we must be perfectly clear in our minds with regard to this person—who He is and therefore what He has done. 'But,' someone may ask, 'if that is what he is concerned about, why does he drag in this idea about coming not by water only but by water and by blood?'

Here again there have been many different views with regard to that. There are those who tell us that this reference to the water and the blood is simply a reminder of what John reports at the end of his Gospel. He tells us about the crucifixion, that when the spear was thrust into Christ's side, there came out blood and water. Obviously, they say, he is just referring back to that. Yet it seems to me that that is quite impossible as an explanation. To start with, John, in the Gospel, refers to 'blood and water'; this is a reference to 'water and blood.' Not only that, but he goes out of his way to say, 'Not by water only, but by water and blood.' In other words, he is not so much referring to blood and water as to water and blood: they are separate, and they are distinct, and they must be held apart. Thus I cannot accept the explanation that this just refers to the blood and water that came from the pierced side of our Lord.

Then there are others who tell us that this has reference to the two sacraments—the sacrament of baptism and the sacrament of the Lord's Supper. Here, again, is something that cannot be made to sit easily upon what we are considering together. John has made no reference to the sacraments; he is, rather, concerned with objective witness to the deity and the uniqueness of the person of our Lord and Saviour Jesus Christ.

So again we must ask the question, what does he mean by saying this? Well, it seems that the best way to approach the subject is to look at it like this: John is concerned to establish the reality of the incarnation, to prove that Jesus Christ is really the Son of God incarnate, in the flesh. I believe that he was anxious to do so in order to correct a heresy that was very prevalent at that time, which we have had occasion to mention previously. It taught, let me remind you, something like this: Jesus of Nazareth was a man, but when He was baptised by John in the Jordan, the eternal Christ came upon Him and entered into Him, so that from the moment of the baptism the eternal Christ was dwelling in the human Jesus. And He continued to do so until just before the crucifixion took place. Then the eternal Christ went back to heaven, and it was only the man Jesus who was crucified.

Now that was a very common heresy in the first centuries, and it is a heresy that has also been prevalent during these past centuries. This whole trouble during the last hundred years or so about the person of Christ has been nothing, in a sense, but a recapitulation of that ancient heresy; it puts a wedge between the man Jesus and the eternal Christ. And here John is concerned to assert this mighty fact, that the baby in the manger is the God-Man, 'Jesus Christ,' and not Jesus only. The incarnation is a reality, and the one who died upon the cross was not only the man Jesus—it was the God-Man who died. And I believe that John mentions this testimony and witness of the water and the blood in order to establish the unity and the oneness of the person; not two persons, but one person with the two natures.

That, it seems to me, is the main division of these verses, but we shall go on to show how John, in a still more detailed way, maintains that there are these three witnesses to this unique person. We shall see how he demonstrates that the water and the blood, in addition to the Spirit, assert this, and he assures us that the one in whom we repose our faith is none other than the only begotten Son of God.

We must be certain of these things, and it is in order to give us that certainty that the Apostle has thus written.

7

THE THREE WITNESSES

This is he that came by water and blood, even Jesus Christ; not by water only, but by water and blood. And it is the Spirit that beareth witness, because the Spirit is truth. For there are three that bear record in heaven, the Father, the Word, and the Holy Ghost: and these three are one. And there are three that bear witness in earth, the spirit, and the water, and the blood: and these three agree in one.

1 JOHN 5:6-8

IN THIS SECTION (1 John 5:6-12), John is dealing with the great doctrine of belief in Jesus Christ as the Son of God, and we suggested that it could be divided roughly into three divisions: the claim that is made (vv 6-8); the witness that is borne, and, in verses 9 and 10, the reason we are to accept this witness and this claim; and in verses 11 and 12, the consequences of believing the testimony. We also indicated that the whole object, generally, is to establish faith and give us certainty—to have this faith in Jesus Christ as the Son of God, to be certain of Him, and to know exactly in whom we have this belief. So John takes up this theme of the person of our Lord, and we saw that, having in mind the heresy that would put a wedge between Jesus the man and Jesus the eternal Christ, John is arguing for the unity of the person. Jesus Christ is one person. It is the Son of God who was born as a baby, and it was the Son of God who died on the cross—not only the man, but the God-Man.

But this is not the only object of John's statements. Indeed, I would say that it is not even his main or particular object. I think his main object is to show that Jesus, the Son of God, is the Christ of God, the one who came to do what was so necessary for mankind and its salvation. Indeed, this is the only way in which we can understand these difficult verses. John is concerned particularly here to establish the fact that Jesus is the Christ, the Messiah, the long-expected Saviour, the long-awaited deliverer of His people.

He is stressing this for two main reasons. The first is that we are driven to that conclusion by the changing of the terminology in verses 5 and 6: 'Who is he that overcometh the world, but he that believeth that Jesus is the Son of God?' (v 5); 'This is he that came by water and blood, even Jesus Christ' (v 6). You see, it is no longer Jesus is 'the Son of God,' but Jesus is the 'Christ'; and I suggest that when John varies his expression like that, he has a very deliberate object in mind. He does it not just for the sake of doing so, but because he is bringing out some additional meaning.

There is a second reason for arguing that this is right. It is the very interesting word *came*—'This is he that *came*.' It is also a significant word, because 'coming' carries with it not merely the fact that He has come, but the purpose of His coming. We can follow this word as it is used in the Scriptures. Take, for instance, the question set to our Lord by John the Baptist: 'Art thou *he that should come*?' Now that was a phrase among the Jews; the Messiah was the one who was to come and do certain things.

Take also the statement by John in the first chapter of his Gospel— 'For the law was given by Moses, but grace and truth came by Jesus Christ' (1:17). 'Grace and truth came'; He is the one who brought, He is the conveyor of, grace and truth; and there are other instances of the same expression. In other words, John is not only referring to the birth of our Lord Jesus Christ in a literal sense, but also to the coming of the one who has brought and was to bring certain benefits to mankind. He is coming as the Messiah, so that in effect what John is saying is this: 'He is coming to us as a Messiah by water and blood; not with water only, but with blood'; there is the clue to the understanding of these verses that have so often perplexed people.

We have seen that we could not completely understand this as a reference to the blood and water that came from His side when He died. We also indicated that it is surely not right to say that the water and the blood referred to the sacraments of baptism and the Lord's Supper. If you consider the various suggestions that have been made, you will be driven to the conclusion that the references to water and blood are references to the baptism and the death of our Lord. How do we fit these in together? Well, let us look at it like this:

The great business of the Messiah who was to come was to deliver the people from the thraldom and bondage of sin and its consequences. Men and women, as a result of their sin, were under the wrath of God. They needed to be delivered from the power of the world, the flesh, and the devil—the power of sin both inside and outside. So the Messiah, the Saviour, had to make expiation for our sin and set us free from its power. This was His great task. And John tells us that Jesus Christ came as the Messiah and has done that, and we see Him doing it as we look at His baptism and as we see His death on the cross. His baptism, in a sense, is the beginning of His power as the Messiah—He came as the Messiah by 'water.' Through that He identifies Himself with our sin, and it is upon the cross that He deals with it, expiates it, and delivers us from the wrath of God and therefore from the power of sin and the power of the world, the flesh, and the devil.

Now I think we see why John does not refer to Christ's birth in his Gospel. He has been pointing to Christ as the Messiah, fixing his attention upon that, that Jesus is the Son of God. So he does not refer to the birth; but he does refer to the baptism. And so I think we see very clearly why it is that we have the phrase 'not by water only, but by water and blood.' The Lord Jesus Christ did not merely identify Himself with us and our sins—He went further; He dealt with it not in water only, but also in the blood. His death is an absolute essential in addition to the baptism.

That, therefore, I suggest to you, is the statement that John makes. He is not only interested in the person of our Lord, but in the work also. John was never interested in our Lord, if I may so put it, in a mere theoretical manner. He wanted to help these people. He wanted them to know that what our Lord had done applied to their immediate condition and to their immediate need. It is only, therefore, as we say, 'This is our Messiah' that we can be delivered from and overcome the power of the world, the flesh, and the devil and everything that is set against us.

The next phrase is, 'it is the Spirit that beareth witness, because the Spirit is truth.' This is, I think, a reference to the particular testimony that is borne to all of us by the Holy Spirit, a testimony to the saving

work of Christ. How does the Holy Spirit do this? John is referring to
the descent of the Holy Ghost on the Church on the Day of Pentecost
at Jerusalem and the consequences that followed. He is primarily interested in objective witnesses, and so his emphasis is that the Holy Spirit
is bearing final testimony to the fact that Jesus is the Christ. John says
that the Spirit is the truth. He is the Spirit of God; He is God; and so
there is the final proof that Jesus is the deliverer, the Messiah. Let us then
examine the details of this extrordinary statement.

The peculiar and special matter with which the Apostle is dealing is
this description of our Lord and Saviour as the emancipator, the Saviour
who has come to take away the sins of the world; but that leads him to
make a further statement. In verse 8 John says, 'And there are three that
bear witness in earth, the spirit, and the water, and the blood: and these
three agree in one.' The proof is in His suffering. 'This is he that came
by water and blood, even Jesus Christ,' and the Spirit bears witness to
this, and that makes John think in terms of the witnesses that are
borne—'the spirit, and the water, and the blood.'

What does he want to prove by that? What is it that we, as believers,
need to know? I think the best way to answer these questions is to remind
ourselves of what was after all the essential and characteristic thinking of
the Apostles. What exactly was their message? In Acts 17 we read this:
'And Paul, as his manner was, went in unto them, and three sabbath days
reasoned with them out of the Scriptures. Opening and alleging, that
Christ must needs have suffered, and risen again from the dead; and that
this Jesus, whom I [Paul] preach unto you, is Christ' (vv 2-3).

In other words, the Apostles set out to do two things: they had to
prove that the long-awaited Messiah must of necessity suffer, that He
would be put to death; and the second thing they had to do was to prove
that Jesus was the Messiah. So the things we find John emphasising here
are the things that Paul emphasised, three things that bear witness—'the
spirit, and the water, and the blood.' How do they do so? There are certain headings I will give you that you can work out for yourselves. Take
first this witness or testimony. How did the Spirit bear testimony to the
fact that Christ was the Son of God, the Messiah?

First, in the baptism you remember that John told the people, 'I
knew him not: but he that sent me to baptize with water, the same said
unto me, Upon whom thou shalt see the Spirit descending, and remaining on him, the same is he which baptizeth with the Holy Ghost' (John

1:33). He therefore bore witness and testimony to the fact that Christ is the Lamb of God. But not only that; the Holy Spirit also bears witness to Him in His life. Look at the words of our Lord, and look at His works. How can you explain Him? How can you explain these things in Him? There is only one answer. 'God giveth not the Spirit by measure unto him' (John 3:34). He is filled with the Spirit, and thus He is able to speak His words and do His perfect works. Indeed, Paul says that He is 'declared to be the Son of God with power, according to the spirit of holiness, by the resurrection from the dead' (Rom 1:4).

But then the next great way in which the Spirit bears this witness is in what happened on the Day of Pentecost, which shows that Christ is in particular the Messiah in His sending of the gift of the Spirit to the Church.

The Spirit bears this witness in the Church herself and in the testimony of the life of the Church. Peter says to the Jewish rulers, 'And we are his witnesses of these things; and so is also the Holy Ghost, whom God hath given to them that obey him' (Acts 5:32). There is the witness and testimony of the Holy Spirit, and in all these ways he testifies to the fact that Jesus is the Christ.

How next does the water, the baptism, bear witness? Well, we have emphasised the descent of the Holy Ghost upon Christ; there He is, being baptised in the Jordan, and the Spirit in the form of a dove descends upon Him. And we read that a voice spoke from heaven saying, 'This is my beloved Son, in whom I am well pleased' (Matt 3:17). In the baptism God bears witness and testimony to the fact that this is the Christ, this is the Messiah, this is the one who is come to do the work that has been allotted to Him. 'The spirit, and the water'—the testimony of the two are the same and bring us to the same conclusion.

But the last witness is centred on Christ's death on the cross. How does this bear witness? Why is John so anxious to emphasise it? Not the water only, but the blood—how does this prove that Jesus is the Christ and that He must suffer and be slain to save us? In the first place like this: the very fact that the death led to the resurrection is proof that Jesus is the Son of God. It was the resurrection that established it, and the death is the ultimate proof. But that is not the most important. It is as we look at the death that we see He is the Christ and the Saviour. The Jews had a false view of the Messiah. He was to them a man who was to emancipate them politically and militarily. But He did not do this, and so they crucified Him. They jeered at Him and despised Him and said, 'Why not come to Jerusalem and be crowned? If you are the Messiah why not declare yourself?' A Prince? No! That was their error; but 'it behoved Christ to suffer' (Luke 24:46).

That was the preaching of the Apostles, and it was not merely *their* preaching—it was the very thing our Lord Himself had taught. He wanted to show the disciples that all He had done was the work that His Father had sent Him to do. The Old Testament Scriptures show us that everything that happened to Him was a fulfilment of the old prophecies. And when the Apostles preached this, they were after all doing nothing but repeating His own words to them. 'And he said unto them, These are the words which I spake unto you, while I was yet with you, that all things must be fulfilled, which were written in the law of Moses, and in the prophets, and in the psalms, concerning me. Then he opened their understanding, that they might understand the Scriptures, and said unto them, Thus it is written, and thus it behoved Christ to suffer, and to rise from the dead the third day: and that repentance and remission of sins should be preached in his name among all nations, beginning at Jerusalem. And ye are witnesses of these things. And, behold, I send the promise of my Father upon you: but tarry ye in the city of Jerusalem, until ye be endued with power from on high' (Luke 24:44-49).

What does He mean? Again, you see, it is that the Messiah was to suffer. They all said He was to suffer and die. The Messiah, the Christ, was to be the suffering servant, and one on whom the sins of the world are laid and who is punished. 'Don't be depressed by the death on the cross,' he said in effect to his disciples; 'it was only by dying that I could set you at liberty.'

So the death—the blood—is the ultimate establishment of the fact that He is the Christ, the deliverer, the Messiah. He said it, and He proved it, and it was the burden of the apostolic preaching.

So, then, I look at Him dying and ask myself, 'If He is the Son of God, why this?' Because it was the only way in which the Son of God could save us. It was the only way in which the Son of God could emancipate us and set us free. It had to be. I look at Him on the cross, and I listen, and hear Him say, 'It is finished' (John 19:30). What is finished? The work the Father had given Him to do; the work for which He was baptised and the work for which he died; the work for which He became the Messiah. The special work of the Messiah, the Christ, the Saviour, had been fully accomplished. This is the fact to which the three bear witness. That is the fact about which the three agree—that Jesus is the Christ and that Christ must suffer.

What do *we* say about it? As I look and listen to the evidence of the three witnesses I repeat the words of Peter: 'Lord, to whom shall we go? thou hast the words of eternal life. And we believe and are sure that thou art that Christ, the Son of the living God' (John 6:68-69). He is the one who gave Himself to the work of His Father and to the death on the cross. If He had not died, I would not be forgiven, I could not be saved. Jesus is the Son of God. Jesus is the Christ of God.

8

Eternal Life

If we receive the witness of men, the witness of God is greater: for this is the witness of God which he hath testified of his Son. He that believeth on the Son of God hath the witness in himself: he that believeth not God hath made him a liar; because he believeth not the record that God gave of his Son. And this is the record, that God hath given to us eternal life, and this life is in his Son. He that hath the Son hath life; and he that hath not the Son of God hath not life.

1 John 5:9-12

WE LOOK ONCE MORE at these words, in this vitally important and interesting paragraph running from the sixth verse to the end of the twelfth verse. The Apostle is really bringing to a conclusion the subject matter of his letter, and he ends with this great statement concerning the person of our Lord and Saviour Jesus Christ. Now let me remind you, I have suggested that the most convenient way of subdividing this matter is that in verses 6, 7, and 8 he is stating a claim; in 9 and 10 he gives the reasons for believing it; and in 11 and 12 he reminds us of the consequences of belief.

We have already considered verses 6 to 8 and have seen how John shows that the Messiah, long expected, is none other than Jesus of Nazareth, the Son of God. Now here, in verses 9 and 10, he gives us various reasons for believing that, and we must, therefore, consider them together.

These verses can be subdivided into two divisions, and it might be well to take them together and indicate three reasons why we should accept this testimony concerning Jesus as the Son of God and the Saviour. After all, someone may say, 'You exhort us to believe that Jesus is the Christ and the Son of God. Why should we? On what grounds?'

The first answer is, the nature of the evidence. You may look at this if you like in a different way. In a changing, uncertain world we need something certain; and John wants people to have this certainty. The first element is that there is objective, external evidence provided for us. 'If we receive the witness of men, the witness of God is greater: for this is the witness of God which he hath testified of his Son. He that believeth on the Son of God hath the witness in himself . . .'

John there is surely saying that the witness to which we have been paying attention—namely the Spirit, the water, and the blood—is none other than the testimony of God Himself. This is a matter of which we are quite certain. We have the evidence from the baptism, the evidence of the death on the cross and the Day of Pentecost, and the subsequent evidence of the events of the Church; the three agree in one.

Now, it is the custom of natural man to accept the evidence of two or three witnesses—people and witnesses who can be relied upon. If you have two or three such people bearing the same testimony, you accept them. Therefore, says John, if we accept the witness of man, 'the witness of God is greater.' And this is the witness of God: it was *God* who was testifying in the baptism that Jesus is the Christ. It is God who has provided that evidence. It is God, likewise, who has provided the evidence of the blood in Christ's death on the cross. It is *God* who is doing this, and He further did it by raising Christ from the dead. It is through the resurrection that He has declared Christ to be the Son of God, His Son. And the evidence of the Holy Spirit is the evidence of God because He is God. He is the third person in the Trinity.

So why should I believe on Jesus Christ? Well, if you have no other answer, God has told you that this is the Messiah. It is not merely the testimony of man, but the testimony of God, and over and above all other testimony our case rests on this fact—that this is a revelation from God. This is not a philosophy. This is not something that man thinks. It is not human imagination; it is not a myth. We claim that we have here a revelation from God, and the reason for believing this message is that it is the witness and testimony of God Himself. But John puts it negatively as well as positively: 'He that believeth not God hath made him a liar; because he believeth not the record that God gave of His Son.'

This is a terrifying thought, and I wonder whether we realise it as we should. Not to believe the gospel and the Christian message is to say that God is a liar. Is there anyone uncertain about these things, anyone who talks about difficulties and says, 'My mind is not fully satisfied'? If there is such a person I have great sympathy with you. But I would remind you that this statement comes from *God*; God Himself is giving testimony. But quite apart from your difficulties, so-called, I would remind you that this is a question of accepting testimony and witness. God has said, '*This is my beloved Son*, in whom I am well pleased; hear ye him' (Matt 17:5). Am I to refuse Him? Well, the terrifying thing is that if I do, I am saying that God's pronouncement is not true. That is the position in which it involves us; for here we start on a different level. It is a revelation from God. It is the Almighty Himself who tells us this, and it is not a question of pitting our minds against a human teaching. It is a statement from Heaven, and to reject it is to say that God is a liar.

The second argument is this: in addition to the external evidence there is also the subjective or internal evidence. John puts it in this way: 'He that believeth on the Son of God hath the witness in himself . . .' So we are dealing here with these two different stands—the external and the internal, and this is a very great and important subject. I am not at all sure but that this is not the most vital of all the parts of the subject. It was a great matter to the minds of the Reformers. They clearly defined this matter. The believer is confronted by two great sources of certainty, one outside and one inside—*Spiritus Externus* and *Spiritus Internus*.

But perhaps the best way to understand this is to ask ourselves, 'How may I know that the Bible is the Word of God?' There are two main ways. There is the Word itself—the testimony of the Holy Spirit, and the agreement of the books written within it. This general consensus, the internal unity of the Bible, and various other arguments—this is the *Spiritus Externus*—the outside testimony. But according to the Reformers, that is not enough to give people certainty. They need something inside as well, and the Holy Spirit also gives them that internal certitude—the *Spiritus Internus*. Let me put this personally. There was a time when I read the Bible and thought it was a wonderful book; I felt it was a unique book and that I could not compare it with any other book. But then the time came when I was confronted with the great evidence given to me in the Gospels and the Old and New Testaments, and I had a feeling within me that this was the Word of God. That is what it means—this internal evidence.

Paul, in 1 Corinthians 2, refers to 'the princes of this world' (v 8), these wise men who all looked at Jesus Christ and failed to recognise that He was the Lord of glory. They lacked the Spirit who enables us to understand the great things of God that have been given to us. But 'He that believeth on the Son of God hath the witness in himself,' and it is important that we should bear this in mind—this internal certainty first that Jesus is the Christ, and second that I myself am a child of God.

So am I happy in my Christian life? Do I know in whom I have believed? Am I ready to meet all the contingencies that may come to me? Does a possible war, illness, or trouble distress me? In death, in that unknown future, how do I stand with respect to these things? Now, it is just at this point that this element of certainty comes in. There is all the difference in the world in accepting the Word of God and knowing for certain that these things are true. There have been many who have gone through a lifetime, thinking they have this belief in God and in His Word, living the Christian life; and yet when they came to their deathbeds they felt lonely and deserted. They had no certainty just when they needed it. In other words, I am sure that without this witness in ourselves there is no peace and no real satisfaction. We are provided with everything we need; we are not asked to rest alone on something external. If you believe this, you will have the witness within yourself as well.

Of course, there are certain difficulties to which I must refer. How is this certainty to be obtained? Here is the most important principle, and we must observe the order in which these things come: the objective must come first. We try to have the subjective, but notice the order. First I am to receive the witness of God, and it is only after I have that that I am likely to have the evidence and the witness within myself. There is a statement in Psalm 34 that says, 'Taste and see that the Lord is good' (v 8). The trouble is, we want to see before we have tasted. No! Taste and then you will see that the Lord is good. Or take the way the Lord Himself put it in his teaching. He said, 'If any man will do his [God's] will, he shall know of the doctrine' (John 7:17). So if you want to be certain, believe first, and then you will be certain.

So this question of the order is a vitally important one. Believe God, and then have the belief within yourself. To reverse the order would be insulting to God. Someone may say, 'Well, I will only believe if I have proof.' But God says, 'I ask you to believe because I am speaking'; so not to believe is dishonouring to Him. To try to insist that you must have proof is to detract from His glory. So first I must believe because God is the witness; and if I do, then I shall have the witness of the Spirit within myself.

The other practical thing, of course, is just to learn exactly what believing His evidence means, and here John puts it in a very few words: 'He that believeth on the Son of God hath the witness in himself.' Oh, what important words these are; what an important word is that little word 'on'! John does not mean us to say, 'Well, on the whole I am satisfied with the evidence, and I am prepared to believe that Jesus of Nazareth is the Son of God.' So I put down my book and prepare to argue with my friends and we can all meet and have a discussion. And after a long discussion, we come to the conclusion that we are satisfied that the claim made does really convince us that Jesus is the Son of God.

That is not it! 'He that believeth on the Son of God . . .' Such a person has abandoned himself to Him. He has surrendered to Him. He is the man who says, 'I look on Him, and I see the Saviour, the Son of God, sent by God. I am under the wrath of God. I am a doomed, guilty, foul sinner, and there He is—the one who can deliver me. So I cast myself upon Him, "just as I am without one plea."' You can give your intellectual assent to the truth perhaps sitting comfortably or in a discussion, but you can only believe on the Son of God on your knees. You may not realise the full implications of the statement, but you hand over your whole life into the strong arms of the Son of God. And you will very soon have the witness. You will know who He is, and all your uncertainties will have gone. Jesus is not only the Christ, He is the Son of God, the Messiah, the deliverer of the world.

And that brings us to the last great argument, in verses 11 and 12, which is that we are to believe it because of the consequences that follow. It is not only that we are to be certain of eternal life. 'God hath given to us eternal life, and this life is in His Son. He that hath the Son hath life; and he that hath not the Son of God hath not life.' We are considering all this because our eternal future depends on these things. We either have life or we are dead, and to come out of this world spiritually dead means to go out to the wrath of God, to go out into an eternity of darkness and death.

Our Lord has said, 'This is life eternal, that they might know thee the only true God, and Jesus Christ, whom thou hast sent' (John 17:3). Do you know God? I do not ask you if you say your prayers. Do you know that He has loved you with an everlasting love? Do you know that He is yours? Can you say, 'My God'? Do you know He is your Father? If you know Christ, you know God, for you know Jesus whom He has sent. You are full of a new life. 'Christ liveth in me.' Can you say that?

To be a Christian is not merely to hold certain Christian philosophies. It is more than that. You are able to say, 'I am a new man or woman. I am not what I was. I, yet not I. God is dwelling in me.' And John emphasises this. Why is it so important that I should be clear about Jesus Christ? Why is it I should be certain He is the Son of God, the Christ, the Messiah? 'This is the record, that God hath given to us eternal life, and this life is in his Son.' If you have not the Son, you have not life. 'This is my beloved Son, in whom I am well pleased,' God said at His baptism. He has put it all into Him. Life is entirely, exclusively, solely in the Son of God, so that if I am not clear about these facts—that Jesus is the Son of God, and that Jesus is the Christ—then I have not life. Eternal life is only available as I believe—if I go to Jesus Christ for it. So unless I can say, 'and of his fulness have [I] received, and grace for [or upon] grace' (John 1:16), I am without life, I am dead. In other words, it is not my belief alone that saves me. I have received the gift of life, and I can face death and judgment with this evidence that I am a child of God, because in Jesus Christ I have received eternal life, the life of God Himself, in my own soul.

9

CERTAIN KNOWLEDGE

*These things have I written unto you that believe on the
name of the Son of God; that ye may know that ye have
eternal life, and that ye may believe on the name of the Son
of God.*

1 JOHN 5:13

IT IS GENERALLY AGREED that the right translation of this verse is
more like this: 'These things have I written unto you, that you may
know you have eternal life, that believe on the name of the Son of God.'
The meaning is exactly the same in both cases, because those who do
believe on the name of the Son of God may *know* that they have eternal life.

This obviously is a very important verse, perhaps the most important in the entire epistle, for in it the Apostle is looking back. He has finished his letter, and here he looks back and summarises what he has been
saying and reminds the people of his object when he began to write.

He has said that he was anxious that they might have fellowship
with him and with the other Apostles, because the fellowship was with
the Father and with his Son Jesus Christ. John was particularly anxious
that these people to whom he had been writing should be clear as to the
central purpose of his letter. That is something that is very necessary,
because our danger is to miss the forest because of the trees. It is absolutely necessary to be clear about everything, but we must also bear in
mind the purpose of it all; and the Apostle reminds us of his ultimate
object, which is that those who are Christians, those who believe on the

name of the Son of God, might know that they have eternal life. 'These things have I written unto you . . . that ye may *know* . . .'

Now there can be no question that this is the most important statement that could ever be made to a company of men and women. In John 17 this is emphasised from beginning to end. There was our Lord, immediately prior to His death on the cross, reviewing His life and praying not concerning the world, but concerning those whom God had given Him, and He says exactly the same thing. His prayer was that men and women might know God and Jesus Christ whom He had sent. He had come to bring eternal life, and in that prayer He goes on repeating His desire that the men and women whom God had given Him might possess this full knowledge and glory in it.

We have been repeating that as we have worked our way through this epistle. This is the essence of the Christian life, that we might have the full knowledge of God and that we may know we have it. In the immediate context we see that John has been emphasising and stressing a prior knowledge—that Jesus of Nazareth is really the Son of God and the Messiah. He wants the people to know for certain the truth concerning Him—that they might know for certain that they possess eternal life and the full knowledge of God. So it is important for us to understand exactly what the Apostle is telling us here, and we can look at it in a number of propositions.

This knowledge that we have eternal life is something that is possible to us. That is something that needs to be emphasised. There are those who would tell us that eternal life is something to which we attain only when we come to die and leave this world and go into the next. They suggest that it is wrong for anyone to claim that he *has* eternal life. Such people dislike the doctrine of assurance. 'We do not know,' they say, 'and we must not seek to know. Faith means that you are always grasping at it, but it is something you cannot actually have while you are in this world.'

But that is a philosophical concept of faith that is not in accordance with what we have here. John says, 'My whole object in writing to you now is that you may know you have eternal life and know it certainly. I want you to *know* that you possess it.' You find the other Apostles saying the same thing. What was more characteristic of the Apostle Paul than this assurance? In Romans 8 he says, 'For I am persuaded, that neither death, nor life, nor angels, nor principalities, nor powers, nor things present, nor things to come, nor height, nor depth, nor any other creature, shall be able to separate us from the love of God, which is in Christ Jesus our Lord' (vv 38-39). 'I know whom I have believed,' he writes to Timothy (2 Tim 1:12). 'I *know*,' he says. There is no uncertainty about it.

So it seems to me that to interpret faith as a kind of constant uncertainty is to deny the teaching of the Word of God that we are His children. Indeed, 'the Spirit itself beareth witness with our spirit, that we are the children of God' (Rom 8:16). Such knowledge is possible to us. We ought to be in a position of knowing that we have eternal life, that we know God, and that we know Christ.

The second proposition is that this is not only possible, but it is possible to all of us. I have often met people who have taken up a position like this: they say that there are some special men and women who do have this certain knowledge. Yes, John wished everybody to have it, but, of course, he was in that position. So was Peter. They were unique men; they were apart. The spiritual can attain to this knowledge, but it is not meant for us all.

But the answer to that is to repeat the Scripture. There is no such distinction drawn in the New Testament. John is desirous that all these people to whom he writes may share the knowledge that has been given to him. 'That which we have seen and heard,' he says at the beginning of his letter, 'declare we unto you, that ye also may have fellowship with us: and truly our fellowship is with the Father, and with his Son Jesus Christ' (1:3). And here he puts it quite as strongly: 'These things have I written unto you that believe on the name of the Son of God; that ye may know . . .'

In the same way the Apostle Peter, writing to the early Christians, said that they obtained 'like precious faith with us' (2 Pet 1:1)—that is, not a lesser faith, but the same faith. And precisely the same is taught in all the epistles of the Apostle Paul. Yet the Roman Catholic teaching has always divided people into two groups—those who are saints and those who are not. But we are all called to be 'saints' according to the New Testament, and I sometimes think that we rob ourselves of some of the most glorious blessings the New Testament has to offer. There is no such thing as an 'ordinary Christian.' There is a division of labour, but here we are dealing with basic Christian experience. Every Christian is meant to have this certain knowledge of eternal life, this immediate fellowship and communion with God. It is possible for all.

Then the third step is this: it is the duty of all to possess it, and I argue that in this way: it is obvious that God means us to have it. Our Lord Himself says that is why He came into the world. The work that He has now finished is to enable us to have eternal life, to make it possible for us to enter into this blessed and amazing knowledge of God. And, therefore, I argue that it is dishonouring to God for us not to possess it. Indeed, it can be said that we have no right *not* to have this knowledge.

But an argument put forward by people who say that they would not like to presume that they have salvation or that they know they have eternal life is that such a statement makes us Pharisees and makes us say, 'Thank God we are not as other men.' Yet it should not do so, because eternal life is something that we receive from God as a gift. He has offered it to us, and He sent His Son to a cruel death on the cross that we might receive it. So I repeat, we have no right not to have it. If Christian people are uncertain as to the fact that they have eternal life, they are dishonouring God, and they are bearing a very poor witness and testimony to the power of salvation.

Then let me come to a more practical and personal reason why we should have it. It is that if I am uncertain of my position and of salvation, I shall probably spend most of my time putting myself right. How can the blind lead the blind? My first business is to get right myself. In my reading of Scripture and in meditation I then shall have to be centring on myself. I am lacking in power and witness and effective testimony. The only way to be strong is to be certain about all this, and the history of the Church bears out that statement abundantly.

Read the stories of the martyrs and confessors; read the stories of those men and women who gave their lives for their beliefs, those who went to the stake and died for the truth. What was their secret? What made them so strong? The answer is that these men and women *knew* in whom they believed. They possessed eternal life, and the only effect of the death at the stake was to usher them into salvation and to bring them face to face with their Lord Jesus Christ. If they had been uncertain of all this, they could not have faced such a trial.

It is equally essential now. You cannot really know the joy of the Lord until you are perfectly certain that all is well between you and God. And the way to have this joy is to have this eternal life, which means fellowship with God and with His Son, Jesus Christ. This knowledge is possible, and possible for all; and it is our duty to have the knowledge before we take any other step. Therefore, let me ask you another simple question: do you know that you have eternal life; have you this knowledge? This is what is offered. This is what we are meant to have. It is this that makes a brighter and more confident testimony. Can we say, 'I know that I have eternal life'?

So let us do what John invites us to do. Let us remind ourselves of the way in which we can have this certain knowledge that we do really possess eternal life. John has gone on repeating it, and I have reminded you of it, but let us say it all once more. How do I know I have this?

Before I touch on any difficulties there are certain tests by which, if we apply them to ourselves, we may know that we have this knowledge of God. The first is our belief concerning the Lord Jesus Christ Himself. John started and ended with this: 'That which was from the beginning, which we have heard, which we have seen with our eyes, which we have looked upon, and our hands have handled, of the Word of life; (For the life was manifested, and we have seen it, and bear witness, and shew unto you that eternal life, which was with the Father, and was manifested unto us).' That is how he began the letter. He was referring to the Lord Jesus Christ, and in this chapter he says, 'He that hath the Son hath life; and he that hath not the Son of God hath not life.'

In other words, this is something basic; we need not consider any other question if we are not right about this. The first question I must answer is: what is Jesus Christ to me? What do I think of Him? What is my view of this person, Jesus of Nazareth, the one of whom we read in the pages of the four Gospels? The whole point of this is to show that if I have any uncertainty about Him, I have no eternal life. There is no such thing as a knowledge of God apart from Jesus Christ; we never arrive at God truly unless we come through Him.

Therefore, Jesus Christ is absolutely essential to me. He is essential in my scheme and outlook. I have come to see my own unworthiness, my sinfulness, and my smallness. I have seen it deeply and can do nothing to save myself. But God has sent His only begotten Son into the world to do what I cannot do myself. How can I face God? I have but one hope, and that is that God sent His Son. He satisfied God and gave His whole life absolutely, perfectly; He has dealt with the problem of sin. Here is one who has taken my very sins and died for them on the cross, and in Him God forgives me. That is the first essential of this sure knowledge that I have eternal life. Unless I am resting my faith solely in Jesus Christ and His perfect work, I have no life, because the only way to God is in Him.

This leads me to the second test. If I believe all that, I must of necessity come to love God. As I look at Jesus Christ, I see there is only one explanation of this. Jesus Christ is the Son of God, and He has eternal life. 'In this was manifested the love of God toward us, because that God sent his only begotten Son into the world, that we might live through him. . . . We love him, because he first loved us' (1 John 4:9, 19). So this is my second test: what is my attitude towards God? Is He a hard taskmaster? Let me ask myself this question: do I harbour harsh thoughts of God? Do I say when things go wrong, 'God is against me'? But if I believe in the love of Jesus Christ, I believe that God sent Him. So I believe on Him and in the love of God.

But, also, John is very fond of putting this in terms of our attitude towards the world in which we live. 'Love not the world, neither the things that are in the world. If any man love the world, the love of the Father is not in him. For all that is in the world, the lust of the flesh, and the lust of the eyes, and the pride of life, is not of the Father, but is of the world. And the world passeth away, and the lust thereof: but he that doeth the will of God abideth for ever' (1 John 2:15-17).

What is my view of the world when I know for certain that I have eternal life? What is my attitude to the world in which we are all living, the world as we see it in the newspapers—is that what interests me? What am I anxious to obtain? Or am I more interested in these other things—these spiritual things? According to John, Christians are men and women who have come to view the world in an entirely new manner. They see that it is governed by sin. They have come to regard it as a place in which evil forces are at work and whose whole mind is but the working of the spirit of the world. They know that it is something they have to fight, something to withstand, and they realise that unless they do so they will be defeated by it.

Do I hate the world? A good way of answering is this: the Apostle Paul, looking at his surroundings, said, 'For which cause we faint not; but though our outward man perish, yet the inward man is renewed day by day. For our light affliction, which is but for a moment, worketh for us a far more exceeding and eternal weight of glory; while we look not at the things which are seen, but at the things which are not seen; for the things which are seen are temporal; but the things which are not seen are eternal' (2 Cor 4:16-18). In looking at 'the things which are seen,' how much time do I spend in thinking about the Lord God? How much do I think about the glory which is with Him? Which do I meditate upon most—the eternal or the world?

John goes further and says that people who are truly Christians are those who overcome the world. They rise above it; they conquer it. They are in the world, but no longer of it. They are in it, but above it. They may fall into sin, but they do not dally in it; they do not gloat over it. They have been delivered out of this evil world, having been translated out of the kingdom of darkness into the Kingdom of God's dear Son. So what do I really want? Do I want to cling to this world, or do I want to know God whatever it may cost me? Can I answer these questions honestly? Those who have eternal life want more of it.

Then, thirdly, as we have seen, John constantly keeps before us the importance of keeping God's commandments, those commandments which are 'not grievous.' And, finally, we come to the last great test, which is the test of loving the brethren. John says repeatedly that men and women who are Christians will recognise other Christians; they will love them, they will realise that they belong with them, and they will realise that essential unity with them of which our Lord spoke in that great prayer in John 17. Here, then, is a very great test: do we love the brethren? I have sometimes put it like this: if I had the choice of spending an afternoon with a humble saint or with some great earthly personage, which would I choose? Do I want to be where God's people are gathered together? Is that the kind of society that I desire, or is it the other society with all its show and pomp? Love of the brethren is crucial! These tests are very searching, and if we honestly apply them to ourselves we will know where we stand.

Your eternal future depends on this. You have eternal life in this world. It is received here. If you have it, you are destined for glory; but if you die without it, you are destined for perdition. Have you got this life? What is Jesus Christ to you? What is God to you? Do you want to be righteous and holy? Do you want to be like Christ, and do you love the brethren? These are the tests. Our Lord said, '. . . that they may know thee the only true God, and Jesus Christ, whom thou hast sent' (John 17:3). I am not asking what you believe about God. I am asking, do you *know* Him? Do you believe Him to be your Father? Can you say honestly, 'The Lord is my shepherd, I shall not want' (Psa 23:1). Can you say, 'My God'? Is He yours? Can you say, 'My Jesus, I love Thee, I know Thou art mine'? Do you know in whom you have believed? Have you received this divine gift?

If you have, God bless you, and may you have it more and more. If you feel honestly that you cannot say that, then what you have to do is very simple. Tell God that you are not certain, that you do not know, and that you desire that knowledge above all else. And ask Him, by His Holy Spirit, to enable you to see your true helplessness, and ask Him to give you the gift. I assure you that if you do, He will not reject you, because He has said, 'Him that cometh to me I will in no wise cast out' (John 6:37). If you have not possessed this, ask Him, believing His own promise, and I assure you that He will answer your prayer. He will give you the gift, and you will *know* you have eternal life.

10

THE LIFE OF GOD

These things have I written unto you that believe on the name of the Son of God; that ye may know that ye have eternal life, and that ye may believe on the name of the Son of God.

1 JOHN 5:13

I COME AGAIN TO THIS VERSE because it does seem to me that it is such a vitally important one that we must try to gain the full benefit we were intended to gain from it. We have looked at it in general, from the merely mechanical standpoint, a kind of summary in and of itself of the entire teaching of the Apostle. We have reminded ourselves that John here is saying, "That is why I have written the letter, in order that you might have this certain knowledge that you possess eternal life'; and we have considered John's own particular tests and applied them to ourselves in order to make sure that we really do possess this eternal life about which he is writing.

Now I repeat, this matter is of vital importance. Indeed, it would not be an exaggeration to say that it is the great theme, the *greatest* theme even, in the New Testament itself. It is the whole object of the New Testament, and it is extraordinary, is it not, how constantly we seem to forget that. We are interested in forgiveness, we want to know that our sins are forgiven and that we do not go on to punishment and perdition, and we are interested in living a good life. But for some remarkable reason we tend to persist in forgetting that the ultimate thing that is offered us in the New Testament is nothing less than this very quality of eternal life. The New Testament is really a book that is, in a sense, just meant to tell us that this is what God offers us in Jesus Christ. Is not that the real object that every part of the New Testament has in view?

Why, for instance, do you think that the four Gospels were ever written? Why did the early church not just go on preaching the message of salvation and leave it at that? Now, there can be only one real answer to that question, and it was the answer given by John towards the end of his own Gospel. Having written it, he sums it up like this: 'And many other signs truly did Jesus in the presence of his disciples, which are not written in this book: but these are written, that ye might believe that Jesus is the Christ, the Son of God; and that believing ye might have life through his name' (John 20:30-31). That was why John wrote his Gospel; he was led by the Holy Spirit to do so for that reason.

And what is true of John is equally true of the writers of the other three Gospels. They wrote them not only to give a portrait of the Lord Jesus Christ, but also in order to give this proof and demonstration that Jesus of Nazareth is none other than the Son of God and is indeed the Christ of God, the Messiah, the one who has come into the world bringing life to men and women. You find this as a theme running right through the Gospels. Take that great word which our Lord said to the people: 'I am come that they might have life, and that they might have it more abundantly' (John 10:10); nothing less than that. So we must be clear about the fact that He is the Son of God and that He is the one who brings life.

In the same way the book of Acts is designed to do the same thing. It has that great evidence about His ascension and about the sending of the Holy Spirit on the early church. That is the final proof, as we have already seen, of the fact that He is the Son of God, the Messiah, the promise of the Father about which the Old Testament speaks so much. At last the promise has come to us, and this is the promise of the Holy Spirit, that by Him and through Him we receive this eternal life. And all the records that you have in the Acts of the Apostles are nothing but an elaboration of that one theme. Those first preachers went around saying that they were witnesses of these things; they said, 'We heard His preaching, we saw His crucifixion, we saw Him buried, we saw the stone rolled over the mouth of the grave. But we saw Him risen again, we saw the empty grave, we saw Him ascend, and we received this gift of the Holy Spirit.' That is the testimony!

The Apostle Paul was as 'one born out of due time' (1 Cor 15:8). He had not been one of the disciples; he had not heard Christ's teaching in that sense. But he was given a special sight of the risen Lord in order that he might bear his witness to the fact that Jesus is the Christ, the Son of God, the one, therefore, who gives more abundant life to mankind. Furthermore, as I am never tired of pointing out, that is the great object that lies behind the writers of the New Testament epistles. These letters were written to people who had already believed the gospel. They were written to churches; they were not open letters to the world, but particular letters to groups of Christian people or to individual Christian believers. But why were they written? They were written because all these Christians lived in a difficult and gainsaying world. They had their difficulties; they were tempted perhaps at times to doubt; they were sometimes defeated by Satan and were falling into temptation. Various things were going wrong in various ways, and the letters were written to them in order that they might be strengthened and encouraged and helped to go forward on their journey.

And the great message to all of them is just this self-same message, that everything they need is in the Lord Jesus Christ; that they have but to realise that it is His life that they need and that without it they can do nothing. So the argument of the New Testament from beginning to end is just that Christ Jesus, the Son of God, came into the world to give us this eternal life, and this is the most momentous and the most important thing that has ever come to mankind.

In other words, we must once and for ever get rid of this idea that the New Testament is but a book that contains an exalted teaching that we are meant to practise and to put into action. Not at all! It is not an exhortation to us to rise to the level of some wonderful teaching; it is an announcement, it is a proclamation! It calls itself 'good news,' and the amazing good news is that God is giving this gift of eternal life to all those who have realised their need of it and are ready to receive it. That is the whole argument, and it is one that is based very solidly upon facts. So the Gospels and all the details were written in order to demonstrate to us that this is not some wonderful idea, some great dream, or some sublime thought. No; this is something concrete: a person has appeared in this world who is, in and of Himself, the bearer of this eternal life that God is giving to mankind. So the one thing to be certain about is that we know Him.

In a sense, therefore, the New Testament says that the greatest tragedy that can ever happen is that anyone should be uncertain about this, that anyone should go on still searching or hoping or saying, 'Of course I am not to have that while I am in this life and world; perhaps after death . . . ?' 'Not at all!' says John; 'these things I have written unto you that believe on the name of the Son of God, that ye may know that ye have eternal life'—now, not at some future time.

Now, I put it like that in order that I may lead up to this question: why is it that there is anyone who is at all in difficulty about this subject? We have looked at some of what I would call the purely theological reasons. Some people, because of their view of faith, seem to think that this is impossible, and we showed how that contradicted the New Testament teaching. But I want now to give some more practical difficulties that I often find mentioned when people discuss this together. There are those who seem to be in trouble about this matter and uncertain as to whether they have eternal life or not, because they will persist in thinking of it in terms of experience, or in terms of feeling, rather than in the terms that are indicated here. That very often happens in this way. There is always this fatal tendency to standardise the experience of certain notable or outstanding incidents and illustrations.

This is something, I suppose, that is more or less inevitable. There is a tendency in mankind to pay great attention to and to concentrate upon the unusual and the spectacular. We seem to do that instinctively; I suppose it is one of the results of the Fall. Anything unusual or exceptional always attracts attention much more than the usual and the ordinary; that is why some sort of calamity or extraordinary thing in nature always attracts and interests us much more than the perpetual and wonderful things of nature from day to day. Wordsworth discovered that when he said about himself at the end of his great Ode:

> To me the meanest flower that blows can give
> Thoughts that do often lie too deep for tears.

That is right, and we ought all to put it like that. But the trouble with most of us is that because it is always there we do not marvel at it; that little flower in the hedgerow does not give rise in us thoughts that 'lie too deep for tears.' But if we see a tree struck by lightning we are interested because it is unusual, because it is exceptional.

Now, we tend to do that self-same thing in the whole matter of Christian experience. I attribute this to the Fall, and, of course, one must point out in passing that this is something that tends to be organised and often becomes a business. Those who produce books know that the spectacular always appeals to the mind; so they pick out these exceptional cases and give them great publicity. So we ordinary people who read about them say, 'That is marvellous. If only that had happened to me, then I should know that I have eternal life.' But it has not, and therefore the query arises in my mind as to whether I have eternal life or not. This is the tendency to think of it in terms of experience or feeling, something that comes to us suddenly. I may have gone on for months and years living at a certain level, and suddenly I get some thrilling experience, and I know that from then on all is well. Thus we tend to say that is the only way in which this certainty is to be obtained, and we may well spend a lifetime in waiting for the unusual and the spectacular.

But all that, of course, is just to contradict the essential New Testament teaching. The New Testament never lays stress upon the way in which this comes to us; what it is interested in is the fact that it *has* come. How often, in dealing with enquirers after salvation, does one have to point out that the New Testament never says, 'Whosoever feeleth shall be saved,' but 'whosoever believeth.' People often say, 'In a sense I do accept that teaching; but, you know, I cannot say that I have felt anything.' To which the simple reply is that the New Testament does not insist upon feeling. It says, do you believe; are you prepared to venture your all upon this? So it is sufficient for you to say, 'I live by this; whether I feel or whether I do not does not matter; we are not saved by feeling but by believing.'

And it is exactly the same in this matter of assurance, with this question of knowing that we have eternal life. Let me use an illustration that I once heard an old preacher use. He pointed out that two men may arrive at the end of a journey with their clothes wet all through. But if you enquired as to how it happened to the two men, you might find that it happened in a different way in each case. One man might say that he set out on the journey with the sun shining brilliantly. He had not brought an umbrella or a macintosh as there was no suggestion it was going to rain; but halfway along the road, suddenly the clouds gathered and a veritable downpour took place, and in a moment he was soaked through. The other man's story is a very different one. There was a kind of drizzle all the way through the journey, so he could not tell you when he got wet. The first man could, and the second man could not, but what really matters is not *how* the two men got wet, but the fact that they *are* both wet all through. Whether it happened suddenly or imperceptibly is utterly irrelevant.

So, the vital question is not whether I can point to some vital experience in my life in which I was given certain assurance. The vital question for me is this: as I face these tests in this first epistle of John, do I know that I have life? Whether I have the same experience as somebody else or not, as I examine the tests of life that are given can I say that in spite of my not having had that climactic experience or that thrilling feeling I must have life or I could not say yes to these questions?

Now thinking of it in terms of experience and feeling is a very common cause of trouble. God grant, if there is anyone who has been held in bondage by that kind of difficulty, that they may see the folly of it and may see that what matters, if I may so put it, is not precisely how and when we were born, but the fact that we are alive!

But the second difficulty is this: there are those who feel that before they can say they have eternal life, they ought to be perfect and sinless. They say, 'It is a very great thing to claim that I know I have eternal life, but surely before I can claim that, I ought to be in a position to say that there is no sin and no failure in my life. After all,' they say, 'eternal life is a very wonderful thing, but I cannot say I have it. I am conscious of the fact that I fall and fail and sin; and surely while I am in that condition I cannot make the claim that I have it.' That view, again, is very common.

The simple reply is that John has already dealt with that in the first chapters of this very epistle where he has gone out of his way to say, 'If we say that we have no sin, we deceive ourselves, and the truth is not in us. If we confess our sins, he is faithful and just to forgive us our sins, and to cleanse us from all unrighteousness. If we say that we have not sinned, we make him a liar, and his word is not in us' (1:8-10). The whole of the New Testament, in a sense, is constantly repeating this self-same argument. I wonder whether I can help with regard to this particular difficulty by putting it like this: not only does the New Testament not tell us that we must be able to claim sinless perfection before we can claim we are the possessors of eternal life, but I go so far as to assert that the New Testament itself teaches us quite plainly and clearly that the fact that there is a real struggle in our lives is proof in and of itself of life. 'For the flesh lusteth against the Spirit, and the Spirit against the flesh: and these are contrary the one to the other; so that ye cannot do the things that ye would' (Gal 5:17).

Now, I know that this is teaching that we may wrest to our own confusion, but it is New Testament teaching, and there is a sense in which all New Testament teaching is dangerous. I mean that its teaching is so deep that if we want to misuse it we can do so; hence you have antinomianism. So it means this: before we receive the gift of eternal life, we are dead in trespasses and in sin. There is a stage in which we are at peace; there is no struggle. Of course, we may have heard the moral teaching that is glibly applied by the world, and in our own way we may be concerned and may be striving to reach up to a certain level. But that is not the struggle the New Testament speaks of. The New Testament says that when we receive the gift of eternal life, a new man comes into us, so that we are now two men, and the two are different and contrary—the spirit and the flesh—and there is a struggle and a conflict.

Now those who are aware of that, who though they sin and fail are aware of the fact that there are these two men in them, that there is a struggle between the two—these people have given proof positive that they have received the gift of eternal life. There is no spiritual struggle in the life of unbelievers. There may be a moral struggle, there may be a struggle to live up to a certain code that they have set up, they may struggle to do certain things and if they do not achieve them they are ashamed of themselves—but I am not referring to that. I am referring to a spiritual struggle, to those who are aware of a conflict between two essential things, the one of God and the other of themselves. So you must not allow the devil to depress and discourage you because you occasionally fall into sin or because you say, 'I am not satisfied with my achievements.' If there is this struggle in a spiritual sense, then, according to the New Testament, that of itself is proof that you have eternal life.

Or, to put it slightly differently, there are many who do not say that we must be sinless and perfect before we can make this claim, but after reading the lives of some of the outstanding saints they look at themselves and say, 'Can I claim that I have eternal life when I look at that man or woman?' You must have had that experience; after, for example, reading the life of a man like Hudson Taylor[1] you may have felt you were never a Christian at all. If you have not, there is something wrong with you, for I would regard that as the normal reaction of any Christian. You contrast yourself and you say, 'How can I say I have eternal life when I see such a difference between that man and myself?' and the devil would have us believe that we have no life at all.

Well, again, if we believe that, we are just flying in the face of plain, clear New Testament teaching. The Scripture tells us that we are born into this Christian life as babes, babes in Christ. John in this epistle has been writing to 'little children,' 'young men and old men'; he has a classification and a division (see the second chapter). All that development is possible in this life, so that I think we can answer this particular difficulty by saying, and thank God for this, that a little life is nevertheless life. The baby that was born an hour ago is as much alive as I am; the fact that he is a baby does not mean he is not alive. He is not full-grown, he is not developed, he cannot think and reason, he cannot speak and express himself, but he has life. The babe is as much alive as the old man, and that is the New Testament teaching. So do not let the devil discourage you and rob you in that way; if you are alive at all, you have life.

One of the most gracious words, I think, in the Gospels is that precious word spoken by our Lord where he quotes Isaiah and says, 'The smoking flax he will not quench.' When you look at that flax you may wonder whether there is any fire there at all; it seems absolutely lifeless. But it is all right—there is fire, there is something there; and the smoking flax He will not quench. He will, rather, fan it until it becomes a flame. Though you may have but little life, hold on to the fact that you have life, and thank God for it.

But to sum it all up, we fail to remember that this thing is life, and life is something that shows itself in different ways. Life does not only show itself in feeling and experience—it does so in performing some of the most ordinary common tasks in life; and that is a true test to apply to one's profession of faith. If I have this manifestation of life that John has indicated, I am not interested in feelings, I am not interested in other people's experiences. I face the tests of life, and I see that these things are in me; therefore I must be alive, for a dead man cannot do things like that and would not be like that.

So I would put it in a practical form at this low level. If you are concerned about this question of eternal life, if you feel you have not got it and if it is your greatest ambition to know that you have got it, then you may know that you have got it or you would not have this desire. If you feel that you are empty, if you feel you are nothing, if you feel you are poor and wretched and blind, if you hate your inclination to sin and have any suspicion of a feeling of self-loathing and hatred, you can take it from me that you have eternal life, for no one ever experiences such things until the life of God comes into his or her soul.

There are some further reasons why we should make sure that we have this eternal life. If only we realised the value of this, we would not rest for a moment until we were absolutely certain. Here are some of the reasons: the life that is offered us is nothing less than the life of Jesus Christ; the life you see in Him is the life that He offers. 'I am come,' he says, 'that they might have life, and that they might have it more abundantly' (John 10:10). It is His own life; He gives Himself for the life of the world. We must eat of His flesh and drink of His blood; that means we partake of Him, not the sacrament—we take of *Him*. 'The words that I speak unto you, they are spirit, and they are life,' He says (John 6:63).

In other words, the life that is offered us is the life of God Himself. What an amazing, what a wondrous thought! Yes, but let me go further and say that this life that is offered us is an everlasting life. I know we are often told that eternal life means a quality of life, but it also means duration, and thank God that it does. 'Eternal' includes everlasting, and that means that it is a life that, once I have it, can never be taken away from me. Read the tenth chapter of John. If God gives me His life, and if His life enters into my life, if I am born again of that divine seed, that is an action that is irreversible. Our Lord says of His sheep, 'My Father, which gave them me, is greater than all; and no man is able to pluck them out of my Father's hand' (John 10:29). To me, that is one of the most glorious and amazing things we can ever know, that already there is started in us here something that will go on for ever and ever.

Paul says the same thing, in Romans 8:38-39: 'I am persuaded, that neither death, nor life . . . shall be able to separate us from the love of God, which is in Christ Jesus our Lord.' This is something no one can rob us of, so that whatever may happen to us in this life and world, we have this grand and glorious security. We may be tried and tested and feel ourselves shaking and almost going under, but we have this eternal guarantee behind us.

The work which His goodness began
The arm of His strength will complete,
His promise is yea and amen
And never was forfeited yet.

AUGUSTUS TOPLADY

This is a life that will go on to all eternity; so what we are offered here is a foretaste—these are New Testament terms. We taste the first fruits, so that here on earth, according to this promise, I can begin the great feast that will keep me through the countless ages of all eternity. What a wonderful truth, that here in this world of time I can already sit at the banqueting table and begin to partake and go on without end.

But let me remind you again of what this means. To have eternal life means, as John has reminded us in the third chapter, that I shall see God. If I have this life, I shall see Him; I shall see Christ as He is, and I shall stand in His presence. It is only those who have His nature and share His life and who have been born again who will go on to that; and those who have it will see Him and will be like Him, and they will spend their eternity in glory with Him, enjoying it in His glorious presence.

I remind you of these things, my friends, in order that I may urge anyone who is uncertain to make certain. Would you not like to know you are destined for these things; would you not like to enjoy them here and now? 'That is what is offered,' says John, 'that you may know it now and not lose a second.' But it also helps us in a very practical sense in that if I know I have eternal life already, then I know there is a great life principle working in me. 'Work out your own salvation,' says Paul, 'with fear and trembling: for it is God which worketh in you . . .' And if He is in me in this life, He is working in me 'to will and to do of his good pleasure' (Phil 2:12-13). He is sanctifying me; He is getting things out of my life because He has destined me for that glory; and having destined me for that glory, He will fit me for it.

I have the assurance, therefore, that if this work has begun, the work will end. I 'know' that if I have eternal life, I shall stand one day faultless and blameless, without spot and blemish, in the presence of God's glory. So as I meet temptation and sin in this world, I realise that I am not left to myself. I cease to feel helpless and frustrated. I say, 'If God is in me, if God has destined me for that, then He will come and hold me though all hell and the devils be opposed to me.' That was the mighty argument of a man like Martin Luther. It was because he knew he had eternal life that he could defy all those enemies the way he did, and all those who have this hope in them can say the same thing.

> *And were this world all devils o'er*
> *And watching to devour us,*
> *We lay it not to heart so sore;*
> *Nor they can overpower us.*

If we have eternal life and know that we have it, we know that God's work in our souls will be carried on until it eventuates in that ultimate perfection and glory. As Paul puts it in that mighty bit of logic in the middle of the eighth chapter of Romans, 'Whom he called, them he also justified; and whom'—you see the jump—'he justified, them he also glorified.' If He starts, He will finish, so that if the life is in me, I can be certain of the glory. Far from presuming on that in order to sin, while I am in this life and world I rather say with John, 'Every man that hath this hope in him purifieth himself, even as he is pure' (1 John 3:3). God grant that having listened to these great inducements we all may know for certain that we have eternal life, the life of God in our souls.

11

PRAYER WITH CONFIDENCE

And this is the confidence that we have in him, that, if we ask any thing according to his will, he heareth us: And if we know that he hear us, whatsoever we ask, we know that we have the petitions that we desired of him.

1 JOHN 5:14-15

CLEARLY IN THESE TWO VERSES we have what we may accurately describe as a kind of postscript to the letter. The Apostle has already told us in the thirteenth verse the reasons that prompted him to write his letter at all, and he really had finished it at the end of that verse. But like many another letter writer, he felt it was essential to write a postscript. That, of course, happened because John was so concerned about the condition and the happiness and the welfare of the people to whom he was writing.

That is the great difference between the Scriptures and a work of art. Artistically, I suppose, a postscript is not a good thing, but the men who wrote these epistles were not interested in the art of writing as such. It was not the form that mattered—it was the content and the truth, Knowing the hard life of these people, John is anxious for them, and so he adds a postscript. In his great wisdom he wants to draw certain deductions from what he has already been saying. So what we have in these verses from the fourteenth to the end is just a series of these deductions. It is a sign, again, of a very good teacher that he summarises all he has been saying. These, he says, are the things that we can therefore proceed to act upon as a result of all that we have been laying down.

His first deduction is this whole subject of confidence in prayer. 'This is the confidence that we have in him'—in the light of all we have been saying—'that, if we ask any thing according to his will, he heareth us.' I am sure we need take no time in emphasising the vital importance of this whole subject of prayer. In many ways there is nothing more important for us in this life and pilgrimage than that we should be well instructed in this matter. I have the authority of our Lord Himself for saying that prayer is absolutely essential; He said that 'men ought always to pray, and not to faint' (Luke 18:1), the suggestion being that if you do not pray, you will faint. Prayer is essential to every pilgrim whose face is set upon glory and eternity, and without it we cannot live. Our Lord Himself spent much time in prayer, 'rising up a great while before day,' we read (Mark 1:35), for prayer.

Prayer is vital, and so the Apostle, not unnaturally, draws this as his first deduction or conclusion. 'One of the most wonderful things about all this,' says John in effect, 'is that it enables us to pray with confidence and gives us assurance in our petitions at the throne of grace and of mercy.' He has already mentioned this in passing in the third chapter, in verses 21 and 22: 'Beloved, if our heart condemn us not, then have we confidence toward God. And whatsoever we ask, we receive of him, because we keep his commandments, and do those things that are pleasing in his sight.' And here he tells us once more that nothing is more important than our prayer life and that therefore we should be certain in our minds and in our hearts with regard to this great biblical teaching with regard to prayer.

Yet there is nothing perhaps that seems to give people so much trouble and perplexity as this very question. There is nothing that leads to so much misunderstanding, and I believe that every minister and every pastor would agree in saying that he is probably questioned more frequently about this matter of prayer than about any other single subject. People seem to be in difficulty about it, and the difficulties are almost endless. I shall not deal with them all now; I am simply reminding you of the extraordinary confusion that does seem to obtain with regard to this most vital and central subject. There are those, on the one hand, who seem to feel that prayer is quite unnecessary; they say that in light of the doctrine of the sovereignty of God, how can prayer be possible? If God knows all things and everything is appointed and determined, what is the value of prayer?

But then, at the other extreme, there are people who in a spirit of fanaticism take certain biblical and scriptural statements right out of their context. They fix upon certain particular words and, on the strength of that, pray for and expect and even demand things that are almost ridiculous and thereby bring grievous distress to themselves and even ridicule upon the Christian gospel. There are people who take certain verses, which I shall quote later, and say that on that basis we are entitled to ask and to demand anything; so they try to put God to the test, as it were, and make extraordinary claims. The whole procedure leads to nothing but disappointment and perhaps a shaking of their own faith life.

We find, therefore, that the subject often presents itself as difficult and perplexing to many people. The people of whom I have just been speaking, for instance, are very fond of taking a verse like the fifteenth verse here: 'If we know that he hear us, whatsoever we ask, we know that we have the petitions that we desired of him'; and on the strength of that, they make ridiculous demands. So what do we do in the light of all this? Well, it seems to me that the first rule should be that we must observe carefully and closely what the Scripture really does show, and what the Scripture teaches concerning this subject.

The second is that we must be exceptionally careful in this matter of comparing Scripture with Scripture. The Bible never contradicts itself; therefore, in considering a subject like this, it is a good and a wise thing to gather together everything that Scripture has to tell us about the subject. We must never base our doctrine upon one statement only; or to put it in another way, our doctrine must never be so formulated as to be in conflict with any other statement of Scripture or to contradict any other clear and obvious scriptural teaching. Then, having done that, we come to certain conclusions. One conclusion is, and let me state it before I go any further, that there is an element of mystery about this question of prayer; it is one of those aspects of God's gracious dealings with us that is beyond our understanding. Now I feel like saying, 'Thank God for that!' I mean that in an ultimate and absolute sense you and I simply cannot reconcile God's omniscience and foreknowledge and sovereignty with this fact of prayer that we find so clearly taught in Scripture.

But there are so many other things one cannot understand. I cannot understand how a holy God would ever forgive or can ever forgive a single soul. I cannot understand it, but thank God, I believe it! I cannot understand the eternal mind and heart, but I thank God for a revelation that assures me that God can be just and a justifier of the ungodly. And there are many other instances and illustrations that I could give of exactly the same thing, and this question of prayer is one of them. In an ultimate philosophical sense there is an element of mystery about it, but, praise God, we are not left with philosophy. We have a gospel that comes to us in its simplicity and tells us what to do; so though our little minds cannot understand it philosophically, there is nothing that is so plain and clear in Scripture as that we are taught and exhorted to pray. Go through the Scriptures and notice the frequency of the exhortations to pray.

Not only that but, as I have already reminded you, one sees the very Son of God Himself at prayer. So if you are interested in that philosophical aspect of prayer, go immediately to the case of our Lord Jesus Christ. There is the only begotten, the eternal Son of God; there is the one who says of Himself that though He is upon earth, He is still in heaven; there is the one who says, 'I and my Father are one' (John 10:30). Why had He any need to pray; why, before choosing His disciples, did He spend all night in prayer? If you are interested in philosophical problems answer that; why was it ever necessary for the Son of God to pray so much while He was here on earth? And yet He did.

In other words, the Scripture teaches that prayer is essential and vital to us, and everywhere we are exhorted to it. Not only that, but if you read the lives of God's greatest saints in the long history of the Church, you will find that they were men and women of prayer. I believe I am right in saying that John Wesley used to say that any Christian worthy of the name should spend at least four hours every day in prayer, and he tended to judge his people by that. There has never been a man or woman of God who has been singularly used of God in this world, but that they spent much time in prayer. The nearer people are to God, the more they pray to Him; so that the testimony of the Christian Church supports the teaching of Scripture itself.

Furthermore, we have numerous incidents in Scripture of what

God has clearly done by way of answer to prayer, and it seems to me that the explanation ultimately is not really difficult. The God who determines the end determines the means; and if God in His infinite wisdom is determined that He is going to bring certain things to pass as a result of and in answer to the prayers of His people, I ask with reverence, why shouldn't He? And it is there that I see the infinite condescension and kindness of God. It is His way of bringing us into and giving us a share in the work and in the glory. If you read Paul's epistle to the Philippians, you will find this. He explicitly tells them that God is doing this 'through your prayer' (Phil 1:19), so that they may come in for a share of the glory and rejoicing; and thus it was that the great Apostle who knew the mind and will of God and was so happy in the hands of God nevertheless pleaded with the Philippians to pray for him and for his release from prison.

This is God's way of doing things. As He has decided to order and maintain the creation through various laws that He has put into nature, so he has decided to work in the spiritual realm through prayer. God could maintain the universe without the laws of nature, but He does not choose to do it in that way. This is cause and effect; instead of doing things directly, He does them indirectly. And it seems to me that prayer is involved in some such way as that. However, we must not be concerned or bothered about the philosophical aspect; it is for us to observe the plain injunctions and exhortations of the Scriptures. It is for us to observe the lives of the saints and to see that prayer was the very breath of their life; and if we would follow the way the Master went, we likewise must spend much time in prayer.

I am concerned, therefore, only to look at a certain number of principles concerning this matter that seem to me to be obvious in the light of the teaching of these two verses. The first is that if we want to have real confidence in prayer, then we must know that we ourselves are accepted by God. If I have any doubts in my mind as to whether I am accepted by God, then prayer will be useless. I cannot pray about any particular thing if I am unhappy about myself or if I am doubtful as to whether God is there and whether He is listening to me and is prepared to accept my person. I must start with that. 'Now,' said John, 'this is one of the most glorious things of all. These things have I written unto you . . . that ye may know that ye have eternal life; and if you know that you have that, then this is the confidence that we have in him, that if we ask any thing according to his will, he heareth us.' You see the argument. If I know that I have eternal life, then I know I am a child of God; and if I know I am a child of God, then I know that God is my Father. God is not some abstract X away in the heavens; God is not just some great force spelt with a capital F; He is not some great potentate away in the eternity of holiness. If I know I have eternal life and am a child of God, God is my Father, and I then know that He hears me.

This is a most interesting statement—'he heareth us.' Now obviously, hearing is not something mechanical, because in that sense God hears everybody. No; this word '*heareth*' is a very special one and is full of great meaning. It means that His ears are open to us; it means that His heart is enlarged towards us. There used to be a saying that so-and-so was 'the King's favourite' and that the favourite always 'had the King's ear.' That does not mean that the King could not physically hear other people who spoke to him; it meant that the man who was a favourite of the King would be especially heard by him. And that is what John means; if we have eternal life, if we are His children, we, I say it with reverence, have the ear of God—we can be confident that He is always waiting to listen to us. This was put very clearly by the blind man who was healed by our Lord. After he had been healed, the Jews questioned him as to who had done this, almost trying to prove to him that it could not have happened like that, because, they said, 'This man is a sinner.' So he replied, 'Now we know that God heareth not sinners; but if any man be a worshipper of God, and doeth his will, him he heareth' (John 9:31). 'I know,' said the blind man, 'that God has heard this man; otherwise I would not have been healed. So he cannot be a sinner because God does not hear sinners.'

What he meant was that God is not ready to do what sinners ask of Him, that God's ear is not open to them, that His heart is not enlarged towards them. But if you have accepted the whole of the teaching of this epistle and have applied the various tests propounded by John to yourself, and if as the result of all that, you know you have eternal life, then you know God is always ready to listen to you. He is always ready to receive you in audience; you need never have any doubt about that. He is your Father, and He loves you with an everlasting love. The very hairs of your head are all numbered; He is concerned about you. Think of an earthly father's love and multiply that by infinity, taking all sin out of it, and that is God's attitude towards you.

Christian people, we should always approach the throne of God with confidence and, of course, always with reverence and godly fear, because He who is in heaven is our Father. Yes, but always with assurance, always with what the author of the Epistle to the Hebrews calls a holy 'boldness' (Heb 10:19). So if you like, we can translate verse 14 like this: 'This is the boldness we have with respect to Him.' Let us, therefore, never be uncertain; get that settled before you offer a single petition. Start by thanking Him that you are His child, that He has adopted you, and that you are in Christ, and therefore He delights to see you come and to hear you offering up your prayers and your petitions. We are a favourite of the King if we have eternal life.

The second principle I deduce is this: we must not only know that we ourselves are accepted—we must also know that our prayers are accepted. 'This is the confidence that we have in him, that, if we ask any thing according to his will, he heareth us. And if we know that he hear us, whatsoever we ask, we know that we have the petitions that we desired of him.' This is a really important principle. It is at this point, of course, that the danger of excess and fanaticism comes in, and it always does so because people will not observe the conditions that are laid down so plainly in the Scriptures. Let me, then, remind you of some of the conditions, and as I am trying first to make a brief comprehensive statement, I shall merely give you some headings at this point.

What, then, are the conditions that must be observed before we can be confident and assured that our prayers are accepted by God? The first is that our motive in praying must be a correct and a true one. 'Ye ask, and receive not, because ye ask amiss, that ye may consume it upon your lusts' (Jas 4:3). 'You are complaining to me,' says James, 'that your prayers are not answered, and I tell you that this is the reason.' I think we all know what is meant by that. Our prayers can be unutterably selfish; we want a blessing for ourselves or for our family—not for the glory of God, but for ourselves. It is possible for a man to ask for his ministry to be blessed so that he may consume it upon his own lusts, his own self-esteem, and he must not be surprised if his prayers are not answered. A man may ask that souls may be given as a result of his preaching, but they are not given because if they were he would be still more inflated with his own pride. Are you troubled because your prayers are not answered? Well, search your heart. Why are you praying? Why do you want your prayers to be answered? What is the reason for that particular petition; is it something purely selfish, something you can consume upon your own lusts, your own self-love? The motive must be right and clean and pure.

The second condition is faith and believing. These words were uttered by our Lord Himself: 'And all things, whatsoever ye shall ask in prayer, believing, ye shall receive' (Matt 21:22). Or listen again to James: 'If any of you lack wisdom, let him ask of God, that giveth to all men liberally, and upbraideth not; and it shall be given him. But,' says James, 'let him ask in faith, nothing wavering: for he that wavereth is like a wave of the sea driven with the wind and tossed. For let not that man think that he shall receive any thing of the Lord' (Jas 1:5-8). There is no writer in Scripture who is more maligned than James. There is nothing, quite honestly, that so frightens me as I read Scripture as the place given to faith in the writings of James. Take his statement about the prayer of faith healing the sick (5:6). Without faith, says James, your prayers will not be answered.

Again, let us examine ourselves when we are on our knees in prayer. Do we really believe, or is it a desperate cry in the dark, in the words of the poem, speaking to 'whatever gods may be'? Is it some desperate experiment, doubtful of an answer? If it is, we must not be surprised if our prayers are not answered. There must be no doubt; we must be clear about God and our relationship to Him. Our prayers must be believing and in faith.

Another condition laid down in Scripture is that we must abide in Christ and be obedient to God. Here are the words of our Lord: 'If ye abide in me, and my words abide in you, ye shall ask what ye will, and it shall be done unto you' (John 15:7). 'If ye abide in me'—the condition is there. Or you remember what John said earlier in chapter 3 of his first epistle, verse 22: 'And whatsoever we ask, we receive of him, because we keep his commandments, and do those things that are pleasing in his sight.' We must be obedient to God and His holy laws; we have no right to expect our prayers to be received and answered if we are living in known sin, or if we are doing anything that we know to be contrary to the will of God. We must keep His commandments; we must abide in Him, and His words must abide in us. Or take the condition that is given us in this verse that we are now considering: 'This is the confidence that we have in him, that, if we ask any thing according to his will, he heareth us'—it must be according to the will of God.

The last condition is that our prayers must be in the name of Christ. He Himself said, 'Whatsoever ye shall ask in my name, that will I do' (John 14:13); and, '. . . that whatsoever ye shall ask of the Father in my name, he may give it you' (John 15:16). And again, 'No man cometh unto the Father, but by me' (John 14:6). There is no value in prayer unless it is given in the name of the Lord Jesus Christ. This is an absolute, essential condition. We have no right to expect prayer to be answered otherwise; we have no reason to believe it is acceptable in the sight of God. Of course, psychologists will tell you that prayer does you good; but when you regard prayer as nothing but a psychological exercise, you are persuading yourself, and I am not talking about that. I am talking about having an audience with God the Father and having a sure knowledge that He hears and receives us.

But let me go on to the third principle. To pray with assurance, we must not only know that we are accepted and that our prayers are accepted, we must believe—indeed, we must have confidence—that our petitions are granted if we observe the conditions we have just laid down. Now this is a very striking thing. 'If we know that he hear us, whatsoever we ask, we know that we have the petitions that we desired of him.' He does not say, 'We *shall* have'; he says, we '*have* them'; we have already got them, we already possess them. This is a very remarkable and astounding statement. The people who pray truly in this world can be certain that they already have the petitions they have desired of God.

Here again, I feel, is a statement that has often been misinterpreted. People say, 'When you offer a petition to God, if you can really persuade yourself that you have already got it, you have got it.' But that, I say again, is nothing but sheer psychology; not only is it psychology, it is something even worse. It ultimately means that what determines God's answer to my prayer is my persuading myself that I have already got it. That is not the teaching of the Scripture! The teaching of Scripture is, rather, something like this: take that famous statement in Mark's Gospel, chapter 11 and verse 24 (this is the favourite text of those who misinterpret this teaching of prayer): 'What things soever ye desire, when ye pray believe that ye receive them, and ye shall have them.' 'Now,' they say, 'the only thing to do is this: persuade yourself that you receive them and you shall have them.' And they are there on their knees agonising and trying to persuade themselves that they have got it, and then in the end they find it has not happened; they persuade themselves and yet it does not take place. They ask, 'What has happened? God has broken His word,' and their whole faith is shaken.

What, then, is wrong with that interpretation? Well, I think we should interpret Mark 11:24 by considering Romans 8:26 and 27 where we read this: 'Likewise the Spirit also helpeth our infirmities: for we know not what we should pray for as we ought: but the Spirit itself maketh intercession for us with groanings which cannot be uttered.' Then notice: 'And he that searcheth the hearts knoweth what is the mind of the Spirit, because he maketh intercession for the saints according to the will of God.' So if you take those two statements together, I think that it comes to this: Mark 11:24 seems to me, in the light of Romans 8:26, to mean that when I feel a desire and a prompting and an urge to pray, if I know and believe that I have received that from God through the Holy Spirit, I can be confident that I shall have my desires and my requests.

Is that not exactly what Paul is teaching in Romans 8? So often 'we know not what we should pray for as we ought,' says Paul. So what happens? 'The Spirit itself maketh intercession for us with groanings which cannot be uttered,' and here are we just groaning and sighing in the presence of God. What is a sigh? It is something created in you by the Spirit, and the Spirit knows the mind of God, and He always prompts and urges according to the will of God. And the promise is that 'if we ask any thing' according to the will of God He hears us; and we know that if He hears, 'we have the petitions that we desired of him.' It works like this, you see: when you believe that your prayer comes to your heart from the Spirit of God, you may be sure that an answer to your prayer will also be given from God. If I am surrendered to God, and if my one concern is to please Him, as I pray I feel and know that this petition has come to me from God, and I pray with confidence, I pray with assurance.

Is that not your experience? Do you not know something of what I am trying to say? There are times when I am led to pray; I am prompted or urged to pray, and as I pray I know I have my petition, I have already received my answer. The actual answer, in practice, may not come for weeks, for years even, and yet I know I have received it. That, it seems to me, is the plain, clear teaching not only of these words but also of those parallel passages. This is often illustrated in the lives of God's saints. They may have prayed, for instance, for physical healing, and they have prayed with confidence; they have felt led and prompted to do so, and healing has taken place. Then there has been another occasion in their experience where somebody dear to them has been taken ill. They do not feel the same urge to pray, but they do pray, and the loved one is not healed. That is the sort of thing I mean; the Holy Spirit lays these things upon the hearts of men and women and works within, 'with groanings which cannot be uttered.' We do not know how to pray—there is this sort of sigh; but if you know that the Spirit is within you, you can be certain you have your answer. The Spirit will never lead you to pray about anything but that God has, in a sense, granted you that thing.

Now this just means in practise—and oh, how comforting this is— that these are the kind of things we can pray for with absolute confidence. We can pray that all the precepts, all the promises, and all the prophecies with respect to ourselves may be fulfilled in us. 'This is the will of God, even your sanctification' (1 Thess 4:3); and if you pray for sanctification, you can be sure that God will sanctify you. It is God's will that we may know His love; ask Him therefore to reveal His love to you by the Holy Spirit, and you can be certain He will do so. And the same with all these various other promises that are in the Scriptures: 'Ask, and it shall be given you; seek, and ye shall find; knock, and it shall be opened unto you' (Matt 7:7).

Are you concerned that you do not love as much as you ought? Tell Him about it, ask Him to shed His love abroad in your heart, and He will do so. Are you concerned about some sin that casts you down? Pray this confident prayer; it is the will of God that you should be delivered from sin, so pray for it. Are you concerned that your heart shall be clean? Well, offer David's prayer ('Create within me a clean heart, O God; and renew a right spirit within me,' Psa 51:10), and I assure you, on the Word of God and on His character, that He will answer you, and the blood of Christ will cleanse you from all sin and all unrighteousness. Go through your Bible and make a list of the promises of God to you; then take them to God, use them in His presence, plead them, and you can be quite certain that you have your petition. You already possess it, and in His own time and way God will give you a full realisation of it and a full enjoyment of it.

That, then, is the first deduction that we draw from this blessed knowledge that we have eternal life and that we are children of God. It transforms prayer; prayer no longer becomes an uncertain experiment, something done in desperation. No! We get down on our knees, and we know we speak to our Father, the Father of our Lord Jesus Christ, the one who loved us so much as to send His Son to the death of the cross for us. We come to Him knowing that; and then, knowing that our prayers are according to His will, we pray with confidence. We believe we have the answer, and we rise up calm and quiet and rejoicing and go on our way, leaving it to Him to grant us the precise performance of the petition in practice, but being certain that He has not only heard us, but that He has even answered us.

May God grant us this assurance, this holy boldness in prayer so that whatever our condition, we may take it to the Lord in prayer and do so confidently.

12

PRAYER FOR THE BRETHREN

If any man see his brother sin a sin which is not unto death, he shall ask, and he shall give him life for them that sin not unto death. There is a sin unto death: I do not say that he shall pray for it. All unrighteousness is sin; and there is a sin not unto death.

1 JOHN 5:16-17

WE HAVE HERE THE second of the deductions that the Apostle draws from this great doctrine of the assurance of salvation and the possession of eternal life. He has told us, you remember, in the thirteenth verse that this is the great concern that he had in mind when he came to write the letter—the controlling thought. The most important thing in this life and world, according to John, is that we should know that we have eternal life; that has been the great theme that he has demonstrated in various ways. But here the Apostle puts it especially in terms of this confidence and assurance in prayer; and as we saw in our consideration of verses 14 and 15, he there drew the first deduction about our own personal, private prayer, when we ourselves are faced with difficulties and problems in a world like this—a world that, he is going to remind us again in the nineteenth verse, lies in wickedness or in the wicked one. When we are beset by trials and temptations, what can be more important than that we should know the way into the presence of the Father and should go there with confidence?

That is John's first deduction, and we have worked that out. But now he goes on to a second, and this has a reference to our prayers for one another, our prayers for the brethren. 'If any man see his brother sin a sin which is not unto death, he shall ask . . .' Now one cannot really look at this statement without again being impressed by the writer's method; we have already seen it so many times, and here is another example of it. John, in his whole thinking and outlook, was clearly controlled by certain basic principles and considerations, and he moves naturally and inevitably from the one to the other. You see, he cannot talk about our personal prayer without immediately thinking of prayer for the brother or sister also; how often have we seen him doing exactly this same thing.

In other words, the tests of life are not only that I should be in the right relationship to God, but that I should also be in the right relationship to my brother—brotherly love once more. After my love to God and my relationship to Him comes my relationship to the brethren. Of course, this is a great, central biblical doctrine: 'Thou shalt love the Lord thy God with all thy heart, and with all thy soul, and with all thy strength, and with all thy mind; and thy neighbor as thyself' (Luke 10:27). It is all there, but here, in particular, the reference is to the Christian brethren, those who are members of the same household of faith and of the same family of believers. And here that is what John is concerned to emphasise; he is controlled by these things.

Let me put it to you like this in a picture: we are among a number of Christian people in a world like this. We know that we are of God and that the whole world lies in the evil one, and we are a company of people marching through this wilderness. Now, we are in fellowship with God; we are walking with Him; we have fellowship with the Father and His Son, Jesus Christ, and with one another. And as we go on, nothing is more important than that these relationships should be maintained in the right way. We are concerned, obviously, about our own condition; we must be sure that we are right with God. But our concern does not stop at that—we must be concerned about the whole family. We must have this view of ourselves as Christian people, God's people—as members of the Church, in which we see ourselves as God's household, God's family. We must have a great and jealous concern about that family; our desire should be that everybody in it should be enjoying the full benefits of this great salvation and are marching together to Zion with God. So we should be very concerned that we ourselves do not fall, and we should be equally concerned that our brother or sister should not fall.

That is the New Testament concept; it is this wonderful picture of a family of people and every one of them concerned about the other. Now in this particular connection, John is concerned to emphasise the importance of prayer for a brother who may fall or fail. And once more his great doctrine is the assurance with which we should offer such a prayer, having already emphasised that we should be certain that our petitions are granted to us personally if they are in accordance with the will of God. But now he makes a tremendous claim and says that if we truly pray for this brother who has fallen into 'the sin not unto death,' we shall give him life as it were—a wonderful statement showing the effectiveness of prayer that is truly prayed on behalf of the brethren.

But I need scarcely remind you that the Apostle puts this statement, this doctrine, in such words and in such language that its main effect has often been to cause perplexity and considerable misunderstanding and trouble in the minds of many individuals in the Church. These words have often engaged the attention of men and women. What exactly do they mean, 'a sin unto death' and 'a sin not unto death'?

Now here again it seems to me that I must make one glancing comment as I pass on. Have you noticed how it happens that some of these most thorny problems in connection with the life of faith, the Christian life, are to be found in the writings of John? Take, for instance, the particular ones we have discovered in working through this epistle. How often has that first chapter been a bone of contention over the words, 'If we say that we have no sin, we deceive ourselves' and so on. Then take some of those statements in the third chapter where he says, 'Whosoever is born of God doth not commit sin'; all the argument about perfectionism really comes from that. And then we have had those various statements that we have been considering recently in this fifth chapter about the three witnesses. And it is interesting to observe that some of these difficult problems seem to have arisen from various statements made in the writings of John rather than in the writings of the Apostle Paul.

I mention this in passing merely so that those who are interested in these matters, as I think we all should be, and those who are especially interested in the question of inspiration, might pause and just ponder it. What is the precise relationship of that fact to the doctrine of inspiration? Why should these statements almost invariably be things said by John rather than by one of the other writers? It does not invalidate for a moment the doctrine of inspiration, but it does show very clearly that the doctrine of verbal inspiration does not mean a mere mechanical dictation. The personality of the writer is left as it was, and the individual characteristics of style and mode of thought remain, whereas the truth is guaranteed and controlled. There are these interesting variations. I have often queried whether it is right at all to compare and contrast the writings of these different writers, but people have done so. They say that John is more profound than Paul, and I mention this word in passing to people who hold that view: this way of putting things *is* more profound than the other way, and the logic of the great Apostle to the Gentiles is not something superior, if we can make such comparisons, to this more poetical, mystical style of the Apostle John. However, that point is not vital to salvation, nor is it vital as a doctrine, though it is a matter of interest.

So then, seeing that we have here once more one of those typical statements by this particular writer, let us be careful how we approach it. And again the whole secret is that we should observe carefully what he does and what he does not say. Instead of rushing off into particular theories and views, let us clearly observe the statement of the Apostle. So let me put it in the form of a question: what are the conditions of effectual prayer for the brethren? That is the theme, and we must never lose sight of it. And here, as I see it, are the answers. The first is that we must be in right relationship with the brethren; and the first thing here, obviously, is that we must realise that he is a brother. You see, here is the picture: there is the infant church to which John is writing. He is an old man, and he is about to leave them, and he is concerned about their welfare and happiness. 'Now,' he says, 'in a sense you must look after one another's interest. Remember, you are brethren; so if you see anyone who is a member of the church fall into sin, pray. He is a brother, not an outsider. If you believe you have eternal life, if all these others have the same life, you must be brothers.'

That is the deduction; it is a perfect theological deduction. Once more, Christian people are not merely a collection of individuals who may hold certain views in common and come together for certain purposes. Not at all! According to the New Testament we are to realise we are brothers and sisters; we belong to the same Father; we are partakers of the same divine nature; we have this intimate relationship of blood, as it were, than which nothing can be deeper or stronger. So we must look at one another as brothers and sisters; this is a family relationship. And that, of course, leads in turn to this: we must be concerned about one another; we should be exercising a watchful care and interest in one another; we should have a real concern about one another.

Of course, John does not mean by that that we should be busybodies; that is condemned in the New Testament. But it does mean that as members of a family we are not unnatural. As we are naturally interested in one another and love one another and are concerned about one another's welfare, so it should be with the members of the Christian Church. It should be a matter of great concern to all of us if any one of us is falling into sin, not only because it brings the Christian gospel into disrepute, but because our very love for that brother should make us concerned about him. We should be sorry; we should be grieved that he is missing so much and that he is bringing unhappiness upon himself and is putting himself into the wrong relationship to God and that he is likely to experience chastisement and punishment. We should be deeply and gravely concerned about him. We should not be impatient; we should not say, 'Why does this fellow let us down? Let him reap the consequences of his own actions.' Let us not say, 'We will carry on whatever he may do.' No; 'bear ye one another's burdens,' said the Apostle Paul (Gal 6:2), meaning exactly the same thing. Or again, 'Look not every man on his own things, but every man also on the things of others. Let this mind be in you, which was also in Christ Jesus' (Phil 2:4-5); Christ did not consider Himself but considered you. That other man is a brother, and we must be greatly concerned for him and his welfare.

And then the next thing John tells us in this reference to the brother is that we shall 'ask' for him before God. Now this word '*ask*' is a very strong one. 'If any man see his brother sin a sin which is not unto death, he shall ask, and he shall give him life for them that sin not unto death.' The word really means 'beseech'; it means that we should be urgent in prayer, that we should always be in an agony of prayer; it should be a fervent prayer. Now we all know what that kind of prayer is for ourselves. When we are in some desperate plight or condition we do not merely ask, we beseech—we agonize before Him. 'Do that for your brother,' says John; 'implore; be urgent and fervent.

Do not cease, as it were, until the brother is restored.' That is the way to pray for the brethren.

So there, I say, we have this wonderful picture of the life of the Church; that is John's conception of a Church.

> *Brother clasps the hand of brother,*
> *Stepping fearless through the night.*
>
> BERNHARDT INGEMANN

Christians are meant to be realising their unity, their oneness, their relationship—knowing something of the glory to which they are marching—bound together by this great love not only for the Father and the Son and the Holy Spirit, but for one another also. Because of their privileged and unique position, they exercise this watchful care; and if a brother falls, they 'restore such a one in the spirit of meekness,' remembering that they also have their weaknesses. They bear one another's burdens remembering while they do so that 'Every man shall bear his own burden' (Gal 6:1-5); they bear one another's sin. The New Testament is full of that—this oneness, living in this great concern and this great fellowship of prayer for one another. That is the relationship that must be personal before our prayers for one another can be efficacious.

But now let us turn to the second principle, which is the difficult one. The second great principle controlling this matter is that we must have a clear view of the nature of sin. We must be perfectly clear about this because John immediately introduces qualifications: 'If any man see his brother sin a sin which is not unto death'—he must know what is meant by that—'he shall ask, and he shall give him life for them that sin not unto death.' Then, 'there is a sin unto death: I do not say he shall pray for it. All unrighteousness is sin: and there is a sin not unto death.' Let us, then, approach these statements one by one. Here, it seems to me, is what we can say with confidence about the nature of sin. First, 'all unrighteousness is sin'; anything that is not righteous is sin. Anything that is not living according to God's way of life for us is sin; anything that is a departure from God's will and purpose and desire for us is sin.

Now, John undoubtedly makes that statement because, once more, he is anxious to counter the false doctrines of perfectionism and antinomianism that he has dealt with so frequently. He was concerned about those people who say, 'Because I am a Christian, because I have the love of God in my heart, I no longer sin; I am free from it.' 'All unrighteousness is sin,' says John; 'do not listen to people who talk like that. If you see your brother doing something that is patently wrong, that is sin, and he needs your prayer.' Likewise with the people who are guilty of antinomianism, who say that such things do not matter to the Christian, and who say that because they are Christians, their actions, as it were, are irrelevant—that it is the flesh that sinned, not themselves. 'Oh no!' says John; 'all unrighteousness is sin; anything which we ourselves recognise as unworthy or imperfect is sin and nothing else. You must not call it weakness or indiscretion—it is sin; it is a violation of God's law, and anything that is a violation of God's law is sin.' He has told us, you remember, in the third and fourth chapters[1] that the seed of unrighteousness is sin. There is no need to argue about this, he says; all that is the simple truth concerning us; we know that sin is the transgression of the law—those are his various statements. That is the first thing.

The second statement about sin is this: all sin interrupts the life of fellowship with God. I test that in this way: 'If any man see his brother sin a sin which is not unto death, he shall ask, and he shall give him life for them that sin not unto death.' So it is obvious that this brother, who has sinned 'a sin which is not unto death' has somehow or another interrupted his life of fellowship with God. And the result of our prayer for such a man, says John, is that in effect we are going to be able to give back to him this life that has been interrupted—from which I draw the negative deduction that all sin interrupts our life of fellowship with God. The normal Christian life is a life of uninterrupted fellowship and communion with Him. 'This is life eternal, that they might know thee the only true God, and Jesus Christ, whom thou has sent' (John 17:3). The moment we sin, there is a cloud, as it were, over that knowledge; there is a losing of God's face for the time being, and the fellowship has been interrupted. You find that in the first chapter of this epistle: 'God is light, and in him is no darkness at all. If we say that we have fellowship with him, and walk in darkness, we lie, and do not the truth' (1:5-6). That is always the effect of sin; it interrupts this blessed communion and fellowship, and for the time being we seem to be lifeless and cold.

I need not press this; we all must know it in experience, and it is perhaps one of the most delicate and sensitive tests of whether we are Christians or not. When we fall into sin, what grieves us most of all is not the sin we have done, but the fact that we have hurt the Person. An interruption has come into the fellowship, and we, as it were, feel we are dead and have lost the face of God. What a terrible statement about sin; what an exhortation to us to watch and pray; what an urge to us to be wary and to walk circumspectly in this world! That is what sin does; it comes between you and the one who loves you with an everlasting, eternal love. It is the thing that will rob you of the smile and the face of God; oh, what a horrible, foul, ugly thing it is.

That is always the effect of sin, but that brings us to the crucial statement: 'there is a sin unto death.' What is this? Now, it is here that the discussion has arisen. I do not think that we need to spend much time with it because the main points can be reduced to a very small compass. There are those who suggest that the whole thing is quite simple and that John is merely referring to what the Apostle Paul speaks of in the passage on the communion of the Lord's Supper. He exhorts the people, when they come to the Table of the Lord, to examine themselves, and he gives various reasons for this. One is that it is because some people do not examine themselves that 'many are weak and sickly among you, and many sleep' (1 Cor 11:30); and 'sleep' there means death. There are those, says the Apostle Paul, who in a sense are dead because of this lack of self-examination. So these people say that is what John is referring to here. He is referring to the people who have sinned in such a way that it leads to their physical death.

Now that seems to me to be an utterly impossible and a totally inadequate explanation, because when John talks of giving life to the brother who has not sinned unto death, he is not thinking of physical life. He is obviously thinking of spiritual life, and the whole context and connotation, therefore, must be determined by that. He is referring to spiritual death and not physical death, and I can prove that still further. I am told that I must pray for the man who has sinned not unto death; but John tells me, 'I do not pray for the man who has sinned a sin unto death.' Well, if sinning unto death means physical death, how do I know the man is going to die? What is the point of telling me to pray for a man who is not going to die? Clearly, therefore, it is a useless commandment. No; this has reference beyond any doubt to a spiritual condition, a spiritual condition that you and I are capable of praying about.

'There is a sin unto death,' says John, and surely it must be that to which he has referred so frequently in his letter. It is the doctrine of the antichrists, the thing he has been emphasising so much. 'Beloved,' he says, 'believe not every spirit, but try the spirits whether they are of God: because many false prophets are gone out into the world. Hereby know ye the Spirit of God: Every spirit that confesseth that Jesus Christ is come in the flesh is of God: And every spirit that confesseth not that Jesus Christ is come in the flesh is not of God: and this is that spirit of antichrist, whereof ye have heard that it should come; and even now already is it in the world' (4:1-3). And, you remember, he has also already dealt with this at great length in the second chapter: 'Little children, it is the last time: and as ye have heard that antichrist shall come, even now are there many antichrists; whereby we know that it is the last time.' Then he says, 'They went out from us, but they were not of us; for if they had been of us, they would no doubt have continued with us: but they went out, that they might be made manifest that they were not all of us' (2:18-19).

That is it; that is what he is talking about. There were people in the early church who claimed to be Christian members of the church, but they had gone out. They had left the church; they had denied this doctrine concerning Jesus as the Son of God and Jesus as the Christ. And that is why, in a sense, John writes his letter to safeguard against that. It is a terrible thing that a man should deny that Jesus is the Son of God. In other words, it seems perfectly clear to me that John here is simply repeating that teaching of the Lord concerning blasphemy against the Holy Ghost of which we read at the beginning of Matthew 12 and in the sixth chapter of the Epistle to the Hebrews. It is a wilful rejection of the teaching of the Holy Spirit as to the true nature and Messiahship of Jesus, the denying of Christ as to His true nature. That is what is meant by the sin against the Holy Ghost, and that is what John means by 'a sin unto death.'

Now let me elaborate that a little more closely, because it has so often caused people grievous trouble. Clearly this is something that cannot exist in unbelievers generally. Unbelievers are not wilful, they are not deliberate—they are just blind and ignorant. There are many in the world today who say, 'I do not believe this gospel about Jesus being the Son of God'; they are incapable of the sin against the Holy Ghost. The people who sin against the Holy Ghost are people like the Pharisees—people who claim a knowledge and an interest and an understanding; people like those described in Hebrews 6, who had been in the church and had experienced, in general, certain of the operations of the Holy Spirit and then had turned against the gospel—they denied and denounced it and said, 'Jesus is not a man—perhaps He's even an imposter.'

That is it. These are those who come into that category of having 'tasted the good word of God, and the powers of the world to come' (Heb 6:5) and then deny them—those who claim to know and yet wilfully and deliberately denounce and reject it all; those who refuse this testimony of the Holy Spirit with regard to the Son of God. We have already seen this in this chapter; John puts it like this: 'He that believeth on the Son of God hath the witness in himself; he that believeth not God hath made him a liar; because he believeth not the record that God gave of his Son' (v 10). And God gave record of the Son, he said, through the 'water,' through the 'blood,' and through 'the Holy Ghost'; to deny this witness and evidence of the Holy Spirit with regard to Jesus of Nazareth is to make God a liar, and obviously this is an unforgivable sin.

But let me be still more particular and practical. Who are the people who are *not* guilty of the sin against the Holy Ghost? I deliberately put this negatively. Let me answer like this: those who believe they are guilty of the sin against the Holy Ghost are obviously not guilty of it. If you are afraid, my friend, that you have committed the sin against the Holy Ghost, on the basis of this exposition I say to you that you can be absolutely certain you are not guilty. To be afraid that you are guilty of it is proof that you are not. The people who are guilty are people like the Pharisees, who ridicule Jesus with contempt, who are self-satisfied and dismiss Him and say, 'This is the devil, and He is doing what He does by means of Beelzebub' (compare Mark 3:22). They were arrogant, self-satisfied, self-assured; so if you are very unhappy about this thing, you are opposite to the people who are guilty of the sin against the Holy Ghost.

But take the second thing: to be assailed by doubts and evil thoughts about the Lord Jesus Christ is not to be guilty of the sin against the Holy Ghost, and for this reason: that comes from the devil. It is a temptation; it was the sort of temptation with which the devil tempted our Lord. He said, 'If thou be the Son of God . . .' (Matt 4:3). Now this is the way you can settle that: do these evil thoughts trouble you; do you regret them; do you say, 'What can I do to get rid of them?' If you do, then you are as far away from the sin against the Holy Ghost as anyone can ever be. The people who sin against the Holy Ghost are not worried or troubled;

they are absolutely certain they are right, and they pour contempt on the truth. To be worried about doubts and evil thoughts, to hate them means, I say, that you are not guilty of the sin against the Holy Ghost; you have not sinned the sin unto death—you are the very opposite of it.

Also, the people who feel terribly unworthy and who are concerned about the fact that they are not more worthy as Christians, they, again, are not those who have committed the sin against the Holy Ghost. And lastly I would say that those who are trying to find God and wish to be found of Him, those who pray and go the place of prayer, those who delight to hear the gospel—all these are not guilty of this sin. I put it like that because I once received a letter from an anonymous writer that went as follows: 'How does one know if he or she has sinned against the Holy Ghost? Would one try to find God or to be found of God, or pray, or come to the place of prayer? Would a person who has sinned against the Holy Ghost,' asked this writer, 'do such things?' And the answer is, 'No!' Would a person who has committed this dreadful sin like to attend evangelistic meetings or bring other people to them? Would such a person ever be touched by a soul-searching sermon and have to fight the tears that will sometimes come and, when tempted to commit suicide, fear to do so because of the hereafter? And the answer in every single case is again a confident and assured, 'No!'

The people who have sinned against the Holy Ghost have gone out, said John, and they do so positively and with assurance. These are the people who have sinned the sin unto death; but troubled, tormented, humble souls who are unhappy about this thing and hate these ugly, foul thoughts, who are harassed by them and long to get rid of them, who are troubled about the imperfection of their lives and love—such people are as far away from the sin against the Holy Ghost or the sin that is unto death as it is possible for a person to be. The people who are guilty of this sin are arrogant and self-satisfied; they dismiss the gospel and do not want to hear God. That is the character of such a person, and that brings me to my final deduction.

All sin that is short of that is sin for which we can pray and pray with confidence, not only in ourselves, but in any other person. 'There is a sin not unto death'; 'the sin unto death' is that which crucifies Christ afresh, saying that He is not the Saviour, saying that His blood shed upon the cross is not the only way. That alone is 'the sin unto death,' and anything short of that is not. And when men and women have not sinned that sin, with love and compassion, with concern and with urgency we not only *can* pray for them—we *should* pray for them. And we have this blessed assurance that if we pray thus with faith, knowing the access we have to Him, we shall be able, as it were, to restore that brother and sister; God will see that our prayer is the means of restoring them to the full life of fellowship. They will continue with us in this glorious march towards Zion, and we shall rejoice together more than ever at the wondrous grace of God that not only forgives us at the beginning, but that continues to forgive us and to heal our backsliding and to restore us to the joyous life of fellowship.

13

SAFE IN THE ARMS OF JESUS

We know that whosoever is born of God sinneth not; but he that is begotten of God keepeth himself, and that wicked one toucheth him not.

1 JOHN 5:18

WE COME HERE TO the first of three statements that are made by the Apostle John in this postscript to his letter, each of which starts with this confident assertion 'we know.' He has been dealing with prayer, our own personal private prayer and our prayer for others; and having said all that, he comes to this statement of the eighteenth verse. You will see, in a manner that is very characteristic of himself, that the Apostle takes up a thought and expounds it. I have often pointed out as we have worked through this letter that really the way to understand John is to remember that his method is rather that of the poet or musician than that of the logician or one who uses the more orthodox type of reasoning. He never seems to start out by laying down a number of propositions and then treating them one by one. He rather takes up a theme and, in dealing with that, mentions a certain aspect, and that, as it were, suggests another major theme to him, so he takes it up.

Now here is a perfect illustration of that. John is really setting out to take up the theme of praying for one another and the thought in particular of praying for brothers and sisters when they fall into sin. But that raises a question in his mind. He has said in verse 17 that 'all unrighteousness is sin,' and that 'there is a sin not unto death,' and so you must pray for a man who is in that condition. But then he says to himself, 'I must qualify that a little; I must make sure they are still clear about this whole question of sin in the life of a Christian.' So he gives a special statement: 'We know that whosoever is born of God sinneth not; but he that is begotten of God keepeth himself, and that wicked one toucheth him not.'

Now we must stop, just for a moment, at this affirmation, 'we know.' There are certain things, according to this writer and according to the whole of the New Testament, about which there is no need for discussion; there are certain things, as it were, that are axiomatic in the Christian life. You remember the axioms in your books on geometry? There are certain things laid down, and then you build your propositions on them; but these things themselves are basic postulates and propositions. And here are some such things, according to John; and, therefore, as Christian people we must never be in doubt about them. These are the things that we as Christian people 'know,' so that in a sense we can say that if we do not know, we are not Christians. 'Whatever may happen to you,' says John, 'wherever you may find yourselves, here are things that are simple absolutes in your life—*we know*!' We know this first; we know in the next place 'that we are of God, and the whole world lieth in wickedness [or, in the wicked one]'; and we also know that 'the Son of God is come, and hath given us an understanding, that we may know him that is true; and we are in him that is true, even in his Son Jesus Christ. This is the true God, and eternal life.'

Now it is, of course, a most excellent and valuable thing to isolate great principles like these. There are many points that are debatable and disputable in the Christian life and experience, but there are certain things that can always be isolated and extracted and laid down as postulates, and here are some. And surely we misunderstand the whole message of this epistle if by now we have not come to see that these things are absolutes. So here we come then to the first of them—the Christian and sin.

Once more I must indicate that this subject has caused a great deal of confusion and misunderstanding. It has led to a great deal of disputation—very largely, again, because of the way in which this particular writer states his case. We have already seen in passing how it is interesting to observe that some of these thorny points of dispute in connection with the Christian life do arise from statements made by John rather than by the Apostle Paul, and this is entirely due, as I suggested, to that extraordinary type of thought and mind that he had. It is simply a question of the natural personality of the writer that was used by the Holy Spirit; the truth is clear and plain, but we have to pay attention to the form in which it is conveyed.

So there is a difficulty here. The whole doctrine of perfectionism has often been based upon this particular verse and upon its parallel statement in the ninth verse of chapter 3, which reads like this: 'Whosoever is born of God doth not commit sin; for his seed remaineth in him: and he cannot sin, because he is born of God.' That is the great text of perfectionists throughout the centuries, with this one to support it because it is virtually a repetition of the same thing. So it is necessary once more that we should pay close attention to exactly what the Apostle does say. Not only that; we must be exceptionally careful to take the context into consideration.

Nothing, incidentally, is more dangerous in reading or interpreting Scripture than to take a single statement right out of its context and elaborate a theory or doctrine upon it. That has generally been what has happened in every heresy and in every error in the long history of the Church. It is this fatal habit of men and women of jumping on to texts, as it were, and saying, 'The Bible says this—therefore . . . ' And they forget the context; they forget that Scripture must always be compared with Scripture; that Scripture never contradicts itself, and that there is a homogenous collation and unity about the message of the Bible from beginning to end. So it is important that we should bear that in mind as we come to this particular verse that is engaging our attention now.

So let us look at this first thing about which John tells us, 'We know; we are certain beyond dispute.' It is a comprehensive statement and obviously divides itself into three subsidiary statements. There is no difficulty about subdividing this verse—it does it for us itself. The first statement that he makes is this: 'Whosoever is born of God sinneth not.' 'We know that,' John says; 'there is no need to argue—there is no need for you to stop and consider it—we know it.' But the question is, what exactly is it that we thus 'know'? Well, it is the same thing as he tells us in chapter 3, verse 9.

Let me suggest what it does *not* mean. It cannot mean that whoever is born of God is incapable of sin. At first sight it looks as if John is indeed saying that whosoever is born of God does not sin—'sinneth not'—which has led many of the perfectionists to say they cannot sin. John uses that term in chapter 3, where he says that he does not sin because 'his seed remaineth in him.' So people have argued and said, 'As a Christian I cannot sin. John does not say I must not, but that I cannot. Therefore, I am incapable of sin as a Christian; it is impossible to me.' And they would therefore explain away in terms of the flesh various things that are pointed out to them that they have done and that are clearly a transgression of the law.

But surely the answer to all that, in this verse here, is just the context. If it is true to say that a Christian is one who is born again, who is born of God and is incapable of sin, why should John, as it were, have wasted his breath in the two previous verses by exhorting us to pray for our brother who *does* fall into sin? Such an exhortation is ridiculous if he is here saying that the Christian is incapable of sin. So it cannot mean that.

'Well,' says somebody else, 'I wonder whether it means not so much that the man who is born of God is incapable of sin, but that he does not fall into sin. It is possible, but he just does not do it. It is not that he has been made so absolutely perfect that he cannot sin, but that he is placed in a position in which it is possible for him not to sin.' Now there are two little Latin phrases: *non posse peccare* and *posse non peccare*, which mean either it is not possible for a Christian to sin or it is possible for him not to sin, and you can see the difference between the two. Is John saying that a Christian is someone who in actual practice and as a matter of fact does not sin? And once more it seems to me that the answer is precisely the same—that if the Christian does not sin, it would be unnecessary to exhort us to pray for the brethren who do fall into sin. Now the power that is offered to us in the Bible can keep us from sin—that is a different thing. But all I am concerned to indicate now is that John does not say that the Christian, the one who is born of God, does not fall into or commit particular acts of sin.

So what does he say? Well as I understand it, the only conceivable way of understanding the whole of this epistle is to repeat what I said when we considered chapter 3, verse 9.[1] What John means is that whosoever is born of God does not go on continuing in a state of sin; he does not continue practising sin. He is not interested in action at this point; he is interested in *condition*. He is concerned about the state of the Christian, not in the particular action of the Christian. And what he is asserting, therefore, is that whosoever is born of God is in a different condition with respect to sin from whosoever is not born of God. Men and women who are not born of God lie 'in the wicked one,' in the evil one. They are in the dominion of Satan. Their whole life is a life of sin; they dwell in it, it is their realm, and they inhabit it. But those who are born of God are no longer in that state; they have been taken out of it.

Look at this in terms of what John has told us in the first chapter; he is very fond of thinking in this way. He says that the man or woman who is not born of God is one who walks, or lives, in the realm of darkness; but the one who is born of God walks in the light with God. That is the first thing that John has in mind here. He says that those who are begotten of God do not continue in a state of sin; they may fall into sin—he has just been reminding us that the brethren, alas, do this—but they do not dwell there; that is not their condition. That surely is the only adequate explanation of this statement.

The way to look at this is to think of it as the two realms, the realm of darkness and the realm of light, the dominion of Satan and the kingdom of God and of His Christ. Or if you prefer it, I sometimes like to think of it in the sense of being down or being up. The men and women who are not born of God are those who live on a low level in life. They make occasional efforts to improve themselves, and they attempt to raise themselves for a while; but back they go. That is their level, down there. But Christians, those who are born of God, have been elevated; they have been raised up by Christ to a new height, so that the level of life on which they are living is up there. Now, unfortunately, they occasionally fall into sin; but that does not mean they continue to live down there. They fall, they repent, and they are received back again to the height and the level of their life.

So what John is concerned to emphasise is the level of life on which we are living. And his assurance is that those who are born of God no longer live on the sinful level, but on the higher level. Their whole realm is different and is changed; that is the position to which they belong. Alas, they may fall, they may lapse, but they do not continue on the ground, as it were. They belong to that other realm; that is their native sphere. He 'sinneth not' in the sense that he does not continue in sin, he does not keep on; or to use John's favourite word, he does not 'abide' in sin. The apostle is interested in character, not in particular action and conduct, at this point.

Perhaps I can put it again in the form of an illustration. I happened to be talking to a minister recently, and he was telling me about his two little children. He was telling me, with shame, how these little children could be a bit of a trial when he was trying to prepare his sermons. He said, 'You know, before my conversion I had a very bad temper, and it was a great trouble in my life—I could not control it. But I thought that once I was converted I would get rid of that for ever. But,' he said, 'I find myself still falling into it.' He is no long a bad-tempered man, he has been delivered out of that; but he continually has to watch it—there is a tendency to fall back into it. But he does not stop there; the thing that grieves him is that he ever loses his temper at all. Before his conversion he was doing nothing else; it was then his natural state and condition. But it is now an exception; he is living on a new level. He does not abide in this state of irritability; it is not his character any longer. 'Whosoever is born of God does not continue in sin'—does not abide in sin. That is the real meaning of the word, and that is the first thing of which we can be certain and which we 'know.'

But let me go on to the second statement, which is much more difficult. 'We know that whosoever is born of God sinneth not; but [or because] he that is begotten of God keepeth himself.' Now here again is a statement that is difficult, not, if I may so put it, in a doctrinal or theological sense, but simply as a matter of exposition; and it is entirely due, once more, to the whole question of the difference in the various texts of the New Testament. You remember that we have already had occasion to emphasise the difference between textual criticism of the New Testament and the so-called higher criticism. There are a number of manuscripts, and there are minor differences that do not affect ultimate truth, but they do affect the interpretation of a particular statement.

Here is an example of this. The Revised Version here reads, 'He that was begotten of God keepeth him.' Can you see the difference? The Authorised Version seems to suggest that 'whosoever is born of God does not sin because he keeps himself'—he looks after himself. But the other version suggests that 'whosoever is born of God does not sin because he that was begotten of God keeps him.'

Now I think there can be very little doubt but that in this instance the Revised Version is probably right, because it seems to me to be more in accord with what we have in the whole text here, with the whole object that John has in mind, and, indeed, with the teaching of the whole of the New Testament. It is not that these different versions contradict each other at all; they are both true in a sense, but it is just a question of what John is emphasising at this point. 'Whosoever is [has been] born of God sinneth not.' Why? Because 'he that *was* begotten' now 'is begotten'; John has changed his tense. Now surely this change is important, and that is why we must accept the translation of the Revised Version at this point. 'He that was begotten' stands alone and is none other than the Son of God, our Lord and Saviour, Jesus Christ.

Then again, we have another difference. 'He that was begotten of God,' says the Revised Version, 'keepeth *him*,' not 'himself.' Once more this is purely a question of these different manuscripts; but if 'was begotten' is a reference to the Lord Jesus Christ, I think we must agree that 'him' is correct here. So it comes to this: the Authorised Version suggests that the begotten of God does not sin because he keeps himself, while the Revised Version suggests that he that is born of God does not sin because the Son of God keeps him. Now this word *keepeth* is very important, and it is a great word. It means that He watches over him, takes care of him, keeps His eye on him; it means that He observes him attentively. Now I am sure that that is what the Apostle wanted to say at this point. He was writing, an old man, to these people who were tempted and tried and harassed with troubles outside and inside the Church. And this is what he wanted them to know—that the only begotten Son of God is watching over them; He is keeping them in that sense. He is the watchman of Israel; He is never asleep but always awake.

Let me show you that this must be what John is anxious to convey here. This statement is repeated in John 17; it is the same writer, and I am sure he had the same idea in his mind here. But we have it in his Gospel even before that, where our Lord Himself says about His sheep, 'Neither shall any man pluck them out of my hand' (John 10:28). He is going to keep them. But then listen to Him in His high priestly prayer: 'Holy Father,' He says, 'keep through thine own name those whom thou hast given me' (John 17:11)—keep them. Then He goes on to say, 'While I was with them in the world, I kept them in thy name: those that thou gavest me I have kept'—in effect, 'I have looked after them'—'and none of them is lost, but the son of perdition'—that is prophecy, he has gone. 'I pray not that thou shouldest take them out of the world,' He adds, 'but that thou shouldest keep them from the evil' (which means, 'from the evil one') (vv 12, 15)—the very thing John says in this verse. Surely, then, we are confronted here by that statement. It is the same thing of which Jude reminds us: 'now unto him that is able to keep you from falling, and to present you faultless before the presence of his glory with exceeding joy' (Jude 24). That is it!

This is the thing you find so constantly in our hymns—the celebration of the fact that the God who has kept and held His people in the past is still our God.

> Guide me, O Thou great Jehovah,
>   Pilgrim through this barren land;
> I am weak, but Thou art mighty,
>   Hold me [or keep me] with Thy powerful hand.
>
> WILLIAM WILLIAMS

Augustus Toplady's confidence, too, is that Christ is his keeper; He looks after him:

> A sovereign Protector I have,
>   Unseen, yet for ever at hand,
> Unchangeably faithful to save,
>   Almighty to rule and command.
> He smiles, and my comforts abound;
>   His grace as the dew shall descend,
> And walls of salvation surround
>   The soul He delights to defend.

This is the other side of the prayer,

> I need Thee every hour;
>   Stay Thou near by.

Why?

> Temptations lose their power
>   When Thou art nigh.
>
> ANNIE SHERWOOD HAWKS

This is one of the great consoling, comforting doctrines that we find in the New Testament—praise God! When we realise our weakness and helplessness in this difficult contradictory world, what is our final consolation save this that the Apostle Paul writes in Romans 5:10: 'For if, when we were enemies, we were reconciled to God by the death of his Son; much more, being reconciled, we shall be saved by his life.' If He died to save us, He will keep us, He will look after us; 'He that was begotten of God keepeth him.' 'Let us remember that then,' says John; 'let us be so certain of it that we can use the claim that we know it.' Let us be sure that wherever we are and however hard pressed and difficult our circumstances, we know that the Son of God is the shepherd and the guardian of our souls; that He is watching over us, He is keeping His eye upon us, He will not suffer us to be tempted above that we are able to bear but always 'will with the temptation also make a way to escape' (1 Cor 10:13)—thank God for that! He who was begotten of God is keeping us; that is why we do not dwell or continue or abide in a state of sin.

But that brings us to the last statement, the third great term: 'that wicked one [or evil one] toucheth him not.' Once more we have to be careful about a word, and here it is the word '*toucheth.*' Now, what one normally means by touching is putting your hand lightly upon somebody; but that is not the meaning of this word. The commentators all point out, very rightly, that John only used this word in one other connection, and you will find it in the twentieth chapter of his Gospel and the seventeenth verse, where, after His resurrection, our Lord was recognised by Mary. Mary took hold of Him, and He said to her, according to our translation, 'Touch me not.' He said, 'Don't keep clinging to me, Mary; don't hold on to me, for I am not yet ascended to my Father.'

Now, that is what John says here. 'That wicked one' does not get hold of those who are born of God; that evil one does not cling to them, does not get them into his embrace; he does not get them back into his clutches. Again, what a wondrous promise this is! You see how it fits in with the previous doctrine? If we just think of that word 'toucheth' with its usual connotation, it would virtually be saying that a Christian cannot be tempted, but that would patently be wrong. John does not say that we know that because we are born again we will never be touched in that sense. No, the devil will tempt us, that wicked one will try us; he may torment us, he may make us wretched and miserable. He will do his best to depress us and make us unhappy. Yes; but he will never get us back into his clutches. That is what John is saying. He can do many things to us, but he will never hold us again.

'They overcame him,' says the book of Revelation, 'by the blood of the Lamb, and by the word of their testimony' (Rev 12:11). He tried to get them back, he almost persuaded them, but he could never get them back into his grip—they 'overcame.' Yes, he can tempt us, he can even entice us in our folly to fall into acts of sin; but never again will we be held by him. Redemption cannot be undone; we have been delivered— we have been emancipated and set free. We belong to Christ, and we are children of God. We belong to the heavenly family, and though in our weakness and frailty we may often listen to Satan and his insinuations and suggestions, let us never forget that great word of John: 'that wicked one' will never get us back; he will never cling to us and embrace us.

The next verse says the whole thing: 'We know that we are of God, and the whole world lieth in wickedness,' in the arms of Satan. But you and I, beloved friends in Christ, will never be back there again—it is impossible. We are safe in the arms of Jesus, beyond the furthest reach of Satan; he cannot finally rob God of His possession. 'No man shall pluck them out of my hand.'

That, then, is the first thing we are to 'know,' and may God grant that we know it—that being born of God, we do not continue in sin. May God grant that we know that the Son of God is keeping an eye on us and is watching over us and is protecting us. May God grant that we may always know, when tempted by Satan, that we do not belong to him, that we need not be frightened of him, that we can resist and defy him. May we know that we can have this assurance that we are beyond his reach and his clutches, because we belong to God our Heavenly Father, to the Lord Jesus Christ, His precious Son and our Saviour, and to the Holy Ghost, whom He has given us to form Christ in us and to prepare us for the glory that awaits us.

14

THE LIFE OF THE WORLD

And we know that we are of God, and the whole world lieth in wickedness [the wicked one].

1 JOHN 5:19

WE LOOK TOGETHER NOW at the second of these three confident affirmations that the Apostle gathers together here in the postscript to his letter. And this second statement follows, I think we must agree, logically from the first. John, in emphasising the fact that whosoever is born of God does not sin because he is kept by the Son of God, ended by remarking that because of all that, he could not get into the clutches of the evil one again. And that suggests this second statement to him, that we are of God, but the whole world lies in the clutches of that evil one.

Looked at from any angle, this is a most important and vital statement. It is a statement of the Christian's view of life in this world, and surely nothing can be more important than that. The celebrated preacher Robert Murray McCheyne said of this verse—his advice to his congregation—'Never rest until you can say this.' Certainly, whatever our particular view may be of the statement, we must admit that it is very typical and characteristic of the New Testament. You find it everywhere; there is a very definite view of this world in the Gospels, in the book of Acts, and in the various epistles.

Take, again, for instance, our Lord's high-priestly prayer in John 17, and you will find that it is just an elaboration of this particular statement.

Our Lord there divides His people from those who are of the world. He says He does not pray for the world, but for those whom God has given Him out of the world; and His prayer is that His people might be kept from certain influences in that world. And you will find that implicitly in our Lord's teaching everywhere. And again, you will find it running right through the epistles. Take the famous Hebrews 11 with its portraits of the great heroes of the faith and the old dispensation; what we are told about them all is really that these men and women were declaring plainly that they were seeking another country. They were a people apart— unique people who had an utterly different view of life from all others. They were men and women who regarded themselves as pilgrims and strangers and sojourners in this world; it is the same distinction.

And you find this sometimes as an explicit exhortation: 'Come out from among them, and be ye separate, saith the Lord' (2 Cor 6:17); 'what communion hath light with darkness?' (2 Cor 6:14); and so on. In those places it is as an explicit injunction or exhortation. And as we have seen repeatedly in our study of this epistle, this is a distinction that runs right through the whole letter; it is, in a sense, a kind of basis on which John elaborates the whole of his argument. And that is why, when we began to study this letter together,[1] we started with this verse, because I tried to show that there is a sense in which if we do not understand this verse, we cannot understand the whole of the epistle; so we took it as an intro- duction. And we are back to it now, not to repeat what we said then, but to expound it in its particular context here in this postscript.

This is, therefore, a typical New Testament statement, but you will find exactly the same thing if you consider the subsequent history of the Christian Church after the end of the New Testament canon. I suggest to you that every period of reformation, every great time in the movement of the Holy Spirit, has been an era when this particular world view has been prominent and has been emphasised. Monasticism, for example, degenerated into something that became evil, but the original idea behind its message was based upon this clear-cut division of God's people.

Then you get it emphasised particularly at the time of the Reformation, and it was obviously the very essence of the doctrine that was emphasised by the Puritans—hence, partly the reason why they were given that name. They were not only interested in liturgical reform—they were particularly interested in this way of life which the Christian should live. Perhaps we can summarise it all by saying that this is obviously the controlling idea of *Pilgrim's Progress*. John Bunyan has once and for ever voiced the whole teaching of this verse; *Pilgrim's Progress* is nothing but a great allegory on it. So then, we see that this is one of the great basic and controlling concepts of Christian history.

Or if you prefer to look at this from the practical standpoint, I think you will have to agree again that it is of supreme importance, because it is a verse like this that really determines our attitude towards what is happening in the world at the present time. We all must be concerned with our present situation, and the problem that must arise in our mind is why the world is as it is. Now, whether we believe this verse or not determines our view of, or reaction to, the present scene; are we surprised at it, or do we expect it? Are we baffled by it, or is it in accordance with our whole outlook on the course of life in this world?

But still more personally, it is my attitude towards this verse that determines my own conduct and behaviour. I am in a world that is speaking to me and addressing me constantly in its newspapers, its books, its whole organisation of life, and its outlook. It is always making suggestions to me; its advertisements, the people with whom I speak and with whom I mix—all these are making appeals to me. So my response and reaction to all this will be determined by the fact of whether I agree with the doctrine of this verse or not.

So from every standpoint this is one of the most basic and vital statements that we must consider and that we must face. And you see at once that it confronts us with a very striking situation. Look at all the parallels in similar New Testament statements; look at those great lives in the Church in every time of revival. They all imply a clear-cut division and distinction between the Christian and the non-Christian. According to the New Testament, it should not be difficult to tell who is a Christian, for Christians are not merely people who are slightly better than others. They are not merely people who have added something to their lives. They belong to a different realm, to a different organisation; they are utterly different: 'We are of God, and the whole world lieth in wickedness.' You cannot imagine a greater contrast. Now that is the New Testament emphasis everywhere; the Christian and the non-Christian are altogether different. It is not some subtle, slight difference or change; it is a cleavage that is as clear-cut and as absolute as anything can be.

So it is obvious that what determines our view of the statement of this verse, what decides whether we can apply this verse to ourselves or not, whether we feel, like Robert Murray McCheyne, that this is the most important thing I can ever say about myself, what determines all this is clearly our view of the world and our view of the Christian. Now there are many people who are in trouble about this whole statement. There are those who feel that it implies an air of superiority and boastfulness and pride. There are people who say, 'I cannot make a statement like that; does it not suggest that you are looking down with derision upon everybody? If you say that, are you not being like the Pharisee who said, "God, I thank Thee that I am not as other men are—like this publican?" Is this not the very essence of the Pharisaical spirit of boastfulness, pride, arrogance—indeed worse, of superiority? I do not like it,' they say.

But surely that is completely to misunderstand this statement. There was nothing further from the mind and the heart and the spirit of this Apostle. He, above all others, liked to preach the doctrine of love. The spirit here is not one of pride and arrogance; it is, rather, one of profound gratitude. The statement is one of thanks to God, and it is said with humility. Yet it must be said. And if we are in any trouble or confusion in our minds with regard to this statement, it must be due to the fact that there is something wrong in our view of the world, or something wrong in our view of the Christian, or perhaps both. That is why we must consider these two things about which the Apostle has written so frequently in this letter; and if our view of them is not in accordance with the New Testament, then we must recognise the absolute cleavage, this utter distinction.

Now I am prepared to say that perhaps the thing above everything else that is most responsible for the present state of the Christian Church is the failure to maintain this distinction. The line between the Church and the world is becoming increasingly indistinct; they are becoming so much one for many reasons. And this accounts for the weakness of the Church, her unhappiness, and her failure to influence the life of the world. Because the attitude of the man of the world is virtually, 'What have you got that I have not?' he says, 'What is the difference between us? Why should I come amongst you?'

Or put it another way: I think you will find that at every period of revival and reformation, the Church has stood out distinct and apart. That is always the way; when the Church is unique, she has the greatest influence upon the world. The tragedy of the twentieth century especially has been that the Church in her folly has been trying to accommodate herself to the world, thinking that by so doing she could attract it. But the world expects the Christian to be different, and it is right—this is the New Testament emphasis. It is nothing but a departure from New Testament doctrine that ever tries to make the Church ingratiate herself to the world; the Church is meant to be, and is, essentially different. So this means that we must go back and consider the Christian view of the world and the Christian's view of the Christian.

First, let us look at the Christian view of the world. 'The whole world,' says John, 'lieth in wickedness [or, the wicked one].' Now as we have pointed out in our study of the second chapter,[2] by 'world' John does not mean the physical organisation of the world. What the Bible always means by 'the world' is life as it is organised without God—the outlook and the mentality of mankind that is exclusive of thoughts of God; life in the world as it is controlled without, or apart from, God. Now that, you see, is a very comprehensive definition. It includes the whole life of the world, and I would emphasise this. John says *the whole world*,' and he means it. 'The whole world' does not only mean those who dwell in the gutters of sin; it is inclusive of all life that excludes God, at its very best and highest as well as at its very worst and lowest. It is very important that we should maintain that in our minds. So then, what is our view of life in this world defined in that way?

Now, the whole object here is to emphasise the uniqueness of the Christian view, and perhaps we can do that best by putting it negatively. Let us look at some of the other views of the world, and life in the world as it is today, in order that we may emphasise and stress and contrast this uniqueness.

There are many who take a biological view of life. If you go to these people and ask them how they explain the state of the world—why it is so troubled and unhappy, what has gone wrong with it, and what is its real need—their answer is purely biological. They say that it is just a part of this process of evolution, part of the development, the growing pains that always accompany growth. You cannot expect, they say, to advance and develop without a certain amount of conflict and reaction. There are forces that have to be overcome, and these troubles in the world are but a manifestation of that. It is all right, they maintain; there is nothing to be alarmed about; childhood and youth are often a period of strain and crisis, but they are part of the inevitable process as we advance.

But to others it is purely a question of economics. There was a great deal of talk before the Second World War of 'the psychology of the economic mind.' This is a century of economics, as last century was a century of the biological; the great thing in this century is economic force. Life in this world, they say, is entirely governed and controlled by capital and labour. Indeed, there are some who think they can explain it all in terms of food! It is a question of food and an attempt to satisfy the fundamental needs of man—economics.

But then there are others who describe the whole thing in terms of politics. 'No,' they say, 'the real trouble with man is that he is a political animal, and these associations in life always need a certain amount of organisation. We have done very well, but we obviously have not perfected it, and there are certain nations that are backward, politically immature, and they need to be developed and trained.' So they, too, exhort us to be patient, because they assure us that as man is more trained politically he will solve his problems.

But still another group says that the whole problem is one of intellect. In other words, the real trouble with the world and all the troubles of mankind, they say, are due to the fact that people do not use their brains. They are foolish enough to live too much like the animal; they are not sufficiently developed. That was the great theory preached by men like H. G. Wells; that was his creed. Such people assure us that if only we gave men and women better knowledge and education, we could solve our personal problems, our national problems, and indeed our international problems.

Then the last view is what we might call the moral view. 'No,' say these last people, 'the problem of life in this world is not biological or economic or political or intellectual; the problem of life in this world is a moral one. People are taking a far too materialistic view in these days, rather than considering man in his relationship to man, man in his conception of good and evil, man in his conception as to how life should be lived. So the moral problem is the real problem for us.' Now you will notice that I am putting this moral view in the same category as the others because I am anxious to show that, in a sense, that is as far removed from the Christian view as is the biological or any of the others.

There, then, are some of the most common ideas with respect to life in this world that are current today; but there are others. Some of them may actually claim to be religious, but we have seen that to have a religious view of the world is not the same thing as to have a Christian view.

So let us turn now to this view that is entirely different from all the others. The Christian, New Testament view of life in this world is spiritual, and it is essentially different even from the moral view. Here it is: 'The whole world lieth in wickedness.' In other words, according to this view the trouble with the world is not that it just lacks certain qualities; it is not simply that it ought to be better than it is. Rather, the life of this world is controlled entirely and absolutely by an evil power, by the one who is described here as 'the wicked one.' That is what I mean when I say it is the spiritual view of life in this world.

In other words, we are facing here the biblical doctrine of sin and the biblical doctrine of the devil. Here again is something you find running through Scripture. Our Lord speaks about 'a strong man armed,' keeping his goods and palace at peace (Luke 11:21). That is typical; in other places he talks about 'the prince of this world' (John 12:31). We find this also in Ephesians 2:2, where Paul talks about 'the prince of the power of the air'; or again we find such terms as 'the god of this world' (2 Cor 4:4), or the adversary and 'the accuser of our brethren' (Rev 12:10). So my point is that if we accept the biblical view of life in this world, to believe in Satan is an absolute necessity, for the Christian view of life is a spiritual view.

We can put it like this: there is an evil person, according to the Bible, who is controlling the life of this world. We are told about him in the Old Testament. God made man perfect, and He made the world perfect—it was called Paradise. What went wrong? Well, an evil person came in— an angel of exceptional brightness and glory who had rebelled against God and set himself up against Him and attacked the very being and power of God. He, the devil or Satan, came into God's universe and tempted man; and man listened and fell. That is the cause of the trouble, according to the Scriptures. When man listened to the suggestions and insinuations of Satan, he handed himself and his world over to the dominion of Satan. And, according to this view, ever since the fall of man into sin, the devil, who is described in the categories I have mentioned, is controlling life in this world. The whole world lies in the power of the evil one. It is lying in his bosom; he is there clasping it, and he is controlling its whole outlook and all its activities and everything that happens in it.

That is the Christian view. Is that not the explanation of our ills and troubles? It is not the economic view, nor the political view. The problem is not our intellectual lack or our lack of culture; it is not even that we are not striving to be as moral as we ought to be. It is that we are controlled and the life of the world is controlled by Satan; the god of this world has blinded men and women. It is the devil who has a stranglehold upon the whole outlook and mentality and upon the whole organisation of life in the world. In other words, the world, according to Scripture, is positively evil; it is being governed by this unseen spiritual power who holds it in its grasp.

You cannot read the New Testament without coming across this concept. 'For we wrestle not against flesh and blood, but against principalities, against powers, against the rulers of the darkness of this world, against spiritual wickedness in high places' (Eph 6:12). Read about these dominions and thrones and principalities and powers that are so constantly mentioned; look at the Book of Revelation with its great struggle. What does it mean? What is behind this evil power, these figures that are used, such as beasts and others? They are but a representation of this malign power of Satan, the devil, the god of this world.

So according to this statement and according to the whole biblical teaching, the world is as it is today because it is being controlled by the devil. You remember how, when he tempted our Lord in the wilderness, one of the temptations he put before Him was this: he took Him to a high mountain and showed Him all the kingdoms of this world, and he said in effect, 'Bow down and worship me, and I will give it all to you' (Matt 4:8-9). He was making there a claim for himself, and that claim, in this spiritual sense, is true. He has mastered life in this world; he holds man under his control; 'the whole world lieth in the wicked one.'

Now I emphasise this because I know full well that there are many who not only dispute this, but who dislike it. 'Clearly,' they say, 'that is ridiculous. It is something that we can understand in a book that was written, most of it, two thousand years ago; it is typical of primitive society and primitive mentality. We can even understand it and believe it about people a hundred and fifty years ago. But how can you still go on preaching a doctrine like that? Look at the improvements in this world. Look how much less suffering and cruelty there is. Look at the factory acts and so on. Look at the care we are giving to the aged and to the ill and to the infirm. Look at our great advance and development. Are you asking us to believe that this world is under the control of the evil one and in the grasp of the devil?'

To which surely the answer is perfectly simple. Let us look at the so-called improvements. We are well aware that the acts of Parliament that have been passed in the last hundred years or so have righted many wrongs; but I would ask you to remember that they have, all of them, without a single exception, resulted directly from Christian activity. None of these things have been automatic. Take the movements for better education; take the hospitals; take the interest in health or the care for the aged, the abolition of slavery, the passing of factory acts—every one of these things has emanated from Christian sources. It has not been a development. No; these things have come from work organised by Christian men and women, often against violent opposition from those who were not Christians. We must always remember when we look at the life of this world that the world has been very ready to borrow from Christianity when it has suited it to do so. It has rejected the doctrine, but it has often accepted the improved state of life. One thinks of a man like Mr. Ghandi who was avowedly not a Christian, but who was always ready to borrow Christian teaching when it suited him; and there are others who do the same thing. People who believe in other religions borrow from Christianity, and there have been improvements that have resulted in that way.

But that is not the whole of my answer. I suggest to you that the improvements of which we hear so much are general and superficial. Can we still go on boasting of improvements as we look at the state of the world in general? Do we still boast of progress in this twentieth century after our two world wars and all the uncertainty that characterises life; is that advance? Look at the state of society on a smaller scale. We say man is improving, but has there ever been so much selfishness manifested in the life of the nation as there is today, a self-centredness as well as a self-seeking? It is the only explanation of the appalling increase in divorce; it is the whole explanation of the spirit of greed; it is the whole basis of the attitude of the average person towards work—I do the minimum, I get the maximum—greed, self-centredness, the increasing rudeness in life, the increasing lack of consideration for others, the appalling suffering that is caused to innocent little children through the sheer selfishness of parents. The whole attitude towards life today as looked at in every respect is one that is showing this self-centredness. We do certain things on the surface, but man as man is still this selfish creature.

To put it finally, you see the truth of our doctrine most of all in the attitude of the world towards God. That is the ultimate way of testing the spirit of man or the spirit of the world. The devil, as we have seen, is one who hates God, and his primary concern is that God should be attacked and that the world should be kept from Him. The devil cares very little what men and women may be like, so long as they do not believe in God. It is not a question of culture, because people may be highly cultured and yet godless. This is where all of us are so polite when we look at things superficially and say the world is improving. The ultimate test is the attitude of men and women towards God, and in particular their attitude towards the Lord Jesus Christ. The final test is not how cultured or how polite they may be superficially, but whether they are still opposed to God; whether they hate God and do not believe on the Lord Jesus Christ. And I think that if we view it in that way, we will have to admit that the world is as much in the power of the evil one today as it has ever been. Some of the most educated men and women have been the most prominent in their hatred of God, in their scoffing at religion, in their ridicule of the supernatural and the miraculous, in their refusal to believe on the Lord Jesus Christ, and in their antagonism to the Cross and to the blood of Christ shed for man's sin. It is this that supremely proves that 'the whole world lieth in the wicked one.'

That, according to Scripture, is the view of life in this world. Men and women were made for God and were meant to serve God and enjoy Him; but they are in the grip of Satan. So they hate the name of God, and because of this they are unhappy. They are unhappy within themselves; they cannot find satisfaction; they are unhappy with other people because they blame them for their trouble. They do not say that it is in themselves—they are all little gods fighting with one another, jealous and envious of one another. That is the meaning of the state of the world according to the Bible. 'From whence come wars and fightings among you?' The answer is: 'Come they not hence, even of your lusts . . . ?' (Jas 4:1).

It is this enmity towards God, this failure to worship God and reverence Him, that is the problem. Those who are in the hands of Satan must be unhappy, and this is the meaning of everything in life. The life of men and women in this world, according to the Bible, is suicidal; they are destroying themselves and marring their own true destiny. They are as they are and behave as they do and their world is as it is because Satan is governing and controlling and keeping them from God, who is waiting to bless them. So here we are abounding in misery, overwhelmed by trouble, denying our God and refusing salvation and bliss with the Lord Jesus Christ.

That is the biblical view of life in this world. The problem is not an 'evolutionary lag'; it is not economic or political problems; it is not a mere matter of education and knowledge and culture; it is not that we need to be taught higher morality or appealed to to be honest and kind. It is none of these things. The trouble is spiritual; men and women must be converted in their relationship to God, and they must see that they are in the grip of God's greatest enemy, who is blinding them and restraining them lest they should turn to God in repentance and worship Him and know Him and the Lord Jesus Christ, His Son, who has come even into the world to save it and who alone can conquer Satan.

Oh, may God grant us this increasing spiritual insight into the life of the world, that we may not only see it and flee from it and fight it, but above all that we may work without ceasing to deliver others out of it and to bring them to a knowledge of the glorious liberty of the children of God.

15

OF GOD

And we know that we are of God, and the whole world lieth in wickedness [the wicked one].

1 JOHN 5:19

WE HAVE FOUND THAT if we are to come into this position into which John is so anxious that these people should come—namely, that we should be walking with God, experiencing this rich fellowship with Him and with His Son Jesus Christ, and rejoicing in the benefits of joy that result from it—then it is obviously essential that we should be very clear as to the condition and the state of this world in which we live. And it is still more important that we should know who we are and what we are and what the things are that are possible to us and for us as Christians and as children of God.

So we have looked at this definition of the world as something that 'lieth in the wicked one.' We have seen that the ultimate object of the devil is always to get us to turn away from God, and always to hold us in a kind of thraldom to this world and to ourselves—to do anything, in other words, that would distract our attention away from God, anything that would disturb our relationship and our fellowship with Him. 'The world,' we saw, is a very inclusive term; but it is ultimately anything that tries to make us feel satisfied without fellowship and communion with God.

That, then, is the world. Now let us look at what John has to tell us about Christians themselves—Christians' view of themselves in contradistinction to their view of the world. And what John tells us about our-

selves is this: '*we are of God.*' Surely we must at times be astounded at
these laconic statements of the Scriptures. 'That is the whole truth about
you,' says John, 'you are of God.' Now again I would remind you that
the Apostle says that we 'know' this; we must know it—it is the essential thing that we are to grasp and understand; it is a confident affirmation. 'These three things,' says John, 'that I am here underlining for you
are things about which there should be no doubt and no discussion. This
is not something at which you hope to arrive; no, we are confident, we
are assured, there is utter, absolute certainty about this—we *know* that
we are of God.' This has been, as we have seen so repeatedly, the great
theme of the entire epistle. That is the knowledge to which John was
bringing them—'These things have I written unto you that believe on the
name of the Son of God; that ye may know that ye have eternal life' (v
13). There it is, the same thing. So I ask once more, do we know this;
are we able to say it?

What, then, does John mean by saying that 'we are of God'? Well,
obviously it is a complete contrast to the other statement that 'the whole
world lieth in the wicked one.' And it is not only a complete contrast to
it—it is the only possible contrast. Here, in other words, we are once
more looking at one of the great, characteristic New Testament definitions of the Christian; that is the great theme of the New Testament.
Obviously Christians are not just good people, not even just moral people. Let us go further: Christians are not even just religious people. You
can be good, you can be moral, you can even be religious and still not
be a Christian. So John's definition of Christian men and women is not
that they are benefactors, not even those who are highly moral and have
noble ideas; not people who are religious and give their whole life to religion. Christians are those who are '*of God*'; nothing less than that. So
let us start by some negative definitions of what John means.

To say that Christians are 'of God' means that they have been taken
out of the clutches of the wicked one. You notice that in dealing with
this verse I have started with the end rather than with the beginning: 'We
know that we are of God, and the whole world lieth in the wicked one.'
I had a reason for that—it helps us to understand what is meant by being
'of God.' We are all born in the world and in the clutches of the wicked
one; we are all born, as Paul puts it in writing to the Ephesians, 'the children of wrath' (Eph 2:3); we are all born in sin and shapen in iniquity
(Psa 51:5). So we all start our lives in this world 'in the wicked one,' in

his grasp, belonging to that kingdom of the devil and under his dominion. To be 'of God,' then, obviously means that we are taken out of the clutches of sin; we are no longer lying 'in the wicked one.'

Now the New Testament is fond of saying this. Paul, for instance, in writing to the Galatians, bursts out at the beginning in a hymn of praise as he mentions the name of the Lord Jesus Christ: 'who gave himself for our sins, that he might deliver us from this present evil world' (Gal 1:4). That is it! We were in this present world and in its chains and shackles, but Christ has offered Himself and has died for us and thereby has delivered us. Or listen to Paul again in writing to the Colossians: 'who hath delivered us,' he says, 'from the power of darkness, and hath translated us into the kingdom of his dear Son' (Col 1:13). That is simply a repetition of what John is saying here. Everything, we have seen, is under the power and the dominion of Satan; but now we have been moved, transferred into the kingdom of God's dear Son.

Or take another statement that Paul makes in writing to the Romans when he says, 'Sin shall not have dominion over you' (Rom 6:14). Why? Because you are taken out of his dominion. You no longer belong to that realm; you are no longer citizens of such a kingdom. The Apostle Peter says exactly the same thing: 'which in time past were not a people, but are now the people of God; which had not obtained mercy, but now have obtained mercy' (1 Pet 2:10). He has brought us, he says, 'out of darkness into his marvellous light' (1 Pet 2:9). All these are but different ways of expressing what John is saying here. So that to be 'of God' means negatively that we are no longer lying 'in the wicked one'; we have been brought out, emancipated, set free. Describe it as you will, it is a marvellous way of looking at it. And the negative is almost as good as the positive at this point. I say almost because it is not as good. But it is a great thing to know that we have been taken out of that kingdom and dominion.

What, then, does it mean positively to say that we are 'of God'? Well, we can sum it up by saying that we belong to God, to His realm, to His kingdom. This is a complete antithesis of everything that we saw in the other statement. But let us analyse it; it is such a rich statement that, in a sense, we cannot analyse it too much. It means, of necessity, that we must have been forgiven by Him, because as long as we belong to the realm and the dominion of Satan, we are enemies of God. Satan is the archenemy of God; he is everything that represents enmity against

God, and all in his kingdom are enemies of God and under His wrath. So to be 'of God' means that we have been reconciled to God; we have come into an entirely new relationship to Him.

But it does not stop at that, of course, because it must mean also that we have received life from God. We are 'of God' in the sense that we are born of God, 'partakers of the divine nature,' as Peter says (2 Pet 1:4); we have received the life of God Himself. We are 'of God' in the sense that we have come out of God, and the life we now have is the life that is derived from Him. We are of God by the new birth. But it also means that our very existence and continuance is by God and of God; we not only receive this divine life once, but we go on receiving it. We are 'of God' in the sense that our whole being is dependent upon Him, that our sustenance, our everything, is derived from Him.

Let me, then, sum it up by saying, as I have already suggested, that it means that we belong to God and to the family of God. Have you thought of it in terms of 'party'? It means that we belong to God's party. We are no longer of the party of Satan and everything that represents; we now belong to God's party. We belong to God's family and are thus in this intimate relationship to Him. This is not merely an intellectual relationship; it is not even a faith one. It is more than that; we have become the children of God, and we belong to Him in that family sense.

But, of course, having said that, we must go on to say certain other things because John is always interested in the practical application. If we are 'of God' in that sense, it means also that we delight in God and we rejoice in Him. The natural man, the man who belongs to the world, does not delight in God; the natural man is, according to Paul, His enemy, and that is absolutely true. There are many people in this world who say they believe in God, but let something go wrong with them and they soon show how they are at enmity with Him. Indeed, the world would be very glad if someone could prove there is no God; that is its attitude. In the depths men and women do not delight in God; they do not rejoice in Him. But we are 'of God'; God is the centre not only of the universe, but of our whole life and outlook.

And that in turn must mean that we who are 'of God' are controlled by Him and by His Spirit. We have seen that those who are in the world and of the world are controlled by Satan and are governed by him; that is the terrible part of that life. Our Lord put it in a terrifying picture when He said, 'When a strong man armed keepeth his palace, his goods are in peace' (Luke 11:21). There is a terrible kind of peace under the dominion of Satan. It is the peace of men and women who are not allowed to do anything. They are hemmed in; they are held there. Why don't people believe the gospel? asks Paul in writing his second letter to the Corinthians. And the answer is this: 'The god of this world hath blinded the minds of them which believe not' (4:4). They cannot believe. The devil is preventing them; he is controlling them. But Christians, who do believe, are opposite to that. They are 'of God'; they are directed and governed by God.

And that in turn comes to this, that they are people who are living for God; it is their desire to live for Him. Let me put it like this: we saw, in considering the case of those who belong to the world, that ultimately it comes right back to slavery; the devil holds men and women in his own grasp by persuading them that it is to their own best and highest interest. The principle that is governing the world is self-centredness, selfishness, and self-seeking; to be of God, therefore, obviously means that we no longer live for self or Satan, but we live for God, and our supreme desire is to please Him. We are 'of God.' That is our party; that is our interest. He is our Father. As Philip Doddridge wrote:

> *'Tis to my Saviour I would live,*
> *To Him who for my ransom died.*

Ah yes, but it must mean also that if I am 'of God,' in the sense that I am born of Him and am a partaker of the divine nature, there must be some signs of this in my life. The New Testament is always very careful to press this and to press it very strongly. As John reminds us in the first chapter, 'If we say that we have fellowship with him, and walk in darkness'—what is the truth about us? Well, we are liars, says John; 'we lie, and do not the truth' (v 6). It is no use saying you are 'of God' and then showing that you live under the dominion of Satan, in the life of Satan as it were. That would be a contradiction, a lie; if we are 'of God,' we must have certain manifestations to the effect that the life of God is in us. What are these? We have repeatedly reminded one another of them as we worked our way through this epistle. The tests that John applies are: keeping His commandments; loving the brethren; believing the truth about the Lord Jesus Christ; these are the tests of life.

Or if you like, you can state this in terms of what the Apostle Paul calls 'the fruit of the Spirit.' In other words, if the Spirit is in you, if the life of God is in you, certain fruits will begin to appear. What are they? 'Love, joy, peace, longsuffering, gentleness, goodness, faith, meekness, temperance' (Gal 5:22-23). This is inevitable, and the great teachers of the Church throughout the ages have generally emphasised that one of the most important and vital tests is the test of humility. The great St. Augustine said that the first test of the Christian life, and the second, and the third is humility. 'Be clothed with humility,' says Peter (1 Pet 5:5), and that must be the test because there is nothing that stands out more gloriously in the life of our blessed Lord Himself than just that. Though He was God and equal with God, He thought it not something to be clutched at; He humbled Himself. 'Let this mind be in you also,' says Paul (Phil 2:5); 'who,' says Peter, 'when he was reviled, reviled not again; when he suffered, he threatened not; but committed himself to him that judgeth righteously' (1 Pet 2:23).

This must be the ultimate test because the worldly spirit is the very antithesis of this—pride, arrogance, self-confidence, and assurance. The world is full of it. Look at your newspapers—it is there shouting at you. The worldly are always praising us, making us believe we are wonderful. And look at men and women in their speeches. Listen to them—the self that is being manifested. In its psychological training the world would encourage you to rely upon yourself, to believe in yourself. It says that nothing is impossible if you believe in yourself; always self—that is the spirit of the world. The world, in a sense, knew nothing about true humility until Christ came into it. That is the ultimate test. We show signs of His life in us in that way, and one of the most delicate and subtle tests is just this test of humility, the very antithesis of everything that the world represents and stands for.

But the last way in which I define this being 'of God' is that we are destined for God. We are returning to God; we are making our way to Him. We are going to eternity with Him and shall spend it in His presence. I like to think that Christians, in a sense, are men and women who have a label on them; their destination is booked, they are marked. They are 'of God,' and they are for God. They are going to God; they have a new name written upon them, and it is *God*. They are God's property; you and I are 'of God' in that sense. 'The whole world lieth in the wicked one'; it is the devil's property, his luggage, and it is destined for destruction and perdition. It is destined for the lake of fire that burns without ceasing for ever and ever; that is its destiny—that is the destiny of the devil, and it goes with him. But we are 'of God.' We are destined for God; we are meant for Him. We belong to God, and we shall spend eternity with Him.

That, then, is something of what the New Testament teaching means by the use of this term 'of God.' But remember, we say that Christians realise this is all true of them not as a result of anything they are, not as a result of anything they have done, but entirely and solely as the result of the grace of the Lord Jesus Christ, because of His coming into this world and the perfect work that He has accomplished for us. We are 'of God' because He has bought us and ransomed us and delivered us by taking hold of us and translating us into His own kingdom.

So we can see that the way in which we read a verse like this is of vital importance. I started by saying that there are many people who dislike this sort of statement and feel that it suggests an arrogance if we say, 'We are of God, and the whole world lieth in the wicked one.' They say that suggests a kind of censorious spirit, a lack of charity with regard to those who are not Christians. But I hope that nobody feels like that about this statement now. We have looked at what it means to be 'in the wicked one,' and we have considered what it means to be 'of God.' How does one say this? Well, there is no arrogance or pride or boasting. The people who say this truly, as we have seen, are those who say it with a deep and profound sense of gratitude; it is all of Christ. We were hell-deserving sinners and were destined for it; but Christ has saved and rescued us, and we say it with a sense of wonder.

I believe increasingly that the most delicate test we can ever have of the fact that we are Christians is that we are amazed and surprised at that fact, that we never cease to wonder at ourselves. We have a sense of escape, of having been delivered. We have a deep consciousness of the privilege and a consciousness of the responsibility. We look at ourselves and say, 'Am I of God in that sense? Is that true of me? Is it possible that I am going to be with Him and in His presence for all eternity? Is it possible that such a worm as I should be able to say, "Abba Father" and know that the eternal everlasting God is my Father in the Lord Jesus Christ?' We are 'of God'—oh, the wonder and amazement of it all, the surprise and the gratitude, the praise and the thanksgiving, the privilege and the high responsibility! That is the way such a statement is to be said.

But let me go further and say that if you cannot say this and if you feel that objection to saying this, it is because your idea of a Christian is wrong. The people who do not like this statement are those who think that they are Christians because of what they do; and then it would indeed be boasting. If I say it because I am such a wonderful man or woman, that is the height of pride and arrogance. But if I say it like this: 'By the grace of God I am what I am' (1 Cor 15:10) and 'there but for the grace of God go I,' then there is no pride. Arrogance and boastfulness are removed because we realise that we are what we are solely because of God's wondrous love and His amazing grace in the Lord Jesus Christ.

What, then, are the views of Christian people in the light of these two definitions?

Well, in general we see that the world is not something that is gradually improving. Indeed, we go further and say that the world cannot be improved in an ultimate sense. In the last analysis, any hope of this world ever being improved or reformed or Christianised is nothing but a simple denial of the most essential and primary New Testament message. Anything that 'lieth in the wicked one' can never be improved ultimately.

But wait a minute! I have not finished my statement—that is only the first step. My second is that all the same, evil must be controlled and kept within bounds. The world cannot be improved in an ultimate sense, but that does not mean that we do not do our utmost to control evil and its manifestations and its effects in it. It is God's world, and God has appointed kings and governments and magistrates, according to the Scriptures, so that evil and its effects may be kept within bounds and a limit put upon them. The forty-fifth chapter of the prophecy of Isaiah makes the statement that God said, 'I create evil' (v 7), which in one sense means that He controls it. He has it within His grasp, and it will not be allowed to proceed beyond a certain limit.

Then my third step is that evil is something that will finally be judged and damned. 'Love not the world,' says John in this epistle, 'neither the things that are in the world.' Why? 'The world passeth away, and the lust thereof' (2:15, 17). The world is doomed; judgment is coming for certain. History is working up to a grand climax, and the climax will be the return of Christ and the judgement of the world in this particular spiritual sense. Satan and all who belong to him will be finally condemned and destroyed. The world as we know it, without God and without Christ, is but awaiting the end that is surely coming. If reform were possible, reform would take place; but there is no ultimate reform—the world will be destroyed.

That is the view of the world in general. But what about people who are in the world? Well, the Christian's view of the people in the world is that we must regard them as being in a desperate and dangerous position. They belong to a kingdom that is already doomed and will be condemned and destroyed, and they need to be rescued. They need to be delivered, to be emancipated. We know they can be, and that is the whole point in preaching the gospel. We know that 'we are of God, and the whole world lieth in the wicked one'; it lies in him, but it can be brought out of him! We were all there to start with, but we have been taken out. We are now 'of God,' so that our view of those who are in this world and who belong to it is that they are in this dangerous condition, and our hearts should be filled with compassion. We should have great concern and anxiety, and we should be doing everything we can to bring them out of that dominion. We should tell them of the gospel and show them the Redeemer, that they may be brought from that position in the wicked one and be translated into the kingdom of God and of His dear Son. That is our view of people in the world.

Lastly, what is our view of ourselves, as we still live and exist in this world? Well, here is the New Testament teaching: the world is something that is actively hostile to us in a most subtle manner; it is doing its utmost to separate us from God. That is Satan's whole object and intention. He is 'the accuser of our brethren' (Rev 12:10); he is the adversary of our souls. The world we are living in is something that is extremely dangerous to us, something that is all the time trying to infiltrate us. It is always making suggestions to us; it suggests that its life is a larger and a bigger and a freer life—the subtle antagonism of the world to us—the flesh warring against the spirit.

So we can say that the world in its spirit is a thing that we are to avoid. 'Pure religion and undefiled before God and the Father is this, To visit the fatherless and widows in their affliction, and to keep himself unspotted from the world' (Jas 1:27). Never forget that; it is a great statement. You have to work in this world, but while you are doing that, you must be careful to keep yourself unspotted from it. Jude in his epistle says the same thing, that we must save those who have gone back into sin but watch ourselves so that our garments do not become spotted by that evil (v 23). The world is something to be avoided; we must do everything we can to restrain evil. The Christian is a citizen in this world; but let us be careful that the world does not enter into us again and get us back. We are to avoid this spirit of the world.

The last thing, therefore, is this: the world is something from which we are constantly needing to be cleansed. As we walk in it and thus are actively busy in it, we constantly become defiled by it, and we need constant cleansing from the stain of the world and its sin. But thank God, the provision is perfect. John, you remember, has told us that in the first chapter: 'If we walk in the light, as he is in the light, we have fellowship one with another, and the blood of Jesus Christ his Son cleanseth us from all sin. . . . If we confess our sins, he is faithful and just to forgive us our sins, and to cleanse us from all unrighteousness' (vv 7, 9). The defilement is there, and the sin; but, my dear friend, do not be depressed. Immediately confess the sin, and acknowledge it, and ask God to cleanse you again and renew you; He has promised to do so. 'If any man sin, we have an advocate with the Father, Jesus Christ the righteous: and he is the propitiation for our sins: and not for ours only, but also for the sins of the whole world' (1 John 2:2).

What a tremendous statement that is, and how important! You and I are 'of God,' strangers and pilgrims in this world—a colony of heaven, says Paul to the Philippians, and we are far from home. But we are going towards home in an alien land, and we have to remember that and bear it in mind. 'We are of God, and the whole world lieth in the wicked one.' Let us have a right view of the world; let us have a right view of its history; let us understand what is happening to the world at this present time; let us look ahead and see what it is destined for; let us never rest our affection on it. And as we go on, let us remember its subtle insinuations, and let us beware of its defilement and sin. But let us ever remember that whenever we may fall or be conscious of defilement, the blood of Christ still avails; we can be washed, we can be cleansed anew. We can continue to walk in blessed fellowship with the Father and with His Son, Jesus Christ. 'We are of God'—amazing! But 'the whole world lieth in the wicked one,' so let us have pity, mercy, and compassion upon others and tell them of the way of escape.

16

UNDERSTANDING

And we know that the Son of God is come, and hath given
us an understanding, that we may know him that is true;
and we are in him that is true, even in his Son Jesus Christ.
This is the true God, and eternal life.

1 JOHN 5:20

THIS IS THE THIRD and the last of the three confident affirmations that
we find here in the postscript to this first epistle of John. It is interesting
to observe the sequence that was obviously in the Apostle's mind as he
uttered these three affirmations. His main concern is, of course, the
whole problem of sin and evil. This is the great theme of the entire Bible;
how are men and women to live in this world in a godly manner and in
a manner that is well-pleasing in God's sight? That is the great problem
of life and existence according to the Bible. Its view of life, as we have
seen repeatedly, is a spiritual view; and so this is especially the question
that should be uppermost in the minds of all those who call themselves
Christian.

Now John has been giving these great assurances that those who are
born of God do not continue in a state of sin, that being 'of God' and
having been translated from the kingdom of Satan into the kingdom of
God's dear Son we are in this unique and separate position. But he still
feels that something else is necessary, and that is what we have in this
twentieth verse. He is still thinking in terms of the world that is around
and about us and of that wicked one, that evil power that is set against
us; that is our problem, and we must never lose sight of it. Our life in

this world is a spiritual warfare, whether we want it or not; it is inevitably so, because of Satan.

You see that clearly in the life of the Son of God Himself, how constantly He was attacked and besieged by Satan. Satan only left Him for a season after the temptation in the wilderness; then he came back. Because Satan is the god of this world and governs and orders it, the whole life of the Christian is, of necessity, one of spiritual conflict. Yet John has reminded us, as we have seen, of certain things that are a great comfort and consolation to us, and now here is the last of these, one which is a great comfort. It is that we have an *'understanding,'* that we are able to see this thing.

The tragedy of those who are not Christians is that they are not only blinded by sin, but that they are unaware of that fact. That, according to the Bible, is the real tragedy of mankind when it is not in relationship to God. It goes through life in this world and persuades itself that all is well, that it is fairly happy, not realising the terrible doom that is awaiting it. It lacks an understanding; it does not know. Before one can ever wage a successful warfare against these powers of evil and darkness that are around and about us, we must be aware of their existence. We must know something about them, and we must know some of the resources that are available for those who are anxious to overcome them. And here, says John, is something again that we know and for which we can thank God: 'We know that the Son of God is come, and hath given us an understanding, that we may know him that is true.' We are able to differentiate between the truth and lies, between light and darkness; not only are we not in the clutches of Satan, but we know God, we are 'of God,' and we belong to Him. We are in Him and in His Son, Jesus Christ.

That, then, is the connection between these three confident affirmations that are made here by the Apostle; and, surely, we must agree with him that nothing is more important than that we should know these three things for certain. So let us concentrate now upon what it is that enables us to know them. We do not 'think'; we are not on the whole persuaded or have some misgivings or are nearly sure. No; *we 'know'*! The Christian position is one of certainty—no doubt, no hesitation; it is a clear-cut position. This is something, as we have already considered, that you find running through the Bible. There is this great division going on from beginning to end—Noah and his family in the ark, the rest of the world outside; God's people and those who are not

God's people. And the great characteristic of the people of God is that they 'know' certain things.

That, of course, is the whole secret of their life; that is the argument, for instance, of that great eleventh chapter of Hebrews concerning the heroes of the faith. Why was it that those men and women behaved as they did? What made Abraham leave his country and go out? What was it that made Moses, who had the prospect of being adopted by the daughter of Pharaoh, with a wonderful career before him in the court of Egypt—what made him reject it all and become a mere shepherd and endure the adversity that he experienced for so long? What was the secret of all those people? Well, according to the writer of the epistle to the Hebrews, it was just that they knew certain things. They had their eye on 'the recompense of the reward' (v 26); they had a particular view of this world and of life in this world, and therefore they preferred 'to suffer affliction with the people of God, than to enjoy the pleasures of sin for a season' (v 25). And that is the great case of the Bible everywhere.

Now there are so many things in the modern world that ought to enable us men and women in this generation to see these things with a particular clarity. In many ways I thank God that I am preaching this gospel now rather than in the nineteenth century, and I say that because though I know it was then the popular thing for people to go to a place of worship—Christianity was, in a sense, fashionable and it paid to be a Christian—in spite of all that, it seems to me that it was more difficult to see the true nature of life in this world then than it is now. People harboured those great illusions about a perpetual state of peace and prosperity and progress and development. There had not been a war of any magnitude since the Napoleonic, and they had great confidence and optimism. They seemed to have lost sight of the fact that Satan is the god of this world and that you cannot by human effort and endeavour produce a perfect society in a world like this while sin is sin and men and women are governed by sin.

But today that should be painfully obvious to all of us with the things that we have experienced in this century. Surely we of all people ought to be seeing so clearly that we are surrounded by evil powers and forces that the one thing that should be concerning us is, what can we do in a world like this? How can we master and conquer it; how can we avoid being engulfed in the vortex and being drowned in this terrible world? Well, the answer is to be found here in this one verse, and it obviously has a very direct reference to what happened at Pentecost.[1] The whole secret is that we may have 'an understanding,' and the message is that 'the Son of God is come, and hath given us an understanding,' so that we may have a right view of all these things.

In other words, this reference to the 'understanding' in this text is nothing but a very direct piece of teaching with regard to the Holy Spirit. For what John says is that the Son of God has come and has done something to our minds. He has not merely come and revealed and displayed the Father to us and told us certain things about Him. No; He has done something more than that, something that, in a sense, is even more vital than that: He has enabled us to understand these things. 'Understanding' means the mind, the depth of the mind, that rational part of our being that enables us to grasp the truth; and, therefore, it is clearly a reference to the work of the Holy Spirit and what He enables us to do.

The first thing, therefore, that we can lay down is that the Holy Spirit is the gift of Jesus Christ. 'We know,' says John, 'that the Son of God is come, and hath given us an understanding.' Now this is something of supreme importance. Whit-Sunday, this day on which we remember together what happened at Jerusalem on that great Day of Pentecost, is of vital importance in Christian doctrine and in an understanding of the Christian truth. We must always be clear and certain as to what took place on that occasion. There, as was expounded by the Apostle Peter, something happened that had long been promised by God. 'Therefore,' he says, 'being by the right hand of God exalted, and having received of the Father the promise of the Holy Ghost, he hath shed forth this, which ye now see and hear' (Acts 2:33). 'What has happened today,' said Peter in effect to that assembled concourse, 'is nothing but a fulfilment of the prophecy that you find in the Old Testament.' He had already put it in terms of the fulfilment of the prophecy according to Joel.

In other words, the ultimate purpose of the coming of the Lord Jesus Christ into this world was to send this gift of the Holy Spirit upon His people. Must we not agree that there is a tendency for us to forget that? Is there not a tendency on our part to stop with the life and example and teaching of Jesus Christ, or to stop only with His work upon the cross, as if to say that the whole purpose of the coming of the Son of God into this world was to purchase pardon and forgiveness for us and nothing more? Thank God that we do emphasise that, and it is ever central, and must be; but the work of the Lord Jesus Christ does not end at that point. His work in the resurrection is equally vital for us; His ascension, too, is equally important; and, above all, this great event that took place on the Day of Pentecost at Jerusalem.

The way in which the Bible puts it is this: what people needed was a new spirit; they needed this new relationship to God, this understanding that could only be given to them by God. And running through the Old Testament there is a promise of this. There is a contrast between the giving of the law through Moses and this further new understanding that was to be given. The law was given by Moses on stones; it was given externally. The law was given to men and women, and they were told to read that law and try to put it into practice, 'which if a man do, he shall live in them,' said God (Lev 18:5). But the prophecy was that a day would come when God would make a new covenant with men and women. He would write His law in their minds and place it in their hearts. The law would no longer be something external; it would be something that would be put right into them, into their very essence. So they would no longer look at the law and painfully try to keep it and fail. They would want to keep it, they would love to keep it; it would be something working within them. That was the great promise; that was something to which the people of God looked forward. So the New Testament refers to it as 'the promise of the Father' (Acts 1:4).

Now this was what the world needed, and according to this Scripture, Jesus Christ, having come into the world, has made that possible. He came into the world; the Son of God became incarnate. He took upon Himself the form of man and the likeness of sinful flesh, and the Holy Spirit was given to Him in all His fulness. Look at Him and watch His life, and you will see that there was never a life like this. He was free from sin; He was able to master and to conquer Satan. He had unusual powers that enabled Him to control the elements of nature and to work His wonderful miracles. It is a life apart, and it is a life that is to be explained, according to the Scripture, in terms of the Holy Spirit. Though He was the Son of God, He humbled Himself; He did not make use of the prerogatives of His Godhead. That is the meaning of His self-humbling, that He lived life as a man; He was given the gift of the Holy Spirit, and He depended upon Him, and this is the result. As we look at that life, we say, 'Oh that we could live such a life! Oh, that it were possible for us to live in that way!'

And the answer of the Bible to us is that it is possible; that He, having come thus into the world and having rendered perfect obedience to God's law, went even to the death of the cross. There He made Himself responsible for our guilt and for our sin; the thing that stood between mankind and God was there removed. He has thus, by dying upon the cross, purchased our pardon; He has made Himself our Redeemer and Rescuer. Then He ascended into heaven and presented Himself and His perfect offering; He presented His own blood as an expiation for all sin, and God received Him. And—this is the wonderful sequence—because of what He has done, God has given to Him the gift of the Holy Spirit to give us. By dying thus, Peter argued on the Day of Pentecost, exalted by God, He has received 'the promise of the Father.' God, as it were, rewarded Him for the work He had done for mankind by giving Him this gift of the Holy Spirit to give to us, and there on that Day of Pentecost at Jerusalem He showered forth this gift that He had received from the Father.

'You cannot understand it,' says Peter to that assembled concourse in Jerusalem; 'you are amazed at the fact that we are able to speak in other tongues. Some of you have suggested we are drunk, but that is impossible because it is only the third hour of the day. You are bewildered and amazed by what you see, and you ask, What is this that you are doing, what is this power? Well,' says Peter, 'this is just the fulfilment of prophecy. Jesus of Nazareth, whom you crucified, is none other than the only begotten Son of God. He, by doing what He has done, has become the Prince and Saviour of Israel. God has given Him this gift, and He has showered it forth upon us. That is why we are what we are. This is that which was spoken of by the prophet Joel; this is the promise of the Father.' Therefore, what happened on the Day of Pentecost at Jerusalem is nothing but a fulfilment of those ancient prophecies—that prophecy of Joel, that prophecy of Jeremiah about the new covenant and about the writing of the laws in the mind and upon the heart (Jeremiah 31:31-34).

Indeed, this is the perfect fulfilment of that which we find in John 7:39. Our Lord said to the people in Jerusalem, 'If any man thirst, let him come unto me, and drink' (v 37). 'If there is anybody amongst you,' says Christ in effect, 'who is conscious of weakness and tiredness, if there is anybody who has been battling against sin and is conscious of defeat, if there is any man who needs a power that will enable him to overcome, let him come unto me and drink. And,' He said, 'if he does so, from his inward parts shall flow rivers of living water (v 38). He will not simply be filled—he will overflow; this great power will come upon him from Me; if he is thirsty and drinks of Me, that will be the result.' Then says John in recording all this, 'this spake he of the Spirit, which they that believe on him should receive; for the Holy Ghost was not yet given' (v 39). Christ, says John, was speaking at that point of what the Holy Spirit was going to do when He would come; and on the Day of Pentecost at Jerusalem, that very thing happened. He poured forth His Holy Spirit upon the assembled church.

There were one hundred and twenty people in the upper room waiting. He had told them to do that, and He had said, 'I will pour out my Spirit upon you, and then you will be My witnesses. You cannot do it without this gift.' And the gift came, they began to witness, and prophecy was fulfilled. So the Holy Spirit is the gift of the Lord Jesus Christ. You remember how, even before the Day of Pentecost, when He appeared to the disciples in the upper room, we are told that He breathed upon them and said, 'Receive ye the Holy Ghost' (John 20:22) He gives us the Spirit; the Spirit is the gift of the Father to the Son as the triumphant mediator, the Redeemer and Saviour, and He in turn gives the Spirit to His people. 'We know,' says John, 'that the Son of God is come, and hath given us this gift of the Holy Spirit.'

That, then, leads to the second principle, that it is through this gift of the Holy Spirit alone that we have or can have any spiritual knowledge and 'understanding.' This, of course, is obviously the central doctrine in these matters. What we need is understanding. If the world is, as the Bible tells us, under the control of Satan, and if we are all helpless face-to-face with Satan, the one thing we need is knowledge and enlightenment. And according to the Scripture, that is only possible as we receive the gift of the Holy Ghost. The trouble with the world apart from the Holy Spirit is that, as Paul puts it in writing to the Ephesians, non-Christians are living 'in the vanity of their mind, having the understanding darkened' (Eph 4:17-18). There is a kind of shutter that has come down on their minds. As we have seen, the god of this world has blinded them, as Paul says in writing to the Corinthians; the world by nature lacks a spiritual faculty and understanding.

Now surely we all must recognise the importance of this. Let me put it in this way: Are you surprised at the state of the world or of society? Does it come to you sometimes with astonishment that the world is as

it is, that men and women can be so carefree? Is it not a remarkable thing
that, having had two world wars and all the continuing uncertainty in
the world, our newspapers can be filled with trivial things? Does it not
seem incredible? And yet that is a fact. How do you explain that in the
face of many tragic possibilities the world can laugh and joke and enjoy
itself and be apparently carefree; what is the explanation?

There is only one adequate explanation. It is that the world's understanding is darkened. It does not see what is happening; it is not aware
of the tragedy. This is only possible because the minds of men and
women are blinded, and that is precisely what the Bible says about them.
The trouble with people in this world is that they are fooled by Satan.
Satan persuades them, 'Eat, drink and be merry, for tomorrow you die.
What is the use of worrying about any possible catastrophe? All the
worry in the world will not affect it; it will come soon enough without
going to meet it. So have a good time; turn your back upon it!' That is
the philosophy of the devil that the world believes; that is the tragic condition, and nothing will awaken men and women out of this but this
enlightenment that comes alone by the Holy Spirit. We have received 'an
understanding,' and our minds are awakened because the Son of God
has come and has given us the gift of the Spirit.

You find this everywhere in Scripture. Take, for instance, the
account of the Apostle Paul preaching for the first time in Europe. Is it
not interesting to observe what we are told about the first convert to
Christianity? She was a woman named Lydia living in a place called
Philippi. The Apostle Paul went there to preach the gospel, she and others listened to him, and she believed the things that were told her. She
came to see that you must believe and accept the gospel and give yourself to it, and her life was transformed by it. And the Scripture says that
it happened because the Lord 'opened' her heart, that she might believe
(Acts 16:14). If the Lord, through the Holy Spirit, had not opened her
heart she would never have believed, for what the Holy Spirit does is to
enlighten our spiritual faculty. He awakens certain things that are dormant in us and makes us understand.

Again, take the case of Nicodemus. He was a man who was a master in Israel, a teacher of the people. Here was a man of great reputation, a man of erudition and learning, a man who was an expert in the
Old Testament and a teacher of the people in these matters. But having
looked at Jesus Christ and having watched Him and having seen His

miracles, he felt that here was someone whom he could not understand, someone who had a power greater than he or any other teacher in Israel had. And so he went one night and sought an interview with Jesus. He said to Him, 'Master, You must be a teacher sent from God, for no man could do the things that You do except God be with Him.' And immediately our Lord interrupted him and said, 'Verily, verily, I say unto thee, Except a man be born again, he cannot see the kingdom of God.' Poor Nicodemus began to expostulate, and our Lord replied again, 'Except a man be born of water and of the Spirit, he cannot enter into the kingdom of God' (John 3:2-5).

What does that mean? It means this: Nicodemus was trying to understand these things, and our Lord said to him in effect, 'My dear man, you cannot understand them. You are a master in Israel, but you must be born of the Spirit. You have to have this enlightenment that the Holy Ghost alone can give. You cannot advance from Judaism to Christianity; you must be born again. You need a new faculty, as it were, and the Holy Ghost alone can give it.'

'The wind,' said our Lord, 'bloweth where it listeth, and thou hearest the sound thereof, but canst not tell whence it cometh, and whither it goeth: so is every one that is born of the Spirit' (John 3:8). 'You must have this gift of God,' He said, 'and then, and then only, will you understand these things.'

And the Apostle Paul has put this more explicitly still in writing to the Corinthians. It is only the man who is spiritual, he says, who can understand these things. When Christ, the Prince of Glory, was here, said Paul, the princes of this world did not know him, for had they known Him, 'they would not have crucified the Lord of glory.' But we know Him because God has given us His Spirit, and 'the Spirit searcheth all things, yea, the deep things of God' (1 Cor 2:8, 10). Only men and women of understanding know the things of the Spirit of God because they have to be spiritually understood, and the others lack that faculty. 'We have received, not the spirit of the world, but the Spirit which is of God; that we might know the things that are freely given to us of God' (1 Cor 2:12). It is only the Holy Spirit who can give us this understanding.

But, says the Apostle John here, 'we know that the Son of God is come, and hath given us an understanding.' He has given us the gift of the Spirit. Now John has already emphasised this, you remember, in the second chapter, where he says, 'Ye have an unction from the Holy One, and ye know all things. . . . But the anointing which ye have received of him abideth in you, and ye need not that any man teach you: but as the same anointing teacheth you of all things, and is truth, and is no lie, and even as it hath taught you, ye shall abide in him' (vv 20, 27).

This is the great teaching throughout the Bible. It was only as they were enlightened by the Spirit of God that those people of the Old Testament understood the truth as they did. Look at those prophets of Israel who not only prophesied to their own generation, but who predicted things that were coming, who told of the coming of Christ, where He would be born, and all these things—how did they do it? Peter answers that by telling us that 'no prophecy of the Scripture is of any private interpretation.' He says that these men did not write these things because they thought them out or because they suddenly got an idea from their own reasoning. Not at all! 'Holy men of God spake as they were moved [carried along, enlightened] by the Holy Ghost' (2 Pet 1:20-21). The Holy Spirit came in that way; the power of the Holy Spirit enlightened their understanding and guided them how to write. And the same thing is always true. It is only as we receive this gift of the Spirit that we shall understand; without that we remain in spiritual darkness. We are dead in trespasses and sins; we need to be quickened, enlightened in power and understanding, and then, and then alone, we have true spiritual knowledge.

And that brings us to the last word—what is this knowledge? Well, John summarises it once more, and I need only to give you headings therefore. The first thing that the Holy Spirit enables us to see and understand is the fact concerning Christ Himself. The world is not interested in Him and would explain Him away as a man; it is only those who have this spiritual understanding that know Him to be the Son of God, the Saviour of the world. Indeed they not only know things about Him—they know Him. 'We . . . know him,' says John.

And the same is true of God the Father. 'We know that the Son of God is come, and hath given us an understanding, that we may know him that is true'—that is, God the Father. Again, we not only know things about God—we know God. That is what John is emphasising. The Jews knew about God; the Mohammedan also knows things about God. But 'we . . . know him that is true.' We know Him as Father; we are in this relationship to Him. We have that knowledge of Him that enables us to cry out, 'Abba Father'; and this makes our prayer possible. But we not only know God—we know also that we are in God; and not only are we in God, but in His Son Jesus Christ also.

In other words, here at the end of the epistle John comes back to the thing with which he started. He started off, you remember, by saying that he is anxious that these people to whom he is writing may share in that fellowship that he and the Apostles are enjoying. 'Truly,' he says, 'our fellowship is with the Father, and with His Son Jesus Christ.' And the way that is made possible, he says, is: 'That which was from the beginning, which we have heard, which we have seen with our eyes, which we have looked upon, and our hands have handled, of the Word of life; (For the life was manifested, and we have seen it, and bear witness, and shew unto you that eternal life, which was with the Father, and was manifested unto us)' (1 John 1:1-3). He has come and has given us life, says John; and here he ends on exactly the same note. For by giving us the Holy Spirit, he has not only given us the faculty and understanding and the knowledge, but He has given us life itself. We are in Christ and in God, and God and Christ are in us.

If you read chapters 14, 15, and 16 of John's Gospel, you will find that there our Lord promises all that. He said to those people, 'I would tell you more, but you cannot bear it now. But after I have gone, I will send the gift of the Holy Spirit, and He will lead you into all truth—He will remind you of the things I have spoken unto you. Not only that, He will come and dwell in you, and He will be with you; and the Father will come, and the Father and I will make our abode with you, you in us and We in you.' Those are the essential things we are promised, so that even in this world we are given this 'understanding' by the Holy Spirit.

As Christian people we are not fooled by the world and its gaudy prizes; we are not for a moment misled by its supposed happiness, which we know is utterly artificial. We have been given 'an understanding'; we know something about the nature of sin in us and in the world around and about us. We have been given a knowledge of God and a relationship with Him; we have been given a knowledge concerning Christ as our Redeemer and Saviour; we have been given life by Him, so that we are in fellowship with God. We see the truth in contrast to evil; we are aware of that which is eternal in contra-distinction to the temporal. And being in God and in His Son Jesus Christ, we have a power, a might, and a strength that are more than enough to conquer Satan, so that we can look at the world and all its evil without fear. 'We know that the Son of

God is come, and hath given us an understanding, that we may know him that is true. This [the Son] is the true God, and eternal life'; and having Him and knowing Him, we need have no fear. Thank God for the gift of the Holy Spirit; thank God for that which happened on the Day of Pentecost.

Have you this understanding; are you clear about your life in this world and of the victory that is possible to you? Have you this unction, this anointing about which the Apostle speaks; have you received the Holy Spirit? Those are the questions. If you have, you have nothing to do but to praise God and to yield yourself increasingly to Him and to ask that you may be filled with His Spirit more and more. If not, I repeat to you the word of the Lord Jesus Christ Himself: 'If ye then, being evil, know how to give good gifts unto your children; how much more shall your heavenly Father give the Holy Spirit to them that ask him' (Luke 11:13). We have but to ask, to seek, to knock and we shall receive. It is God's desire that we receive this gift; therefore, if we feel we lack the understanding, if we lack the power, if we lack the joy and happiness and the peace and the abounding life that the Holy Ghost gives, we have but to go to God in simplicity. We have but to confess our need and lack and ask Him for the gift of the Holy Spirit, and He is pledged to answer and to give us the gift. And having received the Holy Spirit, we shall have this understanding and begin to produce the fruit of the Spirit in our daily lives.

17

IDOLATRY

Little children, keep yourselves from idols. Amen.

1 JOHN 5:21

WE THUS ONCE MORE and for the last time in this series consider the message of the first Epistle of John. For those who may be interested in statistics, it is actually the sixty-seventh time[1] that we have looked at this epistle together; and now here are the last words. They are John's final advice, his final warning to these people whom he loved so truly and whom he constantly addressed as 'little children.' That does not mean, you remember, that they were literally little children because, as we saw in the second chapter, he addresses them in different categories—'little children,' 'young men,' and 'fathers.' But it is his custom to use this term of endearment with regard to the whole body of people, and this is what he does here.

There are authorities who would say that these are probably the last words in the entire Scripture, if you take Scripture in chronological order. This point cannot be proved, but there is a good deal to be said for it. In any case, these are the last words of this old man who was so concerned about the life and the future of these Christians to whom he was writing. The words of an old man are always worthy of respect and consideration; they are words that are based upon a long lifetime's experience. The last words of all people are important, but the last words of great people are of exceptional importance, and the last words of an Apostle of the Lord Jesus Christ are of supreme importance.

So here we have this Apostle looking back across a long life, having had many and varied and strange experiences himself, a man who has looked back at a wonderful three years spent in the actual presence and company of the Son of God, who heard all His addresses, who saw His miracles and was with Him on every special occasion. Here is a man out of this great and mighty experience saying a last word. He is an old man; he knows the end is at hand, and he sees this group of people in a hostile world, and he wants them to live a life of victory. He wants them to have a joy that may be full, and this is his final word to them: 'Little children, keep yourselves from idols.'

Now in ending on this note John is doing something that is very characteristic of himself. We have seen repeatedly, as we have gone through this epistle together, his liking for contrast. He is very fond of comparing—light and darkness, love and hate, that which is true and that which is false. His mind instinctively seems to think in terms of these great contrasts, and he ends on that. The previous verse has told us that 'we know that the Son of God is come, and hath given us an understanding, that we may know him that is true; and we are in him that is true, even in His Son Jesus Christ. This is the true God, and eternal life.' Then he adds, 'Little children, keep yourselves from idols'—the false; this is a contrast between the true and the false.

Or we can put it like this: John was also very fond of negatives; he never contented himself with the positive only. So he generally puts his positive first and then his negative, and this is what he does here. We are not only told that we must keep the commandments and be perfect; we are also told that we must not sin. Here we see the negative in relation to the one and only true and living God—the avoidance of idols.

Or to put it yet another way, John always warns us. Now most people do not like warnings, and we instinctively do not like them, because we are sinners. We do not like to be told not to do something; we always feel that this is insulting because it proves that we need the warning. But John, out of his long experience, knew the importance of warnings. How often he warns these people to be aware of the world, of the antichrists, these false teachers, and of false doctrines; to be aware of claiming great things in theory and forgetting to put them into practise. He warns them that it is useless to say you love God and yet to hate your brother; to give the impression of unusual devotion and yet not to be true in the ordinary details of your life.

John is full of warnings of that kind, and he actually ends this wonderful epistle, in which he has led us to the very highest heights of doctrine and of truth, on this note. Some might regard this as being methodical, but it is obviously not this, because John had a practical interest; there is nothing more dangerous than a theoretical interest in truth. John never wrote this letter merely to give a knowledge of truth as such; his object from the beginning was essentially practical—he wanted to help these people in their daily life and in their battle against the forces that are set against them in this world. So he is not concerned about stopping; he does not lead to a great oration and then suddenly stop. No; he is as practical as this: 'Little children, keep yourselves from idols'; that is his last word.

Now the way in which he uses this is of real interest. The great thing and the supreme thing is that we may know the only true and living God; that was the third of his great affirmations—'that we may know him that is true.' That is the thing that you must hold on to, says John, in spite of everything; the one thing that matters in this life and world is to know God. 'This is life eternal,' said our Lord himself, 'that they may know thee the only true God, and Jesus Christ, whom thou hast sent' (John 17:3). If we haven't that knowledge, says John, if we haven't that understanding, then we are not aware of the spiritual problems in which we are set, and we are obviously going to be defeated. And this knowledge of God is only to be obtained in Jesus Christ, who Himself is God; and if we know Him we have eternal life, as John has repeatedly reminded us.

So then, the vital thing is to know God, to walk with Him, and to abide in Him and in that knowledge. Nothing can ever go wrong with us if we are in that position, if we but walk in fellowship with God. That is what John is so anxious for these people to have—'that ye also may have fellowship with us: and truly our fellowship is with the Father, and with his Son Jesus Christ.'

'All right,' says John, 'that is the positive aspect of the truth. But if you want to make absolutely certain that you will be in that condition, keep yourselves from idols.' There are constantly things in this life and world that threaten to come between us and that knowledge of God. In other words, whether we like it or not, it is a warfare, it is a fight of faith; there is an enemy set against us. We have just been reminded of that—'that wicked one' that John speaks of towards the end of the letter; and the supreme object of that evil one is to come between us and this knowledge. And the way he does that, of course, is to try to get us to fix our mind and our attention and our heart upon something else. So it is in order to warn us against that terrible danger that John ends on this note. Let me, therefore, put this in the form of three propositions. The first is that the greatest enemy that confronts us in the spiritual life is the worshipping of idols. The greatest danger confronting us all is not a matter of deeds or of actions, but of idolatry. That may sound strange to some. They may think that above all we need to be warned not to do certain things, and there are indeed great warnings like that in Scripture. But let us never forget that before we are told what not to do, we are always told what we *are* to do. Take the Ten Commandments—positive, then negative; they follow exactly the same procedure as John does here. Our deeds and actions are always the outcome of our attitudes and our thoughts. 'As a man thinks, so he is'; and if, therefore, you carefully scrutinize a man's life, it is not at all difficult to discover what he really believes. Actions are always the expression of a point of view, and that is why the actions always proclaim the man. So the thing to concentrate on is the outlook, the philosophy, the belief; and that is emphasised everywhere in the Bible.

Now it was the cardinal error of the Pharisees that they were so interested in the details of the 614 points of the law on which they were so expert that they constantly forgot the great *principles* of the law. They showed that on one occasion when they went to our Lord and asked Him the question, 'Which is the first commandment of all?' They had been having a disputation amongst themselves with regard to this matter, just as people still like to argue whether one sin is greater than another. Our Lord replied, 'Thou shalt love the Lord thy God with all thy heart, and with all thy soul, and with all thy mind, and with all thy strength: this is the first commandment. And the second is like, namely this, Thou shalt love thy neighbour as thyself' (Mark 12:30-31). That is the principle, for if that comes first, then our actions and our conduct and our behaviour are likely to look after themselves. So the Scriptures always start with this, and that is why the greatest danger in the spiritual life, therefore, is always idolatry.

What does this mean? What is idolatry? Well, an idol can be defined most simply in this way: an idol is anything in our lives that occupies the place that should be occupied by God alone. Anything that holds my life and my devotion, anything that is central in my life, anything that seems to be vital, anything that is essential to me; an idol is anything by which

I live and on which I depend. Anything that moves and rouses and attracts and stimulates me is an idol. An idol is anything that I worship, anything to which I give much of my time and attention, my energy and my money; anything that holds a controlling position in my life is an idol.

Now when we look at it in that way, we see how practical this advice of the Apostle is. The commentators have expended a good deal of time and energy in dealing with the question of what John meant when he said this. There are those who say this is perfectly simple. John was writing to people who had been pagan and who were still set in a pagan society, where idols had literally been made out of silver and gold and wood and stone and various other things, and he was just telling them not to go back and worship them. But surely that is an impossible suggestion; that was not the danger confronting these people. The danger was the teaching of the antichrists and the dangers that still confront Christian people always, everywhere. There is no suggestion in the New Testament that any of those people were liable to go back to literal idolatry in that sense.

The Protestant Fathers were, of course, very anxious to interpret these words in terms of the gross errors and the superstitions and the idolatry of Roman Catholicism, and of course an idol may indeed be an actual idol. But it does not stop at that; would to God it did! No; idolatry may consist of having false notions of God. If I am worshipping my own idea of God and not the true and living God, that is idolatry. That is something about which John is very concerned. These antichrists had been denying the teaching that Jesus Christ is come in the flesh. They had been denying that Jesus of Nazareth is the Son of God. And therefore, says John, if you claim that, and if your idea of God is not the biblical idea, if you have a false conception of Him and are worshipping such notions and conceptions, according to the Scripture that is simply idolatry.

So then, this may take the form of worshipping images and everything that is true of the Roman Catholic teaching—the worship of the Virgin Mary, the worship of the saints and praying to them; that is a form of idolatry. God alone is to be prayed to; God alone is to be worshipped—God the Father, God the Son, and God the Holy Spirit. He is the only true and living God—God in three Persons; no one else is to receive our devotion. That is the teaching of Scripture, and anyone to whom we give devotion beyond that makes us guilty of idolatry.

But let me go on to point out that idolatry can take many other forms. It is possible for us to worship our religion instead of worshipping God. How subtle a thing this idolatry is! We may think that we are worshipping God, but really we are simply worshipping our own religious observances and devotions. It is an error always of every Catholic type of religion that lays stress upon doing particular things in particular ways, such as getting up and going to early-morning Communion. The emphasis may be more upon the observance of this rather than upon the worship of God.

I give that as but an illustration. It is not confined to the Catholic type; it is also found in the most evangelical circles. It is possible for us to worship not only our own religion but our own church, our own communion, our own religious body, our own particular community, our own particular sect, our own particular point of view—these are the things we may be worshipping. Theology has often become an idol to many people; they have really been worshipping ideas and not worshipping God. What a terrible thing this is; and yet, and I am sure we all must agree, how easy it is to forget the person of the Lord Jesus Christ and to stop at the ideas and the theories and the teaching concerning Him. How easy it is to stop, for instance, at the very doctrine of the Atonement and to forget the blessed person and what He suffered for me that I might be saved—and that is idolatry! Anything that occupies this central position rather than God Himself is idolatry. Also, there are people who worship their own experiences; they do not talk about God, they talk about themselves and what has happened to them—always self in the foreground rather than God.

Further, the idol in the case of some people is their own country; there are people who worship it. Are we guiltless of that? There are people who worship the state, or certain people in the state; there is a kind of mysticism that has often been developed. It was something of which the Stuart Kings became guilty, this almost deifying of the sovereign. And we have seen it in recent years in the dictatorships on the continent of Europe. But there are people still who worship the state—the power of the state and what the state can do for them; they live for it—it is their idol, their god.

But come, let us be still more careful in our self-examination—our idol may very well be another person. A man may make an idol of his wife; a wife may make an idol of her husband. Parents may really worship their children; the children may occupy in their minds and hearts the place that should be occupied by God. They give more time and attention and more thought to them; they are more concerned about them, and everything else, even attendance at church, may be put on one side because of the children. Any person that occupies in my life the place God should occupy I have turned into an idol; I have allowed that person to become an idol to me.

There are many people who worship their work, their profession. They live for it, they sacrifice all for it; God is pushed on one side in order that they might get on in their profession and their status. The position— this big thing, this thing they want above everything else, this thing for which they live—any such thing that occupies the place of God is idolatry. There is no difference in any sense between that and making a god out of gold or silver or wood or stone. You may say that is ridiculous, but it is the same thing. They did it with the hands, we do it in the spirit; and I am not sure but that our sin is worse than theirs.

But perhaps the supreme idol is self, for I suppose that in the last analysis we can trace all the others back to self. The people, for instance, who worship their country do so because it is *their* country. They do not worship another country, and that is for one reason only: they happen to have been born in this one rather than in that one. It is really themselves, and the same is true with children; it is because they are *your* children. And this other person? Well, it is the relationship in which that one person is something to *you*—it is always self. All the saints throughout the centuries have recognised this. The ultimate idol about which we have to be so careful is this horrible self—this concern about myself, putting myself where God ought to be. Everything revolving around *myself*, *my* interest, *my* position, *my* development, myself and all the things that result from that.

'Little children, keep yourselves from idols.' Beware that you do not put yourself in the place of God. The greatest danger in the spiritual life is idolatry, and it comes into all our activities. It comes into our Christian work; it is the greatest danger confronting a man standing in a pulpit preaching, a concern that he should preach in a particular manner. It comes into the activities we are engaged in. Let us examine ourselves as we think about these things. Idolatry—it is the greatest danger of all in the spiritual life.

So the second principle is that we must guard ourselves against this.

'Keep yourselves,' says John, which really means that we must guard ourselves as if we were in a garrison against this horrible danger of idolatry. Now you will notice that John tells us this is something that *we* have to do; it is not done for us. 'Keep yourselves from idols.' You do not 'Let go and let God.' No; you are always on guard—you watch and pray. You realise this terrible danger; *you* have to do it. At first sight John seems to be contradicting himself, because in the eighteenth verse he says, 'We know that whosoever is born of God sinneth not; but he that is begotten of God keepeth him, and that wicked one toucheth him not.' Oh, the comfort we derived as we considered that together; we know that everyone that is born of God does not go on sinning because He is kept by the Lord Jesus Christ. And yet here John is saying, 'Little children, *keep yourselves* from idols.' Is he contradicting himself? No; these things form the perfect balance that we always find in Scripture from beginning to end. It is simply John's way of saying, 'Work out your own salvation with fear and trembling: For it is God which worketh in you . . .' (Phil 2:12-13).

It is the same thing you find in the Old Testament, which says, 'Thou wilt keep him in perfect peace, whose mind is stayed on thee' (Isa 26:3). It does not stop at 'Thou wilt keep him in perfect peace'; He will do that, but only if the believer's mind is 'stayed' on Him. He will keep us, and the evil one will never get us back into his clutches; yes, that is true, but only if we keep ourselves from idols.

In other words, we must keep ourselves in right relationship to Him. If you and I keep our minds on the Lord Jesus Christ by the Holy Spirit, we need not worry. The Son of God will keep us, and the evil one will not be able to touch us. We do not have to meet the evil one in single combat; I am not fighting the devil directly, as it were. What I do is I keep myself in that right relationship with Christ, and He will defeat the enemy for me. I must be careful that some idol is not receiving my time and energy and the things that should be given to God. I must be constantly on the watch. I must beware, for there is an enemy with evil darts throwing these things at me. And realising all this, I must guard myself. I must guard my mind and understanding; I must watch my spirit and my heart. This is the most subtle thing in the world. It is the central temptation, so that I constantly have to watch and pray and ever and always be on my guard.

But that brings me to the last proposition, which is essentially practical. How is this to be done? How am I thus to guard myself from idols? It seems to me that the principles are quite simple.

The first thing we must always do is to remember the truth about ourselves. We must remember that we are God's people, that we are those whom Christ has purchased at the price and cost of His own precious blood. We must remember our destiny and the kind of life in which we are engaged and in which we walk. We must remember, as John has reminded us in the nineteenth verse, that 'We are of God, and the whole world lieth in the wicked one.' In other words, if we are of God and belong to God, then we must live for God, and we must not live for any of those other things. It does not matter what they are—I must not live for anything in this life and world. I can use them but not abuse them. God has given me these gifts; but if I turn any of them into my god, I am abusing them—I am worshipping the creature rather than the Creator. Oh, the tragedy that we should be doing that! The way to avoid that is to realise what I am; I am to exercise this 'understanding' that Christ has given me through the Holy Spirit, as we saw in verse 20. I am to remember that I am not of this world, and therefore I must not live for or worship anything that belongs to it.

Or we can put that in the form of a second principle: I must remember the true nature of idols. That is the way to avoid worshipping them and a very good way of guarding yourself against idolatry. Just look and consider what they are, and there again is something we need to be reminded of constantly. Look at the things to which we tend to give our worship and our adoration; even if we put them at their highest and their best, are they worthy of it? Is there anything in this world of time which is worthy of our worship and our devotion? We know full well there is not. There is nothing in this world that lasts; everything is only temporary, everything is moving on to an end. There is nothing lasting and eternal; they are thus unworthy of our worship. They are all gifts given to us by God, so let us use them as such; let us not regard them as worthy of our entire devotion. Is it not tragic to think of a human soul worshipping money, possession, position, success, any person, children, or anything else of this life and world? It is all passing away. There is one alone who is worthy, and that is God.

And that is the last thing to remember. The way ultimately to keep ourselves from idols is to remember the truth about God and to live in communion with Him. Whenever we are tempted to engage in idolatry, let us think again of the nature and the being of God. Let us remember that the privilege that is offered to us is to worship Him and to walk with Him, to know Him and to commune and converse with Him, to be a child of God and to go on and spend eternity in His holy presence.

> *The dearest idol I have known,*
> *Whate'er that idol be,*
> *Help me to tear it from Thy throne,*
> *And worship only Thee.*
>
> WILLIAM COWPER

How right he is! It is as we realise this wondrous possibility of knowing God that everything else should pale into insignificance. In other words, the Apostle's final advice, it seems to me, can be put like this: we must strive, without ceasing, to realise the presence and the fellowship and the communion of God. There was a prayer that Hudson Taylor, the great pioneer missionary to China, was very fond of, and we cannot do better than follow in the steps of that saintly, mighty man of God. After his death they found a sheet of paper in his diary on which he had written these words, and he obviously moved it from day to day as his diary went along. This, according to Hudson Taylor, was the most important thing in life for him:

> *Lord Jesus make thyself to me*
> *A living bright reality,*
> *More present to faith's vision keen,*
> *Than any outward object seen,*
> *More dear, more intimately nigh,*
> *Than e'en the sweetest earthly tie.*

That is it. To realise His nearness and His presence, to realise His companionship, to know that we are with Him and in Him, and to see to it always and ever that nothing and no one shall ever come between us and Him.

NOTES

CHAPTER 1: THE NEW TESTAMENT DEFINITION OF A CHRISTIAN

1 Cf. *The Love of God* (Crossway Books, 1994).

CHAPTER 2: THE WHOLENESS OF THE CHRISTIAN LIFE

1 For a further treatment of this, cf. *Fellowship with God* (Crossway Books, 1993).
2 See *The Love of God* (Crossway Books, 1994).
3 *Ibid.*
4 See *ibid.*

CHAPTER 5: HOW FAITH OVERCOMES

1 This sermon was preached during the 1950 election campaign in Britain.
2 Cf. *Walking with God* (Crossway Books, 1993).

CHAPTER 10: THE LIFE OF GOD

1 The founder of the China Inland Mission, now the Overseas Missionary Fellowship.

CHAPTER 12: PRAYER FOR THE BRETHREN

1 See *Children of God* and *The Love of God* (Crossway Books, 1993 and 1994 respectively).

CHAPTER 13: SAFE IN THE ARMS OF JESUS

1 Cf. *Children of God* (Crossway Books, 1993).

CHAPTER 14: THE LIFE OF THE WORLD

1 Cf. *Fellowship with God* (Crossway Books 1993).
2 Cf. *Walking with God* (Crossway Books, 1993).

CHAPTER 16: UNDERSTANDING

1 This sermon was preached on Whit Sunday, 1950.

CHAPTER 17: IDOLATRY

1 The other sermons in this series are to be found in the first four volumes (*Fellowship with God, Walking with God, Children of God,* and *The Love of God,* published by Crossway Books).

Wearing rose-colored glasses may seem to make the world a happier, easier place to live, but denial simply postpones dealing with the realities of life. The Apostle John's first epistle shatters any illusions that we may have about sin, salvation, loving the world, prayer, false spirits, and much more. While opening our eyes to these great truths, he brings encouragement and conviction, understanding and confidence to our spirits.

From the mind and pen of Martyn Lloyd-Jones comes a prayerful contemplation of this marvelous book of the Bible. Chapter by chapter he eloquently takes you through an in-depth study and careful application of truths that will challenge and enlighten you. These valuable insights on God's holiness and love, Christ our Advocate, and the work of the Holy Spirit are strategic to strengthening your spiritual understanding so that you can best live out your faith.

Previously released in five volumes, this comprehensive study and application of I John is now gathered together in one book.

MARTYN LLOYD-JONES (1899-1981), minister of Westminster Chapel in London for 30 years, was one of the foremost preachers of his day. His sermons and books have challenged and enriched millions of Christians worldwide.

BIBLICAL STUDIES / COMMENTARY

ISBN-13: 978-1-58134-439-4
ISBN-10: 1-58134-439-2

CROSSWAY

www.crossway.com

52499

9 781581 344394

U.S. $24.99